MW01484925

Temple and Worship in Biblical Israel

TEMPLE AND WORSHIP IN BIBLICAL ISRAEL

Proceedings of the Oxford Old Testament Seminar

EDITED BY

JOHN DAY

t&t clark

Published by T&T Clark
A Continuum imprint
The Tower Building, 11 York Road, London SE1 7NX
80 Maiden Lane, Suite 704, New York, NY 10038

www.continuumbooks.com

First published in hardback as volume 422 of the Library of Hebrew Bible/Old Testament Studies, 2005

This edition published, 2007

British Library Cataloguing-in-Publication Data
A catalogue record for this book is available from the British Library

Typeset by Forthcoming Publications Ltd
Printed and bound in Great Britain by Antony Rowe Ltd., Chippenham, Wiltshire

ISBN-10: PB: 0-567-04571-4
ISBN-13: PB: 978-0-567-04571-3

CONTENTS

Part III
The Temple in Late Second Temple Judaism
and in the New Testament

PREFACE

This volume contains twenty-three essays which were originally delivered as papers to the Oxford Old Testament seminar between January 2001 and November 2003, and which have subsequently been revised and often expanded. The essays, which make a major contribution to the subject of Temple and worship, range over a wide field, stretching from the ancient Near East, through the Old Testament and Late Second Temple Judaism and into the New Testament.

I am extremely grateful to all the contributors to this work who have helped make it a success, many from within Oxford, others from elsewhere in the United Kingdom, and yet others who have travelled vast distances from overseas in order to address the Oxford seminar. Yet again, I am indebted to one of the participants, Professor John Barton, for facilitating the project by enabling me to take over for such a long period the organization of the deliberations of the seminar which he normally convenes. I also wish to thank T. & T. Clark International for publishing this work and express gratitude to all their staff who have been involved with its production. A special word of thanks is due to Dr Duncan Burns, who has acted not only as copy-editor and typesetter, but has also undertaken the laborious task of compiling the indexes.

This is now the third series of published proceedings of the Oxford Old Testament seminar which have appeared under my editorship. The first volume to appear was *King and Messiah in Israel and the Ancient Near East* (JSOTSup, 270; Sheffield: Sheffield Academic Press, 1998). A second volume, based on an Old Testament seminar series running concurrently with that appearing here, has recently been published as *In Search of Pre-Exilic Israel* (JSOTSup, 406; London and New York: T. & T. Clark International, 2004). A fourth seminar series and volume, *Prophecy and the Prophets in Ancient Israel*, is proposed for the future and is currently at the planning stage.

John Day

LIST OF CONTRIBUTORS

John Barton, Oriel and Laing Professor of the Interpretation of Holy Scripture, University of Oxford, and Fellow of Oriel College, Oxford

Elizabeth Bloch-Smith, Senior staff member on the Tel Dor excavations

George J. Brooke, Rylands Professor of Biblical Criticism and Exegesis, University of Manchester

John Day, Professor of Old Testament Studies, University of Oxford, and Fellow and Tutor of Lady Margaret Hall, Oxford

Susan Gillingham, Fellow and Tutor of Worcester College, Oxford, and Lecturer in Theology (Old Testament) in the University of Oxford

Martin Goodman, Professor of Jewish Studies, University of Oxford, and Fellow of Wolfson College, Oxford

Anselm C. Hagedorn, wissenschaftlicher Assistent in Old Testament/Hebrew Bible at the Humboldt-Universität, Berlin; previously Kennicott Hebrew Fellow, Oxford University

C.T.R. Hayward, Professor of Hebrew, University of Durham

Victor Avigdor Hurowitz, Professor of Bible and Ancient Near Eastern Studies, Ben-Gurion University of the Negev, Beer Sheva, Israel

John Jarick, Tutor in Old Testament, St Stephen's House, Oxford

Philip S. Johnston, Tutor in Old Testament and Hebrew, Wycliffe Hall, Oxford

Paul M. Joyce, Fellow and Tutor of St Peter's College, Oxford, and Lecturer in Theology (Old Testament) in the University of Oxford

Michael A. Knibb, Samuel Davidson Professor Emeritus of Old Testament Studies, King's College, University of London

Larry J. Kreitzer, Fellow and Tutor in New Testament, Regent's Park College, Oxford, and Research Lecturer in Theology in the University of Oxford

Jill Middlemas, Liddon Research Fellow in Theology, Keble College, Oxford, and Hebrew Lector, The Oxford Centre for Hebrew and Jewish Studies

Deborah W. Rooke, Lecturer in Old Testament Studies, King's College, University of London

Christopher Rowland, Dean Ireland's Professor of the Exegesis of Holy Scripture, University of Oxford, and Fellow of The Queen's College, Oxford

Simcha Shalom Brooks, Freelance scholar working in London

Mark S. Smith, Skirball Professor of Bible and Ancient Near Eastern Studies, New York University

Stuart Weeks, Lecturer in Old Testament and Hebrew, University of Durham

H.G.M. Williamson, Regius Professor of Hebrew, University of Oxford, and Student of Christ Church, Oxford

Ian Wilson, Freelance scholar working in Cambridge. Life member of Clare Hall, Cambridge

Molly M. Zahn, Doctoral student in the department of Theology, University of Notre Dame

ABBREVIATIONS

AAR	American Academy of Religion
AAR.SR	American Academy of Religion. Studies in Religion
AASOR	Annual of the American Schools of Oriental Research
AB	Anchor Bible
ABD	David Noel Freedman (ed.), *The Anchor Bible Dictionary* (6 vols.; New York: Doubleday, 1992)
Abr-N	*Abr-Nahrain*
AcOr	*Acta orientalia*
AfO	*Archiv für Orientforschung*
AGJU	Arbeiten zur Geschichte des antiken Judentums und des Urchristentums
AHw	Wolfram von Soden, *Akkadisches Handwörterbuch* (3 vols.; Wiesbaden: Harrassowitz, 1959–81)
AJSL	*American Journal of Semitic Languages and Literatures*
ANEP	James B. Pritchard (ed.), *Ancient Near East in Pictures Relating to the Old Testament* (Princeton, NJ: Princeton University Press, 2nd edn, 1969)
ANET	James B. Pritchard (ed.), *Ancient Near Eastern Texts Relating to the Old Testament* (Princeton NJ: Princeton University Press, 3rd edn with supplement, 1969)
AnOr	Analecta orientalia
ANTC	Abingdon New Testament Commentary
AOAT	Alter Orient und Altes Testament
ArOr	*Archiv orientální*
ARTU	J.C. de Moor, *An Anthology of Religious Texts from Ugarit* (Leiden: E.J. Brill, 1987)
ARW	*Archiv für Religionswissenschaft*
ASOR	American Schools of Oriental Research
ATSAT	Arbeiten zu Text und Sprache im Alten Testament
ATD	Das Alte Testament Deutsch
AUSS	*Andrews University Seminary Studies*
BA	*Biblical Archaeologist*
BARev	*Biblical Archaeology Review*
BASOR	*Bulletin of the American Schools of Oriental Research*
BBB	Bonner biblische Beiträge
BCAT	Biblisches Commentar über das Alte Testament

BDB	Francis Brown, S.R. Driver and Charles A. Briggs, *A Hebrew and English Lexicon of the Old Testament* (Oxford: Clarendon Press, 1907)
BETL	Bibliotheca ephemeridum theologicarum lovaniensium
BHS	*Biblia hebraica stuttgartensia*
Bib	*Biblica*
BibInt	*Biblical Interpretation: A Journal of Contemporary Approaches*
BibRes	*Biblical Research*
BiOr	*Bibliotheca Orientalis*
BKAT	Biblischer Kommentar: Altes Testament
BL	H. Bauer and P. Leander, *Historische Grammatik der hebräischen Sprache des Alten Testaments* (Halle: M. Niemeyer, 1922)
BN	*Biblische Notizen*
BR	*Bible Review*
BTB	*Biblical Theology Bulletin*
BWANT	Beiträge zur Wissenschaft vom Alten und Neuen Testament
BWAT	Beiträge zur Wissenschaft vom Alten Testament
BZ	*Biblische Zeitschrift*
BZAW	Beihefte zur *ZAW*
CAD	Ignace I. Gelb *et al.* (eds.), *The Assyrian Dictionary of the Oriental Institute of the University of Chicago* (Chicago: Oriental Institute, 1956–)
CAT	Commentaire de l'Ancien Testament
CBC	Cambridge Bible Commentary
CBQ	*Catholic Biblical Quarterly*
CBQMS	*Catholic Biblical Quarterly*, Monograph Series
CBSC	Cambridge Bible for Schools and Colleges
CDA	Jeremy Black, Andrew George and Nicholas Postgate (eds.), *A Concise Dictionary of Akkadian* (Wiesbaden: Otto Harrassowitz, 1999)
CID	*Corpus des inscriptions de Delphes*
ConBNT	Coniectanea biblica, New Testament
ConBOT	Coniectanea biblica, Old Testament
CRAIBL	*Comptes rendus de l'Académie des inscriptions et belles-lettres*
CSCO	Corpus scriptorum christianorum orientalium
DJD	Discoveries in the Judaean Desert
DNEB	Die neue Echter Bibel
DNWSI	J. Hoftijzer, K. Jongeling *et al.*, *Dictionary of the North-West Semitic Inscriptions* (2 vols.; Handbuch der Orientalistik, 1.21; Leiden: E.J. Brill, 1995)
EBib	Etudes bibliques
EHAT	Exegetisches Handbuch zum Alten Testament
EncJud	*Encyclopaedia Judaica*
EncMqr	*Encyclopedia Miqrait* (9 vols.; Jerusalem: Bialik, 1950–88)

ET	English translation
ExpTim	*Expository Times*
FAT	Forschungen zum Alten Testament
FDelphes	*Fouilles de Delphes*
FRLANT	Forschungen zur Religion und Literatur des Alten und Neuen Testaments
GAT	Grundrisse zum Alten Testament
GKC	*Gesenius' Hebrew Grammar* (ed. E. Kautzsch, revised and trans. A.E. Cowley; Oxford: Clarendon Press, 1910)
HALAT	Ludwig Koehler *et al.* (eds.), *Hebräisches und aramäisches Lexikon zum Alten Testament* (5 vols.; Leiden: E.J. Brill, 1967–1995)
HALOT	L. Koehler, W. Baumgartner, J.J. Stamm *et al.*, *Hebrew and Aramaic Lexicon of the Old Testament* (trans. and ed. M.E.J. Richardson; 5 vols.; Leiden: E.J. Brill, 1994–2000)
HAR	*Hebrew Annual Review*
HAT	Handbuch zum Alten Testament
HBT	*Horizons in Biblical Theology*
HeyJ	*Heythrop Journal*
HKAT	Handkommentar zum Alten Testament
HNT	Handbuch zum Neuen Testament
HSM	Harvard Semitic Monographs
HSS	Harvard Semitic Studies
HThKAT	Herders theologischer Kommentar zum Alten Testament
HTR	*Harvard Theological Review*
HUCA	*Hebrew Union College Annual*
ICC	International Critical Commentary
IDB	George Arthur Buttrick (ed.), *The Interpreter's Dictionary of the Bible* (4 vols.; Nashville: Abingdon Press, 1962)
IDBSup	*IDB*, Supplementary Volume
IEJ	*Israel Exploration Journal*
IG	*Inscriptiones Graecae*
Int	*Interpretation*
ISBE	Geoffrey Bromiley (ed.), *The International Standard Bible Encyclopedia* (4 vols.; Grand Rapids: Eerdmans, rev. edn, 1979–88)
ITC	International Theological Commentary
IVP	InterVarsity Press
JAOS	*Journal of the American Oriental Society*
JB	*Jerusalem Bible*
JBL	*Journal of Biblical Literature*
JBLMS	*Journal of Biblical Literature Monograph Series*
JBTh	*Jahrbuch für biblische Theologie*
JCS	*Journal of Cuneiform Studies*
JETS	*Journal of the Evangelical Theological Society*

JHS	*Journal of Hebrew Scriptures*
JJS	*Journal of Jewish Studies*
JM	P. Joüon, *A Grammar of Biblical Hebrew* (trans. and rev. T. Muraoka; Rome: Pontificio Istituto Biblico, 1991)
JNES	*Journal of Near Eastern Studies*
JPOS	*Journal of the Palestine Oriental Society*
JPS	*Jewish Publication Society*
JQR	*Jewish Quarterly Review*
JRS	*Journal of Roman Studies*
JSJ	*Journal for the Study of Judaism in the Persian, Hellenistic and Roman Period*
JSNT	*Journal for the Study of the New Testament*
JSNTSup	*Journal for the Study of the New Testament*, Supplement Series
JSOT	*Journal for the Study of the Old Testament*
JSOTSup	*Journal for the Study of the Old Testament*, Supplement Series
JSPSup	*Journal for the Study of the Pseudepigrapha*, Supplement Series
JSS	*Journal of Semitic Studies*
JTS	*Journal of Theological Studies*
KAR	E. Ebeling (ed.), *Keilschrifttexte aus Assur religiösen Inhalts* (Leipzig: J.C. Hinrichs, 1919–23)
KAT	Kommentar zum Alten Testament
KHAT	Kurzer Hand-Kommentar zum Alten Testament
KTU	M. Dietrich, O. Loretz, J. Sanmartín, *The Cuneiform Alphabetic Texts from Ugarit, Ras Ibn Hani and Other Places (KTU: Second Enlarged Edition)* (Münster: Ugarit-Verlag, 1995). 2nd edn of M. Dietrich, O. Loretz, J. Sanmartín, *Die keilalphabetischen Texte aus Ugarit* (Neukirchen–Vluyn: Neukirchener Verlag, 1976)
LCL	Loeb Classical Library
LSCG	*Lois sacrées de cités grecques*
LSS	*Lois sacrées supplément*
LXX	Septuagint
ML	R. Meiggs and D.M. Lewis, *A Selection of Greek Historical Inscriptions to the End of the Fifth Century B.C.* (Oxford: Oxford University Press, 2nd edn, 1988)
MT	Masoretic Text
NCB	New Century Bible
NEB	*New English Bible*
NF	Neue Folge
NICOT	New International Commentary on the Old Testament
NIDOTTE	Willem A. VanGemeren (ed.), *New International Dictionary of Old Testament Theology and Exegesis* (5 vols.; Grand Rapids: Zondervan, 1997)
NJB	*New Jerusalem Bible*
NRSV	New Revised Standard Version
NS	New Series

NTS	*New Testament Studies*
OBO	Orbis biblicus et orientalis
OED	*The Oxford English Dictionary*
OLP	*Orientalia lovaniensia periodica*
OLZ	*Orientalistische Literaturzeitung*
Or	*Orientalia*
OTG	Old Testament Guides
OTL	Old Testament Library
OTM	Old Testament Message
OTP	James Charlesworth (ed.), *Old Testament Pseudepigrapha*
OTS	*Oudtestamentische Studiën*
PEFQS	*Palestine Exploration Fund, Quarterly Statement*
PEQ	*Palestine Exploration Quarterly*
PIBA	*Proceedings of the Irish Biblical Association*
PNTC	Pelican New Testament Commentaries
QD	Quaestiones disputatae
RB	*Revue biblique*
REB	Revised English Bible
REJ	*Revue des études juives*
RevQ	*Revue de Qumran*
RGG^2	H. Gunkel, L. Zscharnach et al. (eds.), *Die Religion in Geschichte und Gegenwart* (5 vols.; Tübingen: J.C.B. Mohr [Paul Siebeck], 2nd edn, 1927–31)
RHR	*Revue de l'histoire des religions*
RSV	Revised Standard Version
RTU	N. Wyatt, *Religious Texts from Ugarit* (Sheffield: Sheffield Academic Press, 1998)
Sam. Pent.	Samaritan Pentateuch
SAOC	Studies in Ancient Oriental Civilization
SB	Sources bibliques
SBAB	Stuttgarter biblische Aufsatzbände
SBL	Society of Biblical Literature
SBLDS	SBL Dissertation Series
SBLMS	SBL Monograph Series
SBLSCS	SBL Septuagint and Cognate Studies
SBS	Stuttgarter Bibelstudien
SBT	Studies in Biblical Theology
SCM	Student Christian Movement
SCSS	Septuagint and Cognate Studies Series
SEL	*Studi epigrafici e linguistici*
Sem	*Semitica*
SHCANE	Studies in the History and Culture of the Ancient Near East
SJLA	Studies in Judaism in Late Antiquity
SJOT	*Scandinavian Journal of the Old Testament*
SJT	*Scottish Journal of Theology*

SNTSMS	Society for New Testament Studies Monograph Series
SOTSMS	Society for Old Testament Study Monograph Series
SPCK	Society for Promoting Christian Knowledge
SR	*Studies in Religion/Sciences religieuses*
ST	*Studia theologica*
STDJ	Studies on the Texts of the Desert of Judah
SVTP	Studia in Veteris Testamenti pseudepigrapha
TA	*Tel Aviv*
TBü	Theologische Bücherei
TDNT	Gerhard Kittel and Gerhard Friedrich (eds.), *Theological Dictionary of the New Testament* (trans. Geoffrey W. Bromiley; 10 vols.; Grand Rapids: Eerdmans, 1964–)
TDOT	G.J. Botterweck and H. Ringgren (eds.), *Theological Dictionary of the Old Testament*
TGUOS	*Transactions of the Glasgow University Oriental Society*
THAT	Ernst Jenni and Claus Westermann (eds.), *Theologisches Handwörterbuch zum Alten Testament* (Munich: Chr. Kaiser, 1971–76)
ThWAT	G.J. Botterweck and H. Ringgren (eds.), *Theologisches Wörterbuch zum Alten Testament* (Stuttgart: W. Kohlhammer, 1970–)
ThWNT	G. Kittel and G. Friedrich (eds.), *Theologisches Wörterbuch zum Neuen Testament* (10 vols.; Stuttgart: W. Kohlhammer, 1932–74)
TLOT	E. Jenni and C. Westermann (eds.), *Theological Lexicon of the Old Testament* (2 vols.; trans. M.E. Biddle; Peabody, MA: Hendrickson, 1997)
TOTC	Tyndale Old Testament Commentaries
TS	*Theological Studies*
TU	Texte und Untersuchungen zur Geschichte der altchristlichen Literatur
TZ	*Theologische Zeitschrift*
UCOP	University of Cambridge Oriental Publications
UF	*Ugarit-Forschungen*
VT	*Vetus Testamentum*
VTSup	*Vetus Testamentum*, Supplements
WBC	Word Biblical Commentary
WMANT	Wissenschaftliche Monographien zum Alten und Neuen Testament
WO	*Die Welt des Orients*
WUNT	Wissenschaftliche Untersuchungen zum Neuen Testament
ZABR	*Zeitschrift für Altorientalische und Biblische Rechtsgeschichte*
ZAH	*Zeitschrift für Althebraistik*
ZAW	*Zeitschrift für die alttestamentliche Wissenschaft*
ZDPV	*Zeitschrift des deutschen Palästina-Vereins*
ZNW	*Zeitschrift für die neutestamentliche Wissenschaft*
ZTK	*Zeitschrift für Theologie und Kirche*

Part I

Temples and High Places in Israel and the Canaanite World

Like Deities, Like Temples (Like People)

Mark S. Smith

This investigation addresses literary temples and not actual temples. My interest in literary temples involves deities more broadly, especially in the Late Bronze Age texts discovered at Ugarit. One Ugaritic text cited many times in the following discussion is the Baal Cycle (*KTU* 1.1–1.6), which narrates three episodes about the divine king, Baal: his victory over the cosmic waters personified (Yam); the building of the god's (temple) palace on his mountain; and his struggle against his enemy, Death personified (Mot). I am not interested in focusing simply on Baal, however. Instead, I wish to inquire into the meanings of temples and the relation of those meanings to divinities and divinity in general. The scope of this investigation may be broadened by recourse to the Bible[1] (especially Gen. 2–4; Exod. 24.10; 1 Kgs 5–8; Ezek. 28; Ps. 29 and the Song of Songs) as well as other West Semitic texts (for example, Lucian of Samosata's *De Dea Syria* and Philo of Byblos's *Phoenician History*). From this West Semitic literature I would like to try to abstract some sense of *how* deities and their characteristics are expressed or mediated through temples as well as the various *means* of how the ancients posited their relationships to deities *via* temples. Four such means are evident: intersection, recapitulation, participation, and analogy (or homology). The four means of positing relationships are not separate from one another; at times it is difficult to ascertain whether a given predication is to be assigned to only one of these four categories. Moreover, these terms do not belong to the indigenous vocabulary of Levantine cultures, and therefore represent an abstraction. Nonetheless, such a classification may serve as a useful heuristic exercise. Following the discussion of these four categories illustrated with examples, the closing remarks briefly address the *content* shared by deities. Such an effort at synthesis is necessarily built on many observations (some very well known) made by numerous scholars. It is my hope that by situating these points in a larger framework, their significance will become clearer.

1. *Intersection: Life, Fertility, Revelation and Presence*

The relationship between the divine and the human most widely embodied in ancient Levantine texts is intersection. At its core, temples serve as points of

1. I would like to mention a general methodological consideration—the occasional insistence on distinguishing some strain of biblical tradition from the rest of the ancient Near East (e.g. Mendenhall 1985).

intersection between divine presence (theophany) and human presence (pilgrimage). At the core of intersection is ritual, which provides the context for divine presence with blessing from the divine side and human presence of priests and pilgrims with their offerings from the human side. Such ritual activity in biblical texts has been the subject of many important studies reaching an apex in the commentaries on Leviticus and Numbers in the 1990s, produced by B.A. Levine, J. Milgrom and others.[2] Similarly, Levine, sometimes in conjunction with Jean-Michel de Tarragon, has helped to generate interest in Ugaritic ritual, the study of which has reached a new level with D. Pardee's magnificent edition of the ritual texts discovered at Ras Shamra (2000).[3] Association of a deity with a ritual site, often with implications of intersection, is perhaps best known by a series of roots expressing various aspects of property and/or architecture: foundation (**ysd*), establishment (**kwn* in the D-stem) and choice (**bḥr*); building (**bny*) and raising (**rwm* in the D-stem); dwelling (**yṯb*) and tenting (**škn*); agriculture (**nṭ'*); and, finally, attachment (* *'hb*). These terms predicate intersection by relating the deity to temple structures.

Instead of focusing on divine intersection at the ritual sites or the roots used to denote such divine activity, I would like to look into what such activity was thought to yield from the deity. Perhaps foremost, intersection issues in expressions of divine fertility and life. The Baal Cycle temple narrative uses an architectural detail in order to express the god's fertility and life, specifically the image of the cosmic window in the clouds that allows Baal to project his holy voice and to provide the water that will fructify the earth. Before Baal's palace is built, Athirat expresses hope for its construction, with the attendant natural effects associated with the storm god, Baal (*KTU* 1.4 V 6-9):

> So now may Baal fructify (*'dn*) with his rain (*mṭrh*),
> May he enrich (*y'dn*) richly (*'dn*) with watering (*ṯrt*[!]) in a downpour (*glṯ*)
> May he give voice (*ql*) in the clouds,
> May he flash (*šrh*) to the earth lightning-bolts (*brqm*).[4]

C. Virolleaud and T.H. Gaster viewed *'dn* as the abundance provided by Baal's rain, citing Ps. 36.9 (ET 8; Virolleaud 1932: 133, 141):[5] 'They fill up on the rich (fare) of Your house, and You give them drink with the stream of your abundant

2. For listings, see the bibliographies in Levine 1993 and Milgrom 1991.
3. See also his English edition Pardee 2002.
4. For a preliminary discussion, see Smith 1994: 53, 66.
5. T.H. Gaster (1933: 119 n. 1) likewise argued for this proposal based on South Semitic cognates (see Arab *ġadan*, 'dainties' and Early South Arabian * *'dn*, 'well-being', cited in Biella 1982: 354, and biblical Hebrew *'dn*, as in Ps. 36.9, ET 8). The etymological issue with the Arabic cognates with *ghain* rather than *'ayin* are unexpected given the Ugaritic usage. McCarter points to the XII-stem of Arabic **ġdn* applied to luxuriant hair, suggesting a rather restricted usage and attestation; perhaps its connection with the West Semitic * *'dn* is to be suspected. Other scholars take *'dn* as 'time, season' based on Akkadian adanu/adannu and Aramaic *'iddana* ('time') as well as Arabic *'addana* ('to fix the time of public distribution'). See Gordon 1965: 19.1823; Cross 1973: 149; Caquot, Sznycer and Herdner 1974: 207-208; Gibson 1978: 60. For further discussion of the cognates, see entry *'addana* in Leslau 1987: 56. This is not to preclude that Ugaritic * *'dn* elsewhere may refer to 'time'; cf. *KTU* 1.12 II 52-53.

(things) (*naḥal ʿᵃdāneykā*)'. The name of Eden (*ʿdn*) in Gen. 2.15 is also interpreted along these lines (BDB: 727; Greenfield 1984; Millard 1984: 103-106). The Akkadian–Aramaic Tell Fekheriyeh bilingual inscription evidently confirms this view (Greenfield 1984).[6] The opening list of titles and common attributes in the Akkadian text calls the storm god Hadad (a cognomen of Baal in the Ugaritic texts) *mutaḫḫidu kibrati*, the one 'who makes the whole world luxuriant', paralleled in the Aramaic by *mʿdn mt kln* the one 'who makes all lands luxuriant'. This passage applies *ʿdn*, 'to make luxuriant, abundant, to fructify' to the West Semitic storm god, as in the Baal Cycle: Baal-Hadad is said to luxuriate with the rain, and through these rains, the storm god provides, as it were, 'Eden' or 'abundance, fertility', a notion that is reinforced later in the Baal Cycle. El knows that 'the heavens rain oil, And the wadis [*nḫlm*] run with honey' (*KTU* 1.6 III 12-13); compare the use of *naḥal* in the 'stream of your abundant (things)' (*naḥal ʿᵃdāneykā*) in Ps. 36.9 (ET 8).

The storm god's temple is the focal point for the delivery of his rains. The ancient Middle Eastern parallelism between the heavenly palace of the storm god and his earthly temple is expressed in part by the vocabulary that they share; house (*bt*) and palace (*hkl*[7]) apply to both cosmic palace and terrestrial temple. The earthly temple provides the location to express cultic devotion to the storm god, while the heavenly palace serves as the storm god's home. One form of intersection between the two is expressed by the palace's window in the clouds, from which the storm god is conceived as manifesting his power in lightning and thunder and his blessing in the rains. Accordingly, Baal's window in his house, when complete, is called a 'break in the clouds' (*bdqt ʿrpt*, *KTU* 1.4 VII 19, 28). His palace is thought to be located in the clouds that cover the top of his mountain, Mt Ṣapan (cf. biblical *ṣāpôn* in Ps. 48.3, ET 2). Similarly, 2 Kgs 7.2, 19 note how 'Yahweh makes windows in the heavens' (*yahweh ʿōśeh ʾᵃrubbôt baššāmayim*). Solomon is promised a divine blessing of rain when he properly prays at the Temple (1 Kgs 8.35-36). Malachi 3.10 correlates the exchange of divinely given rains from the heavenly window and the humanly provided tithe to the temple (cf. Deut. 28.12); see also *ʾᵃrubbôt mimmārôm* in Isa. 24.18. The mythology of the cosmic window perdures, perhaps in coalesced form, with the image of the floodgates of Gen. 7.11 and 8.2 (Weinfeld 1977–78). The rains are also experienced in the context of the temple, dramatized in Psalm 29 as Yahweh's easterly procession. This storm issues in the community's recognition of the theophany indicated by *kābôd* ('effulgence', usually rendered 'glory'[8]) in v. 9.

Connected in the Baal Cycle with the fertility of the divine palace is knowledge of this reality. The divine sanctuary as the point of intersection for revelation is a biblical theme: 'For instruction shall come forth from Zion' (*kî miṣṣîyôn tēṣēʾ tôrâ*, Isa. 2.3; cf. divine instruction in Pss. 50 and 81). Yet, the Bible holds no

6. See also Greenfield and Shaffer 1983.

7. See also BH *hêkal*, Syriac *haykla* and Akkadian *ekallu* separately deriving from Sumerian E.GAL, 'big house'.

8. For *ûbᵉhêkālô kullô ʾōmēr kābôd* in Ps. 29.9c, understood to mean 'and in his temple, all of it, effulgence is visible', see Smith 2001a: 160-61.

monopoly on the revelation of divine knowledge from the temple site. Indeed, divine revelation lies at the heart of temple narrative, and in the case of the Baal Cycle, the message of divine revelation (*KTU* 1.3 III 20-31) proceeds from 'the midst of my mountain, Divine Ṣapan (*'il ṣpn*). On the holy (*qdš*) mount of my heritage (*nḥlty*), On the beautiful (*n'm*) hill of my might (*tl'iyt*)'. This turning point in the Baal Cycle reveals the storm god's impending revelation to take place at the mountain site of his temple-palace. The nouns here predicated of Baal's mountain will be discussed later.

2. *Recapitulation: Divine Narrative*

Temple architecture embodies and conveys various divine narratives, and in this way, temples may recapitulate the understanding of deities. In the case of the Jerusalem Temple, E.M. Bloch-Smith[9] has cogently suggested how the cultic accoutrements of the Jerusalem Temple (1 Kgs 6–8) communicate the narrative of Yahweh's victory over the sea, his acceptance of the people's offerings, the accession (or re-accession) to the divine throne within the divine house and the blessing of the people (Bloch-Smith 1994). The courtyard symbols perhaps conveyed Yahweh's triumphant enthronement. Upon defeating the chaotic forces of nature, as represented by 'the molten sea', the god of the Israelites accepted the sacrificial offerings and entered the Temple bestowing blessings on the king and the people, as recorded on the pillars flanking the Temple entrance (named Jachin and Boaz), plausibly to be construed as a single sentence, specifically a blessing formula. The reading of the formula **yākîn bᵉ'ōz*, 'May he [Yahweh] establish [the temple/king/people] in strength', compares well with Ps. 29.11a: *yahweh 'ōz lᵉ'ammô yittēn*, 'May Yahweh give strength to his people'. This narrative of the god's march and resumption of his throne appears in texts such as Psalm 29, and it lies at the heart of the Baal Cycle: victory followed by temple building, offering of food and drink to the divine family, and fertility to the earth with the rains. Like Baal's throne in his heavenly palace on Mt Ṣapan, Yahweh was perceived as assuming his superhuman sized throne in his palace on his mountain, Jerusalem (to be discussed in section 4 below).

Another form of recapitulation, marked by the presence of objects or cultic actions, would suggest that the Jerusalem Temple expressed the model of the divine king ruling over the subjects, both divine and human. Many studies have pointed out the royal terms of the Temple as the palace of the divine king who receives tribute (*minḥâ*) and other sacrificial tokens modelled on royal motifs (e.g. the *šᵉlāmîm* offering).[10] Furthermore, the Temple is the home of the god; there is no place like home, and home implies family. This is no less true for deities as it is for humans. Baal's complaint that he lacks a house mentions that not only he, but also his household, needs a house. Temples may convey a model of divine households generally headed by a leading male, not just in the Ugaritic

9. See also her contribution in Smith 1997: 84-86.

10. On the secular background of these two terms, see Levine 1974: 16-17, 27-35. See also Anderson 1987: 27-34 and Smith 1997: 124-25.

texts, but also for Israel. The tour of Ezekiel 8–10 may suggest such a model of divinity for the temple. The presence of the asherah in the Temple, as supposed by many scholars, would point to the family model of divinity; in Yahweh's house there were many rooms, including room for his alleged consort, Asherah (symbolized by the asherah; see below). Such a divine home would convey the well-being desired by the family household, in short, prosperity, or in religious terms, blessing and fertility. Concerns over blessing and fertility would continue to be expressed in the Second Temple, as shown in Haggai 1 and Malachi 3. Yet, the picture of home changed. With the asherah and other signals of other deities removed, the Second Temple perhaps expressed the viewpoint of its priestly groups, arguably by realigning various sorts of monisms into expressions of oneness:[11] in short, one deity, one Temple, one people, one priesthood, one prophet, one teaching.

An aesthetic sensibility of the Jerusalem Temple was expressed in the literary presentation of the garden of Eden. The Jerusalem Temple evokes not only a statement of power, but also one of Edenic beauty, as noted by Bloch-Smith (1994: 27): 'Solomon's choice of palmette and cherubim motifs to adorn the walls and doors conveyed to Temple visitors that the Temple proper recreated or incorporated the garden of Eden, Yahweh's terrestrial residence'.

In addition to these explicit markers of garden imagery in the Temple, Bloch-Smith observes further (Bloch-Smith 1994: 27): 'The molten sea perhaps symbolized secondarily the primordial waters issuing forth from Eden (Genesis 3.10), and the twin pillars modeled the trees (of life and knowledge) planted in the garden'. Bloch-Smith's observations about the Jerusalem Temple as the divine garden known also from Genesis 2–3 stand in a long line of scholarship.[12] The Jerusalem Temple embodies several mythological notions of divine garden or 'paradise' known from Genesis 2–3 and Ezekiel 28: the divine mountain, home of the patron divine king, source of cosmic fertility and abundance, the basic meaning of the biblical word *'dn*. Jerusalemite texts likewise evoke the Eden theme of fertility and abundance, by using the same root, as expressed in Ps. 36.9 (ET 8; noted above): 'They feast on the rich fare [lit. "oil"] of your house, and from the wadi of your abundant provisions (*'ᵃdāneykā*) you give them drink'.[13]

Yet such themes of abundance found in the Baal Cycle and Genesis 2–3 are not specific to Baal's house, but may be located against a broader backdrop of West Semitic divine abodes, including that of El, a point noted by H.N. Wallace (1985: 28-29). Other scholars, notably T. Stordalen (2000) and L.E. Stager (1999), have highlighted the role of the garden imagery in divergent ways that

11. For these conceptual 'monisms' informing Ugaritic polytheism, see Smith 2001b: 41-66.

12. A sampling of this massive literature includes (by year): Begrich 1932; Widengren 1951; Clifford 1972; Bogaert 1983; Wallace 1985; Smith 1987b: 40-47; Batto 1991; Morris and Sawyer 1992; Wright 1996; Stager 1999; Callendar Jr 2000; Stordalen 2000; McCarter 2001. See also Andrae 1952.

13. For the image of the wadi running with such fertility, compare El's vision of the cosmic fertility in *KTU* 1.6 III 6-7//12-13: 'The heavens rain oil, the wadis run with honey'. For the translation of *'ᵃdāneykā* as 'abundant provisions', and for the temple and its gardens as a source of abundant provisions, I am indebted to a talk by McCarter (2001, cited gratefully with permission).

cast further light on Genesis 2–3. Stordalen highlights the imagery of the temple *qua* garden in both the Baal Cycle and the Jerusalem Temple, while Stager argues for the goddess's tree(s) as a seminal feature of the garden imagery. Finally, S.M. Olyan has insightfully observed that *ḥawwâ* (Eve) may echo a title of the goddess; for this point, Olyan (1988: 71 n. 4) cites *rbt ḥwt 'lt* attested in *KAI* 89.1. Putting together these cultural clues, one might see behind Genesis 2–4 not simply an attestation of the garden similar to or echoing that of El; it may involve either echoing of or a polemic against the Jerusalem Temple as the garden-home of the divine couple to which the king has access, perhaps after his 'birth' (i.e. his coronation, for example in Ps. 2.7).[14] If this background were correct, several features would gain in understanding: the tree of knowledge echoes the asherah; the snake hints at the goddess's emblem animal; the name of Eve (*ḥawwâ*) may echo a title of the goddess; and the choice of verb in Eve's statement in Gen. 4.1 (*qānîtî 'îš 'et-yhwh*) might be explained by recourse to Asherah's title, *qnyt 'ilm* (or perhaps, the title of her consort El, **qny 'rṣ*, which is not only in Late Bronze Age material, but also known in biblical tradition, attached to the founding myth of Jerusalem in Gen. 14) (see Miller 1980). On this reading, Gen. 4.1 might have presupposed and perhaps even polemicized against the following rendering of an older royal garden myth, with implicit cultural understandings added:

> And the male [i.e. the god El] knew [in 'sacred marriage'] Hawwat [the goddess], and she bore and she conceived…and she said: 'I have created (**qny*) a man [i.e. the newly crowned human king] with DN [here said to be Yahweh, but formerly, El, secondarily identified as Yahweh].

All of this is terribly hypothetical and badly in need of real evidence, but such details in the narrative call for the unpacking of cultural understandings that the text's audience may have taken for granted.

However such details are to be understood, the traditions behind the Eden thematic complex can be traced to the late third millennium. In an important study, P. Kyle McCarter (2001) has suggested that the Eden theme associated with a sanctuary tradition in the Lebanon and Anti-Lebanon ranges was a particularly old West Semitic tradition,[15] reflected in native West Semitic sources such as the Ugaritic Baal Cycle and the Bible, but also in Mesopotamian and Egyptian royal narratives concerning the acquisitions of cedars. To turn first to Mesopotamia, the wealth of the mountains is a traditional literary image with a long history, noted nicely by N. Waldman (1981) and V.A. Hurowitz (1992: 171-223). McCarter (2001) believes that behind these reports stands an old local Levantine sanctuary tradition, or to use his phrase, 'a cultic reality'. This tradition is reflected also in the Old Babylonian version of the Gilgamesh story, which locates the mount of assembly in the cedar forest, specifically Lebanon. In an old West Semitic tradition now embedded in Mesopotamian lore, the cedar mountain is called 'the

14. See also Wyatt 1986.
15. Cf. already Lipiński 1971.

abode of the gods',[16] as well as 'the secret dwelling of the *Anunnaki*'.[17] The second of the two passages further specifies the location in Saria (biblical Sirion) and Lebanon.

This constellation of temple themes is illustrated also by the Ugaritic Baal Cycle.[18] The palace narrative, especially in *KTU* 1.4, contains many of the temple themes identified in Genesis 2–3, Ezekiel 28 and many psalms. The wood for Baal's palace also is obtained through a journey for cedars in Lebanon and brought to Baal's mountain where the palace is to be constructed (*KTU* 1.4 VI 16-21). Precious metal and stone are likewise to come from a distance, from mountains (*KTU* 1.4 V 12-18). Like the divine abode mentioned in the critique of Tyre in Ezekiel 28 (cf. Gen. 2.11-12), Baal's heavenly palace consists of gold and precious stone (specifically, lapis lazuli, the stone associated with the heavenly palace in Exod. 24.9-11) (see Smith 1987a). In sum, the Baal Cycle embodies traditional themes of the temple as royal garden-sanctuary. Above it is noted how the name of Eden expresses the notion of abundance or fertility associated with both the Baal palace and the Jerusalem Temple.

For a Phoenician attestation of this tradition, McCarter points to the critique of Tyre in Ezekiel 28, which assumes this local tradition of the divine garden located on the god's mountain graced with cedar, gold and precious metal. To McCarter's observations concerning Tyre, it may be added that like their Mesopotamian and Egyptian counterparts, Phoenician kings sent missions to the Lebanon for cedar (citing Menander, Josephus, *Ant.* 8.145; cf. *Apion* 1.118).[19] Philo of Byblos also attests to the Phoenician tradition of the northern mountains as the home of the sanctuary. He comments on the northern mountains (in Eusebius, *Praeparatio Evangelica* 1.1.9), Mt Casios (= Mt Ṣapan), the Lebanon, the Anti-Lebanon and Mt Brathy: 'From these...were born Samemroumos, who is also called Hypersouranois'.[20] The first term has long been understood as Phoenician **šamim ramim*, 'high heavens' (Hypersouranios appearing to be a Greek translation). Philo then informs readers that Hypersouranios settled Tyre. Samemroumos has long been connected with *rmm šmm* mentioned in a Sidonian inscription (*KAI* 15),[21] which Moshe Weinfeld (1991: 99-103, esp. 100) understands as a reference to a temple. Weinfeld senses a sanctuary sensibility in 'Samemroumos' (cf. Hebrew equivalent *rāmîm* in the description of the Jerusalem Temple in Ps. 78.69, so Weinfeld 1991: 99-103, esp. 100 n. 12).[22] In sum, Phoenician temple

16. Tablet V, (i), l. 6; *ANET*, 82.

17. The so-called Bauer fragment; Tablet V, C, reverse, l. 20; *ANET*, 504. For an iconographic representation of the cedars in the conflict of Gilgamesh and Enkidu vs. Huwawa, see Lambert 1994: 55 fig. 9. For a brief discussion in the site's relation to West Semitic tradition, see Smith 1994: 112.

18. For these themes in both the Jerusalem Temple and the temple narrative of the Baal Cycle, see Bloch-Smith 1994: 19-23.

19. Thackeray and Marcus 1934: 648-49. For *Apion* see Thackeray 1926: 210-11.

20. For the text and translation of these lines see Attridge and Oden 1981: 42, 43. For text and translation of Philo of Byblos throughout this paper, see Attridge and Oden 1981.

21. Eissfeldt, 'Schamemrumim', pp. 123-26, cited in Attridge and Oden 1981: 82 n. 56.

22. Weinfeld notes also the name of the queen Semiramis, identified with Sammuramat, the queen mother of Adad-nirari III (810-782), attested for example in Lucian of Samosata's *De Dea Syria* 14

traditions appropriated the old notion of the sanctuary located in the northern mountains. The site of Jerusalem in turn inherited this long tradition, and here McCarter notes 'the House of the Forest of the Lebanon' in 1 Kgs 7.2. Following a long line of scholarship, McCarter (2001) notes that Ps. 48.3 (ET 2) represents a Jerusalemite appropriation of this constellation of themes in identifying the city as 'the recesses of Ṣapon' (*yark*^{e}*tê ṣāpôn*); the latter word being arguably the same as the name of Baal's mountain. Whether one regards the word more generically in its biblical meaning 'north' or the name Ṣapon itself (many prefer the second alternative), McCarter (2001) observes that the allusion in Ps. 48.3 (ET 2) evokes an older West Semitic tradition of the special divine abode located in the northern mountains of Lebanon. It is not difficult to imagine that the transference of the northern traditions to Jerusalem was mediated by Tyrian influence deriving from the relationship between Hiram (Ahiram) and Solomon (1 Kgs 5.26, ET 12; 9.11), which gave the latter's workers access to wood in the Lebanon (1 Kgs 5.27-29, ET 13-15) and brought Phoenician craftsmanship for the construction of the Jerusalem Temple (1 Kgs 5.32, ET 18).

In addition to the witness to such old northern traditions for Jerusalem, the Bible evidently preserved alternative traditions of the northern sanctuary. The storm theophany in Psalm 29 progresses over the 'waters' (the Mediterranean) and across the Lebanon and Sirion mountain ranges (with the cedars mentioned in v. 5) and culminates with the experience of this divine 'effulgence' or 'glory' (*kābôd* in v. 9). From the northern geographical references, it is evident that this psalm provides an attestation of the northern temple site independent of Jerusalemite tradition. Similarly, I wonder if Song 4.8-16 evokes the northern mountains in its stirring invitation for the bride to come from Lebanon, Amana, Senir and Hermon. The description of the bride accordingly compares her to the garden, with fragrant woods.[23] Song of Songs 7 also evokes the distant north. Is this passage drawing on the old sanctuary tradition of the northern mountains? The Song of Songs as a whole might be seen as evoking the northern sanctuary reflected in the description of the bride. Accordingly, the bride figured in northern terms 'becomes' the Shulammite, a feminine term perhaps designed to play on Solomon's own name as well as the name of Jerusalem (issuing in a marriage of the north and the south, expressive of the ideal of the united monarchy?).

3. *Participation: Power, Eternity and Holiness*

Just as the king may participate in the power of the god, so too the sanctuary site participates in the power of the deity. (Here I am thinking of the mediaeval metaphysical concept of ontological participation, but in ancient Near Eastern

and 39; for text and translation, see Attridge and Oden 1976: 20-21, 48-49. According to the first passage, Semiramis' mother is known as Derketo. Both names are reminiscent of Anat's titles in *KTU* 1.108.6-7, *b'lt drkt b'lt šmm rmm* (cf. reading *rḫpt* [bšm] *rm* <*m*>, so *KTU* 1.108.9-10).

23. See the discussion of geographical allusions by Pope 1977: 474-500; see also the observations of Wright 1996: 320. Pope saw a Syrian goddess behind such allusions (1977: 477), a possibility to consider if the northern sanctuary tradition was fully known or transmitted, at least in its essentials.

terms, participation does not involve 'Being' and 'beings', but power.) Baal's mountain is the site of 'victory' (*tl'iyt*) according to *KTU* 1.13 III 31 and 1.10 III 31. Similarly, the deity's strength is manifest in the tradition of Jerusalem's strength (Ps. 46). Its titles include terms of power and security, 'refuge and stronghold' (*maḥᵃseh wā'ōz*, Ps. 46.2, ET 1) and 'haven' (*miśgāb*, Pss. 46.8, ET 7; 48.4, ET 3). Great size is also an element of this discourse of strength (to be discussed in section 4 below). Given the widespread nature of this discourse of power in biblical texts, this feature might be regarded as one of the more dominant shared predications made between deities and their temple-mountains. Just as the deity guarantees the security of their mountain, the mountain manifests the deity's power. To walk about the city and to see its ramparts is to have a sign of the god's strength (Ps. 48.13-15, ET 12-14). (A full listing of pertinent texts is beyond the scope of this discussion.) One might add that the temple-city is to be established by the deity also *'ad-'ôlām* ('forever', Ps. 48.9, ET 8), partaking of the deity's own eternity.

A further expression of power involves holiness. Temples are generally regarded as holy, consistent with the holiness of the deities. They themselves are marked for holiness, reflected by their general designation as 'holy ones' (*bn qdš*),[24] literally 'sons of holiness' or possibly 'sons of the Holy One'[25] (*KTU* 1.2 I 20-21, 38; 1.17 I 3, 8, 10-11, 13, 22; cf. 1.2 III 19-20; cf. *KAI* 4.4-5 referring to the deities as the 'holy ones', *qdšm*. Israelite texts also mention the Holy Ones as a divine body or assembly led by Yahweh, their king. Psalm 89.6-8 (ET 5-7) is often cited in this regard, with its reference to 'the assembly of the Holy Ones' (*qᵉdōšîm*). Zechariah 14.5 assumes a similar view: 'And Yahweh my God will come, with all Holy Ones (*qᵉdōšîm*) with You'.[26]

In the West Semitic world, holiness was a general characteristic adhering also to material *realia* and religious processes in shrines, including theophanies. By definition, divinity is observable in some sense in these places. They are marked and demarcated for holiness, and divinity is perceived to partake fully of holiness. In turn, the presence of divinity imparts holiness to those places. By extension not only deities' sanctuaries, but also their dwellings on mountains partake of holiness. So Baal's mountain, Mt Ṣapan, is called 'holy' (*KTU* 1.3 III 30; 1.16 I 7) as well as 'divine' (*KTU* 1.3 III 29). So, too, Yahweh's dwelling-place is called 'holy mountain' (*har-qodšô*, Ps. 48.2, ET 1) and 'the holy dwelling place of the Most High' (*qᵉdōš miškᵉnê 'elyôn*; Ps. 46.5, ET 4). Temples as well as their mythic expressions as sacred garden participate in the deity's holiness.[27]

In a sense, to call deities 'holy ones' may seem to constitute a sort of tautology, but further study of the words for 'holy' and 'holiness' helps to turn up the underlying root metaphor. As discussed by K. van der Toorn, one of the main

24. See Smith 2002b: 144, and the secondary literature cited there.

25. In the second translation *qdš* might be regarded as the title of a specific deity (perhaps El, but Athirat is the usually cited possibility here), but this view is debated. For discussion, see Smith 1994: 294-95; Merlo 1997: esp. p. 50.

26. For the divine retinue, see Smith 2002b: 122-23 n. 64.

27. As noted by Wright 1996: 305-29.

Akkadian terms for 'holy', namely *ellu*, denotes not only holiness, but also cleanliness.[28] Here cleanliness in its profane sense is not simply the absence of dirt, but also brilliance and luminosity (what in older American English is suggested by the phrase 'sparkling clean'). So the brickwork of Baal's palace on his mountain, consisting of gold and silver and even lapis lazuli, is called *ṭhrm* (*KTU* 1.4 V 19), referring to its brilliance and luminosity. Similarly, the brickwork of the divine palace on the holy mountain is called *ṭhr* (Exod. 24.10): *wayyir'û 'ēt '^{e}lōhê yiśrā'ēl w^{e}taḥat raglāyw k^{e}ma '^{a}śēh libnat hassappîr ûk^{e} 'eṣem haššāmayim lāṭōhar*, 'and they saw the god of Israel, and beneath his feet was like sapphire brick-work, and like the very heaven with respect to brilliance'.[29] The brilliance of the stonework is a motif of the heavenly temple running at least from the Baal Cycle to the book of Revelation. After Rev. 21.1-4 introduces three great themes known from the Baal Cycle (the victories over Sea and Death, and the appearance of the heavenly palace, here understood as the heavenly Jerusalem), the chapter continues with its description of this heavenly palace in v. 11 (NAB): 'Its radiance was like that of precious stone, like jasper, clear as crystal' (Smith 1994: xxvii, 355-56; 1987a). To be cultically holy (or pure) is based analogically on the profane notion of cleanliness, both in its negative understanding as free of dirt and in its positive connotation of brilliance (van der Toorn 1985: 23). Both senses are germane to the human experience of deities: theophanies characteristically transpire in places regarded as clean from a cultic perspective, namely spaces ideally uncontaminated by human sin or impurity; and theophanies are often marked by the brilliance of the deity's presence.

Divine holiness and its associated numinous characteristic are well attested in the Bible and other ancient Near Eastern texts.[30] Divine holiness as experienced and expressed in cult is associated with shaking, whether of places of theophany (*KTU* 1.4 VII; Ps. 114) or people who experience it (*KTU* 1.4 VII; Isa. 6.4). The divine 'holy voice', whether belonging to Yahweh or Baal, signals a theophany, which may wreak destruction (Ps. 29) or revelation (as in Num. 7.89); it induces flight and fear on the part of the god's enemies (*KTU* 1.4 VII 29). Similarly, sanctuaries can be regarded as awe-inspiring like the deities who own and inhabit them (Jacobsen 1976: 16). It has been common for students of ancient religion to understand this experience of the holy in terms of awe and fear. In the modern Western discussion of religion, this idea is customarily traced to the theologian Rudolf Otto, who characterized this confrontation with the divine as *mysterium tremendum et fascinosum*. The great Sumerologist Thorkild Jacobsen (1976: 3) followed Otto explicitly in stressing the 'wholly other' character of the numi-

28. These points are made in van der Toorn 1985: 28-29; 1989: 339-56. It is claimed that the Akkadian word related to the Hebrew words for 'holy' and 'holiness' (**qdš*) means 'to be clean' (so *AHw* II, 891a). However, such usage is rarely, if ever, attested, according to van der Toorn 1985: 28. For clarifications of the Mesopotamian evidence, see Geller 1990.

29. For discussion of both this Ugaritic passage and Exod. 24.10, see Smith 1985: 321-22. See also Smith 1987b.

30. To be sure, Otto's *mysterium tremendum et fascinosum* has been influential in the analysis of other religions. For only one example, see Zaehner 1966: 86.

nous.[31] By the same token, such a view requires some comment. Because such experience is mediated by human experience and language, it is not by definition entirely 'Wholly Other'. It may be recognizable in natural effects of the rainstorm or dream experience at night. In these experiences, the completely 'other' partakes of the here and now. Moreover, as the opening parts of this section indicate, divinity throughout the ancient Middle East is also experienced personally, and not entirely as 'other'. Indeed, anthropomorphism is a hallmark of the classic deities of the pantheon as opposed to divine monsters in many Mesopotamian and Syro-Palestinian myths of primordial conflict (Wiggerman 1992: 151-54; Smith 2001b: 27-40). The view of ancient Middle Eastern religion (and conesquently divinity) fostered by Otto's notion of *mysterium* captures one side of the perception of the divine. The *mysterium* was simultaneously 'other' and not 'other', as recently underscored by K. van der Toorn (1985), and it is this combination which helps make it, to repeat Otto's expression, *tremendum et fascinosum* (see Merkur 1996).

The 'this-worldly' quality of holiness is not merely a theoretical matter. To come full circle to a point raised at the beginning of this section, deities and their holiness are not only served by their servants, priests and kings; deities also serve priests and kings, and by definition, the public sacred spaces serve both as well. As the historian of religion S. Guthrie has emphasized, the category of holiness is also a delimitation and expression of the power of those who maintain such spaces.[32] Guthrie stresses that in Israel holiness attaches to the elite and the monarch, and the point may apply as well to Ugarit. He comments how the radiance of the deity became associated with the power of the king (Guthrie 1996: 135): 'Holiness here is ideology, and designed to serve a particular social system'. In his discussion of sacred order, another historian of religion W.E. Paden remarks in a related vein (1996: 15):

> Power and order are intertwined and mutually conditioning elements of religious world-building. Each is a premise of the other. The gods presuppose the very system that invests them with their status as gods, even though the world-order may itself be perceived as a creation of the gods.

Paden further comments (1996: 13): 'The rites for honoring a religious leader or a king and those for honoring a god are often hard to distinguish'. Paden sees rites honoring a human figure as honouring a divine one as well. It may be said that myths arguably achieve the opposite effect: in honouring a deity explicitly, they thereby honor a king or priesthood implicitly. Accordingly, it may be thought that holiness appeared to ritual participants as a top-down phenomenon from gods to kings and priests to people. In contrast, it may be argued that the practice underlying such presentations of holiness serves to focus the holiness of the whole people into their experience of the divine in temples, mediated by priests and sponsored by kings. In other words, the holiness of a place expressed relationships of power and status in the form of a bottom-up social investment

31. A similar view of the divinity as numinous has been forwarded by de Vito 1993: 256-57.

32. For the ideological use of 'holiness' of temples and other sacred spaces, see Guthrie 1996.

undergirding a praxis that was understood and marked as emanating from the top-down.

As many scholars have noted (see BDB: 871-74), holiness in ancient Israel developed a nuance in the notion of 'apartness'. The origins of this particular connotation are unclear, but they might be traced to the development of priestly notions about separation of the holy from the profane, represented systematically, for example, in Genesis 1. The Israelite priesthood apparently came to define divine holiness specifically as a separation from death and sex. Indeed, the presentation of Yahweh generally as sexless and unrelated to the realm of death would appear to have been produced precisely by a priesthood whose central notion of Yahweh as holy would view this deity as fully removed from realms of impurity, specifically sex and death (Frymer-Kensky 1992: 189-90; Gerstenberger 1996: vi, 90; Wright 1996: 314). There are several prohibitions governing the impurity of sexuality[33] and death (Num. 19.11, 14-19; 31.19). The priesthood is restricted in their selection of a spouse specifically because of the issue of holiness (Lev. 21.7). The priesthood was specially restricted also in their contact with the dead.[34] Unlike the other priests, the chief priest is even more restricted in not being permitted contact with any dead (Lev. 21.11-12) and in being permitted for a wife only a woman who has not yet had children (*b^e^tûlâ*, Lev. 21.13-14). As the single human permitted to enter it, the chief priest is to approach the holiness of the divine sanctuary.[35] Accordingly, a working hypothesis about the deity's holiness in the context of Israel's priestly culture might be entertained: holier than the holy of holies, the deity of the priesthood came to epitomize the fullest possibilities of sacredness and separation in avoiding sexuality and death. It may be that older mythologies involving divine death and sex did not survive, and here we might compare mythologies of sex and death in Lucian of Samosata's *De Dea Syria* 53-54, even though the priesthood there is said to observe purity rules involving the deceased and food.[36] The loss of divine sex and death mythology in Judah may not have transpired only because the priesthood might have actively censored such views (although such a situation is theoretically possible). Instead, such mythologies did not cohere with the emergent Priestly tradition's normative understanding of the divine (nor the Deuteronomic view of the divine), and so as part of an explanation for their absence from biblical literature, perhaps they fell into disuse in these traditions (Smith 2002b: 205-206).

The biblical record, even as it might afford some comparisons,[37] largely demurs from visual association with the phallus or its further meaning. Yet this

33. Sexual impurity includes menstruation (Lev. 15.19-30; 18.19), pregnancy (Lev. 12), a male's emission of semen (Lev. 15.1-18). The connection between these sorts of impurity and the holiness of Yahweh is made explicitly in Lev. 15.31.

34. For restrictions on priestly contact with the dead, see Lev. 21.1-3, 11; 22.4b; Num. 6.6-7. The statement in Lev. 21.3 stands in tension with 22.4b. See Bloch-Smith 1992: 222-23, who emphasizes the financial benefit gained through these prohibitions.

35. For the degrees of holiness between the people, the priesthood and the chief priest, see Milgrom 1976.

36. For text and translation, see Attridge and Oden 1976: 56-57.

37. Burkert (1979: 42) draws into his discussion the stele of Bethel in Gen. 28.

lack should not divert attention from the wider fund of sexual physicality attested in Ugaritic and Phoenician material, however much the former may be overlaid with royal thematics or the latter refracted by the euhemeristic lens of Hellenistic tradents. El's sexual invitation to Athirat seems so conventional in the Baal Cycle temple narrative (*KTU* 1.4 IV 38-39) that divine mating may have served as common material for temple stories. The royal cult as expressed in *KTU* 1.23 likewise assumes recollections of divine sexuality. In a different vein, Philo of Byblos (in Eusebius, *Praeparatio Evangelica* 1.10.29) tells of a cult site commemorating Ouranos's castration by his son Elos (El) identified in the source as Kronos. (This theme has its background perhaps not in traditional West Semitic traditions; rather, its closer echoes are Anatolian.[38]) Divine sexuality may have been accorded a broad place in temple myth in West Semitic cultures, with the exception of the very rare expressions found in that lengthiest of West Semitic mythic material, the biblical record. It would seem that the biblical records' tradents did not preserve such a rendering for Israel's deities. One might base such a possible reconstruction on a combination of putative evidence and apparent displacements. Largely inspired by the Kuntillet 'Ajrud inscriptions that refer to 'Yahweh...and his asherah', it is commonly argued that Asherah was worshipped as a goddess in Jerusalem (perhaps even in the Jerusalem Temple, in the form of the symbol of the asherah).[39]

A number of scholars, myself included,[40] dispute this reading of the ancient evidence. Instead, the asherah by the eighth century may have been viewed as something that as the inscriptions say, is 'his', namely a symbol of fertility and perhaps even female sexuality associated with Yahweh without referring to a goddess as such. On this point, Z. Zevit correctly asks (2000: 403 n. 10, *italics* Zevit's): 'What would it have meant to say that the goddess *belonged to* or was *possessed by* Yahweh?' This female imagery may be related to later descriptions of the temple-city as the bride of the deity, even possibly as a literary displacement of such cult (Frymer-Kensky 1992: 168-78). From these materials, it might be argued that the imagery of divine sexuality was indeed known for the First Temple, only to be displaced or omitted from the ancient record some time

38. See Kirk 1970: 215-20, and note also Tamil Hindu temple myths where the god's blood reveals the shrine. Comparable, though later, influence may lie behind the castration of the priestly Galli in putative imitation of Attis and the castration story of the mythical cult founder, Combabus, mentioned in *De Dea Syria* 15-27: 'This sort of love' between women and *castrati*, we are told, 'exists in the Holy City even to this day. Women desire the Galli, and the Galli go mad for a woman. Yet, no one is jealous, for they consider the matter quite holy' (Para. 22, Attridge and Oden 1976: 33). As in such stories, sexual mythology may at times relate to mythology's priestly authority and at least in this case, the cult myths of the founder and the personnel in their phallic focus comport with one aspect of the reported cult iconography, namely the 1800 foot double phalluses which stand in the gateway of the cultic complex (*De Dea Syria* 28) and attract cultic activity from what *De Dea Syria* 29 calls 'Phallus-Climbers'. Whether Anatolian or West Semitic or both, this expression of gender-crossing is anomalous for the West Semitic record.

39. E.g. Ackerman 1992: 37-66. See also the discussions of Dijkstra 2001: 118 and Hadley 2001: 201-202.

40. E.g. Miller 1986; Korpel 2001: 145-50; Smith 2002b: 108-37; Lang 2002: vii.

already during the First Temple period. Indeed, the priestly avoidance of sexuality noted above may suggest a competing view of the divinity as sexless. The First Temple debate may not have involved simply a goddess in the Temple, as many scholars have supposed especially since the discovery of the Kuntillet ʻAjrud inscriptions. Instead, the putative association of the asherah with a goddess in passages such as 1 Kgs 15.13, 2 Kgs 21.7 and 23.4, 6 may represent a polemic against any sexual view of the deity associating Yahweh with the asherah symbol of sexuality and fertility.[41] (This would explain the vast preponderance of references to the symbol over and against the goddess, and it would also help to explain the references to the goddess in the later parts of 2 Kings.) For this reason, one might think it less likely to suppose (as argued in the secondary literature) that Israel never knew such divine sexual themes.

4. *Analogy (and/or Homology*[42]*): Size and Attractiveness*

Baal and Yahweh are both the subject of super-sized descriptions, with temples and temple accoutrements as the point of comparison. In the Ugaritic Baal Cycle, Baal is the focus of such expressions of strength and size. By implication, Baal's throne and footstool are superhuman in size. They are so large that not even another divine warrior, Athtar, can measure up: 'his feet do not reach the footstool, his head does not reach the head-rest' (*KTU* 1.6 I 59-61). Elsewhere, Baal's palace is understood to be superhuman in scale; it is to cover 'a thousand *šiddu*, ten thousand *kumanu*' (1.4 V 56-57). It is from this palace that the super-sized god is to process across tens of towns in a victory march (1.4 VII 7-14), and that an aperture is created for the projection of the god's voice, which conveys thunderously (1.4 VII 25-39). Evidently, this is the sort of super-sized palace befitting a deity, since it is precisely the same scale marking the lengths which divinities travel (1.4 V 22-24), bow down from (1.1 IV 1-3, V 13-17; 1.3 VI 17-20; 1.4 VIII 24-29), or are perceived from (1.3 IV 37-40). Baal's edifice and its accoutrements denote not just the majesty of the divine in general terms; it further evokes the super-size of the deity. This concept of the divine palace as housing a superhuman-sized god is replicated in Syrian temple architecture in the early first millennium. As many studies have now noted, the meter-long footsteps carved into the portal and thresholds leading into the cult niche of the temple at Ain Dara suggest a deity of superhuman size.[43]

41. Regarding 2 Kgs 23.4, Day (2000: 42-43) considers 'Contra Mark S. Smith', that 'it would be extremely forced not to understand Asherah here as the name of the deity likewise'. Although I continue to harbor doubts for reasons that go unanswered by Day, I grant that it could be the name of the goddess. Unfortunately, Day does not consider the larger cultural issue of whether polemic is involved in these passages and, if so, whether scholars should presume that the cult of the goddess Asherah was a historical reality in the seventh century.

42. Levenson 1988: 82, 84, 88.

43. See Abū ʻAssāf 1990: 13-16; Bloch-Smith 1994: 21-25; Smith 1997: 85, 87. For pictures of the foot impressions, see Lewis 1998: 40. For an older discussion of deities' super size, see Smith 1988.

Superhuman divine size was also a feature of Israel's cultural heritage. Israel understood its deity and cultic appurtenances devoted to the deity in superhuman terms.[44] According to 1 Kgs 6.23-28, the throne built for Yahweh in the Temple's 'Holy of Holies' or 'backroom' (*d^ebîr*) was 10 cubits high and 10 cubits wide (c. 5.3 m square). It was a deity superhuman in scale who was thought to assume such a throne. The Temple's courtyard items were also of unusually great size, and in the case of the tank and stands, significantly larger than the commonly adduced ancient Middle Eastern parallels. The pillars, Jachin and Boaz, rose a total of 23 cubits (c. 12.2 m), consisting of a five cubit high capital atop an 18 cubit high stem. The immense tank, ten cubits in diameter (c. 5.3 m), is estimated to have held nearly 38,000 litres. Including the height of the wheels and the band that supported the basin, each stand ('laver') measured 4 cubits square (c. 2.1 m) and 7 cubits high (c. 3.7 m). The basin supported by each of the ten stands had a capacity of 40 baths (c. 920 litres). The exaggerated size of the structures in the Solomonic Temple courtyard would suggest that they were not intended for human use, but belonged to the realm of the divine, as noted by Bloch-Smith (1994). Accordingly, a sort of homology between the size of the deity and temple is assumed. Such a homology between the divinity and the temple functions to increase the identification of the two, to use the temple to house not just the deity, but the deity's story and to use the deity to express the social and political importance of the house.[45]

Ancient texts likewise render divinity and temples in terms of attraction. In this context, the well-known biblical female personification of the temple-city (Jerusalem) (e.g. Ezek. 16; 23; Lam. 1) immediately comes to mind, but this notion of the god and temple-city as a male and female should not divert attention from older notions surrounding the temple (or temple-mountain) as expressive of the god's attractiveness. The lexicon of both deity and temple includes terms of beauty. In Ugaritic, deities are called 'lovely, pleasant' (*n'm*) and 'beautiful, attractive' (**wsm*). In *KTU* 1.14 III 41-42 (paralleled in 1.14 VI 26-28), Anat is characterized generally as *n'm*, and in the same passage, Athtart is said to have *tsm* (<**wsm*), 'beauty' (followed by a description of eyes like lapis lazuli and alabaster). The newborn gods of *KTU* 1.23 are called *'ilm n'mm* (*KTU* 1.23.1 [largely reconstructed], 23, 58 [partially reconstructed], 60, 67). The same gods are called *ysmm* (<**wsm*, *KTU* 1.23.2). Unnamed gods in *KTU* 1.5 III 15 are also called *n'm 'ilm* (if correctly understood). In general, *n'm* seems to be regarded as a standard feature of West Semitic divine appearance.

44. For the following points, see Bloch-Smith 1994. See also her contribution in Smith 1994: 84-85, 86.

45. A further development of the homology of god and house involves the well-known representation of the temple as cosmos representation. This particular homology between temple and cosmos in Priestly works of the Bible (Gen. 1 and Exod. 39-40) has been addressed by Weinfeld (1981: 501-12), Levenson (1988: 78-87) and Janowski (1990). This move reflects a long-standing tendency to relate temple to cosmos and vice versa. The associations of cosmic creation and tent-shrine and temple represent a Priestly take on the more general theme of cosmos and sacred spaces. This particular topic lies beyond the scope of the discussion.

The same terms apply analogically to other features of deities, for example, El's years (*KTU* 1.108.27). Baal's *n'm* is predicated of his capacity as a provider of water, understood anthropologically as a quality of his voice in *KTU* 1.19 I 42-46. This quality of Baal's voice is in turn said to be good for the earth in *KTU* 1.16 III 4-11. Biblical contexts for divine *n'm* are more restricted, but it would seem that both the presence of the deity and the name of the deity also enjoy this attractive dimension. Yahweh's name has *n'ym* (Ps. 135.3), and Yahweh is said to have *n'm* which can be dispensed to humans who pray to the deity (Ps. 90.17). The temple-mountains of the gods also have *n'm*. In a passage (*KTU* 1.3 III 30-31; see also 1.10 III 31) cited above (in section I), Baal's mountain is said to have holiness (*qdš*) and victory (*tl'iyt*) as well as attractiveness (*n'm*). The first two features are regarded as derivative of the god. Just as Baal is the god of victory, victory is associated with his mountain; similarly, Baal's mountain is regarded as holy because it is associated with the god. Given that *n'm* appears in the same string of terms for the god's mountain, it follows that the mountain is regarded as having *n'm* because it partakes of the god's *n'm*. Of course, a given mountain might have been so selected because of its own natural attractiveness or because it matches the description of the god in other ways, for example, Ṣapan as Baal's mountain because it is high and cloud-covered. Nonetheless, it would appear that just as other features of the mountain were thought of as deriving from the god, so the feature of attractiveness did as well. The materials associated with the temples in Ugaritic myth and biblical narrative, namely of cedars, gold and silver, both in Baal's house and Solomon's temple, involve both luxury and aesthetics. Similarly, the heavenly palace of Baal, like that of Yahweh, involves brickwork of precious stone, lapis lazuli in the case of Baal (*KTU* 1.4 V 19), sapphire in the case of Yahweh (Exod. 24.10). (It is possible that this specific detail should be further located in the category of homology, of temple *qua* cosmos [Levenson 1988: 82, 84, 88], but even so it may betoken an aesthetic sensibility.) In sum, the mountain participates in the *n'm* of the god, and the *n'm* of the god is manifest terrestrially in his mountain.

Similarly, it would seem that *n'm* is a feature associated with the house of Yahweh or at least the god's presence in the house in Ps. 27.4.[46] The two are difficult to distinguish. Psalm 16.11 discusses *n'm* in connection with the deity, apparently in a sanctuary context, perhaps by a priest.[47] Moreover, Jerusalem, the holy mountain of Yahweh, is called **ypy* ('beautiful') in a number of phrases: *y^epēh nôp m^eśôś kol-hā'āreṣ* ('beautiful of height, joy of all the earth', Ps. 48.3, ET 2); and *miklal yōpî* ('perfect of beauty', Ps. 50.2). The personification of Jerusalem as a woman in Ezekiel 16 apparently relates to the notion of the place's beauty, since **ypy* in vv. 13-14 (cf. Song 4.7) is used with **kll* just as it is in

46. For a different understanding of **n'm* in this context and in other psalms, see Levenson 1985. Levenson does not mention that *n'm* is one of terms used for the inheritance of the god in *KTU* 1.3 III 28-31. The usage of *KTU* 1.3 III 28-31 also suits the sanctuary-context of Ps. 27.13, as noted by Greenfield 1990: 164.

47. E.g. van der Toorn 1996: 210-11 and Tournay 2001: 21-25. See also Rodríguez 1993 and Spronk 1986: 334-38.

Ps. 50.2. Yet it would seem that this personification was not produced casually; the sense of attractiveness of the temple-mountain and its relationship to the attracting god may have been involved in this development, one related not only to the literary personifications of Jerusalem in the prophetic corpus, but perhaps also to the presentation of the female protagonist in the Song of Songs (alluded to above). Finally, the divine dwelling in Jerusalem (Ps. 84.2, ET 1) is regarded *y^e^dîdôt* ('lovely', NJPS), and an object of yearning (Ps. 84.3, ET 2). In short, the vocabulary of attraction for the temple-mountain includes language of desire, though without any explicit sexualization.

One Ugaritic text, *KTU* 1.101 (on its obverse) describes Baal enthroned on his mountain, Ṣapan,[48] in such a way so as to evoke an aesthetic analogue between Baal and the peak:

Baal sits (enthroned) like the sitting of a mountain,	*b'l yṯb kṯbt ġr*
Hadad...like the (cosmic) ocean,	*hd r*[ ] *kmdb*
In the midst of his mountain, divine Ṣapan,	*btk ġrh 'il ṣpn*
In [the midst of?] the mount is victory,	*b*[tk] *ġr tl'iyt*
(With) seven lightning-flashes,	*šb't brqm* [ ]
Eight store-houses of thunder (?).	*ṯmnt' iṣr r't*
A tree-bolt of lightning.[..].	*'ṣ brq y*[ ].
His head is adorned (?),	*r'išh tply*
With dew between his eyes	*ṭly bn 'nh*
...at his base,	*'uz'rt tmll 'išdh*
...the horn[s]...on him (?),	*qrn*[m] *b(?)t 'lh*
His head with a downpour from the heavens	*r'išh bglṯ bšm*[m]
...is watering,	[ ] *ṯr 'iṯ*
His mouth like two clouds (?)...	*ph kṯ*[t] *ġbt*[...]
Like wine is the love of his heart...	*kyn ddm lbh*

On the whole, this passage identifies the god's super-sized features with those of his mountain (Pope and Tigay 1971: 122; Irwin 1983: 54-57). The homology between the god and his temple-mountain further conveys the power of his enthronement and meteorological weaponry in the first part of the poem. The second part continues with images of precipitation, ending in a personal envisioning of the god's mouth in a way that is perhaps[49] suggestive of love-making (implying the image of his lips kissing). This last image perhaps smacks of Song 1.2, *yiššāqēnî minn^e^šîqôt pîhû kî-ṭôbîm dōdeykā miyyāyin* ('May he kiss me with

48. For text, translation and notes, see Pardee 1988: 119-52. See also Pope and Tigay 1971; Irwin 1983: 54-57; Wyatt 1998: 388-90. Pardee sees *ṭly* as a reference to the goddess Dewy associated with Baal, which is possible. Pardee rightly compares *glṯ* and *ṯr* in this text with *glṯ* in the Baal Cycle (*KTU* 1.4 V 6-9) cited above. The word *ṯkt* in the latter context is accordingly to be emended to *ṯrt*.

49. Pardee (1988: 124, 125) reconstructs 'lips' before the simile *kyn ddm*, hence 'lips like wine-jars', and he takes *lbh* with what follows in the lacuna. This approach is philologically possible, since *ddm* may be either 'jar' (e.g. *dd šmn gdlt*) or 'love' (//) *'hbt'//yd* in *KTU* 1.3 III 6-7; cf. Akkadian *dadu*. This approach is, however, less likely syntactically. With Pardee's rendering, one would expect instead **kdd yn*. Or, perhaps assuming 'lips' is to be reconstructed, perhaps *kyn ddm lbh* is an extended simile, 'like the wine of the love of his heart' (this translation assumes enclitic mem on *ddm*).

the kisses of his mouth, for your love is sweeter than wine') (Irwin 1983: 57). That this notion is the import of the final lines of *KTU* 1.101 might be reflected by the reverse of the tablet, which tells how the goddess Anat 'sings the love of Mighty Baal' (*tšr dd 'al*['iyn] *b'l*—paralleled in the Baal Cycle, in *KTU* 1.3 III 5-6). In short, the end of the obverse may hint at divine eroticism within a complex of temple-mountain images. *KTU* 1.101 encapsulates the major themes associated with the god as known from the Baal Cycle, yet it may further preserve explicitly what many temple texts perhaps only imply or presuppose, namely that the god's erotic magnetism is conveyed through the literary presentation of the human experience of his temple-mountain.

This survey of texts and iconography suggests something of the range of traditions inherited by the Jerusalem Temple to convey its royal divine power and Edenic beauty. The language of aesthetics served as a powerful force for distinguishing Jerusalem and perhaps capital cities more generally. The language of aesthetics was not only lavished on Jerusalem because the city was lavished with public works, in particular palace and Temple (other cities received such works). It would seem that the application of the language of beauty, attested, for example, in Pss. 48.3 (ET 2) and 50.2, was a means of presenting divine association with the city beyond traditional terms such as divine establishment, planting, ownership or choice. These traditional terms for divine association with a site evoke the terms of sanctuary, and many of these were applied to Jerusalem, but the language of beauty is not generally attested for sites of local sanctuaries. Accordingly, such language may belong to the literatures patronized by the monarchy. Such aesthetic language is common to the broader ancient Near Eastern genres of temple hymns and temple narratives, sponsored by local kings. In short, the vocabulary of aesthetics might be viewed as a discourse of royal power. The place and the deity not only focus attention on one other; nor is their power merely part of their attraction. Their attractiveness may powerfully provide sense and order, symmetry and identity, at least for priestly and royal echelons of Levantine societies. By lining the dominant discourse of power with the vocabulary of attraction, the discourse of power is made beautiful and thereby even more powerful. In short, attractiveness of deity and temple involves a reciprocal social power, perhaps even seduction.

5. *Further Thoughts*

In the West Semitic context, temples focus public attention on deities, more specifically on the connections between human celebration and problems on the one hand, and the perceptions of divine presence and aid on the other hand. Out of the various sorts of relations discussed above, five divine characteristics associated also with temples in West Semitic culture stand out: strength and size; fertility and beauty; holiness; immortality and knowledge. For heuristic purposes, these categories may be correlated to different aspects of the human condition, as understood in the ancient Levant.

Human Problems	*Human Contradictions*	Divinity	*Temple*
powerlessness	*limited human power, but experience of suffering and evil people*	strength, size	*strength, size*
lack of prosperity infertility	*experience of divine presence and divine absence*	sexuality/love, beauty	*channel of blessing, beauty*
unholiness	*knowledge and experience of self as both wrong (sinning) and whole (holy)*	holiness	*intersection, transition*
mortality	*limited time, but intuiting eternity*	eternity	*duration*
ignorance	*limited knowledge of the world/ God, but experience of disorder and unintelligibility*	wisdom and knowledge	*source of divine revelation*

Temple ideologies in West Semitic cultures were encoded in texts and in iconography. In these forms, temples tell not only where deities are, but what and how they are. Bringing deities and people to one another, temples focus on a variety of relationships between divinity and humanity. Accordingly, the crucial term in this presentation is the word 'like', which expresses the fulcrum-point between similarity and difference, connection and disjunction. This word conveys the fundamental point that visible yet inert buildings marked as temples and mostly imperceptible yet animate deities enjoyed little public life apart from one another on the extra-familial levels of social and political organization.[50] The mediating power of sacred places and spaces both captured and expressed the relations between themselves and their deities; they received ritually what they perceived as beyond them, in modes that they likened to themselves and their human interactions.

In closing, a final remark. This approach to temples holds ramifications for understanding later tradition. Over the past two decades, the later literature associated with temple mysticism of Jewish Kabbalah has been traced back to the *Songs of the Sabbath Sacrifice* discovered among the Dead Sea Scrolls. In turn, scholars have detected visionary mysticism in priestly works in the Bible not only in Ezekiel 1–3, but also in briefer glimpses such as Exod. 24.9-11 and Ezekiel 28 (Smith 1987a). It requires another step to situate the literature of temple 'mysticism' in the Bible and later Judaism (in other terms, priestly mystical literature perhaps as part of traditional secret knowledge) within the larger context of earlier West Semitic religious literature, such as the Baal Cycle or perhaps better, *KTU* 1.101.[51] In time, biblical tradition would differentiate and dissociate itself from the monistic polytheism of the earlier non-Israelite literature (as expressed in the concepts of the divine council and the divine family)[52] to

50. Wright insightfully observed that divine–human interaction is regularly set in sanctuary or other ritual contexts. See Wright 2001: 47.

51. The anthropomorphism of the super-sized deity explicit in the Ugaritic texts has been connected with both the protagonists of the Song of Songs as well as the presentation of the deity in a Jewish mystical text such as *Shi'ur Qomah*. So Pope 1988: 323.

52. For these conceptual 'monisms' informing Ugaritic polytheism, see Smith 2001b: 41-66.

which biblical literature was—often unknowingly—indebted and attracted. In the late monarchy and afterwards, when Israel preserved various fragments of older ideas about divinity in its later version of a monotheistic Divine King with angelic hosts and other divine servants, this record of Israel's collective memory would retain some features of the Godhead that Israel had forgotten (Smith 2002a).

Bibliography

Abū 'Assāf, A.

1990 *Der Tempel von 'Ain Dārā* (Damaszener Forschungen, 3; Mainz: Philipp von Zabern).

Ackerman, S.

1992 *Under Every Green Tree: Popular Religion in Sixth-Century Judah* (HSM, 46; Atlanta: Scholars Press).

Anderson, G.A.

1987 *Sacrifices and Offerings in Ancient Israel: Studies in Their Social and Political Importance* (HSM, 41; Atlanta: Scholars Press).

Andrae, W.

1952 'Der kultischen Garten', *Die Welt des Orients* 1: 485-94.

Attridge, H.W., and R.A. Oden, Jr

1976 *The Syrian Goddess (De Dea Syria) Attributed to Lucian* (Texts and Translations, 9; Greco-Roman Religion, 1; Missoula, MT : Scholars Press for the Society of Biblical Literature).

1981 *Philo of Byblos—The Phoenician History: Introduction, Critical Text, Translation, Notes* (CBQMS, 9; Washington, DC: Catholic Biblical Association of America).

Batto, B.

1991 'Paradise Reexamined', in K.L. Younger *et al.* (eds.), *The Biblical Canon in Comparative Perspective* (ANET, 11; Lewiston, NY: Edwin Mellen Press): 33-66.

Becking, B. *et al.* (eds.)

2001 *Only One God? Monotheism in Ancient Israel and the Veneration of the Goddess Asherah* (Biblical Seminar, 77; Sheffield: Sheffield Academic Press).

Begrich, J.

1932 'Die Paradieserzählung. Eine literargeschichte Studie', *ZAW* 50: 93-116.

Biella, J.C.

1982 *Dictionary of Old South Arabic; Sabaean Dialect* (HSS, 25; Chico, CA: Scholars Press)

Bloch-Smith, E.M.

1992 'The Cult of the Dead in Judah: Interpreting the Material Remains', *JBL* 111: 213-24.

1994 '"Who is the King of Glory?": Solomon's Temple and its Symbolism', in M.D. Coogan, J.C. Exum and L.E. Stager (eds.), *Scripture and Other Artifacts: Essays on the Bible and Archaeology in Honor of Philip J. King* (Louisville, KY: Westminster/John Knox Press): 18-31.

Bogaert, P.-M.

1983 'Montagne sainte, jardin d'Eden et sanctuaire (hiérosolymitain) dans un oracle d'Ezéchiel contre le prince de Tyr (Ez 28,11-19)', in H. Limet and J. Ries (eds.), *Le mythe, son langage et son message: Actes du colloque de Liège et Louvain-la-Nueve 1981* (Homo Religiosus, 9; Louvain-la-Neuve: Centre d'histoire des religions): 131-53.

Burkert, W.
1979 *Structure and History in Greek Mythology and Ritual* (Berkeley: University of California Press).

Callendar, D.E., Jr
2000 *Adam in Myth and History: Ancient Israelite Perspectives on the Primal Human* (HSS, 48; Winona Lake, IN: Eisenbrauns).

Caquot, A., M. Sznycer and A. Herdner
1974 *Textes ougaritiques*, I. *Mythes et legendes* (Littératures anciennes du Proche-Orient, 7; Paris: Cerf).

Clifford, R.J.
1972 *The Cosmic Mountain in Canaan and the Old Testament* (HSM, 4; Cambridge, MA: Harvard University Press).

Cross, F.M.
1973 *Canaanite Myth and Hebrew Epic* (Cambridge, MA and London: Harvard University Press).

Day, J.
2000 *Yahweh and the Gods and Goddesses of Canaan* (JSOTSup, 265; Sheffield: Sheffield Academic Press).

Dijkstra, M.
2001 'El, the God of Israel—Israel, the People of YHWH: On the Origins of Ancient Israelite Yahwism', in Becking *et al.* (eds.) 2001: 81-126.

Frymer-Kensky, T.
1992 *In the Wake of the Goddesses: Women, Culture, and the Biblical Transformation of Pagan Myth* (New York: Basic Books).

Gaster, T.H.
1933 'The Ritual Pattern of a Ras-Shamra Epic', *ArOr* 5: 118-23.

Geller, M.J.
1990 'Taboo in Mesopotamia: A Review Article', *JCS* 42: 105-17.

Gerstenberger, E.S.
1996 *Yahweh the Patriarch: Ancient Images of God and Feminist Theology* (trans. F.J. Gaiser; Minneapolis: Fortress Press).

Gibson, J.C.L.
1978 *Canaanite Myth and Legends* (Edinburgh: T. & T. Clark, 2nd edn).

Gordon, C.H.
1965 *Ugaritic Textbook* (AnOr, 38; Rome: Pontifical Biblical Institute).

Greenfield, J.C.
1984 'A Touch of Eden', in *Orientalia J. Duchesne-Guillemin Emerito Oblata* (Hommages et Opera Minor, 9; Leiden: E.J. Brill): 219-24.
1990 'The "Cluster" in Biblical Poetry', in E.M. Cook (ed.), *MAARAV* 5–6, *Sopher Mahir: Northwest Semitic Studies Presented to Stanislav Segert*: 159-68.

Greenfield, J.C., and A. Shaffer
1983 'Notes on the Akkadian–Aramaic Bilingual Statue from Tell Fekherye', *Iraq* 45: 109-16.

Guthrie, S.
1996 'The Sacred: A Skeptical View', in Idinipulos and Yonan (eds.) 1996: 124-38.

Hadley, J.M.
2001 *The Cult of Asherah in Ancient Israel and Judah: Evidence for a Hebrew Goddess* (UCOP, 57; Cambridge and New York: Cambridge University Press).

Hurowitz, V.A.
1992 *I Have Built You an Exalted House: Temple Building in the Bible in Light of Mesopotamian and Northwest Semitic Writings* (JSOTSup, 115; JSOT/ASOR Monographs, 5; Sheffield: Sheffield Academic Press).
Idinipulos, T.A., and E.A. Yonan (eds.)
1996 *The Sacred and the Scholars: Comparative Methodologies for the Study of Primary Religious Data* (Numen, 73; Leiden: E.J. Brill).
Irwin, W.H.
1983 'The Extended Simile in RS 24.245 obv', *UF* 15: 53-58.
Jacobsen, T.
1976 *Treasures of Darkness* (New Haven and London: Yale University Press).
Janowski, B.
1990 'Tempel und Schöpfung. Schöpfungstheologische Aspekte der priesterschriftlichen Heiligtumskonzeption', *Jahrbuch für Biblische Theologie* 5: 37-69.
Kirk, G.S.
1970 *Myth: Its Meaning and Function in Ancient and Other Cultures* (Sather Classical Lectures, 40; London: Cambridge University Press; Berkeley and Los Angeles: University of California Press).
Korpel, M.C.A.
2001 'Asherah Outside of Israel', in Becking *et al.* (eds.) 2001: 127-50.
Lambert, W.G.
1994 'Gilgamesh in Literature and Art: The Second and First Millennia', in J. Maier (ed.), *Gilgamesh: A Reader* (Wauconda, IL: Bolchazy-Carducci): 50-62.
Lang, B.
2002 *The Hebrew God: Portrait of an Ancient Deity* (New Haven and London: Yale University Press).
Leslau, W.
1987 *Comparative Dictionary of Ge'ez (Classical Ethiopic)* (Wiesbaden: Otto Harrassowitz).
Levenson, J.D.
1985 'A Technical Meaning for *N'M* in the Hebrew Bible', *VT* 35: 61-67.
1988 *Creation and the Persistence of Evil: The Jewish Drama of Jewish Omnipotence* (San Francisco: Harper & Row).
Levine, B.A.
1974 *In the Presence of the Lord* (Leiden: E.J. Brill).
1993 *Numbers 1–20* (AB, 4; Garden City, NY: Doubleday).
Lewis, T.J.
1998 'Divine Images and Aniconism in Ancient Israel', *JAOS* 118: 36-53.
Lipiński, E.
1971 'El's Abode: Mythological Traditions Related to Mt. Hermon and the Mountains of Armenia', *OLP* 2: 13-69.
McCarter, P.K.
2001 'The Garden of Eden: Geographical and Etymological Ruminations on the Garden of God in the Bible and the Ancient Near East' (unpublished paper presented to the Colloquium for Biblical Research, Duke University, 19 August 2001 [cited with permission]).
Mendenhall, G.E.
1985 'The Worship of Baal and Asherah: A Study in the Social Bonding Functions of Religious Systems', in A. Kort and S. Morschauser (eds.), *Biblical and Related Studies Presented to Samuel Iwry* (Winona Lake, IN: Eisenbrauns): 147-58.

Merkur, D.

1996 'The Numinous as a Category of Values', in Idinipulos and Yonan (eds.) 1996: 104-23.

Merlo, P.

1997 'Note critiche su alcune presunte iconografie della dea Ašera', *SEL* 14: 43-64.

Milgrom, J.

1976 'Israel's Sanctuary: The Priestly "Picture of Dorian Gray"', *RB* 83: 390-99. Reprinted in J. Milgrom *Studies in Cultic Theology and Terminology* (Leiden: E.J. Brill, 1983): 75-84.

1983 *Studies in Cultic Theology and Terminology* (Leiden: E.J. Brill).

1991 *Leviticus 1–16* (AB, 3; Garden City, NY: Doubleday).

Millard, A.R.

1984 'The Etymology of Eden', *VT* 34: 103-10.

Miller, P.D.

1980 'Creator of Earth', *BASOR* 239: 43-46.

1986 'The Absence of the Goddess in Israelite Religion', *HAR* 10: 239-48.

Morris, P., and D. Sawyer (eds.)

1992 *A Walk in the Garden: Biblical, Iconographical and Literary Images of Eden* (JSOTSup, 136; Sheffield: JSOT Press).

Olyan, S.M.

1988 *Asherah and the Cult of Yahweh in Israel* (SBLDS, 34; Atlanta: Scholars Press).

Paden, W.E.

1996 'Sacrality as Integrity: "Sacred Order" as a Model for Describing Religious Worlds', in Idinipulos and Yonan (eds.) 1996: 3-18.

Pardee, D.

1988 *Les textes para-mythologiques de la 24e campagne (1961)* (Ras Shamra–Ougarit, IV; Mémoire, 77; Paris: Editions Recherche sur les Civilisations).

2000 *Les textes rituels* (Ras Shamra–Ougarit, XII; Paris: Editions Recherche sur les Civilisations).

2002 *Ritual and Cult at Ugarit* (Writings from the Ancient World; Atlanta: Scholars Press).

Pope, M.H.

1977 *Song of Songs* (AB, 7C; Garden City, NY: Doubleday).

1988 'Metastases in Canonical Shapes of the Super Song', in G.M. Tucker and D.L. Petersen (eds.), *Canon, Theology, and Old Testament Interpretation: Essays in Honor of Brevard S. Childs* (Philadelphia: Fortress Press): 312-28.

Pope, M.H., and J.H. Tigay

1971 'A Description of Baal', *UF* 3: 117-30.

Rodríguez, A.A.

1993 *Tú Eres Mi Bien: Análisis exegético y teológico del Salmo 16. Aplicación a la vida religiosa* (Madrid: Clarentianas).

Smith, M.S.

1985 'Kothar wa-Hasis, the Ugaritic Craftsman God' (unpublished PhD dissertation, Yale University).

1987a 'Biblical and Canaanite Notes to the Songs of the Sabbath Sacrifice from Qumran', *RevQ* 12: 585-88.

1987b *Psalms: The Divine Journey* (New York and Mahwah, NJ: Paulist Press).

1988 'Divine Form and Size in the Ugaritic and Pre-Exilic Israelite Religion', *ZAW* 100: 424-27.

1994 *The Ugaritic Baal Cycle*, I. *Introduction with Text, Translation and Commentary of KTU 1.1–1.2* (VTSup, 55; Leiden: E.J. Brill).

1997 *The Pilgrimage Pattern in Exodus* (JSOTSup, 239; Sheffield: Sheffield Academic Press).

2001a *Untold Stories: The Bible and Ugaritic Studies in the Twentieth Century* (Peabody, MA: Hendrickson).

2001b *The Origins of Biblical Monotheism* (Oxford: Oxford University Press).

2002a 'Remembering God: Collective Memory in Israelite Religion', *CBQ* 64: 631-51.

2002b *The Early History of God: Yahweh and the Other Deities in Ancient Israel* (Grand Rapids: Eerdmans, 2nd edn).

Spronk, Klaas

1986 *Beatific Afterlife in Ancient Israel and in the Ancient Near East* (AOAT, 219; Kevelaer: Butzon & Bercker; Neukirchen–Vluyn: Neukirchener Verlag).

Stager, L.E.

1999 'Jerusalem and the Garden of Eden', *Eretz-Israel* 26 (Frank Moore Cross Volume): 183-94.

Stordalen, Terje

2000 *Echoes of Eden: Genesis 2–3 and Symbolism of the Eden Garden in Biblical Hebrew Literature* (Contributions to Biblical Exegesis and Theology, 25; Leuven: Peeters).

Thackeray, H.St.J.

1926 *The Life/Against Apion* (LCL; London: Heinemann; Cambridge, MA: Harvard University Press).

Thackeray, H.St.J., and R. Marcus

1934 *Josephus V: Jewish Antiquities, Books V–VIII* (LCL; London: Heinemann; Cambridge, MA: Harvard University Press).

Tournay, R.J.

2001 'A propos du Psaume 16, 1-4', *RB* 108: 21-25.

Toorn, K. van der

1985 *Sin and Sanction in Israel and Mesopotamia: A Comparative Study* (Studia Semitica Neerlandica, 22; Assen: Van Gorcum).

1988 'La pureté rituelle au proche-orient ancien', *RHR* 206: 339-56.

1996 *Family Religion in Babylonia, Syria and Israel: Continuity and Change in the Forms of Religious Life* (SHCANE, 7; Leiden: E.J. Brill).

Virolleaud, C.

1932 'Un nouveau chant du poème d'Alein-Baal', *Syria* 13: 133-41.

Vito, R.A. de

1993 *Studies in Third Millennium Sumerian and Akkadian Personal Names: The Designation and Conception of the Personal God* (Studies Pohl: Series Maior, 16; Rome: Pontificio Istituto Biblico).

Waldman, N.

1981 'The Wealth of the Mountain and Sea: The Background of a Biblical Image', *JQR* 71: 176-80.

Wallace, H.N.

1985 *The Eden Narrative* (HSM, 32; Atlanta: Scholars Press).

Weinfeld, M.

1977–78 'Gen. 7.11, 8.1-2 against the Background of Ancient Near Eastern Tradition', *WO* 9: 242-48.

1981 'Sabbath, Temple and the Enthronement of the Lord—The Problem of the Sitz im Leben of Genesis 1.1–2.3', in A. Caquot and M. Delcor (eds.), *Mélanges bibliques et orientaux en l'honneur de M. Henri Cazelles* (AOAT, 212; Kevelaer: Butzon & Bercker; Neukirchen–Vluyn: Neukirchener Verlag): 501-12.

1991 'Semiramis: Her Name and Her Origin', in M. Cogan and I. Eph'al (eds.), *Ah, Assyria...: Studies in Assyrian History and Ancient Near Eastern Historiography Presented to Hayim Tadmor* (Scripta Hierosolymitana, 33; Jerusalem: Magnes Press): 99-103.

Widengren, G.
1951 *The King and the Tree of Life in Ancient Near Eastern Religion (King and Saviour 4)* (Uppsala Universitets Årsskrift, 4; Wiesbaden: Lundequistska Bokhandeln and Otto Harrassowitz).

Wiggerman, F.A.M.
1992 *Mesopotamian Protective Deities: The Ritual Texts* (Cuneiform Monographs, 1; Groningen: Styx & PP).

Wright, D.P.
1996 'Holiness, Sex, and Death in the Garden of Eden', *Bib* 77: 305-29.
2001 *Ritual in Narrative: The Dynamics of Feasting, Mourning, and Retaliation Rites in the Ugaritic Tale of Aqhat* (Winona Lake, IN: Eisenbrauns).

Wyatt, N.
1986 'The Hollow Crown: Ambivalent Elements in West Semitic Royal Ideology', *UF* 18: 421-36.
1998 *Religious Texts from Ugarit: The Words of Ilimilku and His Colleagues* (Biblical Seminar, 53; Sheffield: Sheffield Academic Press).

Zaehner, R.C.
1966 *Hinduism* (Oxford and New York: Oxford University, 2nd edn).

Zevit, Z.
2000 *The Religions of Ancient Israel: A Synthesis of Parallactic Approaches* (New York: Continuum).

MAṢṢĒBÔT IN THE ISRAELITE CULT: AN ARGUMENT FOR RENDERING IMPLICIT CULTIC CRITERIA EXPLICIT

Elizabeth Bloch-Smith

1. *Introduction*

Recent debate over the use of symbols and images in the Israelite cult calls for reassessing archaeological examples of *maṣṣēbôt*, hereafter to be called standing stones. A perusal of relevant literature, both biblical and archaeological, reveals a lack of explicit criteria; stones achieve cultic status by virtue of having been so designated by the excavator. Not until criteria for identifying *maṣṣēbôt* are made explicit, and standardized, may stones merit certain, probable/plausible, possible, or unlikely *maṣṣēbôt* status. Only then may meaningful debate proceed on the practice of erecting *maṣṣēbôt* and their place in the Israelite cult. This essay proposes criteria and then subjects three commonly accepted examples of *maṣṣēbôt* to reappraisal. The varying results demonstrate the need to reopen discussion on defining and identifying cultic elements.

Cultic Criteria

In his book *The Archaeology of Cult*, Colin Renfrew (1985: 16-18) identifies three aspects of sacred ritual: (1) focusing attention on the divine/transcendent, (2) establishing a connection between the human and the transcendent realms, and (3) worship or acknowledging divine power. These three aspects translate into distinctive spatial arrangements and material remains created by humans acting on their religious beliefs. Material correlates might include demarcated sacred space or a mechanism for focusing attention, a representation of the transcendent or a symbolic focus, and the accoutrements for distinctive behaviours appropriate to the sacred or liminal zone (e.g. offerings).

It is these material correlates arising from behaviours dictated by religious beliefs that we seek to identify: cultic architecture (or designated space), cultic activity, and cultic appurtenances. Multiple criteria for cultic features have been proposed—none apparently necessary or sufficient given the lack of consensus. For virtually each criterion stipulated, other scholars qualify or reject the suggestion. For example, Michael Coogan (1987: 2-3) stipulates a physical separation between holy and profane space, but Tina Haettner Blomquist counters with '"embeddedness" of cult' as in the case of ritual activity within the city gate (1999: 24). Coogan further cites 'exotic materials' as a criterion for assigning a cultic function in the absence of written testimony (1987: 2-3). Considered in isolation, this criterion fails to distinguish cultic from elite objects. Renfrew addressed the 'exotic materials' conundrum by proposing the additional criterion that a possible cultic assemblage 'should not be explicable in secular terms in the light of what we know of the society' (1985: 20-21; *contra* Daviau 1993). However, Renfrew's qualification pertains to assemblages but not individual items and fails in the Levantine context since common domestic activities such as weaving, cooking, and eating transpired in sacred space (see below). Coogan's remaining cultic criteria stipulate continuity in the case of multi-period sites and parallels or comparable occurrences. The conservative nature of ancient Levantine religious expression, evident in architecture, decoration, furnishings, and objects or descriptions thereof, facilitates identifying cultic elements (Coogan 1987: 2-3). Renfrew, however, qualifies Coogan's criterion with the admonition that 'continuity in religious practice does not imply lack of change in that practice, and certainly cannot be taken as evidence of constancy of meaning' (1985: 5). While individual parallels might mislead interpreters, for instance, kings as well as gods sat upon cherub thrones, an aggregate of parallel elements provides a convincing basis for interpretation. Summarizing Coogan's list with Renfrew's discussion, a liminal zone or demarcated space, a high level of workmanship and/or precious materials, continuity, and parallels indicative of patterned ritual behaviour demonstrate sacred space and action. Textual and epigraphic evidence must also be added to the list. The more criteria met, the greater the probability of sanctity.

A sacred architectural plan that evolved in the southern Levant from the Chalcolithic to the Iron Age demonstrates continuity in cultic structures (Ottosson 1980; Amiran 1981; Mazar 1992). The earliest manifestation, from Chalcolithic En-gedi, is a single broadroom, with the focal point in the wall immediately opposite the entrance. With the entrance and niche/focal point positioned along the central axis, light from the opening illuminated the niche where the deity was probably manifest and visible to the worshipper standing in the doorway. This same plan persisted either in a single or side-by-side temples at Early Bronze Age Megiddo Area BB and perhaps at Arad. In the Middle and Late Bronze Ages, the building was elongated by the addition of a forecourt and imposing towers guarding the entrance. This temple, dubbed the 'Migdal Temple' after the biblical reference, restricted access to the focal point now sequestered within a dark, inner room. Shechem, Megiddo Area BB Stratum VII, and Hazor Area H Strata 3-1 present variants of this temple plan (Judg. 9.46). Solomon's Temple, as well as the temples at Ain Dara and Tell Tayinat, exemplify the evolution of this plan in the Iron Age (Abū 'Assāf 1990; Monson 2000). A pillared porch or entrance replaced the imposing towers, but the entire structure was elongated to remove further the focal point from the entrance. The deity, visibly bathed in light in the Chalcolithic temple, moved into a dark inner sanctum, concealed from the entrance by doors and curtains. Sacrifices and other offerings took place at altars, basins, and stands in the temple courtyard, an area accessible to the public and all cultic personnel. This Iron Age tripartite structure is immediately recognizable as a temple. The Arad temple courtyard altar, and broadroom with a niche in the back wall along the central axis conform to this plan (Y. Aharoni 1968).

What attributes or criteria rendered an object cultic in Iron Age Israel? Biblical and epigraphic testimony and continuity of practice attest to cultic function. Exceptional workmanship and elaboration beyond functional needs in addition to the preceding criteria reinforce the identification; without the preceding they are merely suggestive. Cultic objects and iconography, either specified in the Bible or generally attested in southern Levantine cultic contexts, include divinatory instruments such as the High Priest's breastplate with the Urim and Thummim (Exod. 28.15-30), horned headdresses as, for instance, depicted on the Baal Stele (Pritchard 1969: pl. 490), horned altars (1 Kgs 2.28; Amos 3.14; for Beer-sheba see Y. Aharoni 1974: 2-6), (metal) bull figurines (1 Kgs 12.28-29, 32; for the Bull Site see Mazar 1982), ornamental tree representations (1 Kgs 6.29), and composite creatures such as the cherub (though these occur in royal as well as divine contexts) (1 Kgs 6.23-26). Depictions of lions, snakes, the sun, the moon, and the stars in contexts deemed cultic on the basis of other features may also qualify. More problematic is the presumed cultic status of objects sometimes associated with the cult, such as 'incense burners', and elaborate or ornate objects displaying a high level of workmanship or fashioned from a precious material such as metal. For example, decorated or fenestrated tall stands, occasionally with attached bowls, are considered cultic. However, the designation has been extended to tall stands irrespective of context and even some chalices in a variety of contexts. The same applies to 'incense burners', though they surely served multiple functions including hot plate and perfumer/deodorant in both secular and religious contexts (Fowler 1985). Additional objects of disputed cultic function include other animal representations (horses, birds), rattles, miniature furniture, and hollow theriomorphic vessels sometimes called libation vases. While some objects are sufficiently distinctive to be recognizable as cultic no matter what their provenience, such as elaborate metal bull figurines or a depiction that incorporates a horned headdress, others are dependent on context for their cultic classification.

Identifying cultic objects and assemblages is further complicated by the fact that domestic activities such as preparing and consuming food (1 Sam. 9.19-25), processing olive oil (Stager and Wolff 1981), and weaving textiles (2 Kgs 23.7) could also take place in sacred precincts. For example, the Late Bronze II Hazor Shrine 6136 assemblage consisted of predominantly common domestic items. From a total of 69 artifacts and architectural features, P.M. Michèle Daviau counted 68 per cent typical domestic objects, mainly for food preparation, consumption, and storage, in addition to 34 per cent specialized items not typically found in domestic settings (e.g. basalt slabs, glass sceptre, bronze cymbals, offering table, statuettes). Daviau further determined that the number of bowls and chalices far exceeded the number ordinarily recovered from domestic contexts (Daviau 1993: 224-27). The Hazor assemblage included a preponderance of common domestic items, but, the architectural plan, the significant number and range of specialized items, and the atypical percentage of select vessel types confirm the cultic identification. In contrast to Hazor, the Megiddo Shrine 2081 and Tel Taanach 'Cultic Structure' vessels and objects associated with common domestic activities were ascribed cultic status based on a small number of associated, alleged cult objects; nothing marked the architectural setting as cultic. The archaeological presumption of cultic status for an entire assemblage when conferred by individual 'cult' items must be made explicit and requires corroborating evidence for a persuasive attribution.

Sanctity by association is tendentious, at best, whether it is based on a small number of cult items in a large assemblage or cultic space rendering the associated objects sacred. Sanctity by association is also susceptible to circular reasoning. An alleged cultic object confers sacred status on the associated assemblage, which in turn renders the space sacred, which bestows *maṣṣēbôt* status on any appropriately shaped stones in the vicinity. The alleged *maṣṣēbôt* found in the Megiddo 'Shrine' and Building 2081, the Taanach 'Cultic Structure', and the Jerusalem Ophel 'Ceremonial Structure' all exemplify the chain of presumptions beginning with or confirmed by associated 'cultic' objects. In her article 'Israelite Cult Elements in Secular Contexts of the 10th Century B.C.E.', Ora Negbi maintained, 'spatial and architectural data are the definitive criteria for determining whether the context is sacred or secular' (1993: 221). Cultic identification is best determined not by any one trait but by a convergence of factors including specific objects, the total assemblage, and the general context.[1]

Criteria for Identifying Israelite Maṣṣēbôt

Israelite *maṣṣēbôt* are not labelled or in any way marked as such; the classification in each case entails recognizing patterned behaviour in an appropriate context. Other than noting that Jacob erected a stone used as a pillow to be a *maṣṣēbâ* (Gen. 28.18), the Bible provides no physical description or prescription. Without biblical specifications, what criteria apply in the identification of archaeological examples of stones *functioning* as Israelite *maṣṣēbôt*? Archaeologically attested stones in cultic contexts, such as the Middle Bronze Age *Temple aux obélisques* in Byblos (Dunand 1950: pls. XX-XXXV) and the Late Bronze Age Shrine 6136 in the Hazor rampart (Yadin 1958: 87-88), corroborate the presumed contours of the biblical example. These second and first millennium BCE stones stood taller than they were wide, resting on a wide base that tapered towards a rounded top. In general, the stones displayed a flat or flattened face while the back was more rough or convex. Short stones measuring no more than 0.3 m high did not stand alone but beside larger more prominent stones.

One further criterion probably distinguishes *maṣṣēbôt* from utilitarian stones. In additional to the stipulated shape and size, no sacred stone should allow for a functional or structural identification, since sacred stones presumably tolerated

1. Uzi Avner identified *maṣṣēbôt* in the Negev and Sinai which purportedly stood alone or clustered in groups of 2, 3, 5, 7, or 9, combined broad and narrow stones, and typically faced east (Avner 1984; 1990; 1993). Close examination of published photographs suggests that many examples are misattributed fragmentary (round) house walls and the alleged significant number of standing stones discounts additional fallen, shorter, or slightly displaced stones clearly associated with those being counted. Given the doubts regarding the examples published with photographs, Avner's results are not included in this study.

little or no ambiguity in recognition. To avoid ambiguity the following criteria are proposed: (1) the stone's shape and size conform to expectations (generally, height exceeds width, though in substantial, isolated stones the width may equal or slightly exceed the height), (2) the stone does not bear a striking resemblance to a functional item such as a grinding stone, a stand, a constructional stone in a basin or wall, or a structural pillar, and (3) the context and accompanying assemblage support the identification *if the stone is functioning as a maṣṣēbâ*; a stone identical to nearby house pillars in a location where one might expect a house pillar or a grinding-shaped stone found among kitchen vessels in a domestic setting invite misattribution and so should be excluded from discussion. Based on both biblical and archaeological evidence, Carl Graesser defined a *maṣṣēbâ* as 'a plain stone set up by human activity so that it stands higher than it is wide' (1969: 296). Even this vague definition fails to include the 'Bull Site' stone and, of greater consequence, allows for functional items such as structural pillars and grinding stones. The criteria suggested above allow for individual variation yet preclude ambiguity in identification.

The proposed criteria are largely based on stones erected in public sacred space, which risks excluding variant practices from private or non-traditional sacred contexts. In fact, several short squat stones, measuring 0.3 m high or less, were deemed *maṣṣēbôt* though retrieved not from a temple or shrine but instead were found in a courtyard (Tel Rehov), a gateway (Beth-saida), along the city wall (Tel Dan), in a presumed cultic storage room (Tel Taanach), or buried in a pit in a pathway (Tel Lachish). If one accepts that the identification of *functioning maṣṣēbôt* is largely context dependent, then examples outside of or in a non-traditional sacred context *without further corroborating evidence* should be regarded as tentative.

2. *Iron Age* 'Maṣṣēbôt' *Re-assessed According to the Proposed Criteria*

Commonly accepted *maṣṣēbôt* from Iron Age Arad, Megiddo, and Hazor are now to be re-examined in the light of the proposed criteria. Of these three cases, one meets the criteria, a second fails, and a third is inconclusive. This disparity in results highlights the importance of explicitly stating criteria for interpreting physical remains.

Arad

Within the Judahite administrative fortress at Arad, one limestone *maṣṣēbâ*, perhaps in conjunction with two additional stones of flint, stood in the elevated niche of a temple. Yohanan Aharoni, director of the excavation, identified the temple on the basis of multiple features. Sacrifices were made on an altar (2.40 × 2.20 × 1.5 m high) built of unhewn stones in conformance with the biblical description (Exod. 20.22; Deut. 27.5-6; Josh. 8.31) in the temple courtyard (12.0 × 7.5 m). From the courtyard, one proceeded into a narrow broadroom (10.5 × 2.9 m) furnished with stone and mud benches. An elevated niche was constructed in the rear wall of this broadroom, on the central axis of the building. Apparently within the niche lay an arched limestone stele (0.9 m high) with remnants of red paint adhering to its short end (cf. Deut. 27.4-8). Two carved incense altars with burnt organic remains on top, measuring 0.50 m and 0.30 m high, rested on the step leading into the niche. Aharoni attributed the temple to Strata XI-VII (late tenth to the seventh centuries BCE). According to his historical reconstruction, the altar was decommissioned with Hezekiah's cultic reforms (Stratum VIII) and the temple finally destroyed during Josiah's reforms (Stratum VII) (Y. Aharoni 1967 and 1968). Preliminary reports and excavation team members' subsequent reports[2] prompted scholarly challenges to the stratigraphic determinations and consequent dating, and to the number of *maṣṣēbôt* standing in the niche.[3]

Most recently, Ze'ev Herzog led a team in the re-examination of the temple stratigraphy and associated pottery, to clarify the relevant strata and dates of temple use (Herzog 2001). Herzog restricted the life of the temple to Strata X and IX (late ninth to eighth century BCE), rather than Aharoni's significantly longer Strata XI-VII. Germane to our discussion, Herzog discounted the possibility that the two large flint slabs incorporated into the niche walls once functioned as *maṣṣēbôt*. Rather, he regarded them as construction stones. Conclusive determination is not possible from the published photographs or descriptions. Regarding the temple's demise, Herzog's team concluded that the temple was not destroyed in two stages; in fact, it was not destroyed at all. It was buried in the eighth century BCE and the destruction debris, which filtered into the temple remains, originated in a later stratum. Having limited the temple to the late ninth to eighth century BCE, Herzog confidently attributed its dismantling and burial to Hezekiah's religious reforms (Herzog 2001). Poor preservation and limitations of the excavation and publication preclude conclusive dating. Pottery analysis supports an eighth-century date for the temple (Herzog 2002; Singer-Avitz 2002). All that can be argued with conviction is that the temple existed for an indeterminate period between the tenth or ninth century and the early sixth century, most likely through the second half of the eighth century. A *maṣṣēbâ* stood in an official shrine niche down at least to the end of the eighth century.

Fulfilling all criteria cited above, the Arad stone convincingly functioned as a *maṣṣēbâ*. It stood with accompanying incense altars, in an elevated niche centrally positioned in the back wall of the inner room, fronted by a courtyard with an altar for animal sacrifices.

Megiddo

The Megiddo Shrine 2081 pair of pillars (early tenth century BCE, Stratum VA) fails to meet the proposed criteria for *maṣṣēbôt*. Two square stone pillars, each 1.5 m high, stood side-by-side in the entrance into the interior rooms of a large

2. Y. Aharoni 1967; M. Aharoni 1981; Herzog, M. Aharoni, Rainey, and Moshkovitz 1984.
3. Yadin 1965; Cross 1979; Mazar and Netzer 1986; Ussishkin 1988.

building designated Shrine 2081. This entryway opened out on to locus 2081, identified by the excavator Gordon Loud as a possible forecourt, which yielded an extensive assemblage including cultic vessels. At the time of excavation Loud wrote, 'The presence of cult objects in locus 2081 arouses the suspicion that two upright stones at the entrance to the central room north of it may, despite their perfect structural positions, bear some cult significance' (1948: 45). A later generation more inclined to identify archaeological examples of *maṣṣēbôt* instead argued that the position of the pillars demonstrated their cultic rather than structural function (Y. Aharoni 1968: 19; 1975: 31). Nothing distinguishes these pillars from structural pillars of comparable size and shape in the adjacent structure(s) to the west: the pair in locus 2112 and the single doorway pillar in locus 2162 (Loud 1948: fig. 388). Negbi also argued against a cultic attribution, instead stressing the 'secular affinities' of the building: the location among private houses in a residential quarter, the elaborated 'four-room' house plan, and the building size and contents commensurate with the residence of a prosperous owner (1993: 221). Clearly, these pillars fail one identification criterion; their resemblance to nearby structural pillars and location where pillars might be expected render them liable to being mistaken for house pillars rather than sacred stones.

Furthermore, neither context nor accompanying assemblage secures the identification. While Loud proposed that locus 2081 might function as a forecourt for the building with the pillared entryway, the forecourt designation is tentative, as most of the ground surface, the south-eastern corner of the court, and the southern closing wall are all reconstructed. Cultic objects lay jumbled among household pots, tools, and personal items scattered throughout the adjacent open area and were concentrated in a corner of the reconstructed courtyard. Two limestone horned altars (one large and one small), two offering stands (one large and one small), a tall fenestrated stand, and a 'steleform' stone comprised the cultic assemblage. The two altars and one incense stand lay in the 'courtyard' corner among common domestic items including several jars, limestone objects, a jug, and a chalice. Generally overlooked is the fact that the vast majority of the more than one hundred courtyard objects and vessels were typical household items: 36 jugs, 16 bowls, seven jars, two chalices, one cooking bowl, one lamp, four steatite scarabs or scaraboids, three stamp seals, bone objects (whorl, handle, awl, spindles, miniature mallet), bronze items (toggle pin, fibula, bracelets, finger ring), iron pieces (five arrowheads, an axe), two faience Eyes of Horus, beads, a basalt mortar and pestle, basalt vessels, clay stoppers, two basalt stone rubbers, and sheep/goat or perhaps pig astragali in a bowl from an undefined location in the courtyard (Loud 1948: 161-62). The range of items indicative of hunting, processing grain, cooking, and spinning more likely derive from a domestic than a cultic context, though processing olive oil, weaving textiles, and preparing and consuming foodstuffs were cultic as well as domestic activities. The assemblage may be interpreted in various ways. Perhaps some objects considered 'cultic' by virtue of their form or high value (e.g. tall stands for bowls and incense stands) were actually 'elite'. Alternatively, as proposed by Walter Rast in the case of the

Tel Taanach Cultic Structure assemblage, 'cultic' objects found in secular settings may have been ritual objects entrusted to priests or artisans for storage, repair or maintenance (1994: 361). Whether the altars and stands in locus 2081 are elite rather than cultic, or cult items stored among secular items in a domestic setting, these few items do not indicate that the location was cultic or that the pillars functioned as *maṣṣēbôt*.

In the case of the pair of pillars in the entryway to the building opening into locus 2081, neither their architectural position, context within the structure, shape and size, nor associated assemblage suggests they functioned as *maṣṣēbôt* or would have been recognized as such. Yigael Shiloh expressed this opinion already in 1979 (1979: 147).

Hazor

The mid-eleventh century BCE Area B Stratum XI *maṣṣēbâ* exemplifies a stone whose cultic assignation remains indeterminate. Interpretation premised on patterned behaviour precludes categorizing distinctive occurrences such as the Hazor stone with its atypical shape, in a unique architectural setting. Yigael Yadin's excavation in the 1950s revealed portions of a building's internal rooms: the southern end of a paved room containing the 'bamah' and '*maṣṣēbâ*' (locus 3283) and paved surfaces of adjoining rooms (loci 3275, 3279, 3307). Limited exposure precluded determining the building's overall function. At the southern end of the preserved room, a low, narrow (0.2–0.3 m) ledge ran around a low, very wide platform or 'bamah'. A large, banana-shaped stone found recumbent presumably stood, propped up, as a *maṣṣēbâ* on the bamah (Yadin 1958: 84-87; Ben-Tor 1996: 266-68).

Objects found in the vicinity were adduced in support of cultic activity. A one-handled, plain grey jug filled with bronzes including a Late Bronze Age seated male figurine lay buried beneath the floor near the platform. Even as the figurine lends cultic status to the room, the aggregate bronzes require explanation. In addition to the figurine, the jug contained an axe, two swords/blades, two javelin butts, a needle, a wire, two javelin heads, two possible fibulas, a bracelet, a bent rod, and a lump (Yadin 1961: pl. CCV). While possibly cultic, the bronzes are arguably scrap metal to be smelted and recast (so also Uehlinger 1997: 104). Within the room on the floor lay basalt vessels, a chalice, various types of mortars and pestles, a bronze toggle-pin(?), a bronze arrowhead, and a bone handle, nothing definitively cultic. On the pavement outside the cult room to the south (locus 3275), excavators uncovered a complete 'incense burner' on a fenestrated stand and fragments of an additional stand, together with a faience bead and a bronze arrowhead. Two more stands lay on the pavement outside the cult room to the north-east (locus 3307) (Yadin *et al.* 1961: pls. XXXVII-XXXVIII, CCIII-CCVI; Ben-Tor 1989: 80-81, plan XVIII; Ben-Tor personal communication). The concentration of stands, the buried bronze hoard, the perimeter ledge and platform/bamah, and the peculiarly shaped stone all deviate from attested public, private, and governmental assemblages, and so arguably served a cultic function.

3. *Conclusions*

Colin Renfrew argued for a 'framework of inference' that allows for the reconstruction of cult practice and religious belief based on material remains. Archaeologists operate on the presumption that religious beliefs, recorded in texts, precipitated actions that produced the material remains (Renfrew 1985: 11-12). Each excavator and subsequent interpreter's 'framework', with its underlying interpretative principles and assumptions, must be made explicit for others to evaluate the plausibility of any interpretation.

Considering the specific case of *maṣṣēbôt*, whether or not a stone functioned as a *maṣṣēbâ* is a matter of interpretation as *maṣṣēbôt* lacked distinctive identifying markings. This article proposes criteria for identifying stones that *functioned* as *maṣṣēbôt*; in cases where the stone was discarded or placed in storage, neither the context nor the accompanying assemblage necessarily supports the *maṣṣēbâ* identification, and therefore its cultic status remains tentative. The identifying criteria address both the physical specifications and the perception of the stone as a cultic marker: (1) the stone's shape and size conform to expectation; generally, height exceeds width, (2) the stone does not bear a striking resemblance to a functional item such that its cultic status is not evident, and (3) the context and accompanying assemblage support the identification *if the stone is functioning as a maṣṣēbâ*.

Applying the proposed criteria to published examples of Israelite *maṣṣēbôt*, a surprising number lose their sacred status, others are relegated to possible *maṣṣēbôt*, and the rest merit plausible or certain status. Stones in the following settings lose their sacred status because they resemble functional stones—structural pillars, grinding stones, or stands—found in a context appropriate to their functional or structural purposes: Megiddo Shrine 2081 (Stratum VA, early tenth century BCE) (Loud 1948: 45); Megiddo Building 338 Stratum VA-IVB, tenth century BCE) (Schumacher 1908: 110-24); Tel Taanach 'Cultic Structure' (second half of the tenth century BCE) (Lapp 1964: 26-28); Lachish Cult Room 49 (Stratum V, 1000–925 BCE) (Y. Aharoni: 1975: 26); Jerusalem 'Ceremonial Structure' (Phase 2C, late ninth century BCE) (Kenyon 1964: 9); Lahav 'Shrine' (Stratum VIB, late eighth century BCE) (Borowski 1995: 151-52); and the Beth-shemesh 'betyls' (seventh century BCE) (Mackenzie 1912: 174). The gateway stone at Tell el-Far'ah (N) (Niveau 3; Period VIIb–VIIe, eleventh or tenth to the seventh century BCE) (de Vaux 1951: 428) may be a *maṣṣēbâ*. More plausible or probable examples include Shechem Temple I (twelfth to eleventh century BCE) (Wright 165: fig. 28); the Bull Site (twelfth to eleventh century BCE) (Mazar 1982: 33-36); Hazor Bamah (Stratum XI, mid-eleventh century BCE) (Ben-Tor 1996: 266-68); Lachish locus 81b and favissae stones (Strata V-III, tenth to eighth century BCE) (Y. Aharoni 1975: 28-32); Tel Rehov courtyard bamah (Phase E-1a-b, tenth or ninth century BCE) (Mazar 2000: 44-45); Tel Dan gateway *maṣṣēbôt*—some more plausible than others (Strata 3-2, first half of the ninth to the second half of the eighth century BCE) (Biran 1998: 42-45); and Beth-saida gateway—some more plausible than others (Level 5b-a, 850-732 BCE)

(Arav 2001). Only the Arad fortress temple (Strata X-XI) (Y. Aharoni 1967) provides an undisputable example of an Israelite *maṣṣēbâ*. This survey highlights the need for explicit cultic criteria, ideally widely adopted, to facilitate meaningful discussion on *maṣṣēbôt* in the Israelite cult.

BIBLIOGRAPHY

Abū 'Assāf, 'Alī

1990 *Der Tempel von 'Ain Dārā* (Damaszener Forschungen, 3; Mainz: Philipp von Zabern).

Aharoni, Miriam

1981 'Preliminary Ceramic Report on Strata 12-11 at Arad Citadel', *IEJ* 15: 181-204 (Hebrew).

Aharoni, Yohanan

1967 'Excavations at Tel Arad: Preliminary Report on the Second Season, 1963', *IEJ* 17: 233-49.

1968 'Arad: Its Inscriptions and Temple', *BA* 31: 20-32.

1974 'The Horned Altar of Beer-sheba', *BA* 37: 2-6.

1975 *Investigations at Lachish, The Sanctuary and the Residency (Lachish V)* (Tel Aviv: Gateway Publications).

Amiran, Ruth

1981 'Some Observations on Chalcolithic and Early Bronze Age Sanctuaries and Religion', in A. Biran (ed.), *Temples and High Places in Biblical Times* (Jerusalem: Nelson Glueck School of Biblical Archaeology of the Hebrew Union College–Jewish Institute of Religion): 47-53.

Arav, Rami

2001 'Bethsaida, 2000', *IEJ* 51: 239-46.

Avner, Uzi

1984 'Ancient Cult Sites in the Negev and Sinai Deserts', *TA* 11: 115-31.

1990 'Ancient Agricultural Settlement and Religion in the Uvda Valley in Southern Israel', *BA* 53: 125-41.

1993 '*Mazzebot* Sites in the Negev and Sinai and the Significance', in Biran and Aviram (eds.) 1993: 166-81.

Ben-Tor, Amnon

1966 'Tel Hazor, 1996', *IEJ* 46: 262-69.

Ben-Tor, Amnon (ed.)

1989 *Hazor III-IV: An Account of the Third and Fourth Seasons of Excavations, 1957–1958: Text* (Jerusalem: Israel Exploration Society and Hebrew University of Jerusalem).

Biran, Avraham

1998 'Sacred Spaces of Standing Stones, High Places and Cult Objects at Tel Dan', *BARev* 24.5: 38-45, 70.

Biran, A., and J. Aviram (eds.)

1993 *Biblical Archaeology Today, 1990: Proceedings of the Second International Congress on Biblical Archaeology* (Jerusalem: Israel Exploration Society).

Blomquist, Tina Haettner

1999 *Gates and Gods: Cults in the City Gates of Iron Age Palestine: An Investigation of the Archaeological and Biblical Sources* (ConBOT, 46; Stockholm: Almqvist & Wiksell).

Borowski, Oded
1995 'Hezekiah's Refom and the Revolt Against Assyria', *BA* 58: 148-55.
Coogan, Michael D.
1987 'Of Cults and Cultures: Reflections on the Interpretation of Archaeological Evidence', *PEQ* 119: 1-8.
Cross, Frank M.
1979 'Two Offering Dishes with Phoenician Inscriptions from the Sanctuary of 'Arad', *BASOR* 235: 75-78.
Daviau, P.M. Michèle
1993 *Houses and Their Furnishings in Bronze Age Palestine: Domestic Activity Areas and Artefact Distribution in the Middle and Late Bronze Ages* (JSOT/ASOR Monograph Series, 8; Sheffield: Sheffield Academic Press).
Dunand, Maurice
1950 *Fouilles de Byblos*, II (Paris: Atlas).
Fowler, Mervyn D.
1985 'Excavated incense burners: A Case for Identifying a Site as Sacred?', *PEQ* 117: 25-29.
Graesser, Carl
1969 'Studies in *Maṣṣēbôt*' (unpublished PhD dissertation, Harvard University).
Herzog, Ze'ev
2001 'The Date of the Temple at Arad: Reassessment of the Stratigraphy and the Implications for the History of Religion in Judah', in A. Mazar (ed.), *Studies in the Archaeology of the Iron Age in Israel and Jordan* (JSOTSup, 331; Sheffield: Sheffield Academic Press): 156-78.
2002 'The Fortress Mound at Tel Arad: An Interim Report', *TA* 29 (2002): 1-109.
Herzog, Ze'ev, Miriam Aharoni, Anson F. Rainey and S. Moshkovitz
1984 'The Israelite Fortress at Arad', *BASOR* 254: 1-34.
Kenyon, Kathleen M.
1964 'Excavations in Jerusalem, 1963', *PEQ* 96: 7-18.
Lapp, Paul W.
1964 'The 1963 Excavations at Ta'annek', *BASOR* 173: 4-44.
Loud, Gordon
1948 *Megiddo II, Seasons of 1935–39* (Oriental Institute Publications, 62; Chicago: University of Chicago Press).
Mackenzie, Duncan
1912 'The Excavations at 'Ain Shems, June–July 1912', *PEFQS*: 171-78.
Mazar, Amihai
1982 'The Bull Site—An Iron Age I Open Cult Place', *BASOR* 247: 27-42.
1992 'Temples of the Middle and Late Bronze Ages and the Iron Age', in A. Kempinski and R. Reich (eds.), *The Architecture of Ancient Israel: From the Prehistoric to the Persian Periods* (Jerusalem: Israel Exploration Society): 161-87.
Mazar, Amihai, and John Camp
2000 'Will Tel Rehov Save the United Monarchy?', *BARev* 26.2: 38-51, 75.
Mazar, Amihai, and Ehud Netzer
1986 'On the Israelite Fortress at Arad', *BASOR* 263: 87-90.
McCown, Chester C.
1950 'Hebrew High Places and Cult Remains', *JBL* 69: 205-19.
Monson, John
2000 'The New 'Ain Dara Temple: Closest Solomonic Parallel', *BARev* 26.3: 20-35, 67.

Negbi, Ora

1993 'Israelite Cult Elements in Secular Contexts of the 10th Century B.C.E.', in Biran and Aviram (eds.) 1993: 221-30.

Ottosson, Magnus

1980 *Temples and Cult Places in Palestine* (Uppsala Studies in Ancient Mediterranean and Near Eastern Civilizations, 12; Uppsala: Uppsala University).

Pritchard, James B. (ed.)

1969 *Ancient Near East in Pictures Relating to the Old Testament* (Princeton, NJ: Princeton University Press, 3rd edn with supplement).

Rast, Walter

1994 'Priestly Families and the Cultic Structure at Taanach', in M.D. Coogan, J.C. Exum and L.E. Stager (eds.), *Scripture and Other Artifacts: Essays on the Bible and Archaeology in Honor of Philip J. King* (Louisville, KY: Westminster/ John Knox Press): 355-65.

Renfrew, Colin

1985 *The Archaeology of Cult: The Sanctuary of Phylakopi* (British School of Archaeology in Athens Supp., 18; London: British School of Archaeology in Athens and Thames & Hudson).

Schumacher, Gottlieb

1908 *Tell el-Mutesellim I* (Leipzig: Haupt).

Shiloh, Yigael

1979 'Iron Age Sanctuaries and Cult Elements in Palestine', in F.M. Cross (ed.), *Symposia Celebrating the Seventh-Fifth Anniversary of the Founding of the American Schools of Oriental Research* (Cambridge, MA: ASOR): 147-57.

Singer-Avitz, Lily

2002 'The Iron Age Pottery Assemblages', *TA* 29 (2002): 110-214.

Stager, Lawrence E., and Samuel R. Wolff

1981 'Production and Commerce in Temple Courtyards: An Olive Press in the Sacred Precinct at Tel Dan', *BASOR* 243: 95-102.

Uehlinger, Christoph

1997 'Anthropomorphic Cult Statuary in Iron Age Palestine and the Search for Yahweh's Cult Image', in Karel van der Toorn (ed.), *The Image and the Book: Iconic Cults, Aniconism, and the Rise of Book Religion in Israel and the Ancient Near East* (Leuven: Peeters): 97-155.

Ussishkin, David

1988 'The Date of the Judaean Shrine at Arad', *IEJ* 38: 142-57.

Vaux, Roland de

1951 'La Troisième Campagne de Fouilles à Tell el-Far'ah, près Naplouse', *RB* 58: 393-430.

Wright, G. Ernest

1965 *Shechem: The Biography of a Biblical City* (New York: McGraw–Hill).

Yadin, Yigael

1958 *Hazor I: An Account of the First Season of Excavations, 1955* (Jerusalem: Magnes Press).

1965 'A Note on the Stratigraphy of Arad', *IEJ* 15: 180.

Yadin, Yigael, Yohanan Aharoni, Ruth Amiran, Trude Dothan, Immanuel Dunayevsky and Jean Perrot

1961 *Hazor*, III–IV. *An Account of the Third and Fourth Seasons of Excavations, 1957–1958: Plates* (Jerusalem: Magnes Press).

From Gibeon to Gibeah: High Place of the Kingdom*

Simcha Shalom Brooks

The biblical sources have seriously neglected Saul's origins and reign. His biography is so brief that it is difficult to evaluate his place in Israelite history. There is no clear statement as to how long he reigned. The dominant impression is that Saul was a failure. Only scattered hints give the indication that Saul was a strong military leader of political and religious importance. Yet this way of presenting Saul was not from a lack of availability of material, but due to a deliberate and selective editing by the pro-Davidic writers in order to legitimize David's accession to the throne of Israel. My aim in this article is to examine the sources, both textual and archaeological, in order to find out whether it is possible to extract any information that might then bring to light some aspects of Saul's origins and reign which have not been considered before. The purpose of exploiting the textual and archaeological material is neither to force archaeological data into proving the biblical events, nor to force the biblical account to interpret the archaeological data. Rather, it is to see whether there could be a 'dialogue' between the two, and whether that 'dialogue' can shed light on the events discussed within the context of this article.

This paper divides into two main sections. Section 1 concentrates on the city of Gibeon. It is my primary hypothesis that Gibeon was already a major cultic centre *before* the reign of Solomon, and in particular in the time of Saul. Secondly, that Gibeon was Saul's ancestral home from where he emerged to kingship. Section 2 concentrates on the possibility of Gibeah, Saul's capital city, being identified with Tell el-Ful.

1. *Gibeon*

Biblical Gibeon has been identified with modern el-Jib, 9 km north of Jerusalem. The first proper scientific identification with modern el-Jib was in 1838 by Edward Robinson (see also Pritchard 1962: 24-52). During the archaeological excavations of 1956, 1957 and 1959, directed by J.B. Pritchard, this identification was confirmed by the discovery of thirty-one jar handles inscribed with the name

* My special thanks are extended to Nancy Lapp for her kind permission to use her illustrations (figs. 3 and 4), and for allowing me access to the Tell el-Ful pottery; to Professor S. Gitin for his kind welcome to the Albright Institute in Jerusalem, and for arranging access to the pottery from Tell el-Ful in April 1994; to Dr Shimon Gibson for his kind permission to use his topographic map of Tell el-Ful (fig. 2) and to Professor John Day for his useful comments on this paper.

gb'n. These inscribed jar handles date from the end of the Judaean monarchy. A. Demsky (1971) and S. Yeivin (1971) have demonstrated that there is a link between Saul's genealogy lists in 1 Chronicles (8.29-40; 9.35-44) and the names inscribed on the jar handles. The studies of these genealogies by Demsky and Yeivin provide some evidence relating to the Benjaminites' settlement in their territory. Demsky attests that these lists present at one and the same time the history of the branch of the Ner family, and the clans and villages that depended on Gibeon both culturally and administratively. These lists also illustrate the relationship of the clans to each other and to Gibeon which would not have changed from the time of the initial Benjaminite settlement to the exile (see Demsky 1971). Yeivin suggests (1971: 145) that after the Benjaminites' penetration there must have been a considerable integration with the local inhabitants, mainly through marriage, the results of which are reflected in the genealogical lists in Chronicles. These lists are not concerned with the Gibeonites of Gibeon, but with the Benjaminite group which came to settle at Gibeon in the course of time. Their eponymous ancestor is called 'the father of Gibeon' in 1 Chron. 8.29-40 and its duplicate in 9.35-44. In the first list his personal name is not given, whereas in the second list he is named Yehiel.

The most interesting aspect of these lists is the naming of the wife of 'the father of Gibeon' as Maacah (Yeivin 1971: 151). This name does not appear as an Israelite name, but is the name of an Aramaean principality in the Golan. When it appears as a personal name it always represents a non-Israelite or someone of non-Israelite descent (Yeivin 1971: 151).[1] This reference to the non-Israelite Maacah may indicate one element of the penetration into Gibeon which expressed itself in intermarriage with the local women. Such intermarriages probably resulted in acquisition of rights of heritage and property. The title 'the father of Gibeon' could indicate a head of a large family, probably quite wealthy and influential. Three generations after settling there that family produced Saul the son of Kish as the first Israelite king. Indeed, Saul's ancestors are recorded as Kish, Ner...and Benjamin, i.e. in ascending order from the smaller to the larger unit (Demsky 1971: 17). Also in 1 Sam. 9.1, Kish, Saul's father, is described as *gibbôr ḥayil*, which is also taken to mean a man of wealth.

Gibeon might well have been a prosperous city; the flat land around Gibeon was suitable for agricultural production and the slopes beyond were suitable for vineyards. The Karstic[2] character of the soil meant there were many springs of which the largest was at Gibeon. This richness in water sources and agricultural land indicates a flourishing economy as evidenced by the large number of pots found as well as by the frequent occurrences of wine cellars. About forty such cellars have been discovered. These were cistern-like constructions, each 2 m deep and dug out of the rock. The jars inside each cellar held about 45 litres of wine; sixty-six such cellars were unearthed and should give an idea of the economic prosperity of Gibeon.

1. E.g. 2 Sam. 3.3; 1 Kgs 2.39; 1 Chron. 27.16.

2. Karstic topography is rocky type of countryside found in limestone areas. Ground water makes its way through the rock and dissolves it, and streams flow below the surface (Watt 1982).

However, there are scholars who reject the connection between Saul and Gibeon because they claim that the reference in Chronicles is late and unreliable. But that argument stands on weak ground; the studies by Demsky and Yeivin are more convincing, demonstrating that these genealogies had been composed before the area was depopulated and that the relationship of these clans to Gibeon would not have changed radically from the time of the initial settlement in the area until the exile (Demsky 1971: 17; see also Blenkinsopp 1972: 61-62).

The archaeological excavations also indicate that the site was not occupied at all prior to the period of the settlement, i.e. the Iron I period (Pritchard 1976: 449-50). R.B. Coote and K.W. Whitelam (1987: 128) argue that 'the fact that such sites as Jericho, 'Ai and Gibeon, key cities in the biblical account of the "conquest", provide no archaeological evidence of occupation during this period...forces the search for alternative explanations'. It is not my intention to discuss the 'conquest' period here, nor Ai or Jericho. But, as far as Gibeon is concerned, here is the alternative explanation demanded by Coote and Whitelam. Thus no trace of Late Bronze Age settlement was discovered at Gibeon because there was no Hivite settlement there, despite the statement in Joshua. In the following Iron I period, Gibeon was *first* settled by the Benjaminites. The name 'Gibeonites' should not be understood as the name of an ethnic group, but merely as a name given to the inhabitants of Gibeon. There was no pre-Israelite, i.e. Hivite group there, contrary to what is suggested in Joshua 9. This story of the Gibeonites was a later addition to Joshua designed to provide a background to and justification for David's slaughter of Saul's family in 2 Samuel 21.

Now I would like to consider the text. We are told that Gibeon was the largest and best known of the Benjaminite cities, and is described as 'a large city, like one of the royal cities...' (Josh. 10.2). The biblical text indicates a number of cultic centres used by the Israelites during this period. These are Shiloh, Gilgal, Mizpah and Bethel (Fig. 1). Until the reign of Solomon there seems to be no mention of Israelites worshipping at Gibeon. My suggestion is that, although Gibeon is not specifically mentioned before Solomon, it was probably already the largest place of worship in the time of Saul. 1 Kings 3.2 states that 'The people were sacrificing at the high places, however, because no house had yet been built for the name of the Lord'. Furthermore, Solomon went to Gibeon to offer the sacrifices: 'The king went to Gibeon to sacrifice there, for that was the principal high place; Solomon used to offer a thousand burnt offerings on that altar' (1 Kgs 3.4).

The presentation in this text of the importance of the sanctuary at Gibeon has been explained as reflecting a desire to relate the old to the new way of worship about to begin (de Vaux 1960: II, 126, ET 1961: 297); others, however, reject it as a fabrication by the narrator of Kings intended to justify Solomon's inaugural visit to Gibeon and to bring his action into line with the Priestly law in Lev. 17.8-9 (Williamson 1982: 130-31). But these explanations must now be revised and Gibeon should be seriously considered as having played an important role in Israelite cultic life in the time of Saul. My view is based on several considerations. First, it is implausible that Gibeon was insignificant throughout the period

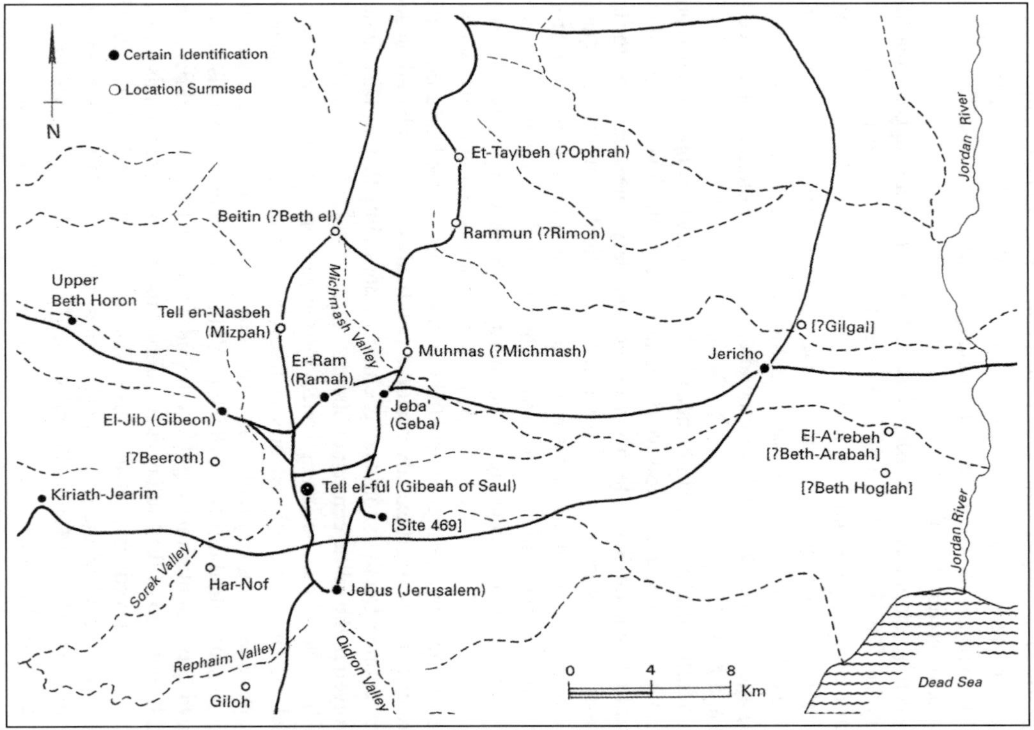

Figure 1. *The Central Highlands (The Territory of Benjamin and South Ephraim): Iron Age I Main Sites and Internal Routes (Shalom Brooks 1998)*

between Samuel and Saul and David; its cultic popularity does not make sense unless the sanctuary had a long history behind it (de Vaux 1960: II, 138, ET 1961: 306). It could not have suddenly emerged as so important in the reign of Solomon. Secondly, the description of worship at Gibeon makes sense and is quite convincing since Gibeon is described as a Levitical city (Josh. 21.17). Moreover, according to the Chronicler the 'Tent of Meeting' (*'ōhel mō'ēd*) was there (1 Chron. 16.39; 21.29; 2 Chron. 1.3). Gibeon probably served as a major cultic place from the early days of the Israelite settlement there. The main reason for the lack of emphasis upon Gibeon in the text is probably because Saul's family is strongly associated with Gibeon.

This can be supported by J. Blenkinsopp (1974: 1), who suggests that the sanctuary that David visited (2 Sam. 21.1) was at Gibeon. He also argues that the first altar (*'eben gᵉdōlâ*) that Saul built to Yahweh (1 Sam. 14.33) was in the Gibeonite region and must be the 'great stone' which is at Gibeon (2 Sam. 20.8). According to Blenkinsopp, this stone has cultic significance (Josh. 24.26; 1 Sam. 6.14-16) and may be identified with the altar on which Solomon sacrificed at Gibeon in 1 Kgs 3.4.

If we return to the reference in Joshua (21.17) in which Gibeon is listed as one of the Levitical cities, a question would be raised as to the involvement of the Benjaminite group, i.e. Saul's family, with the sanctuary. The sources for the list of the Levitical cities are not clear. Joshua lists forty-eight towns divided equally among the tribes, though this list is repeated with some variations in 1 Chron. 6.39-66. On the one hand, Deuteronomy describes these Levites scattered throughout the land as depending on the charity of those who possessed wealth (de Vaux 1960: II, 225, ET 1961: 366-67). On the other hand, Levitical towns are described as important centres, where the Levites controlled the land around. It is therefore difficult to assert exactly what the Levitical system was based on and how it functioned, but this should not exclude the possibility that the Kish family was involved in the cultic centre at Gibeon.

This hypothesis can be strengthened by the reference to the incident in 1 Samuel 13, where Saul offered the sacrifice without waiting for Samuel and is thus regarded as doing so illicitly, as well as by the reference to Saul's taking part in an ecstatic ritual in 1 Sam. 10.9-11. Within the context of this discussion the following two quotations might be relevant: Deut. 33.12 states, 'of Benjamin he said: the beloved of the Lord rests in safety—the high God surrounds him all day long—the beloved rests between his shoulders'; and Ps. 68.27-28 (ET 26-27) declares, 'Bless God in the great congregation, the Lord, O you who are of Israel's fountain! There is Benjamin, the youngest, in the lead…' However, with the emergence of the monarchical office there may have been demands to separate it from the religious institution, a problem well expressed in the tension between Saul and Samuel.[3]

3. K. van der Toorn (1993) argues that the rule under Saul meant a break from the old order, that the religion of the Saulide state began in the army, since warfare in the ancient world was not purely a secular matter (p. 528), and also that Saul chose Yahweh as the patron god of the state (p. 541).

An additional reason why the sources are silent about Gibeon as a major cultic place could be that the intention is to draw attention away from the significance of David's action regarding the transfer of the ark to Jerusalem. But the reference to the location of the ark at Kiriath-jearim is dubious and needs careful examination. In Josh. 9.17 Kiriath-jearim is cited as one of the four Gibeonite cities[4] and located 10 km north-west of Jerusalem. Kiriath-jearim is also referred to in the incident described in Joshua 10; again, in 1 Samuel 6 Kiriath-jearim is associated with the return of the ark from the Philistines, after the battle at Ebenezer (1 Sam. 6.21–7.1a). It is stated:

> So they sent messengers to the inhabitants of Kiriath-jearim saying, 'the Philistines have returned the ark of the Lord. Come down and take it up to you'. And the people of Kiriath-jearim came and took up the ark of the Lord, and brought it to the house of Abinadab on the hill.

It should be noted that there seems to be a contradiction in connection with the location of Kiriath-jearim. According to the story in Joshua 9–10 and 18.14, Kiriath-jearim is located in Benjamin. Yet the Chronicler (probably as part of his tendency to Judaize everything) places Kiriath-jearim in Judah (1 Chron. 13.6). This cannot be correct, because the Chronicler based his location on 2 Sam. 6.2, which in itself is a distorted verse and does not, in any case, indicate with any clarity that Kiriath-jearim is in Judah. Finally, the Israelites gathered for worship at several places such as Gilgal, Mizpah, Bethel and most probably at Gibeon as well. Significantly, the editor of Josh. 18.14 was probably aware of the contradiction and therefore, in an attempt to correct it, added that Kiriath-jearim is a town belonging to Benjamin. L. Rost (1926: 6, ET 1982: 7) tried to solve this problem by suggesting that Baalah (2 Sam. 6.2) is another name for Kiriath-jearim.

By rejecting the location of Kiriath-jearim in Judah, and placing it instead near Gibeon, I would still argue that the ark could not have been placed at Kiriath-jearim. The issue which still remains is that Kiriath-jearim does not play any role in the life of the Israelites. After all, it was a Hivite settlement, not an Israelite one. My suggestion is that it is possible that the ark had been placed at the great cultic centre that was at Gibeon. There is no other suitable place for it. This claim can be supported by the following two quotations:

> For the tabernacle of the Lord, which Moses had made in the wilderness, and the altar of burnt offering were at that time in the high place at Gibeon. (1 Chron. 21.29)

> Then Solomon and the whole of the assembly with him went to the high place that was at Gibeon; for God's tent of meeting, which Moses the servant of the Lord had made in the wilderness, was there. But David had brought out the ark of God up from Kiriath-jearim to the place that David prepared for it... (2 Chron. 1.3-4)

Most commentators overlook the significance of David's removal of the ark from Kiriath-jearim, and instead focus their attention on its destination, Jerusalem (see, e.g., Jones 1993: 36; Williamson 1982: 192-94). But one must realize

4. The others are Chephira, Beeroth and Kiriath-jearim. They are close to each other in distance and are situated in Benjaminite territory.

that readers would expect the ark to be at Gibeon because the high place and the Tent of Meeting (*'ōhel mō'ēd*) were there. Therefore it is more logical that the ark should be there too, since the Tent of Meeting and the ark are inseparable. It could be argued, of course, that the ark and the tent were originally separate and came together at a certain point later. My suggestion would then be that once they came together they became inseparable.

G. von Rad (1958: 109-29, ET 1966: 103-24) showed that the relationship between the 'ark of the Lord' and the 'Tent of Meeting' is very close. The notion that Yahweh dwells in the tent is clearly found in P. This is mainly because of the frequent use of the phrase 'before the Lord' in cultic activities, for example in the offering of sacrifices, and in slaughtering, making atonement and laying shew-bread. All these activities take place 'before' the God who is thought of as being in the tent (e.g. Lev. 1.5; 14.23). It should be mentioned that the date of P is disputed, many considering that it comes from the post-exilic period; if that view is correct, evidence from P could not be used here, but nevertheless, there are also scholars who think that P rests on earlier practices. According to Lev. 4.7, the altar of incense stood before the Lord. There is an opposing view to this which suggests that the Lord does not dwell in the tent, but appears there from time to time (e.g. Exod. 16.10). But whether Yahweh dwelt in the tent or appeared there from time to time, the close connection between the ark and the tent remains. This connection shows why the ark could not be placed separately in Kiriath-jearim and that it is more likely to have been situated at Gibeon with the tent.

As far as Deuteronomy is concerned, however, the ark has no cultic significance, nor any relation to sacrificial worship, nor is it the dwelling place of Yahweh (de Vaux 1960: II, 131-32, ET 1961: 301). Consequently, every trace of magical belief is omitted and the ark becomes merely the place where the tablets were kept (see Deut. 10.1-5). Moreover, what is striking in Deuteronomy is the absence of the tent and its association with the ark. There is, however, one mention of the tent in Deuteronomy (31.14), but it is attributed to the Elohistic commentators. In my view, these accounts regarding the ark and the tent should not be seen as a contradiction but as a development in the religion of Israel. The ark and the tent played a major role in the cultic life of Israel for many generations. Evidently this changed later, possibly after the building of the Temple, or by the time of the Deuteronomist when their function was unknown, except for the ark which merely provided a safe place for the tablets of the law. One may also assume that Deut. 31.14 was written during or after the exile, in which case the ark would have been lost anyway. However, the description of the ark and an understanding of its function and place in Israelite cultic practice in the period of Saul would give great insight as to its significance and would explain why it was so important for David to remove the ark from Gibeon (or Kiriath-jearim). David not only wanted complete control over Israel through the monarchical and religious office, he also wanted to eliminate any attachment of the people to the old rule of the house of Saul.

If we return to the Tent of Meeting at Gibeon, it would seem that the ark and the tent are inseparable. So the ark could not in any way be located at Kiriath-jearim, but only at Gibeon. Thus the reference in 2 Chron. 1.14, which suggests that David brought the ark from Kiriath-jearim to Jerusalem, is intended partly to justify this transfer and to diminish Gibeon as an important Benjaminite cultic city.

2. *Gibeah of Saul*

The search for Gibeah began in the 1840s and since then its identification with the site of Tell el-Ful (Arabic translated as 'hill of beans') has provoked hot debate among biblical scholars and archaeologists. One of the reasons for the uncertainty about the identification of Gibeah is the story in Judges 19–21, which indicates that Gibeah existed before the monarchy. However, the chronology of Gibeah in this story and the later identification of Gibeah as Saul's city do not correlate with the archaeological finds at this site; therefore, scholars argued in favour of placing Gibeah at a number of other ancient ruins.[5] My aim in this section is to discuss the arguments for the identification of Gibeah with modern Tell el-Ful and to re-examine and reconstruct the archaeological data which may have been misinterpreted.

Gibeah was the central city in the territory of Benjamin, and the royal capital at the time of Saul. It was located on the main road from Judah to Mt Ephraim (Judg. 19.11-13), near the Jerusalem–Shechem road. The territory of the tribe of Benjamin is characterized by a hilly terrain. Therefore, the biblical sources relating to this territory contain a large number of place names based on the root *g-b-'*, the stem for the Hebrew word meaning 'hill'. These include the names Gibeon (modern el-Jib), Geba (Jaba', 1 Sam. 14.5) and Gibeah (Judg. 19.12; 1 Sam. 14.2), the last named thought to be Tell el-Ful. There are also longer terms such as Geba of Benjamin (1 Sam. 13.16), Gibeah of Benjamin (13.2) and Gibeath Haelohim (10.5). In addition Mizpah (10.17) and Ramah (22.6) are also included in this territory: although these place names are not based on the same root, they do have a similar meaning, Mizpah meaning 'observation place' and Ramah meaning 'high (or elevated) place'.

The modern site of Tell el-Ful is situated 5.5 km north of the Damascus Gate in Jerusalem. It is located on the crest of the watershed, with deep wadis extending to the east and west (Fig. 2 [next page]). The hill rises with steep terraces on the east, south and north, but on the west the slope is more gradual. The slopes have a steepness of about 30 degrees or more, which made travel from north to south quite difficult. The ancient road from Judah to Mt Ephraim ran along the base of the tell. This was the main north–south route of central Palestine and the tell, 840 m above sea level, commanded it. The top was relatively flat, about 150 m (north–south) by 90 m (east–west). The north-west corner is the highest area of the mound (Lapp [ed.] 1981: 1).

Tell el-Ful overlooks a wide area in all directions. To the south-east, the Dead Sea is visible on clear days, as well as the mountains of Moab and Ammon. To the north-east Jaba' (Geba) and Mukhmas (Michmash) are in view. The Ramallah

5. See, e.g., Albright 1924: 4; Birch 1914: 43; Conder 1877; Demsky 1973; Mackenzie 1911.

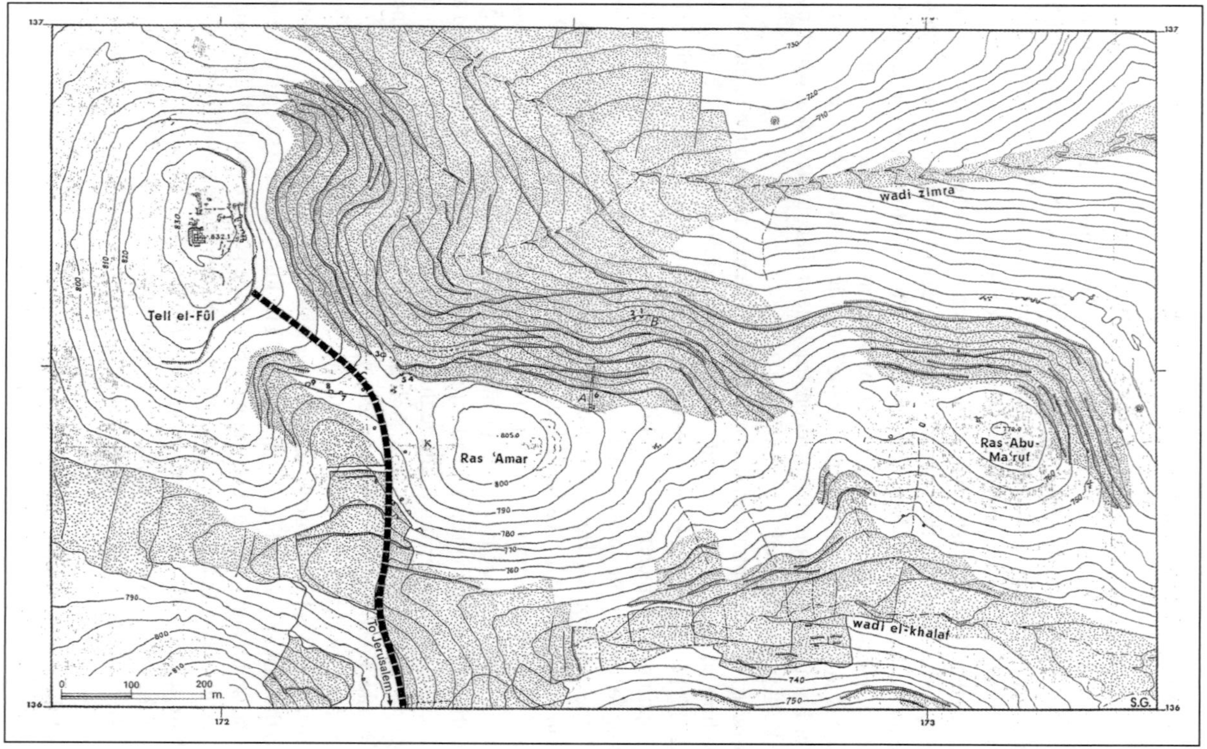

Figure 2. *Topographic Map of Tell el-Ful and Its Vicinity (Gibson 1995)*

ridge to the north-west is high and limits the view in that direction. To the west, Nebi Samwil dominates the horizon, and to the south Shu'afat and Jerusalem are located. Because of its height, the temperatures are never very hot and can be bitterly cold in winter. All these natural factors made Gibeah quite important strategically and politically.

a. *The Identification of Tell el-Ful with Gibeah of Saul*

Edward Robinson (1841: 14-15) first identified Gibeah with modern Jaba', but later changed his mind and identified it with Tell el-Ful.[6] Although the identification of Gibeah with Tell el-Ful is generally accepted, there were and still are scholars who challenge this view. This is mainly due to the fact that Gibeah belongs to a group of sites whose precise location was already lost in ancient times. C.R. Conder (1877) claimed that Geba was the name preserved in that of the modern village of Jaba' and that Geba referred to the surrounding district. Tell el-Ful, he claimed, may have been the site of Ophni, a town in Benjaminite territory, though this identification provoked further debate.

About thirty years later W.F. Birch (1911) renewed the argument. He argued that Gibeah was located at Khirbet Adaseh, 3 km north-west of Gibeon. However, the careful examination of Khirbet Adaseh did not reveal any ceramics earlier than the Byzantine period (Mackenzie 1911). Birch, nevertheless, was not convinced and continued to insist that Khirbet Adaseh was the true site of Gibeah (1913). He translated Judg. 19.14, which reads 'The sun went upon them near Gibeah', as 'the sun went for them by the side of Gibeah' (1914: 43). This he took to mean that Gibeah, like the sun, must have been to the west. Therefore, Gibeah could not possibly have been at Tell el-Ful towards the east, on their right.

More recently, scholars such as J.M. Miller (1975), P.M. Arnold (1990) and A. Demsky (1973) have challenged the identification of Gibeah with Tell el-Ful. In reviewing the literary material and the archaeological evidence, Miller proposed that Gibeah, Geba, Geba of Benjamin, Gibeah of Benjamin, Gibeah of Saul, and probably also Gibeath Haelohim were all identical. He identifies all these names with Geba (modern Jaba'). But he distinguishes Geba from Gibeon and Gibeath Kiriath-jearim as separate places. The Geba form of the name is related to the appellative 'Gibeah' (*haggib'â*) form in the same way that Ramah relates to *hārāmâ* and Mizpah relates to *hammiṣpâ*. Hence, the inconsistent usage of Geba and Gibeah in Judges 19–21 and in 1 Samuel 13–14 should be explained on literary and textual grounds rather than supposing that actions shifted back and forth between different Benjaminite villages (Miller 1975: 165). Miller also argues that the archaeological evidence from Tell el-Ful does not provide specific evidence to identify it with Gibeah of Saul. On the contrary, the preconceived idea that Tell el-Ful is ancient Gibeah has influenced the interpretation of the material found there.

6. It would be interesting to mention some recent new information. In an excavation 1.5 km east of Tell el-Ful directed by Ronny Reich (Israel Antiquities Authority) an ostracon has been discovered. Details of its content have not yet been published, but there appears to be a list of names of the sites in the vicinity, names which are from the time of Josephus, first century CE; one of the names is that of Gibeah.

Arnold's argument very much follows Miller's view. He examines the various forms of the name Gibeah in the biblical text. In the second chapter of his study he considers the geographical and archaeological situation of Gibeah and suggests that the evidence produced severely undermines the identification of Gibeah with Tell el-Ful. Arnold (1990: 60) also suggests that this site probably served as a Judaean military watchtower-settlement known as Eleph. Arnold proposes that Gibeah and Geba are two names of the same place located at Jaba'. But at the same time Arnold is aware that the surface of Jaba' revealed ceramics of Iron II as well as Persian sherds, but none from Iron Age I.

Demsky (1973: 26) has a different approach. He suggests that the *g-b-'* root place names can be reduced to three: Geba, Gibeah and Gibeon. Using the archaeological data (discussed in section 1 of this paper) Demsky suggests that Saul's ancestral home was not at Gibeah (Tell el-Ful) as is generally accepted, but rather at Gibeon. However, he claims that it is more likely that after the Philistines had discovered the secret of Saul's coronation, he was forced to remove himself to a new base. Saul therefore chose Gibeah of Benjamin, which was outside the Philistine sphere, and there he established his capital city. With reference to Gibeah of Benjamin and Geba-Benjamin, Demsky (1973: 29) suggests that the author of the Saul cycle used Geba (Gibeah) of Benjamin (1 Sam. 13.3, 16) when referring to Jaba'. This is because Geba (Jaba') absorbed part of the displaced population after the destruction of Gibeah (Geba) of Benjamin described in Judg. 21.23.

In view of this debate, Miller and Arnold's proposal that the *g-b-'* rooted place names, except Gibeon and Gibeath Kiriath-jearim, are various names of the same place cannot be fully accepted. This is because Isa. 10.29 (in describing Sennacherib's journey through the region north of Jerusalem) describes the journey in north to south order and clearly distinguishes Geba from Gibeah of Saul. This verse implies that Geba is between Michmash and Ramah (fitting well with the location of modern Jaba'), and Gibeah of Saul to the south of Ramah, which is consistent with the identification of it with Tell el-Ful. Furthermore, Miller and Arnold's proposal that the location of Gibeah/Geba is at Jaba' must be rejected for the following reasons. First, Gibeah is one of the many sites which lost their original ancient name. This is a phenomenon well affirmed in the study by Yeivin (1971: 142) 'whereby in later periods settlements moved down from the hill tops by carrying with them their older names, while the ruins of the older settlements took on other designations' (see Yeivin 1971: 142 n. 15). It is possible, therefore, that already in ancient times the name Gibeah was transferred as Geba to the place name known today as Jaba'. Secondly, there is no archaeological evidence to support Miller or Arnold in placing Gibeah/Geba at Jaba'. Jaba' revealed ceramics of Iron II as well as Persian sherds, but none from Iron Age I. A recent survey of Jaba' and its vicinity by Gibson and Bargouth in 1993 (Negev and Gibson 2001) has also concluded that no Iron Age I remains exist at Jaba'. Tell el-Ful not only produced evidence from Iron Age I, but also all the evidence shows that Tell el-Ful was an extremely strong and important site. In addition to the archaeological evidence, the view from the summit of Tell el-Ful covers a very wide area. The strong fortress (or tower) on the summit is also situated on the main trade routes leading from Jerusalem to the north and from the coast in the west, to Moab and Ammon in the east. No other proposed site for Gibeah has these advantages.

b. *The Archaeological Excavations at Tell el-Ful*

Tell el-Ful was one of the first sites to be excavated in Palestine (Albright 1924: 3), and three main excavations have been carried out there. The first two (by the American School of Oriental Research) were directed by W.F. Albright in 1922–23 and in 1933. The third took place in 1964 and was directed by Paul Lapp (it was a joint excavation between the American School in Jerusalem and the Pittsburgh Theological Seminary headed by J.L. Kelso). Five periods of occupation were uncovered, dating between the twelfth century BCE and the first century CE. Albright stated that no Bronze Age ceramics were found at Tell el-Ful, but, in Lapp's later excavations a few Middle Bronze sherds and a mace-head were actually found. In the more recent excavations by Gibson and Greenhut in 1995, a Middle Bronze IIA settlement was found on the lower slope and a burial cave on the south-eastern slope (see also Gibson 1988).

However, the phase of occupation most relevant to our topic is the first phase. It was concentrated on the summit of the mound in the ruins of what Albright called a fortress. This phase of occupation was divided into three, as follows:

Period I: miscellaneous constructions antedating the foundation of the fortress (which do not belong to the fortress at all), destroyed by fire.

Period II: Fortress I, the first fortress, also destroyed by a massive fire.

Period II: Fortress II, a second fortress which was a reconstruction of the first one, following nearly the same plan. This fortress was abandoned without any trace of destruction by fire, but there are signs that this fortress underwent a rebuilding phase.

Originally Albright dated the foundation of Tell el-Ful to 1230 BCE or a little later, and the fortress to 1200 BCE (1924: 45). Albright was convinced that the archaeological results supported the story as it appears in Judges 19–20, that of the concubine of Gibeah. He dated the destruction of Gibeah in this story to 1130–1120 BCE, basing this on the assumption that the Benjaminite war must have occurred long enough before Saul for the recollection of that event to have been erased. The ceramic evidence covered a period extending over more than a century, from the destruction of Gibeah to the erection of Saul's fortress.

The second period, Fortress I, was assigned to the time of Saul on the basis of evidence of potsherds attributed to the last phase of Iron I and before the transition to the Iron II period in the tenth century (Albright 1933: 8). The stones employed in the first fortress are fairly large: 70 × 30 cm, 65 × 45 cm and 45 × 35 cm. Owing to their massive character, the walls of some of the rooms (Fig. 3 [next page], rooms A, C1 and C2) stood to a height of 180–220 cm. Albright concluded that since Tell el-Ful represents Gibeah, this was probably the residence of Saul, who reigned about 1020–1000 BCE.

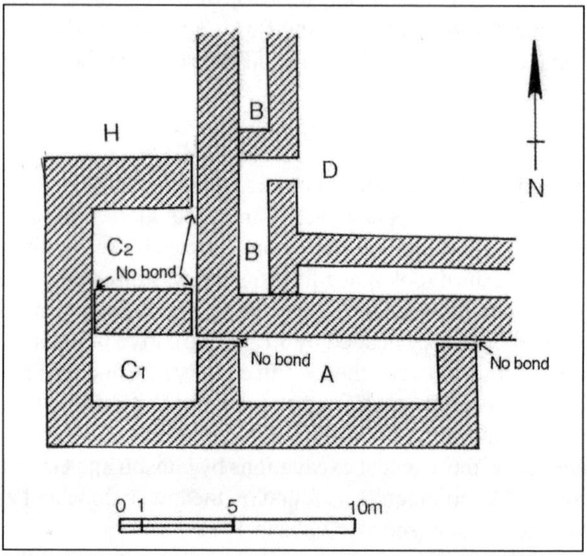

Figure 3. *Reconstructed Plan of Albright's Fortress I (after Lapp [ed.] 1981)*

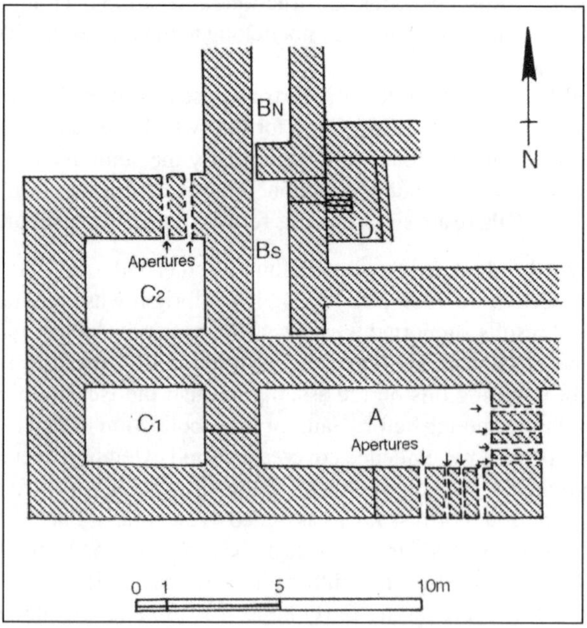

Figure 4. *Reconstructed Plan of Fortress II (after Lapp [ed.] 1981)*

The reconstruction of the second fortress in Period II followed the exact plan of the first fortress, using its wall as a foundation (Fig. 4). A layer of ashes representing woodwork was found in the remains of the foundation. This layer appeared at a height of 50–150 cm from the ground (in rooms B, D, H). However, there were major differences in the construction techniques. The second fortress was more elaborate and carefully constructed than the previous one. Albright suggested that this fortress belonged to a person of importance, and therefore ascribed it to Saul. Here the tower was bonded to the main fortress wall and there were straight joints visible in the middle of the walls. This fortress had a massive staircase leading from the first to the second storey and was found resting on the burnt level. There are no differences in the pottery of the two phases. The duration of this fortress is not known. It was abandoned early in the tenth century, c. 1000–990 BCE (Sinclair 1960: 11).

P. Lapp's excavation was a salvage operation, since King Hussein of Jordan was planning to build a palace on top of the mound. The results of his excavations basically agreed with and confirmed Albright's stratigraphy, though Lapp could not date precisely the foundation phase but placed it between the late eleventh and mid-tenth centuries BCE (Lapp [ed.] 1975: 84). However, Lapp's main objection to Albright's earlier result was the suggestion that during Period II at Tell el-Ful an entire fortress was built, and that the tower which Albright had unearthed served as the south-west corner (Lapp [ed.] 1981: 79). Albright also suggested that similar towers were built on the corners of the fortress which, when reconstructed measures 62 × 57 m, when in actual fact the contour of the mound precludes such an extension of the fort eastwards (Lapp [ed.] 1975: 85).

The tower which Albright discovered stood to a height of 3 m and was well preserved. Hence, it is not clear why so few traces of the fort have been discovered elsewhere on the site. All the evidence unearthed so far indicates clearly that there was one massive tower, not a fortress, at Tel el-Ful in Period II (the period of Saul). In my view, it is possible that at the time of Saul only the tower on the summit was necessary, and that walls were added later. If future excavations on the eastern slope of Tell el-Ful should reveal the actual settlement, we should perhaps envisage a solitary tower on the summit of the mound.[7]

The pottery discovered at Tell el-Ful is typical of the Iron Age I. The pottery from Period II, Fortress I and II is identical and cannot easily be distinguished, among which were cooking pots, and storage jars with long collared rims dating to the twelfth century (Fig. 5 [next page]). Jars with short collared rims also appeared in the twelfth century and continued into the tenth century (Lapp [ed.] 1981: 79), i.e. before the transition to Iron II. This pottery is contemporary with the latest pottery from Shiloh of Iron I, which dates from about 1050 BCE. The rims of the heavy storage jars (pithoi) are typical of this period. The rims are

7. At the time of my visit to Tell el-Ful in the autumn of 1996 new excavations concentrated on the Middle Bronze II Period. However, the abundance of Iron Age I pottery remains on the eastern slope of the hill strongly indicates that the rest of the settlement lies beneath the terraces on the eastern slope, somewhere between the area of Lapp's excavations and the eastern edge of the summit.

thickened and rounded and have sloping shoulders with little or no neck. Sherds of the white painted ware imported from Cyprus were also found.

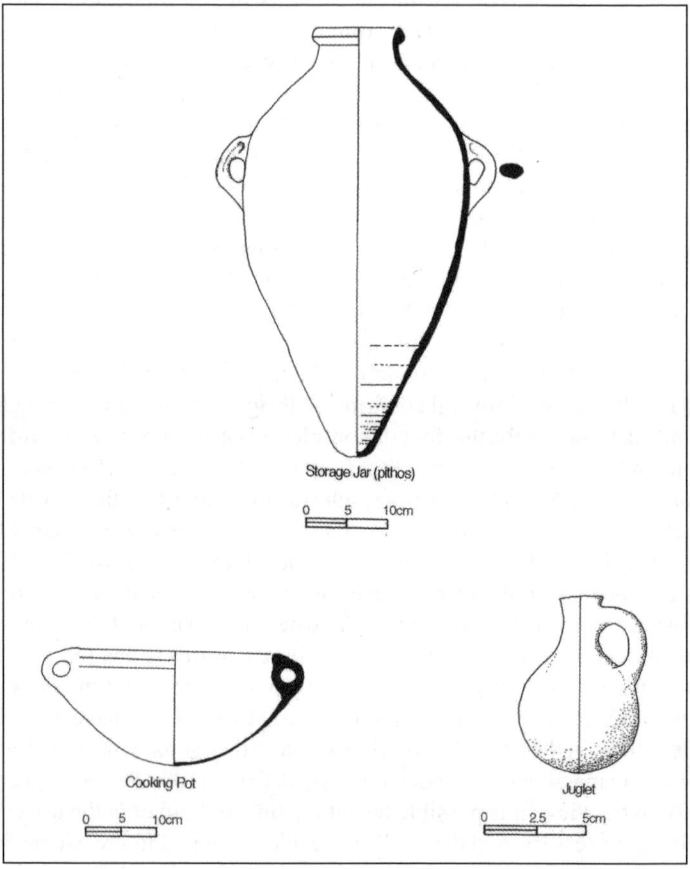

Figure 5. *Representative Iron I Ceramic Vessels from Tell el-Ful, Periods I and II (Shalom Brooks 1998)*

The collared-rim pithoi are large vessels (about 1.2 m high) and ovoid in shape. They were used for the storage of oil, wine and water and were very common in central Palestine during Iron Age I. D.L. Esse (1992) has claimed that the distribution of the collared-rim pithoi was most likely the product of a specific potting tradition. If this is accepted, then judging by the significant quantity of evidence and its distribution throughout the core highland areas, the potters were either Israelites or at least the Israelites were their best customers. Esse further claimed that the commerce between these areas (Israelite in the highlands and Canaanite in the lowland) was relatively free and open. In addition, he argued that although there are references in the biblical text (i.e. 'the song of Deborah' in Judg. 5.1-31, and 'the blessing of Jacob' in Gen. 49.14-15) which reflect a conflict between the Israelite and Canaanite groups, the cross-ethnic economic ties proved stronger than the ethnic differences between them, and these were further strengthened by intermarriages between the groups.

The archaeological finds at Tell el-Ful did not produce much evidence for reconstructing the economy of the inhabitants. However, the quantity of pottery found in the debris of Period II does perhaps indicate a measure of rural luxury. Fragments of about thirty cooking pots, identical in dimension, were found. An iron plough tip, numerous fragments of hand-mills for grinding corn, rubbing-stones and spindles would reflect domestic activities.

c. *Dating Tell el-Ful Periods I and II*

It appears that the archaeological data from the various excavations of sites in the hill country do not provide enough substantial evidence from which more accurate chronology can be deduced. However, consideration should be given to A. Mazar's dating of Giloh as a helpful starting point.[8] The site of Giloh shares common characteristics with Tell el-Ful. Both of these are close to the 'City of David', about 5–6 km away, and both are situated at a height of 840 m with an excellent view over a wide area, and have no natural sources of water or fertile land for agricultural produce. Not surprisingly therefore, both these sites produced similar ceramic wares. In the building remains of the Iron I period at Giloh sherds of collared-rim jars and cooking pot types from this period were unearthed.

The ceramic finds from Giloh date the settlement to the early Iron Age or even to the Late Bronze Age, when many Canaanite towns were destroyed. A good example of one of these cities is Lachish. The latest excavations there show that Lachish was destroyed in the reign of Rameses III, c. 1184–1153 BCE, i.e. in the first half of the twelfth century (Ussishkin 1993: 904).[9] It would seem that the settlement at Giloh started during that time. However, it has not been possible to determine whether this was a few years before the destruction or after it. Some of the vessels which appear at Giloh have parallels at Lachish, but other types, especially the collared-rim jars and some of the cooking pots, do not appear at Lachish.

Taking into consideration Mazar's dating of the settlement at Giloh, one can assume that Giloh was constructed some time around 1153 BCE at the latest. Giloh is also contemporary with Period I at Tell el-Ful, even though there is no clear indication as to how long the Period I settlement survived or how many years elapsed between Period I and Period II at Tell el-Ful.

Lapp's excavation results allowed Period I about fifty years, from c. 1200 to 1150 BCE (Lapp [ed.] 1981: XVII). I propose a slight modification of this. Since Period I at Tell el-Ful is contemporary with Giloh, we should allow fifty years from 1153 BCE, and place the beginning of Period II (Saul's period), roughly about 1100 BCE.

8. Giloh is the name of a new modern suburb of Jerusalem. It is situated south of the valley of Rephaim and north of the town of Beit Jala. The site is situated at the centre of this suburb, hence the name. The biblical city of Giloh is most probably located further south, as described in Josh. 15.51. See Mazar 1981: 16-17.

9. The dating for Rameses III is based on the lower chronology given for Lachish by D. Ussishkin.

It is generally accepted that Saul reigned for a period of about twenty years. I have also argued elsewhere (Shalom Brooks 1996–97) that there was a gap of at least seventeen years in Israel before David ascended the throne. Hence, taking away about forty years from c. 1100 BCE brings us closer to the date of c. 1060–1050 BCE, the time which marks the end of the rule of the house of Saul, contrary to the generally accepted dates for Saul, i.e. c. 1025–1005 BCE.[10]

The main reason for the uncertainty in dating the early archaeological periods at Tell el-Ful stems from the attempt which had been made to correlate the archaeological material with the biblical story in Judges 19–20, the 'concubine of Gibeah' story. This story describes a real town with houses, streets and fortifications, whereas the archaeological finds from Iron I have not produced anything at all like this. It is reasonable therefore to assume that the story may not be historical (Mazar 1990: 137-38). However, some historical elements can be deduced from this narrative. It does reflect a civil war between the Israelite tribes, though the circumstances in the narrative may have been altered; it may have been the war fought between David's followers and the house of Saul after the battle at Gilboa (Shalom Brooks 1996–97). The hatred between the two groups is reflected in the degree of destruction evident in the first fortress.

Scholars, in an attempt to match the biblical narrative with the finds at Tell el-Ful, have allowed an excessive gap of about one hundred years between Period I and period II (Saul's period). This was in an attempt to allow for the time span between the events in Judges 19–20 and the rise of Saul to power. This length of time was given for two specific reasons: first, it gives the tribe of Benjamin, which was almost exterminated by the events, enough time to repopulate; secondly, as Albright put it, it allows 'enough time to erase the keen edge of Israelite recollection of the atrocity' (Albright 1924: 49-50).

In the light of the discussion so far, the following hypothesis may be proposed in order that the archaeological material can be better understood. Period I at Tell el-Ful (most possibly a Philistine post, which was defeated by Saul as described in 1 Sam. 13–14), ended some time before or around 1100 BCE, and it ended by fire, but on a small scale. The site was later probably taken by Saul. It is possible that Saul built the big tower (Period II, Fortress I), which ended with a violent destruction after his death on Mt Gilboa. The second fortress (Period II, Fortress II) was built almost immediately after the first one was destroyed, and was a rebuilding of the first fortress. This fortress, according to the archaeological finds, survived for a short period of about ten years. Because the fortress was built immediately after the first one was destroyed, and the building followed exactly the same plan, the builder was possibly closely connected with Saul. That person was either Abner, Saul's uncle or Ishbaal, Saul's son. Is it possible that they tried to rebuild Saul's tower in order to resettle in Saul's town? Abner was murdered a few years later (2 Sam. 3.27), which might explain why fortress II was abandoned.

10. This dating seemed reasonably acceptable to Professor Amihai Mazar during a conversation at the Institute of Archaeology, Jerusalem, 26 April 1994.

The archaeological evidence shows that Gibeah stood in ruins until the eighth century BCE. No attempt was made to rebuild or inhabit the site. Perhaps it was during this period that the story in Judges 19–21 was written to explain why Gibeah had been sacked. The story was also written as propaganda against the house of Saul which also represented the northern kingdom of Israel.

3. *Conclusions*

In the light of this discussion it becomes apparent that Gibeon and Gibeah were two very important Benjaminite cities in the time of Saul. It is quite possible that Gibeon played an important political, economic and religious role in the life of the Israelites at the time of Saul. It is also possible that Saul grew up in Gibeon and that after he became king he moved to Gibeah. Then Gibeah became his capital and was renamed after him as Gibeah of Saul. If further archaeological excavations are carried out on the eastern slope of Tell el-Ful they will most probably produce further evidence not only to support its identification as Gibeah of Saul, but also to enhance our understanding of the events surrounding Saul and his reign in that period.

BIBLIOGRAPHY

Albright, W.F.

1924 *Excavations and Results at Tell el-Ful (Gibeah of Saul)* (AASOR, 4; New Haven: ASOR).

1933 'A New Campaign of Excavation at Gibeah of Saul', *BASOR* 52: 6-12.

Arnold, P.M.

1990 *Gibeah: In Search of a Biblical City* (JSOTSup, 79; Sheffield: JSOT Press).

Birch, W.F.

1911 'Gibeah of Saul and Zela: The Site of Jonathan's Home and Tomb', *PEFQS*: 101-109.

1913 'Gibeah and Adaseh', *PEFQS*: 38-42.

1914 'The Site of Gibeah', *PEFQS*: 42-44.

Blenkinsopp, J.

1972 *Gibeon and Israel* (SOTSMS; Cambridge: Cambridge University Press).

1974 'Did Saul Make Gibeon his Capital?', *VT* 24: 1-7.

Conder, C.R.

1877 'Gibeah of Saul', *PEFQS*: 104-105.

Conder, C.R., and H.H. Kitchener

1883 *The Survey of Western Palestine* (London: Palestine Exploration Fund).

Coote R.B., and K.W. Whitelam

1987 *The Emergence of Early Israel* (The Social World of Biblical Antiquity, 5; Sheffield: Almond Press).

Demsky, A.

1971 'The Genealogy of Gibeon (1 Chronicles 9.35-44): Biblical and Epigraphic Considerations', *BASOR* 202: 16-23.

1973 'Geba, Gibeah, and Gibeon—An Historical-Geographic Riddle', *BASOR* 212: 26-31.

Esse, D.L.

1992 'The Collared Pithos at Megiddo: Ceramic Distribution and Ethnicity', *JNES* 51: 81-103.

Gibson, S.

1988 'Ras 'Amar', *IEJ* 38: 80-82.

Jones, G.H.

1983 *1 and 2 Chronicles* (OTG; Sheffield: JSOT Press).

Lapp, N.L. (ed.)

1975 *The Tale of the Tell* (Pittsburgh: Pickwick Press).

1981 *The Third Campaign at Tell el-Ful: Excavations of 1964* (AASOR, 45; Cambridge, MA: ASOR).

Mackenzie, D.

1911 'Report from Dr. Mackenzie on Adaseh', *PEFQS*: 97-100.

Mazar, A.

1980 'An Israelite Site Near Jerusalem', *Qadmoniot* 13: 34-39.

1981 'Giloh: An Early Israelite Settlement Site Near Jerusalem', *IEJ* 31: 1-36.

1990 *Archaeology of the Land of the Bible 10,000–586* BCE (The Anchor Bible Reference Library; New York: Doubleday).

Miller, J.M.

1975 'Geba/Gibeah of Benjamin', *VT* 25: 145-66.

Negev, A., and S. Gibson (eds.)

2001 *Archaeological Encyclopedia of the Holy Land* (New York: Continuum).

Pritchard, J.B.

1962 *Gibeon, Where the Sun Stood Still: The Discovery of the Biblical City* (Princeton, NJ: Princeton University Press).

1976 'Gibeon', in M. Avi-Yonah and E. Stern (eds.), *Encyclopedia of Archaeological Excavations in the Holy Land* (4 vols.; Oxford: Oxford University Press): II, 446-50.

Rad, G. von

1958 *Gesammelte Studien zum Alten Testament* (Munich: Chr. Kaiser Verlag). ET *The Problem of the Hexateuch and Other Essays* (trans. E.W.T. Dicken; London: Oliver & Boyd, 1966).

Robinson, E.

1841 *Biblical Researches in Palestine, Mount Sinai and Arabia Petraea: A Journal of Travels in the Year 1838* (Boston: Cracker & Brewster).

Rost, L.

1926 *Die Überlieferung von der Thronnachfolge Davids* (BWANT, 3.6; Stuttgart: W. Kohlhammer). ET *The Succession to the Throne of David* (trans. M.D. Rutter and D.M. Gunn; Introduction by E. Ball; Historic Texts and Interpreters in Biblical Scholarship, 1; Sheffield: Almond Press, 1982).

Shalom Brooks, S.

1996–97 'Was there a Concubine at Gibeah?', *Bulletin of the Anglo-Israel Archaeological Society* 15: 31-40.

1998 'King Saul: A Re-Examination of his Reign and its Effect on Israel Down to the Schism' (Unpublished PhD thesis, University of London).

Sinclair, L.A.

1960 *An Archaeological Study of Gibeah (Tell el-Ful)* (AASOR, 34-35; New Haven: ASOR).

Toorn, K. van der

1993 'Saul and the Rise of Israelite State Religion', *VT* 63: 519-42.

Ussishkin D.
1993 'Lachish', in E. Stern (ed.), *The New Encyclopedia of Archaeological Excavations in the Holy Land* (4 vols.; Jerusalem: Israel Exploration Society and Carta): III, 897-911.

Vaux, R. de
1958–60 *Les Institutions de l'Ancien Testament* (2 vols.; Paris: Cerf). ET *Ancient Israel: Its Life and Institutions* (trans. J. McHugh; London: Darton, Longman & Todd, 1961).

Watt, A.
1982 *Longman Illustrated Dictionary of Geology* (Harlow: Longman).

Williamson, H.G.M
1982 *1 and 2 Chronicles* (NCB; London: Marshall, Morgan & Scott).

Yeivin, S.
1971 'The Benjaminite Settlement in the Western Part of their Territory', *IEJ* 21: 141-54.

Part II

Temple and Worship in the Old Testament

YHWH'S EXALTED HOUSE—ASPECTS OF THE DESIGN AND SYMBOLISM OF SOLOMON'S TEMPLE*

Victor Avigdor Hurowitz

An Introductory Caveat

Doubts have been cast in recent times on the Bible's attribution of building the Temple in Jerusalem to Solomon.[1] Not only do no archaeological remains confirm the biblical account, but many scholars claim that in the tenth century BCE during the supposed time of Solomon there was no monumental building in the eastern Mediterranean basin, and that Solomon could not have built such a luxurious Temple and grand palace as described in Scripture.

These claims have increased in recent years with the ascendance of archaeology as a factor in writing history of the land of Israel in the Iron Age, yet they are actually not new, even though they are informed now by new methodologies and *Zeitgeist* (Handy 1997). In fact, some of the current trends were adumbrated long ago and subsequently forgotten because they were not yet in fashion. Six decades ago L. Waterman (1943; 1947; 1948), using literary-historical criticism of 1 Kings 6–7, suggested that Solomon built only storerooms, and after several generations these storerooms were converted into a Temple, and their structure was expanded accordingly. More recently K. Rupprecht (1977), on the basis of tradition criticism, contended that the Bible preserves no ancient, authentic tradition from the time of Solomon accrediting him with founding of the Temple and building it *ex novo*. All specific statements to this effect are deemed products

* The architecture and design of Solomon's Temple, also known as the First Temple, has been a perennial subject of scholarly interest and has enjoyed several major studies in recent years including Avigad 1964; Busink 1970; Garber 1951; Gutmann 1976; Herzog 2000; Möhlenbrink 1932; Ouellette 1976; Parrot 1954, ET 1957; Yadin 1956; Yeivin 1968; Zwickel 1999, and others. The symbolism and religious significance of the Temple has been studied by Bloch-Smith 2002; Lundquist 1983; Uffenheimer 2000; Wright *et al.* 1960. These studies are to be supplemented by numerous encyclopaedia articles on the temples in ancient Israel and the ancient Near East, and the recent critical commentaries on the books of Kings and Chronicles, including in recent years Cogan 2001; Hurowitz, Oded and Avramsky 1995; Hurowitz, Oded and Garsiel 1994. This article is a greatly revised and updated English version of Hurowitz 2000 (see also Hurowitz 1994, and 1998 for briefer, more popular forms). In all these articles an attempt was made to combine architectural reconstruction of the Temple based on the biblical descriptions and relevant extrabiblical sources with illuminating its symbolism and religious significance. The present article has made no attempt to be bibliographically exhaustive.

1. For the problems of the Solomonic age in current research, see the essays collected in Handy (ed.) 1997. For various possibilities of bridging the biblical attribution of the Temple to Solomon and the absence of archaeological evidence, see Ussishkin 2003: 114.

of late, Deuteronomic scribes. Rupprecht suggested that the Temple was originally a Jebusite sanctuary, and Solomon merely made some alterations to make it suitable for worship of YHWH, God of Israel.

These claims, each with its own methodology, have, of course, not gone unchallenged, but every refutation meets in turn with a rebuttal. W.F. Albright suggested that the land of Israel did not lack monumental architecture at the beginning of the first millennium BCE, so building a Temple and palace by Solomon would not contradict any archaeological evidence (Albright 1959; Dever 1982, 1990, 1997). However, Albright's 'accepting' approach to the tenth century and the biblical record is in hot dispute nowadays, and his once authoritative voice is no longer heard uncritically. The question of architecture aside, Helga Weippert (1992) has shown that the water wagons (*m*[e]*kōnôt*) described in 1 Kgs 7.27-37 accord with art of the beginning of the first millennium BCE. Alan Millard (1997) has argued that many of the elements of Solomon's Temple described in 1 Kings and considered imaginative by scholars, such as the lavish use of gold, are in fact in accord with the reality of Solomon's supposed age. The Temple gates described in Ezek. 40.6-15, 24-30 resemble city gates from Gezer, Hazor and Megiddo, and if Ezekiel's vision is based on similar gates he knew from the First Temple, this would indicate that elements of architecture from Solomon's day indeed adorned the building attributed to him. These approaches and finds would indicate that the Bible's portrait of the Temple reflects some elements of the actual material culture at the time when the Temple was reportedly built.

Waterman's suggestion is based on a mistaken understanding of the description of the Temple, and on an unjustifiable reconstruction of its literary history, and was rejected from the very outset be G.E. Wright (1948).

Rupprecht's contention that the Temple of Solomon was connected from the point of view of its building history (*Baugeschichte*) to a Jebusite shrine is possible theoretically, but it is in fact irrelevant to Solomon's contribution as described in the biblical sources. One cannot rule out that Solomon located the Temple on a site where a temple already stood (assuming that 2 Sam. 24, which mentions no temple, has no relevance to the Temple's building history), and removed the original building before founding his own. Even if it is possible that the Temple was constructed on a site occupied by a previous sanctuary, there is no evidence that Solomon did not erect a completely new edifice. Not unexpectedly, Rupprecht's questionable proposal was rejected initially by several scholars (Rimbach 1978; Soggin 1979; Saebø 1982; Tomes 1996: 43). Nonetheless, Knauf (1997: 85 n. 17), relying on Rupprecht, declares: 'It is well established by now that Solomon did not build the Temple of Jerusalem; he rather redecorated it, suffice it to recall 2 Sam. 12.20 (and 2 Sam. 5.9?)'.

As for the claim made by Rupprecht and many others that the literary material and the traditions reflected in 1 Kings 6–7 do not date back to Solomon, careful examination of the building narrative raises the possibility that ancient literary elements have been incorporated into a more recent narrative framework, including some contemporary with Solomon and deriving from the building process itself (Hurowitz 1992: 311-21). Van Seters (1997) and Na'aman (1997: 67, 74;

cf. McCormick 2002: 97-106) deny the existence of such material, claiming that ancient Near Eastern royal building accounts do not contain detailed descriptions of the buildings. But they ignore the existence of detailed descriptions in archival (as opposed to monumental) documents, as well as the contention that it was this type of material that entered the biblical account, being integrated as a building block into the main narrative. In other words, they agree that 1 Kings' account of building the Temple has literary parallels in the Mesopotamian building stories, but do not give proper attention to the form-critically composite nature of the biblical narrative. One must exercise caution, therefore, before summarily dismissing the biblical tradition according to which Solomon founded the Temple and built it in its entirety, as a completely new building.

Given the complexity of the issues, and the fact that new finds, interpretations and methodologies constantly demand revisions in historical reconstruction, the present study will ignore the problems of the historicity of the biblical narrative and of the Temple itself, and focus on understanding what is described.[2] Denying that it was Solomon who built the Temple does not imply that the Temple itself never existed. In fact, it makes no difference for its essence whether Solomon built it or someone else; nor is it of any significance whether it rose in one fell swoop in a single building project or whether it grew in stages over several generations. But even if the Temple presented in the Bible is no more than a literary creation, with no roots in physical reality, it expresses an ancient author's coherent conception of what the Temple in Jerusalem looked like, and reflects what he thought it would have symbolized. The biblical description itself, whatever its referent be, and historically reliable or not, is an authentic product of ancient Israel to be elucidated by comparison with physical and literary remains of the period from which it purports to be derived. Although available to us only as a literary work, the First Temple of the Bible will be treated as if it were an artifact. Physical artifacts are studied and described, compared with other ancient objects, dated and explained; so the Temple of 1 Kings 6–7 will be translated from the Bible's words into our own, thus enabling visualization of what the author saw in his mind's eye, compared with other texts and relevant artifacts, and analysed. Some may question whether the Bible reflects ancient Israelite reality; none can doubt that it expresses ancient Israelite belief.

1. *The Sources*

Nothing remains of Solomon's Temple nor has anything from it been discovered,[3] so to visualize it and understand its meaning one must rely solely on

2. Nor will it discuss the question of when and why the description of the Temple in 1 Kgs 6–7 was composed (cf. Tomes [1996] and Van Seters [1997] who place it, respectively, in the exile and the late pre-exilic period). Let it be pointed out, nonetheless, that I take it to reflect the Temple at the time of Solomon and not at a later phase. This is because the changes made in the Temple, as discussed below in this article, seem not to be reflected in this account.

3. A small ivory pomegranate with a broken inscription perhaps associating it with the Jerusalem Temple (Avigad 1989) is now considered a modern fake. For supposed remains of some architectural

the written sources. Assistance may be drawn, of course, from other ancient temples discovered in excavations in the land of Israel and adjoining areas, but such finds are very few and their testimony is not always clear or unambiguous (Davey 1980; Fritz 1987). In fact, only two ancient temples have been revealed offering significant architectural parallels to the Solomonic Temple. One is in Tell Tayinat, Syria, discovered in 1936 (McEwan 1937: 9; Hurowitz 1994: 28-29; cf. Ussishkin 1996), and the other is in Ain Dara, also in Syria, unearthed between 1980 and 1985 (Abū ʻAssāf 1990; Monson 1996, 2000; Stager 2000). These temples, dating to the early first millennium BCE, are not identical, but both display certain striking similarities of architecture and design features with the Jerusalem Temple. There is an Iron Age temple from Arad in the land of Israel that excavator Yohanan Aharoni claimed bore great resemblance to both the Temple of Solomon and the Tabernacle, but his attempt at stuffing three distinct structures into a single template seems questionable (Aharoni 1971; 1973), and the architecture and date of the Arad temple remain problematic (Ussishkin 1988).

In contrast to architectural parallels that are few in number, there is a wealth of artifacts and iconographic finds from the land of Israel and neighbouring areas that can illuminate individual features in the décor and furnishing of Solomon's Temple. There are also many texts from the ancient Near East describing temples and palaces that enhance the visual evidence and add a crucial interpretative dimension, offering important information about how the physical structures were conceived.

Not only is relevant archaeological evidence meagre or spotty; it is limited in what it can actually show. It is useful for illustrating and concretizing reconstructions based on the biblical record, and it can be suggestive for understanding obscure passages, filling gaps in the reconstruction, and creating links between the written sources and ancient reality. But all this is possible only to the extent that there are congruencies between the finds and the written evidence, for incongruities are of little illustrative or explanatory value. Most important, however, one must not force the interpretation of the biblical text or impose upon it the archaeological evidence. To be sure, one of the most important innovations in archaeology of recent times is the realization that archaeological finds, if properly interpreted, may have their own story to tell which is not necessarily similar to what Scripture has to say.

The Bible contains two detailed descriptions of Solomon's Temple, one in 1 Kings 6–7 and the other in 2 Chronicles 3–4. Reconstructing the original form of the Temple must be based primarily on the description, or 'verbal icon' (cf. McCormick 2002: 112-47), found in the book of Kings. The picture portrayed by Chronicles is to be dealt with separately. Admittedly, it describes a complete building, but the building described differs in certain details from the one

components, see Laperrousaz 1987 and Kaufman 1998. The sensational inscription published in 2003, supposedly being of Jehoash and describing the repairs to the Temple as reported in 2 Kgs 12 and 2 Chron. 24, has been determined to be a modern forgery.

depicted in 1 Kings, and, as it turns out, is replete with obvious changes of explanatory, tendentious, and intentional natures (Hurowitz, Oded and Avramsky: 1995). So, for instance, the curtain made of blue, red, crimson, and white and decorated with cherubs (2 Chron. 3.14) is an invention of the Chronicler, using late Biblical Hebrew and intent on bringing Solomon's Temple into line with the desert Tabernacle, which had a curtain made of 'blue and red and scarlet and woven linen', and decorated with cherubs (Exod. 26.31). This is the case of the cherubs carved into the walls of the outer sanctum (2 Chron. 3.7). Overlaying the walls of the *'ûlām* (forecourt) with gold (v. 4) and the *hêkāl* with 'precious stone for glory' (v. 6) has no basis in the reality of the First Temple, and actually reflects an erroneous understanding of the *'ûlām*, conceiving it as a full room and not a forecourt (see below). From the mention of upper chambers overlain with gold above the *d*ᵉ*bîr* it seems that the author was of the opinion that the Holy of Holies was not elevated off the ground but was at ground level. He is apparently right, but his testimony relies not on personal observation, nor on a reliable ancient source, but on logic. There is no mention of cedars, and it even is stated that Solomon overlaid the *hêkāl* with cypress wood; and it seems as if the intention was that the walls were covered with cypress and not only the floors, as reported in the book of Kings. It is possible that for this detail and some others the Temple of Zerubbabel is in the background, for it did not possess the grandeur of the First Temple (cf. Hag. 2.3).[4]

Chronicles' description of the Temple has most value as a textual witness, because the account in Kings is in some places corrupt and occasionally the text can be restored with the help of Chronicles. The most important addition in Chronicles in contrast to Kings is the description of the bronze altar (2 Chron. 4.1). This verse, the style of which diverges from that of the rest of the description and is not typical of the Chronicler, may have been deleted from the book of Kings because of homoioteleuton or homoiarcton. It is hard to imagine that the Chronicler had available another reliable and authentic description of Solomon's Temple, differing from the one in Kings, and it goes without saying that he did not see the First Temple with his own eyes. His testimony is that of an exegete and not of an eyewitness.

In addition to these two descriptions of the Temple, Ezekiel portrays a Temple the Israelites are commanded to build 'when they will be ashamed of their sins' (Ezek. 40.1–43.12; cf. 43.10-11). This Temple, described in painstaking detail and extreme precision, is commonly held to reflect in form the First Temple during its final days and as seen by the prophet. This opinion, which has a certain amount of validity, led some scholars to utilize the description liberally to fill gaps in the portrait of Solomon's Temple; in particular they conjectured that the thickness of the walls in the Temple was 6 cubits. And here lies the problem! Ezekiel's Temple is, all things considered, an ideal, visionary Temple that mixes reality with imagination. Ezekiel's Temple with all its courts, gates and chambers

4. A problem unto itself is the referent of the plan of the Temple described in 1 Chron. 28.11-19, which seems to have items not found in the description of the Temple in 2 Chron. 3–4.

is square and symmetrical. It does not reflect some true reality, but is a figment of the imagination of a prophet who was able in another place to divide all of the mountainous land of Israel, crisscrossed by ravines and valleys, into rectangular parcels with parallel sides and right angled corners, totally ignoring the natural topography. In order to arrive at the desired geometrical symmetry the prophet was forced to add cubits here and there, evidence for which we can cite the width of the *'ûlām*, to which Ezekiel added a cubit (40.49). The reason for this addition is clear: he wanted to assure that the outer dimensions of the Temple would be exactly 100 × 50 cubits, in a clean ratio of 2:1. To do so he widened the *'ûlām* by 1 cubit, and it is most likely that the wall of 2 cubits thickness, dividing the outer from the inner sanctum (41.3), also resulted from the prophet's expansion and was not in Solomon's Temple precisely the way it is described in the text. Moreover, the Temple Ezekiel knew had already undergone the alterations to be discussed below. Therefore, even when Ezekiel did not add anything on his own one cannot rely on his description to reconstruct the Temple in its pristine form. All things considered, Ezekiel's Temple must be viewed with suspicion, and used for filling gaps only with utmost care, and in places where the proposed filling of the gap can draw on corroborating evidence. At the same time, however, Ezekiel's vocabulary has undoubted lexical importance as a rich reservoir of rare and enigmatic architectural terms, some of which are used in 1 Kings 6–7.

Additional, albeit indirect, evidence for the structure of the Jerusalem Temple comes from the description of the Tabernacle (Exod. 25–31; 35–40). The Pentateuchal Priestly source, when describing the Tabernacle that stood in the centre of the Israelite camp during the desert wanderings, envisioned it in the form of the Jerusalem Temple he knew in his day (Haran 1978: 187-204).[5] The image of the Tabernacle probably represents a phase in the Jerusalem Temple, between its original form, as described in Kings, and its final form, as reflected in Ezekiel's description. In fact, its form was probably fixed in the image of the Temple at the time of King Ahaz.

Considering the limitations enumerated here, the discussion below relies mainly on the description of the Temple found in 1 Kings 6–7, with material being adduced from the other sources only in accordance with these strictures. It should be added, in concluding this survey of sources, that post-biblical, rabbinic and mediaeval exegetical tradition relating to the First Temple, even when insightful, must be used with great caution because it is harmonistic and anachronistic. On the one hand later exegesis views several biblical sources as if of one cloth. On the other hand, it imposes on the First Temple features of the Second Temple. In any case, it is highly doubtful whether if preserves any authentic, independently derived information.

5. Alexander Rofé has argued that P stems from Bethel rather than Jerusalem. Even if he is right, this does not detract from the obvious similarities in form and décor between the Tabernacle and the First Temple, and does not diminish its value in understanding the design and symbolism of Solomon's Temple. It would at most indicate that there was a concept of an ideal Temple in ancient Israel that was more widely held than otherwise thought.

2. *The Temple from Without*

Solomon's Temple was constructed of full, unhewn stone (1 Kgs 6.7). By building it so, the king applied to it the custom reflected in the ancient 'altar law' (Exod. 20.22): 'and if you make me an altar of stones, do not build it of hewn stones; for by wielding your tool (lit. your sword) upon them you have profaned them'; and Deut. 27.5-6: 'There, too, you shall build an altar to the Lord your God, an altar of stones. Do not wield an iron tool over them; you must build the altar of the Lord your God of whole stones' (cf. also Josh. 8.30-31). Even so, the building's foundations were of hewn stone (1 Kgs 5.31, ET 17) as was the paving of the courtyard (7.9bβ).

The external dimensions of the Temple are not given, and 1 Kgs 6.2, 'sixty cubits was its length and twenty its width and thirty cubits its height', records the internal dimensions. Furthermore, these measurements themselves are schematic, as we will see below. In Ezekiel's Temple, the external measurements were 100 cubits long and 50 cubits wide, but they are not to be imposed on Solomon's Temple. They are based on the addition of 1 cubit to the width of the *'ûlām* and perhaps some addition to the wall between the *hêkāl* and the *dᵉbîr*, as explained above, and to the thickness of the other walls.

The entry to the Temple was on its eastern end, and the building's axis ran east to west. The Temple was situated higher than the royal palace as indicated by several verses which speak of ascending from the king's house to the Temple (1 Kgs 12.11; 22.4; Jer. 26.10) or going down from the Temple to the king's house (2 Kgs 11.19; Jer. 36.12). The experience of the masses ascending to the Temple on pilgrimages (Pss. 24.3; 122.4, etc.), and any spiritual uplifting that may have inspired in the pilgrims, is perhaps behind the eschatological vision in Isa. 2.1-4 (cf. Mic. 4.1-5; Ezek. 40.2; Zech. 14.10a) in which the Temple mount itself is to be higher than all the hills (Schwartz 1998: 14).

In front of the Temple was the *'ulām*, or forecourt, a broad-room structure with internal dimensions of 10 cubits deep and 20 cubits wide (like the width of the building, 1 Kgs 6.3). There are those who connected the term *'ûlām* (also spelled *'ylm*) with the Akkadian word *ellamu*, meaning 'before'; but this comparison is doubtful because in Akkadian itself the word is used only in adverbial combinations, with both temporal and spatial meanings, but it has no architectural usages. The height of the walls of the *'ûlām* is not specified, and the version of 2 Chron. 3.4 according to which it was 120 cubits high is certainly some sort of textual error (but cf. Yeivin 1964). Some hold that the walls of the *'ûlām* were 30 cubits high, matching the vertical dimension of the rest of the building, while others set them at 25 cubits, following the Septuagint. Carol Meyers (1983a) has proposed that the *'ûlām* was a type of low forecourt at the entrance to the building, surrounded by a low wall like the other courts of the Temple and palace. According to 1 Kgs 6.36 and 7.12 these walls consisted of three courses of hewn stones and one course of cedars (Thompson 1960). Those who set the heights of these walls as 30 or 25 cubits contend accordingly that the *'ûlām* had a roof that was supported by the pillars Jachin and Boaz, while those who lower the walls hold that the *'ûlām* was open from above and the pillars had no architectural function and were purely decorative and symbolic.

The continuation of the description of the forecourt states: *wayya'aś labbayit ḥallōnê šeqāpîm 'aṭumîm* (1 Kgs 6.4). Many scholars follow Rashi's opinion that these words describe windows that were wide from without and narrower from within. Targum Jonathan and Radaq have a slightly different interpretation, according to which the windows were narrow from without (*setîmān milibārā*) and broad from within (*petîḥān milgaw*). Y. Yadin pointed out that this type of window was prevalent in the land of Israel and Syria, as is indicated by engraved ivories showing windows having interlocking, stacked frames, one deeper than the next (Yadin 1956; Karageorghis 1970: fig. 80). More recently, the temple at Ain Dara has been cited as having had such windows (Monson 1996; Stager 1998).

According to another suggestion (Ouellette 1968, 1976) these words do not designate windows but rather a type of building designated in Assyrian sources *bīt ḫilāni*, and recognized as a type of building in the Hittite, or western style. According to this suggestion, a *bīt ḫilāni* was a broad room structure with two chambers that stood in front of the main building. The first room was a porch, in which stood two or three pillars. In front of the pillars were a few steps, and a staircase at the side of the building led to a second storey (Weidhass 1939; Hrouda 1972–75). Interpreting *lbyt ḥlny* (1 Kgs 6.4) as a *bīt ḫilāni* requires interpreting *šeqāpîm* as a threshold (cf. Hebrew *mašqōp*, Aramaic *'aśqûppâ*, Akkadian *askuppu, askuppatu*), and *'aṭumîm* as a term for pillars, connected perhaps with Akkadian *dimmu/timmu* (cf. Ouellette 1974).

If we interpret the verse in this way, then the forecourt in front of the Temple would have been a *bīt ḫilāni*, but this proposal still faces several significant difficulties. On the one hand, it is hard to define precisely what the ancient texts mean by *bīt ḫilāni*, and on the other hand it remains difficult to draw an exact correlation between this type of structure and the still enigmatic biblical evidence concerning the form of the forecourt. Moreover, Ezekiel (40.16) speaks of *ḥallōnôt 'aṭumôt* in the gate chambers of the visionary Temple. Now it is difficult to separate Ezekiel's term from the one in Kings, but it is also certain that a *bīt ḫilāni* type structure does not suit the context. We can maintain Ouellette's suggestion only by assuming that Ezekiel's terms are homonyms, sounding like those in Kings, but are not identical to them.

The two chambers of the Temple (excluding the *'ûlām* which was not properly a room) were surrounded by structures designated *yāṣîa'* and *ṣelā'ôt*. Scholars have had trouble explaining these terms (Kitchen 1989). Most hold that the structure so designated was a type of three-storied side building, made of stone, which surrounded the building on its two sides and rear and was divided into rooms or chambers. The bottom storey, 5 cubits in width, was narrower than the middle storey, the width of which was 6 cubits, and this in turn was narrower than the 7 cubit wide third storey. The walls of the Temple were stepped and the *yāṣîa'* rested on *migrā'ôt*, or recesses, forming shelves in the wall formed by the stepping. Some scholars contend that the *yāṣîa'* was some sort of structure on the roof of the Temple (Ouellette 1972).

But more preferable, in our opinion, is Haran's (1996: 212) suggestion that the *ṣᵉlā'ôt* and *yāṣîa'* were not a stone side structure divided into cells, but a sort of wooden crate which enveloped the building from without. In Haran's opinion, based on other usages of the words involved, the *ṣᵉlā'ôt* were wooden panels which stood erect around the building, while the *yāṣîa'* was a set of three horizontally lain wooden panels which joined the *ṣᵉlā'ôt* to the Temple and by means of which the *ṣᵉlā'ôt* were supported by the shelf like *migrā'ôt*. This wooden envelope hid the Temple that was constructed of non-hewn stone.

Support for this reconstruction comes from v. 10, which states: *wayye'ᵉḥōz 'et-habbayit ba'ᵃṣê 'ᵃrāzîm*. Translated literally, this would mean 'and it/he held on to the building with cedar wood', which would seemingly contradict the end of the previous verse (v. 6) which says *kî migrā'ôt labbayit sābîb ḥûṣâ lᵉbiltî 'ᵃḥōz beqîrôt habbāyit*, 'for recesses he placed in the Temple all around outside so as not to hold on to the walls of the Temple'. But the verb *wy' ḥz* should be vocalized differently from the Masoretic vocalization, not in the qal theme, but as *wayyᵉ'aḥēz* in the piel theme. The statement would then read *wayyᵉ'aḥēz 'et-habbayit ba'ᵃ ṣê 'ᵃrāzîm*, 'he caused the Temple to be inlaid with cedar wood', and be interpreted that Solomon built the stone structure of the Temple in such a way that it could be held onto by the cedar wood of the erect panels (*ṣᵉlā'ôt*), namely, he decorated it with cedar. A similar use is found in the cognate Akkadian verb *aḫāzu* (G, 'to grasp') or *uḫḫuzu* (D, 'to decorate, inlay') in many Akkadian texts dealing with items that were 'made to grasp', i.e. decorated or overlain with precious stones, metals, and even wood (cf. *CAD* A/1, 179 *s.v. aḫāzu* 8a).

The newly discovered temple at Ain Dara has been cited as offering a parallel to the *yāṣîa'* and *ṣᵉlā'ôt*, for its main rooms are surrounded on the sides and back by a narrow corridor or series of chambers (Monson 1996, 2000; Stager 1998). This parallel is most interesting, and deserves consideration. But, it should not be adduced to reject my contention that the side structure on the Jerusalem Temple was made of wood rather than stone. We should remember that the Tell Tayinat temple, which is still closer to Solomon's Temple in basic structure and proportions, has no side structure at all, showing that such a feature was optional, and nothing in any case would preclude Solomon having made a side structure of wood rather than stone.[6] The Jerusalem Temple may represent an intermediary step in architectural development, standing between the temple with no side structure as found at Tell Tayinat, and the temple with stone side structure found at Ain Dara.

It is possible that this wooden envelope played only an aesthetic, decorative role as covering and hiding the whole, unhewn stones, which were certainly not very attractive. On the other hand, enveloping the Temple in cedar wood may

6. My colleague Professor Shmuel Aḥituv has raised the objection (orally) that a wooden structure would not have withstood the climatic conditions of Jerusalem, a mountainous region with cold, windy, wet winters. I assume, nonetheless, that proper means would have been discovered for making the wood impervious to such conditions.

have had some symbolic function. As is well known, the mountains of Lebanon were considered sacred by the peoples of the region and were even thought of as a divine dwelling place (Clifford 1972: 132; M. Weippert 1980–83: 648).[7] Covering the Temple with cedar wood, both from within and without, would suggest that the Temple was the natural habitat of the deity in residence, and by doing so the resident deity's natural home is transferred to the new location.

But the side structure also had a practical function. According to v. 8, it was possible to enter the space between the *ṣᵉlā'ôt* and the stone wall through an opening in the eastern end of the Temple (the *ketep habbayit;* Haak 1983), to the right of the entrance. Through this entrance one entered the middle *ṣela'* (some read *hayyāṣîa'*), namely the corridor between the middle wooden panel and the lower wooden panel. Once inside it was possible to ascend to the upper corridor or descend to the lower corridor by means of *bᵉlûllîm* (cf. Gil 1972). This word has usually been taken as a *hapax legomenon*, *lûllîm*, with a prefixed instrumental *bet*, but Elisha Qimron (1974) has demonstrated on the basis of the lexeme in good manuscripts of the Mishnah that the *bet* is not a preposition but part of the word. Three interpretations have been offered: trap doors or entrances; (spiral) staircases of ladders; or a closed passageway within a building.

Whatever the precise meaning of *bᵉlûllîm* is, their function is clear: they made it possible to reach all parts of the multi-tiered side structure. The fact that these structures were readily and freely accessible indicates that they served more than an aesthetic role. It is possible that they were used for storing cultic paraphernalia or Temple treasures which would have included presents dedicated to God which were to remain 'before YHWH' (*lipnê yhwh*) as a reminder (*zikkārôn*) of the contributor. Such objects were obviously not just thrown haphazardly into the side structure as in a traditional Jewish Genizah, but would have been displayed in an orderly fashion. The inside of the structure with all the items stored away may have resembled a sort of museum (and cf. *bêt nᵉkôt* of Hezekiah and *bêt kēlāyw*) where he stored the treasures of the king and could display them to the emissaries of Merodach-baladan, king of Babylon (2 Kgs 20.13; Isa. 39.2; Mankowski 2000: 101-102).

The roof (*sippûn*) of the Temple was constructed of cedar wood beams lain widthwise and lengthwise (*gēbîm* and *śᵉdērôt*).[8] It may be assumed that shorter cedar beams (*gēbîm*) were lain the length of the building, stretching from side to side, while longer cedar beams (*śᵉdērôt*) were lain perpendicularly above them along the width of the building, stretching from front to back.[9]

7. An inscription of Nebuchadrezzar II calls the Lebanon *qištu ellu*, 'holy/pure forest', and another one calls it *qišāti Marduk*, 'the woods of Marduk' (Langdon 1911: 174, IX, 16). Its trees are called *tarbît Anim*, 'growths/plantings of Anu' (and cf. Num. 25.6)

8. *Qôrôt hassipûn* should be read in 1 Kgs 6.15 (cf. 16) rather then the slightly corrupt and nonsensical *qîrôt hassippôn* of MT. Yeivin 1954 prefers Radaq's explanation that the *śᵉdērôt* were the beams, while the *gēbîm* were the depressions between the beams when laid side by side.

9. For roofing buildings in wood in the ancient Near East see *CAD* G, *s.v. gušuru*; Ṣ *s.v. ṣullulu*; *AHw*, *s.v. tarbaṣu*.

3. *Inside the Temple*

Within the Temple were two rooms, both designated by the common word for house, *bayit*. The anterior room was called specifically the *hêkāl*, a word of probable Sumerian origin (*é.gal*) meaning big (*gal*) house (*é*), and palace in particular (Mankowski 2000: 51-52). The etymology of this word may actually have been known somehow to the Chronicler, who in 2 Chron. 3.5 dispenses with the word *hêkāl* and calls it *habbayit haggādôl*, 'the big room'. This word was also borrowed into Akkadian as *ekallu* ('palace') and is known in other Semitic languages as well. In Biblical Hebrew it is used only rarely to mean palace (2 Kgs 2.1; 20.18 = Isa. 39.7; 2 Chron. 36.7; Isa. 66.6; Nah. 2.7, ET 6; Pss. 45.16, ET 15; 144.12; Dan. 1.4, etc.), and in these cases mostly designates a foreign palace. The vast majority of its appearances is in connection with the Temple in Jerusalem, and usually refers to the Temple in its entirety. In Ugaritic myths it is used for Baal's heavenly palace, and in biblical poetry it designates YHWH's heavenly abode (Pss. 11.4; 18.7, ET 6 = 2 Sam. 22.7; cf. Hab. 2.20). This room, of the long room variety, was 20 cubits wide, 40 deep, and 30 high.

The inner room was called *d^ebîr*, which is glossed as *qōdeš haqq^odāšîm* (Holy of Holies, most holy; 1 Kgs 6.16; 7.50; 8.6). The origin and meaning of the term are obscure. Some (BDB) have explained it as 'hindmost chamber', 'innermost room', on the basis of Arabic *dubur* meaning 'back' or 'rear'. It has more recently been proposed to derive it from Egyptian *dbr* (Coptic *tabir*), which designates a wooden object, made by a carpenter—perhaps a wooden division, and secondarily the area behind a division (Yeivin 1948: 8-11; Ouellette 1970; Mulder 1982; Tvedtnes 1982). In fact, the *d^ebîr* was a wooden cubical structure, measuring 20 cubits on each side.

The height of the *d^ebîr* was less than the height of the *hêkāl*, so a question arises about how it was situated. Did the *d^ebîr* rest flat on the ground leaving a space of 10 cubits above, between it and the Temple roof, or was it suspended or elevated so that its top was flush with the roof of the Temple and its floor was higher than the floor of the *hêkāl*? The first possibility can be supported by the fact that no steps are mentioned leading to the *d^ebîr*, so its entrance had to be at ground level. Even Ezekiel, who takes care to point out steps (*ma'^alôt*) wherever they were, does not mention any between the *hêkāl* and *d^ebîr*. Similarly, 2 Chron. 3.9 mentions in relationship with the Holy of Holies '...and the upper chambers (*hā'^aliyyôt*) he covered with gold', namely he plated with gold the chambers above the Holy of Holies.[10] But, the second possibility can also draw significant support. First of all, in ancient Near Eastern temples it was customary to elevate

10. Rashi on 2 Kgs 11.2 interprets the *ḥ^adar hammiṭṭôt* ('bedroom') in which Jehoash son of Ahaziah was hidden as 'the loft above the Holy of Holies', but Radaq contends that the reference is to a room in the Court of Levites of Priests. M. Weinfeld (1996) suggests that in the 'bedroom' a sacred marriage rite between YHWH and his female consort, Asherah, was performed. Margueron (1999a) suggests that second storeys may have been a regular feature of ancient Near Eastern buildings, including temples, and that they may have been used for overnight lodging by people such as priests who had to be on the temple premises on a daily basis.

even if slightly, the place upon which the divine symbol stood, be it an idol, or a pillar, or something else. Since the *d^e^bîr* was the place where the symbols of YHWH's presence stood—the two cherubs and the ark—one can expect it to be elevated as well. Secondly, 1 Kgs 6.30 says about the floor of the *d^e^bîr* 'and the floor/ground of the room (*bayit*) he overlaid with gold inside and outside (*lipnîmâ w^e^laḥîṣôn*)', implying that the wooden floor of the *d^e^bîr* was plated with gold on both sides, above within the room, and below, underneath and outside the room, as the roof of the space under the *d^e^bîr*![11] Furthermore, it is possible that the great height of the *d^e^bîr* as opposed to that of the *hêkāl* is alluded to in Isaiah's throne vision (6.1): '...and I saw YHWH sitting on a high and exalted throne, and his skirts filling the *hêkāl*'. Apart from these two possibilities, it is possible that the *d^e^bîr* was suspended between the ground and the roof with chambers above as suggested by Chronicles and a cavity below as implied in v. 30. This would explain the seemingly contradictory evidence.

Even so, the first possibility seems more likely, namely, that the *d^e^bîr* stood firmly on the ground with space only above. As for the words *lipnîmâ w^e^laḥîṣôn*, they apparently infiltrated the text by accident of a vertical dittography of the words *millipnîm w^e^laḥîṣôn* in the previous verse. If these words are excised, no sign will remain of the cavity below the *d^e^bîr*, and without such explicit testimony that the *d^e^bîr* was raised, there remains only the other evidence indicating that it was not. One should note that although the Arad temple had steps leading up to the cult niche, there are no such steps at Tell Tayinat.

The internal walls of the *hêkāl* were covered with cedar wood, while its floor was of cypress (1 Kgs 6.15). The two side walls as well as the front wall through which one entered the *hêkāl* were decorated with 'carvings of gourds and calyxes' (*miqlā'ôt p^e^qā'îm ûp^e^ṭûrê ṣiṣṣîm*; Strange 1985; Goldman 1997). These three walls were overlain with gold, and the gold covered the decorations as well.

As for the *d^e^bîr*, all four internal walls, as well as its floor, were of cedar wood. The decorations in the *d^e^bîr* were more ornate than those in the *hêkāl*. All around on the walls of the *d^e^bîr* were 'engraved carvings of cherubs, palms and calyxes' (*pittûḥê miql^e^'ôt k^e^rûbîm w^e^timōrōt ûp^e^ṭûrê ṣiṣṣîm*, 1 Kgs 6.29)—palms instead of gourds, and the addition of cherubs.[12]

It seems that the wall between the two chambers was decorated on both sides with the decorations of the inner chamber, the *d^e^bîr*. This is indicated by the words *millipnîm w^e^laḥîṣôn* that mean 'both on the side of the wall within the *d^e^bîr* and the side of the wall outside the *d^e^bîr*, within the *hêkāl*'.[13] If so, the back wall of the *hêkāl*, through which one entered the *d^e^bîr* and which one would see

11. The possibility of Solomon having access to the enormous amounts of gold needed for the Temple as described in 1 Kings has been defended by Millard 1997: 38-42.

12. The word *habbayit* in vv. 29-30 refers only to the *d^e^bîr*, and not the Temple in its entirety, as many scholars incorrectly assume. This interpretation eliminates an imagined duplication in the description of the Temple.

13. All scholars take the words *millipnîm w^e^laḥîṣôn* in v. 29 and *lipnîmā w^e^laḥîṣôn* in v. 30 to be referring to the inner room (*d^e^bîr*) and outer room (*hêkāl*), but this explanation yields an extraneous duplicate.

when facing the *d^e^bîr*, differed in appearance from the three other walls of the *hêkāl*.

As for the plating, all the internal walls of the *d^e^bîr* were covered with *zāhāb sāgûr*.[14] The floor of the *d^e^bîr* was overlain with *zāhāb*. The wall dividing the *hêkāl* from the *d^e^bîr* was plated on both sides with *zāhāb sāgûr* (v. 20), so that in this feature as well it was different from the other walls in the *hêkāl*.

In the entrance to the *hêkāl* hung two doors of cypress wood (1 Kgs 6.33-35). Each door was made of two *ṣ^e^lā'îm*, or broad planks. These planks were not flat but rounded (*g^e^lîlîm*).[15] The doors were engraved with cherubs, palms and calyxes and plated with gold that covered the decorations as well. The doorframes were made of 'oil-wood',[16] and their form is described with the enigmatic term *mē'ēt r^e^bi'ît*, 'quadruple(?)'. Some scholars hold that the frame of the entrance was rectangular, with four sides; others contend that the doorframe was made of four stepped, interlocking frames, one inside another and deeper than the next.[17] Both with regard to the decorations engraved on the doors and the use of oil-wood for the doorposts, the entryway to the *hêkāl* has some of the ornamentation of the *d^e^bîr*.

In the entrance to the *d^e^bîr* were two doors of 'oil-wood' (1 Kgs 6.31-32). These doors are not made expressly of 'rounded planks', so it must be assumed that each consisted of a single plank, and was flat. Broad planks of oil-wood such as these may not have been as ornate as the others, but they certainly came from huge trees that had reached a very advanced age, so the doors would have been extremely costly. Similarly, it would have been necessary to work the wood in a special procedure to prevent warping. These doors too were decorated with cherubs, palms and calyxes.

The doorframe in this entrance is described with the words *hā'ayil m^e^zûzôt ḥ^a^mišît*.[18] The word *ḥ^a^mišît*, resembling *r^e^bi'ît* morphologically, has been taken by some to designate a pentagonal, five-sided shape of the doorframe, that would not have a horizontal lintel but one which came to a point. Others explain it as indicating a doorframe of five interlocking doorposts or frames. Those favouring

14. For this term, see Akkadian *ḫurāṣu sakru* (*CAD* S: 81b), which designates gold that has been smelted in a particular way.

15. According to Yeivin (1968: 339) the *g^e^lîlîm* were the door axes. For the Temple doors see Millard 1989. He contends that the terms *r^e^bi'ît* and *ḥ^a^mišît* designate the proportional width of the doors in relationship to the width of the walls. The width of the door to the *hêkāl* would have been 5 cubits, and to the *d^e^bîr* 4 cubits.

16. *'ēṣ šemen*, 'oil wood', is mentioned in Neh. 8.15 along with olive, and it was usually interpreted as an olive tree or a wild olive (so Targum Jonathan and Rashi; and see also Isa. 41.19). But Radaq and Ralbag, in their commentaries on 1 Kgs 6.23 suggested that *'ēṣ šemen* is a type of cedar. Y. Felix suggested that it is Jerusalem pine, called in the Aramaic of the Jews of Kurdistan *'a'ā' d^e^mišḥā'*, i.e. oil wood. In Akkadian *šamnu* designates the sap of certain types of trees, so it may be assumed that *'ēṣ šemen* is any type of tree that drips sap.

17. For such an entry in a grave from Tamasus in Cyprus, see Shiloh 1979: pl. 18. See also the stone capital with ornamentation in the form of the front of a temple found at Byblos, and a discussion of the stepped entryway in Stern 1991: 256-61.

18. For the meaning of *'ayil*, see below.

the first explanation point to a coin from Byblos from 218 BCE bearing the image of a temple with such an entrance. Advocates of the latter interpretation draw support from the temple of Tell Tayinat with an entrance surrounded by a frame consisting of interlocking doorposts. Similar entry ways have been discovered in graves on Cyprus, and also resemble the window frames found on various engraved ivories. Interestingly, such frames are depicted on the so-called *kudurru* stones, well known from Mesopotamia. These stones bear divine symbols consisting of a stylized temple topped by the attribute of a particular deity. The temple is stylized by reducing it to a depiction of the stepped doorframes of the entrance. The same convention is found on the Louvre stele of Hammurabi which shows the sun-god Shamash sitting on a stylized temple with a five-framed entrance.

There has been considerable debate over the nature of the divider separating the *hêkāl* and the *dᵉbîr*. According to some it was a stone wall; others suggest that the two chambers were separated only by a thin wooden partition of negligible thickness. Those who claim there was a stone wall point to Ezekiel's Temple, in which a wall of 2 cubits thickness separated the two chambers (Ezek. 41.3), and the Tell Tayinat temple that also contains a true wall between the inner and outer rooms. These scholars assume that the overall dimension of 60 cubits given for the length of the Temple is a schematic number, not resulting from measurement but from calculation, arithmetically adding the 40 cubits of the *hêkāl* to the 20 of the *dᵉbîr* to yield 60. It is not unreasonable that the description will contain a schematic detail, because the description of the bronze basin (*yām*) also contains such a datum (1 Kgs 7.23; see below). Moreover, in the book of Ezekiel the word *'ayil* indicates the wall at the side of a passageway formed by the end of the wall through which it passes (see below), implying thereby some true thickness.

Proponents of the second interpretation hold that the 60-cubit dimension is not a schematic one but an accurate designation of the total, internal dimensions of the Temple, taking in both rooms. In their opinion Ezekiel's Temple does not truly reflect Solomon's (see above), and they point to many Canaanite temples consisting of a single room. The five-tiered doorpost is explained according to this approach as only an engraving in the wood of the wall suggesting such a frame, as we find on the ivories, while the word *'ayil* is interpreted as a pilaster protruding from the wall.

In my opinion, the word *'ayil* is decisive. It cannot be denied the meaning demanded of it by its use in the book of Ezekiel (40.9, 10, 14, etc.). In Ezekiel's vision the *'êlîm* are the short walls between the chambers (*tā'îm*) in the gates to the right and left of one who goes through the passage. They are adorned with palms (*timōrîm*), they have windows, and their widths vary between 2 and 6 cubits. It is difficult to assume that a term describing such an architectural feature would also designate a mere pilaster protruding from the wall, and there is actually no justification for such an interpretation. I conclude, therefore, that the word *'ayil* indicates the end of the wall separating the *dᵉbîr* and the *hêkāl*, and the existence of an *'ayil* indicates the existence of the wall.

An example of a decorated *'ayil* has been found in the excavations at Hazor. Discovered there were gates with chambers; the walls between the chambers (*'êlîm*) are decorated with pilasters sunk into the wall and protruding from it, bearing proto-aeolic capitals, or *timōrîm* (Shiloh 1979: 21-25). The *'ayil* mentioned in Solomon's Temple, which is actually a broad doorpost, was divided into five doorposts, as is the *'ayil* from the Tell Tayinat temple. It is not impossible that the total thickness was 2 cubits, just like the *'ayil* between the *hêkāl* and the *d^ebîr* in Ezekiel's vision, although one may not exclude the possibility that Ezekiel added a bit to the thickness in order to get to 100 cubits as the length of the Temple, as suggested above.

I discussed above whether the Temple had windows, concluding that it probably did, in which case it would have been illuminated during the day by natural light. At night lighting was provided by lamps on the ten lamp stands. However, this applies only to the *hêkāl*. The Holy of Holies, on the other hand, seems to have had no windows or lamps, and would have been dark within. That this is so is indicated by Solomon who declares in his dedication prayer (1 Kgs 8.12), *yhwh 'āmar liškōn bā'^arāpel*, 'The Lord decided to dwell in thick darkness'. This resembles statements in Mesopotamian texts describing temples as dark inside. In particular, a hymn to Ekur, the temple of Enlil in Nippur states (*ANET*, 582-83, ll. 1-5):

> The House of Enlil—it is a mountain great
> The House of Ninlil—it is a mountain great.
> The House of Darkness—it is a mountain great.
> The house which knows no light—it is a mountain great.

Likewise, in the famous composition known as the 'Curse of Agade', when Narām-Sîṇ desecrates the temple one of the disastrous effects is that 'The people now saw its cella, the house that knew not light' (*ANET*, 649, l. 128).

4. *The Temple Vessels and Furnishings*

The Temple of Solomon had two assemblages of vessels. In the courtyard stood enormous, impressive bronze vessels, made by the Tyrian artisan Hiram. In the *hêkāl* were cultic furnishings and implements, reportedly manufactured by Solomon himself (Hurowitz 1995a). The description of the bronze implements is long and quite detailed (1 Kgs 7.13-47), while those of gold are hardly described at all but only listed in a short, inventory-like passage (7.48-50). Nonetheless, as far as the cultic importance and even indispensability are concerned, the bronze vessels are of far less significance than the golden ones. In fact, the Temple could function quite well without the pillars, and with more modest implements for water, but the golden vessels were indispensable, for without them the vital cultic activities performed in the *hêkāl* could not take place.

A bronze implement standing in the court, which was indispensable, was the bronze altar. Curiously, this crucial piece of cultic paraphernalia does not appear among the vessels enumerated in 1 Kings 7. However, it does occur in 2 Chron. 4.1, and its description was inadvertently deleted, as suggested above. This altar is mentioned in connection with dedicating the Temple in 1 Kgs 8.64, and the small implements used with the altar (pots, pans, and pouring vessels) are mentioned at the end of the description of the bronze implements (7.45).[19]

Another item in the Temple whose manufacture was not mentioned was, of course, the ark, which was not made by Solomon. In fact, this most holy symbol of divine presence was in existence for generations, was believed to have been produced by Moses himself (Deut. 10.1-5, etc.), and stood previously at Shiloh, Kiriath-jearim, and the temporary tent David provided it in Jerusalem. It was subsequently brought to the Temple and installed in its place, as is described in 1 Kgs 8.1-13.[20]

The Outer Implements

In the Temple courtyard, before the Temple building, stood several enormous water vessels: the Sea (*yām*) and ten 'stands' (*m*ᵉ*kōnôt*) bearing basins (*kiyyōrôt*). In the forecourt, but outside the Temple building itself, were two immense, bronze pillars, Jachin (*yākîn*) and Boaz (*bō'az*).

The Sea (1 Kgs 7.23-26, 39) was a round water container, made of bronze, standing upon twelve bronze cattle, three facing in each direction of the compass. The Sea measured 10 cubits in diameter and 5 cubits tall (Bagnani 1964). According to v. 23 its circumference ('and a line...could encircle it round about') was only 30 cubits rather than the 31.4...cubits it must have been according to the laws of geometry. It seems, therefore, that this detail was not derived from measuring but from calculation and gross approximation based on the mistaken concept that $\pi = 3$ (Hollenback 1999, 2001).[21]

There are those who compare the Sea to a large water vessel, made of soft limestone, found in Amathus in Cyprus, 2.20 m in diameter and 1.85 m high (Parrot 1954: 32-34, ET 1957: 45-47). On the edge of this basin are reliefs of four handles, each one in the form of a bull. Another illustrative find is a large basin mounted on four lions found at Ebla. Others compare the Sea with water containers called *apsû* mentioned in several Akkadian texts (cf. Burrows 1932). One should also mention a square basalt water trough from the time of Sennacherib discovered at Assur (Andrae 1977: 34) measuring 1.8 m high and 3.12 m on each side. It is surrounded with reliefs of mythical *apkallu* figures indicating that it is

19. For bronze implements (*yā'îm*, 'pans') found alongside the altars in the excavations at Tel Dan, see Biran 1985: 184 and pl. 22 a-b. Probably the head of the jar filled with ashes found imbedded in the earth south of the altar is to be compared with the 'place of ashes', *m*ᵉ*qôm haddešen*, mentioned in the Priestly laws in Lev. 1.16 (cf. also Lev. 6.3).

20. Richard Elliot Friedman has made the astonishing suggestion that the desert Tabernacle was set up in the Holy of Holies. Although Friedman stubbornly persists in this theory (Prov. 26.11), having repeated it most recently in his popular commentary on the Pentateuch, it is disdainful of the biblical text and the Hebrew language. The detailed refutation offered by Hurowitz 1995b has been ignored by Friedman and his student Homan (2000: 25, 55), but was accepted by Cogan (2001: 279), who calls the criticism 'stinging', and J. Milgrom in his commentary on Leviticus (Milgrom 2001: 2453) retracts his previous approval of the theory.

21. The use of calculation rather than measurement is said to be the origin as well as the discrepancy between Kings and Chronicles on the volume of the Sea, the former setting it at 2000 baths, the later at 3000 (Wylie 1949).

related to the cosmic sea, or *apsû*, from which these primordial sages ascended in ancient times, bringing with them the secrets of culture. The *apkallu* were often associated with Ea, god of crafts and purification rituals, and equivalent of Canaanite El, a god of wisdom and syncretized with Ea in later periods (see below).

The function of the Sea is not entirely clear. According to 2 Chron. 4.6 it was 'for the priests to wash in'. If this is the case, then it served the same purpose as the *kiyyôr* in the Tabernacle, in which the priests washed their hands and feet before performing their ministrations (Exod. 30.18-21; 40.31-32). But this Sea was quite high and hard to access, and it is difficult to imagine that such a vessel would serve only for simple ablutions. It is possible that the priests immersed in it before performing certain ceremonies (cf. Lev. 16.4: 'and he will bathe his body in water'; and also Exod. 29.4; Lev. 8.6), because it was deep enough to cover a man's entire body. If so, it must be assumed that a priest wishing to bathe would use a ladder or some other device at the side of the basin to reach its upper edge.

The mᵉkōnôt ('stands') were bronze, wagon-like implements that carried smaller water vessels (1 Kgs 7.27-39). The ten stands stood in parallel rows, five to the right and five to the left of the Temple entrance. Each *mᵉkōnâ* was a square wagon standing on four wheels. The diameter of the basins was 4 cubits, equalling the side dimension of the stands, and each basin rested atop the stand on a small collar-like attachment called a 'mouth' (*peh*). The description of these stands is very detailed and extremely difficult to understand, but it is clear nonetheless that these stands lined up in front of the Temple were very similar in structure and appearance to large and small stands found in excavations at Larnaka and at Enkomi in Cyprus, and even at Hafaja in the area of the Diyala river which flows into the Tigris north of where it bends and approaches the Euphrates (Yadin 1956: 185-86; Burney 1903, facing p. 91; H. Weippert 1992; Hurowitz, Oded and Garsiel 1994). Later parallels from third-century BCE Sidon have been suggested to be connected to Asherah worship (Zwickel 1987).

According to 2 Chron. 4.6, the basins served for washing the burnt offerings. It is quite reasonable that the Chronicler depicts the true function of the basins, but most likely his comment is based mainly on Lev. 1.9, 13, according to which the entrails and the hindquarters of the sacrificial animals were to be washed in water. Albright compared the basins with *egubbû* vessels, i.e. portable water containers that served in numerous Mesopotamian purification rituals (Albright 1969: 144-45). For the most part, *egubbû* vessels were used for purifying human beings, divine statues or buildings; but according to one text (Thureau-Dangin, *Rituels accadiens* 5.iii 21) it was also used for washing cuts of sacrificial flesh.

The supposed symbolic and cosmic significance of the Sea and the twelve cattle upon which it stood has been explained in various ways, but some of them are mere conjectures. The Sea in Solomon's Temple should be connected, perhaps, with the sea in the divine dwelling of the Canaanite god El. El's dwelling is described in Ugaritic mythology as *mbk nhrm//qrb apq thmtm*, 'at the well springs of the rivers//amidst the course of the two seas' (Clifford 1972: 35-57, 168-72). The same idea appears in the Bible (Ezek. 28.2), where the ruler of Tyre boasts 'I am El! In the dwelling of the gods I dwelt in the midst of the seas'. If Solomon's molten bronze Sea represents this same sea, which is probably the Mediterranean Sea off the coast of Lebanon, then we have an additional example of transferring the natural divine habitat to Jerusalem. One should also note that the water trough from Assur mentioned above seems to have been associated with Ea, and that Ea is a partial Mesopotamian counterpart of El (cf. Day 2000: 13-41, esp. 26-35).

It was suggested recently that the bronze Sea symbolizes the Sea vanquished by YHWH during his primordial war with the chaotic forces of nature (Bloch-Smith 1994; cf. Day 1985: 97-101). This was an Israelite echo of the ancient Near Eastern theomachy myth exemplified variously by Marduk's war with Tiamat described in *Enūma Eliš*, Baal's war with Prince Sea (*zbl ym*) of Ugaritic mythology (Bordreuil and Pardee 1993), or Adad's war with the Sea alluded to in a letter from Mari (Durand 1993). A corollary of this suggestion relates the *m*ᵉ*kōnôt* to YHWH's triumphal procession into the Temple following the battle. In any case, following this interpretation, the bronze items would represent vanquished enemies doing permanent obeisance to YHWH and divine victory trophies displayed in the palace to commemorate the great event. Corroboration for this interpretation might be found in the Sumerian mythical composition *An-gim-dim-ma* (*Ninurta's Return to Nippur*), in which Ninurta, returning from battle, sets up his victory trophies in his temple, Ekur. Lines 152-58 read (translation from Electronic Text Corpus of Sumerian Literature):

> Let my father therefore bring in my battle trophies and weapons for me. Let Enlil bathe my heroic arms. Let him pour holy water on the fierce arms which bore my weapons. Let him set up a holy dais in the throne room for me. Let him set my heavenly chariot upon a pedestal. Let him tether my captured warriors there like butting bulls. Let him have my captured kings make obeisance to me there, as to the light of heaven.

This passage is probably an aetiology of actual divine trophies displayed in Ekur, and can serve as a model for Bloch-Smith's suggestion.[22]

A quite different, inner-biblical hint of the meaning of the Sea derives from Ezekiel's vision of the City and Temple of the future. Ezekiel, to be sure, makes no mention of a Sea, wagons or basins. In their stead he tells of 'water coming out from under the Temple towards the east...and the water flowing down from the right façade of the Temple from south of the altar' (Ezek. 47.1-2). The place from which this water emerges is, so it seems, the very place where the Sea had stood in Solomon's Temple (1 Kgs 7.39; 'and the Sea he placed on the right side of the Temple, at the south-east [corner]').[23] The water flowing from Ezekiel's eschatological Temple is to be a source of fertility, healing and life. These waters are also parallel to the river that flowed out of the garden of Eden (Gen. 2.10; cf.

22. It was suggested above that the cedar wood of the Temple's interior and exterior are reminiscent of the Lebanon as a divine dwelling place, but by the same token it should be pointed out that the Lebanon was also known as a venue of divine battles (Clifford 1972: 132). This idea as well would be congruent with Bloch-Smith's interpretation of the Temple furnishing's significance.

23. In both passages describing the placement of the Sea, the left–right orientation is of one standing inside the Temple looking out.

Levenson 1976: 7-36; Mazor 2003). Since the envisioned water replaces the Sea and basins that Solomon made, it becomes clear that these bronze vessels symbolized the river that flowed from the garden of Eden.

The bronze vessels on the one hand and the water flowing from Ezekiel's Temple on the other are both to be compared with streams and rivers mentioned in Mesopotamian inscriptions as parts of temples or royal palaces.

Assurnasirpal II, in his famous banquet stele describes the water for the new royal palace in Kalhu:

> The canal comes rushing above to the orchard; the paths [are full] of scent; the channels of water flow like the stars of heaven in the garden of pleasure; the pomegranate trees which are clothed with clusters like vines, make the wind rich in the garden of... (Postgate 1973: 239 n. 266; cf. *ANET*, 558-61)

Even more interesting is an inscription of Ilūšuma king of Assyria (Grayson 1987: 17) stating:

> The god Assur opened up for me two wells in Mount Ebiḫ [= the ancient mountain of the city of Assur], and I struck bricks for a wall by the wells. One well, its waters flow to the Anšum Gate; and the second well, its waters flow down to the Wertim gate.

Unlike Assurnasirpal II and Ezekiel who tell of one river (cf. Joel 4.18, ET 3.18), this text speaks of two rivers flowing forth from the temple. We are reminded on the one hand of Zech. 14.8, which tells of two rivers flowing forth from Jerusalem, one to the eastern (Dead) sea, and one to the western (Mediterranean) sea, and on the other of the two rows of water-wagons in Solomon's Temple. We are also reminded of the water trough from Assur mentioned above, which is decorated not only with the *apkallu* figures already discussed, but also with divine creatures carrying jugs from which flow multiple streams of water.

The *m*ᵉ*kōnôt* have additional symbolic meaning as well. We have just seen that they represented the rivers flowing out of the divine residence giving fertility to the surrounding countryside. This symbolic meaning is enhanced by the decorations on the wagons. According to 1 Kgs 7.29, the wagons were decorated with 'lions, cattle and cherubs'. This combination of wild and domestic beasts and *Mischwesen* creatures typifies the divine realm. Precisely such a combination of life-forms characterizes the divine gardens of the ancient Near Eastern mythology. The Sumerian myth of Enki and Ninḫursag (ll. 11-16) describes Dilmun, the pure land where Enki makes love with Ninsikila (translation according to Electronic Text Corpus of Sumerian Literature):

> In Dilmun the raven was not yet cawing, the partridge not cackling. The lion did not slay, the wolf was not carrying off lambs, the dog had not been taught to make kids curl up, the pig had not learned that grain was to be eaten.

But we are reminded in particular of Isa. 11.6-9:

> The wolf shall dwell with the lamb,
> The leopard lie down with the kid;
> The calf, the beast of prey, and the fatling together,
> With a little boy to graze them.

> The cow and the bear shall graze,
> Their young shall lie down together;
> And the lion, like the ox, shall eat straw…
> In all of my sacred mount
> Nothing evil or vile shall be done;
> For the land shall be filled with devotion to the Lord
> As water covers the sea.

All having been said, the Temple, the garden of Eden, and the Assyrian palaces and temple are on mountains that are divine residences, and all are surrounded by gardens through which rivers flow. Since Jerusalem has no natural river, and even the Gihon spring is not on the Temple grounds, Solomon made a bronze Sea and the water wagons in order to provide the necessary water, and symbolize the life-giving river flowing forth from the garden of God. In the future, these man-made implements are to be replaced by natural ones, miraculously made.

The Pillars Jachin and Boaz. In the *'ûlām* or forecourt stood two enormous pillars (7.15-22; cf. 2 Kgs 25.15-17; Jer. 52.21-23), given the names Jachin (*yākîn*) and Boaz (*bō'az*). Opinions vary with regard to the form of the pillars, their function, and the meaning of their names (Yeivin 1959; Meyers 1983a; Görg 1991a, 1991b).

According to the description in the book of Kings, the pillars were 18 cubits high and 12 cubits in circumference. The diameter of the pillars would have been, therefore, 3.82 cubits, and together they would have covered nearly a third of the façade of the Temple inside the *'ûlām*. On the tops of the pillars were placed capitals, 5 cubits in height (or three according to 2 Kgs 25.17; cf. Fritz 1992). According to v. 19 it seems as if the height of the capital was 4 cubits. On this basis some scholars have assumed that each pillar had two capitals, while others claim that this verse deals with the capitals of other pillars whose description mistakenly infiltrated and contaminated this context. But it is more likely that the 4 cubits were the height of the *šôšan* ('lotus' or 'lily'; Goldman 1997), and that the girdle, or 'belly' (*beṭen*) at the bottom of the capital, under the lotus, was 1 cubit high. Also, the total height of the pillars together with the capitals is in doubt. The capitals may have rested on top of the pillars, in which case the total height would be 23 cubits. But it is also possible that the top of the pillar was inserted and swallowed up into the capital, in which case the total height could have been between 23 and 18 cubits. It is likely that the *beṭen* was the part of the capital that encircled the top of the pillar, in which case the total height of the pillar was 22 cubits. According to the description in the book of Jeremiah the pillars were hollow (*nābûb*), and their walls were 'four fingers/thick'.

Many scholars tend to the opinion that the pillars served no architectural function, that they were free-standing, and did not support any roof. After all, the height of the Temple was 30 cubits, while these pillars were no more than 27, even according to those claiming that there were double capitals standing one atop the other. This is certainly correct according to the approach claiming that the *'ûlām* was a small, low walled open-roofed forecourt (Meyers 1983a). Nonetheless, it is possible that the pillars supported not a full roof but a canopy that would have been suspended from the façade of the Temple (as suggested by Oullette 1968).[24]

Some scholars have attributed to the pillars cultic functions, such as large altars for burning sacrificial fat, or large torches whose smoke could be seen at great distances. But it seems more likely that these pillars had some sort of symbolic meaning. Carol Meyers suggested that the pillars designated the building as a divine residence, and that they perpetuated the memory of YHWH's entry into his Temple on the day of its dedication when the ark was brought into it in a pompous procession and popular celebration (Meyers 1983a). This opinion can draw support from comparison of the two pillars of the Temple with pairs of pillars that symbolized complete temples and divine residences in ancient Near Eastern iconography from the Sumerian period to the neo-Assyrian period. David Hawkins has suggested (orally) that the gigantic footprints leading into the Holy of Holies in the temple at Ain Dara were also intended to commemorate the resident deity's entry. A similar suggestion was made by Barnett (1981) who, comparing Ezek. 43.4-7, proposed that some Hittite and neo-Hittite reliefs decorating temple gates depict the celebrations marking the god's entry into the temple.

By naming the pillars, Solomon followed an ancient, widespread custom of giving names to cultic vessels and parts of buildings (Gelb 1956). In the Bible itself, Jacob set up an altar and called it *'ēl 'elōhê yiśrā'ēl* (Gen. 33.20); and Moses built an altar and called it *yhwh nissî* (Exod. 17.15). As for the names, one of the most likely proposals, although not in all its details, is the suggestion of R.B.Y. Scott (1939) that the words *yākîn* and *bō'az* are the first words in inscriptions inscribed on the pillars and which contained prophecies of blessings for the royal dynasty. He would reconstruct the blessing something like *yākîn yhwh kissē' dāwid ûmamlaktô 'ad 'ôlām*, 'may YHWH found with strength the throne of David and his kingdom to his descendants forever', and *be'ōz yhwh yiśmaḥ melek*, 'by might of YHWH may the king rejoice'. Such beatific names were given to secular and religious buildings in Mesopotamia. Hammurabi, king of Babylon, built a wall in Sippar and called it 'by command of the god Shamash, Hammurabi has no rival'. Nebuchadrezzar, king of Babylon, called his new palace 'Long live Nebuchadrezzar; may the patron of Esagila grow old'. Most interesting is the name Sennacherib gave one of the gates of Nineveh, 'Enlil makes firm the regnal period' (*Ellil mukīn palê*).

A parallel to the description of the pillars, lending support for Scott's suggestion, is provided by a small tablet discovered at Assur, dating apparently from the time of Tukiltī Ninurta I in celebration of the dedication of several wooden pillars to a temple in the new city of Kār-Tukultī-Ninurta (Weidner 1954–56; Hurowitz 1992: 257-58). The document contains two parts. The first describes the pillars and their capitals, specifying their length, thickness and quality of workmanship. The second part states that they were inscribed with a royal dedicatory

24. Terra cota miniatures of buildings (probably temples) found in the land of Israel display both free-standing columns as well as columns which support roofs.

inscription, that they were brought from Assur to Kār-Tukultī-Ninurta, and erected in the temple on the fifth day of the month of Qararatu when the king offered a sacrifice. If so, this tablet describes the pillars, their capitals, their length and thickness, the place where they stood and the inscriptions they bore. It is quite reminiscent of the detailed description of Jachin and Boaz that also contains the length of the pillars, their thickness, the place where they stood and the capitals upon them. Continuing with the parallel we find that the designation of the names in the biblical passage parallels the note in the Assyrian inscription that the pillars were inscribed.

Finally, we must bear in mind that the columns were topped with capitals bearing floral and arboreal elements (*šûšan*, 'lily'; *rimmōnîm*, 'pomegranates'; *ś^ebākîm*, 'tangled branches'). They are, in fact, stylized trees. To be sure, columns at the entrances of temples are referred to in ancient Near Eastern literature[25] and depicted on numerous terra cotta temple models found in the land of Israel. I would like to conjecture, however, that in the context of a Temple reflecting a divine garden, these two treelike columns, standing at the entrance to the Temple in the middle of the court, may have represented the two trees which, according to the tradition reflected in J, were at the middle of the Garden of Eden (Gen. 2.9b, translating according to the Masoretic accentuation and Onqelos): 'And the Tree of Life was in the middle of the garden, as was the Tree of Knowledge of Good and Evil'.

The Inner Furnishings and Implements

The gilded furnishings standing in the *hêkāl* (1 Kgs 7.48-90) were identical in kind, if not in all details of number and design to the guilded furnishings found in the Tabernacle (Hurowitz 1995a). Similar furnishings could be found apparently in Israelite temples predating the Jerusalem Temple. Solomon's Temple housed a golden altar, a table for displaying bread, and ten lamp stands.[26] The golden altar (1 Kgs 6.20, 22; 7.48; cf. also Isa. 6.6) served certainly for burning incense, as was done in the Tabernacle. A table for displaying bread was also found in the Tabernacle. There is testimony that a bread offering was practised in the temple in Nob (1 Sam. 21.4-7), and it is most reasonable to assume that there would have been a table for displaying it before YHWH. Also Mesopotamian temples, where sacrifices were not offered by burning them on altars, contained tables (*paššuru*) for displaying various types of offerings to the gods. In the Tabernacle was a single lamp stand with seven branches, and in Shiloh there was a 'lamp of God' (*nēr *'^elōhîm*, 1 Sam. 3.3) that burnt in the temple during the night until burning out before dawn. Just as in the Tabernacle and the other ancient Israelite temples, so in Solomon's Temple these were the main cultic furnishings upon which the priests performed their daily duties as YHWH's household servants.

25. Herodotus (*Histories* 2.44) describes the Melqart (Herakles) temple at Tyre, saying that in front of it stood two pillars, one of gold and one of emerald which gleamed in the dark. There is no indication that they were treelike, although this possibility is not to be excluded.

26. Bloch-Smith (2002: 88-89) has suggested possible astral significance for the Temple lamp stands. She seems to assume that the ten lamp stands of the Temple were each seven branched, as was the lampstand in the Tabernacle.

Along with these implements, which we call 'furnishings' because they were bulky, and stood immovable on the ground on permanent display, there were supplementary, smaller implements necessary for performing the cultic rituals. Literary analysis of this list (1 Kgs 7.48-50) and comparison of the implements here with the same or similar paraphernalia mentioned in other biblical passages shows how the minor cultic vessels were associated with the three major furnishings (Hurowitz 1995a). The 'flower' (*peraḥ*), lamps and tongs (*melqāḥayim*) were associated with the lamp stands (cf. Exod. 25.37-38). The spoons (*kappôt*) and fire pans (*maḥtôt*) were associated with the incense altar (cf. *maḥtôt* in Lev. 10.1; 16.12; *kappôt* in Num. 7.14, etc.). There remain *sippôt*, *m^{e}zamm^{e}rôt* and *mizrāqôt*. The *sippôt* were vessels for holding liquids and beverages, as we learn from Akkadian texts such as the instructions of the daily offerings in the temple of Anu in Uruk, where it is written: 'Every day...eighteen *sappu* vessels of gold you will arrange on the table of Anu' (Thureau-Dangin, *Rituels accadiens* 75.2). The *sippôt* in the Temple correspond to the *q^{e}śôt hannesek* found on the table of shewbread in the Tabernacle (Exod. 25.29). The *mizrāqôt* were, perhaps, vessels for presenting vegetable offerings (cf. Num. 7.13) or drink (cf. Amos 6.6), or a receptacle for liquids as were the *sippôt*. In contrast to the prevalent scholarly opinion, the *m^{e}zamm^{e}rôt* were not scissors or shears for trimming the wicks of the oil lamps, but musical instruments, as already understood by the Jewish mediaeval exegetes. Musical performance was probably associated with the table of shewbread, upon which the divine repast would have been served. One can illustrate this with an Akkadian text reflecting the daily ritual, and describing in particular the tenth day of the month of Tishri (Thureau-Dangin, *Rituels accadiens* 92.12-14):

> The main meal of the morning will be served, the musicians will play. The meal will be removed, the second meal will be served, and the meal will be removed; the main meal of the evening will be served and the musicians will play. <The second meal of the night will be served>, the second meal of the evening will be removed, and the gate will be locked.

At the end of the list of small golden implements we find reference to 'the *pōtôt* of the doors of the inner room, i.e. of the Holy of Holies; (and) of the doors of the chamber of the *hêkāl*' (1 Kgs 7.50b). All modern commentators interpret the *pōtôt* as door sockets (as in rabbinic Hebrew), or as plating of the doors, but this would be quite out of place. After all, this list of minor cultic implements is hardly the place for such architectural details, whereas the doors and their decorations were already described in 1 Kgs 6.31-35. Now Rashi makes here a fascinating comment: '*happōtôt* (means) keys (*maptēḥôt*); I have heard that one seduces [deriving *m^{e}pattîn* from *pth*, seduce, and also alluding to *pōt*, pudendum] with them the lock'. It turns out that Rashi, perceptive as always, has hit upon the simple meaning of the text, and that the *pōtôt* are indeed keys to the inner and outer doors. It is appropriate, however, to emend slightly and read the graphically similar *pōt^{e}ḥôt* or even *pōtēaḥ*, and it is likely that such a reading was known to the Chronicler, where in 1 Chron. 4.22 MT reads 'and the entrance (*ûpetaḥ*) to the house: the doors of the innermost part of the house, the Holy of Holies, and the doors of the great hall of the house, of gold'. We should clearly revocalize the word and read *ûpōtēaḥ*, leaving us with a word for key.[27]

A reference to keys in the list of the minor cultic implements implies that ceremoniously opening the doors to the Temple was part of the daily ritual. To be sure, we find in 1 Sam. 3.15: 'Samuel lay there until the morning; and then he opened the doors to the House of the Lord'. Opening the gates in the Second Temple is described in great detail in Mishnah, *Tamid* 3.6-7. Similarly, opening the temple doors in the morning and locking them at night was part of the daily ritual in Mesopotamia and Egypt as well (*ANET*, 325-26).

The most sacred part of the Temple was the *d^{e}bîr*, also known as the Holy of Holies. Within the *d^{e}bîr* stood two gigantic cherubs, each one occupying half the width of the chamber, made of oil-wood and overlain with gold. These items are not described, apart from their wings. According to 2 Chron. 3.10 they were *ma'^{a}śēh ṣa'^{a}ṣu'îm*, an enigmatic term interpreted by traditional commentators as baby-faced (a supposed by-form or variant of *ṣe'^{e}ṣā'* meaning offspring), but now taken to mean 'sculpted work' and the like. It is clear, however, that they were *Mischwesen* resembling winged quadrapeds known throughout the ancient Near East, be they griffins, sphinxes, winged bulls and lions, or the like (Albright 1961). They served as YHWH's throne, just like the royal thrones decorated with cherubs known from various places in the ancient Near East (Haran 1959, 1978: 246-59).

Under the outstretched wings of the cherubs stood the *'^{a}rôn*, ark—the wooden box that had previously stood in the temple of Shiloh and was brought to Jerusalem by David. According to the biblical tradition about the sojourn in the desert, the conquest and the settlement, the ark was made by Moses at Mt Sinai, and accompanied the Israelites in their wanderings. Many scholars today cast doubts on the very existence of a desert period in Israelite history, and it is therefore obviously impossible to connect the origins of a cultic implement with a period that never was. According to this approach (which has not convinced all scholars) the traditions about the wandering ark must be seen as retroversions into the past of the custom of taking the ark out of the Temple into the battlefield or into the military camp as a symbol of YHWH's presence (cf. Num. 10.35-36; 1 Sam. 4). They could also reflect the use of the ark in cultic processions during the time of the First Temple. In any case, when the ark is in the Temple it is considered to be YHWH's footstool; and it is possible that it was considered his palanquin when it was taken into the field or on parade.

Although 1 Kings offers no explanation for the cherubs within the Holy of Holies, 1 Chron. 28.18 calls them *tabnît hammerkābâ*, a model of the Chariot, indicating that the gigantic cherubs in the Temple represented the divine Chariot seen by Ezekiel, using the term for this employed in rabbinic Hebrew (Mishnah, *Ḥagigah* 2.1, etc.).

27. In the light of this interpretation, Milard's well intentioned attempt to defend gold door sockets on the basis of Mesopotamian door sockets covered with gold foil is unnecessary and beside the point (Millard 1997: 35).

The ark housed the tablets of the Covenant. This was in keeping with a well-known custom in the ancient Near East, by which copies of international treaties were deposited under the feet of the gods in their temples. There were probably not cherubs on the ark, and its original form when introduced into the Temple would have been like that described in Deut. 10.1-3. According to the Priestly conception, the ark was covered by a lid called a *kappōret*, out of which extended two cherubs (Exod. 25.10-22; 36.1-9). This Priestly ark apparently never existed as such, and its form derived from an artificial merging (for purposes of mobility[28]) of the ark-less cherubs and the cherub-less ark which stood in the Temple from the time of Solomon until they disappeared, being either removed by Manasseh (according to Menahem Haran) or utterly destroyed by the Babylonians (e.g. John Day).[29]

5. *The Temple as a Divine Residence and Garden*

The decorations in the Temple and their distribution were significant and logical. It seems as if the Temple was not merely YHWH's residence, but a divine garden on earth (Wenham 1986; Stager 1998; Bloch-Smith 2002; Mazor 2003). We have already seen how this idea is expressed in the bronze implements of the courtyard that represent the Sea and rivers of the divine residence, the natural tranquility of the holy mountain, and possibly the Trees of Life and of Knowledge. But it also explains the vegetable motifs engraved on the walls and doors of the Temple building. Bloch-Smith (2002: 87) explains the palmettes as stylized sacred trees resembling those well known from ancient Near Eastern iconography, and recreations of the garden of Eden. The cherubs engraved on the doors symbolize cherub guards, similar to those stationed 'east of the garden of Eden to guard the way to the tree of Life' (Gen. 3.24; according to a suggestion of John Strange [1985], all the vegetable motifs in Solomon's Temple were connected with eternal life and fertility). The cherubs incised on the back wall of the *hêkāl* also guard the door to the *d^ebîr*, resembling the guards whom Jehoiada the priest stationed 'from the right shoulder of the Temple to the left shoulder of the Temple' in order to keep watch over the king (2 Kgs 11.11; Cogan and Tadmor 1988: *ad loc.*). This is to say, these cherubs were the private honour guard of the Temple's divine resident. The cherubs engraved on the inner walls of the *d^ebîr* represented God's retinue consisting of servants, advisors and courtiers stationed to praise the divine king, similar to the the host of heaven in the vision of Micaiah son of Imlah (1 Kgs 22.19), the sons of God in the Job 1–2, and the seraphim Isaiah saw in his throne vision (Isa. 6.2-3). There are no cherubs

28. Other examples of changing of the Tabernacle's equipment for purposes of mobility are the laver and the lamp stand (*m^enôrâ*). In the Temple there were a bronze Sea atop twelve cattle as well as ten water wagons (*m^ekōnôt*) bearing basins (*kiyyôrôt*). These were merged in the Tabernacle into a single *kiyyôr* standing on a *kan* (Exod. 30.18; 38.8). In the Temple there were ten lamp stands, while the Tabernacle had only one.

29. For the theories of the fate of the ark, see John Day's contribution to the present volume (pp. 250-70).

engraved in the front and side walls of the *hêkāl*, because that is where YHWH's human servants, the priests, ministered (for the priest as an angel see Mal. 2.7, and cf. Zech. 3.7).[30]

The overall symbolism of the Temple's décor may be illuminated by a passage from the Sippar Cylinder of Nabonidus, king of Babylon, in which he describes the restoration of Eḫuḫul, the temple in Harran of the moon god Sin (Langdon 1911: 222, Nabonid Nr. 1, Col. II 10-17):

> Long beams of cedar, growths of the Amanus mountains, I spread over it.
> Doors of sweet smelling cedar I erected in its gates.
> I plated its walls with silver and gold and made it as bright as the sun.
> A wild ox made of bright *zaḫalû* mightily goring my enemies I stood in its holy of holies.
> Two guardian *laḫmu*-deities made of *ešmaru* silver, vanquishing my enemies
> I directed to the right and left of the eastern gate.

According to this passage, Nabonidus set up mythological images at the entrance of the temple and in its innermost cella. The statues are described as goring his enemies and vanquishing his foes, and it is clear that they are assigned with guarding the temple. Moreover, stipulating the place where the cedars grew as the Amanus mountains directs the mind of the reader to the holy mountain, dwelling-place of the gods, and reminds one that the temple is a copy of that residency. From comparison of the form of the Temple in Jerusalem with the temple described in this inscription, and many other texts like it, we see that Solomon's Temple was not much different from the neighbouring temples as far as its basic conception was concerned.

6. *The Material and Technological Gradation*

Another important factor in the design of the Temple was the material and technological gradation in its components and appurtenances. Menahem Haran (1978: 158-65) has already explained in great detail how, in the Tabernacle, the deeper one penetrates towards the innermost part, the more valuable and more technologically sophisticated its components become. The increase in value of materials and sophistication of design corresponds with an ascending holiness and increasing severity of restriction upon who may enter. In the margins of his study Haran suggested that a similar gradation characterizes Solomon's Temple as well (Haran 1978: 190 n. 2-3), and this idea may be explored further here:

1. All the vessels standing in the courtyard were made of bronze. In the *hêkāl* there were furnishings covered with gold, and the cherubs in the *d*ᵉ*bîr* were also covered with gold. There was nothing of gold in the court, nor was anything within the building of bronze.

30. In Ezekiel's visionary Temple the decorations in the *hêkāl* and *d*ᵉ*bîr* are identical (Ezek. 41.18-21). Both rooms were adorned with cherubs and palmettes, but there is no mention of calyxes. In the Tabernacle too there were cherubs on the walls (side curtains) of the 'Holy' and the 'Holy of Holies', so that the decorations of both rooms were identical. It is possible that the walls of the Temple were redecorated at the time of Jehoash when the Temple was repaired.

2. The golden altar for incense in the *hêkāl* was made of cedar but the cherubs in the *d^ebîr* were made from 'oil-wood'. All the walls in the Temple, both in the *hêkāl* and the *d^ebîr*, were panelled in cedar wood. However, the floor of the *hêkāl* was made of cypress wood, while the floor of the *d^ebîr*, as the *d^ebîr* in its entirety, was apparently made of cedar.
3. The floor of the *d^ebîr* was also plated in gold, but not the floor of the *hêkāl*.[31]
4. The walls of the *hêkāl* were engraved with gourds and calyxes, but the walls of the *d^ebîr* and the innermost wall of the *hêkāl*, shared by the *hêkāl* and the *d^ebîr*, displayed palms instead of gourds, and there were also cherubs.
5. The cherubs in the *d^ebîr* were made of 'oil-wood', which was apparently a most valuable wood. The doors of the *d^ebîr* were also made of this type of wood, but the doors of the *hêkāl* were made of cypress, and only their doorposts were of 'oil-wood'.
6. The doors differ from each other in their craftsmanship as well. The doors of the *hêkāl* were made of two boards, while the doors of the *d^ebîr* were of only one. This would seem to show a preference for the outer door, the one to the *hêkāl*, but, as was pointed out above, it was certainly most difficult to create a large plank of 'oil-wood', so such a plank would be most expensive and impressive.[32]
7. The doorposts of the *hêkāl* were *r^ebi'ît* (perhaps in place of *mē'ēt r^ebi'ît* in 1 Kgs 6.33 one should read *m^ezûzat r^ebi'ît*), while the doorposts of the *d^ebîr* were *m^ezûzat ḥ^amišît*.
8. There may have also been a difference in the method by which the gold was applied to the doors. Concerning the doors to the *hêkāl* we read: *w^eṣippāh zāhāb m^eyuššār 'al-hamm^eḥuqqeh*, 'and he overlaid it with gold, straightened(?) on the engravings/carvings',[33] while the doors to the *d^ebîr* are described *w^eṣippāh zāhāb wayyāred 'al-hakk^erûbîm w^e 'al-hattimōrôt 'et-hazzāhāb*, 'and he plated (the doors) with gold and hammered(?) the gold onto the cherubs and palms', and it is most likely that *rdd* expresses a more sophisticated type of craft than *yšr*.

In summary, this survey of the materials and workmanship in the Temple shows that the principle of gradation found in the Tabernacle characterized the design of the Solomonic Temple as well. The purpose of the material and technological gradation was certainly to inspire a feeling of increasing holiness and grandeur while approaching the most sacred spot, and focusing attention on YHWH who sat enthroned in the *d^ebîr*. The results are summarized in the following chart.

31. 1 Kgs 6.30 relates only to the *d^ebîr*. For the words *lipnîmâ welaḥîṣôn*, see above.

32. We should remember that even in modern times, solid wood furniture is much more valued than plywood, sandwich board, pasteboard and the like.

33. *m^eḥuqqeh*, from *ḥqh*, a by-form of *ḥqq*.

The Décor of the Temple

CHAMBER	*Hêkāl*	*D^{e}bîr Qōdeš haqq^{o}dāšîm*
DOORS		
Type of wood	Cypress	Oil Wood
Number of boards	2	1
ṣ(q)^{e}lā'îm	each rouded? *g^{e}lîlîm*	
Plating material	Gold	Gold
Method of plating	*M^{e}yuššār 'al-hamm^{e}huqqeh*	*wayyāred 'al-hakk^{e}rûbîm w^{e}hattimōrôt*
Engraving	*k^{e}rûbîm*	*k^{e}rûbîm*
	Palmettes *timōrôt*	Palmettes *timōrôt*
	Calyxes *p^{e}ṭûrê ṣiṣṣîm*	Calyxes *p^{e}ṭûrê ṣiṣṣîm*
FRAMES/DOORPOSTS—Form	*r^{e}bi'ît*	*'ayil m^{e}zûzôt ḥ^{a}mišît*
Type of Wood	Oil wood	???
FLOOR—Type of wood	Cypress	CEDAR
CEILING—Type of wood	Cedar	Cedar
WALLS		
Type of wood	Cedar	Cedar
Engraving	Gourds *p^{e}qā'îm*	PALMETTES *timōrôt*
	Calyxes *p^{e}ṭûrê ṣiṣṣîm*	Calyxes *p^{e}ṭûrê ṣiṣṣîm*
	----------	*k^{e}rûbîm*
Plating	Gold	Gold
FURNISHINGS	Incense altar	Huge *k^{e}rûbîm*
	Table of shewbread	ARK
	Ten Lamp stands	
Type of wood	Cedar	OIL WOOD
Plating	Gold and *sāgûr* gold	GOLD

7. *Architectural Growth of the Temple*

According to the biblical narrative, the Temple in Jerusalem was built by King Solomon. Its foundations were reportedly laid during the king's fourth year (c. 964 BCE?), and the building was completed seven years and six months later, during his eleventh year (1 Kgs 6.1, 37-38). These data do not necessarily aim at reflecting the authentic chronology of events. Rather, they are based on a common literary topos, on the one hand, and a 'typological' number, expressing an ideal time span, on the other.[34] As for founding the Temple in the king's fourth year, one may conjecture that this particular year was actually Solomon's first year as an independent sovereign, after he had served as prince regent during his ailing father's final three years (Yeivin 1976). If so, this number may be regarded

34. Casperson (2003) has recently suggested that the delay in constructing the Temple until Solomon's fourth year was so that it would coincide with the sabbatical or jubilee year. In fact, he claims that all Temple building and rebuilding activity between 1000 BCE and 500 BCE were timed to commence during jubilee years.

as a biblical expression of a concept the likes of which are attested in ancient Mesopotamian royal inscriptions. According to this conception, it is fitting to attribute to the king in his first year some impressive feat on behalf of his god, and in particular the building of a temple (Cogan 1985: 207-209). The three year co-regency may also be a typological number. As for completing the construction in seven years, periods of seven units of time were considered in ancient Near Eastern literature as ideal spans of time. Moreover, in the Bible itself we find that constructing the Tabernacle extended over seven months, while in the Ugaritic Baal epic, Baal's palace is said to have emerged on its own from a fire that had burned seven days (*KTU* 1.4 VI 22-35).

The plan to build the Temple was allegedly raised by David, as reported in detail in 2 Samuel 7, and alluded to briefly in 1 Kgs 5.17-19 (ET 3-4); 8.15-21. YHWH rejected this initiative through the agency of Nathan the prophet, for reasons that remain enigmatic (cf. Dirksen 1996). According to the book of Chronicles, David made many preparations for building the Temple (1 Chron. 28–29). He financed the building fund largely from his own pocket, encouraged popular contributions, and prepared everything necessary for the project both in resources and manpower. He commanded Solomon to build the Temple, and even transferred to him the written plans that had been revealed to him prophetically by God himself. All these details notwithstanding, we should certainly accept the common scholarly opinion completely rejecting the Chronicler's version of events, regarding it at most as an attempt on the part of the author to fill in literary and historical gaps in the account of building the Temple, such as explaining how Solomon knew what God had instructed David to build, and aggrandize the beloved King David, even at the expense of dimming the lustre of Solomon (Hurowitz, Oded and Avramsky 1995; Throntveit 1997). One has the feeling that had the Chronicler been granted the privilege to determine the course of history, he would have made David builder of the Temple rather than Solomon; but since even he was limited in what he could get away with, he sufficed with attributing to David everything save the physical labour of putting the pieces together.

At the same time, however, one need not dismiss out of hand the tradition found in the Former Prophets crediting David with the desire to build the Temple and reporting the rejection of this initiative by a divine spokesman. In fact, Mesopotamian inscriptions provide several examples of kings wanting to build temples to their gods, and the gods denying permission to do so, as was their prerogative (Hurowitz 1993: 160-63). Moreover, it has been suggested that building a temple by a founder of a royal dynasty was typical royal behaviour in antiquity, so that David's attempt to build a temple as part of stabilizing his royal house did not diverge from usual and expected conduct (Meyers 1987a; cf. Meyers 1983b). Furthermore, transferring the ark of YHWH to Jerusalem would necessitate, earlier or later, providing a permanent domicile, so that suggesting to build a Temple as a natural next step is not at all surprising. We may never know whether it was David who first thought of building a Temple in Jerusalem, but there is nothing in his recorded behaviour deviating from common ancient Near Eastern practice.

According to biblical tradition, the Temple was built on the site of a threshing floor owned by the Jebusite Araunah. David bought the threshing floor and some cattle for fifty shekels of silver; he built an altar on the site and sacrificed the cattle (2 Sam. 24.18-25). 2 Chronicles 3.1 identifies the site as Mt Moriah, where Abraham had bound his son Isaac to sacrifice him as the Lord had commanded, until an angel stopped him (Gen. 22). Later tradition tries to lend antiquity and authenticity to the site by saying that Noah, Cain and Abel, and even Adam had also sacrificed there, and that the dust from which Adam was created was taken from there (Kalimi 1990).

The Temple was burnt down on 7 Ab, 586 BCE by Nebuzaradan, chief of the guards, officer of Nebuchadrezzar II, king of Babylon (2 Kgs 25.8; cf. Jer. 52.12, according to which the Temple was burnt on the tenth of the month). At that time, the Babylonians took as booty all the bronze, silver and gold implements remaining in the Temple (2 Kgs 25.13-17; cf. Jer. 52.17-23).

The Solomonic Temple is said to have stood, therefore, close to three hundred and eighty years. During this period it did not remain static in architecture or décor. Instead, it underwent no small amount of changes in physical structure and appearance as well as in functioning and its religious, national, and social role. One may learn about the changes that occurred in the Temple either from explicit references or from comparison of the description of specific items at different times.

1 Kings 6.36 reports that Solomon 'built the inner courtyard', while 1 Kgs 7.8, 9, 12 mention the 'other courtyard' and '(the) great courtyard'. These descriptions imply that the Temple was surrounded originally by a single courtyard (*ḥ^{a}ṣar bêt yhwh*). A second, larger courtyard (*heḥāṣēr hagg^{e}dôlâ*), encompassed all the Solomonic buildings, taking in the Temple and its court as well as the royal buildings, but it was not properly a court of the Temple. One should note that the Tabernacle, which reflects certain aspects of the First Temple, had only one court. This would imply that only one court had significant cultic function, and perhaps at the time the Tabernacle account was composed there was indeed only one court considered belonging to the Temple.

On the other hand, 2 Kgs 21.5 (see also 23.12) reports 'he (Manasseh) built altars to all the host of heaven in the two courts of the House of YHWH'. Ezekiel, in describing the abominations done in the Temple on the eve of its destruction (Ezek. 8–10), mentions the 'inner court of the Temple of YHWH' and 'the outer court', and refers to the entire Temple compound as *ḥ^{a}ṣērôt*, courtyards (in plural). The Temple described in the great vision concluding the book of Ezekiel is also surrounded by two courtyards; and in Solomon's Temple itself, as described in 2 Chron. 4.9, there was a 'priests' court' (*ḥ^{a}ṣar kōh^{a}nîm*) and a 'great court' (*'^{a}zārâ g^{e}dôlâ*), but it is not speaking of a new court.

In fact, there is no essential difference between 1 Kings 6–7 and the later sources, but we must assume that at some time before the days of Manasseh the large court was appropriated for Temple use. It is not impossible that at the same time certain structural modifications were introduced; and perhaps the expansion of the Temple grounds is to be associated with the enigmatic note in 2 Kgs 16.18:

'and the Sabbath passage (? *mûsak*/*ysk haššabbāt*) which they built in the Temple and the outer king's entrance he directed towards the Temple because of the king of Assyria'.

The description of the Temple as built (1 Kgs 6–7) makes no mention of service chambers (*lᵉšākît*)—i.e. cells, rooms or storerooms—which served various administrative and cultic needs of the community, the workers in the Temple and royal officials (Kellermann 1984, ET 1997).[35] At the same time, however, the chambers of certain dignitaries who frequented the Temple are mentioned in 2 Kgs 23.11 and Jeremiah 35–37, and these chambers assume great prominence in Ezekiel's visionary Temple (Ezek. 40.17, 44, etc.). Although all references to these chambers are concentrated in depictions of the Temple during the last years of its existence, one should not exclude the possibility that at least some were present earlier, even from the time of Solomon. It is reasonable to assume that every temple would be in need of such facilities, even if they are not mentioned explicitly. In fact, we find that there was a *liškâ* in the high place at Ramah (1 Sam. 9.22), where Samuel 'blessed the sacrifice' offered in the city. Perhaps even in connection with the temple at Shiloh we should read in 1 Sam. 1.18: 'and the woman went on her way and she entered the *liškâ* and ate with her husband and drank', following LXX, and it has been suggested emending v. 9 and reading: 'and Hannah got up after eating in the chamber (*balliškâ* rather than *bᵉšilōh*) and after drinking'. The temple at Dan possessed a room the excavator calls a *liškâ* (Biran 1985, 1986, 1987). Even so, it is likely that with the expansion and growing influence and importance of the Jerusalem Temple from the time of Hezekiah until Josiah, and with its elevation to sole place of legitimate worship, activity intensified and many chambers were added.

Repair of damage and wear to the Temple is reported twice: first at the time of King Jehoash and Jehoiadah the priest (2 Kgs 12.7-17; Cogan and Tadmor 1988: 135-41; Hurowitz 1986; Greenfield 1985), and again in the time of King Josiah and Hilkiah the priest (2 Kgs 23.9-13). It is likely that these repairs were needed to fix damages rendered by Queen Athaliah or King Manasseh and his son Amon, rulers who were portrayed as antagonistic to worship of YHWH and promoters of foreign, even idolatrous practices. It is possible, therefore, that certain changes were religiously motivated, either to restore the situation to what it had been previously, or to remove something that could become part of illegitimate worship (cf. 2 Kgs 18.4 from the time of Hezekiah). At the same time, however, both stories explicitly indicate that the Temple had to be maintained and kept in good repair constantly, and that repair and upkeep were both funded and provided with manpower (Hurowitz 1986). From all that has been said, it is possible to assume that the kings of Judah cared for the Temple and its maintenance, and we may conjecture that in the course of running repairs, occasionally changes were made in the structure of the Temple and in its appurtenances.

35. The etymology of the Hebrew term has eluded scholars (cf. Kellermann 1997). In my opinion it is to be related to Akkadian *ašl/rukattu* ('storeroom for grain', 'lobby', 'hallway in temple'), which, according to *AHw* (82b) is a loanword of unknown background.

From time to time substantial alterations were made affecting the cult that were religiously, politically or aesthetically motivated. Of these alterations, most prominent are a series of changes introduced by King Ahaz, with the active participation of Uriah the priest (2 Kgs 16.10-18). He replaced the bronze altar, which had stood in the Temple court since the days of Solomon, with a new 'large altar', designed after the form of an altar he had seen in Damascus when he met King Tiglath-pilesar III of Assyria. The old altar he placed to the north of the new one. Recently M. Cogan and H. Tadmor (1988: 135-41) suggested that replacing the old altar with a new one reflects a fashion prevailing at the time throughout the Assyrian empire of imitating Aramaean art. Perhaps this one is reflected in Ezek. 43.13-17, where he recommends for the future a stepped altar resembling in architecture and echoing some terminology of the Mesopotamian ziggurats (cf. Albright 1969: 150-52). At the same time, Ahaz cut up some of the large bronze implements—the water wagons and the small basins and the bronze oxen statues supporting the bronze 'Sea'-basin, and he most likely sent them as tribute to Tiglath-pileser (v. 8). Hezekiah beat out the bronze serpent Moses had made and displayed in the Temple (2 Kgs 18.4). He cut up the 'doors of YHWH's outer sanctum' and the 'doorposts' (? *'ōmᵉnôt*) which he had plated, and sent them to Sennacherib as part of the heavy tribute he paid (v. 16), and we may assume that it was not the doors themselves he cut up and sent but the gold with which they were overlain. It goes without saying that even though the items removed and shipped away were not cultic items *per se*, their removal would have effectively scrambled and rendered incoherent the symbolism of the design and décor discussed above.

There is evidence that from time to time new structures were introduced into the Temple, but their identity, nature and function are not clear.

1 Kings 10.12 reports that Solomon made the *'almuggîm* (a type of wood; cf. Akkadian *elamakku;* Greenfield and Mayerhoffer 1967) that the fleet of Hiram had brought from Ophir into 'decorations (*mis'ad*) in the house of the Lord and in the royal palace and for harps and lyres for the musicians'. It is difficult to know whether the *mis'ad* was part of the building with an architectural role in strengthening (on the basis of the parallel *hēkîn sā'ad*) or a portable furnishing, such as a dining table (on the basis of the meaning of Hebrew *s'd* and the fact that some Akkadian texts refer to tables made of *elamakku* wood).

Jotham, son of Uzziah built the 'upper gate of the Temple of YHWH' (2 Kgs 15.35). This gate may be mentioned in the book of Jeremiah, either as 'the upper Benjamin gate that is in the Temple of YHWH' (Jer. 20.20) or 'the New gate of (the Temple of) YHWH' (Jer. 26.10; 36.10) which was in the Upper Court. It has even been identified with the enigmatic *ša'ar sûr*, mentioned a single time in 2 Kgs 11.6.

2 Kings 16.12 recalls 'the loft of Ahaz' (*'ᵃliyyat 'āḥāz*) on top of which stood altars, obviously for astral worship (many Akkadian texts mention rituals performed at night on roofs). Since this structure occurs within a list of abominations performed in the Temple, there is room to assume that it too was part of the

Temple. This structure is mentioned in Isa. 38.8, according to the large Isaiah scroll from Qumran where we find *b^ema ʿ^alôt ʿ^aliyyat ʾāḥāz* (and cf. 2 Kgs 20.11, *b^ema ʿ^alôt ʾāḥāz*). Y. Yadin (1959; cf. Iwry 1957) suggested that the steps of this structure served as a sort of giant sundial. Such a use was destined obviously to misuse in astral worship; but originally the loft of Ahaz and its steps were part of the innovations that Ahaz made in the Temple, which were acceptable to Uriah the priest and which were not condemned by members of the Deuteronomic school, editors of the book of Kings. It must be assumed that a sundial was set up for a reason, and it is possible that its original purpose was to fix precisely when sacrifices and other cultic activities were to be performed.

But the most significant alterations in the Temple were made at the time of Manasseh. According to 2 Kgs 21.7 (cf. also 23.6), he set up the statue of the Asherah in the Temple, and by doing so he changed the Temple from being a house of YHWH to the house of a different deity. Whether he removed the ark of YHWH is a question still debated. According to M. Haran (1978: 276-88), it was Manasseh who removed from the Temple the ark of the Covenant; and, to be sure, it is no longer mentioned except in popular longings, as mentioned in Jer. 3.16: 'and when you increase and are fertile in the land, in those days—declares the Lord—men shall no longer speak of the ark of the Covenant of the Lord, nor shall it come to mind. They shall not mention it, or miss it, or make another.' Jeremiah's prophecy, as well as the fact that the ark is missing from the list of booty the Babylonians took and is not even mentioned in Ezekiel's restoration vision, indicate that Josiah did not return the ark when he purified the Temple. Haran therefore assumed that it disappeared or was destroyed in the time of Manasseh. It is also possible that the disappearance of the ark at that time contributed to the new theological development of the author of the Deuteronomic source and the redactors of the book of Kings according to which YHWH does not dwell in the Temple but, instead, his name alone is called upon it (see further, below).

John Day, on the other hand (in his contribution to the present volume, pp. 250-70), rejects this thesis. He sees the loss of YHWH's footstool (*h^adōm raglāyw*) in Lam. 2.1 as referring to the ark. He also claims that since Asherah was YHWH's consort (a matter known to scholarship only after the recent discoveries at Kuntillet ʿAjrud, etc. and subsequent to Haran's formulation of his view), Manasseh would have seen the two as compatible and would not have to remove the symbol of the one in the face of the other.

Manasseh is also said to have built altars to all the astral deities in the two Temple courtyards, and was probably responsible for 'all the vessels made for the Baal and the Asherah and all the Host of Heaven' which were located in the *hêkal yhwh*, as well as 'the houses of the *q^edešîm* in the Temple where woman would weave clothing for the Asherah' (2 Kgs 23.4, 7). All these 'improvements', some of them decorative, others architectural, were removed by Josiah, but only in his eighteenth year, and it seems unlikely that the Temple would have or could have been restored to its pristine state.

8. *Divine Presence in the Temple*

Over the nearly four centuries of its existence, the Temple built by Solomon not only changed its physical shape and appearance, but its conceptual nature also evolved (cf. Uffenheimer 2001).

The temple as a religious phenomenon was not a native Israelite invention, but one of the many institutions that the people of Israel borrowed from neighbouring cultures (Haran 1978, 1988; Huot 1999; Margueron 1999b). It is only natural, therefore, that the essential significance of the Temple was not determined within the confines of Israelite religion but by the previous peoples who had initiated it. In fact, we find that ancient Near Eastern temples were thought of primarily as places of earthly residence among men for the gods, their families, and their divine subordinates (Wright *et al.* 1960). Every temple housed a divine cult statue or some other physical embodiment of the deity. The gods ate, drank, slept, and even cohabitated and carried on family life in their houses, or temples; and if the deity's worshippers regarded him or her as a king or queen or some other potentate, then the temple would be the equivalent of the sovereign's residence and governmental offices. Anyone wishing to offer homage to the god, ask a question, or make a request, would visit him at his home. There the person could address the deity directly or through agency of a lower ranking member in the divine pantheon, all depending on the circumstances and the rank of the petitioner.

Despite whatever deep differences may have existed between the religion of ancient Israel and those of surrounding peoples, the Israelite temple, at the outset of its development, was still nearly identical in basic conception to that of the others. It seems as if in Israel as well the house of YHWH was considered to be his place of residence, or, at least, a place of special and permanent presence of the God of Israel. Just as the gods of the gentiles were not confined and restricted to their temples, or one single temple, so YHWH was not limited exclusively to a single domicile. But just as among the surrounding peoples, he was always found within his temple in some form or another, and anyone who sought him out would always find him available on the premises.

The Israelite temples that antedated the one in Jerusalem housed tangible symbols of YHWH's presence: the ark (a divine footstool, throne and chariot), a pillar (abstract representation of divine presence), an ephod (divine garment), or even a cult statue (cf. Niehr 1997; Na'aman 1999). God was also conceived of as being present in the Temple in a supernatural but perceivable form as well, in the *kābôd*, or Majesty. Accordingly, when the ark of YHWH from Shiloh was captured, the wife of Phinehas the priest and mother of Ichabod wailed '*kābôd* has been exiled from Israel' (1 Sam. 4.21; on the *kābôd* as a physically perceivable entity see below).

The Jerusalem Temple was conceived of and planned initially as a place of residence for YHWH, as indicated by the Temple's cultic implements which are essentially household furnishings (lampstands, a table with dishes, and incense altar). In the Holy of Holies stood two gigantic cherubs that were YHWH's throne.

When the Temple was dedicated the ark was installed.[36] The ark served as God's palanquin, borne by priests, when he was outside the Temple (Num. 10.35, 36; 1 Sam. 4.4)[37] and his footstool when he was inside. According to an ancient poetic passage, perhaps cited from the enigmatic *sēper hayyāšār* (or *sēper haššîr* on the basis of LXX), Solomon announced before YHWH on the occasion of dedicating the Temple: 'I have surely built for you an exalted house, a firm place for your eternal dwelling' (1 Kgs 8.13). Isaiah, in his famous throne vision, sees YHWH 'sitting on a high and uplifted throne, and his skirts fill the *hêkāl*' (Isa. 6.1); while in his end of days vision he describes the mountain (of the house of) YHWH and the Temple of the God of Jacob as a courthouse to which nations in conflict will come so that YHWH can instruct them in his ways and judge between them (2.2-4; Schwartz 1998). Particular evidence of the belief that God was present in the Temple, where his presence can be enjoyed, comes from the book of Psalms, which contains chapters of prayer and reflection expressing the feelings of those who ascend to Zion and visit the Temple. According to Psalm 132, David swears to find 'a place for YHWH, a dwelling place for the Mighty One of Jacob', and he invites YHWH, 'Arise, O YHWH to your resting place, you and the ark of your might'. As reward for David's acts of kindness and appropriate intentions God chooses Zion and swears: 'This is my resting place for ever, here I shall dwell for I am desirous of it'. And Psalm 84 states:

> How beloved is your dwelling place, O YHWH of Hosts
> My soul yearns and longs for the courtyards of YHWH...
> Blessed are those who dwell in your house...
> Blessed is the man...who appears before God in Zion... (vv. 2, 3, 5, 8, ET 1, 2, 4, 7)

These verses, and others like them (Pss. 23.6; 27.4-5; 122, etc.), demonstrate that one who made a pilgrimage to the Temple felt that when visiting the Temple he was standing really in the immediate presence of YHWH; from this we learn that YHWH's presence in the Temple was extraordinary, perceptible, and unique in comparison with his presence in any other place.

The thought that God could somehow be limited to a single place did not sit well in certain circles, and towards the end of the days of the First Temple a controversy developed, the purpose of which was to define more precisely the nature of YHWH's presence in the Temple. Although this argument was never decisively settled, it left its mark on circles and thinkers of the period of restoration and thereafter. The so-called Deuteronomic school which stood behind the writing of the book of Deuteronomy (Deut. 26.15) and the redaction of the books of the Former Prophets, and who composed most of Solomon's Temple Dedication Prayer (1 Kgs 8.15-61), preferred the ancient, widespread idea that YHWH sat in

36. There have been recent suggestions that the Jerusalem Temple originally possessed a cult statue (Niehr 1997), but there is no textual indication that this was ever the case, and the suggestions have been soundly refuted (Na'aman 1999).

37. The ark serving as a war palanquin should be compared to the use of the chair, *kussû*, on the war campaign by Sennacherib in his fifth campaign (cf. Luckenbill, *Sennacherib* 36, 4). For faster, air transportation God rode on a cherub which represented a chariot (2 Sam. 22.11; Ps. 18.11, ET 10; 1 Chron. 28.18).

his heavenly abode and looked down upon the earth (cf. 2 Sam. 21.8-10) but he went to the extreme, claiming both that YHWH does not dwell and is unable to dwell on the earth, within the confines of the Temple. He 'places' his name or 'causes his name to dwell' (Zakovitch 1972), or calls his name on the Temple, and looks at it more than upon any other place on the surface of the earth; but he was not tangibly, physically attached (von Rad 1952; Mettinger 1982; Richter 2002).[38] The ark, considered by earlier generations as an item to which God was linked, was redefined as the ark of the Covenant, as representing the special legal relationship existing between YHWH and the people of Israel. God was 'kicked upstairs', so to speak, and the Temple itself became a sort of gigantic 'switchboard' through which all prayers and requests were redirected toward him who dwells on high. Building the Temple was aimed at guaranteeing that YHWH's blessing will be upon the king who built the Temple. But it loses its traditional, accepted significance, so that God's blessing for the people and the royal dynasty is now conditional on keeping covenant promises on the part of God and fulfilling certain religious obligations on the part of the people and king (Hurowitz 1992: 285-300).

Members of the Jerusalem priesthood, on the other hand, held that YHWH dwells in the Temple, and that the Temple was permeated by a dangerous, contagious sanctity emanating from the divine Majesty, *kābôd*, present therein (Exod. 29.23-44). They did not express their opinion in a description of the Jerusalem Temple, but did so circuitously in the so-called 'Priestly source' (P) preserved in the Pentateuch. Also, Ezekiel son of Buzi the priest, descended from the Jerusalem Priestly line, expresses the views of the Priestly school in his vision of wicked Jerusalem in chs. 8–11, as well as in the visionary law code which concludes his book. The Priestly source describes in great detail the Tabernacle that the Israelites erected in the desert, but it is quite likely that it imposes on the Tabernacle, which stood at Shiloh, a new form that is none other than that of the Jerusalem at the time of Ahaz or Hezekiah. According to the conception of the Priestly source, the Tabernacle (and the Jerusalem Temple that it reflects) was filled by the divine *kābôd* from the time of its completion and dedication (Exod. 30.34-35; Lev. 9.4, 6, 22, 23; Num. 7.89); and by virtue of YHWH's *kābôd* filling the Tabernacle he *ipso facto* dwelled in the midst of the people of Israel (Exod. 25.9; 29.46).

38. Richter's thesis, which cannot be addressed here in any detail, disputes the commonly accepted idea of 'Name theology' as a belief in some sort of divine presence embodied or hypostasized in the divine name. She posits instead that *šakkēn šēm* in Hebrew is to be interpreted as equivalent of *šūma šakānu* in Akkadian, as reflecting the concept of the Temple as a sign of YHWH's victorious domination of the land. An alternative new interpretation of the Deuteronomic idiom was presented by John Van Seters at the 2003 International Meeting of the Society of Biblical Literature in Cambridge, England. He relates the idiom to the Akkadian *šūma šaṭra šakānu*, and claims that it refers to placing a copy of the Deuteronomic legislation in the Temple. Both new suggestions seem problematic, but deserve wider scholarly discussion (see reviews, Hurowitz 2004–2005; Mettinger 2003; Van Seters 2003). Neither of them, in any case, contradicts the fact that the *kābôd* is not part of Deuteronomic theology, and must explain how Name placing, whatever it means, supplants it.

K^{e}*bōd YHWH*, which is an essential component in Priestly thought, is no abstract concept. This divine Majesty was a perceptible entity, visible, and blatantly anthropomorphic, and has been compared with the divine aura called *melammu* and *puluḫtu* know from Mesopotamian writings (Weinfeld 1971).[39] From afar the Majesty looked like a consuming fire impossible to view, but seen up close one could perceive through the radiance an anthropomorphic appearance. Ezekiel witnesses the *kābôd* leaving the Temple prior to its destruction (Ezek. 8.1–11.23) and envisions it returning to the Temple to be built in the future (43.2-4). Nor was the concept of the *kābôd* an invention of the Jerusalem priesthood, but it was most likely known already at Shiloh, as mentioned above. The *kābôd*'s entry into the Temple of Solomon is also mentioned in the (pre-Priestly) description of dedicating the Temple in 1 Kgs 8.10-11: 'When the priests came out of the sanctuary—for the cloud had filled the house of the Lord and the priests were not able to remain and perform the service because of the cloud, for the presence of the Lord filled the house of the Lord'.

These two approaches, one with an imminent view of YHWH and the other transcendental in outlook, lived on into the time of the Second Temple. Haggai and Zechariah disagreed over precisely the issue of divine presence in the Temple, and the dispute continued on after them. They neither initiated nor finally settled the debate. To be sure, the argumentation is expressed subtly, but it may be discerned by careful analysis of some crucial verses. Zechariah's position is stated clearly in Zech. 2.9, where we read:

> Jerusalem will dwell like the un-walled city…,
> and I myself, declares the Lord, will be a wall of fire all around it,
> and I will be a glory (*kābôd*) inside it.

Later on we find (2.14; cf. 8.3 as well):

> Shout for joy, Fair Zion!
> For lo, I come; and I will dwell in your midst (*w*^{e}*šākantî b*^{e}*tôkēk*)
> —declares the Lord.

The prophet, using P's idiom, agrees here with Ezekiel (43.1-3; 44.4), who, as noted, envisages the return and re-entry of YHWH's radiant *kābôd* to the Temple of the future, the same *kābôd* which he saw depart in ch. 10 and encountered wandering about homelessly in ch. 1. The fire around the city and the *kābôd* within reflect as well the Priestly view of the Tabernacle as found in Exod. 40.34-38, in which a cloud covers the Tabernacle while the *kābôd* surrounded by fire are within. In other words, Zechariah carries forward and applies to the rebuilt Jerusalem traditional Priestly theology known from P of the Pentateuch and 1 Kgs 8.11, Ezekiel, and other sources.

Haggai's position, in contrast, is profoundly different, and is expressed in two verses. In Hag. 1.8, YHWH commands:

39. The concept of divine radiance in the Bible and the ancient Near East is the topic of a University of Pennsylvania dissertation presently being written by Shawn Aster under the direction of Jeffrey Tigay.

> Go up to the hills and get timber,
> and rebuild the house;
> then I will look on it with favour and I will be glorified (*w*^{e}*'ekkāb*^{e}*dâ*),
> said the Lord.

This verse should be compared with Exod. 25.2:

> Tell the Israelite people to bring me gifts…,
> and let them make me a sanctuary
> that I may dwell among them.

Each of these commands has three parts that may be paraphrased as follows: (1) gather materials for building a Temple; (2) build God a Temple; (3) God's anticipated reaction. Comparison of the passages juxtaposes and equates Haggai's *w*^{e}*'erṣeh bô w*^{e}*'ekkāb*^{e}*dâ* with P's *w*^{e}*šākantî b*^{e}*tôkām*. To be precise, Haggai's *w*^{e}*'ekkāb*^{e}*dâ*, 'I will be glorified', substitutes for P's 'I will dwell among them', and indicates a deliberate change in the concept of *kābôd*. The Priestly *kābôd* present in the Tabernacle is God's visible aura, whereas Haggai's *kābôd* is God's glorious reputation gained by glorious acts.[40] The relationship between Haggai's statement and the absence of *kābôd* is correctly perceived and hinted at by the rabbinic comment (*b. Yoma* 21b; cf. Rashi, *ad loc.*) that the missing *he* (cohortative ending) indicates five things which were present in the First Temple but absent in the Second, namely the ark and cherubs; fire (on the altar); divine presence (*Shekinah*); the Holy spirit; Urim and Thummim. The first three of these items are related directly to God's presence in the Temple. In other words, Haggai's use of *kbd* here is correctly understood to be an allusion to the *kābôd* with the expected meaning 'divine substance and aura', but it has been demythologized.

Another set of references to Haggai's revised *kābôd* occurs in 2.6-9:

> For thus said the Lord of Hosts:
> In just a little while longer I will shake the heavens and the earth, the sea and the dry land;
> I will shake all the nations. And the precious things of all the nations shall come [here],
> and I will fill the house with glory (*kābôd*), said the Lord of Hosts.
> Silver is mine and gold is mine—says the Lord of Hosts.
> The glory (*kābôd*) of this latter house shall be greater than that of the former one, said the Lord of Hosts;
> and in the place I will grant prosperity—declares the Lord of Hosts.

In this passage, the word *kābôd* appears with the meaning 'wealth' as it does in numerous other biblical passages. Once again Haggai has retained the term *kābôd*, the presence of which is necessary for a functioning Israelite temple, but has employed it with a totally different meaning, again demythologizing it. By use of word-play, Haggai has his cake and eats it too, maintaining the *kābôd* in the Temple, even while changing its essence.

This dispute continued on after the prophets contemporary with the rebuilding of the Temple. Trito-Isaiah, in Isa. 60.1, an eschatological vision, speaks of

40. For *k-b-d* in the niphal theme with God as subject, see Exod. 14.4, 17, 18; Ezek. 28.22; 39.13.

YHWH's *kābôd* shining upon Israel, perhaps echoing Zechariah and Ezekiel and certainly reflecting the ancient meaning. But in v. 12 he predicts:

> The glory (= wealth; *kābôd*) of Lebanon shall come to you—
> Cypress and pine and box together
> —to adorn the site of my Sanctuary,
> to glorify (*ʾakabbēd*) the place where my feet rest.

This verse clearly incorporates Haggai's dual interpretation of *kābôd* as 'wealth' in the first instance and 'glory' in the second, but by mentioning God's feet (see Isa. 66.1) he may allude to Ezek. 43.6.

Finally, in Ezra 6.16-18, describing the dedication of the rebuilt Temple, no ark is installed (cf. 1 Kgs 8.1-9), there is no mention of the *kābôd* entering (cf. Exod. 40.34-38; 1 Kgs 8.11), and there is not even a divine promise that the divine Name will be placed on the Temple (cf. 1 Kgs 9.3). The entry of the deity into the Temple, which constitutes the central act of temple dedication ceremonies in the Bible and throughout the ancient Near East (Hurowitz 1992: 260-84), is nowhere to be found.[41] In fact, the Temple appears to be no more than a place of sacrifice. Even though, as at the time of dedicating the Tabernacle, priests and Levites are installed (cf. Lev. 8; Num. 8.5-26) and sacrifices are made for the twelve tribes (cf. Num. 7), the *kābôd* is absent, even in allusion. The retrospective historian, so it seems, accepts neither Haggai's nor Zechariah's views, and the Temple has profoundly changed its essence.

BIBLIOGRAPHY

Abū 'Assāf, A.
1990 *Der Tempel von 'Ain Dārā* (Mainz: Philipp von Zabern).
Aharoni, Y.
1971 'The Israelite Sanctuary at Arad', in D.N. Freedman and J.C. Greenfield (eds.), *New Directions in Biblical Archaeology* (Garden City, NY: Doubleday): 28-44.
1973 'The Solomonic Temple, the Tabernacle, and the Arad Sanctuary', *Beer Sheva* 1: 79-86, 240-41 (Hebrew with English Abstract).
Aḥituv, S., and A. Mazar (eds.)
2000 *The History of Jerusalem: The Biblical Period* (Jerusalem: Yad Izhak Ben-Zvi)
Albright, W.F.
1942 'Two Cressets from Marisa and the Pillars of Jachin and Boaz', *BASOR* 85: 18-27.

41. The absence of divine presence in the Second Temple as seen in the account of the dedication festivities contrasts with the implication of the Cyrus decree in Ezra 1.3, where the king commands building *bêt yhwh ʾelōhê yiśrāʾēl hûʾ hāʾelōhîm ʾašer bîrûšālayim*, 'a house of YHWH, God of Israel, he is the God who is in Jerusalem', for which we can compare Cowley (1923) no. 30.5, 6 which refers to *ʾlhʾ ḥnwb zy byb byrtʾ* and especially *yhw ʾlhʾ zy byb byrtʾ*. These identical locutions reflect the same commonly held belief that a deity was present in a certain city, i.e. in the temple of that deity, in which case, there is a clear conceptual difference between the two parts of the account of rebuilding the Temple.

1959 'Was the Age of Solomon without Monumental Art?', in M. Avi-Yonah, H.Z. Hirschberg, Y. Yadin and H. Tadmor (eds.), *Eretz-Israel* 5 (Benjamin Mazar Volume; Jerusalem: Israel Exploration Society, Hebrew University, Bialik Institute): 1*-9*.

1961 'What Were the Cherubim?', in G.E. Wright and D.N. Freedman (eds.), *The Biblical Archaeologist Reader* (3 vols.; Garden City, NY: Doubleday): I, 95-97.

1969 *Archaeology and the Religion of Israel* (Garden City, NY: Doubleday, 5th edn).

Andrae, W.

1977 *Das Wiedererstandende Assur* (ed. B. Hrouda; Munich: C.H. Beck, 2nd edn).

Avigad, N.

1964 'The Temple of Solomon' (Lecture at the Eighty-Third Meeting of the Bible Study Group in the President's Residence), *Beth Miqra* 17: 4-25 (Hebrew).

1987 'The Inscribed Pomegranate from the "House of the Lord"', *Israel Museum Journal* 8: 7-16.

Bagnani, G.

1964 'The Molten Sea of Solomon's Temple', in W.S. McCullough (ed.), *The Seed of Wisdom: Essays in Honour of T.J. Meek* (Toronto: University of Toronto Press): 114-17.

Barkai, G.

1997 'The *M^{e}gērâ* and the *Ṭ^{e}pāḥôt*', *Shnaton* 11: 32-45 (Hebrew).

Barnett, R

1981 'Bringing the God into the Temple', in A. Biran (ed.), *Temples and High Places in Biblical Times: Proceedings of the Colloquium in Honor of the Centennial of Hebrew Union College–Jewish Institute of Religion, Jerusalem, 14–16 March 1977* (Jerusalem: The Nelson Glueck School of Biblical Archaeology of Hebrew Union College–Jewish Institute of Religion): 10-20.

Ben-Tor, A., J.C. Greenfield and A. Malamat (eds.)

1989 *Eretz-Israel* 20 (Yigael Yadin Volume; Jerusalem: Israel Exploration Society, Hebrew University, Hebrew Union College–Jewish Institute of Religion).

Biran, A.

1985 'Tel Dan 1984', *IEJ* 35: 186-89.

1986 'The Dancer from Dan, the Empty Tomb and the Altar Room', *IEJ* 36: 168-87.

1987 'The Head of a Scepter and the *Liškâ* of Amadyaw at Dan', *Qadmoniyot* 21: 11-17 (Hebrew).

Bloch-Smith, E.

1994 '"Who is the King of Glory?": Solomon's Temple and its Symbolism', in M.D. Coogan, J.C. Exum and L.E. Stager (eds.), *Scripture and Other Artifacts: Essays on the Bible and Archaeology in Honor of Philip J. King* (Louisville, KY: Westminster/John Knox Press): 18-31.

2002 'Solomon's Temple: The Politics of Ritual Space', in Gittlen (ed.) 2002: 83-94.

Bordreuil, P., and D. Pardee

1993 'Le combat de Ba'lu avec Yammu d'après les textes ougaritiques', *MARI* 7: 63-70.

Burney, C.F.

1903 *Notes on the Hebrew Text of the Books of Kings* (Oxford: Clarendon Press).

Burrows, E.

1932 'Problems of the Abzu', *Or* NS 1: 231-56.

Busink, T.A.

1970 *Der Tempel von Jerusalem von Salomo bis Herodes*. I. *Der Tempel Salomos* (Leiden: E.J. Brill).

Casperson, L.W.

2003 'Sabbatical, Jubilee, and the Temple of Solomon', *VT* 53: 283-96.

Clements, R.E.

1965 *God and Temple: The Idea of the Divine Presence in Ancient Israel* (Oxford: Basil Blackwell).

Clifford, R.J.

1972 *The Cosmic Mountain in Canaan and the Old Testament* (HSM, 4; Cambridge, MA: Harvard University Press).

Cogan, M.

2000 'The Chronicler's Use of Chronology Illuminated by Neo-Assyrian Royal Inscriptions', in J.H. Tigay (ed.), *Empirical Models for Biblical Criticism* (Philadelphia: University of Pennsylvania Press): 197-209.

2001 *1 Kings: A New Translation with Introduction and Commentary* (AB, 10; New York: Doubleday).

Cogan, M., and H. Tadmor

1988 *II Kings: A New Translation with Introduction and Commentary* (AB, 11; New York: Doubleday).

Cowley, A.E.

1923 *Aramaic Papyri of the Fifth Century B.C.* (Oxford: Clarendon Press).

Davey, C.J.

1980 'Temples of the Levant and the Buildings of Solomon', *TynBul* 31: 107-46.

Day, J.

1985 *God's Conflict with the Dragon and the Sea: Echoes of a Canaanite Myth in the Old Testament* (UCOP, 35; Cambridge: Cambridge University Press).

2000 *Yahweh and the Gods and Goddesses of Canaan* (JSOTSup, 265; Sheffield: Sheffield Academic Press).

Dever, W.G.

1982 'Monumental Architecture in Ancient Israel in the Period of the United Monarchy', in T. Ishida (ed.), *Studies in the Period of David and Solomon and Other Essays* (Winona Lake, IN: Eisenbrauns): 269-306.

1990 'Of Myths and Methods', *BASOR* 277/278: 5-22.

1997 'Archaeology and the "Age of Solomon": A Case Study in Archaeology and Historiography', in L.K. Landy (ed.), *The Age of Solomon: Scholarship at the Turn of the Millennium* (Leiden: E.J. Brill): 217-51.

Dirksen, P.B.

1996 'Why was David Disqualified as Temple Builder? The Meaning of 1 Chronicles 22.8', *JSOT* 70: 51-56.

Durand, J.-M.

1993 'Le mythologème du combat entre le dieu de l'orage et la met en Mésopotamie', *MARI* 7: 41-62.

Fritz, V.

1987 'Temple Architecture: What can Archaeology Tell us about Solomon's Temple?', *BARev* 13.4: 38-49.

1992 'Die Kapitelle der Säulen des salomonischen Tempels', in E. Stern and T. Levi (eds.), *Eretz-Israel* 23 (Abraham Biran Volume; Jerusalem: Israel Exploration Society, Hebrew Union College–Jewish Institute of Religion): 36*-42*.

Garber, P.L.

1951 'Reconstructing Solomon's Temple', *BA* 14: 2-24.

Gelb, I.J.

1955 'Names of ex voto Objects in Ancient Mesopotamia', *Names* 4: 65-69.

Gil, M.

1972 'The *lûllîm* in the Temple', *Beth Miqra* 17: 297-301 (Hebrew).

Gittlen, B.M. (ed.)

2002 *Sacred Time, Sacred Space: Archaeology and the Religion of Israel* (Winona Lake, IN: Eisenbrauns).

Goldman, Z.

1997 'The Sign of the Lily and its Roots, Significance and History in Antiquity, Part 1', *Shnaton* 11: 197-221 (Hebrew).

Görg, Manfred

1991a 'Jachin und Boas; Namen und Funktion der beiden Tempelsäulen', in *Aegyptiaca–Biblica: Notizen und Beiträge zu den Beziehungen zwischen Ägypten und Israel* (Ägypten und Altes Testament, 11; Wiesbaden: Otto Harrassowitz): 79-98.

1991b 'Die "ehernen Säulen" (I Reg 7,15) und die "eiserne Säule" (Jer 1,18); ein Beitrag zur Säulenmetaphorik im Alten Testament', in R. Liwak and S. Wagner (eds.), *Prophetie und geschichtliche Wirklichkeit im alten Israel: Festschrift für Siegfried Herrmann* (Stuttgart: W. Kohlhammer): 134-54.

Grayson, A.K.

1987 *Assyrian Rulers of the Third and Second Millennia BC (to 1115 BC)* (Royal Inscriptions of Mesopotamia: Assyrian periods, 1; Toronto: University of Toronto Press).

Greenfield, J.C.

1985 'The Meaning of *TKWNH*', in A. Kort and S. Morschauser (eds.), *Biblical and Related Studies Presented to Samuel Iwry* (Winona Lake, IN: Eisenbrauns): 81-85.

Greenfield, J.C., and M. Mayerhoffer

1967 'The 'Algummim/'Almuggim Problem Reexamined', in G.W. Anderson *et al.* (eds.), *Hebräische Wortforschung: Festschrift zum 80. Geburtstag von Walter Baumgartner* (VTSup, 16; Leiden: E.J. Brill): 83-89.

Gutmann, J. (ed.)

1976 *The Temple of Solomon: Archaeological Fact and Medieval Tradition in Christian, Islamic and Jewish Art* (AAR and SBL, Religion and the Arts, 3; Missoula, MT: Scholars Press).

Haak, R.D.

1983 'The 'Shoulder' of the Temple', *VT* 33: 271-78.

Handy, L.K. (ed.)

1997 *The Age of Solomon: Scholarship at the Turn of the Millennium* (SHCANE, 11; Leiden: E.J. Brill).

Haran, M.

1959 'The Ark and the Cherubim: Their Symbolic Significance in Biblical Ritual', *IEJ* 9: 30-38, 89-94.

1978 *Temples and Temple-Service in Ancient Israel* (Oxford: Oxford University Press).

1984 'Ezekiel 40–48', in G. Brin (ed.), *Ezekiel* (Encyclopaedia Olam Ha-Tanakh, 12; Ramat Gan: Revivim): 200-47 (Hebrew).

1988 'Temple and Community in Ancient Israel', in M.V. Fox (ed.), *Temple in Society* (Winona Lake, IN: Eisenbrauns): 17-25.

Herzog, Z.

2000 'The Temple of Solomon: Reconstruction of its Plan and its Archaeological Parallels', in Aḥituv and Mazar (eds.) 2000: 155-74 (Hebrew).

Hess, R.S., and G.J. Wenham (eds.)

1999 *Zion City of Our God* (Grand Rapids: Eerdmans).

Hollenback, G.M.

1998 'The Value of "pi" and the Circumference of the "Molten Sea" in 3 Kingdoms 7,10', *Bib* 79: 409-12.

2000 'The Dimensions and Capacity of the "Molten Sea" in 1 Kgs 7,23.26', *Bib* 81: 391-92.

Homan, M.M.

2000 'The Divine Warrior in His Tent: A Military Model for Yahweh's Tabernacle', *BR* 16.6: 22-33, 55.

Hrouda, B.

1972–75 'Ḫilāni, bīt B', in D.O. Edzard (ed.), *Reallexikon der Assyriologie und vorderasiatischen Archäologie* (Berlin and New York: W. de Gruyter): IV, 406-409.

Huot, J.-L.

1999 'In Search of the Earliest Temples', *The World of the Bible* 1: 11-17.

Hurowitz, V.A.

1986 'Another Fiscal Practice in the Ancient Near East (LAS 277)', *JNES* 45: 289-94.

1992 *I Have Built You an Exalted House: Temple Building in the Bible in Light of Mesopotamian and Northwest Semitic Writings* (JSOTSup, 115; ASOR Monograph Series, 5; Sheffield: Sheffield Academic Press).

1994 'Inside Solomon's Temple', *BR* 10.2: 24-37, 50.

1995a 'Solomon's Golden Vessels (I Kings 7.48-50) and the Cult of the First Temple', in D.P. Wright, D.N. Freedman and A. Hurvitz (eds.), *Pomegranates and Golden Bells: Studies in Biblical, Jewish, and Near Eastern Ritual, Law, and Literature in Honor of Jacob Milgrom* (Winona Lake, IN: Eisenbrauns): 151-64.

1995b 'The Form and Fate of the Tabernacle: Reflections on a Recent Proposal', *JQR* 86: 127-51.

1998 'Ascending the Mountain of the Lord: A Glimpse into the Solomonic Temple', in J.G. Westenholz (ed.), *Capital Cities: Urban Planning and Spiritual Dimensions: Proceedings of the Symposium Held on May 27-29, 1996, Jerusalem, Israel* (Bible Lands Museum Jerusalem Publications, 2; Jerusalem: Bible Lands Museum): 215-23.

2000 'The Temple of Solomon', in Aḥituv and Mazar (eds.) 2000: 131-54 (Hebrew).

2004–2005 Review of Richter 2002, *JHS* 5 (<http://www.arts.alberta.ca/JHS/reviews/review 157.htm>)

Hurowitz, V.A., B. Oded and S. Avramsky

1995 '2 Chron. 2-7.11', in G. Galil (ed.), *2 Chronicles: Olam Ha-Tanakh* (Tel Aviv: Davidson-Atti): 18-52 (Hebrew).

Hurowitz, V.A., B. Oded and M. Garsiel

1994 '1 Kgs 5.15-9.25', in M. Garsiel (ed.), *1 Kings: Olam Ha-Tanakh* (Tel Aviv: Davidson-Atti): 60-91 (Hebrew).

Iwry, S.

1957 'The Qumran Isaiah and the End of the Dial of Ahaz', *BASOR* 147: 27-33.

Kalimi, Y.

1990 'The Land of Moriah, Mount Moriah, and the Site of Solomon's Temple in Biblical Historiography', *HTR* 83: 345-62.

Karageorghis, V.

1970 'Chronique des fouilles et découvertes archéologiques à Chypre en 1969', *Bulletin de correspondence héllenique* 94: 191-300.

Kaufman, A.S.
1998 'The Temple and Subterranean Structures in the Temple Area', *BDD. Bekhol Derakhekha Daehu. Journal of Torah and Scholarship* 7: 15-29.
Kellermann, D.
1984 '*liškâ*', in *ThWAT*: IV, 606-11, ET *TDOT*: VIII (1997), 33-88.
Kitchen, K.A.
1989 'Two Notes on the Subsidiary Rooms of Solomon's Temple', in Ben-Tor, Greenfield and Malamat (eds.) 1989: 107*-12*.
Knauf, E.A.
1997 'Le Roi est mort, vive le Roi! A Biblical Argument for the Historicity of Solomon', in L.K. Handy (ed.), *The Age of Solomon: Scholarship at the Turn of the Millennium* (SHCANE, 11; Leiden: E.J. Brill): 81-95.
Knoppers, G.N.
1995 'Prayer and Propaganda: Solomon's Dedication of the Temple and the Deuteronomist's Program', *CBQ* 57: 229-54.
1997 'The Vanishing Solomon: The Disappearance of the United Monarchy from Recent Histories of Ancient Israel', *JBL* 116: 19-44.
Langdon, S.
1911 *Die neubabylonischen Königsinschriften* (Vorderasiatische Bibliothek, 4; Leipzig: J.C. Hinrichs'sche Buchhandlung).
Laperrousaz, E.M.
1987 'King Solomon's Wall Still Supports the Temple Mount', *BARev* 13.3: 34-44.
Lundquist, J.M.
1983 'What is a Temple? A Preliminary Topology', in H.B. Huffmon (ed.), *The Quest for the Kingdom of God: Studies in Honor of George E. Mendenhall* (Winona Lake, IN: Eisenbrauns): 205-19.
Levenson, J.D.
1976 *Theology of the Restoration of Ezekiel 40–48* (HSM, 10; Atlanta: Scholars Press).
McCormick, C.M.
2002 *Palace and Temple: A Study of Architectural and Verbal Icons* (BZAW, 313; Berlin: W. de Gruyter).
McEwan, C.W.
1937 'The Syrian Expedition of the Oriental Institute of the University of Chicago', *American Journal of Archaeology* 41: 8-16.
Mankowski, P.V.
2000 *Akkadian Loanwords in Biblical Hebrew* (HSS, 47; Winona Lake, IN: Eisenbrauns).
Margueron, J.-C.
1999a 'A Storey for the Temple Personnel', *The World of the Bible* 1: 22-23.
1999b 'The Origins of Holy Places', *The World of the Bible* 1: 18-22.
Mazor, L.
2002 'The Correlation between the Garden of Eden and the Temple', *Shnaton* 13: 5-42 (Hebrew).
Mettinger, T.N.D.
1982 *The Dethronement of Sabaoth: Studies in the Shem and Kabod Theologies* (ConBOT, 18; Lund: C.W.K. Gleerup).
2003 Review of Richter 2002, *JBL* 122: 753-75.
Meyers, C
1983a 'Jachin and Boaz in Religious and Political Perspective', *CBQ* 45: 167-78.
1983b 'The Israelite Empire: In Defense of King Solomon', *Michigan Quarterly Review* 23.3: 412-28.

1987 'David as Temple Builder', in P.D. Hanson *et al.* (eds.), *Ancient Israelite Religion: Essays in Honor of Frank Moore Cross* (Philadephia: Fortress Press): 257-76.

Milgrom, J.

2001 *Leviticus 23–27* (AB, 3b; New York: Doubleday).

Millard, A.R.

1989 'The Doorways of Solomon's Temple', in Ben-Tor, Greenfield and Malamat (eds.) 1992: 135*-39*.

1997 'King Solomon in His Ancient Context', in L.K. Handy (ed.), *The Age of Solomon: Scholarship at the Turn of the Millennium* (SHCANE, 11; Leiden: E.J. Brill): 30-53

Milson, D.

1986 'The Design of the Royal Gates at Megiddo, Hazor and Gezer', *ZDPV* 102: 87-92.

Möhlenbrink, K

1932 *Der Tempel Salomos: Eine Untersuchung seiner Stellung in der Sakralarchitektur des alten Orients* (BWANT, 4.7; Stuttgart: W. Kohlhammer).

Monson, J.H.

1996 'Solomon's Temple and the Temple at 'Ain Dara', *Qadmoniyot* 29: 33-38. (Hebrew)

2000 'The New 'Ain Dara Temple: Closest Solomonic Parallel', *BARev* 26.3: 20-35, 67.

Mulder, M.J.

1982 'Exegetische Bemerkungen zum Tempelgebäude I Kön 6.5-10', *JNSL* 10: 83-92.

Na'aman, N.

1997 'Sources and Composition in the History of Solomon', in L.K. Handy (ed.), *The Age of Solomon: Scholarship at the Turn of the Millennium* (SHCANE, 11; Leiden: E.J. Brill): 57-80.

1999 'No Anthropomorphic Graven Images: Notes on the Assumed Anthropomorphic Cult Statues in the Temples of YHWH in the Pre-Exilic Period', *UF* 31: 391-415.

Niehr, H.

1997 'In Search of YHWH's Cult Statue in the First Temple', in K. van der Toorn (ed.), *The Image and the Book: Iconic Cults, Aniconism, and the Rise of Book Religion in Israel and the Ancient Near East* (Contributions to Biblical Exegesis and Theology, 21; Leuven: Peeters): 73-95.

Ouellette, J.

1969 'Le vestibule du Temple de Salomon: Etait-il un Bīt-Ḫilani?', *RB* 76: 365-78.

1970 'The Solomonic *Debîr* according to the Hebrew Text of 1 Kings 6', *JBL* 89: 338-43.

1972 'The *Yāṣīa'* and the *Ṣᵉlā'ōt*: Two Mysterious Structures in Solomon's Temple', *JNES* 31: 187-91.

1974 '"Atumîm" in 1 Kings 6.4; a Dravidian Origin', *Bulletin of the Institute of Jewish Studies. London* 2: 99-102.

1976 'The Basic Structure of Solomon's Temple and Archaeological Research', in J. Gutmann (ed.), *The Temple of Solomon: Archaeological Fact and Medieval Tradition in Christian, Islamic and Jewish Art* (AAR and SBL, Religion and Arts, 3; Missoula, MT: Scholars Press): 1-20.

Parrot, A.

1954 *Le Temple de Jérusalem* (Cahiers d'archéologie biblique, 5; Neuchâtel: Delachaux & Niestlé). ET *The Temple of Jerusalem* (trans. B.E. Hooke; Studies in Biblical Archaeology, 5; London: SCM Press, 1957).

Postgate, J.N.
1973 *The Governor's Palace Archive* (Cuneiform Texts from Nimrud, 2; Hertford: Stephen Austin and Sons; British School of Archaeology in Iraq).

Qimron, E.
1974 '*Lwl* and *blwl*', *Leshonenu* 38: 225-27 (Hebrew).

Rad, G. von
1953 'Deuteronomy's "Name Theology" and the Priestly Document's "Kabod" Theology', in *idem*, *Studies in Deuteronomy* (trans. D. Stalker; London: SCM Press, 1953): 37-44.

Renger, J.
1972–75 'Ḫīlānī, bīt', in D.O. Edzard (ed.), *Reallexikon der Assyriologie und vorderasiatischen Archäologie* (Berlin and New York: W. de Gruyter): IV, 405-406.

Richter, S.
2002 *The Deuteronomistic History and the Name Theology: lᵉšakkēn šᵉmô in the Bible and the Ancient Near East* (BZAW, 318; Berlin: W. de Gruyter).

Rimbach, J.A.
'Review of Rupprecht: 1977 (*Der Tempel von Jerusalem*)', *JBL* 97: 379-80.

Rupprecht, K.
1977 *Der Tempel von Jerusalem: Grundung Salomos oder jebusitisches Erbe?* (BZAW, 144; Berlin: W. de Gruyter).

Saebø, M.
1982 Review of Rupprecht: 1977 (*Der Tempel von Jerusalem*), *VT* 32: 371-73.

Schwartz, B.
1998 'Torah from Zion: Isaiah's Temple-Vision (Isaiah 2.1-4)', in A. Houtman, M.J.H.M. Poorthuis and J. Schwartz (eds.), *Sanctity of Time and Space in Tradition and Modernity* (Jewish and Christian Perspectives Series; Leiden: E.J. Brill): 11-26.

Scott, R.B.Y.
1939 'The Pillars Jachin and Boaz', *JBL* 58: 143-49.

Shiloh, Y
1979 *Proto-Aeolic Capital and Israelite Ashlar-Masonry* (Qedem, 11; Jerusalem: Israel Exploration Society).

Soggin, J.A.
1978 Review of Rupprecht: 1977 (*Der Tempel von Jerusalem*), *BiOr* 36: 83-84.

Stager, L.E.
1999 'Jerusalem and the Garden of Eden', in B.A. Levine, P.J. King, J. Naveh and E. Stern (eds.), *Eretz-Israel* 26 (Frank Moore Cross Volume; Jerusalem: Israel Exploration Society, Hebrew University, Hebrew Union College–Jewish Institute of Religion): 183*-94*.

Stern, E.
1992 'The Phoenician Architectural Elements in Palestine During the Late Iron Age and Persian Period', in A. Kempinski and R. Reich (eds.), *The Architecture of Ancient Israel from the Prehistoric to the Persian Periods: In Memory of Immanuel (Munya) Dunayevsky* (Jerusalem: Israel Exploration Society): 302-309.

Strange, J.
1985 'The Idea of Afterlife in Ancient Israel: Iconography in Solomon's Temple', *PEQ* 117: 35-40.

Thompson, H.C.
1960 'A Row of Cedar Beams', *PEQ* 92: 57-63.

Throntveit, M.A.

1997 'The Idealization of Solomon as the Glorification of God in the Chronicler's Royal Speeches and Royal Prayers', in L.K. Handy (ed.), *The Age of Solomon: Scholarship at the Turn of the Millennium* (SHCANE, 11; Leiden: E.J. Brill): 411-27.

Tomes, R.

1996 '"Our Holy and Beautiful House"; When and Why was 1 Kings 6–8 Written?', *JSOT* 70: 33-50.

Tvedtnes, J.A.

1982 'Egyptian Etymologies for Biblical Cultic Paraphernalia', in S. Israelit-Groll (ed.), *Egyptological Studies* (Scripta Hierosolymitana, 28; Jerusalem: Magnes Press): 218-22.

Uffenheimer, B.

2000 'Religious Significance of the Temple and Jerusalem', in Aḥituv and Mazar (eds.) 2000: 175-94 (Hebrew).

Ussishkin, D.

1966 'Building IV in Hamath and the Temples of Solomon and Tell Tayanat', *IEJ* 16: 104-10.

1988 'The date of the Judaean Shrine at Arad', *IEJ* 38: 142-57.

2002 'Solomon's Jerusalem: The Text and the Facts on the Ground', in A.G. Vaughn and A.E. Killebrew (eds.), *Jerusalem in the Bible and Archaeology: The First Temple Period* (SBL Symposium Series, 18; Atlanta: Society of Biblical Literature): 103-15.

Van Seters, J.

1997 'Solomon's Temple: Fact and Ideology in Biblical and Near Eastern Historiography', *CBQ* 59: 45-57.

2003 Review of Richter 2002, *JAOS* 123: 871-72.

Vaux, R. de

1945 'Notes sur le Temple de Solomon', *Kedem: Studies in Jewish Archaeology* 2: 48-58 (Hebrew).

Waterman, L.

1943 'The Damaged "Blueprints" of the Temple of Solomon', *JNES* 2: 284-94.

1947 'The Treasuries of Solomon's Private Chapels', *JNES* 6: 161-63.

1948 'A Rebuttal', *JNES* 7: 54-55.

Weidhaas, H.

1939 'Der bīt ḫilāni', *ZA* 45: 108.

Weidner, E.

1954–56 'Säulen aus Nahur', *AfO* 17: 145-46.

Weinfeld, M.

1972 'Presence, Divine', in *Encyclopedia Judaica* (Jerusalem: Keter): XIII, 1015-20.

1996 'Feminine Features in the Imagery of God in Israel: The Sacred Marriage and the Sacred Tree', *VT* 46: 515-29.

Weippert, H.

1992 'Die Kesselwagen Salomos', *ZDPV* 108: 8-41.

Weippert, M.

1980–83 'Libanon', in D.O. Edzard (ed.), *Reallexikon der Assyriologie und vorderasiatischen Archäologie* (Berlin and New York: W. de Gruyter): VI, 641-50.

Wenham, G.J.

1986 'Sanctuary Symbolism in the Garden of Eden Story', in *Proceedings of the Ninth World Congress of Jewish Studies, Jerusalem 1985, Division A: The Biblical Period* (Jerusalem: Magnes Press), English part: 19-25.

Wright, G.E.
1948 'Dr. Waterman's View Concerning the Solomonic Temple', *JNES* 7: 53.
Wright, G.E., *et al.*
1961 'Significance of the Temple in the Ancient Near East', in G.E. Wright and D.N. Freedman (eds.), *The Biblical Archaeologist Reader* (Garden City, NY: Doubleday): I, 145-200.
Wylie, C.C.
1949 'On King Solomon's Molten Sea', *BA* 12: 86-90.
Yadin, Y.
1956 'The First Temple', in M. Avi-Yonah (ed.), *Sefer Yerushalayim* (Jerusalem: Bialik Institute): I, 176-90 (Hebrew).
1959 'The Steps of Ahaz', in M. Avi-Yonah, H.Z. Hirschberg, Y. Yadin and H. Tadmor (eds.), *Eretz-Israel* 5 (Benjamin Mazar Volume; Jerusalem: Israel Exploration Society): 27-33.
Yeivin, S.
1948 'Linguistic Notes', *Leshonenu* 32: 5-11 (Hebrew).
1958 '*gab*', in *EncMqr*: III, 394 (Hebrew).
1959 'Jachin and Boaz', *PEQ* 91: 6-22.
1964 'Was there a High Portal in the First Temple?', *VT* 14: 331-43.
1968 'Temple of Solomon', in *EncMqr*: V, 328-46 (Hebrew).
1976 'Solomon', in *EncMqr*: VII, 693-99 (Hebrew).
Zakovitch, Y.
1972 'To Cause His Name to Dwell There; To Place His Name There', *Tarbiz* 41: 338-40 (Hebrew).
Zevit, Z.
2002 'Preamble to a Temple Tour', in Gittlen (ed.) 2002: 73-81.
Zwickel, W.
1987 'Die Kesselwagen im salomonischen Tempel', *UF* 18: 459-61.
1999 *Die salomonische Tempel* (Mainz: Philipp von Zabern).

The Prophets and the Cult

John Barton

Two issues are involved in speaking of 'the prophets and the cult'. First, what did the so-called classical prophets think about the practice of the cult in Israel in both pre- and post-exilic times? Secondly, how far were people who can be identified as 'prophets' actively involved in the Israelite cult, again, in various periods? In this article I shall try to clarify some of the issues, and to comment on possible wider implications for our understanding of both prophecy and cult. (For recent discussion of these issues see Ernst 1994.)

To begin with what can be known for certain about these matters: the evidence tends in two opposite directions. On the one hand, the books ascribed to the prophets of the eighth and seventh centuries—Amos, Hosea, Micah, Isaiah, and Jeremiah—attribute to them hostility to the cultic religion practised by their contemporaries, and especially to the sacrificial element in it. The relevant passages are very well known.

First, Amos 4.4-5 derides the sacrificial cult at Bethel and Gilgal by sarcastically telling the people to heap up their sacrifices ('Come to Bethel, and transgress, to Gilgal, and multiply transgression; bring your sacrifices every morning, your tithes every three days', and later in the book is presented as denouncing the festivals (5.21-22):

> I hate, I despise your festivals,
> and I take no delight in your solemn assemblies,
> even though you offer me your burnt-offerings and grain-offerings
> I will not accept them,
> and the offerings of well-being of your fatted animals
> I will not look upon.
> Take away from me the noise of your songs,
> I will not listen to the melody of your harps.
> But let justice roll down like water,
> and righteousness like an ever-flowing stream.

Hosea denounces mainly what he presents as a highly Baalized cult, but he seems like Amos also to have been against all cultic expressions, as in the famous passage in Hos. 6.6, 'I desire steadfast love and not sacrifice, the knowledge of God rather than burnt-offerings'.

Micah has one passage that can be read as opposing sacrifice, in Mic. 6.6-8:

> With what shall I come before the Lord,
> and bow myself before God on high?
> Shall I come before him with burnt-offerings,
> with calves a year old?

> Will the Lord be pleased with thousands of rams,
> with ten thousands of rivers of oil?...
> He has shown you, O mortal, what is good,
> and what does the Lord require of you
> but to do justice, and to love kindness,
> and to walk humbly with your God.

Isaiah presents the same theme:

> What to me is the multitude of your sacrifices?
> says the Lord.
> I have had enough of burnt-offerings of rams
> and the fat of fed beasts;
> I do not delight in the blood of bulls,
> or of lambs, or of goats...
> Bringing offerings is futile;
> incense is an abomination to me.
> New moon and Sabbath and calling of convocation—
> I cannot endure solemn assemblies with iniquity. (Isa. 1.11-13)

Jeremiah is similarly recorded as opposed to the sacrificial cultus, and, like Amos, maintains that it did not form any part of the worship of Yahweh in ancient times: 'On the day that I brought your ancestors out of the land of Egypt, I did not speak to them or command them concerning burnt-offerings and sacrifices' (Jer. 7.22). Cf. Amos 5.25, 'Did you bring to me sacrifices and offerings the forty years in the wilderness, O house of Israel?', a question evidently expecting the answer 'No', and by implication rejecting sacrifice as a late and improper addition to the worship of Yahweh. Both these passages are regarded by some as Deuteronomistic (Wolff 1975: 309, ET 1977: 264), but they are *prima facie* evidence of prophetic opposition to the cult.

On the other hand, several post-exilic prophetic books record prophetic approval for the sacrificial cult, though sometimes criticizing its existing form. Haggai and Zechariah are presented as being strongly in favour of the rebuilding of the Temple, which is hard to imagine if they were opposed to the sacrificial rituals which were housed in it. In this they may have been opposed to a possibly contemporary source, Isa. 66.1, which seems to reject the Temple in the manner of the pre-exilic prophets: 'Heaven is my throne, and the earth is my footstool; what is the house that you would build me, and what is the place of my rest?' Malachi criticizes those who offer deformed or defective animals in sacrifice: 'When you offer blind animals in sacrifice, is that not wrong? And when you offer those that are lame or sick, is that not wrong?' (Mal. 1.8)—which makes sense only if he approves in principle of offering animals to God. Similarly Mal. 3.3-4 speaks of offerings that will be 'refined', and so will be acceptable. Joel laments the fact that the sacrifices in the Temple have ceased for lack of any food-stuffs to offer, as a result of natural disaster: 'Grain-offering and drink-offering are withheld from the house of your God' (Joel 1.13). He approves strongly of the 'calling of assemblies', denounced by Isaiah, and thinks that there should be one to lament for the current state of famine and drought, and to entreat the favour of God: 'Blow the trumpet in Zion, sanctify a fast, call a solemn assembly' (2.15). (There are a few post-exilic passages opposed to the cult, for example Isa. 58 against fasting; Joel's 'Rend your hearts and not your clothing', 2.13, has also been taken as anti-cultic.)

Typically this difference between the pre- and post-exilic classical prophets has been explained in one of two ways, or by a combination of the two. First, from the time of Wellhausen at least it has been normal to see the post-exilic prophets as having accepted the codification of the Torah, with its detailed ritual regulations, and so as having turned their backs on the radical rejection of the cult by earlier figures such as Amos and Isaiah. This is a part of the 'establishment' attitude of post-exilic prophecy, representing a sharp break with the 'anti-establishment' stance of the pre-exilic prophets. Secondly, it has often been suggested that the post-exilic prophets were actually 'cultic prophets', officially employed by the Temple, as opposed to the great eighth- and seventh-century prophets who were independent figures in the mould of Elijah, appearing from the margins of society and denouncing it from outside. In this they may have been a throwback to the circles of prophets common in the pre-exilic period to which, for example, Elisha probably belonged, who were professionals at oracular guidance and in some cases may have been on the staff of temples. But whatever explanation is given, it is a fact that we have pro-cultic statements in the books attributed to some post-exilic prophets, and anti-cultic ones from those attributed to the pre-exilic prophets.

This stark opposition strikes some scholars as rather worrying or implausible. This may be either because it suggests an inconsistency in the biblical witness which is a theological problem for them, or because, as a matter of historical development, they think it unlikely that the single institution of prophecy could have included within itself such a diversity of approach. The opposition may be mitigated by casting doubt on one or other of its poles. Either the anti-cultic stance of the pre-exilic prophets or the pro-cultic stance of the post-exilic ones may be played down or softened.

To begin with the first of these: it may be argued that the pre-exilic prophets were in reality far less badly disposed toward cultic religion than the texts, taken at face value, might seem to suggest. One line of argument, which I want to take up again later, is that it is simply not conceivable that anyone in ancient Israel could have been so radically anti-ritualistic as the texts seem to imply. Religion, it is suggested, was so intimately bound up with sacrifice and ritual that no-one could have opposed them per se without stepping outside the culture altogether. Sometimes this point is linked to the speculation that finding anti-ritualistic attitudes in the prophets reflects a characteristically Protestant agenda: that issues to do with disputes between Protestants and Catholics are being read back into the Old Testament, and this is anachronistic. There is not much doubt, for example, that Wellhausen's opposition to ritual in religion, which he regarded as a somewhat degenerate phenomenon, is linked to his liberal Protestantism.

Similarly, Jewish scholars sometimes see the emphasis on the anti-ritualism of the prophets as part of a general Christian opposition to the ritual side of Judaism, proceeding from a contrast between a dead religion of external works and a living religion of the heart, which they feel is a denigration of Judaism that looks for support from the prophets but in the process remakes the prophets in its own image. Probably the easiest way to reconcile such a defence of ritual in religion with what the prophets appear to be saying is to argue that they were not speaking against cultic ritual in principle, but rather wanted to introduce an order of priorities. Sacrifice is not unacceptable in itself, but is simply of a lower order of importance than social justice or heartfelt repentance. Thus we read Hosea's 'I desire steadfast love and not sacrifice' as 'I desire steadfast love in first place and sacrifice only in second place', 'I desire steadfast love *more than* I desire sacrifice, though it goes without saying that I do also desire sacrifice'. Similarly, Joel's 'Rend your hearts and not your clothing' means 'Rend your hearts as well as your clothing', 'Let your torn clothing represent true inward contrition—but tear them all the same'. This is far from impossible, and would be reminiscent of what Jesus is reported as saying in Matthew's Gospel (23.23): 'Woe to you, scribes and Pharisees, hypocrites! For you tithe mint, dill, and cumin, and have neglected the weightier matters of the law: justice and mercy and faith. It is these you ought to have practised *without neglecting the others*.' Both–and, rather than either–or, would be the essence of the prophetic message on this interpretation.

Another possible line of argument is that the prophets were opposed to ritual when offered by those with hands polluted by crime, rather than in itself. This can claim some support from Isa. 1.15, 'When you stretch out your hands I will hide my eyes from you; even though you make many prayers I will not listen; *your hands are full of blood*'. This does not imply a root-and-branch opposition to the cult, but only the (surely widely shared) belief that those who offer sacrifice must be in a state of purity, and moral transgression—especially such sins as murder or theft—pollute the would-be worshipper just as much as offences against purity regulations do, and make his sacrifices unacceptable. So in Mal. 3.3-4 the offerings need purification, but there is no question of opposition to religious ritual as such.

Thirdly, it may be suggested that the prophets were in any case cultic officials themselves, so that it is inconceivable that they could have opposed the sacrificial cultus as such, and hence some other explanation must be found for their condemnations of sacrifice. This has been a characteristic argument in Scandinavian scholarship, where a cultic setting for much in the Old Testament has been more popular than typically in the German or Anglo-Saxon realms. One might think, for instance, of Hans Barstad's work on Amos, *The Religious Polemics of Amos* (Barstad 1984), which thinks of Amos as a cult-prophet rather than as the outsider to Israelite institutions postulated by traditional German-speaking scholarship. It is of a piece with this that when faced with Amos 5.25, 'Did you bring me sacrifices and offerings forty years in the wilderness?', Barstad argues that the emphasis must fall on 'me': 'Was it *to me* that you offered your sacrifices during the forty years in the wilderness?' No, it was to other gods. Thus the prophetic polemic against sacrifice is really a polemic against *false* worship. This is frequently so in Hosea, as I suppose most would agree, but Barstad sees it as normal throughout the prophetic corpus. Prophetic opposition to sacrifice is thus opposition to syncretism, not to cultic activity as such.

The problem with this is that it does not seem to do justice to the assertion in Jer. 7.21-23 that Yahweh had never commanded sacrifice at all, nor to Amos's own insistence that he hated Israel's feasts not because they were celebrated in honour of the wrong god but because they were unaccompanied by justice and righteousness. (It may also be noted that in Amos 5.25 the words 'to me' do not come first in the Hebrew, as one might have expected if Barstad's exegesis were correct.) As many scholars have argued, it is hard to defend the picture of Amos as actually a cultic prophet when so much that he says tends to undermine not just a syncretized cult but any cult at all. The relation between cultic prophets, if any, and the classical prophets such as Amos will, however, concern us again later.

So much, for now, for attempts to reduce the anti-cultic appearance of the pre-exilic prophets. The equal and opposite approach is to try to reduce the pro-cultic appearance of the post-exilic prophets. I cited Joel earlier as an example of a prophet who is, *prima facie*, well disposed to cultic worship. He laments the fact that because of the famine there are no materials to offer to God in sacrifice, and he calls for a cultic assembly of the people, just the kind of thing that Isaiah was apparently opposed to. For anyone who has a large investment in the prophets as proponents of non-cultic religion Joel is something of a problem. This can be seen most clearly in the commentary on Joel by Hans Walter Wolff (Wolff 1975, ET 1977).

Wolff notes that Joel seems to take cultic forms as a given: it would be hard to deny this. 'To be sure, Joel treats the established worship (with its customs and traditions and the ministry of the priests) as something to be taken for granted and, in itself, unassailable (1.9, 13-14, 16; 2.15-17)' (Wolff 1975: 13, ET 1977: 13); or again, in reference to fasting and the use of sackcloth, 'Joel has no objection to the customary rituals' (p. 58, ET p. 49). But he is at pains to stress that Joel places no ultimate confidence in the ritualized cult of his day: 'Ultimately he regards it as merely temporary and transient, something that will be overtaken by new, final acts of God' (p. 13, ET p. 13). This is true, in that Joel thinks *everything* will ultimately be overtaken by God's intervention, but perhaps is not strictly relevant to the matter in hand: it does not in any way delegitimize the cult for the present. 'The expectation is a warning against regarding cultic restoration and life under the canonized Torah in the Jerusalem of the fourth century as the goal of God's ways' (p. 79, ET p. 67). Surely this *is* an expression of a Protestant unease about cultic matters, and about life under the Law, rather than having much to do with the text of Joel?

More than this, Wolff actually identifies trust in the cult, as directed by the Torah, as precisely the sin of which Joel's community needed to repent: 'Joel can hardly belong to the circles that take their stand upon the canonized Torah and see in liturgical compliance with it the ultimate will of the God of Israel' (Wolff 1975: 12, ET 1977: 15)—where the use of the word 'ultimate' of course skews the argument in Wolff's favour and exonerates one from asking whether he did not see in liturgical compliance at least the will *for the time being* of the God of Israel. 'Israel', Wolff writes, 'is awakened from its Torah-contentedness to a life anticipating the coming free acts of God's compassion' (p. 16, ET p. 15); but

'Torah-contentedness' is a deliberately tendentious way of describing a concern for liturgical observance. Wolff concedes that 'We sense nothing in Joel of that critical disposition towards the cultus, and especially towards its customary fasting rituals, which we find in Jeremiah (14.12), Trito-Isaiah (58.1-14) and Zechariah (7.5-7). At the same time, though, the instructions regarding the cultus are by no means his real concern' (p. 38, ET p. 33). And again, 'an extremely critical word is spoken in veiled manner against the cultic community of Jerusalem which has constituted itself theocratically' (p. 41, ET p. 36). Where, we might ask?

Wolff's wider concern emerges clearly when he writes,

> In the history of the new Jerusalem, too [he means the Church], the voice of Joel remains relevant. All too frequently a well-functioning churchliness is considered the goal of faith... Self-assured and secure churchliness has to experience, first, then, that its last two props—the natural craving for piety on the part of weak persons and the political acts of helping that spring from ambiguous interests—can quickly be broken. It can march on into the future only with its eye upon him who has put his seal on Joel 2.13b ['Return to the Lord your God, for he is patient and merciful, etc.]. (Wolff 1975: 63, ET 1977: 53)

This is standard Lutheran polemic against a religion of works, and I am far from wanting to oppose it in itself. But I find it hard to see it as anchored very much in Joel, of all prophets, and think that Wolff's concern to get all the prophets to speak with one voice on such issues has led him to try to read a characteristically pre-exilic prophetic message into a post-exilic prophecy that will not sustain it.

So much, then, for attempts to mitigate the tension in the prophetic corpus about the legitimacy of cultic activity. Something can be done to bring about some rapprochement between different attitudes, but on the whole it seems to me that there remain differences of opinion among the various prophets represented in the Old Testament. Justice needs to be done to this at least apparent diversity, and this is surely best achieved by considering each book on its merits, and not, for the sake of a unified 'prophetic message', adopting a Procrustean approach which forces either pre-exilic or post-exilic classical prophets to conform to the image of the other.

The discussion so far has thrown up a number of issues which still need clarifying, and I want to look briefly at five of these.

1. Was it in fact possible for people in ancient Israel to be as anti-cultic as Amos, Isaiah, and Jeremiah appear to have been, or is it historically inconceivable that they could really have meant it when they appear to have said that Yahweh had no interest whatever in cultic offerings? Two considerations, one empirical and the other theoretical, make me think that this was indeed a possible attitude, and that—whether or not the prophets actually did oppose all religious ritual—they certainly could have done so.

The empirical consideration is the existence of Psalm 50:

> I will not accept a bull from your house,
>   or goats from your folds.
> For every wild animal of the forest is mine,
>   the cattle on a thousand hills.

> I know all the birds of the air,
> and all that moves in the field is mine.
> If I were hungry, I would not tell you,
> for the world and all that is in it is mine.
> Do I eat the flesh of bulls,
> or drink the blood of goats? (Ps. 50.9-12)

I cannot see that this can be interpreted other than as a total opposition to the practice of sacrifice in itself (even though, oddly, the psalm begins by calling for the assembling of 'those that made a covenant with me by sacrifice'). Of course we do not know that it is as early as the eighth century prophets, but it certainly comes from ancient Israelite culture in some period, and is not a later interpolation into the Psalter. Its critique of sacrifice is very similar to the critique of idolatry in Deutero-Isaiah—putting, as it were, the worst and most trivial possible interpretation on the practice as an attempt to feed God. But it makes sense only if the author was capable of getting outside the institution and asking about its validity in principle. It shows that anti-ritualism could exist in ancient Israel, and gives the lie to suggestions that it is simply inconceivable.

For the theoretical consideration I go, as Old Testament scholars do in times of need, to the work of Mary Douglas, and especially to her *Natural Symbols* (Douglas 1970, 1996). There she deals at length with the phenomenon of anti-ritualism in religion, and shows that it is by no means a product only of a modern, secularized culture, but occurs equally in what she there still refers to as primitive societies. It is not in the least unusual to find groups living within, or alongside, a highly ritualized society that reject virtually all ritual activities or reduce their ritual to a bare minimum, stressing inner experience and freedom of religious expression. This is true, according to her, of the religious culture of pygmies as against that of the groups with which they coexist. Those who thus reject ritual are characteristically those who are alienated from the values of the larger group, but this may be because they are outcasts or of low social status (low grid, low group in Douglas's terms), or because they are highly distinctive individuals who as it were plough their own furrow (high grid, low group), and perhaps attract a following which picks up and imitates their own anti-ritualistic cast of mind.

> We are able to see that alienation from the current social values usually takes a set form: a denunciation not only of irrelevant rituals, but of ritualism as such; exaltation of the inner experience and denigration of its standardized expressions; preference for intuitive and instant forms of knowledge; rejection of mediating institutions, rejection of any tendency to allow habit to provide the basis of a new symbolic system. (Douglas 1970: 40, 1996: 20)

That the classical prophets of Israel could be seen in this light seems clear enough, and it is not necessarily an anachronism to paint them in the colours of Protestant reformers: there is a clear similarity in some of their attitudes.

Douglas also points out that anti-ritualism may go hand-in-hand with a stress on the superior importance of 'good works' in the sense of a commitment to charity and to social justice. Her particular example is taken from London life in the 1960s, when in the wake of the Second Vatican Council Catholic clergy were often themselves somewhat anti-ritualistic, and spent much energy in trying to persuade their people that such ritualized observances as Friday abstinence from meat should be replaced with acts of generosity to those in need—the kind of 'true fast', in fact, proposed by Trito-Isaiah in Isaiah 58. This plea was unheeded, in fact virtually unheard, by Irish manual workers who, in their exile in alien London, held fast to Friday abstinence as a defining mark of their Catholic culture, and resisted the attempts by the Catholic intelligentsia to deritualize their religious practice. No doubt the lines of this discord have changed greatly in the intervening forty years or so, but Douglas's point, which is that ritualistic and anti-ritualistic opinions can occur within the same general religious culture, remains an effective one. Her own sympathies are very much with the Irish labourers: she has little time for a 'prophetic' religion that would remove people's ritual markers. But she is quite clear that prophetic types of religion do indeed occur within traditional cultures, and—though she does not directly refer to the Old Testament prophets—her arguments support the theoretical possibility that they could have been as anti-cultic as they appear to be. Nothing in cultural anthropology precludes the possibility.

2. A second area of uncertainty is the existence of 'cultic prophets' in ancient Israel; and, if they did exist, of the relation of the classical prophets to them. This question cannot be said to have been resolved. In the 1950s and 1960s much was made of the existence of cultic prophets, in the British Old Testament scene especially by Aubrey Johnson (see Johnson 1962; cf. Johnson 1979), yet the evidence always remained circumstantial. The groups of prophets described in the books of Samuel and Kings seem often to have had an association with a cultic centre, but how far they actually engaged in strictly 'cultic' activity remains a matter of conjecture. The idea that they gave oracles during liturgical observances is mainly based on form-critical arguments about the Psalms, rather than on direct evidence. Here the common phenomenon of a change of tone from entreaty to thanksgiving within a single psalm was thought by many to imply that someone gave a favourable oracle, no longer present in the text, to which the thanksgiving was a response; and the best candidate for giving such oracles was a 'cultic prophet'. Psalm 20 seems to imply such a scenario, and Ps. 60.8-10 (ET 6-8) may indeed be an example of such an oracle. It was also held that oracles against foreign nations, of which the earliest extant example is Amos 1–2, probably rested on cultic practice: ritual denunciation of the enemies of Israel as a means of ensuring their downfall (see Bentzen 1950). If so, then Amos was in a way parodying such a practice by constructing a chain of oracles that culminated in the downfall of Israel itself. But real concrete evidence for all this is hard to come by, and the relation of the classical prophets to such cultic prophets if they did exist remains desperately unclear. The classical prophets—who never apply to themselves the title *nābî'* apart from the heavily disputed texts in Amos 7.14 and Jer. 28.8—refer disparagingly to 'the prophets' as a group distinct from themselves (note that the Hebrew does not say 'false prophets', a term not found

before Josephus); but whether these are 'cultic' prophets remains uncertain. Of course there are many ancient Near Eastern parallels to the activities supposed to have been performed by cultic prophets, but whether such activities occurred in Israel, and, if so, whether a *nābî'* was the proper person to perform them, we really do not know.

3. A further complication is that what we call 'the classical prophets', that is, those people who have one of what we call the prophetic books named after them, may not form a homogeneous group. In an important article Richard Coggins (1982) returned to an older distinction between those of the biblical prophets who were active in the cult, such as, probably, Nahum, Joel, and Obadiah, and those who produced freely composed oracles later compiled into what, on the basis of Arabic comparisons, older scholars called the *diwan* type—loosely linked sayings on all manner of subjects. The latter were, on this view, certainly not cultic figures, but poets who stood well outside the settled orders of Israelite society and commented on it from a detached position. Attempts (like that by Wolff surveyed earlier) to include a prophet such as Joel in the 'true' tradition of classical prophecy, by making him as critical of the established cultic institutions as Amos or Isaiah, would thus be radically misconceived. Joel was not a 'prophet' in that sense at all—or, perhaps we should say instead, Joel was a prophet but Amos and Isaiah were not: some other term ought really to be found for them. They were, as E.W. Heaton (1961) put it, 'laymen', not part of the religious institutions of Israel at all. On this view Amos's *lō' nābî' 'ānōkî* means what it appears to mean, 'I am not a prophet': I am an outsider, alienated from your religious culture. The question of whether the prophets were prophets remains still unresolved.

4. I have spoken so far of prophets opposing or supporting 'the cult', and that way of putting it has been common in Old Testament study. It is, however, not a very precise way of speaking. 'The cult' can include many things: sacrifices, which in ancient Israel were of many types and achieved many different purposes; sacred song and possibly dance; fasting accompanied by ceremonies of lamentation; possibly sacred drama of some kind. Being 'against the cult' or 'for the cult' might discriminate among these different elements of public liturgy. To take one example, the pre-exilic prophets who are opposed to sacrifice seem to me to be overwhelmingly concerned with the kind of sacrifice which accompanies feasting, probably the *šᵉlāmîm* type, offered with rejoicing and thanksgiving in mind. Among the pre-exilic prophets only Micah, in Mic. 6.6, speaks unequivocally of sacrifice *for sin* ('Shall I give my firstborn for my transgression, the fruit of my body for the sin of my soul?'), whereas the others seem more concerned with sacrifices accompanying feasts and celebrations.

That could mean that at least some of the anti-sacrifice polemic in, say, Amos and Isaiah is linked to their disapproval of feasting and self-indulgence, rather than to questions of what for us would be strictly questions of religious ritual observance. One of the features of eating meat in pre-exilic Israel, as we can infer from the change brought about by Deuteronomy, was that it entailed sacrifice: *zbḥ* means, indifferently, to slaughter and to sacrifice. But that point can be stood on its head. Sacrifice involved eating meat, and thus having a feast; not in the metaphorical sense in which the Christian calendar contains so-called 'feast' days, but in the quite literal sense of having a lot of meat to eat—'a feast of rich food, a feast of well-matured wines, of rich food filled with marrow', as Isa. 25.6 expresses it. A prophet could well be opposed to that kind of thing in what for him was a time of desperate national crisis, as Isaiah was according to Isa. 22.12-13—'the Lord God of hosts called to weeping and mourning, to baldness and putting on sackcloth, but instead there was joy and festivity, killing oxen and slaughtering sheep, eating meat and drinking wine'—without thereby being 'anti-cultic' as such. After all, he was obviously in favour of 'weeping and mourning', cutting off hair as a sign of penitence and supplication and 'putting on sackcloth', and in our terms those are equally 'cultic' activities. It is only with Trito-Isaiah and Zechariah that we get equivalent condemnations of religious observances that were not enjoyable for the people who practised them, such as fasting and lamenting (Isa. 58; Zech. 7.1-7). To condemn fasting as self-indulgent (of all things) does start to lead us into the world of anti-ritualism as constructed by Mary Douglas, where the opposition is to external rites as contrasted with internal contrition. The pre-exilic prophetic opposition to sacrifice, on the other hand, might be mainly part of the prophets' condemnation of excessive luxury, display, and self-indulgence.

I do not want to press this further, but simply note that 'the cult' is a rather slippery term, which perhaps needs closer definition before we can be sure what we are talking about.

5. There remains, finally, the question of how far the prophets opposed cultic observance per se and how far they thought it was unfitting for those who were embroiled in activities that to them seemed sinful, such as oppression of the poor and perversion of the course of justice. The majority of prophetic condemnation does seem to concern the offering of sacrifice or (in the case of Isa. 58) the practice of fasting by those who are morally compromised. The way to please Yahweh, the prophets argue, or the way to be forgiven for one's sins, is to engage in moral reform. Until that is done, practising cultic observances compounds the insult being offered to God.

However, there do remain a few passages that seem hostile to sacrificial activity in itself. Against Barstad, I would think that this is the case in Amos 5.25 (whether or not it actually goes back to Amos), the logic of which is that, since Israel offered no sacrifices during the time in the wilderness, and that time was (as Jeremiah would later express it) the time of its honeymoon with Yahweh (Jer. 2.1-3), therefore sacrifice cannot be what Yahweh requires. It is the same in Jer. 7.22: Yahweh had no thought of imposing a sacrificial form of religious observance on Israel when he brought them out of Egypt: sacrificial rites have crept in since then. The people might just as well stop distinguishing between sacrifices burnt wholly to Yahweh and those in which the worshippers share, and simply eat the whole animal, because Yahweh is not honoured in any case. This is surely moving in the direction of Psalm 50, with its root-and-branch rejection of sacrifice as such. It is strict anti-ritualism as described by Mary Douglas, in which religion is defined as consisting in quite other duties than the observance of ritual stipulations. Maybe the sinfulness of the worshippers makes the sacrifices *worse* than useless, but essentially they are useless anyway. The heart of religion consists instead in right social interaction.

The nineteenth-century scholars who first saw clearly that the prophets had been revolutionary in their turning away from the sacrificial cultus thus seem to me in essence to have been right; and I do not think the fact that they were liberal Protestants, who were therefore very happy to find their own ideas about the character of true religion endorsed by the prophets, vitiates the essential truth of their perception. It is a condition of seeking the truth about other cultures that we do not predetermine what we are going to find there, and if what we think we find is congenial to us, we should be suspicious. But our suspicion should not be absolutized to the point where we come to think we are bound to be wrong whenever we feel we have recognized a kindred spirit in a past culture. If Douglas is right, Protestantism and the kind of anti-ritualism that can be found in the prophets genuinely do share certain features in common. That is easier to accept once we have seen, with her, that anti-ritualism is an option in a number of different societies, than it would be if we thought it was a unique insight of the prophets, which the Reformation recaptured for the first time. Rather, the tension between those who seek formal observance in matters of religion, and those who are scornful of established custom and seek the freedom of the spirit, can be found in many religious cultures. So can the tension between those for whom true religion is *religio*, public observance, and those for whom it is, in the words of the Epistle of James, 'to care for orphans and widows in their distress, and to keep oneself unstained by the world' (Jas 1.27). To recognize such tensions in ancient Israel is to see it as a culture like many others. The pre-exilic classical prophets belong on one side of those divides, the priests largely on the other, just as was being said well over a hundred years ago.

BIBLIOGRAPHY

Barstad, H.M.
1984 *The Religious Polemics of Amos* (VTSup, 34; Leiden: E.J. Brill).

Bentzen, A.
1950 'The Ritual Background of Amos 1.2–2.16', *OTS* 8: 85-99.

Coggins, R.J.
1982 'An Alternative Prophetic Tradition?', in R.J. Coggins, A. Phillips and M.A. Knibb (eds.), *Israel's Prophetic Heritage: Essays in Honour of Peter R. Ackroyd* (Cambridge: Cambridge University Press): 77-94.

Douglas, M.
1970, 1996 *Natural Symbols: Explorations in Cosmology* (London: Penguin Books, 1st edn; London: Routledge, 2nd edn).

Ernst, A.B.
1994 *Weisheitliche Kultkritik: Zu Theologie und Ethik des Sprüchebuchs und der Prophetie des 8. Jahrhunderts* (Biblisch-theologische Studien, 23; Neukirchen–Vluyn: Neukirchener Verlag).

Heaton, E.W.
1961 *The Old Testament Prophets* (Baltimore: Penguin Books).

Johnson, A.R.
1962 *The Cultic Prophet in Ancient Israel* (Cardiff: University of Wales Press, 2nd edn).
1979 *The Cultic Prophet and Israel's Psalmody* (Cardiff: University of Wales Press).

Wolff, H.W.
1975 *Dodekapropheton*. II. *Joel and Amos* (BK, 14.2; Neukirchen–Vluyn: Neukirchener Verlag, 2nd edn). ET *Joel and Amos: A Commentary on the Books of Joel and Amos* (trans. Waldemar Janzen, S. Dean McBride and Charles A. Muenchow; Hermeneia; Philadelphia: Fortress Press, 1977).

TEMPLE AND WORSHIP IN ISAIAH 6

H.G.M. Williamson

In recent years, discussion of the nature of the pre-exilic Jerusalem Temple and of the forms of worship which were practised there has become complicated by the increased awareness of the extent to which much of the literature of the Hebrew Bible has been influenced by post-exilic institutions and points of view. The aim of this contribution to the present volume is to inquire to what extent oblique light may be shed on the topic by way of an approach from one part of the writings of the eighth-century prophet Isaiah.

The possibility that this approach may bear fruit is to be expected, given the fact that Isaiah is one of the few witnesses available to us who was both resident in or near Jerusalem in the eighth century and whose recorded words have much to say about the city and its state apparatus. Nevertheless, two brief preliminary remarks need to be made in order to define our procedure more closely.

In the first place, the extent to which Isaiah himself may or may not have subscribed to the so-called Zion theology, in which the Temple had a central role to play, is disputed (contrast, for instance, Wildberger 1982: 1596-602, ET 2002: 579-85 and Clements 1980: 72-89). Fortunately, however, this problem need not detain us, since our interest is not in what Isaiah himself believed but rather in what he presupposes as given. And as we shall see, the text clearly indicates the distinction between the two.

Secondly, it will always be possible to challenge the results of such an inquiry by querying whether the text discussed is indeed from the time of Isaiah himself. Since that has been the subject of a separate series of Oxford Old Testament Seminars, including attention to the problems raised specifically by the book of Isaiah (see Williamson 2004), I may perhaps be forgiven for not devoting much attention to it here. Suffice to say that the part of the text which will claim most of our attention is recognized to be Isaianic by even the most rigorous of minimalists (e.g. Becker 1997: 79-81, with whom orally O. Kaiser has recently expressed agreement in this regard; only Gosse 1992 differs, but on weak grounds, in my opinion).

Without further ado, therefore, I turn to Isaiah 6 itself. The first issue requiring attention arises from the fact that some commentators insist that what Isaiah describes here is not directly related to the Jerusalem Temple at all, but is set entirely, rather, in the heavenly palace or court.[1] If that were the case, we

1. This seems already to have been the understanding of the Targum, which glosses the throne of v. 1 with 'in the heavens of the height', and in v. 3 this is in turn contrasted with 'the earth, the work

obviously could not use the passage for our present purposes without serious qualification. It is true that one might argue that his conception of the heavenly sanctuary would inevitably be coloured by his knowledge of the earthly, but in fact it seems that resort to this device is unnecessary.

It is important that the implications of a response to this argument be not misunderstood. It is clear that certain aspects of Isaiah 6 are envisaged as taking place in the heavenly court, and of course it is now generally accepted that there is a considerable degree of overlap between the earthly and heavenly sanctuaries; Metzger's 1970 article is widely cited in this regard, and Jeremias (1996: 252) more or less summarizes the position by implying that this is a distinction without a difference:

> this alternative is artificial and inappropriate. The eyes of the prophet in the vision and of the reader in the text are, rather, constantly redirected...between the heavenly...and the earthly temple because we are not dealing here with two different holy places but rather of dimensions of God's single dwelling place where the heavenly community joins in praise with the earthly.[2]

However, even in accepting that position, it remains legitimate to inquire after what might be termed the basic standpoint from which Isaiah witnesses the proceedings; was he, so to speak, present (either physically or in his imagination) in the Jerusalem sanctuary, from where he was caught up into the heavenly, or *vice versa*? And as soon as the question is posed in those terms, a decision swiftly comes down in favour of the former. There are several reasons for this conclusion.[3]

First, it seems rather obvious that from Isaiah's perspective both God's throne and, indeed, the figure of God himself tower way above him. Not only is the throne 'high and lifted up', but God's *šûlāyw*[4] alone filled the sanctuary. This could clearly not apply to the heavenly sanctuary; the image rather is of the divine presence being uncontainable in the sanctuary of which the text speaks,

of his might'; among more recent commentators, see, for instance, Feldmann 1925: 69-70; König 1927: 89; Fohrer 1991: 95. Wildberger (1980: 245-46, ET 1991: 262-63) is ambivalent, but in some respects is close to this view.

2. The German original, which I have translated above, reads: 'diese Alternative künstlich und unsachgemäß ist. Vielmehr werden das Auge des Propheten in der Vision und dasjenige des Lesers im Text ständig zwischen himlischem...und irdischem Tempel...hin und hergeführt, weil es nicht um zwei verschiedene heilige Orte handelt, sondern um Dimensionen des einen Wohnortes Gottes, dem die himmlische Gemeinde zusammen mit der irdischen zujubelt'.

3. Among many discussions, I have found especially helpful Keel 1977: 47-56 and Hartenstein 1997: 63. Keel in particular argues point by point against those who have maintained that the Jerusalem Temple is not in view.

4. There is now considerable doubt about the meaning of this word. I still take it to mean the bottom edge of a garment (though clearly not the 'train' of the traditional English renderings), as in Exod. 28.33-34 and 39.24-26, though other types of lower extremities are theoretically possible. The argument above holds on any of the views which have been suggested; cf. Hehn 1916–17; G.R. Driver 1971; Eslinger 1995; Podella 1996: 51-53 and 189; Hartenstein 1997: 56-57. I discount the suggestion of A. Shaffer, as reported by Hurowitz 1989: 42 n. 3, that *šûlayim* is cognate rather with Akkadian *šamallû* (which came into Aramaic as *šwly'*) meaning 'minor assistants'.

and that must therefore be the earthly sanctuary. That imagery of a super-human sized God can be combined with a physical earthly temple has recently been nicely illustrated by the imprint of outsized feet on the steps leading into the Iron Age temple at Ain Dara (Abū ‘Assāf 1990: 14 and pl. 11; for general comments on the representation of God as very large in the ancient Near East, including Israel, see Greenfield 1985 and Smith 1988).

Second, while it is certainly the case that sometimes God’s throne and sanctuary are said to be in heaven, there are some architectural terms used in this passage which would be unprecedented in that regard. ‘The doorposts of the threshold’ (if that is what v. 4 refers to; at least ‘threshold’ is not in doubt[5]) and

5. LXX καὶ ἐπήρθη τὸ ὑπέρθυρον was probably influenced by comparison with Ps. 23 (24).7, 9 (cf. Ziegler 1934: 108; Seeligmann 1948: 72), and it seems that the Vulgate (*superliminaria cardinum*) followed suit. Targum’s *'lwt sypy hykl'* (‘posts of the Temple thresholds’) is more plausible, and Rashi and Kimhi interpret as door-posts. *Sap* is the more transparent of the two words, and in the singular seems to have the sense of threshold (see especially Judg. 19.27; more precisely, the outward-facing side of the threshold, according to Zwickel 1993), most often in connection with the Temple. Indeed, its single most frequent use is in expressions for Temple door/threshold-keepers (though for palace guards, see Est. 2.21; 6.2). In Ezek. 43.8 it seems to be distinguished from the door-posts, and in Amos 9.1 from the capital (see too *mašqôp* for lintel in Exod. 12.7). Although the Akkadian cognate *sippu* had a wider connotation with reference to different parts of the door frame or, indeed, the frame as a whole (cf. *CDA*, 324; Salonen 1961: 62-66; there is a useful discussion in Paul 1991: 275), there is no firm evidence to contradict the view that in North-West Semitic it acquired a narrower focus (cf. *DNWSI*, 796-97) and more recent evidence from Qumran also supports this conclusion (for references, see Meyers 1986: 899, ET 1999: 297; see too Hess 1996: 283). The less common use of the plural form might be thought to pose a difficulty for this view and open the way for a wider sense in Hebrew, but such a conclusion would be hard to defend in view of the Chronicler’s use of the plural several times in place of the singular form in Kings for the ‘keepers of the threshold(s)’. *'Ammôt* is even more obscure. There is no philological justification for connecting it with *'ēm*, ‘mother’ (so rightly Dillmann 1890: 58), and so to suggest that it refers either to the foundations (the attempt by Görg 1991: 222 to defend this understanding by appeal to Akkadian *ammatu* II [cf. *CDA*, 15] founders on the uncertainty of the meaning of the latter owing to its very sparse attestation; cf. Hartenstein 1997: 124), which in all other respects would be most attractive (Delitzsch 1889: 126, ET 1894: 183, and many others), or to the sockets in which the door-pivots were sunk; indeed, Exod. 12.22 may even indicate that *sap* itself could refer to this latter, though it is ruled out in any case as an unsuitable subject for ‘shook’. The proposal of Hitzig (1833: 63) and Dillmann (1890: 58) to link with *'mm* = ‘precede, be in front’, and so to mean ‘cornice, moulding’, is not very appropriate in context and has not attracted more recent support. A connection with *'ammâ* = cubit (and once, ‘mother city’) does not look promising either, unless we think that ‘forearm’ could give rise to the meaning ‘upright’ (Blenkinsopp 2000: 223), which is conceivable, though in fact *'ammâ* never has the meaning ‘forearm’ in the Hebrew Bible. Wildberger (1980: 232, ET 1991: 249, following Halévy 1887: 151-52; likewise Procksch 1930: 55) supposes (but does not strictly justify) that the reference is to the *Zapfen der Türflügel*, by which I presume he means the poles to which the doors themselves were attached and which, being stood in their sockets in the threshold, could allow the door to be opened. One could imagine that they might shake in their sockets, though if something more violent is envisaged (and it frequently is, both because it is thought that there is an earthquake/theophany reference here, and because there may be a conscious allusion to Amos 9.1, which has *r'š*; see n. 6 below), then a reference to something structural would be more appropriate (the calculations of the weight involved in shaking the door-poles by Hartenstein 1997: 124 as a defence of this understanding does not, therefore, really answer the point). A final possibility is to revert to an old emendation which seems to have been completely forgotten in the meantime, namely *'ōm^{e}nôt*; the

the altar with its glowing coals are obvious examples, and perhaps more significantly, the heavenly sanctuary is never referred to as God's 'house' (*bayit*, the term used in v. 4b). Moreover, as Hartenstein (1997: 63) observes, there is a logical progression from inside the most holy place outwards in a manner that suggests the physical Temple rather than the heavenly, where such a progression is not normally mentioned; thus, we have the throne in what would elsewhere be called the *d^ebîr* (the inner sanctuary, or holy of holies, v. 1a), then the *hêkāl* (the main sanctuary, or nave, v. 1b) with its entry threshold (*sap*, v. 4a), and lastly the *bayit*, referring to the building complex as a whole (v. 4b).

Finally, the consciousness of the prophet's and his people's sin also points in the same direction; to quote Gray (1912: 104), 'It is indeed the very fact that he sees Yahweh holding court in Jerusalem that gives full point to his alarm; it is the actual presence of the Holy One of Israel in the midst of Israel and not remote in heaven that spells doom to the unclean people'. This might well be supported by the closely parallel vision in Amos 9.1 (on which some scholars think that Isaiah was dependent for the phraseology of his vision), where Amos reports that 'I saw the Lord standing over the altar' (*rā'îtî 'et-'^adōnāy niṣṣāb*: note the identical construction with Isa. 6.1 and 8, as discussed below) of what was clearly the physical shrine at Bethel and which was about to be destroyed in judgment (Gray 1908: 540).[6]

On the assumption, then, that Isaiah's description has the Jerusalem Temple in view, it is necessary next to analyse the syntax of this passage, since this is a great help in distinguishing between the given and the innovative. What follows represents my own analysis, though it agrees with what has emerged in recent years as something of a consensus, with only minor variations, among those who have given attention to the matter (e.g. Irsigler 1991; Müller 1992: 163-66; Hartenstein 1997: 31-37).

The narrative progression through the account of Isaiah's vision is clearly marked by the use of the *waw*-consecutive verbal forms. The first and most obvious division of the chapter comes at v. 8, with its close parallel with v. 1:

> *wā'er'eh*[7] *'et-'^adōnāy yōšēb* ('I saw the Lord sitting', v. 1)

loss of a *nun* by haplography either following a *mem* in Palaeo-Hebrew or before a *waw* in square script is highly likely. *'Ōm^enôt* in this sense is a *hapax legomenon* in MT, occurring at 2 Kgs 18.16 where it is associated with the doors of the Temple as something from which Hezekiah stripped precious metal in order to raise tribute. Assuming it derives from *'mn*, 'support', a meaning such as door-posts would be appropriate (cf. Cogan and Tadmor 1988: 229). Clearly, certainty escapes us; the choice seems to be between 'foundation' (contextually attractive, but philologically unsupported) or door-posts/uprights (either by emendation or on the basis of a questionable semantic development of 'forearm').

6. A minority view sees Amos's fifth vision as a later addition to the book and dependent on Isaiah, rather than the other way round; see most recently (with full references to earlier literature) Bergler 2000. Even if this were true, it would still provide more or less contemporary evidence of how Isaiah's wording should be understood.

7. For the use of the *waw*-consecutive after various expressions of time, see GK §111*b*; S.R. Driver 1892 §127*b*; Brockelmann 1956 §123*f*; Waltke and O'Connor 1990: 553; Gibson 1994: 96-98. There is therefore no justification for Whitley's assertion that the verb must originally have stood at

wāʾešmaʿ ʾet-qôl ʾᵃdōnāy ʾōmēr ('I heard the voice of the Lord saying', v. 8)

Each verse begins with a verb of perception, seeing and hearing respectively, and these, of course, are the key verbs which will feature in the hardening saying of vv. 9-10. They are followed by the use of *ʾᵃdōnāy* for the object[8] in preference to the tetragrammaton, no doubt as as a title, 'the Lord', in view of the emphasis on God's royal majesty elsewhere in the passage. That this is likely part of a deliberate structuring device is suggested by its only other use in the chapter, at v. 11, which equally clearly introduces the concluding paragraph of the chapter. Finally, in both verses the reference to God is followed by a descriptive participle. We may conclude, therefore, that the first half of the chapter will be dominated by the description of what Isaiah saw, and the second half by what he heard in his dialogue with God.

Within this broad structure, there are further subdivisions. As our interest relates only to the first part of the chapter, I shall limit the analysis to that. Working backwards, vv. 6-7 are marked out as a unit not only by their subject matter, but also by the initial and then repeated uses of the *waw*-consecutive (and one unmodified *qatal* form). Matching this, the conclusion of v. 5 obviously rounds off the section begun in v. 1 by way of *inclusio*: in the sentence 'for my eyes have seen the king, the Lord of hosts', the recurrence of the verb 'to see' is marked out by the way that it unusually follows its object, and the object itself, 'the king, the Lord of hosts', is resumptive from the point of view of content of *ʾᵃdōnāy* in v. 1.

the start of the sentence and that the date formula has been added later, replacing some alternative introduction (Whitley 1959). Indeed, the use of the perfect tense in such a position (which is apparently what Whitley would have expected had this been a genuine eighth-century composition) is said by GK §111*b* to be found 'only in late books or passages'. In addition, it is likely that the use of the *waw*-consecutive construction was chosen as part of the structuring framework for the passage as a whole, as argued above. 1QIsa[a] omits the initial *waw*. Kutscher (1974: 355) suggests that this may have been because the construction was relatively unfamiliar, but has to concede that the resulting unmodified imperfect does not fit the context. A mechanical scribal error therefore seems more probable, though in view of the fact that the scroll has the shorter form of the king's name (*ʿwzyh* for *ʿzyhw*) this cannot be a simple case of haplography. It is obviously impossible to tell whether the versions read the *waw* or not, but LXX at least probably did because it starts the verse with καὶ ἐγένετο, as though this were the familiar *wyhy* construction. Ziegler (1934: 62) compares Isa. 36.1 with 2 Kgs 18.13 as the basis for proposing that *wyhy* in fact stood in the LXX's *Vorlage*, but this is uncertain; the translator could equally well have been influenced precisely by *wʾrʾh* to assume that this is what was meant.

8. Not surprisingly, many manuscripts here read *yhwh*, which most commentators have long preferred. However, as developed above, Barthel (1997: 67) more plausibly regards the use of the tetragrammaton as secondary on the ground that *ʾᵃdōnāy* occurs at the start of major sections elsewhere in the chapter (see vv. 8 and 11). Interestingly, in 1QIsa[a] the initial *aleph* at least (and possibly one or more letters following) is clearly written as a correction of something else, conceivably the start of the tetragrammaton. If so, it would indicate that the alternatives were already known in antiquity. For the force of this particular title here, see Rösel 2000: 78-110. It is unnecessary for our present purpose to adjudicate on whether the final *yod* is a pronominal suffix or an afformative element (as sometimes in Ugaritic); for a survey of the issues involved, see Eissfeldt 1973: 66-78, ET 1977: 62-72.

Finally, we should note the use of the *waw*-consecutive at the start of both vv. 4 and 5. Verse 5 resumes the first person narrative begun in v. 1 ('And I said'), while *wayyānū 'û* in v. 4 seems to be climactic in a manner yet to be determined.

As will already be obvious from this brief survey, there remains a good deal of material in the first section which is not governed by this narrative format, and it is not difficult to demonstrate that it may all be construed as circumstantial. Thus, after the initial 'I saw' in v. 1, the participle *yōšēb*, 'sitting', clearly describes the Lord's situation at the time he was first seen and throughout the vision. This continues in the second half of v. 1 with the classic form of a circumstantial clause, namely *waw* + subject + participle (e.g. Gibson 1994: 168); whatever this clause describes was therefore also in place before the vision and remained unchanged.

In v. 2 the participle *'ōmᵉdîm* continues the circumstantial construction begun with *wᵉšûlāyw* in v. 1 (e.g. Gibson 1994: 137), while the following phrase, 'with six wings each', is purely descriptive. Then in my view the circumstantial clauses of vv. 1b and 2a are continued by the *waw* + perfects *wᵉqārā'* and *wᵉ'āmar* of v. 3 (so S.R. Driver 1892 §113 [4, *b*]; GK §112*k*; JM §119*v*).[9] The unmodified imperfects in v. 2b (*yᵉkasseh* and *yᵉ'ôpēp*), therefore, seem most likely to be subordinate, describing the uses to which the wings might habitually be put (cf. S.R. Driver 1892 §§31, 33*b*; Müller 1992: 164) and so not necessarily implying that these actions were being undertaken at the time of the vision itself.[10]

Finally, even after the narrative verb at the start of v. 4, we may note that in the second half of that verse we revert to an unmodified *yiqtol* form. The force of this is not agreed, but it seems more likely to describe incipient action ('while the house began to fill with smoke; so Gray 1912: 108, citing S.R. Driver 1892 §§26-27; cf. GK §107*d*; Waltke and O'Connor 1990: 504) than durative action (so GK §107*b*; JM §113*f*);[11] for further discussion, see Hartenstein 1997: 36-37.

The consequence of this analysis is the rather simple point that in the description of his vision Isaiah makes a more careful distinction between what is innovative and what was already in place, so to speak, than might at first have been thought likely. It seems not unreasonable, therefore, to proceed to investigate

9. 1QIsaᵃ reads *wqr'ym* and omits *w'mr*. This undoubtedly indicates the same understanding of the syntax. The use of the plural for MT singular (in itself not an uncommon occurrence; cf. Kutscher 1974: 394-400) will have been exegetically determined (cf. *'mdym* in v. 2 and *zh 'l-zh* immediately following); the same consideration is sufficient to account for the renderings as plural in the versions. It is in many respects the easier reading (and perhaps for that very reason suspect), but unlikely to be original since we should have expected the subject to be expressed before the participle and it would also be difficult to account for the addition of *w'mr* in the MT.

10. If this construal is correct, then *yᵉ'ôpēp* does not directly qualify *'ōmᵉdîm*, and the suggestion that the latter therefore means 'hovering, soaring' (e.g. Dillmann 1890: 55, with the delightful but unimaginative further objection that if *'md* really meant stand, the seraphim would have been standing on God's robe; Delitzsch 1889: 124, ET 1894: 179; Wildberger 1980: 232, ET 1991: 249) should be abandoned.

11. 1QIsaᵃ has *nml'*. This implies an action in sequence ('the house filled with smoke'), and is therefore probably secondary, since as we have seen this chapter is rather careful to use the *waw*-consecutive for this; see differently Kutscher 1974: 42 and 352.

what we might learn of the nature of the Temple and its worship on this understanding.

To begin at the beginning, the clause 'I saw the Lord' is part of the narrative framework and so does not describe the presupposed situation. This suggests that we should be cautious before claiming, as a few have done, that this passage supports the theory that there was a cult statue in the Jerusalem sanctuary.[12] Without going into the broader arguments on which this theory is based, there are two other considerations based upon the present passage which also point towards this negative conclusion. First, the emphasis already noted on the enormous size of God, so that he exceeds by far the confines of the sanctuary, seems easier conceptually to derive from the presence of an empty throne than from one on which there was a cult statue of *ex hypothesi* limited size. Secondly, we have also noted the close phraseological parallel with Amos 9.1, but in that case the question of a cult statue does not seem to arise, given God's position there standing over or above the altar. The use of the Lord as the direct object of the verb 'to see', does not, therefore, necessarily imply that the presence of a statue is demanded.

This conclusion does not, however, apply to the reference to a divine throne in the second half of the verse. The assumption must be that something in the Temple has given rise to this reference, and there is general agreement that it was the ark and its overshadowing cherubim. At that point agreement ceases, for there has been a prolonged debate about such issues as to whether the ark was the throne itself or merely the footstool, whether the wings of the cherubim formed the seat of the throne, whether the whole should not rather be envisaged as the sphinx-thrones of neighbouring countries, whether the inner-sanctuary was elevated or on the same level as the rest of the building, and so on (for a concise and documented survey, see Salvesen 1998: 58-59, and cf. Fabry 1984: 266-70, ET 1995: 253-57). In my opinion, however, it is doubtful whether these debates contribute significantly to the exegesis of Isa. 6.1. As with the figure of God, so with the throne it is clear that, as described here, it exceeds the dimensions of the building, taken from a literalistic point of view (cf. Tengström 1993: 44-45). It is 'high and lifted up',[13] and if merely the edge of the Lord's garment fills the

12. See, for instance, Niehr 1997. The volume in which Niehr's essay occurs serves as a useful introduction also to the wider debate, and may be consulted for further literature; see too Na'aman 1999. The remarks on Isa. 6 made above do not, of course, preclude the existence of other forms of cult statuary in ancient Israel and Judah, a subject to which archaeological discovery is continuing to add new evidence. Nevertheless, so far as the central Jerusalem sanctuary is concerned, I have yet to be persuaded that the more cautious approach of such historians of Israelite religion as Albertz (1992: 101-102, ET 1994: 64-65) and Miller (2000: 16-17, 20-23) is mistaken.

13. In 1QIsa[a] a faint but clear *waw* has been included at the end of *kissē'* as a suffix; since it is followed by a word space, it cannot have been added later, and presumably there was a later attempt to delete it. The matter is of some significance because it suggests that *rām w^{e}niśśā'* following, having no definite articles, was most probably understood to qualify 'the Lord' rather than the throne (contrast LXX; there are two Targum MSS which also include a suffix, *kwrsyh*, and Jacob 1987: 94 suggests that the disjunctive accent under *ks'* indicates that the Masoretes too took the following words separately, so qualifying 'the Lord'). Nevertheless, the natural reading of the text as it stands suggests that the adjectives indeed refer to the throne (and so in a sense secondarily to the one seated on it), even though later the words came to be applied directly to God (cf. Isa. 57.15).

sanctuary, the implications for the size of the throne are obvious. It is further sobering to remember that the ark is nowhere specifically called a throne, and that cherubim are not expressly referred to in the present chapter.

It seems, therefore, that we need to take a slightly different approach to this description. I think that there can be little doubt that in Jerusalem circles generally the ark and cherubim complex was somehow considered to be a divine throne (perhaps with footstool), as the expression 'he who sits (i.e. enthroned, *yōšēb*, as in our verse) [upon] the cherubim', often used in connection with the ark, strongly implies (1 Sam. 4.4; 2 Sam. 6.2; 2 Kgs 19.15; Isa. 37.16; Pss. 80.2, ET 1; 99.1; 1 Chron. 13.6). Precisely how that was conceived is unclear at this stage and immaterial for us. The important point is that it was a trigger for one aspect of Isaiah's vision, and in describing what he saw he accommodates his language not to the *realia* but to his theological understanding of what he saw: hence the characteristically Isaianic 'high and lifted up'[14] (see, e.g., 2.11-15). Whether his vision then was of a sphinx throne is entirely possible, but cannot be determined with any certainty. The important point is that Isaiah now sees the heavenly enthroned king within the Jerusalem Temple, whose physical dimensions are thereby hopelessly breached (Keel 1977: 51-56; Barthel 1997: 97-99). It is a pattern of presentation that we shall see repeated.

We come next to the reference to the seraphim in vv. 2-3. Following the work in particular of Joines (1974: 42-60, developing her earlier 1967 study), de Savignac (1972), Schoors (1977: 95-99) and especially Keel (1977: 70-115), it is widely accepted that these are a developed version of the originally Egyptian uraei, a form of snake with usually two or four wings and also certain human characteristics which, judging by their frequent appearance on seals and the like, were clearly also very familiar in the Levant.[15] In Egypt, these creatures were regularly depicted as royal guardians, sometimes even in connection with thrones, such as the magnificent throne of Tutankhamun:

> Rising vertically on the outsides of the panel and from the back of the seat are two four-winged and crowned uraei. Each arm of the throne is formed by two wings of each uraeus, and the other wings support the cartouche of the king. (Joines 1974: 49, with reference to Carter and Mace 1923, plates LXII, LXIV, and II)[16]

14. Hartenstein (1997: 41-56) rather overinterprets, in my view, when he seeks to establish a link between *rām* and other derivatives of the root *rûm*, such as *mārôm*, in order to trace this element to the Jerusalem cult tradition. Such etymological theologizing on the basis of only one element in what appears to be a fixed pair is hazardous, and the evidence we have points strongly, rather, to the combination 'high and lifted up' as being an Isaianic coinage (the words occur together only twice outside the book which bears his name; the text is uncertain in one case, they are not joined as a pair as in Isaiah, and on neither occasion are there any cultic overtones; cf. Prov. 30.13; Dan. 11.12, and Williamson 1994: 38-41).

15. Morenz and Schorch (1997) suggest an alternative explanation, though their attempt to separate the references in Isa. 6 from those elsewhere is questionable. For a possible Egyptian etymology, see Görg 1991: 211-22; if correct, the link with Hebrew *śārap*, 'to burn', would be at the level of 'folk-etymology' at best.

16. It is by no means clear from the plates that these uraei were four-winged; rather, it appears that their single pair of wings both formed the arms of the throne *and* supported the king's cartouches. Fortunately, this inaccuracy does not materially affect our present discussion.

Despite the fact that Isaiah's seraphim are distinguished by having an unparalleled six wings,[17] there seems to be no good reason not to follow this identification.

The seraphim are nowhere else mentioned in connection with the sanctuary, so that, if our basic approach to Isaiah's vision is sound, we are bound to seek to identify them with something that was already present in the Temple and visible to Isaiah. Two possibilities may be considered. In the first place, the image of Nehushtan, 'the bronze serpent that Moses had made' (2 Kgs 18.4), is often cited. In favour of this identification, it may be noted that in the story in Num. 21.4-9, which lies behind this reference, the bronze serpent which Moses made as the means of deliverance from the snake bites is called a *śārāp* (and the snakes which bit the people are similarly called *hann*ᵉ*ḥāšîm haśś*ᵉ*rāpîm*). In addition, an Egyptian connection would not be inappropriate (and see too Isa. 30.6 for an association of flying seraphim with the way to Egypt).[18] Thus Gray long ago could conclude, 'on this object Isaiah's eye may have been resting just before he fell into ecstasy' (1912: 105; cf. Müller 1992: 176).

There are difficulties for this view, however, not least the fact that Isaiah saw more than one seraph whereas Nehushtan was clearly singular. Furthermore, there is no indication that Nehushtan was winged, whereas it seems that when seraphim had wings or could fly, that point is made specifically; in addition to the present passage, see Isa. 14.29; 30.6.[19]

As an alternative to the trigger for this aspect of Isaiah's vision, it should be recalled that the only objects in the Temple with which wings are elsewhere explicitly associated are the cherubim, both the two associated with the ark and presumably, therefore, those also with which (among other things) the walls of the sanctuary were decorated (cf. 1 Kgs 6.29). Some of these latter will doubtless have appeared to be flying above the ark, so that they would answer well to the position of the seraphim in Isaiah's vision. Since, as we have already noted, the cherubim are, perhaps significantly, not mentioned in the present chapter, the

17. Attention is often drawn to the six-winged genius from Tell Halaf (cf. *ANEP*, no. 655), but (a) this seems to be an exceptional depiction, (b) it is in any case not a seraph and (c) according to Keel (1977: 75) it is by no means certain that the genius is holding serpents in each hand, as many have asserted; he thinks that they are more likely staffs (see too Orthmann 1971: 316), while Day (1979: 150 n. 28) suggests that they might be streams of water. Six-winged guardians of thrones are not uncommon in Mesopotamian iconography, so that the possibility should not be ruled out that in Isaiah's conceptualization there has been something of a fusion of Egyptian and Mesopotamian motifs.

18. Herodotus (*History* 3.109) also speaks of the Egyptian desert as a place of flying serpents.

19. The editor of this volume, John Day, seeks to counter these objections with the observations that although there was only one Nehushtan, Num. 21 makes clear that 'it was made in response to a multitude of seraphim' and that despite the silence of the text, Nehushtan could have had wings, like seraphim elsewhere. As will be seen below, I do not discount the influence of Nehushtan on this aspect of Isaiah's vision, but I should still maintain that it is difficult to see him as the major initial trigger for what Isaiah describes because he was certainly singular, no matter what else he may have represented. Furthermore, if, as this argument supposes, the story of Num. 21 was uppermost in Isaiah's mind (which seems to me uncertain), then it should be noted that *those* seraphim were certainly not winged.

possibility that they are one and the same is enticing.[20] Apart from the Temple, they too seem to have a role as guardians of the divine sphere (cf. Gen. 3.24; Ezek. 28.14-16). The data for identifying the nature of a cherub elsewhere in the Hebrew Bible are sparse and somewhat contradictory (see Freedman and O'Connor 1984, ET 1995), so that it would be difficult to refute the suggestion on the ground of dissimilarity.

Why, then, did Isaiah not simply refer to them as cherubim? Perhaps it was here that Nehushtan also played his part, for the bronze serpent of Num. 21.4-9 was two-edged, so to speak. As Glazov (2001: 121, 133-36 and 161, following Uffenheimer[21]) has recently emphasized, the snakes of which he was a replica were dangerous and threatening (and it was reflection on this that caused Isaiah to cry out in despair, v. 5), whereas Nehushtan himself was life-restoring (something that Isaiah experienced when the seraph purged his impure lips, v. 7). In the fusion of cherubim and Nehushtan, in other words, Isaiah has again given a fresh interpretation in his vision to motifs which were familiar in the Temple setting.

Our previous syntactical analysis has suggested that the cry of the seraphim, the trisagion in v. 3, was also something that Isaiah witnessed as part of the general setting within which various specific acts took place (*w*^{e}*qārā'*, not *wayyiqrā'*). Although I recognize that this is only one argument, and not a decisive one at that, it nevertheless inclines me to favour the view that this may have been based upon some aspect of the regular liturgy of the Temple worship in Isaiah's day.[22] Once again, however, that need not mean that he has recorded it exactly. Although something like it may have been familiar to him, this may once more have served merely as a trigger for what is here recorded. Clearly what is required, therefore, is to inquire what may have been inherited from earlier tradition.

In the first place, it is reasonably certain that holiness was ascribed to God, probably under originally Canaanite influence, in the Jerusalem cult tradition. There is some dispute about the details of this: while there is no doubt that in Ugaritic, as in Hebrew, members of the heavenly court could be designated as

20. They were certainly fused in the later description of Rev. 4.8. I share the view, nevertheless, that Isaiah most probably speaks of only two seraphim, despite the apparent assumption of many commentators that there were many more of them. In v. 3, *zeh 'el-zeh* follows a singular verb, and it is difficult to escape the conclusion that this implies one seraph responding antiphonally to another; as Gray (1912: 107) concludes on the basis of Gen. 29.27, Exod. 14.20 and 1 Kgs 3.23 (and cf. 1 Kgs 22.20; Isa. 44.5; BDB, 260B), 'in similar correlative usages זה refers definitely to *one* of two'. The only possible exception he can find after an extensive discussion is Eccl. 3.19 (he had already dismissed the relevance of Ps. 75.8 [ET 7], on which Irsigler 1991: 144 additionally relies), but even this, as he admits, is 'a somewhat inadequate parallel'. But why should the text not be accepted at face value? It seems to be additionally supported by the singular *haqqōrē'* in the next verse (cf. König 1927: 91).

21. Glazov prefers this explanation to that of Lacheman 1968–69, who suggested that the golden cherubim took on a fiery aspect when the sun shone on them. Lacheman makes no reference to the seraphim in passages other than Isa. 6; his explanation does not appear to fit them.

22. This is the view, for instance, of Hartenstein 1997: 78, who gives further references; contrast Keel 1977: 116-21, who ascribes the whole to Isaiah. Barthel (1997: 100-101) is undecided, but allows the possibility.

‘the holy ones’ or the like,[23] it is less clear whether El himself was entitled *qdš*,[24] though he probably was. Either way, holiness is brought into the closest possible proximity with El-Elyon of Jerusalem in Ps. 46.5 (ET 4), and Schmidt (1968: 136-37, ET 1983: 154) may be right in suggesting that through this route the title ‘Holy One of Israel’ came to be applied by a natural extension to Yahweh. At any rate, the evidence of Pss. 78.41 and 89.19 (ET 18) suggests that this divine title too may have been adapted by Isaiah from the Jerusalem tradition, even though it came to be used far more frequently and with developed meaning by the later contributors to the book of Isaiah as a whole (see Williamson 2001). Although it therefore seems likely that God was always worshipped as holy in Jerusalem, the transition from El to Yahweh in this regard may have been particularly helped by the fact that the ark too had apparently long been associated with the holiness of God (cf. 1 Sam. 6.20). This becomes of further relevance when we recall the strong arguments of Mettinger (1982: esp. 128-35) and Ollenburger (1987) that the divine title used in the trisagion, ‘the Lord of hosts’, was probably not native to Jerusalem, but had its origin in association with the ark at Shiloh. If that be true, then it is attractive to see in the first half of this liturgical formula, in which holiness is so emphatically[25] ascribed to the Lord of hosts, something which reached back to the earliest days of temple worship when Canaanite and native Israelite conceptions of the deity were fused into a new appreciation.

The second half of the acclamation also has parallels elsewhere which suggest that it may have deep roots in the cult tradition, but in this case we find that there is a slight but significant difference. As pointed out by Hartenstein (1997: 101-105), the two most important passages for our concern are Num. 14.21 and Ps. 72.19. Both include an identical clause which is only loosely integrated into its context, so giving the impression of possibly being cited from elsewhere. Numbers 14.21 starts out as a first-person speech by God (see explicitly v. 20), ‘Nevertheless as I live’. Before this speech is resumed in v. 22, however, there is a third-person interruption: ‘and may the whole earth be filled with the glory of the Lord’ (*w^{e}yimmālē’ k^{e}bôd-yhwh ’et-kol-hā’āreṣ*). This uneasy integration

23. E.g. Exod. 15.11(?); Deut. 33.2-3; Zech. 14.5; Ps. 89.6, 8 (ET 5, 7); Job 5.1; 15.15, etc.; cf. Müller 1984: 602, ET 1997: 1112-13.

24. The relevant passages are *KTU* 1.16 I 10-11, 21-22; 1.16 II 49, where Keret is called not only a son of El, but also a *špḥ . lṭpn . wqdš*. There are three principal views on this: (a) usually, it is rendered ‘the offspring of the Gracious and Holy One’ or the like, so that *qdš* refers to El; see most recently Pardee 1997: 339b and 341a. This approach is adopted in particular by Schmidt (1962) in relation to our present discussion; see too Niehr 1984; (b) alternatively, van Selms (1982) follows Ginsberg in rendering ‘an offspring of the Kindly One, and a holy being’, thus attributing the title to Keret himself as ‘a minor god’; (c) finally, it is occasionally suggested that the reference is to Keret’s divine mother: ‘the offspring of Kindly One (‘El) and Qudšu (’Aṯirat)’; cf. Mullen 1980: 250.

25. *Qādôš* is repeated three times to express particular emphasis, similar to the superlative; cf. Jer. 7.4; 22.29; Ezek. 21.32; GK §133*k*. It appears only twice in 1QIsa[a], rather as a repetition was avoided by the scroll in Isa. 6.2 (*šēš k^{e}nāpayim*). While either text is possible, MT is generally preferred (a rare exception is Walker 1958–59 and 1960–61; contrast Leiser 1959–60); if Scoralick (1989) is correct in her understanding that Ps. 99 is based upon Isa. 6, then its threefold *qādôš*-refrain (vv. 3, 5 and 9) would suggest the greater antiquity of MT.

suggests that the clause was not written for its present context but has been cited from elsewhere. The same clause (with *k^{e}bôdô* for *k^{e}bôd-yhwh*) comes in Ps. 72.19 as part of the closing doxology of the Psalm, and perhaps of the whole of the second book of the Psalter, something which makes a liturgical origin highly probable. The fact that two such completely unrelated passages use the same expression indicates that it had a wider currency in ancient Israel. This conclusion is only strengthened by the unusual grammar, at least as provided by the Masoretes, with their vocalization with simple *waw* and the verb in the niphal.[26] Finally, a liturgical origin is also favoured by the recasting of the same formula as an eschatological wish in Hab. 2.14: 'But the earth will be filled with the knowledge of the glory of the Lord, as the waters cover the sea', with which Isa. 11.9 is comparable (though omitting the reference to glory).

The language of the second clause of the trisagion is thus familiar, but its precise formulation is unparalleled. It therefore seems likely that Isaiah has here once again given a characteristic twist to something familiar from the Temple setting. He has turned a verbal clause into a nominal one by the use of the introductory *m^{e}lō'*, and also reversed the order of 'glory' and 'all the earth'. What this may signify, however, is disputed.

The usual, though by no means unanimous, view is that in this nominal clause the predicate precedes its subject, exactly as in the previous clause (see the discussion in Irsigler 1991: 134, and also GK §141*l*; JM §154*e*); hence, 'his glory is the fulness of the earth'. Given that *m^{e}lō'* is the equivalent of 'that which fills' (cf. BDB, 571 for many clear examples; of especial relevance are Isa. 8.8; Pss. 24.1; 50.12; 89.12, ET 11), this may justify the looser but traditional rendering, 'the whole earth is full of his glory', attested already in the versions from the LXX on.[27] It is by no means certain, therefore, that the versions read the verbal form *māl^{e}'â*; still less should we emend (*contra* Nestlé 1905 and, more hesitantly, Gray 1912: 108).

The alternative way of construing the sentence, namely as subject followed by predicate, which is certainly the expected word order when both elements of the sentence are definite, as here (cf. Andersen 1970: 32), unless there are other overriding considerations, is rarely entertained, but has a certain contextual attraction. The matter cannot be decided on any other ground, so that everything depends on whether this alternative approach makes good sense. I have suggested elsewhere (Williamson 1999: esp. 186) that it does, and with one significant modification I briefly repeat the proposal here.

26. GK §121*e* proposes emending to the qal, and this is followed by a number of commentators. Alternatively, the grammar may be explained by appeal to the rare construction where, when an active verb governing two accusatives is turned into the passive, it nevertheless retains the double accusative; so Delitzsch 1883: 519-20, ET 1888: II, 351-52; Gray 1903: 159. JM §129*c*N even speculates that the *'et* might here be used to introduce the subject; although this certainly happens occasionally, it seems unlikely in this case.

27. To that extent, the sharp remarks of Wagner (1989: 182) may not be warranted. The possibility might also be considered that LXX read the word as *mālē'*, and thought that the lack of grammatical concord was acceptable in the case of a verb preceding its subject.

There can be little doubt that the dominant portrayal of God in Isaiah 6 is that of a king. Part of the role of a king in ancient times was to command the army, and there is an apparent hint in that direction here in the use of the divine title 'Lord of hosts', not only in the trisagion itself, but perhaps more significantly as a qualifier of the title king in v. 5 (for a discussion of the semantics of the title, see Mettinger 1982: 123-28). If we then turn with this background in mind to a study of the use of *kābôd* in Isaiah, we quickly come to 8.7, where the invading Assyrian is described as 'the king of Assyria and all his glory', self-evidently a reference to the impressive display of power represented by the Assyrian army.[28] Similarly, at 16.14, 21.16 and 22.18, the 'glory' of a country or prominent citizen occurs in contexts where there is immediate reference to military power. And it seems likely that in such passages as 5.13, 10.3, 16, 18 and 17.4 this same usage is applied metaphorically. My proposal is that in 6.3 the claim is being made that it is 'the fulness of the whole earth' which is the divine king's glory in this sense. What, then, is 'the fulness of the whole earth'?

This use of the construct *m^elō'* is relatively frequent elsewhere in the Hebrew Bible, and in nearly all cases it refers to animate objects which fill the world or some part of it (cf. Snijders 1984: 885-86, ET 1997: 306-307). Without going through every occurrence to support this well-recognized point, attention may be drawn especially to the parallelism in Ps. 24.1, in view of that Psalm's close links with other aspects of Isaiah 6:

> The earth is the Lord's and all *its fullness* (*m^elô'āh*),
> the world, and those who live in it.

Similarly, within Isaiah, sense and parallelism are again telling at 34.1:

> Let the earth hear, and *all that fills it* (*m^elô'āh*),
> the world and all that comes from it (*kol-ṣe'^eṣā'eyhā*).

Jeremiah 8.16, 47.2, Ezek. 12.19, 19.7, Amos 6.8 and Mic. 1.2 are all further clear examples of the same, and it may well be that this phrase was also common in the liturgy with which Isaiah was familiar.

Now, had we been able to ask one of Isaiah's contemporaries what the divine king's 'glory' was, he or she would almost certainly have replied that it was the armies and the might of Israel; indeed, there are those who have sometimes thought that this was the original significance of the word 'armies' in the divine title 'Lord of hosts' itself. Isaiah's vision, it may be suggested, brought him to realize, rather, that the Lord was not so tied to Israel, and indeed that it was 'the fullness of the whole earth' that was at his disposal. It opened the way for the first time, so far as we can tell, for one apparently steeped in the Zion traditions to postulate radically that the divine king had armies available to him not only quite apart from Israel but which, indeed, he could deploy against Israel if the

28. So correctly Wildberger 1980: 326, ET 1991: 345: 'the unheard-of force of the enemy as it storms forward...the splendor of the enemy's external appearance but also its intense inner power'. Wildberger also helpfully recalls the regular Assyrian boast that their 'splendour' had overcome the enemy. See comparably Weinfeld 1984: 25, ET 1995: 25.

need arose. I conclude once again that Isaiah has both bequeathed us something that we should not otherwise have known about the Temple worship in pre-exilic Jerusalem, but also that he has worked creatively with it in order to open up new theological insights of his own.

At this point, the long sequence of circumstantial clauses comes to an end. The only other piece of information (see above n. 5 for discussion of the 'doorposts of the threshold') that we derive from later in the chapter is the presence of an altar to which one of the seraphim could fly (v. 6), so that it was probably inside the sanctuary rather than in the outside court. This points to an incense altar rather than the main sacrificial altar, and it is interesting to note that two small stone incense altars were found on the steps leading to the inner shrine of the Iron Age temple at Arad (the precise date is controversial; cf. Ussishkin 1988). There is reference to an altar at 1 Kgs 6.20, and another to a golden altar inside the sanctuary at 1 Kgs 7.48, but this has often been considered a later addition under the influence of the description of the tabernacle (Exod. 39.38; 40.5, 26; cf. Noth 1968: 166). That may be true in terms of the formulation in Kings, but it may still be claimed on the basis of our chapter that there was indeed some such altar present in the pre-exilic Temple (see further Hartenstein 1997: 187-89).

The 'smoke' mentioned in v. 4 most probably does not relate to this, however, despite a widespread assumption that it does. The word *'āšān* is never once used in association with cultic smoke from sacrifices or incense (North 1989: 440-41, ET 2001: 410-11; Hartenstein 1997: 137); had that been the intention, we should certainly have expected the use rather of *qᵉṭōret* (as at 1.13). Furthermore, when a cloud of incense smoke is mentioned, the phraseology is *'ᵃnan haqqᵉṭōret* (Lev. 16.13; Ezek. 8.11), again never *'āšān*. Rather, if I was right in my preference for understanding the second half of v. 4 as descriptive of incipient rather than durative action, the appearance of smoke will have been closely associated with the trembling in the first half of the verse rather than reflecting any constant state of the sanctuary being filled with the smoke of incense.

This fact draws attention to one final point I wish to make from Isaiah 6, not so much on the basis of a particular phrase, such as has dominated our discussion up until now, but rather on the basis of reflection on the whole of what we have seen. From the movement of the description already noted from the innermost sanctuary to a place just outside the *hêkāl* with its threshold, the implication seems clear that Isaiah's own position, so to speak (whether in reality or in imagination is immaterial), is just in front of the entrance to the sanctuary, presumably therefore in the *'ûlām* ('vestibule, porch') of 1 Kgs 6.3; 7.12, 19, etc. Meyers (1992: 357) describes this as 'a transitional space that shared both in the closed sanctity of the interior and the more open accessibility of the courtyard space surrounding the Temple'. Yet from that vantage point it appears that he can see and hear all that is going on in both the sanctuary and the most holy place. Nothing is said to indicate that this is unusual or remarkable; it is just an accepted part of the stage setting for the visionary action.

The way in which separation was made between the vestibule and the sanctuary and between the sanctuary and the holy of holies is not altogether clear in our sources. 1 Kings 6.31-34 and 7.50 speak of doors at this point, but 2 Chron. 3.14 replaces these with a curtain, at least for the inner set. The Chronicler's version seems likely to reflect tabernacle typology, though according to Mk 15.38 this was also the situation in the Herodian Temple, and so perhaps too for the Temple in the Chronicler's own day. The strange note about the poles of the ark sticking out and so being visible in the sanctuary seems more easily accommodated to the idea of a curtain than doors, assuming the latter could be shut (1 Kgs 8.8; 2 Chron. 5.9), though if, as many think, this note reflects Priestly instruction for the way in which the ark should be carried, it remains unclear whether it also pertained to the *realia* of the First Temple. At all events, the strong impression of our sources that anything beyond the limits of the vestibule was strictly off limits for the laity seems to be belied by the presuppositions lying behind Isaiah 6, and it may well be that this is a case where the influence of the Second Temple has almost completely overshadowed the portrayal of the Solomonic Temple. There may have been doors, but at the least we must assume that they were left open from time to time and that there was no objection to laity witnessing what went on beyond them.

This impression gains strong support from the other main passage in First Isaiah which refers extensively to the Temple cult, namely Isa. 1.11-15. I dealt with this at a previous seminar (Williamson 2004), and so I will merely summarize the relevant conclusions here. The most obvious point of similarity with what we have been discussing, with a textual reflex, is the rereading of an originally qal *lir'ôt pānāy*, 'to see my face', as a niphal (with syncopated *hē*) *lērā'ôt pānāy*, 'to appear before me', in v. 12 (cf. Barthélemy 1986: 3-5). As in Isaiah 6, this seems to imply that lay worshippers had access to the heart of the sanctuary, and this was more than could be accepted in later times; comparable considerations will have determined the Chronicler's rewriting of 2 Kgs 11.4-20 at 2 Chron. 23.1-21 (see Williamson 1982: 315-18). Similarly, some of the terminology used in this passage does not coincide with the later Priestly legislation for sacrifice, and this suggests that the cult may not yet have been so tightly regulated: *'attûdîm* (v. 11), for instance, do not appear in the primary legislation (Lev. 1–7), though they do occur frequently in the descriptive passage in Num. 7.10-88, and still more strikingly *m^erî'îm* are nowhere mentioned in legislative texts, but conversely they are used in association with sacrificial animals only in passages which reflect pre-exilic practice (2 Sam. 6.13; 1 Kgs 1.9, 19, 25; Ezek. 39.18; Amos 5.22). Several other terms developed more specific meanings with the passage of time, but at this stage reflect a less developed theological precision: *minḥâ* (v. 13), for instance, is most easily understood here as carrying its earlier general sense of 'gift' when seeking favour from a superior (and so can be appropriately qualified by *šāw'*: it will not attain what the worshipper intended), but later it came to designate a cereal-offering (Lev. 2); *miqrā'* (v. 13) looks like an early general term for a religious gathering which was later specified in P as a *miqrā' qōdeš* with tighter regulations; and *'^aṣārâ* (v. 13), a certainly pre-exilic term (cf. 1 Kgs 10.20) with probable reference to a general sacred gathering, will have later become the calendrical term *'^aṣeret* which was used for specific days when work ceased for a particularly solemn ceremony.

This greater cultic informality, if it may be so termed, enables us better to understand the force of Isa. 6.4. After the cry of the trisagion, with what I have suggested is a threatening twist given it by Isaiah, it is then precisely something at the threshhold which trembles, and smoke, which nearly always elsewhere is threatening in one way or another, begins to fill the building. I suggest that at this liminal point a barrier, so to speak, descends; the threshold may no longer be passed, and the vision into the sanctuary is hidden from sight. No wonder that at that point Isaiah cries out in despair.[29] The sequence through vv. 3-5 itself

29. Not without reason, G.R. Driver (1960) once wrote an article entitled ‘A Confused Hebrew Root (דמם, דמה, דום)’. Philologists disagree about the number of lexemes that should be ascribed to each of these roots (some of which are clearly related and may simply be by-forms of each other), and this confusion is attested as early as the ancient versions. In the present case, the morphology indicates a niphal of *dmh*, so that attempts to link the word here with *dmm* may be disregarded. (Roberts 1992 observes that before the use of fuller orthography the two forms would have been indistinguishable, and this is the basis for his suggestion that there is a deliberate play on ‘I am undone’ and ‘I am silenced’. I accept the possibility, though doubt whether such ambiguity would have been appropriate in this particular context.) This leaves us with three possibilities. (i) *dmh* = ‘be like, resemble’. The niphal may appear in Ezek. 32.2 (cf. *HALAT*, ET *HALOT*) but not in the absolute sense of ‘be presumptuous’, which would be required here (cf. Zeron 1977; for further analysis of Zeron’s discussion, see Glazov 2001: 130-34). (ii) *dmh* = ‘cease, cut off, destroy’, and so in the niphal (which is well attested) ‘be destroyed, ruined’. This has been the usual rendering in English versions, and is still favoured by many on both philological and centextual grounds. (iii) *dmh* = ‘be silent’, and so here ‘I have been silenced’. This has been favoured of late by a number of commentators because of the reference in what follows to unclean lips, and support has been found from some of the versions (see below). In my view, it remains philologically questionable, however. The presumed roots (ii) and (iii) have no certain cognates, and in some instances they clearly overlap semantically. Furthermore, one of the roots *dmm* certainly means ‘be, become silent’, so that confusion of (iii) with that is not unlikely in some cases. It may, therefore, be a mistake to postulate a *dmh* (iii) in the first place. In addition, to attain sense, since the qal is intransitive, the niphal has to be given the sense of the passive of the causative; though theoretically possible (cf. BL §38*z*’; GK §51*f*), this is improbable given that no piel or hiphil is attested, unlike in other examples of this usage. The appeal to 1QpHab V 10 is beside the point, since if *ndmw* there is a niphal, it is from the root *dmm*, not *dmh* (*contra* Wildberger; cf. Williamson 1977). Finally, Barthel (1997: 68) observes that the verb is equally qualified by the final clause of the verse, ‘for my eyes have seen the king, the Lord of hosts’, so that the context does not point so unambiguously to silence. Given the frequent use of the niphal of *dmh* (ii) (it occurs more than ten times, including elsewhere in Isaiah [15.1]) as well as the uncertainties surrounding the very existence of *dmh* (iii), I conclude that the traditional English rendering is to be preferred. How, then, should we account for the versions? The evidence here is mixed. Several certainly relate the word to silence: Aquila, Symmachus and Theodotion all have εσιωπησα, and Vulgate has *tacui*. LXX (which is clearly followed here by Peshitta) may not be so far removed with κατανένυγμαι, ‘be pricked, goaded; be stupefied’ (see the discussion in Glazov 2001: 136-38, where he combines the notion of silence with the pricking of the conscience towards repentance), but Targum, ‘for I have transgressed; for I am a man who is bound to rebuke’, which at first sight seems further removed from MT, may give us the clue to the earlier renderings as well. The reference appears to be to an old tradition (known already to Jerome in his commentary; see further Ginzberg 1909–38: IV, 63; VI, 359) that Isaiah should have rebuked Uzziah for his presumptuous entry into the sanctuary (cf. 2 Chron. 26.16-21). It seems plausible to conjecture, therefore, that the silence to which the other versions refer is to Isaiah’s silence in this episode and that their knowledge of this tradition led them to confuse *ndmyty* with *dmm* (Gray). It follows that their evidence should not override philological and contextual considerations. Interestingly, even the main rabbinic commentators accept this, despite the targumic rendering.

supports this understanding both of the nature of Temple worship as presupposed in Isaiah 6 and of the development towards a greater separation between laity and divine to which Isaiah contributed and which became normative in post-exilic times. Although the conclusion is hardly startling, our analysis of the first part of Isaiah 6 suggests that it makes a modest contribution to our understanding of the development of a theology of the Temple and of its worship in ancient Jerusalem.

BIBLIOGRAPHY

Abū ʻAssāf, A.
1990 *Der Tempel von ʻAin Dārā* (Damaszener Forschungen, 3; Mainz: Philipp von Zabern).

Albertz, R.
1992 *Religionsgeschichte Israels in alttestamentlicher Zeit.* I. *von den Anfängen bis zum Ende der Königszeit* (GAT, ATD Ergänzungsreihe, 8.1; Göttingen: Vandenhoeck & Ruprecht). ET *A History of Israelite Religion in the Old Testament Period.* I. *From the Beginnings to the End of the Monarchy* (trans. J. Bowden; London: SCM Press, 1994).

Andersen, F.I.
1970 *The Hebrew Verbless Clause in the Pentateuch* (JBLMS, 14; Nashville and New York: Abingdon Press).

Barthel, J.
1997 *Prophetenwort und Geschichte: Die Jesajaüberlieferung in Jes 6–8 und 28–31* (FAT, 19; Tübingen: Mohr Siebeck).

Barthélemy, D.
1986 *Critique textuelle de l'Ancien Testament.* II. *Isaïe, Jérémie, Lamentations* (OBO, 50.2; Freiburg: Editions Universitaires; Göttingen: Vandenhoeck & Ruprecht).

Becker, U.
1997 *Jesaja—von der Botschaft zum Buch* (FRLANT, 178; Göttingen: Vandenhoeck & Ruprecht).

Bergler, S.
2000 '"Auf der Mauer—Auf dem Altar": noch einmal die Visionen des Amos', *VT* 50: 445-71.

Blenkinsopp, J.
2000 *Isaiah 1–39: A New Translation with Introduction and Commentary* (AB, 19; New York: Doubleday).

Brockelmann, C.
1956 *Hebräische Syntax* (Neukirchen–Vluyn: Neukirchener Verlag).

Carter, H., and A.C. Mace
1923 *The Tomb of Tut.Ankh.Amen*, I (London: Cassell).

Clements, R.E.
1980 *Isaiah and the Deliverance of Jerusalem: A Study of the Interpretation of Prophecy in the Old Testament* (JSOTSup, 13; Sheffield: JSOT Press).

Cogan, M., and H. Tadmor
1988 *II Kings: A New Translation with Introduction and Commentary* (AB, 11; New York: Doubleday).

Day, J.
1979 'Echoes of Baal's Seven Thunders and Lightnings in Psalm xxix and Habakkuk iii 9 and the Identity of the Seraphim in Isaiah vi', *VT* 29: 143-51.

Delitzsch, F.

1883 *Biblischer Commentar über die Psalmen* (Leipzig: Dörffling & Franke, 4th edn). ET *Biblical Commentary on the Psalms* (trans. D. Eaton; 3 vols.; London: Hodder & Stoughton, 1887–89).

1889 *Commentar über das Buch Jesaia* (Leipzig: Dörffling & Franke, 4th edn). ET *Biblical Commentary on the Prophecies of Isaiah* (trans. J. Kennedy, W. Hastie, T.A. Bickerton and J.S. Banks; 2 vols.; Edinburgh: T. & T. Clark, rev. edn, 1894).

Dillmann, A.

1890 *Der Prophet Jesaia* (Kurzgefasstes exegetisches Handbuch zum Alten Testament, 5; Leipzig: Hirzel, 5th edn).

Driver, G.R.

1960 'A Confused Hebrew Root (דמם, דמה, דום)', in M. Haran and B. Luria (eds.), *Sepher N.H. Tur-Sinai* (Jerusalem: Kiryat Sepher): 1*-11*.

1971 'Isaiah 6.1 "His Train Filled the Temple" ', in H. Goedicke (ed.), *Near Eastern Studies in Honor of William Foxwell Albright* (Baltimore and London: The Johns Hopkins University Press): 87-96.

Driver, S.R.

1892 *A Treatise on the Use of the Tenses in Hebrew* (Oxford: Clarendon Press).

Eissfeldt, O.

1973 'אֲדֹנָי אָדוֹן', in *ThWAT*, I: 62-78. ET *TDOT*, I (1977): 59-72.

Eslinger, L.

1995 'The Infinite in a Finite Organical Perception (Isaiah vi 1-5)', *VT* 45: 145-73.

Fabry, H.-J.

1984 'כִּסֵּא *kissē*", in *ThWAT*, IV: 247-72. ET *TDOT*, VII (1995): 232-59.

Feldmann, F.

1925 *Das Buch Isaias übersetzt und erklärt* (EHAT, 14; Münster: Aschendorff).

Fohrer, G.

1991 *Jesaja 1–23* (Zürcher Bibelkommentare, AT, 19.1; Zürich: Theologischer Verlag, 3rd edn).

Freedman, D.N., and M. O'Connor

1984 'כְּרוּב *k^erûḇ*', in *ThWAT*, IV: 322-34. ET *TDOT*, VII (1995): 307-19.

Gibson, J.C.L.

1994 *Davidson's Introductory Hebrew Grammar: Syntax* (Edinburgh: T. & T. Clark).

Ginzberg, L.

1909–38 *The Legends of the Jews* (7 vols.; Philadelphia: The Jewish Publication Society of America).

Glazov, G.Y.

2001 *The Bridling of the Tongue and the Opening of the Mouth in Biblical Prophecy* (JSOTSup, 311; Sheffield: Sheffield Academic Press).

Görg, M.

1991 *Aegyptiaca—Biblica: Notizen und Beiträge zu den Beziehungen zwischen Ägypten und Israel* (Ägypten und Altes Testament, 11; Wiesbaden: Otto Harrassowitz).

Gosse, B.

1992 'Isaïe vi et la tradition isaïenne', *VT* 42: 340-49.

Gray, G.B.

1903 *A Critical and Exegetical Commentary on Numbers* (ICC; Edinburgh: T. & T. Clark).

1908 'The Heavenly Temple and the Heavenly Altar', *The Expositor*, 7th series, 29: 385-402 and 30: 530-46.

1912 *A Critical and Exegetical Commentary on the Book of Isaiah I–XXVII* (ICC; Edinburgh: T. & T. Clark).

Greenfield, J.C.

1985 'Ba'al's Throne and Isa. 6.1', in A. Caquot, S. Légasse and M. Tardieu (eds.), *Mélanges bibliques et orientaux en l'honneur de M. Mathias Delcor* (AOAT, 215; Kevelaer: Butzon & Bercker; Neukirchen–Vluyn: Neukirchener Verlag): 193-98.

Halévy, J.

1887 Review of F. Delitzsch, *Prolegomena eines neuen hebräisch-aramäischen Wörterbuchs*, *REJ* 14: 146-60.

Hartenstein, F.

1997 *Die Unzugänglichkeit Gottes im Heiligtum: Jesaja 6 und der Wohnort JHWHs in der Jerusalemer Kulttradition* (WMANT, 75; Neukirchen–Vluyn: Neukirchener Verlag).

Hehn, J.

1916–17 'שולים Is 6, 1 = "Schleppen"? Die Bedeutung von שול und שאול', *BZ* 14: 15-24.

Hess, R.S.

1996 'ספף', in *NIDOTTE*, III: 282-83.

Hitzig, F.

1833 *Der Prophet Jesaja, übersetzt und ausgelegt* (Heidelberg: Winter).

Hurowitz, V.A.

1989 'Isaiah's Impure Lips and Their Purification in Light of Akkadian Sources', *HUCA* 60: 39-89.

Irsigler, H.

1991 'Gott als König in Berufung und Verkündigung Jesajas', in F.V. Reiterer (ed.), *Ein Gott—Eine Offenbarung: Beiträge zur biblischen Exegese, Theologie und Spiritualität. Festschrift für Notker Füglister OSB zum 60. Geburtstag* (Würzburg: Echter Verlag): 127-54.

Jacob, E.

1987 *Esaïe 1–12* (CAT, 8a; Geneva: Labor et Fides).

Jeremias, Jörg

1996 *Hosea und Amos: Studien zu den Anfängen des Dodekapropheten* (FAT, 13; Tübingen: J.C.B. Mohr [Paul Siebeck]).

Joines, K.R.

1967 'Winged Serpents in Isaiah's Inaugural Vision', *JBL* 86: 410-15.

1974 *Serpent Symbolism in the Old Testament: A Linguistic, Archaeological, and Literary Study* (Haddonfield: Haddonfield House).

Keel, O.

1977 *Jahwe-Visionen und Siegelkunst: eine neue Deutung der Majestätsschilderungen in Jes 6, Ez 1 und 10 und Sach 4* (SBS, 84/85; Stuttgart: Katholisches Bibelwerk).

König, E.

1927 *Das Buch Jesaja: eingeleitet, übersetzt und erklärt* (Gütersloh: Bertelsmann).

Kutscher, E.Y.

1974 *The Language and Linguistic Background of the Isaiah Scroll (1 Q Isa^{a})* (STDJ, 6; Leiden: E.J. Brill).

Lacheman, J.

1968–69 'The Seraphim of Isaiah 6', *JQR* NS 59: 71-72.

Leiser, B.M.

1959–60 'The Trisagion of Isaiah's Vision', *NTS* 6: 261-63.

Mettinger, T.N.D.
1982 'YHWH SABAOTH—The Heavenly King on the Cherubim Throne', in T. Ishida (ed.), *Studies in the Period of David and Solomon and Other Essays: Papers Read at the International Symposium for Biblical Studies, Tokyo, 5–7 December, 1979* (Tokyo: Yamakawa-Shuppansha): 109-38.

Metzger, M.
1970 'Himmlische und irdische Wohnstatt Jahwes', *UF* 2: 139-58.

Meyers, C.
1986 'סַף *sap*', in *ThWAT*, V: 898-901. ET *TDOT*, X (1999): 296-98.
1992 'Temple, Jerusalem', *ABD*, VI: 350-69.

Miller, P.D.
2000 *The Religion of Ancient Israel* (London: SPCK; Louisville, KY: Westminster/John Knox Press).

Morenz, L.D., and S. Schorch
1997 'Der Seraph in der Hebräischen Bibel und in Altägypten', *Or* 66: 365-86.

Mullen, E.T.
1980 *The Divine Council in Canaanite and Early Hebrew Literature* (HSM, 24; Chico, CA: Scholars Press).

Müller, H.-P.
1992 'Sprachliche und religionsgeschichtliche Beobachtungen zu Jesaja 6', *ZAH* 5: 163-85.
1984 'קדשׁ *qdš* heilig', in *THAT*, II: 589-609. ET *TLOT*, III (1997): 1103-18.

Na'aman, N.
1999 'No Anthropomorphic Graven Image: Notes on the Assumed Anthropomorphic Cult Statues in the Temples of YHWH in the Pre-Exilic Period', *UF* 31: 391-415.

Nestlé, E.
1905 'Miscellen 13. Zum Trisagion', *ZAW* 25: 218-20.

Niehr, H.
1984 'Bedeutung und Funktion kanaanäischer Traditionselemente in der Sozialkritik Jesajas', *BZ* NF 28: 69-81.
1997 'In Search of YHWH's Cult Statue in the First Temple', in K. van der Toorn (ed.), *The Image and the Book: Iconic Cults, Aniconism, and the Rise of Book Religion in Israel and the Ancient Near East* (Contributions to Biblical Exegesis and Theology, 21; Leuven: Peeters): 73-95.

North, R.
1989 'עָשָׁן *'āšān*', in *ThWAT*, VI: 438-41. ET *TDOT*, XI (2001): 409-11.

Noth, M.
1968 *Könige*, I (BKAT, 9.1; Neukirchen–Vluyn: Neukirchener Verlag).

Ollenburger, B.C.
1987 *Zion, the City of the Great King: A Theological Symbol of the Jerusalem Cult* (JSOTSup, 41; Sheffield: Sheffield Academic Press).

Orthmann, W.
1971 *Untersuchungen zur späthethitischen Kunst* (Bonn: Rudolf Habelt).

Pardee, D.
1997 'The Kirta Epic (1.102)', in W.W. Hallo (ed.), *The Context of Scripture*. I. *Canonical Compositions from the Biblical World* (Leiden: E.J. Brill): 333-43.

Paul, S.M.
1991 *Amos* (Hermeneia; Minneapolis: Fortress Press).

Podella, T.
1996 *Das Lichtkleid JHWHs: Untersuchungen zur Gestalthaftigkeit Gottes im Alten Testament und seiner altorientalischen Umwelt* (FAT, 15; Tübingen: J.C.B. Mohr [Paul Siebeck]).

Procksch, O.
1930 *Jesaia*, I (KAT, 9; Leipzig: Deichert).

Roberts, J.J.M.
1992 'Double Entendre in First Isaiah', *CBQ* 54: 39-48.

Rösel, M.
2000 *Adonaj—warum Gott 'Herr' genannt wird* (FAT, 29; Tübingen: Mohr Siebeck).

Salonen, A.
1961 *Die Türen des Alten Mesopotamien: eine lexikalische und kulturgeschichtliche Untersuchung* (Helsinki: Suomalaisen Kirjallisuuden Kirjapaino Oy Helsinki).

Salvesen, A.
1998 'כִּסֵּא', in T. Muraoka (ed.), *Semantics of Ancient Hebrew* (Abr-Nahrain Supplement Series, 6; Leuven: Peeters): 44-65.

Savignac, J. de
1972 'Les "Seraphim" ', *VT* 22: 320-25.

Schmidt, W.H.
1962 'Wo hat die Aussage: Jahwe "der Heilige" ihren Ursprung?', *ZAW* 74: 62-66.
1968 *Alttestamentliche Glaube und seine Umwelt: Zur Geschichte des alttestamentlichen Gottesverständnisses* (Neukirchen–Vluyn: Neukirchener Verlag). ET *The Faith of Israel: A History* (Oxford: Basil Blackwell, 1983).

Schoors, A.
1977 'Isaiah, the Minister of Royal Anointment?', in A.S. van der Woude (ed.), *Instruction and Interpretation: Studies in Hebrew Language, Palestinian Archaeology and Biblical Exegesis* (OTS, 20; Leiden: E.J. Brill): 85-107.

Scoralick, R.
1989 *Trishagion und Gottesherrschaft: Psalm 99 als Neuinterpretation von Tora und Propheten* (SBS, 138; Stuttgart: Katholisches Bibelwerk).

Seeligmann, I.L.
1948 *The Septuagint Version of Isaiah* (Leiden: E.J. Brill).

Selms, A. van
1982 'The Expression "The Holy One of Israel" ', in W.C. Delsman *et al.* (eds.), *Von Kanaan bis Kerala: Festschrift für Prof. Mag. Dr. Dr. J.P.M. van der Ploeg O.P. zur Vollendung des siebzigsten Lebensjahres am 4. Juli 1979* (AOAT, 211; Kevelaer: Butzon & Bercker; Neukirchen–Vluyn: Neukirchener Verlag): 257-69.

Smith, M.S.
1988 'Divine Form and Size in Ugaritic and Pre-Exilic Israelite Religion', *ZAW* 100: 424-27.

Snijders, L.A.
1984 'מָלֵא *mālē*", in *ThWAT*, IV: 876-86. ET *TDOT*, VIII (1997): 297-307.

Tengström, S.
1993 'Les visions prophétiques du trône de Dieu et leur arrière-plan dans l'Ancien Testament', in M. Philonenko (ed.), *Le Trône de Dieu* (WUNT, 69; Tübingen: J.C.B. Mohr [Paul Siebeck]): 28-99.

Ussishkin, D.
1988 'The Date of the Judaean Shrine at Arad', *IEJ* 38: 142-57.

Wagner, R.

1989 *Textexegese als Strukturanalyse: Sprachwissenschaftliche Methode zur Erschließung althebräischer Texte am Beispiel des Visionsberichtes Jes 6,1-11* (ATSAT, 32; St Ottilien: EOS Verlag).

Walker, N.

1958–59 'The Origin of the "Thrice-Holy"', *NTS* 5: 132-33.

1960–61 'Disagion versus Trisagion', *NTS* 7: 170-71.

Waltke, B.K., and M. O'Connor

1990 *An Introduction to Biblical Hebrew Syntax* (Winona Lake, IN: Eisenbrauns).

Weinfeld, M.

1984 'כָּבוֹד *kāḇôḏ*', in *ThWAT*, IV: 23-40. ET *TDOT*, VII (1995): 22-38.

Whitley, C.F.

1959 'The Call and Mission of Isaiah', *JNES* 18: 38-48.

Wildberger, H.

1980 *Jesaja 1–12* (BKAT, 10.1; Neukirchen–Vluyn: Neukirchener Verlag, 2nd edn). ET *Isaiah 1–12* (trans. T.H. Trapp; Minneapolis: Fortress Press, 1991).

1982 *Jesaja 28–39: Das Buch, der Prophet und seine Botschaft* (BKAT, 10.3; Neukirchen–Vluyn: Neukirchener Verlag). ET *Isaiah 28–39* (trans. T.H. Trapp; Minneapolis: Fortress Press, 2002).

Williamson, H.G.M.

1977 'The Translation of *1QpHab*. V, 10', *RevQ* 9: 263-65.

1982 *1 and 2 Chronicles* (NCB; Grand Rapids: Eerdmans; London: Marshall, Morgan & Scott).

1994 *The Book Called Isaiah: Deutero-Isaiah's Role in Composition and Redaction* (Oxford: Clarendon Press).

1999 '"From One Degree of Glory to Another": Themes and Theology in Isaiah', in E. Ball (ed.), *In Search of True Wisdom: Essays in Old Testament Interpretation in Honour of Ronald E. Clements* (JSOTSup, 300; Sheffield: Sheffield Academic Press): 174-95.

2001 'Isaiah and the Holy One of Israel', in A. Rapoport-Albert and G. Greenberg (eds.), *Biblical Hebrew, Biblical Texts: Essays in Memory of Michael P. Weitzman* (JSOTSup, 333; Sheffield: Sheffield Academic Press): 22-38.

2004 'In Search of the Pre-Exilic Isaiah', in J. Day (ed.), *In Search of Pre-Exilic Israel: Proceedings of the Oxford Old Testament Seminar* (London and New York: T. & T. Clark International): 181-206.

Zeron, A.

1977 'Die Anmassung des Königs Usia im Lichte von Jesajas Berufung', *TZ* 33: 65-68.

Ziegler, J.

1934 *Untersuchungen zur Septuaginta des Buches Isaias* (Alttest. Abhandl., 12.3; Münster: Aschendorf).

Zwickel, W.

1993 'סף II und מפתן', *BN* 70: 25-27.

TEMPLE AND WORSHIP IN EZEKIEL 40–48

Paul M. Joyce

'The vision I saw was like the vision I had seen when he came to destroy the city, and like the vision that I had seen by the river Chebar' (Ezek. 43.3). Chapters 40–48 of Ezekiel, with their vision of the renewed Temple, constitute one of the great set-pieces of the book. Comparable are chs. 8–11, recounting the prophet's journey 'in visions of God' to Jerusalem, and also, in a different way, the remarkable 'divine chariot' vision with which the book opens in ch. 1. Parunak, following rabbinic precedent, treated these visionary sections together (Parunak 1980). And indeed we find in our text, in the words quoted above, a cross-reference, possibly editorial, to both chs. 8–11 and ch. 1.

This block of material at the end of the book has a reputation for being particularly intimidating, on account of its obscurity and difficulty. It has proved a kind of graveyard for commentators. It is interesting that some do not themselves cover these chapters: Bertholet and again Fohrer preferred to leave them to be commented on by Galling (Bertholet [with Galling] 1936; Fohrer [with Galling] 1955); and this pattern has been replicated recently in the ATD commentary on Ezekiel, where Pohlmann hands over to Rudnig for chs. 40–48 (Pohlmann [with Rudnig] 2001). Endings, like beginnings, are often, of course, particularly significant in the impact they have upon the reader. Perceptions of Ezekiel have been heightened by the book's last nine chapters; in particular, prejudice against priests and Priestly concerns has affected discussion of Ezekiel, and not least this final section. J.D. Levenson comments: 'The fact that critical inquiry into biblical tradition was conceived and nurtured mostly by men whose outlook was molded by theologies whose origins lay in the Protestant Reformation has not aided the emergence of a serious and sympathetic appreciation of law and priesthood in the Hebrew Bible' (Levenson 1976: 1). And such prejudice has not been unknown within Britain: in 1928, R.H. Kennett wrote that, whereas 'Jeremiah marked out the way which led to Jesus Christ…of Ezekiel's teaching the almost inevitable outcome was Caiaphas' (Kennett 1928: 58).

But though difficult and sometimes unpopular, these chapters also exercise their own fascination. A series of studies has been devoted to Ezekiel 40–48, not least recently. They cover the spectrum from the stratifying (Gese 1957) to the holistic (Greenberg 1984). The stratifying approach of Gese is followed through in detail by Zimmerli in his commentary (Zimmerli 1979, ET 1983; cf. Zimmerli 1968). Gese saw chs. 40–48 as a confusing structure, with many layers of redaction. His detailed examination of the tradition history of these chapters has dominated their interpretation to a marked extent for more than forty years, whereas study of redaction in chs. 1–39 has seen much more flux over the same period. Rudnig in many ways represents the latest phase of the stratifying approach to chs. 40–48 (Rudnig 2000; Pohlmann [with Rudnig] 2001). His full theory is complex but he identifies two main redactions. The first, dated to the first half of the fifth century, he describes as 'Exile-orientated', having its origins in the real prospect of return and reconstruction. The second main layer is dubbed 'Diaspora-orientated' and is said to derive from later in the fifth century. Rudnig confidently splits individual verses into multiple redactional layers, which he then proceeds to date with some precision.

Others favour a more holistic approach to Ezekiel 40–48, above all Greenberg (Greenberg 1984), with Niditch providing another, less thoroughgoing, example of this trend (Niditch 1986). Greenberg writes that the final long section of Ezekiel:

> ...is arranged according to a design which...follows the principles of composition familiar from other biblical and ancient Near Eastern literature... [I]ts topics cohere and serve a single overriding purpose. The inference from these propositions is that it is the product of a single mind (and hand) and that, as carrying forward ideas and values found in the preceding prophecies, it may reasonably be attributed to their author, the priest-prophet Ezekiel. (Greenberg 1984: 215)

This very characteristic statement from Greenberg rests both on the view that chs. 1–39 derive from the prophet himself and on a particular judgment about the degree of continuity between chs. 1–39 and chs. 40–48.

So scholarship is somewhat polarized on the question of the authorship of Ezekiel 40–48. Rudnig's work represents quite the opposite of the 'holistic' approach championed by Greenberg. If Greenberg fails to engage with the diachronic dimension, it has to be said that Rudnig's refined stratification attempts to demonstrate more than could ever be known about the undoubtedly complex history of the book's redaction. On the issue of authorship and redaction, the most appropriate stance is one of responsible agnosticism. This is not to commend a lazy or casual approach (there can be no escape from wrestling seriously with the detailed case for parts of Ezek. 40–48 being from hands later than Ezekiel's), but rather a rigorous dialectic between what we may reasonably claim and that which is beyond our knowing. In the case of Ezekiel in general we have to take account of a marked homogeneity between Ezekiel and material that may well be secondary. The fact that the 'house style' of Ezekiel is particularly distinctive makes it the more difficult to distinguish between primary and secondary material (Joyce 1995; cf. Niditch 1986: 211). Nonetheless, as well as original material we have to acknowledge the probability of redactional expansion (for example in the more polemical pro-Zadokite verses, 44.15-31 and 48.11); and beyond this we also need to give an account of the coherence of the finished work.

Whether or not it is all from Ezekiel, several factors favour a sixth-century date for Ezekiel 40–48 as a whole. There is nothing that unambiguously refers to events after the sixth century. This is a principle that Clements employs very effectively in his treatment of chs. 1–24 (Clements 1986). Moreover, the fact that

Ezekiel's vision is so divergent from the restoration reality strongly suggests that it predates it (Collins 1993: 96). If the Second Temple had already been inaugurated, it would have been difficult to write in this way; the account would surely have been accommodated to the new reality. This is not an absolutely necessary conclusion (we should not forget the freedom with which the Dead Sea Scrolls and also the Mishnah work with Temple themes). Nevertheless, it must be acknowledged as persuasive.

Much discussion of the dating of our chapters involves comparative work of one kind or another, and yet so much is unknown to us. Given that we do not know what Priestly writings or oral traditions existed prior to Ezekiel, it is impossible to judge the implications of divergences between Ezekiel 40–48 and the Priestly sections of the Torah. Also we do not know precisely what changes had taken place in Solomon's Temple by late pre-exilic times (for example, in the days of Manasseh or of Josiah) and so it is hard to weigh apparent divergences between the account of Solomon's Temple and Ezekiel's. Moreover, it is difficult to know what conclusions, if any, to draw from 'silences' in the Ezekiel account (for example, with regard to the virtual absence of reference to the contents of Ezekiel's Temple).

I have presented a spectrum from the stratifying to the holistic in approaches to the authorship of our chapters. Another spectrum can be discerned with regard to the question of the overall purpose of these chapters. Treatments of Ezekiel 40–48 cover the range from the realistic (Cooke 1936; Wevers 1969) through to the eschatological (Eichrodt 1968, ET 1970) and the utopian (Kasher 1998). This is not the place to attempt to present an exhaustive taxonomy of approaches to these chapters, but further complexity may be hinted at. Scholars often argue or assume that realistic details are a sign of secondary elaboration of an original vision. Zimmerli (1979, ET 1983) provides an example of this general phenomenon. And this can lead scholars to interpret diverse redactional layers (as they perceive them) very differently. Tuell offers a decidedly non-realistic interpretation of what he takes to be the original vision of chs. 40–42 (Tuell 1996), but he is better known for his very realistic reading of the final revision of Ezekiel 40–48 as providing nothing less than a political constitution for Jewish life under the Persians, with the *nāśî'*, 'prince', interpreted as none other than the Persian governor (Tuell 1992).

In fact, I shall argue that Ezekiel 40–48 combines both dream and reality. The interweaving of the richly visionary and the precisely mathematical in these chapters is striking. This apparently future-oriented combination of profound theological questions and minute practical detail can be compared with another text from the exilic age, namely Lamentations, where a retrospective exploration of the tragedy of loss is expounded in meticulously crafted acrostic form. Much in Ezekiel 40–48 exemplifies the concerns and style of the priests (cf. Jenson 1992; Gorman 1990); indeed, without exploring in detail in this context the relative chronology of Ezekiel and the Priestly materials of the Pentateuch, it is clear that both the broad ideological framework of chs. 40–48 and their attention to detail reflect the Priestly tradition within which Ezekiel stood. At the same time this section stands in continuity with Ezekiel's prophetic heritage. The priest-prophet Ezekiel confounds any simple dichotomy between the visionary and the Priestly, such as that once popularized by Plöger and Hanson (Plöger 1962, ET 1968; Hanson 1979). Cook (1995a) showed this convincingly for Ezekiel 38–39, and the same is true of chs. 40–48. The tension between dream and reality is explored with profundity in this final section of the book.

1. *The Literary Context of the Vision*

A word next about the context of the chapters. They form the crown of the second half of the book, which, at ch. 33, turns (broadly speaking) from oracles of judgment of various kinds to oracles of salvation. More immediately, chs. 40–48 follow on from chs. 38–39, the account of the assault by Gog of Magog. Niditch (1986) persuasively argues that the battle scenes of chs. 38–39 provide the prelude to chs. 40–48 in keeping with a familiar ancient Near Eastern model. She finds here reflected a mythic pattern of victory and enthronement of the deity, which appears with variations in the Babylonian *Enuma Elish* and the Canaanite epic of Baal and Anat. At the end of chs. 38–39, in 39.28-29, we read:

> Then they shall know that I am the Lord their God because I sent them into exile among the nations, and then I gathered them into their own land. I will leave none of them remaining among the nations anymore. And I will not hide my face anymore from them, when I pour out my Spirit upon the house of Israel, says the Lord God.

In many ways this functions well as a link into the final chapters of the book. But several scholars have observed that the last section of ch. 37 arguably serves as an even better way into chs. 40–48 (e.g. Lemke 1984; Blenkinsopp 1990: 180). One may note, for example, in 37.26, 'I will set my sanctuary in the midst of them forevermore' and in v. 27, 'when my sanctuary is in the midst of them forevermore'. Moreover in 37.25 we find reference to a *nāśî'*, 'prince', to be an important theme in chs. 40–48. In other ways too, the thought and language of these verses of ch. 37 share much with chs. 40–48. There is a case on these grounds alone for arguing that they once formed the prelude to ch. 40, without the intervention of chs. 38–39. This is the more plausible given the relative independence of chs. 38–39 and the analogy with proto-apocalyptic material such as Isaiah 24–27.

What is probably the earliest Greek text of Ezekiel, P. 967, features precisely this sequence, moving straight from ch. 37 to ch. 40 (with chs. 38–39 preceding ch. 37). Johan Lust has long suggested that this Greek text represents a more primitive witness than our Masoretic Hebrew text (Lust 1980; 1981). He has developed this challenge recently in his Grinfield Lectures on the Septuagint at Oxford. This possibility is intriguing but ultimately not persuasive. Long ago Filson (1943) argued that the arrangement of P. 967 (and various omissions therein) could satisfactorily be explained on the grounds of accidental damage to the text at some early stage. This line was followed by Wevers (1969: 273) too, in spite of his positive attitude to LXX Ezekiel. Moreover, it is interesting that no extant Hebrew text (including the recently published Masada manuscript of Ezek. 35.11–38.14; cf. Talmon 1999) features the sequence of P. 967. Yet although Lust's proposal is not to be followed, there is heuristic value in considering how chs. 40–48 might look if preceded by ch. 37. The pros and cons, similarities and differences between the Greek sequence and that of the Hebrew are worthy of comparison. One can benefit simply from exploring these as different reading options, even though the Hebrew sequence seems historically the more original.

2. *The Vision of the Temple*

And so to chs. 40–48 themselves. Not surprisingly, 40.1-4 is crucial for all that follows, so deserves close attention. It begins with one of the dating formulae characteristic of the book, referring to 'the twenty-fifth year of our exile, at the beginning of the year, on the tenth day of the month, in the fourteenth year after the city was struck down'. The year seems to be 573. This is the last of the sequence of dates in Ezekiel, although the references in 29.17 ('the twenty-seventh year') and 1.1 (the obscure 'thirtieth year') apparently give later dates. There is widespread agreement that the number 25 is significant, being half a Jubilee period, but scholars divide between those such as Van Goudoever (1986), who dates the exile itself as beginning halfway through a Jubilee period and so places this vision at the beginning of a Jubilee year, and the majority, led by Zimmerli, who favour the more likely view that halfway through a Jubilee period Ezekiel is here granted a foretaste of the anticipated release, the end of exile, which will itself come in a Jubilee year (Zimmerli 1979: 995-96, ET 1983: 346). It is interesting to reflect that the Jubilee shares with Ezekiel's Temple vision the question whether it was intended as a realistic provision or whether it was only ever a utopian aspiration. Opinions vary too on whether 'at the beginning of the year' reckons with an autumnal or, as seems more probable in the light of 45.21, a spring new year. But there is growing support for the view that the phrase 'at the beginning of the year, on the tenth day of the month' is the first hint of the relevance of the Babylonian New Year festival to what follows (e.g. Stevenson 1996).

In 40.1-2, we read: 'The hand of the Lord was upon me and he brought me…in visions of God, to the land of Israel'. One is reminded of 8.3, where the prophet is similarly 'brought…in visions of God to Jerusalem'. As is well known, that has been a key text in the debate over the location of Ezekiel's ministry. It is important to take seriously the visionary nature of both references (8.3; 40.1-2), neither of which gives grounds for a view that Ezekiel actually exercised a ministry in Jerusalem. The prophet is not named in these nine chapters (in fact the name Ezekiel only occurs twice in the book, at 1.3 and 24.24); these chapters, like the book as a whole, are couched in autobiographical style, with Ezekiel as the presumed first-person speaker. 'He set me down upon a very high mountain, on which was a structure like a city to the south' (40.2): Jerusalem is not named as such anywhere in Ezekiel 40–48 (nor Zion, which is never used anywhere in the book); but there can be no doubt that Jerusalem is intended by this reference to a city (much as it is clear that 'the place that the Lord your God will choose' in Deut. 12.5 refers to Jerusalem). Note, though, that in what follows the Temple is not in the city, which is located, as here, away to the south; this is a theme to which we shall return. What of the 'very high mountain'? Sinai is surely in mind (so Levenson 1976: 37-49): 'the law of the Temple' is revealed in the course of what follows (43.12). But there are also resonances here of the cosmic mountain of ancient Near Eastern mythology, echoes picked up also in the account of the sacred river in ch. 47. We hear that 'a man was there', an angelic guide (40.3). This figure leads Ezekiel on a tour, the account of which is most sustained in chs. 40–42 but is resumed at various points thereafter. He instructs Ezekiel to pay close attention so that he can declare what he sees to the house of Israel (a motif that recurs, for example, in 43.10).

Verse 5 introduces the first reference to the Temple, and it is a remarkably low-key one, taking the Temple itself for granted: 'Now there was a wall all around the outside of the Temple area'. Significantly, this wall is mentioned again at the end of ch. 42 (v. 20); this 'inclusio' is one of several features that mark chs. 40–42 aside as a distinct section (cf. Tuell 1996). Most of the long ch. 40 is devoted to an account of the Temple area, the gates and the outer and inner courts. But before the chapter ends, we commence a presentation of the tripartite structure of the Temple (*habbayit*) itself. This section extends from 40.48 to the end of ch. 41. The basic structure of the Temple, as it is described, follows the pattern familiar to us from 1 Kings and indeed from the archaeology of the ancient Near East (cf. Hurowitz 1992). At 40.48 we have the *'ulām* or vestibule, at 41.1 the *hêkāl* or nave, and then in 41.3 the *p^{e}nîmâ* or inner room. The word *d^{e}bîr* is not used for the inner room in Ezekiel (as it is in 1 Kgs 8.6) but importantly, in 41.4, Ezekiel's guide declares that this is *qōdeš haqq^{o}dāšîm*, the holy of holies or most holy place, using the important phrase found elsewhere in the Hebrew Bible (including indeed 1 Kgs 8.6). We shall, interestingly, find that phrase also employed differently in our chapters, *qōdeš q^{o}dāšîm* (*without* the article) used more generally of broader areas of special holiness.

Much then about the new Temple envisaged in Ezekiel 40–48 is in continuity with what we read of Solomon's Temple as presented in 1 Kings. But there are discontinuities too. For example, Ezekiel's Temple appears to be all but empty. Virtually all the furnishings of the Solomonic Temple, and indeed the desert tabernacle, go unmentioned. The only interior furniture referred to is the 'altar of wood' in front of the inner room (41.22: 'the table that stands before the Lord'). This is distinct from the stone altar of burnt sacrifice that stands outside the Temple itself (40.47 and 43.13-27). Most notable among these omissions is the ark of the Covenant. Why is Ezekiel's Temple apparently all but empty, and in particular why no ark?

Various attempts have been made to explain the omissions. Greenberg has argued that the implications of the gaps must remain obscure. He writes 'In subsequent divisions of Ezekiel's program…omissions cannot serve as a warrant for negative conclusions—unmentioned therefore absent' (Greenberg 1984: 193). Greenberg's caution here is welcome, for too much should never be made uncritically of silences. But in the case of the ark, the gap is so striking that it is important to enquire further.

Haran grounds the omission of the various items on historical accidents that had befallen the Solomonic Temple. He has in view here, in particular, his hypothesis that the ark was removed by Manasseh, king of Judah, in the seventh century, in connection with the setting up of an image of Asherah in the Holy of Holies (Haran 1978: 276-88). But, even if that particular theory of the fate of the ark were correct, which is doubtful (cf. Day's article in the present volume, especially pp. 256-58), why should Ezekiel's vision be constrained by such historical accidents? After all, the whole Temple was razed to the ground by the Babylonians and yet Ezekiel is able to envisage its restoration. Alternatively, it might be argued that the ark, being more intimately associated with Yahweh than anything else in the Temple, was felt by Ezekiel to be unique and for this reason irreplaceable. This may indeed be the reason the ark was not in fact replaced after its destruction with the Temple in 586 BCE, but, again, a *vision* of restoration such as Ezekiel 40–48 need not be so constrained, particularly when it is so bold in other respects.

We need to press further for positive reasons why Ezekiel has found no place for the ark in his vision. Greenberg entertains the possibility that the house is emptied purposely of all objects contributing to a mythological conception of God. He rejects this as unconvincing, writing that the proposal 'is contradicted by the presence of the wooden altar' (Greenberg 1984: 193). While the exception of the wooden altar remains something of an enigma (cf. Haran 1978: 288), this is not sufficient ground for rejecting this line of explanation, which merits further consideration in connection with an important article by Kasher, who argues that 'Ezekiel's particularly anthropomorphic conception of God dictates his attitude to the Temple, holiness, the cult and even prophecy' (Kasher 1998: 192). He goes on to suggest that 'It would appear that Ezekiel views the entire utopian world built in chs. 40–48 through anthropomorphic glasses, mainly in the sense that he envisages the Temple as God's permanent house or abode' (p. 194). Kasher relates a whole range of features to this, including the omission of the various objects from Ezekiel's Temple (p. 198). While it may be argued that he in some respects overstates the anthropomorphic nature of Ezekiel's presentation of God, much of what Kasher says is very helpful. In a nutshell, when we read in Ezek. 43.5 that 'the glory of the Lord filled the Temple' we can see this as implying that the divine presence renders the ark of the Covenant and other cultic paraphernalia redundant. The statement that the 'glory of the Lord filled the Temple' echoes closely the words of both Exod. 40.34 and 1 Kgs 8.11, so it is necessary to ask further what it is about Ezekiel's conception that might squeeze out cultic objects such as the ark. How might we express the distinctive feature of Ezekiel's theology that is determinative here? A key emphasis within Ezekiel's message of future hope more generally is a stress on the all-sufficiency of God alone. Within ch. 36, for example, Ezekiel's God acts to restore his people for no other reason than that, by doing so, he may be known as he really is. Childs argued long ago that such is this book's focus on God that much else, including historical specificity, recedes out of focus (Childs 1979: 361-62). We are close here to the reason why Ezekiel finds no place for the ark. Such is Ezekiel's focus on God himself, that much else is simply eclipsed.

3. *Cherubim, Sacrifice and Separation*

The Temple decorations described at 41.17-20 contain echoes of chs. 1 and 10, particularly the cherubim. Each cherub has two faces, a human face and the face of a young lion. 'They were carved on the whole Temple all around' (41.19). The bulk of ch. 42 is devoted to the priests' chambers. Before moving to the important words that round off the first section of the Temple vision (chs. 40–42), let us pick up various references to worship matters in these chapters. Ezekiel 40.38-43 refer to a chamber where the burnt offering was to be washed, and tables on which the various offerings were to be slaughtered. Ezekiel 42.13-14 refer to the chambers where the priests shall eat the most holy offerings and also deposit their special vestments before going out into the outer court. Animal sacrifice is, then, to be a feature of Ezekiel's new Temple. There has, of course, been much discussion about what actually happened on the ruined site of the Temple during the years of exile (cf. Jones 1963), but these verses move beyond that situation to envisage a full restoration of the sacrificial system. This may not seem surprising within a Priestly context, but is nonetheless worthy of note, when one thinks of the long-standing prophetic critique of the sacrificial system and also the spiritualizing tendency found in, for example, the bulk of Psalm 51 (itself quite possibly exilic). Moreover, within Ezekiel there is the motif in 11.16 of Yahweh himself becoming a *miqdāš mᵉ'aṭ*, a sanctuary in some measure, to the exiles (a theme to which we shall return). But, for all this, Ezekiel's new Temple will indeed feature the slaughtering of animals and the offering of sacrifices.

That 42.20, the last verse of that chapter, forms an 'inclusio' with 40.5 (with the reference to the wall) was noted earlier. Another feature that highlights the key role of this verse at the end of our first section is the programmatic statement that this wall around the Temple area was 'to make a separation between the holy (*qōdeš*) and the common (*ḥōl*)' (cf. 44.23). We have here a familiar Priestly theme, well expounded by Jenson (1992) in his book *Graded Holiness: A Key to the Priestly Conception of the World* in relation to the Pentateuchal Priestly traditions. This conception is central in Ezekiel 40–48, as is shown by this key statement in 42.20. Division, gradation, degree, access: these are the themes central to the presentation.

4. *The Return of the Glory of the Lord*

Another function of 42.20, besides the look back to the section it closes, is to usher in the crucial event that follows. Chapter 43 begins with a dramatic and powerful scene, the return of the Lord to his sanctuary. Ezekiel is taken to the outer eastern gate of the Temple compound, 'And there the glory of the God of Israel was coming from the east'. Just as Ezekiel witnessed the deity's departure from his sanctuary in ch. 11, so now he sees his return. As has been noted, there is at 43.3 an explicit (if perhaps editorial) cross-reference to ch. 1 as well as chs. 8–11. Bodi (1991) has helpfully highlighted the importance of the Akkadian Poem of Erra for the motif of the absence of the deity. Stevenson (1996) is the latest of several scholars to elaborate the parallels with the Babylonian New Year festival, and in particular the Akitu element, featuring the return of the god to his sanctuary. This is a persuasive case, though a significant divergence is that in Ezekiel the deity is not brought back by a king. More generally, there has of late been much lively discussion of the absence and presence of God in Ezekiel (see, e.g., Block 2000; Kutsko 2000; Tuell 2000a). The culmination of 43.1-5 reads: 'The glory of the Lord filled the Temple'.

The passage that follows is particularly important for Ezekiel's understanding of the divine presence. In v. 7 it is God himself who speaks: 'This is the place of my throne and the place for the soles of my feet, where I will reside among the people of Israel forever'. This verse certainly seems to affirm strongly the divine presence within the sanctuary, and it does so echoing language and imagery (of throne and footstool) used elsewhere of the ark of the Covenant, language that is here reapplied and transformed in a new context, precisely because the ark itself no longer has a place. Such reworking and reapplication of language is characteristic of Ezekiel. A comparable example proposed by Hurowitz is the suggestion that the great metal 'sea' of 1 Kgs 7.23 is reworked symbolically and theologically in Ezekiel 40–48 to become the river flowing from the Temple in ch. 47 (see Hurowitz's contribution to the present volume, especially p. 80).

It is of interest to compare briefly the affirmation of divine presence in Ezekiel 43 with some material in each of the other major prophetic books. One is reminded of Isa. 66.1: 'Heaven is my throne and the earth is my footstool; what is the house that you would build for me, and what is my resting-place?' Ezekiel 43.7 is clearly very different from that. It might even be construed: 'This is the place of *my throne as well as* the place for the soles of my feet'. There is no evidence here of a polemical reaction to Isa. 66.1 (even if relative dating were to allow for that), but Ezek. 43.7 is certainly much more affirmative of the Temple and God's presence within it. As the verse continues: '...where I will reside among the people of Israel forever'.

Perhaps closer to Ezekiel 43 is Jer. 3.16: 'They shall no longer say "The ark of the Covenant of the Lord". It shall not come to mind, or be remembered, or missed; nor shall another one be made.' This is explicit about the end of the ark and possibly more polemical in tone than Ezekiel. But Jer. 3.17 continues, more affirmatively, 'At that time Jerusalem shall be called the throne of the Lord and all nations shall gather to it, to the presence of the Lord in Jerusalem'. The similarity with Ezekiel is significant. Ezekiel 43.7 speaks of the Temple being the place of the divine throne, while Jer. 3.17 comparably says (precisely in the context of an explicit statement that the ark will be no more): 'Jerusalem shall be called the throne of the Lord'. It is intriguing to note in this Jeremiah pericope (3.15-18) several other affinities with Ezekiel (including shepherds, as in Ezek. 34, and the reunification of Judah and Israel, as in Ezek. 37). If Collins is right that the book of Ezekiel reached its final form well before the book of Jeremiah (Collins 1993: 96-97), one wonders whether this Jeremiah pericope may reflect the influence of Ezekiel. Although the inclusion of the nations in Jeremiah 3 is not a theme shared with Ezekiel (Ezek. 44.5, though compare 47.21-23), a theory of possible influence by the final form of Ezekiel need not explain all features of the Jeremiah passage. This is of course speculative, but at the very least the Jeremiah verses would seem to provide a comparable case of accommodation to the loss of the ark.

5. *The Reversal of Ezekiel's Motif of the Departure of the Lord*

The return of the Lord to his sanctuary is one of many satisfying symmetries that the book of Ezekiel features. The book opens, of course, with the great vision of ch. 1, where the throne of God himself is witnessed in far-off Babylonia. The Lord is with his people in exile, no longer tied to the land of Israel. The word used for the throne is the same as in 43.7 (*kissē'*). And when, in the vision of chs. 8–11, the divine throne is seen again, leaving the Temple, it is striking that the term *k^erubîm* (intimately connected with the ark tradition) is associated with Ezekiel's motif of the free and mobile deity. Just as remarkably, we read in 11.16 that the Lord has himself become a *miqdāš m^e'aṭ* to his people; he himself is to be their sanctuary 'in some measure' (Joyce 1996). And then, in the final section of the book, comes the grand return of the deity to his shrine, echoing many ancient Near Eastern models. A pleasing symmetry indeed.

Yet is it not also a disappointment that Ezekiel 43 brings back the deity and shuts him up again in his Temple? Is this return not an undoing of one of the most profound contributions of Ezekiel, whereby the limitations of place are transcended? One might regard the *miqdāš m^e'aṭ* theme as one of the pinnacles of the book, an insight that was to help equip generations of Jews for millennia of diaspora life. If chs. 40–48 were, as many have held, largely secondary Priestly elaboration, one could claim that, while the 'chariot' vision of ch. 1, the departure of the glory in ch. 11 and indeed the *miqdāš m^e'aṭ* theme are all from Ezekiel, the return of the Lord in ch. 43 is from a secondary hand, possibly representing a timid retrenchment on the part of priests lacking the boldness of Ezekiel himself. Yet, while there is doubtless redactional elaboration within Ezekiel 40–48, the theme of the return of the deity cannot be dealt with so easily. Vogt (1981) has advanced a persuasive case for the primary nature of Ezek. 43.4-7a. In the absence of clear evidence that material is secondary, the integrity of the work that is before us must be respected.

The 'chariot' vision of ch. 1, the departure of the glory in ch. 11 and indeed the *miqdāš m^e'aṭ*: all of this needs to be borne in mind when in ch. 43 the glory of the Lord returns from the east and fills the Temple. This return does not undo or erase the motifs of the 'mobile throne' or indeed the *miqdāš m^e'aṭ*. (As I have argued elsewhere, *m^e'aṭ* in 11.16 is not to be understood in a temporal sense, 'for a while' [Joyce 1996].) Rather, the affirmation of 43.7 that 'This is the place of my throne and the place of the soles of my feet' stands within the context of that overarching theology of the freedom of God. The theme of the closed east gate of 44.2 does not run counter to these motifs. The point there is that the gate is hallowed because the Lord has passed through it to return to the place of his special abode. It is not suggested that God is now shut up in his house.

Having abandoned his sanctuary for a time the Lord now commits himself to dwell in his sanctuary permanently. ('Forever' is an important exilic theme: Gen. 9.8-17; Isa. 54.9-10; Ezek. 37.24-28.) But this remains, within the grand architecture of the book of Ezekiel, in tension with the affirmation of his presence with his people in their dispersion, for whom he will himself indeed remain a *miqdāš mᵉ'aṭ*, a 'sanctuary in some measure'. This is a rich theology, with a finely balanced dialectic between the immanence of the Lord and his transcendence, between his presence with his people wherever they are and his honouring of the particular place of the special revelation of his holiness. The deity has indeed returned to his special place, where he will dwell among the people of Israel forever. But his freedom, mobility, transcendence and universalism have also been established forever.

6. *Cult Statues?*

Odell (2004) argues that Ezek. 43.7-9 affords a clear reference to cult statues. Although this text is not usually discussed in connection with Ezekiel 8, a number of clues suggest that it is to be read as its counterpart. As has been noted, 43.3 explicitly links this vision to that of chs. 8–11. More particularly, both 43.7-9 and 8.3-6 revolve around themes of drawing near and distancing. What the people had done in 8.3-6 to draw near to the deity had prompted his departure, while in 43.7-9 the deity's return involves a reversal of those earlier conditions. Furthermore, argues Odell distinctively, both visions refer to the offensive presence of cult statues. In 8.3-6, the statue in question had been the 'image of jealousy', while in 43.7-9, the offensive objects are *pigrê malᵉkêhem*. This Hebrew phrase is rendered in the NRSV as 'the corpses of their kings': 'The house of Israel shall no more defile my holy name, neither they nor their kings, by their whoring and by the corpses of their kings at their death (*pigrê malᵉkêhem bāmôtām*)' (43.7), and again, 'Now let them put away their idolatry (*zᵉnûtām*) and the corpses of their kings (*pigrê malᵉkêhem*) far from me, and I will reside among them forever' (43.9). Odell argues that closer analysis of this phrase *pigrê malᵉkêhem* suggests that it should be understood to refer to statues commemorating offerings to the deity, and more specifically *mlk*-offerings, child sacrifices of the kind proposed by Eissfeldt long ago (Eissfeldt 1935). Without necessarily following Odell in her specific interpretation of the phrase of 43.7, 9 (for in spite of the absence of archaeological evidence to support it, the most natural sense remains the inappropriate location of royal tombs), it cannot be denied that the general parallel with ch. 8 is persuasive.

7. *The Pattern of the Temple and the Law of the Temple*

Ezekiel 43.10-12 is another passage of particular importance as far as the Temple is concerned. Here Ezekiel is told to describe the pattern of the Temple to the people of Israel, 'so that they may observe and follow the entire plan' (43.11).

The key Hebrew words used in vv. 10-11 are rare: *toknît*, 'pattern' (as Ezek. 28.12), *ṣûrâ*, 'plan', and *t^{e}kûnâ*, 'arrangement'. One is reminded of the Exodus narrative, notably Exod. 25.9, 40 (cf. 1 Chron. 28.11-12), which uses the fairly common word *tabnît* for 'pattern' or 'form' (indeed, perhaps unsurprisingly, some wish to emend *toknît* in Ezek. 43.10 to conform to that). A more remote parallel is the Platonic concept of ideals. Some moderns have wished to follow the ancients in suggesting that Greece was indebted to the biblical tradition here. It is unlikely that there is direct influence either way, though the conception is not dissimilar. One can say that the words 'so that they may observe and follow the entire plan' (43.11) seem to imply a definite expectation that the envisaged restoration of the Temple will actually happen and moreover that it will be based on the pattern given to Ezekiel in his vision.

The verse that rounds off this section 43.10-12, namely v. 12, is signalled as especially important since it both begins and ends with the words 'This is the law of the Temple'. It could be that this declaration refers back to the preceding verses, focusing on the pattern of the Temple. But another explanation is more likely. For between the two occurrences of the refrain, which feature like 'bookends' within v. 12, we read 'The whole territory on the top of the mountain all around shall be most holy'. The fact that these words are sandwiched between the double 'This is the law of the Temple' would seem to point to this as the immediate referent. The phrase used for 'most holy' is *qōdeš q^{o}dāšîm*. Here we come to another distinctive feature of Ezekiel 40–48 that demands special attention.

8. *The Diffusion of the Realm of the Most Holy in Ezekiel 40–48*

When our chapters present the three-fold structure of the Temple, the inner room (*p^{e}nîmâ*) is also called in 41.4 *qōdeš haqq^{o}dāšîm*, 'the holy of holies', as elsewhere in the Hebrew Bible. It is interesting then to find that this same phrase (but without the definite article) is used in chs. 40–48 of special areas of holiness in a more general sense. As we have just seen, in 43.12 we read 'The whole territory on the top of the mountain all around shall be most holy'. This of course affirms the holiness of the mountain top, but there is another point here too. The words 'whole' and 'all around' emphasize the breadth of the area of holiness, as though to diffuse the holiness that pertains not so much to the place as to the God who dwells. Elsewhere too we find this generalizing or spreading of the realm of the most holy, which seems surprising in a Priestly context where one expects a very sharp focus upon the defined holy place. At 45.3 we read that a section of the holy district, containing the sanctuary (*hammiqdāš*), is to be measured off, and this area as a whole is described as 'the most holy place', again *qōdeš q^{o}dāšîm* without the article. Another case, perhaps the most striking, is found in 48.12, where the whole special portion of land assigned to the Zadokites is described as 'a most holy place', again *qōdeš q^{o}dāšîm* without the article. (Incidentally, it should be noted that the English versions tend to supply the English definite article or not, according to context, frequently obscuring the particularities of the

Hebrew usage.) Kasher writes: 'This conception of the supreme sanctity of the Temple and its environs is unique to Ezekiel; nowhere else in biblical literature do we find the term 'holy of holies' as a designation for an area outside the Temple proper' (Kasher 1998: 201-202).

Does this recurrent feature (of which a further case will be encountered at the very end of the book) represent a casual or 'fuzzy' attitude to the extent of holiness in Ezekiel 40–48? No, far from it. It is to be seen in the light of Ezekiel's version of the Priestly concept of 'graded holiness'. Our chapters are passionately concerned with the proper separation between holy and common, as we see in 42.20 and 44.23. A key part of this is the notion of degrees of holiness. But in Ezekiel the whole concept is given an added dimension by the radical theocentricity, or God-centredness, of this tradition. The use of *qōdeš q^edāšîm* without the article in the above contexts does indeed take the absolute and exclusive emphasis off the inner room of the Temple as the locus of God's holy presence and this is all of a piece with the fact that it is God himself who is the focus rather than any particular institution.

9. *Altar, Access and Priesthood*

There follow in 43.13-27 the ordinances for the stone altar of burnt offering, in many ways the focus of active worship (cf. 40.47). This great stone altar is located in fact in front of the Temple itself and is to be distinguished from the smaller altar of wood, the table standing before the entrance to the inner room (41.22). The account of the arrangements for the consecration of the great stone altar culminates with the simple but powerful words, couched in classic Priestly language, in 43.27: 'and I will accept you, says the Lord God'. This echoes the strong theology of grace that characterizes the Ezekiel tradition.

Moving on to ch. 44, we read in v. 5: 'Mark well those who may be admitted to the Temple and those who are to be excluded from the sanctuary'. Foreigners, uncircumcised in heart and flesh, are not to be admitted to the sanctuary. This appears to stand in tension with the inclusive emphasis whereby in 47.21-23 aliens are to receive their share in the allotment of territory ('They shall be to you as citizens of Israel'). But the concern there seems to be with pious proselytes and with land tenure, whereas here the concern is with sinful pagans and admission to the sanctuary. The concern here is with preserving holiness and proper separation, a theme highlighted later in this chapter in the Priestly task of teaching the people the difference between the holy (*qōdeš*) and the common (*ḥōl*), the unclean (*ṭāmē'*) and the clean (*ṭāhôr*) (44.23; cf. 42.20).

Chapter 44 is best known as a classic text in discussion of the history of the priesthood. Without exploring this theme in detail in this context, let us at this point summarize the key references to priesthood from our chapters up to this point. Ezekiel 40.46 refers to a chamber 'for the priests who have charge of the altar; these are the descendants of Zadok, who alone among the descendants of Levi may come near to the Lord to minister to him'. In 43.19, at the consecration of the great altar, a bull for a sin-offering is given to the Levitical priests of the family of Zadok, who draw near to minister to God. But it is ch. 44 that develops this theme of the special status of the Zadokites. We read in v. 10 that the Levites went far from God, going astray after their idols when Israel went astray, and so 'they shall bear their punishment' (*wᵉnāśᵉʾû ʿᵃwōnām*). The reference here, historical or intertextual, is unclear; the allusion may be to Numbers 16–18 (Cook 1995b). According to Ezekiel 44, the Levites are to be permitted to serve in the Temple but it is the descendants of Zadok alone (vv. 15-27) who shall enter the sanctuary itself and approach the table, having been faithful. Famously, Wellhausen (1883: 125-57, ET 1885: 121-51) regarded Ezekiel 44 as a key turning point in the history of the priesthood, with P, the Priestly work, being later. This view has remained broadly dominant in spite of numerous critical alternatives, such as Haran's argument for the Priestly work preceding Ezekiel 40–48 (Haran 1978: 147). Most scholars have assumed that the Levites are demoted in some sense here, but this too has been contested. For example, recently Stevenson has argued that the passage is not punitive towards the Levites, but rather a text of political geography about access (Stevenson 1996: 66-78). It may be conceded that the description of the Levites in ch. 44 is ambiguous; they hold responsibilities of some honour (vv. 11 and 14) and some statements about them here are certainly more positive than the dominant theory can fully account for. Nevertheless, the most natural reading remains that the Levites are seriously criticized and indeed in some sense demoted. It could well be that, whereas the distinction between Zadokites and other priests goes back to Ezekiel himself (40.46; 43.18-27), the more polemical references to Zadokite pre-eminence (44.15-31; 48.11) come from redactional elaboration, as is argued even by Niditch, who is generally reluctant to entertain the possibility of secondary addition (Niditch 1986: 210). Interestingly, there appears to be no high priest in this Temple (Rooke 2000: 116-19). It is difficult to weigh the significance of this; is it possibly a case in which we should not make too much of silence, but Kasher has persuasively presented this as a further example of the all-sufficiency of God rendering many institutions redundant (Kasher 1998: 197).

10. *Ezekiel 40–48 and Deviations from Torah*

Another important issue concerns certain alleged deviations from Torah found in Ezekiel 40–48. According to a famous story recounted in the Babylonian Talmud (*b. Šab.* 13b), the book of Ezekiel was in danger of being 'withdrawn', but Hananiah ben Hezekiah ben Garon, a sage of the first century CE, sat in an upper chamber for as long as it took him to explain the text in ways consistent with the Torah. We learn more details elsewhere in the Babylonian Talmud, notably in *b. Men.* 45a. Ezekiel 46.6, for example, says that on the day of the new moon a young bull shall be offered, and six lambs and a ram, whereas Num. 28.11 commands that as well as a ram, *two* young bulls and *seven* lambs be offered. The Talmud reconciles these by saying that if two bulls cannot be found, one must be brought, and similarly, that if seven lambs are not to be found, six must be brought. The other problematic Ezekiel texts mentioned in this section of the Babylonian Talmud are Ezek. 44.31; 45.18, 20; and 46.7.

But it would be a mistake to regard the central issue as concerning whether Ezekiel was worthy of inclusion within the canon of scripture. The question of inconsistency with the Torah is to be seen as an 'inner-canonical' issue. Had it not been for an already established sense that the book of Ezekiel was inspired scripture, inconsistencies between Ezekiel and the Torah would not have been regarded as problematic. Such divergences might well constitute a danger to the uneducated and to that extent justify some restriction of access, but, as Barton has pointed out, the issue can be stated rather more positively: these very inconsistencies constitute 'a signal that the text contains deeper meanings which are best left to the learned' (Barton 1986: 72). With regard to two of the passages where (according to the Babylonian Talmud, *b. Men.* 45a) Ezekiel appears to contradict the Torah (namely 44.31 and 45.18), rabbinic authorities are cited in favour of deferring resolution of the problem until the promised return of Elijah (cf. Mal. 3.23-24, 4.5-6). This may at first appear to be no more than an easy way out of a problem, yet on closer inspection this strategy proves to be a sophisticated hermeneutical tactic, acknowledging an 'excess of meaning' in the text that draws us beyond our present understanding.

11. *Theological Geography*

Significant parts of the latter sections of our text are devoted to the boundaries of the land, the allocation of land to the tribes, to the city, the prince, and related matters. This material is focused in chs. 45 and 48 and might be described as an exercise in theological geography, a map whose heart and focus is the Temple and the worship of the God of Israel. Festival regulations are found in the latter part of ch. 45. A spring new year seems to be assumed (45.21; cf. 40.1). Passover and Booths feature, but not Weeks or the Day of Atonement. (For an important original reading of these and related questions, see Wagenaar 2005). Chapter 46 is the most focused treatment of the *nāśî'*, 'prince'. We discern both continuities with and differences from Davidic monarchy. The *nāśî'* has a significant role in worship, with both duties and privileges (Joyce 1998).

Ezekiel 47.1-12 presents a striking picture of a river flowing from the Temple, and down through the desert to bring life to the Dead Sea. The popular phrase 'River of Life' is actually not used (as indeed 'Chariot' is not used in ch. 1). One is conscious of many biblical echoes: Joel 4.18, ET 3.18; Zech. 14.8; Ps. 46.5, ET 4; even echoes of Eden (Tuell 2000b). But more widely there are resonances with material from Mesopotamia and Canaan, indeed mythological overtones aplenty; here, near the end of the book, one is reminded of the mythological dimension of the reference to the 'very high mountain' at the start of the vision (40.2). But though the canvas is broad, even cosmic in some ways, nevertheless we still encounter detailed measurements here in 47.1-12, and moreover the limits of the vision are those of the land of Israel (Darr 1987).

At 47.13 and indeed for the rest of the book, the reader is thrown back into the 'nitty gritty' of precise theological geography, with the boundaries and tribal allocations. It may be noted that, whereas Joseph has two portions, one each for

Ephraim and Manasseh (47.13), Levi receives no regular tribal territory (cf. 44.28). Instead, Levites and Zadokites each have their special territory in the heart of the land, with the Temple fittingly in the midst of the Zadokite territory (48.8-14).

The book ends on a profound note. After the allocation of the twelve city gates, one to each tribe (48.30-34; Joseph has one gate only, so that Levi can have one), the book concludes (in 48.35) with the statement that 'The name of the city from that time on shall be *yhwh šāmmâ*, "The Lord is There"'. A magnificently theocentric note for this most God-centred of biblical books to end on! 'The Lord is There'. Where? Not the Temple, in this case. That is away to the north, according to Ezekiel's theological geography. Assuming that the reference is indeed to the city itself and that the word *šāmmâ* is not meant to point *away* from the city and to the Temple, this is a final striking case of Ezekiel 40–48 both emphasizing the location of the holy, but also diffusing or spreading it—all within, of course, a highly-ordered theocentric system: *yhwh šāmmâ*, 'The Lord is There'.

Bibliography

Barton, J.

1986 *Oracles of God: Perceptions of Ancient Prophecy in Israel after the Exile* (London: Darton, Longman & Todd).

Bertholet, A. (with K. Galling)

1936 *Hesekiel* (HAT, 13; Tübingen: J.C.B. Mohr [Paul Siebeck]).

Blenkinsopp, J.

1990 *Ezekiel* (Interpretation Commentary; Louisville, KY: John Knox Press).

Block, D.I.

2000 'Divine Abandonment: Ezekiel's Adaptation of an Ancient Near Eastern Motif', in Odell and Strong (eds.) 2000: 15-42.

Bodi, D.

1991 *The Book of Ezekiel and the Poem of Erra* (OBO, 104; Freiburg, Schweiz: Universitätsverlag/Göttingen: Vandenhoeck & Ruprecht).

Childs, B.S.

1979 *Introduction to the Old Testament as Scripture* (London: SCM Press).

Clements, R.E.

1986 'The Chronology of Redaction in Ezekiel 1–24', in Lust (ed.) 1986: 283-94. Reprinted in R.E. Clements, *Old Testament Prophecy: From Oracles to Canon* (Louisville, KY: Westminster/John Knox Press, 1996).

Collins, T.

1993 *The Mantle of Elijah: The Redactional Criticism of the Prophetical Books* (The Biblical Seminar, 20; Sheffield: JSOT Press).

Cook, S.L.

1995a *Prophecy and Apocalypticism: The Postexilic Social Setting* (Minneapolis: Fortress Press).

1995b 'Innerbiblical Interpretation in Ezekiel 44 and the History of Israel's Priesthood', *JBL* 114: 193-208.

Cooke, G.A.

1936 *A Critical and Exegetical Commentary on the Book of Ezekiel* (ICC; Edinburgh: T. & T. Clark).

Darr, K.P.

1987 'The Wall Around Paradise: Ezekielian Ideas About the Future', *VT* 37: 271-79.

Eichrodt, W.

1968 *Der Prophet Hesekiel* (ATD, 22; Göttingen: Vandenhoeck & Ruprecht, 3rd edn). ET *Ezekiel* (trans. Cosslett Quin; OTL; London: SCM Press, 1970).

Eissfeldt, O.

1935 *Molk als Opferbegriff im Punischen und Hebräischen und das Ende das Gottes Moloch* (Halle: Max Niemeyer).

Filson, F.V.

1943 'The Omission of Ezekiel 12 26-28 and 36 23b-38 in Codex 967', *JBL* 62: 27-32.

Fohrer, G. (with K. Galling)

1955 *Ezechiel* (HAT, 13; Tübingen: J.C.B. Mohr [Paul Siebeck]).

Gese, H.

1957 *Der Verfassungsentwurf des Ezechiel (Kap. 40–48) traditionsgeschichtlich untersucht* (Beiträge zur historischen Theologie, 25; Tübingen: J.C.B. Mohr [Paul Siebeck]).

Gorman, F.H., Jr

1990 *The Ideology of Ritual: Space, Time and Status in the Priestly Theology* (JSOTSup, 91; Sheffield, JSOT Press).

Goudoever, J. van

1986 'Ezekiel Sees in Exile a New Temple-City at the Beginning of a Jobel Year', in Lust (ed.) 1986: 344-49.

Greenberg, M.

1984 'The Design and Themes of Ezekiel's Program of Restoration', *Int* 38: 181-208. Reprinted in Mays and Achtemeier (eds.) 1987: 215-36.

Hanson, P.D.

1979 *The Dawn of Apocalyptic: The Historical and Sociological Roots of Jewish Apocalyptic Eschatology* (Philadelphia: Fortress Press, rev. edn).

Haran, M.

1978 *Temples and Temple-Service in Ancient Israel: An Inquiry into the Character of Cult Phenomena and the Historical Setting of the Priestly School* (Oxford: Clarendon Press).

Hurowitz, V.A.

1992 *I Have Built You an Exalted House: Temple Building in the Bible in Light of Mesopotamian and Northwest Semitic Writings* (JSOTSup, 115; ASOR Monograph Series, 5; Sheffield: JSOT Press).

Jenson, P.P.

1992 *Graded Holiness: A Key to the Priestly Conception of the World* (JSOTSup, 106; Sheffield: JSOT Press).

Jones, D.R.

1963 'The Cessation of Sacrifice after the Destruction of the Temple in 586 B.C.', *JTS* NS 14: 12-31.

Joyce, P.M.

1995 'Synchronic and Diachronic Perspectives on Ezekiel', in J.C. de Moor (ed.), *Synchronic or Diachronic? A Debate on Method in Old Testament Exegesis* (OTS, 34; Leiden: E.J. Brill): 115-28.

1996 'Dislocation and Adaptation in the Exilic Age and After', in J. Barton and D.J. Reimer (eds.), *After the Exile: Essays in Honour of Rex Mason* (Macon, GA: Mercer University Press): 45-58.

1998 'King and Messiah in Ezekiel', in J. Day (ed.), *King and Messiah in Israel and the Ancient Near East* (JSOTSup, 270; Sheffield: Sheffield Academic Press): 323-37.

Kasher, R.
1998 'Anthropomorphism, Holiness and Cult: A New Look at Ezek 40–48', *ZAW* 110: 192-208.

Kennett, R.H.
1928 *Old Testament Essays* (Cambridge: Cambridge University Press).

Kutsko, J.F.
2000 *Between Heaven and Earth: Divine Presence and Absence in the Book of Ezekiel* (Biblical and Judaic Studies from the University of California, San Diego, 7; Winona Lake, IN: Eisenbrauns).

Lemke, W.E.
1984 'Life in the Present and Hope for the Future', *Int* 38: 165-80. Reprinted in Mays and Achtemeier (eds.) 1987: 200-14.

Levenson, J.D.
1976 *Theology of the Program of Restoration of Ezekiel 40–48* (HSM, 10; Missoula, MT: Scholars Press).

Lust, J.
1980 'De samenhang van Ez. 36–40. Theologische relevantie van het ontbreken van Ez. 36,23c-38 in enkele handschriften', *Tijdschrift voor Theologie* 20: 26-39.
1981 'Ezekiel 36–40 in the Oldest Greek Manuscript', *CBQ* 43: 517-33.

Lust, J. (ed.)
1986 *Ezekiel and his Book: Textual and Literary Criticism and their Interrelation* (BETL, 74; Leuven: Leuven University Press/Peeters).

Mays, J.L., and P.J. Achtemeier (eds.)
1987 *Interpreting the Prophets* (Philadelphia: Fortress Press).

Niditch, S.
1986 'Ezekiel 40–48 in Visionary Context', *CBQ* 48: 208-24.

Odell, M.S.
2004 'What Was the Image of Jealousy in Ezekiel 8?', in L.L. Grabbe and A. Ogden Bellis (eds.), *The Priests in the Prophets: The Portrayal of Priests, Prophets, and Other Religious Specialists in the Latter Prophets* (JSOTSup, 408; London and New York: T. & T. Clark International): 134-48.

Odell, M.S., and J.T. Strong (eds.)
2000 *The Book of Ezekiel: Theological and Anthropological Perspectives* (SBL Symposium Series, 9; Atlanta: SBL).

Parunak, H. van Dyke
1980 'The Literary Architecture of Ezekiel's *Mar'ôt 'Ĕlōhîm*', *JBL* 99: 61-74.

Plöger, O.
1962 *Theokratie und Eschatologie* (WMANT, 2; Neukirchen–Vluyn: Kreis Moers, Neukirchener Verlag, rev. edn). ET: *Theocracy and Eschatology* (trans. S. Rudman; Oxford: Basil Blackwell, 1968).

Pohlmann, K.F. (with T.A. Rudnig)
2001 *Der Prophet Hesekiel/Ezechiel Kapitel 20–48* (ATD, 22.2; Göttingen: Vandenhoeck & Ruprecht).

Rooke, D.W.
2000 *Zadok's Heirs: The Role and Development of the High Priesthood in Ancient Israel* (Oxford Theological Monographs Series; Oxford: Oxford University Press).

Rudnig, T.A.
2000 *Heilig und Profan: Redaktionskritische Studien zu Ez 40–48* (BZAW, 287; Berlin and New York: W. de Gruyter).

Stevenson, K.R.
1996 *The Vision of Transformation: The Territorial Rhetoric of Ezekiel 40–48* (SBLDS, 154; Atlanta: Scholars Press).

Talmon, S.
1999 'Mas 1043-2220 (MasEzek) (Ezek. 35.11–38.14)', Principal Edition, in *Masada VI: The Yigael Yadin Excavations 1963–1965, Final Reports* (Jerusalem: Israel Exploration Society/The Hebrew University of Jerusalem): 59-75.

Tuell, S.S.
1992 *The Law of the Temple in Ezekiel 40–48* (HSM, 49; Atlanta: Scholars Press).
1996 'Ezekiel 40–42 as a Verbal Icon', *CBQ* 58: 649-64.
2000a 'Divine Presence and Absence in Ezekiel's Prophecy', in Odell and Strong (eds.) 2000: 97-116.
2000b 'Ezekiel 47.1-12 and Gen 2.10-14', in W.P. Brown and S. Dean McBride (eds.), *God Who Creates: Essays in Honor of W. Sibley Towner* (Grand Rapids: Eerdmans): 171-89.

Vogt, E.
1981 *Untersuchungen zum Buch Ezechiel* (AnBib, 95; Rome: Pontifical Biblical Institute).

Wagenaar, J.A.
2005 'The Priestly Festival and the Babylonian New Year Festivals: Origin and Transformation of the Ancient Israelite Festival Year', in R.P. Gordon and J.C. de Moor (eds.), *The Old Testament in its World* (OTS, 52; Leiden: E.J. Brill): 218-52.

Wevers, J.W.
1969 *Ezekiel* (NCB; London: Thomas Nelson).

Wellhausen, J.
1883 *Prolegomena zur Geschichte Israels* (Berlin: G. Reimer). ET: *Prolegomena to the History of Israel* (trans. J.S. Black and A. Menzies; Edinburgh: A. & C. Black, 1885).

Zimmerli, W.
1968 'Planungen für den Wiederaufbau nach der Katastrophe von 587', *VT* 18: 229-55. Reprinted in W. Zimmerli, *Studien zur alttestamentlichen Theologie und Prophetie: Gesammelte Aufsätze II* (ThB, 51; Munich: Chr. Kaiser Verlag, 1974): 165-91. ET: 'Plans for Rebuilding after the Catastrophe of 587', in W. Zimmerli, *I am Yahweh* (ed. W. Bruggemann; Atlanta: John Knox Press, 1982): 111-33.
1979 *Ezechiel* (BKAT, 13.2; Neukirchen–Vluyn: Neukirchener Verlag, 2nd edn). ET: *Ezekiel*, II (trans. J.D. Martin; Hermeneia; Philadelphia: Fortress Press, 1983).

Divine Reversal and the Role of the Temple in Trito-Isaiah

Jill Middlemas

The questions of the authorship and provenance of Isaiah 56–66 have exerted a great deal of influence in Isaiah studies since B. Duhm, noting differences in style and setting, argued in 1892 for the separation of the final eleven chapters from Isaiah 40–55.[1] Among those who accept a Third Isaiah distinct from Deutero-Isaiah, the key issues have revolved around the authorship, its unity[2] or lack thereof,[3] and the nature of the community revealed by the text.[4] The communal concern with the *Sitz im Leben* or, more appropriately, the *Sitz in der Gemeinde*, primarily focuses on a growing division between two distinct groups within the community. Influential in this respect is Hanson, who argues that the struggle for control of the Temple by competing groups plays a central role in the Trito-Isaiah material. With regard to the centrality of the Temple to the issue, he is joined by J. Blenkinsopp (1984: 249-50; 1990), but the attribution of tension to other sources is not uncommon. Alternative suggestions include class conflict (Berquist 1995: 79), the question of possession of the land, the inclusion of foreigners in worship (Sekine 1989; Koenen 1990), competition between syncretistic worshippers of Yahweh and those who worship Yahweh alone (M. Smith 1987: 75-95; Schramm 1995), and inappropriate practices of the priests (Rofé 1985). P.A. Smith (1995) provides a helpful corrective by arguing that a straightforward dichotomy between two distinct groups is too simplistic. Instead, he sees that clear lines cannot be drawn based on the attribution of particular issues to specific parties, but rather, the general nature of the criticism suggests the existence of a pietistic group whose main concern is that the rebuilding of the Temple does not distract from the proper worship of Yahweh. In his view, the construction of the Temple serves as a catalyst for the development of the Isaianic

1. Duhm 1892. Duhm's ascription of Isa. 56–66 to an author separate from that of 40–55 has been widely accepted. However, a minority of scholars continues to raise important arguments that support the unified authorship of chs. 40–66: Torrey 1928; Haran 1963; Smart 1965; Maass 1967; Kaufmann 1970: 68-87; Murtonen 1980–81; Barstad 1997; Holladay 1997; Sommer 1998: 187-92.

2. Elliger 1928, followed by Bonnard 1972; Scullion 1982; Knight 1985. An interesting case has been made for a single author living in exilic Judah by McCullough 1948.

3. Cheyne 1895; Volz 1932; Fohrer 1964; Westermann 1986 (1966), ET 1969; Pauritsch 1971; Sehmsdorf 1972; Vermeylen 1977–78; Sekine 1989; Koenen 1990; Steck 1991; Lau 1994; Berges 1998.

4. Hanson 1975; Blenkinsopp 1984; Sekine 1989; Koenen 1990; Schramm 1995; P.A. Smith 1995.

prophecies. Although all the theories differ in specific points, according to these analyses the central issue at stake in Trito-Isaiah is possession of the Temple. The Temple as the locus for an erupting schism in the community raises questions about its role in Trito-Isaiah, a topic hitherto regrettably unexamined. The following essay hopes to contribute to the current debate about the social setting of the material by focusing exclusively on the use of the Temple in the material ascribed to the Trito-Isaiah tradition.

Even though the material in Trito-Isaiah has been used to support a variety of proposals about the Temple, relatively speaking there are few texts that refer to it outright. Throughout chs. 56–66, the prophet uses multivalent vocabulary when speaking about the central sanctuary. Terms that clearly connote the Temple include 'house' (56.5, 7; 60.7; 64.10, ET 11; 66.1), 'altar' (56.7; 60.7), 'sanctuary' (60.13; 63.18), 'place of Yahweh's feet' (60.13; 66.1), 'courts of my sanctuary' (62.9), and 'Temple' (66.6). More uncertain terms include 'Zion' (59.20; 60.14; 61.3; 62.1, 11; 63.18; 64.9, ET 10; 66.8), 'gates' (62.10), and 'mountain' or 'holy mountain' (56.7; 57.7, 13; 65.11, 25; 66.20[5]). Based on the criterion of vocabulary alone, only one verse specifically mentions the Temple as *hêkāl*. On the whole, prophecies about the sanctuary occupy less pride of place than the main theme of the final chapters of Isaiah which focus on what the Lord is doing and has yet to do in the human realm and how covenant partner, Israel, honours its God in the early return. It is prudent, therefore, to isolate the texts that actually refer to the Temple and assess their importance within the overall message of Trito-Isaiah with particular attention to the question of its role as the focus of competition between two groups in society or within the priesthood.

1. *Non-Temple Texts*

Various analyses include the referents Zion, gates and a high and lofty mountain in discussions about the Temple in Trito-Isaiah. As the following discussion will show, none of these actually refers to the sanctuary.

In his study of Trito-Isaiah, P.D. Hanson, following C. Westermann, notes a nucleus of material in chs. 60–62 that, although strikingly similar to the prophecies of Deutero-Isaiah, nevertheless should be regarded as distinct from them.[6] In these chapters Hanson utilizes the proper noun Zion in a general sense to refer to the city of Jerusalem.[7] Although Hanson is somewhat ambiguous in his use of

5. Isa. 66.20 comes from a third redactional layer (66.18-24) in which the inner-community focus of the prophecies of Trito-Isaiah are expanded to include the theme of the gathering of the nations. Thematically and stylistically it is different and will not be discussed in this paper. See further, Davies 1989; P.A. Smith 1995: 131-32.

6. See Hanson 1975: 59-64; Westermann 1986 (1966): 237-39, ET 1969: 296-300; Elliger 1928; 1931: 112-40; Zimmerli 1963. There is, however, a significant degree of overlap between chs. 60–62 and 40–55. Snaith (1967), argues that chs. 60–62 ought to be attributed to Deutero-Isaiah while Fishbane (1985: 289) highlights the compatibility with the oracles of Isa. 1–39.

7. Zion occurs in the core material in 60.14; 62.1, 11. The MT has 'Zion' in 61.3, but with Hanson (1975: 57) *lāśûm laʾᵃbēlî ṣiyyôn* is to be seen as a gloss clarifying the identity of the mourners in the previous verse. It is not translated in the LXX. Its current placement overbalances the

language in denoting the referent Zion as the city in the core material of chs. 60–62 (Hanson 1975: 72-75), an examination of the parallelism of the texts shows that it is used exclusively for the city.[8] In his analysis, the use of Zion in the material outside chs. 60–62 narrows to refer solely to the Temple. As such, texts including Zion contribute to his argument for the escalating division in the community (Hanson 1975: 92, 95-97, 99, 133-34, 152-53, 180). Though he can argue his case using other language for the Temple, it is not possible simply to read 'Temple' for Zion. A critical study of the texts in which Zion appears reveals that in no way are the two synonymous. Zion occurs in three places outside the nucleus (59.20; 64.9, ET 10; 66.8). In each case Zion appears to represent a geographical location—the city of Jerusalem.

In an oracle predicting the advent of a redeemer, Zion in Isa. 59.20 represents the city of Jerusalem. The reference to Zion occurs in a salvation oracle (vv. 15b-21) that closes a statement of judgment in which a communal lament has been inserted (vv. 1-15a). In it the prophet assures the community that 'He will come to Zion as a redeemer and to those who repent of transgression in Jacob' (59.20; cf. 1.27). In the context of vv. 18-20, which portray Yahweh's recompense on foreign nations and Israel, v. 20 provides a fitting conclusion by shifting the focus to Yahweh's purposes for the city of Jerusalem and its inhabitants.[9] In another place, through metaphor, the poet prophesies about the speed with which divine restoration will be brought about by comparing Zion to a mother who gives birth to a nation in an instant (66.7-10). In v. 8, Zion depicted as a mother is really the nation or city which becomes full after the repatriation of the exiles. The call to 'rejoice with Jerusalem' in v. 10 supports an understanding of the city in the preceding one. The clearest example of Zion as city occurs in the communal lament where Zion is directly parallel to Jerusalem in v. 64.9 (ET 10). In 64.9 (ET 10), the community laments the present abysmal state of Zion in vivid language: 'Your holy cities[10] have become a wilderness, Zion has become a desert, Jerusalem a desolation'. Here Zion and Jerusalem are used interchangeably. The community emphasizes the destruction of the land to add weight to their appeal for restoration. The poem is used by Hanson to show a transition to a developing

line and oddly has no accusative for *lāśûm* where one is expected. Besides, it includes the Judahite population in a poem which otherwise deals entirely with the exilic community. There have been numerous attempts to understand its placement in the MT. See Koenen 1988a: 567-68.

8. Zion is used in parallel with 'the city of Yahweh' in 60.14, 'Jerusalem' in 62.1, and the oracle pronounced to Zion in 62.11 is completed in 62.12 with the ascription 'A city not forsaken'.

9. P.A. Smith 1995: 124-25; Blenkinsopp 2003: 196-97.

10. MT *'ārê qodšᵉkā* supported by 1QIsa[a]. The LXX and Vulgate most likely perceived it as a specific reference to Zion and translate in the singular 'your holy city'. The cities of Judah could be referred to as holy. In support, Westermann (1986 [1966]: 315-16, ET 1969: 397-98) and Whybray (1975: 266), point out that Mesopotamian myths depict the whole land as blessed by a sanctuary and the Old Testament, in particular, envisions the whole land as holy (Zech 2.16, ET 12). In this context, it is reasonable to suppose that the community utilizes the image of the cities to convey a sense of the general mass destruction wrought by the Babylonians along with the more particular loss of the nation's political and religious centre as a means to portray the awesome nature of the devastation. Furthermore, destroyed cities of Judah are depicted in Isa. 1.7; Jer. 1.15; 4.7, 16, 26; 5.6, 17; 7.34, etc.; Lam. 5.11.

apocalyptic eschatology that emerges as a reaction to the defilement and the monopolistic control of the sanctuary by a hierocratic party. As we have seen, Hanson's understanding of Zion in this way is not consistent with the representation either in this exilic lament or elsewhere in the material. The Temple cannot serve merely as a substitute for Zion. Zion in the material outside chs. 60–62 corresponds more naturally to the city of Jerusalem (but see Steck 1989).

Another location where the Temple has been understood is Isa. 62.10, where the prophet exhorts the people to clear the way and prepare the highways for the imminent return of the exiles. As part of their task, they are told to 'Go through, go through the gates' and to 'prepare the way of the people' (v. 10). R.N. Whybray argues that the preparation is a symbolic means by which to encourage a way of life devoted to Yahweh. In his reading, the gates are those of the Temple through which one must pass to serve this end (Whybray 1981: 251). It is, however, more natural to understand the whole passage as an exhortation to the citizens of Jerusalem to go out through the gates to prepare the roads leading into the city for the expected returnees (cf. Isa. 40.3; 57.14; Jer. 50.5) (Volz 1932: 252-53; Westermann 1986 [1966]: 300-301, ET 1969: 378-79). Elsewhere in the Isaiah tradition, 'gates' unambiguously represent those of cities (Isa. 14.31; 22.7; 24.12; 26.2; 28.6; 29.21; 45.1; 54.12). Although the use of *'br b^{e}* ('to cross into') connotes the entryway of a city (Judg. 9.26; Ezek. 9.4, 5; Joel 4.17, ET 3.17), it speaks more commonly of marching through a land (Lev. 26.6; Num. 13.32; 14.7; 20.17; 21.22; Deut. 2.27; Judg. 8.21; 34.10, etc.), country (Gen. 41.46; Exod. 12.23; Ezek. 14.15, 17), or territory (Num. 20.21; 21.23; Deut. 2.4; Judg. 11.20) (Delitzsch 1892: 410). F. Delitzsch, therefore, suggests that the more common use, that of passing through a country, provides evidence that the call goes out to the exiles in Babylon encouraging them to go through the gates of that city on their way home. However, the entire poem directs its attention to Zion and the redemption that Yahweh is bringing about. Furthermore, 'gates' are found elsewhere in Trito-Isaiah only in the midst of a poem that is directly addressed to the city of Jerusalem in 60.11 and 18. Their use in these verses illustrates the peaceable city. Within the closely unified section of chs. 60–62 it is more natural to understand Isa. 62.10 as containing a reference to the gates of the city of Jerusalem through which the Judahites are meant to go to prepare the way for the homebound exiles.

In Isaiah, as elsewhere in the Hebrew Bible, the 'holy mountain of Yahweh' or 'my holy mountain' clearly envisions the Temple mount (Isa. 56.7; 65.11, 25; 66.20), but there is one text in Trito-Isaiah which speaks of a 'high and lofty mountain' that is not designated *har qodšî* (57.13) Although a few scholars have equated it with the Temple mount (Hanson 1975: 199-200; Beuken 1986; Sawyer 1989: 100; Ackerman 1992: 113-14; Biddle 1996), it seems likely that this is not the case. In the midst of an indictment against the leaders of the people and the people themselves in 57.3-13,[11] the prophet brings forth the following charge, 'Upon a high and lofty mountain you have made your bed, you surely have gone

11. Understanding the full oracle to begin at 56.9 with Hanson (1975: 186-89).

up to make a sacrifice there' (57.7). Occurring in a speech directed to an anonymous woman, the rebuke extends from vv. 6-13. The unmarked shift in person between vv. 2 and 3 from second masculine plural to second feminine singular suggests that the speaker addresses someone already identified; in this case, the mother of the transgressing children mentioned in v. 3 who is labelled there as a sorceress, an adulteress[12] and a harlot. The use of magical arts and the description of sexual deviance in the context of rebellion (*peša'*) and falsehood (*šeqer*) reveal the issue at stake to be that of apostate worship. In contrast to the marked anonymity of the woman of Isa. 57.3 and 6-13, prophecies addressed to a woman using second feminine forms elsewhere in Trito-Isaiah always mention Zion (60.14; 62.1, 11; 66.8). Moreover, the prophetic oracles directed at Zion figured as a woman are exclusively positive, proclaiming only salvation and redemption, never condemnation as in vv. 12, 20-21. It follows that the mountain in v. 7 is a figurative mountain that takes the place of the true worship of Yahweh,[13] thus eliciting the divine protest in 57.11: 'but me you did not remember, you did not call it to mind'. The rebuke is reminiscent of the charge against those who worship Gad and Meni in 65.11, where the deity declares, 'you are the forsakers of Yahweh, the ones who forget my holy mountain'. The description of the mountain *gābōah w*^e^*niśśā'* in Isa. 57.7 associates it with all the high and lofty things that will be defeated on the day of the Lord as in Isa. 2.12-14 (cf. 5.15; 10.33; and 37.23 of the lofty eyes of Sennacherib) and further distinguishes it from Yahweh who is entitled *rām w*^e^*niśśā'* in 57.15 (cf. 6.1; 33.10; and 52.13 of Yahweh's servant). In stark contrast to the salvation predicted for the Temple and the holy mountain of Yahweh, the fate of the high and lofty mountain raised up in distinction to the proper worship of Yahweh is doom and destruction.[14]

12. MT has *m*^e^*nā'ēp*, piel masculine singular participle 'adulterer'. *BHS* suggests the feminine piel participle. 1QIsa^{a} has a noun and the versions all translate it as a masculine noun. However, the relationship between the substantized participle 'adulterer/ess' and the *waw* consecutive second person feminine imperfect of *znh* suggests that there is something amiss. Like Ackerman (1992: 102), it seems to me that *m*^e^*nā'epet w*^e^*zōnâ* was divided incorrectly as *m*^e^*nā'ēp twznh* which resulted in the further corruption by metathesis of the *waw* and *taw*. This slight emendation yields a list of three feminine participles. The emendation is supported by the fact that the prophet condemns a plural male audience in vv. 3-5 and a single woman in vv. 6-13a, but never a single male. In fact, an oracle of salvation is directed to a single male (57.13b). Further, many of the scholars who translate 'adulterer' here also understand Zion as the referent of the oracle. Yahweh is referred to as father (63.16; 64.7, ET 8) and as the one who will wed Zion (62.4-5). It is surely incorrect to translate 'adulterer' when the complete Trito-Isaiah corpus suggests that Yahweh is the husband of Zion and the father of the community!

13. A variety of proposals have sought to delineate the types of illicit worship practices referred to here. Lewis (1989: 143-58) suggests ancestor worship; Schmidt (1994: 254-59) finds the consistent representation of the worship of Molech; Ackerman (1992: 101-63) argues for a variety of syncretistic practices; Schramm (1995: 131-33) and Nihan (2001) argue along similar lines to Ackerman.

14. Cf. Jones 1963: 18-19: 'The cumulative effect of this passage is to suggest that the superstitious rites, denounced by the prophet, were practised in the favoured old Canaanite sacred places... There is not a hint that any of this was actually attempted in the sacred precincts of the ruined Temple itself.' Middlemas (2003: 96-98, 123-31, 167-77) contains a more complete discussion of the syntax and referents of this text.

Thus far, the elimination of three referents has narrowed the semantic field for the study of the Temple and its role in Trito-Isaiah. References to neither Zion, nor gates, nor the high and lofty mountain of 57.7 can illuminate a discussion about the role of the Temple in chs. 56–66. It remains to consider the texts about the Temple and how they elucidate the use of the sanctuary within the prophecies of Trito-Isaiah.

2. *Temple Texts in the Nucleus*

As previously mentioned, Westermann first isolated a group of oracles linguistically and stylistically similar to the oracles of Deutero-Isaiah in chs. 60–62 (followed by Pauritsch 1971: 241-44; Bonnard 1972: 319; Hanson 1975: 46). The significant amount of overlap in vocabulary and themes with the material in Deutero-Isaiah suggests that the author of the nucleus comes from the same circle as the prophet of the exile. Further, the difference in location and emphasis makes it unlikely that what is known as the 'core nucleus' should be attributed to the same hand as that of Isaiah 40–55.

In spite of the general acceptance of a core nucleus at chs. 60–62, several helpful qualifications have been made. The first is that of P.A. Smith, who persuasively argues on the basis of language and the inseparable nature of restoration from vindication that the nucleus extends to 63.6 (Smith 1995: 38-44). The second point, which is more important for this study, is that although it resembles Deutero-Isaiah, the material also draws heavily upon the prophecies of Isaiah of Jerusalem (Fishbane 1985: 497-99). Finally, B. Schramm reveals that the outlook of the core material is similar to that of Ezekiel 33–37 with the substantial difference that the prophecies remain silent on the issue of the reinstallation of the Davidic dynasty and the reunification of the northern and southern kingdoms (Schramm 1995: 144-45). Although approaches to these chapters vary, there is general agreement that they deal exclusively with the theme of salvation. Moreover, the concentration on unconditional restoration found therein is in stark contrast to the material that surrounds it. Outside 60.1–63.6 the message is one in which the conditions for participation in the community in the salvific era predominate. The difference in the nature and outlook of the nucleus and the outer material is sufficient justification to consider separately the role of the Temple in each, not to mention, of course, that it represents a separate layer of redaction.

Throughout the core material the prophet views the sanctuary in Jerusalem as only a minor detail within the grander scheme of the advent of Yahweh's planned redemption. In fact, the Temple is referred to only three times (60.7, 13; 62.9). The primary focus is on what the deity is doing within Israel and without. The entire message brims with words of salvation, joy, jubilation and blessing, depicted variously as the wealth of nations flowing to Jerusalem, foreign kings bending low in submission and bearing gifts, sacrificial animals leaping upon the altar of the Temple eager to present themselves as offerings, and blessings lavished upon the people. No hint of condemnation appears in these chapters because they focus on a single pervading theme, the fulfilment of expectations based on the promises of Deutero-Isaiah that the advent of the Lord is nigh, bringing with it a great coup in the world of humankind and, through it, the reversal of the dire predictions of Proto-Isaiah (Fishbane 1985: 497-98; cf. Isa. 60.1-2, 17-19 and 9.1-3; 60.3, 5, 14, 17 and 2.1-4; 60.14 and 12.6; 62.4 and 1.7; 62.10-12 and 11.10). The conditions of the past, signified by the judgment of the people, deportation away from the homeland, and servitude to foreign nations, will be overturned. As the people are blessed through Yahweh's intervention, the Temple itself will be blessed.

In the nucleus, the Temple is explicitly referred to twice in ch. 60. The first reference (60.7) occurs in what is more a poem about the day of Zion than the day of Yahweh (Volz 1932: 239). In it the dual imagery of light[15] and movement[16] graphically conveys the sense of the glory of the upcoming eschatological event and Jerusalem's place at its centre. In contrast to the gloom that pervades the preceding chapter (Torrey 1928: 444-45), the light and glory of Yahweh radiate outward from Jerusalem to encompass the entire earth.[17] Although the city of Zion is the main focus of the predictions, part of its transformation from a state of gloom and ruin includes the restoration of the Temple (cf. 61.4). Indeed, in what can only be considered a touch of nationalistic spirit, the prophet declares that 'All the flocks of Kedar will be assembled to you, the rams of Nebaioth will serve you,[18] they will leap up with acceptance[19] on my altar and I will beautify my beautiful house' (60.7; cf. v. 10). The picture is one in which sacrificial animals abound, ready and willing to be offered to the God of Jerusalem who is further depicted as the Lord of all the earth. Foreign peoples in submission travel to the city with tribute to participate in rebuilding the city and the Temple (60.10, 12).

The construction of the Temple is also implied in 60.13: 'The glory of Lebanon comes to you, the cypress, the juniper and the pine together, to beautify the place of my sanctuary. I will make honorable the place of my feet.' Although C.C. Torrey understands the trees as adornment for the city (Torrey 1928: 452; cf. Muilenburg 1956: 703), it is more natural to regard 'the place of my sanctuary' and 'the place of my feet' as references to the Temple. Speaking of the Temple as the throne of Yahweh, Jer. 17.12 has *m*^{e}*qôm miqdāšēnû* ('the place of our sanctuary'). Elsewhere *miqdāš* is used of the sanctuary of Moab (Isa. 16.12), the holy places or the holiest portion of the house of the Lord (Jer. 51.51 and Ezek. 45.3; 48.8, 10, 21 respectively), and of the Temple (Isa. 63.18; Lam. 1.10; 2.7, 20; Ezek. 5.11; 8.6; 9.6; 23.38, 39; 24.21; 25.3; etc.). Although *m*^{e}*qôm*

15. The plethora of words having to do with light include *'ôr*, 60.1 (twice), 3, 19 (twice), 20; *zrḥ*, vv. 1, 2, 3, *nōgah*, v. 3; *nhr*, v. 5; *tip'eret*, vv. 7, 19; *p'r*, vv. 7, 9, 13, 21; *kābôd*, vv. 1, 2, 13 (twice); *gā'ôn*, v. 15. On the centrality of light, see Volz 1932: 243-44.

16. *bô'*, vv. 1, 4 (twice), 5, 6, 11, 13, 14, 20; *qbṣ*, vv. 4, 7; hiphil of *bô'*, vv. 6, 9, 17 (twice). On the emphasis on light and movement as the dual foci of the chapter, see Muilenburg 1956: 697-98; Westermann 1986 (1966): 283-84, ET 1969: 356; Achtemeier 1982: 83-84.

17. On *kābôd* as a term of divine epiphany, see Muilenburg 1956: 697-98, and Isa. 4.4-6; cf. Exod. 24.16-17; Num. 14.10; Deut. 5.23-27; 1 Kgs 8.11; Ezek. 1.1-28; Hab. 2.14.

18. *Y*^{e}*šār*^{e}*tûnek* is attested by MT, Vulgate, Targum, and 1QIsa^{a}, but LXX '(they) shall come'. *BHS* suggests deleting.

19. MT has *'al-rāṣôn mizb*^{e}*ḥî* but 1QIsa^{a}, LXX, Targum and Peshitta read *l*^{e}*rāṣôn 'al-mizb*^{e}*ḥî*, cf. 56.7.

raglay ('the place of my feet') does not occur elsewhere in the Hebrew Bible, the closest parallels speak of the Temple as *hᵃdôm raglāyw* ('his [Yahweh's] footstool', Lam. 2.1) and as *mᵉqôm kappôt raglay* ('the place for the souls of my feet', Ezek. 43.7).[20] Even as the interior of the Temple is glorified by the presence of Yahweh as in v. 7, so the external form of the Temple will be beautified by the types of foreign timber used in its rebuilding.[21] In ch. 60, which serves as the introduction to the central message of the Trito-Isaiah material, the restoration of the Temple is just one consequence of the future advent of Yahweh.

The other reference to the Temple in the nucleus serves as a vehicle to express the renewal of the economic vitality of the people. We read 'But those who reap it will eat it, and they will praise Yahweh; and those who gather it will drink it in my holy courts' (62.9).[22] Instead of sending the choicest of the produce gathered by Jewish workers as tax to an imperial government, the promise insists that the people will be able to celebrate their great feasts within the courts of the Temple (62.8b-9) (Muilenburg 1956: 721-22; Bonnard 1972: 430). It was common practice in the ancient Near East for subject nations to pay a substantial amount of tax, sometimes in the form of foodstuffs, to the imperial government. Since the watchmen in vv. 6-7 are depicted as petitioning on behalf of the people, the vision of celebrating with a cornucopia of food in the Temple is predictive (Hanson 1975: 69). Further, as the grand predictions of Deutero-Isaiah have not yet been accomplished for Jerusalem and the people, the forthcoming salvific intervention of Yahweh is seen as re-establishing normative worship at the Temple. As such the choicest produce will no longer be sent away; rather, it will be enjoyed by a people whose overlord is no human power, but Yahweh alone. In this way, it is perhaps related to the reinstitution of the practice of bringing the first fruits to the Temple during Israel's great pilgrimage festivals (Westermann 1986 [1966]: 300-301, ET 1969: 378; Whybray 1975: 250; Watts 1987: 319).

The future salvation of Jerusalem concomitant with that of the people of Israel results from a divine reversal in every facet of the present circumstances. Although the Temple does not take pride of place in the core material, its physical and spiritual restoration is brought about through the deity's intervention. The blessings of the new age result in the reconstruction of the sanctuary and the resumption of normative ritual practices therein.

3. *Temple Texts in the Outer Material*

The salvific predictions of 60.1–63.6 have been seen to be at odds with the redactional layer that surrounds it. In particular, the prophecies outside Isa. 60.1–63.6

20. This idiom is also thought to refer to the ark of the covenant (cf. Ps. 132.7; 1 Chron. 28.2).

21. Against McCullough (1948: 34-35), who argues that the Temple is standing as a burned out husk, but in need of repair and similarly, against those who see the Temple as rebuilt and that the timber serves only to enhance its external appearance. The same classes of trees are used in 1 Kgs 5.8-10 for the building of Solomon's Temple.

22. Schwarz (1975: 216-17) suggests rearranging the text, 'But those who reap it will eat it, and those who gather it will drink it. And they will praise Yahweh in his holy courts'. His reconstruction has been effectively refuted by Rudolph 1976: 282; Nebe 1978: 106-11; Maier 1979: 126.

are used to provide evidence for a developing schism in the community. It is therefore important to compare this vision with the redaction. Is the role of the Temple in the second redactional layer at odds with that of the core nucleus? References to the sanctuary in the second layer of material occur in Isa. 56.5, 7; 57.13; 63.18; 64.10, ET 11; 65.11, 25; 66.1, 6, and reflect a variety of uses. In so doing, they reveal continuity and discontinuity with the earlier material. Although the primary thrust of 60.1–63.6 portrays an all-encompassing plan of salvation through which the present woeful state of affairs is overturned, the outer material illustrates the current crisis through the depiction of the abysmal state of the Temple, deals with concerns about the make up of the community and access to the Temple, provides a future glimpse of the character of the new age to be inaugurated by Yahweh's salvific intervention, and clearly signifies how this is to come about.

Closely linked to 60.1–63.6 both thematically and semantically,[23] the communal lament of Isa. 63.7–64.11 (ET 12) grapples with a nation's sorrow through an historical recital of Yahweh's mighty deeds (63.7-14) coupled with confession (63.15–64.6, ET 7) and an appeal to the deity for aid (64.7-11, ET 12). Widely regarded as a Judahite liturgical composition stemming from the exilic period, the lament provides a survey of post-587 destruction interspersed with pleas for assistance.[24] Its placement after the grand predictions of 60.1–63.6 suggests that it draws upon an ongoing situation of distress in order to explain why salvation has been delayed (Schramm 1995: 150). In addition, it serves programmatically as an introduction to ch. 65 with its message of salvation for one group and condemnation for another (Hanson 1975: 80-81). In these verses, the present desolate state of the Temple is used to implore the God of Israel to act salvifically. While reflecting on widespread devastation, the lament functions further as a means to comment on the state of the community itself. Like the very physical devastation around them, the people are in ruins.

In the midst of a confession of sin and an appeal for future intervention, the people include the woeful state of the Temple. They cry out, 'For a little while[25] our enemies took possession of your holy mountain,[26] they trampled down your

23. P.A. Smith (1995: 44-47) gives eight examples to indicate that 63.7–64.11 (ET 12) was in the background of the composition of chs. 60–62 and possibly 63.1-6.

24. Volz 1932: 268-69; Janssen 1956: 22; Muilenburg 1956: 729-30; Fohrer 1964: 246-47; Westermann 1986 (1966): 306-307, ET 1969: 386-87; Pauritsch 1971: 169; Vermeylen 1977–78: 491, 503; Williamson 1990; against Hanson 1975: 79-100. Aejmelaeus (1995) dates the composition of the prayer between 530–520 BCE. Goldstein (2001) provides a helpful review of the opinions on the date of the poem and argues for one that is quite late.

25. *Lammiṣ'ār*. Although many people emend on the basis that the period of the existence of the Solomonic Temple could not be described as 'for a little while', Hanson (1975: 84-85) has shown that emendations are not necessary. He is followed by Schramm 1995: 152.

26. *Lammiṣ'ār yārᵉšû 'am qodšekā ṣārênû bôsᵉsû miqdāšekā*, lit. 'For a little while your holy people possessed and our enemies trampled down your sanctuary'. So Vulgate, Targum, and Peshitta, but LXX has ἵνα μικρὸν κληρονομήσωμεν τοῦ ὄρους τοῦ ἁγίου σου οἱ ὑπεναντίοι ἡμῶν κατεπάτησαν τὸ ἁγίασμά σου, 'For a little while they possessed your holy mountain, our enemies trampled down your sanctuary'. It is unusual not to have an accusative for *yrš*. Equally problematic is that the object being possessed is never the Temple, but the land. With the odd temporal use of *miṣ'ār*, most scholars

sanctuary' (63.18) and 'Our holy and beautiful house where our fathers praised you has been burnt by fire and all our precious things have been ruined' (64.10, ET 11). Certain appeals in the lament suggest to Hanson that 'a fatal rift is threatening to divide the community' (Hanson 1975: 92). Against him, Schramm, rightly points out that the text does not reveal a rejection of one group by another, but that of a rejection of the people as a whole by their God. Further, rather than reading the lament metaphorically about exclusion from cultic worship, it shows the destruction of the cult as a consequence of the judgment of Yahweh (Schramm 1995: 152-53). As the predicted reconstruction remains in the future, the lament serves as a plea to Yahweh to intervene. The inclusion of a confession of sin and the response found in ch. 65 in which two groups in the community are clearly delineated according to the measuring line of the exclusive worship of Yahweh suggest that it provides an explanation for the delay in restoration. Salvation remains at bay because the people continue to act in ways that brought about the destruction in the first place!

The sanctuary is used a second way within contexts in which regulations for entry into the Temple precincts and thereby the community are reinterpreted. In particular, the issue of the types of behaviour that make access to the Temple available becomes the main focus in 56.5, 7; 57.13; 65.11. While at the same time showing a remarkable degree of openness in terms of potentially who makes up the community, the prophetic word provides firm guidelines that fundamentally reject certain groups of people based on their behaviour, such as, ongoing participation in idolatrous worship.

In a startlingly inclusive text, it becomes clear that two disenfranchised groups of people, foreigners and eunuchs, garner equal status with the people of Israel. Rather than being based on ethnicity, the requirement for entry to the Temple includes only adherence to Yahweh and the observance of the Sabbath. Although 56.1-8 has been broken up into independent redactional units (Volz 1932: 202-204; Pauritsch 1971: 42-43; Koenen 1990: 11-27; Vermeylen 1977–78: 454-58)[27] and dated as a framework provided by a redactor to a time period significantly later than the rest of the Trito-Isaiah material (Westermann 1986 [1966]: 244-46, 252, ET 1969: 305-308, 315-16; Hanson 1975: 162, 388-89), rhetorical analyses (Muilenburg 1956: 653; Polan 1986: 44-52, 55; P.A. Smith 1995: 51-54) and the reinterpretation of the role of foreigners predicted in the nucleus reveal that these verses should be understood as an integral introduction to chs. 56–66 as a whole.[28] In so doing, they function to introduce two themes found throughout

suggest some type of emendation. Koenen (1988b) restricts the change to *dāšû* for *yārešû*. However, the LXX has been accurate and consistent in its translation of the other occurrences of *har qōdeš* in Isaiah (11.9; 56.7; 57.13; 65.11, 25; 66.20), *'am qōdeš* is unusual in Isaiah, although there is another occurrence in 62.12, and the holy mountain is the object of possession in 57.13, as are 'my mountains' in 65.9. The enemies serve as the subject of both verbs and in both the object is the Temple.

27. Isa. 56.1-8 shares vocabulary with Proto and Deutero-Isaiah, cf. Oswalt 1977; Polan 1986: 58-60.

28. Pauritsch (1971: 243) suggests that 56.1-8 is the motto of the Trito-Isaiah material. As such, it serves as the key to understanding the entirety of the chapters.

Trito-Isaiah: the imminence of salvation and the regulations for a relationship with the deity (Polan 1986: 51-52, 79).

In the second strophe (Isa. 56.3-7), eunuchs and foreigners are welcomed into the covenant community. So long as the eunuchs and foreigners adhere to the commands of Yahweh and observe the Sabbath their place in the Temple is secure (vv. 4, 6; on v. 6, see Van Winkle 1997a). To the eunuchs, who are understandably denied progeny because of physical limitations, v. 5 includes Yahweh's promise that 'I will place[29] for them in my house and among my walls a memorial monument[30] better than that of sons and daughters'. The prediction for 'the children of the foreigner' is even grander in that Yahweh declares, 'I will bring them to my holy mountain and they will rejoice in my house of prayer. Their offerings and sacrifices will be acceptable upon my altar for my house will be called a house of prayer for all peoples' (v. 7). The hiphil of *bô'* ('to bring back') is used elsewhere in Trito-Isaiah to describe the return of the exiles by Yahweh to Jerusalem (60.9; 66.20). In this passage, amazingly, it is used of foreigners. Although not common in the Hebrew Bible, the causative of *bô'* is used in passages that depict Yahweh returning the chosen people to Jerusalem (Exod. 15.17; Jer. 3.14; Ps. 78.53-54; Neh. 1.9). In a radically unique move, the prophet of Trito-Isaiah envisions the inclusion of foreigners within the elect people of Yahweh.[31]

The significance of Isa. 56.1-8 lies not only in the almost 'universalistic'[32] statements about who makes up the covenant community, but its clarification of the message about foreigners promulgated in the nucleus. Linked semantically and thematically to 60.1–63.6, Isa. 56.1-8 provides a corrective to the vision found therein (Van Winkle 1997a). In the nucleus, as we have seen, one of the outcomes of the new age is that foreigners function in a subservient role to the children of Israel (60.10; 61.5). The entirety of Isa. 56.1-8 refutes this position by expanding the role of people considered to be outcasts in the community[33] to include eunuchs and foreigners (56.3). The material in Trito-Isaiah that surrounds the core presents a picture of worship in which proselytes who follow the requirements of the covenant are welcomed fully as participants in the worship of the Temple in the new age. Whereas their kings would serve the Israelites in 60.10 while the Israelites themselves fulfil the role of ministers to the deity (61.6), the correcting vision of the introduction insists that the proselytes will serve Yahweh

29. On the translation, see Scullion 1973.

30. *Yād wāšēm*, lit. 'a hand and a name', but taken as a hendiadys along with Westermann 1986 (1966): 250-51, ET 1969: 314; Pauritsch 1971: 36; Whybray 1975: 198; Polan 1986: 70-71; Van Winkle 1997.

31. Van Winkle (1997b: 241-42) rightly points out the opening verse of the oracle to the foreigners designates them 'my servants', a term used throughout Trito-Isaiah for the faithful members of the community who will exult in the eschaton.

32. The use of the term 'universalistic' has been challenged appropriately by Schramm (1995: 121-24), who argues that the message is not one in which all foreigners come to be part of the community of Israel, but only those who agree to adhere to the stipulations of Yahwistic religion in the early post-exilic period.

33. In Deut. 23.2 (ET 1) eunuchs are prohibited from inclusion in Temple worship; in Exod. 12.43, the foreigner is forbidden from Passover.

(56.6). Similarly, whereas in the nucleus the farm animals of the nations gather to serve Jerusalem and leap up as acceptable sacrifices on the altar, in the outer material it is the offerings made by the foreigners themselves that are acceptable (56.7).[34] The narrow understanding of the restoration community serviced by the nations in the new age is radically reinterpreted by 56.1-8 so that previously disenfranchised peoples who adhere to the worship of Yahweh receive the blessings of the privileged people of God, as well. The criterion for access to the Temple rests on behaviour rather than ethnicity.

With its focus on salvation and judgment, Isa. 57.13, which closes the larger poem of 57.3-13,[35] also clarifies who has access to the Temple. In v. 13, the prophet pronounces judgment on those who have been participating in the idolatrous worship delineated in the preceding verses. Yahweh indicts the sinners while proclaiming salvation for the righteous ones, '[...][36] The wind will carry all of them, a breath will take (them) away, but whoever takes refuge in me will inherit the land and will possess my holy mountain'.[37] In 56.7, as we have seen, Yahweh pledges to bring foreigners to the holy mountain where their offerings will make acceptable sacrifices. Although foreigners and eunuchs who abide by the normative practices of early post-exilic Judaism are enabled to join Temple worship, those who continue to practise what is considered in Trito-Isaiah to be idolatrous worship will not. The two-part focus of the text on judgment for one group and salvation for the other emphasizes the place of both in the grand scheme of things which will follow the advent of Yahweh. In contrast to those who adhere to Yahweh, indeed, to those who take refuge in the God of Israel, to whom a glorious future in Zion including the right to participate in the Temple will be made available, the fate of those whose praxis includes allegiance to other deities is exclusion. Open access to the sanctuary is granted, but only to those who follow the precepts of Yahwistic religion.

Similar in form and content to Isaiah 57, Isa. 65.11 contains another reference to the Temple and predicts judgment for an idolatrous group (Torrey 1928: 469; Hanson 1975: 144). In Isa. 65.11, the prophet condemns a population engaged in apostate worship practices. As part of a larger unit in which salvation and judgment oracles are combined,[38] ch. 65 specifically responds to concerns raised in the exilic lament of 63.7–64.11 (ET 12) (Steck 1991: 217-28, against Hanson

34. P.A. Smith (1995: 59 n. 36) notes that the expression 'to be acceptable on my altar' occurs only at 56.7 and 60.7 in the Hebrew Bible.

35. There is a great degree of disagreement about the coherence of this passage, its relationship to the rebuke of the leaders of 56.9–57.2, and the concluding material of 57.14-21. A helpful summary of the major viewpoints is provided by P.A. Smith 1995: 67-96. His arguments in favour of a unified passage divided into thematic units of 56.9–57.2; 57.3-13, 14-21 seem sound and are therefore adopted in this study.

36. I follow Koenen (1989: 236-39), who, for good reason, places the beginning of v. 13 at the end of v. 12.

37. A number of commentators wrongly attribute v. 13b to a separate redactor who sought to link the judgment of vv. 12-13a to the salvation oracle of vv. 14-21; see the cogent objections by Hanson 1975: 187; P.A. Smith 1995: 78-79, 87.

38. Hanson (1975: 135), followed by Schramm (1995: 154), regards 65.1-25 as a unified prophecy of salvation and judgment. Cf. Webster 1990; P.A. Smith 1995.

1975: 80-81, 134) and thereby functions to clarify who is to be involved in the new Jerusalem to be established by Yahweh. In so doing, it negates the communal appeal based on an exclusive relationship with the deity. The claim 'we are all your people' cannot encourage divine intervention (64.8, ET 9) (Schramm 1995: 155).[39] Indeed, as Schramm notes, 'it is precisely those who raised the lament in 63.7–64.11 who meet with words of judgment in ch. 65' (Schramm 1995: 155; cf. Steck 1991: 401). However, as we shall see, the whole community is not thus envisioned. After a lengthy section of condemnation, the oracle of Yahweh charges the apostates in v. 11: 'But you are forsaking Yahweh, you are the ones forgetting my holy mountain, the ones setting a table for Gad and filling cups of mixed wine for Meni'. The statement of judgment with its predictions of slaughter in the following verse confirms that their fate is sealed (v. 12). In addition to reflecting ongoing cultic abuses,[40] the 'but you' group of vv. 11-12 includes those who are indicted in vv. 3-4 and 7 for sacrificing in gardens and burning incense on tiles, sitting inside tombs, eating the flesh of pigs, and making offerings to gods other than Yahweh, either to the exclusion of the worship of Yahweh or in combination with Yahwistic practice. The dire fate of the anonymous 'you' is consciously connected to that of the redeemed who throughout the passage are consistently labelled 'my servants' (65.8, 9, 13 [emphatic threefold use], 14; cf. 'his servants' in v. 15), 'my chosen ones' (65.9, 15, 22), and 'my people' (65.10, 19, 22). The juxtaposition of oracles of salvation and doom sets up a deliberate contrast whereby judgment and exclusion from the Temple are predicted for some while others await a happy, blessed future in a restored Jerusalem.

A third development in the way the sanctuary is conceptualized in Trito-Isaiah is closely related to the requirements for access to the Temple and the community. In Isa. 65.25 a reference to the 'the holy mountain' occurs in a context which characterizes the features of the new age. A peaceful and just existence belongs to the group for whom Yahweh comes as redeemer. Yahweh's entrance into the sphere of human affairs results in the establishment of a single community of the righteous.

In 65.25 the prophet seemingly portrays an idyllic setting for the new community in the new age, 'The wolf and the lamb shall feed as one; the lion will eat straw like the bullock, and the serpent's food will be dust. They will not harm nor destroy on all my holy mountain. Oracle of Yahweh.'[41] However, through comparison with Isa. 11.6-9, a like text from which it may be drawn, it becomes clear that the imagery points to the promises of a peaceable kingdom for only a portion of the people, while another experiences rejection and condemnation.[42] Although

39. An additional argument in favour of that proposed by Schramm is that ch. 65 also qualifies those who make up the holy people.

40. The repeated use of present participles expresses duration.

41. The verse is commonly thought to be a gloss, but P.A. Smith (1995: 148-49) shows that it is well integrated into the passage.

42. Debate about the relationship of 65.25 to 11.6-9 and the direction of transference continues. *Zᵉ'ēb wᵉṭāleh yir'û kᵉ'eḥād* seems to be a conflation of 11.6a, 7a with the notable change of *kebeś* to

Isa. 11.6-9, too, provides a portrait of an idealized age, it exhibits significant differences from 65.25. Whereas the text from Proto-Isaiah describes the rule of the messianic king (van Ruiten 1997: 36), 65.25 depicts the radical transformation of nature that coincides with the direct intervention and rulership of Yahweh (Whybray 1975: 278-79). During the exilic period, the concept of Yahweh as king takes on greater importance (Ezek. 20.32-44; Pss. 74.12; 102.12; Lam. 5.19; cf. Williamson 1988; Mettinger 1997: 143-54). As such it is quite appropriate that the reference to the 'holy mountain' in the new age is used in conjunction with the sovereign rule of the divine king.

In addition, as J. van Ruiten has pointed out in an intertextual study of Isa. 65.25 and 11.6-9, what is included in the use of Proto-Isaianic material is just as significant as what is left out. Interestingly, while the first two lines of the tricolon portray a carnivorous animal alongside a domesticated one, the final one, in contrast to Isaiah 11 and the previous cola, depicts only the predatory animal, the serpent. The depiction of the serpent alone simultaneously de-emphasizes harmony and stresses the behaviour of the snake, i.e. his 'eating dust'. J. van Ruiten traces the appearance of the serpent and dust to Gen. 3.14, where they appear in the context of a curse, and Mic. 7.17, which likens the humble attitude of the nations to 'licking dust as a serpent'. In his view, the oddly truncated line in which the serpent eats dust draws upon these representations vividly to portray the humble attitude of a hostile group subservient to another (v. 25) (van Ruiten 1997: 41). However, the doomed apostates are never portrayed as serving the faithful community in the new age in the second redactional layer. A better reading would highlight the concept of the curse. Verse 25 summarizes the entire chapter by continuing the intertwining of salvation predicted for one group and judgment for another. Divine rule results in the promise of blessings for the servants of the deity and for the destruction of the wicked (cf. Beuken 1990). As an essential element of the restored Jerusalem, the Temple provides the faithful and true servants of Yahweh a place in which to worship, while simultaneously rejecting the claims of apostate worshippers to be included in the restored community.

The final way the sanctuary appears in the material is to elucidate concretely how Yahweh's divine rule will come about. In what is a much discussed passage, Isa. 66.1 seems to condemn worship in the Temple (Torrey 1928: 471-72; Volz 1932: 289; Westermann 1986 [1966]: 327-28, ET 1969: 412-13) or a specific interpretation of Temple ideology (Smart 1934–35; Muilenburg 1956: 758-60; Pauritsch 1971: 201; Bonnard 1972: 483-86; Hanson 1975: 173-74; Whybray 1975: 279-80; P.A. Smith 1995: 158-59; Watts 1987: 352; Lau 1994: 168). In a divine oracle, a bold statement about the cosmic reign of Yahweh is followed by two questions focused on the Temple: 'Thus says Yahweh: Heaven is my throne

ṭāleh. *Ṭāleh* occurs elsewhere at Isa. 40.11, which suggests that it might be borrowed from the language of Deutero-Isaiah. Except for the addition of *w^enāḥāš 'āpār laḥmô*, the rest of the verse corresponds word-for-word with Isa. 11.7c, 9a. The conflation, literal incorporation, and addition suggest that 65.25 is a reinterpretation of Isa. 11.6-9. So Lau 1994: 140-41.

and the earth is my footstool; where[43] is the house which you would build for me, and where is my resting place?'. The crux of the interpretation of this passage rests with the use of *'ê-zeh*. It is often translated in a condemnatory way 'what is this?' with the sense that no earthly sanctuary is desired by Yahweh. However, the previous discussion has shown that, although the Temple does not occupy pride of place in the prophecies of the two redactional layers of Trito-Isaiah, its restoration and its place as the centre of worship remain a consistent part of the message of salvation. It is inconceivable that the presentation of the Temple as the location for the cultic worship of Israel's deity can lie alongside its condemnation and rejection (Jones 1963; Snaith 1967: 241; Rofé 1985: 213; Beuken 1989; Blenkinsopp 1990: 9; P.A. Smith 1995: 158-59).[44] Therefore, the interpretation of the expression as 'What is this house…' used as a criticism of the sanctuary is untenable. Surely another explanation must be found.

A more likely interpretation of Isa. 66.1 necessitates its placement in its larger setting. The unit to which Isa. 66.1 belongs yields a more likely interpretation. Other scholars have separated the oracle after v. 2 or after v. 4, but I suggest that v. 1 serves as the introduction, indeed, the prism through which v. 6 about the Temple as the location of divine intervention must be read. Verses 1-6 form a unit:[45] vv. 1 and 6 speak of the Temple, vv. 2 and 5 explain the nature of God to have concern for the poor and humble, and vv. 3-4 delineate the judgment of the wicked:

> (1) Thus says Yahweh: 'Heaven is my throne
> and the earth is my footstool;
> where is the house which you would build for me,
> and where is my resting place?
> (2) All these things my hand has made,
> and all of these things came to be,[46] oracle of Yahweh.
> But this is the man to whom I will look,
> he that is humble and contrite in spirit,
> and trembles at my word.

43. The dual use of *'ê-zeh* has been much discussed. The demonstrative adjective *zeh* occurs in the Hebrew Bible as an enclitic to strengthen a question. For examples of this usage, see GKC 136 ch, d. It is found in the Hebrew Bible in a wide range of meanings including 'where is?' (1 Sam. 9.18; Isa. 50.1; Jer. 6.16; Job 28.12, 20; Est. 7.5) and 'which is?' (1 Kgs 13.12; 2 Kgs 3.8; Job 38.19, 24; Eccl. 11.6), with only one example of 'what is?' (Eccl. 2.3) and one of 'how?' (1 Kgs 22.24 = 2 Chron. 18.23). The translation 'what is this house…' in the sense that no Temple is required for correct cultic observance is clearly polemical and is neither consistent with the primary connotation of this expression nor with the rest of the message regarding the Temple in Trito-Isaiah and its place within the deity's restoration plan. Also, inadequate in the context is its use as an urgent inquiry into the whereabouts of the Temple.

44. Schramm (1995: 163-165), further shows that the message of the first layer of material about the Temple is not at odds with that of the prophet Haggai and is in fact consistent with the depiction of Solomon's Temple in 1 Kgs 8.27.

45. Webster (1986) followed by Beuken (1989), argues that the unit extends from v. 1 to 6, against, among others, Torrey (1928: 275, 471) and Volz (1932: 291), who extend the passage to v. 5, and those who divide the unit into independent redactional units, such as Koenen (1990: 183-94) and Vermeylen (1977–78: 500, 505, 514).

46. Reading 'and all these things came to be' with the MT. Cf. Blenkinsopp 2003: 291b.

(3) 'He who slaughters an ox kills a man;
he who sacrifices a lamb breaks a dog's neck;
he who presents a cereal offering offers swine's blood;
he who makes a memorial offering of frankincense blesses an idol.[47]
These have chosen their own ways,
and their soul delights in their abominations;
(4) I also will choose affliction for them,
and bring their terror upon them;
because, when I called no one answered,
when I spoke they did not listen;
but they did what was evil in my eyes,
and chose that in which I did not delight'.
(5) Hear the word of Yahweh,
you who tremble at his word:
'Your brethren who hate you
and cast you out for my name's sake
have said, "Let Yahweh be glorified,
that we may see your joy";
but it is they who shall be put to shame.
(6) "Hark, an uproar from the city!
A voice from the temple!
The voice of Yahweh,
rendering recompense to his enemies!"'

The interpretation of Isa. 66.1 shifts from condemnation to proclamation if read within its wider context to v. 6. Verses 3-4, with their judgment on apostate worship practitioners, are sandwiched between grand oracles of salvation to the poor and lowly of vv. 2 and 5, which are in turn subordinated to the greater issue of the Temple as the place from which Yahweh comes to bring recompense. Thematically, vv. 1-2 parallel the thought of vv. 5-6 by suggesting that although Yahweh is incapable of being contained within a building made by human hands, he is intimately concerned with the affairs of the human realm as evidenced by 'looking' towards the poor or 'the one who trembles at [God's] word' in v. 2 and through the redemption of 'those that tremble at his word' in v. 5. The analysis of J. Blenkinsopp shows that in the Hebrew Bible the expression 'to tremble at the word' of Yahweh is only elsewhere found describing the supporters of Ezra in Ezra 9.4, where they are referred to as 'all who tremble at the words of the God of Israel' (cf. the similar expression in Ezra 10.3, 'Those who tremble at the commandment of our God') (Blenkinsopp 1990: 8). Its infrequent use strongly suggests that the appearance of the expression in vv. 2 and 5 links the two together. Moreover, the references to the Temple in vv. 1 and 6 join the two.

By continuing the vision of the new Jerusalem encountered in 65.17-25 (Muilenburg 1956: 757; Watts 1987: 349-52; Schramm 1995: 163-64; P.A. Smith 1995: 154-55, against Lau 1994: 168), 66.1-6 reveal how this is to come about.

47. The interpretation of the participial phrases in the first half of the verse has occasioned a great deal of discussion. The present translation follows that of Rofé 1985: 205-17; Blenkinsopp 1990: 9-10; 2003: 297-98; Schramm 1995: 162-70. An alternative translation and summary of the discussion can be found in P.A. Smith 1995: 155-57. On the text and its ancient Near Eastern parallels, see Sasson 1976.

The placement of judgment and salvation oracles together, in a pattern previously encountered in the second layer of redactional material, further sandwiched between references to the Temple, is exactly where they should be. It is through the sanctuary that God's retributive activity is mediated. As in the rest of the outer material, this passage is concerned with the character of the community. It further designates the locus through which the divine presence is mediated. Verse 1 introduces this concept and pushes through to v. 6 in which the revelation that God's presence is mediated through the Temple is found. The interpretation of 'where is' in v. 1 cannot be understood apart from this vision.

If the unit is delineated differently, the thrust of the passage is misunderstood. Smith, for example, in his interpretation surveys vv. 1-2 within the larger context of vv. 3-4 and thus argues that the issue at stake is syncretistic worship practices (P.A. Smith 1995: 155-59). Furthermore, the juxtaposition of illicit cultic practices with normative ones in v. 3 suggests that the priests of the Temple are specifically indicted for the worship of other deities. In Smith's view, then, the expression 'where is' raises concerns about the interpretation of the divine dwelling place, particularly, one built by the wicked (cf. Rofé 1985; Blenkinsopp 1990, 2003).

Although the issue of idolatrous worship receives a great deal of attention in the second redactional layer, Smith fails to perceive the connection with the poor and oppressed in v. 2, a theme likewise of interest in the material (Schramm 1995: 165). The two verses are connected in that 'all these things' of v. 2a refers back to the heavens and the earth of v. 1a (Westermann 1986 [1966]: 327, ET 1969: 412; Koenen 1990: 186-87). Moreover, the close assonance of *'ê-zeh* with *'el-zeh* suggests a connection between the questions of v. 1b and the statement of v. 2b. Like Isa. 57.15, where the loftiness of Yahweh is juxtaposed with divine concern for the poor and oppressed, 66.1-2 reveal that although the God of Israel is transcendent and the occupant of a cosmic throne, divine care and attention, indeed, the righteous ruling of Yahweh is concerned fundamentally with the lowly (Koenen 1990; Schramm 1995: 165-66; Ego 1999: 566-67; Albani 1999). Schramm, too, shares this understanding. However, his translation of the expression in the sense of a proclamation of amazement that in spite of Yahweh's greatness, the deity is concerned with the lowly, does not go far enough. The fate of the poor of v. 2 (and one might add at this point v. 5) to whom Yahweh looks is highlighted as a contrast to that of the idolatrous worshippers in vv. 3-4 (Sekine 1989: 55; P.A. Smith 1995: 154-55, against Albani 1999). W.A.M. Beuken has shown that the throne and footstool of the deity have implications beyond the mere place of the governance of Yahweh. They are used throughout scripture in the sense of ruling in justice (Beuken 1989; Lau 1994: 168). As such the deity, though cosmic and beyond any conception of humanity, is inseparably linked with the plight of certain alienated members of the community. The earthly replica of the heavenly Temple of the deity provides a place for divine mediation in the human sphere.

As the place of the righteous ruling of a cosmic deity, the Temple is the locus for the intervention of the divine in history. The coming of Yahweh to bring salvation and judgment is portrayed with battle imagery in Isa. 66.6: 'The sound of a din of battle from the city, a sound from the Temple is the sound of Yahweh bringing recompense to his enemies'.[48] The passage clearly predicts the retributive intervention of the mighty warrior God who comes from the Temple as in other eschatological scenes in the Hebrew Bible (Ezek. 9.4-5; Joel 4.16, ET 3.16; Amos 1.2; Mic. 1.2). Hanson notes that v. 6 is the event towards which the oracle of 66.1-6 has been striving (Hanson 1975: 163). As well as understanding the verse as the climax to the joint oracles of chs. 65 and 66, up to this point, it portrays the fulfilment of the salvation predicted throughout chs. 56–66. The Temple, linked to the advent of divine intervention, becomes the place from which the radical reversal of the present distress stems. The vision depicts Yahweh coming forth from the Temple to judge the enemies within Israel, namely those who have been chastised repeatedly for apostate worship practices, and to save the humble, those who adhere to normative Yahwistic practice.

References to the sanctuary in the second redactional layer reveal a logical progression of ideas. Beginning with the depiction of the present abysmal state of the Temple as a metaphor for the moral turpitude of the people (63.18; 64.10, ET 11), the material delineates who makes up the community and therefore regulates who has access to the Temple (56.5, 7; 57.13; 65.11). Further, it characterizes the community in the new age (65.25) and concludes with a grand theophanic vision which reveals how this is to come about (66.1, 6). In comparison with the message about the Temple in 60.1–63.6, which merely presents a picture of the new age in which the restoration of the Temple features, the second redactional layer further elucidates that vision by explaining the delay in its achievement, defining more clearly the nature and character of the community which has access to the worship of Yahweh in the age of divine rule, and stating how it is to come about. A shift to pragmatic questions regarding who has access to the Temple may indicate that it has been rebuilt by the time of composition of the second redactional layer. However, this is not necessarily so, as Ezekiel 40–48 deals with issues of access and is clearly a future vision, if not an idealistic one (Ezek. 44.5-7, 9).

4. *Conclusions*

In Isaiah 56–66, it has been shown that the Temple appears in two different layers of material that elicit complementary visions of its function as the centre of community life in the post-exilic period and in the divine age. In 60.1–63.6, the sanctuary of Yahweh is treated as only one element of the greater salvific intervention of the God of Israel, albeit a significant one. Normative worship by the Jewish community, the people of Israel, will resume when Yahweh accomplishes the predicted restoration. In the surrounding material in which the vision

48. Not enemies external to Israel such as the foreign nations envisaged by Westermann (1986 [1966]: 332-33, ET 1969: 419) and Pauritsch (1971: 197, 202, 212). Rather, they refer back to the 'brethren' of v. 5 and are thus enemies within the community who are worshipping other deities, as argued by Bonnard (1972: 487), Beuken (1989: 61) and Schramm (1995: 170). Davies (1989: 93-120) focuses on the positive place given to the nations in the book of Isaiah and in chs. 56–66 in particular.

of salvation found in the core is reinterpreted, the prophet seeks to explain the delay in the advent of divine restoration and to exhort the people to align their behaviour with Yahwistic behaviour in preparation for that imminent event.

In so doing, the prophet expands the criteria of who makes up the covenant community, going beyond ethnic identity to include groups previously banned from it, including even foreigners and eunuchs who adhere to Yahweh alone and acknowledge divine sovereignty through the observance of Sabbath worship. Conversely, the worship of other deities through idolatrous or syncretistic practice precludes inclusion in the community, which will joyfully worship its divine king in the new age. The second redaction, therefore, portrays the Temple as the place where Yahweh's righteous governance is mediated. The Temple is the locus of the divine reversal predicted by Deutero-Isaiah and 60.1–63.6. As the place of the righteous king, the sanctuary is the earthly location of the inbreaking of Yahweh's active presence.

Returning to the line of thought that began this inquiry, i.e. the sanctuary as a place hotly contested by divisive groups, it seems that the main point of the material in Trito-Isaiah with regard to the Temple is not that control of the sanctuary is at stake, and certainly not that it is wrested from a prophetic group by a hierocratic Priestly party, but that it has a role within the grander scheme of Yahweh's restoration. In the portrayal of the worshipping community crystallized through its vision of the Temple, Trito-Isaiah maintains a message consistent with that of the Former Prophets. As such, the placement of requirements for joining the chosen people of Yahweh alongside the concept of the cosmic reign of the deity may be another example of the way Isaiah 56–66 draws from and utilizes motifs from Proto-Isaiah and Deutero-Isaiah. In any case, the lack of significant difference between the Temple in the core material and its redaction, as well as the fact that Trito-Isaiah simply enunciates issues important in former prophetic material strongly argue against a clearly defined division in the community along the lines of different ideological perspectives at the time of its composition.

Bibliography

Achtemeier, E.R.
1982 *The Community and Message in Isaiah 56–66: A Theological Commentary* (Minneapolis: Augsburg).

Ackerman, S.
1992 *Under Every Green Tree: Popular Religion in Sixth Century Judah* (HSM, 46; Atlanta: Scholars Press).

Aejmelaeus, A.
1995 'Der Prophet als Klageliedsänger: Zur Funktion des Psalms Jes 63,7–64,11 in Tritojesaja', *ZAW* 107: 31-50.

Albani, M.
1999 'Wo sollte ein Haus sein, das ihr mir bauen könntet? (Jes 66.1): Schöpfung als Tempel JHWHs?', in B. Ego, A. Lange and P. Pilhofer (eds.), *Gemeinde ohne Tempel: Community without Temple* (WUNT, 118; Tübingen: J.C.B. Mohr [Paul Siebeck]): 37-56.

Barstad, H.
1997 *The Babylonian Captivity of the Book of Isaiah: "Exilic" Judah and the Provenance of Isaiah 40–55* (The Institute for Comparative Research in Human Culture; Oslo: Novus).

Berges, U.
1998 *Das Buch Jesaja: Komposition und Endgestalt* (HBS, 16; Freiberg: Herder).

Berquist, J.L.
1995 *Judaism in Persia's Shadow: A Social and Historical Approach* (Minneapolis: Fortress Press).

Beuken, W.A.M.
1986 'Isaiah 56.9–57.13—An Example of the Isaianic Legacy of Trito-Isaiah', in J.W. van Henten, *et al.* (eds.), *Tradition and Re-Interpretation in Jewish and Early Christian Literature: Essays in Honor of Jürgen C.H. Lebram* (Studia postbiblica, 36; Leiden: E.J. Brill): 48-64.
1989 'Does Trito-Isaiah Reject the Temple? An Intertextual Inquiry into Isa. 66.1-6', in S. Draisma (ed.), *Intertextuality in Biblical Writings: Essays in Honour of Bas van Iersel* (Kampen: Kok): 53-66.
1990 'The Main Theme of Trito-Isaiah: "The Servants of YHWH"', *JSOT* 47: 67-87.

Biddle, M.E.
1996 'Lady Zion's Alter Egos: Isaiah 47.1-15 and 57.6-13 as Structural Counterparts', in R.F. Melugin and M.A. Sweeney (eds.), *New Visions of Isaiah* (JSOTSup, 214; Sheffield: Sheffield Academic Press): 124-39.

Blenkinsopp, J.
1984 *A History of Prophecy in Israel: From the Settlement in the Land to the Hellenistic Period* (London: SPCK).
1990 'A Jewish Sect of the Persian Period', *CBQ* 52: 5-20.
2003 *Isaiah 56–66: A New Translation with Introduction and Commentary* (AB, 19B; New York: Doubleday).

Bonnard, P.E.
1972 *Le Second Isaïe, son disciple et leurs éditeurs: Isaïe 40–66* (EBib; Paris: J. Gabalda).

Broyles, C.C., and C.A. Evans (eds.)
1997 *Writing and Reading the Scroll of Isaiah: Studies of an Interpretive Tradition* (VTSup, 70; 2 vols.; Leiden: E.J. Brill).

Cheyne, T.K.
1895 *Introduction to the Book of Isaiah* (London: A. & C. Black).

Davies, G.I.
1989 'The Destiny of the Nations in the Book of Isaiah', in J. Vermeylen (ed.), *The Book of Isaiah/Le Livre d'Isaïe: Les Oracles et leurs reflectures unite et complexité de L'ouvrage* (BETL, 81; Leuven: Leuven University Press): 93-120.

Delitzsch, F.
1892 *Biblical Commentary on the Prophecies of Isaiah* (trans. J. Kennedy, W. Hastie, T.A. Bickerton and J.S. Banks; 2 vols.; Edinburgh: T. & T. Clark).

Draisma, S. (ed.)
1989 *Intertextuality in Biblical Writings: Essays in Honour of Bas van Iersel* (Kampen: Kok).

Duhm, B.
1892 *Das Buch Jesaia* (HAT, 3.1; Göttingen: Vandenhoeck & Ruprecht).

Ego, B.
1998 'Der Herr blickt herab von der Höhe seines Heiligtums: Zur Vorstellung von Gottes himmlischem Thronen in exilisch-nachexilischer Zeit', *ZAW* 110: 556-69.

Ego, B., A. Lange and P. Pilhofer (eds.)
1999 *Gemeinde ohne Tempel: Community without Temple zur Substituierung und Transformation des Jerusalemer Tempels und seines Kults im Alten Testament, antiken Judentum und frühen Christentum* (WUNT, 118; Tübingen: J.C.B. Mohr [Paul Siebeck]).

Elliger, K.
1928 *Die Einheit des Tritojesaja, Jesaja 56–66* (BWANT, 45; Stuttgart: W. Kohlhammer).
1931 'Der Prophet Tritojesaja', *ZAW* 8: 112-40.

Fishbane, M.
1985 *Biblical Interpretation in Ancient Israel* (Oxford: Clarendon Press).

Fohrer, G.
1964 *Das Buch Jesaja* (Zürcher Bibelkommentare, AT, 19.1-3; Zürich: Zwingli Verlag).

Goldenstein, J.
2001 *Das Gebet der Gottesknechte: Jesaja 63,7–64,11 im Jesajabuch* (WMANT, 92; Neukirchen–Vluyn: Neukirchener Verlag).

Hanson, P.D.
1975 *The Dawn of Apocalyptic* (Minneapolis: Fortress Press).

Haran, M.
1963 'The Literary Structure and Chronological Framework of the Prophecies in sa XL–XLVIII', in *Congress Volume, Bonn 1962* (VTSup, 9; Leiden: E.J. Brill): 127-55.

Henten, J.W. van, *et al.* (eds.)
1986 *Tradition and Re-Interpretation in Jewish and Early Christian Literature: Essays in Honor of Jürgen C.H. Lebram* (Studia postbiblica, 36; Leiden: E.J. Brill).

Holladay, W.L.
1997 'Was Trito-Isaiah Deutero-Isaiah after All?', in Broyles and Evans (eds.) 1997: 193-217.

Janssen, E.
1956 *Juda in der Exilszeit: Ein Beitrag zur Frage der Entstehung des Judentums* (Göttingen: Vandenhoeck & Ruprecht).

Jones, D.R.
1963 'The Cessation of Sacrifice After the Destruction of the Temple in 586 BC', *JTS* NS 14: 12-31.

Kaufmann, Y.
1970 *The Babylonian Captivity and Deutero-Isaiah* (trans. C.W. Efroymson; New York: Union of American Hebrew Congregations).

Knight, G.A.F.
1985 *Isaiah 56–66* (ITC; Grand Rapids: Eerdmans).

Koenen, K.
1988a 'Textkritische Anmerkungen zu schwierigen Stellen in Tritojesajabuch', *Bib* 62: 564-73.
1988b 'Zum Text von Jes 63,18', *ZAW* 100: 406-409.
1989 'Zum Text von Jesaja LVII 12-13a', *VT* 39: 236-39.
1990 *Ethik und Eschatologie im Tritojesajabuch: Eine literarkritische und redaktionsgeschichtliche Studie* (WMANT, 62; Neukirchener–Vluyn: Neukirchener Verlag).

Lau, W.
1994 *Schriftgelehrte Prophetie in Jes 56–66: Eine Untersuchung zu den literarischen Bezügen in den letzten elf Kapiteln des Jesajabuches* (BZAW, 225; Berlin: W. de Gruyter).

Lewis, T.J.
1989 *Cults of the Dead in Ancient Israel and Ugarit* (HSM, 39; Atlanta: Scholars Press).

Maass, F.
1967 'Tritojesaja?', in F. Maass (ed.), *Das ferne und nahe Wort: Festschrift Leonhard Rost* (BZAW, 105; Berlin: W. de Gruyter): 153-63.

Maier, J.
1979 'Ergänzend zu Jes 62.9', *ZAW* 91: 126.

McCullough, W.S.
1948 'A Re-examination of Isaiah 56–66', *JBL* 67: 27-36.

Mettinger, T.N.D.
1997 'In Search of the Hidden Structure: YHWH as King in Isaiah 40–55', in Broyles and Evans (eds.) 1997: 143-54.

Middlemas, J.A.
2003 'The Troubles of Templeless Judah' (DPhil thesis, University of Oxford).

Muilenburg, J.
1956 'Isaiah 40–66', in *The Interpreter's Bible* (12 vols.; Nashville: Abingdon Press): V, 199-773.

Murtonen, A.
1980–81 'Third Isaiah—Yes or No?', *Abr-Nahrain* 19: 20-42.

Nebe, G.
1978 'Noch einmal zu Jes. 62.9', *ZAW* 90: 106-11.

Nihan, C.
2001 'Trois cultes en Esaïe 57,3-13 et leur signification dans le contexte religieux de la Judée à l'époque perse', *Transeuphratène* 22: 143-67.

Oswalt, J.N.
1997 'Righteousness in Isaiah: A Study of the Function of Chapters 56–66 in the Present Structure of the Book', in Broyles and Evans (eds.) 1997: 177-91.

Pauritsch, K.
1971 *Die neue Gemeinde: Gott sammelt Ausgestossene und Arme (Jesaja 56–66)* (AnBib, 47; Rome: Biblical Institute Press).

Polan, G.J.
1986 *In the Ways of Justice towards Salvation: A Rhetorical Analysis of Isaiah 56–59* (New York: Peter Lang).

Rofé, A.
1985 'Isaiah 66.1-4: Judean Sects in the Persian Period as Viewed by Trito-Isaiah', in A. Kort and S. Morschauser (eds.), *Biblical and Related Studies Presented to Samuel Iwry* (Winona Lake, IN: Eisenbrauns): 205-17.

Rudolph, W.
1976 'Zu Jes 62.9', *ZAW* 88: 282.

Ruiten, J.T.A.G.M. van
1997 'The Intertextual Relationship between Isa 11.6-9 and Isa 65.25', in Broyles and Evans (eds.) 1997: 31-42.

Sasson, J.M.
1976 'Isa. LXVI 3-4a', *VT* 26: 199-207.

Sawyer, J.F.A.
1989 'Daughter Zion and the Servant of the Lord in Isaiah: A Comparison', *JSOT* 44: 89-107.

Schmidt, B.B.
1994 *Israel's Beneficent Dead: Ancestor Cult and Necromancy in Ancient Israelite Religion and Tradition* (FAT, 11; Tübingen: J.C.B. Mohr [Paul Siebeck]).
Schramm, B.
1995 *The Opponents of Third Isaiah: Reconstructing the Cultic History of the Restoration* (JSOTSup, 193; Sheffield: Sheffield Academic Press).
Schwarz, G.
1975 '...trinken in meinen heiligen Vorhöfen?', *ZAW* 87: 216-17.
Scullion, J.J.
1973 'Some Difficult Texts in Isaiah 56–66 in the Light of Modern Scholarship', *UF* 4: 105-106.
1982 *Isaiah 40–66* (OTM, 12; Wilmington, DE: Michael Glazier).
Sehmsdorf, E.
1972 'Studien zur Redaktionsgeschichte von Jesaja 56–66', *ZAW* 84: 517-76.
Sekine, S.
1989 *Die Tritojesajanische Sammlung (Jes 56–66) redaktionsgeschichtlich untersucht* (BZAW, 175; Berlin: W. de Gruyter).
Smart, J.D.
1934–35 'A New Interpretation of Isaiah lxvi 1-6', *ExpTim* 46: 420-24.
1965 *History and Theology in Second Isaiah* (Philadelphia: Westminster Press).
Smith, M.
1987 *Palestinian Parties and Politics that Shaped the Old Testament* (London: SCM Press, 2nd edn).
Smith, P.A.
1995 *Rhetoric and Redaction in Trito-Isaiah: The Structure, Growth and Authorship of Isaiah 56–66* (VTSup, 62; Leiden: E.J. Brill).
Snaith, N.H.
1967 'Isaiah 40–66: A Study of the Teaching of the Second Isaiah and its Consequences', in H.M. Orlinsky and N.H. Snaith, *Studies on the Second Part of the Book of Isaiah* (VTSup, 14; Leiden: E.J. Brill): 135-264.
Sommer, B.D.
1998 *A Prophet Reads Scripture: Allusion in Isaiah 40–66* (Stanford: Stanford University Press).
Steck, O.H.
1989 'Zion als Gelände und Gestalt: Überlegungen zur Wahrnehmung Jerusalems als Stadt und Frau im Alten Testament', *ZTK* 86: 261-81.
1991 *Studien zu Tritojesaja* (BZAW, 203; Berlin: W. de Gruyter).
Torrey, C.C.
1928 *The Second Isaiah* (New York: Charles Scribner's Sons).
Van Winkle, D.W.
1997a 'An Inclusive Authoritative Text in Exclusive Communities', in Broyles and Evans (eds.) 1997: 423-40.
1997b 'The Meaning of *yād wāšēm* in Isaiah LVI 5', *VT* 47: 378-85.
Vermeylen, J.
1977–78 *Du Prophète Isaïe à l'apocalyptique: Isaïe I–XXXV, miroir d'un demi millénaire d'expérience religieuse en Israël* (2 vols.; EBib; Paris: J. Gabalda).
Volz, P.
1932 *Jesaia* (KAT, 9.2; 2 vols.; Leipzig: A. Deichertsche Verlagsbuchhandlung).
Watts, J.D.W.
1987 *Isaiah 34–66* (WBC, 25; Waco, TX: Word Books).

Webster, E.C.
1986 'A Rhetorical Study of Isaiah 66', *JSOT* 34: 93-108,
1990 'The Rhetoric of Isaiah 63–65', *JSOT* 47: 89-102.

Westermann, C.
1986 [1966] *Das Buch Jesaja: Kapitel 40–66* (ATD, 19; Göttingen: Vandenhoeck & Ruprecht, 5th edn). ET *Isaiah 40–66* (OTL; trans. D.M.H. Stalker; London: SCM Press, 1969).

Whybray, R.N.
1975 *Isaiah 40–66* (NCB; London: Oliphants).

Williamson, H.G.M.
1988 *Variations on a Theme: King, Messiah and Servant in the Book of Isaiah* (Carlisle: Paternoster Press).
1990 'Isaiah 63,7–64,11: Exilic Lament or Post Exilic Protest?', *ZAW* 102: 48-58.

Zimmerli, W.
1963 'Zur Sprache Tritojesajas', in *Gottes Offenbarung: Gesammelte Aufsätze zum AT* (TBü, 19; Munich: Chr. Kaiser Verlag): 217-33.

PLACING (A) GOD: CENTRAL PLACE THEORY IN DEUTERONOMY 12 AND AT DELPHI*

Anselm C. Hagedorn

1. *Prolegomena*

Biblical scholarship on the book of Deuteronomy has long recognized the importance of the centralization of the cult advocated in Deuteronomy 12 and it has recently been argued that this idea of a centralized cult in turn has influenced the shaping of the book as a whole.[1] According to Bernard M. Levinson:

> The authors of Deuteronomy radically transformed the religion and society of ancient Judah… [They] sought to eliminate any vestige of popular piety that could jeopardize their new vision of a homogenous public cultus. Private religion became a matter of public policy in a way that was uncommon in the otherwise religiously tolerant ancient Near East. The authors of Deuteronomy broke down the barriers between public and private and between national and popular religion. (Levinson 1997: 144)

However, surprisingly little attention has been paid to the actual theory and social implications behind Deuteronomy 12. It is here that my investigation will start. It is my aim to evaluate the definition of sacred space and landscape according to Deuteronomy 12. Thanks to the magnificent study of Deut. 12.1–13.1 by Eleonore Reuter we can move quickly from historical-critical questions on to social-scientific interpretation.[2]

After acknowledging the sense of a centre in the ancient world,[3] the starting point for our social-scientific interpretation of Deuteronomy 12 will be Walther Christaller's theory of a *central place* (first developed with regard to mediaeval cities in southern Germany), whose basic function can be defined as a place to provide goods and services for a surrounding tributary area.[4]

* For Joseph Blenkinsopp and Jerome H. Neyrey. I would like to thank the members of the Oxford Old Testament Seminar and the CONTEXT-Group for valuable suggestions and constructive criticism; all remaining faults are of course my own. The following abbreviations of Greek inscriptions are used: *IG* = *Inscriptiones Graecae*; *LSCG* = *Lois sacrées de cités grecques*; *LSS* = *Lois sacrées supplément*; *FDelphes* = *Fouilles de Delphes*; *CID* = *Corpus des inscriptions de Delphes*; ML = R. Meiggs and D.M. Lewis, *A Selection of Greek Historical Inscriptions to the End of the Fifth Century* BC (Oxford: Oxford University Press, 2nd edn, 1988). All translations of Greek authors are taken from the Loeb Classical Library.

1. See Levinson 1997 and Otto 1999a: 341-51.
2. See Reuter 1993 and the critical remarks in Lohfink 1995.
3. See Cohn 1981.
4. See Christaller 1950. This is a restatement of his theory of the central place first developed in 1933. For a much earlier attempt to evaluate the notion of 'centre' and 'periphery' see von Thünen 1930 [1842].

In a second step we need to look at the sacred landscape depicted in Deuteronomy.[5] Rather than just noting the description of landscape in biblical texts and contrasting the portrait found here with the eventual aesthetics of Greek thinking,[6] I will argue for landscape as a cultural construct that embraces more than just a description of nature.[7] Thus, '[a] landscape is a series of named locales, a set of relational places linked by paths, movements and narratives. It is a "natural" topography perspectivally linked to the existential Being of the body in societal space' (Tilley 1994: 34). If that is the case, the landscape depicted in Deuteronomy is much more than the pastoral background that illustrates the verses.[8] If culture shapes the natural landscape to produce a cultural landscape, so that landscape can be seen as a cultural process, we can expect that the description of the sacred landscape in Deuteronomy allows us to interpret the values of the writer(s) of the text.

One further aspect that needs to be considered is the role of the sanctuary during the process of taking possession of new territory.[9] Here the notion of a (central) sanctuary can be employed in two different ways. First of all, an oracle of a central sanctuary such as Delphi can stimulate the foundation of a new settlement (Malkin 1989), as was the case in Cyrene (Hölkeskamp 1999: 165-72). Secondly, the establishment of a cult and a sanctuary in the new terrain consecrated the seizure of the territory;[10] maybe it is no coincidence that legal stipulations regarding the central sanctuary are found at the very beginning of the legal corpus of Deuteronomy *before* the entry into the land (Weinfeld 1988). If that is indeed the case, the building of a sanctuary would precede all other aspects of colonization.[11] The importance of the law regarding the centralization of worship is furthermore emphasized by the formula in Deut. 13.1 which stresses that it is forbidden to change the wording of the law, something that is also found in the Greek world.

If, on the other hand, 'territoriality' is defined 'as the attempt by an individual or group to affect, influence, or control people, phenomena, and relationships, by delimiting and asserting control over a geographic area... Territories require constant effort to establish and maintain' (Sack 1986: 19), we have to relate such a notion of territoriality to our definition of landscape. If a sacred landscape or a sacred territory has to be protected constantly, it is hardly surprising that we find special formulae which aim at such a protection. In Deut. 12.13, 30 we read

5. Generally it can be said that the idea of a central place is often combined with a certain degree of sacredness, as the following quote from Julius Caesar, *De Bello Gallico* 13, shows: '*Hic certo anni tempore in finibus Carnutum, quae regio totius Galliae media habetur, convidunt in loco consecrato*'.

6. For such an approach see Fitter 1995: 53-83.

7. On the problem of 'land into landscape' see Andrews 1999: 1-22.

8. Anthropologists generally differentiate between 'the landscape we initially see and a second landscape which is produced through local practice and which we come to recognize and understand through fieldwork and through ethnographic description and interpretation' (Hirsch 1995: 2).

9. For the Greek world see de Polignac 1995: 98-106 and Malkin 1987: 114-33.

10. Homer, *Odyssey* 6.7-10; Arrian, *Anabasis* 3.1.5; Malkin 1987: 135-86.

11. In a much later period, the prophet Haggai rebukes the Israelites for not rebuilding the Temple first; see Hag. 1.4, 9.

hiššāmer lᵉkā pen and similar phrases of protection can be found, for example, in a so-called sanctuary bye-law from Delos.[12]

I shall have to evaluate the relationship between 'territory' and 'sacred landscape' in the course of this study. Further topics to be addressed will include the relation between a centre and the general notion of the navel of the earth.[13] Greek evidence allows us to conclude that a god located at the centre of the earth is more important than others located at more marginal or peripheral places.[14]

2. *Senses of Centres in the Ancient World*

Before giving some examples from ancient sources regarding the notion of a centre I should emphasize that a 'centre' does not necessarily equal the idea of a navel. When I speak of a 'centre' in the course of this article the term is used more broadly. A centre can literally be off-centre. On the other hand, the centre generally determines the view of the landscape we perceive. Mircea Eliade has drawn attention to the fact that humans are able to use a variety of images to express the 'symbolism of the center' (Eliade 1959: 37), which then symbolizes the link in the communication between the earthly and the heavenly spheres. This place or centre 'constitutes a break in the homogeneity of space' and is therefore a place around which the profane world is ordered (p. 95).

The Hebrew word for 'centre' is *ṭabbûr*, which is only used in Judg. 9.37 and Ezek. 5.5; 38.12,[15] and is translated in the Septuagint by ὀμφαλός.[16] According to Koehler–Baumgartner (*HALAT*) the word *ṭabbûr* is also used in *Jub.* 8.19 and *1 En.* 26.1. The lack of usage, however, does not imply that the world of the Hebrew Bible is unfamiliar with the concept of a centre, and the frequency with which reference is made to Zion might serve as an indicator of that (Isa. 2.2). However, we should be careful not to jump immediately to the conclusion that the myth of the navel of the earth, which is—as we will see below—so prominent in Greek myth, plays a significant, if not identical role in ancient Israel.[17] Shemaryahu Talmon has pointed out that it is virtually impossible to prove, given the paucity of the sources, that the concept of the 'navel of the earth' had a major influence on the Old Testament (Talmon 1993). Therefore, '[i]t is totally unacceptable to hypothesize such cultural transfers except when they can be proven

12. Sokolowski 1962: No 50 (Μὴ πλύεν τὲν κρή[νε]ν | μηδέν, μηδέ κολυμ[θᾶν ἐν τ]* | ε̂ι κρῆνει, μηδὲ [βάλ]λ[εν] κ[α]- | τὰ τὴν κρήν[εν κόπρον μηδ]- | [έ τι ἄλλ]ο. ἐπ[ιζήμια]· δραχμ- | αὶ –[ἱ]ερ[α]ί.); see also *LSCG* 3, 108, 111; *LSS* 4, 24. See also *IG* XII 7.2 where no stranger is allowed to enter the temple of Hera.

13. For a first overview see Roscher 1913 and 1918; Herrmann 1953.

14. See Plato, *Republic* 427c (οὗτος γὰρ δήπου ὁ θεὸς περὶ τὰ τοιαῦτα πᾶσιν ἀνθρώποις πάτριος ἐξηγητὴς ἐν μέσῳ τῆς γῆς ἐπὶ τοῦ ὀμφαλοῦ καθήμενος ἐξηγεῖται, ['For this God surely is in such matters for all mankind the interpreter of the religion of their fathers who from his seat in the middle and at the very navel of the earth delivers his interpretation']).

15. *ṭabbûr* only in Judg. 9.37; Ezek. 38.12; 'highest part', 'centre' (BDB).

16. The LXX uses ὀμφαλός four times: Judg. 9.37; Ezek. 38.12 (for Heb. *ṭabbûr*); Job 40.16 (for *śārîr*); Cant. 7.2 (for *śār*).

17. For such an approach see Terrien 1970.

by evident literary parallels' (p. 75). In the course of this study it will become clear that 'navel' and centre are not necessarily identical. Just because later maps tend to depict Jerusalem as the centre of the earth does not mean that it was always understood like that. Already ancient authors were puzzled by the question whether there was a centre of the world. Plutarch reports a statement of Epimenides of Phaestus, saying:

> οὔτε γὰρ ἦν γαίης μέσος ὀμφαλὸς οὐδὲ θαλάσσης·
> εἰ δέ τις ἔστι, θεοῖς δῆλος θνητοῖσι δ' ἄφαντος [18]
>
> Now do we know that there is no mid-centre of earth or of ocean? Yet if there be, it is known to the gods, but is hidden from mortals.

In the Greek world the centre or 'navel' is called ὀμφαλός,[19] the first occurrence of which is found in the works of Homer, where the 'navel of the sea' can be described as νήσῳ ἐν ἀμφιρύτῃ, ὅθι τ' ὀμφαλός ἐστι θαλάσσης, 'in a sea-girt isle, where is the navel of the sea' (*Od.* 1.50). This is the only occurrence of the word in the Homeric epics describing a navel, but, in the Iliad the round middle part (centre?) of the shield can be described as an ὀμφαλός.[20] With regard to a city, Pindar can use the term to describe the city-centre of Athens:

> Δεῦτ' ἐν χορόν, Ὀλύμπιοι,
> ἐπί τε κλυτὰν πέμπετε χάριν θεοί,
> πολύβατον οἵ τ' ἄστεος ὀμφαλὸν θυόεντ'
> ἐν ταῖς ἱεραῖς Ἀθάναις.[21]
>
> Come to the chorus, Olympians and send its glorious grace you gods who are coming to the city's crowded, incense rich navel, in holy Athens.

In similar manner, Pausanias' *Description of Greece* (2.13.7) can use ὀμφαλός to describe the city of Corinth. Furthermore we have inscriptional evidence from Megara where the word ὀμφαλός is inscribed on an altar, thus denoting that the altar is located at the centre of a temple or a city.[22]

How important such a notion of a centre is becomes clear in the following quotation from Philolaos, where he states that the life of the embryo develops from the navel as the centre of the body:

> κεφαλὰ μὲν νόου, καρδία δὲ ψυχῆς καὶ αἰθήσιος, ὀμφαλὸς δὲ ῥιζώσιος καὶ ἀναφύσιος τοῦ πρώτου, αἰδοῖον δὲ σπέρματος [καὶ] καταβολᾶς τε καὶ γεννήσιος.[23]
>
> The head [is the seat] of intellect, the heart of life and sensation, the navel of rooting and first growth, the genitals of the sowing of seed and generation.[24]

18. Plutarch, *De defectu oraculorum* 409F = Epimenides, *fr.* B11 [Diels].
19. I will only provide a short overview here of the use of the word when it does not refer to the Omphalos at Delphi, since this will be undertaken below (section 4).
20. *Iliad* 13.192 [...δ' ἄρ' ἀσπίδος ὀμφαλὸν οὖτα...]. See also *Odyssey* 19.32 (ἐσφόρεον κόρυθάς τε καὶ ἀσπίδας ὀμφαλοέσσας).
21. Pindar, *fr.* 75.1-4.
22. *IG* VII.53, ll. 11-12.
23. Philolaos, *fr.* 13 [Diels].
24. Translation according to Huffman 1993: 307.

Finally, Josephus states that Jerusalem, as the largest city of the Judaeans, is naturally situated at the centre.[25] However, we should remind ourselves that '[t]he prominent role of Jerusalem, in biblical times as political and cultic centre of Judah and in post-biblical times as a focus of Jewish territorial and spiritual aspirations, makes it easy to forget that this sacred centre was not always sacred or a center for Israel' (Cohn 1981: 64).

3. *Deuteronomy 12*

A fourth superscription within the book of Deuteronomy as a whole marks the beginning of the legal corpus.[26] All previous eleven chapters can be understood as a rather long prologue to Deuteronomy 12–26.[27] The first law which we encounter is that concerning the centralization of the cult, which occupies the whole of ch. 12 (Deut. 12.2-31).[28] The chapter itself is framed by two verses (Deut. 12.1; 13.1) which indicate when and where the laws of ch. 12 are valid and a so-called *Kanonformel*.[29] What follows is labelled *haḥuqqîm wᵉhammišpāṭîm*,[30] which Israel is to observe *after* Yahweh has given the promised land. These stipulations regarding validity will be of crucial importance to my interpretation later on. Within a synchronic reading of the chapter it is possible to distinguish six laws:[31]

I. Deut. 12.2-3
II. Deut. 12.4-7
III. Deut. 12.8-12
IV. Deut. 12.13-19
V. Deut. 12.20-28
VI. Deut. 12.29-31[32]

Thus the two laws regarding foreign cults frame four legal stipulations dealing with the sacrificial cult of Israel.

25. Josephus, *War* 3.52: μεσαιτάτη δ' αὐτῆς πόλις τὸ Ἱεροσόλυμα κεῖτα, παρ' ὃ καί τινες οὐκ ἀσκόπως ὀμφαλὸν τὸ ἄστυ τῆς χώρας ἐκάλεσαν ('The city of Jerusalem lies at its very centre, for which reason the town has sometimes not aptly been called the "navel" of the country').

26. Other such superscriptions can be found in Deut. 1.1; 4.44-45; 6.1; 28.69. All these superscriptions start with a nominal sentence and are followed by a subordinate clause introduced with *ʾᵃšer* which provides the *locale* of the sentence. On the question of the superscriptions see Seitz 1971: 35-44.

27. Wellhausen 1899: 190 remarks: 'Die Gesetze gehn erst Kap. 12 an, vorher will zwar Mose immer zur Sache kommen, kommt aber nicht dazu'.

28. Braulik 1991: 23; Otto 2001: 113 remarks on the character of Deut. 12: 'Legt das dtn Gesetz zur Zentralisierung des Opferkultes...ursprünglich das Altargesetz des Bundesbuches aus, so wird es durch den dtr Rahmen aus Gesetzen zur Zerstörung heidnischer Kulte...in der dtr Hauptredaktion zu einer Auslegung des dekalogischen Fremdgöttergebots'.

29. Lohfink 1991a: 249-55; 1996: 130.

30. The phrase occurs 14 times in Deuteronomy (Deut. 4.1, 5, 8, 14, 45; 5.1, 31; 6.1, 20; 7.11; 11.32; 12.1; 26.16, 17.

31. Lohfink 1996: 130-31 followed by Otto 1999a: 341; slightly different Levinson 1997: 25, who only distinguishes between five laws, since he views Deut. 12.2-7 as a unity.

32. Römer (2000: 210) remarks on Lohfink's proposal: 'Cette proposition...camoufle cependant le fait que Deut. 12 contient une série de répétitions et de réorientations qui déjà au niveau d'une lecture synchronique font apparaître une complexité littéraire dont il s'agit de tenir compte'.

Scholars of Deuteronomy generally assume that the place mentioned in Deuteronomy 12 is Jerusalem.[33] However, the text itself also allows for the interpretation that the creation of a place of centralized worship is possible wherever the conditions of Deuteronomy 12 are fulfilled (Halpern 1981: 34; Norin 2000: 101). Thus it can be read as a document that supports colonization of new territory. Such a view does not necessarily have to argue for a 'northern' origin of Deuteronomy;[34] however I do acknowledge that one of the key terms (*bḥr*) in Deuteronomy 12 generally refers in the Hebrew Bible to Zion/Jerusalem (cf. 1 Kgs 14.21; Ps. 78.68) or the election of the Davidic dynasty which resides in Jerusalem, when a certain place serves as object.[35]

The geographical aspect at the beginning of the chapter is especially interesting. After being concerned with the point in time when the stipulations (*haḥuqqîm wᵉhammišpāṭîm*[36]) will start to become valid, the text states clearly that the utter destruction of the places of worship of the nations is the prerequisite for the setting up of the new, central sanctuary in the land that Yahweh will give Israel to possess.[37] Thus we have in Deut. 12.1-5 the following string of actions:

a. promise of the land;
b. destruction of the places of worship of the nations/taking possession of a new land;
c. election of a central place from among *mikkol šībṭêkem* by Yahweh;
d. sacrifice at the newly established central place.

The taking possession of the land is a forceful action, as the use of the root *yrš* indicates.[38] It seems as if the origin of the central cult and central place is inseparably tied to a conflict, according to Deuteronomy. The peaceful migration into the land followed by the establishment of a cult is thought impossible.

The place Yahweh will choose is one from among the tribes of Israel (Deut. 12.5) and it is only logical that Deut. 12.14 states that the chosen place is then situated in the territory of one Israelite tribe.[39] The chosen place is then the place

33. See *inter alios* Clements 1996: 9-10; Levinson 1997: 23; Maag 1956 with reference to 2 Kgs 23. But see the critical remarks regarding the interpretation of Deuteronomy through the lens of 2 Kgs in Hölscher 1922: 189-90: 'Es ist überhaupt methodisch verfehlt, bei dieser ganzen Untersuchung beständig nach II Reg 22f. hinüberzuschielen; denn es ist eine *petitio principii*, die mit einer rein literarischen Untersuchung nichts zu tun haben darf; erst wenn der Urbestand des Deuteronomiums, ganz ohne Rücksicht auf II Reg 22f., auf rein literarischem Wege festgestellt worden ist, kann das Verhältnis des Urdeuteronomiums zu II Reg 22f. erwogen werden'. The current relevance of Hölscher's verdict can be seen in Otto 1999a: 12-14.

34. For such a view see Rofé 1972.

35. See Lohfink 1991b; Reuter 1993: 115-91, does not find any literary stratum that precedes the linking with Jerusalem.

36. On the phrase as such see Lohfink 1991a: 229-56.

37. This land is normally the land (*'ereṣ* or *'ᵃdāmâ*) which Yahweh has sworn (*šb'*) to give to the fathers and their offspring; see Deut. 1.8, 35; 6.10, 18, 23; 7.13; 8.1; 9.5; 10.11; 11.9, 21; 19.8; 26.3, 15; 28.11; 30.20; 31.7, 23. On the issue of the land in Deuteronomy see Plöger 1967: 60-129 and Perlitt 1994.

38. *lᵉrištāh* plus *'ereṣ* in Deut. 3.18; 4.5, 14, 26; 5.28; 6.1; 7.1; 9.6; 11.8, 10, 11, 29; 12.1; 19.2, 14; 21.1; 23.21; 28.21, 63; 30.16, 18; 31.13; 32.47 and also in Josh. 1.11; Ezek. 9.11.

39. On the chraracter of *bᵉ'aḥad šᵉbāṭeykā* in Deut. 12.14a, cf. Reuter 1993: 65-67.

to which Israel shall come, i.e. a place of pilgrimage[40] or better 'religious travel', since antiquity does not know the concept of the difficult journey to the shrine but simply sees it as a trip to the deity.[41] As such Deuteronomy envisages a certain mobility of its people, when the chapter implies that the Israelites will travel to the sanctuary to offer sacrifices.

The so-called 'centralization formula' occurs 21 times in the book of Deuteronomy[42] and only four times outside the book (Josh. 9.27; Jer. 7.12; Ezra 6.12; Neh. 1.9).[43] Furthermore, within Deuteronomy we can distinguish between a shorter form[44] and a longer version[45] of the formula. Also, the Hebrew verb *bḥr* in Deuteronomy occurs mostly in connection with 'people' (*'ām*) and *māqôm*,[46] thus connecting the central place with the central people. This *māqôm* is clearly a cultic place, as the parallel text in Exod. 20.24-26 emphazises.[47] This cultic place is not necessarily tied to a city and thus the place of worship in Deuteronomy could be regarded as a 'non-urban-sanctuary' in the terms of F. de Polignac.[48] These sanctuaries 'constitute what one might call sanctuaries of territorial sovereignty' (de Polignac 1994: 4). Of course, it is possible that these sanctuaries over a period of time will become part of a city community, such as the cult at Eleusis and Cape Sunion which formed an integral part of the religious life in Athens. The same might be said for Jerusalem, where an original extra-urban sanctuary became integrated in the city as such,[49] so that the extra-urban cult of Yahweh is becoming transformed into a quasi *polis* religion.[50] Furthermore, 'rural sanctuaries often became the site and protectors of practices and institutions of a federal kind in the Archaic and Classical eras' (de Polignac 1994: 15) in ancient Greece. With regard to the taking possession of a new territory, 'the nonurban sanctuaries of the colonial cities were linked first and foremost with the definition of the territory and the political space' (de Polignac 1995: 98). In other words, the setting up of a cult centre consecrated the territory

40. On the anthropological notion of the phenomenon of pilgrimage, cf. Dubisch 1995: 34-48, who notes that '[p]ilgrimage is based on the belief that certain places are different from other places, specifically, that they are in some sense more powerful and extraordinary... This power can not only be experienced by the pilgrim who visits such places; it can also be taken home in one form or another... In addition, a pilgrimage site is connected in complex ways to the non-sacred world around it. It has economic, social and political ramifications...' (pp. 37, 39).

41. I am grateful to Professor R. Parker for drawing my attention to this fact. On the question of 'religious travel' in antiquity see most recently Perlman 2000.

42. Deut. 12.5, 11, 14, 18, 21, 26; 14.23, 24, 25; 15.20; 16.2, 6, 7, 11, 15, 16; 17.8, 10; 18.6; 26.2; 31.11.

43. For more exegetical studies of the formula see Weippert 1980; Lohfink 1991b.

44. Deut. 12.14, 18, 26; 14.25; 15.20; 16.7, 15, 16; 17.8, 10; 18.6; 31.11.

45. Deut. 12.5, 11, 21; 14.23, 24; 16.2, 6, 11; 26.2.

46. But see also Deut. 17.15 (king); 18.5; 21.5 (Levites).

47. Reuter 1993: 123; Otto 1999a: 341-51.

48. See de Polignac 1994: 3-18 and also Jost 1992: 205-39.

49. See 2 Sam. 24.18-25 where the threshing floor of Araunah the Jebusite is outside the city walls; cf. Fritz 1977: 18.

50. For a definition of *polis*-religion in regard to the Greek world see Sourvinou-Inwood 1990: 295-322.

seized (p. 99). Furthermore, we have reports from Greek authors in which, after the arrival of the Greeks, the inhabitants of the land were either expelled or submitted to slavery.[51] At the same time we never really hear what happens to the nations Israel is supposed to expel.

In the course of the legal corpus we find further explicit reference to the central place envisaged in Deuteronomy 12. In the so-called *leges de officiis* (Deut. 16.18–18.22), 17.8-13 refers special cases to the priest(s) at the central sanctuary. These cases (*dābār lammišpāṭ*) are described as too difficult for the local legal authorities to decide. What are envisaged are cases referring to murder, etc. Thus it becomes apparent that the court described in 17.8-13 is not a court of appeal, but rather an authority which can be called upon if the competencies of the local judges are exceeded.[52] Interestingly enough the case of apostasy or idol worship does not seem to rank among the cases too difficult for the local judges to decide (17.8-13), and therefore does not have to be referred to the Priestly judge in the Temple of Jerusalem.

The law regarding the king of Israel (Deut. 17.14-20) also seems to know of a central place. The text states that the king will receive a written copy of the law from the hands of the levitical priests. Since we learn from the same group of laws that there will be no other priests than the ones at the central sanctuary, Deuteronomy assumes that the king will either travel or simply locate his throne in the vicinity of the central place. If that is the case we would have some evidence in 17.14-20 that an originally rural sanctuary becomes transformed into a sanctuary which will start to govern a political entity.

Deuteronomy 12 does not mention priests but 17.9 does know of levitical priests at the central sanctuary and 26.3-4 requires a priest for the offering of the first fruits.

4. *The Apollo Sanctuary at Delphi*

> One would think that if the landscape of Delphi vibrates with such an inner radiance, it is because there is no corner of our land that has been so much kneaded by chthonic powers and absolute light. (Seferis 1997: 84)

The Apollo Sanctuary at Delphi is located on the southern slopes of Mt Parnassos on a fairly narrow natural terrace overlooking a deep river valley.[53] From the sanctuary it is also possible to see the gulf of Itea in the distance. As such Delphi belongs to the Greek district of Phocis, a part of mainland Greece north of Attica, with hardly any urban centres.[54] 'Zeus, according to the Greek legend, once wished to determine the exact centre of the earth. So he released two eagles from

51. See Polybius 12.6.2-5; Polyenus 6.22; Thucydides 6.4.1.

52. In the Greek world inscriptional evidence tells us that it was possible for priests to act as judges if there were no other judges appointed by the community; cf. *IG* IV. 493 (Inscription from Mycenae).

53. On the role of Apollo in the Greek Pantheon, see Burkert 1985: 143-49.

54. The literature on Delphi is literally legion. On the origin of the sanctuary see Parke and Wormell 1956 and Morgan 1990: 106-47. For the oracular responses see Fontenrose 1978.

opposite ends of the world. Flying towards each other they met precisely over Delphi and demonstrated that it was the midmost point.'[55] It is therefore hardly surprising that early Greek maps depict Delphi as the centre of the world. Also Apollo seems to have been a god connected with the notion of centredness since his birth. Greek legend reports that he was born on Delos either near or in a circular lake.[56]

The legend preserved in the Homeric Hymn to Pythian Apollo, a document which probably dates from the early sixth century (Morgan 1993: 30), reports that Apollo himself chose the place of Delphi for his sanctuary and that he himself built the first temple there:

> Ἐνθάδε δὴ φρονέω τεῦξαι περικαλλέα νηὸν
> ἔμμεναι ἀνθρώποις χρηστήριον, οἵτε μοι αἰεὶ
> ἐνθάδ' ἀγινήσουσι τελήεσσας ἑκατόμβας,
> ἠμὲν ὅσοι Πελοπόννησον πίειραν ἔχουσιν,
> ἠδ' ὅσοι Εὐρώπην τε καὶ ἀμφιρύτας κατὰ νήσους,
> χρησόμενοι· τοῖσιν δ' ἄρ' ἐγὼ νημερτέα βουλὴν
> πᾶσι θεμιστεύοιμι χρέων ἐνὶ πίονι νηῷ[57]

> In this place I am minded to build a glorious temple to be an oracle for men, and here they will always bring perfect hecatombs, both they who dwell in rich Peloponnesus and the men of Europe and from all the wave-washed isles, coming to question me. And I will deliver to them all counsel that cannot fail, answering them in my rich temple.

To emphasize the national character of the sanctuary, the text continues stating that the god chose priests from all over Greece, including Crete, to serve at his sanctuary.[58]

By being one of the two main sanctuaries for Apollo—the other one being located at Delos (interestingly the island of Delos served as the central market and common sanctuary of the Cycladic islands)—Delphi occupies a special role in the Greek religious setting as a result of its oracle. Oracular activity at Delphi is attested since Homeric times (*Iliad* 2.519; 9.405), and Apollo and his oracle played an important role in the promulgation of laws. I will only mention here in passing the reforms of Demonax in Cyrene in which the reform is inaugurated by an envoy to Delphi (i.e. Apollo) asking what should be done regarding the order of the state.[59] 'Through the cultic prescriptions emanating from Delphi, the

55. Parke and Wormell 1956: 1. According to Strabo (*Geography* 9.3.6), the myth of the two eagles (or crows) is also told by Pindar. Cf. Plutarch, *De defectu oraculorum* 409F; Plutarch goes on to state that two travellers from opposite parts of the world met precisely in Delphi just like the eagles (ἔτυχον ἄνδρες ἱεροὶ δύο συνδραμόντες εἰς Δελφούς).

56. Aeschylus, *Eumenides* 8-11.

57. *Homeric Hymn to Pythian Apollo* 287-93.

58. *Homeric Hymn to Pythian Apollo* 388-96.

59. Herodotus 4.161: οἱ δὲ Κυρηναῖοι πρὸς τὴν καταλαβοῦσαν συμφορὴν ἔπεμπον ἐς Δελφοὺς ἐπειρησομένους ὅντινα τρόπον καταστησάμενοι κάλλιστα ἂν οἰκέοιεν. ἡ δὲ Πυθίη ἐκέλευε ἐκ Μαντινέης τῆς Ἀρκάδων καταρτιστῆρα ἀγαγέσθαι ('The Cyrenaeans, in the affliction that had befallen them, sent to Delphi to enquire what ordering of their state should best give them prosperity. The priestess bade them bring a peacemaker from Mantinea in Arcadia'). On the reforms of Demonax in general, see Hölkeskamp 1993 and 1999: 165-72.

outlines of a universal morality overriding tradition and group interests may be discerned for the first time among the Greeks' (Burkert 1985: 148). Especially with regard to the regulation about purification following a murder, Delphi became important (in a similar way to Deut. 17.8, where cases *dābār lammišpāṭ bên dām l*ᵉ*dām* are referred to the priests and judge at the central sanctuary). 'Apollo…was a god of oracles who became an authority on murder purification because pollution was an issue on which, like other oracular gods, he was repeatedly consulted' (Parker 1983: 139). However, it remains doubtful if any legal stipulation ever came out of Delphi, since it is more likely that laws were simply sent to Delphi for formal approval by Apollo.[60] This, however, did not prevent the Greeks from seeing Apollo as a lawgiver.[61] 'Apollo was recognized as the god who authorized decisions, interpretations and solutions in the face of changing circumstances; as the source of specific laws; or as the god who provided sanction for the whole social order' (Malkin 1989: 129). It is in that context that we have to see the close connection between various lawgivers such as Solon and Kleisthenes and the Delphic oracle.[62] In general we can say that *poleis* sent envoys to Delphi in times of civil disorder.[63] Also we find dedicatory inscriptions of rulers at Delphi who pride themselves in having ruled by the law.[64]

Stressing the importance of Delphi further, Greek myth tells us that Deucalion landed on Parnassus (a mountain close to Delphi) after the flood.[65] This understanding of Delphi as the centre of the known world is further expressed by the fact that we find the navel of the earth or ὀμφαλός, an egg shaped stone, in the inner sanctuary at Delphi.[66] This stone is frequently mentioned by Greek authors.[67]

Greek tragedy can describe Apollo's shrine at Delphi as μεσομφαλία, i.e. 'in mid-navel' or simply 'central' (translation following LSJ).[68] The whole district of

60. See the excellent discussion of the problem in Parker 1983: 138-43.

61. Plato, *Laws* 624.

62. Parke and Wormell 1956: 110-12. Herdotus 5.66.1 reports that Kleisthenes had bribed the Pythia to deliver an oracle that would suit his need (see Malkin 1989: 141-42).

63. See Tyrtaios, *fr.* 4 [West]; Pindar, *Pythian* 4.5-6.

64. See the so called Daochos Monument and its inscription (*FDelphes* III.4, No. 460).

65. Apollodorus 1.7.3 and see also Roscher 1918: 14.

66. On the location of the ὀμφαλός see Amandry 1992 with reference to *CID* 46 B III ll. 4-5; 49 A I ll. 8-12; 56 A I ll. 30-33; 62 B II ll. 71-80 (also reference to the expression πρόστασις πρὸ τοῦ ὀμφάλου in 56 A I ll. 30-33).

67. The following is a selection of references to ὀμφαλός from Greek authors: Aeschylus, *Choephoroi* 1034-37; *Eumenides* 40 (ὁρῶ δ' ἐπ' ὀμφαλῷ μὲν ἄνδρα θεομυσῆ); *Eumenides* 166-67 (πάρεστι γᾶς ὀμφαλὸν προσδρακεῖν αἱμάτων | βλουσυρὸν ἀρόμενον ἄγος ἔχειν); *Septem ante Thebas* 745-48; Bacchylides 4.4-6 (τρίτον γὰρ παρ' [ὀμφα]λὸν ὑψιδείρου χθονός | Πυ[θ]ιόνικος ἀ[είδε]ται˚ | ὠ[κυ]πόδων ἀρ[ετᾶι] σὺν ἵππων˚); Epimenides in Plutarch, *De defectu orac.* 1 (Οὔτε γὰρ ἦν γαίης μέσος ὀμφαλὸς οὔτε θαλάσσης· εἰ δὲ τις ἐστί, θεοῖς, θνητοῖσι δ' ἄφαντος); Euripides, *Ion* 5.222,414ff., 461f.; *Medea* 667; *Iphigenia* 1251ff.; *Orestes* 325,591; *Phoenissae* 232ff.; Pindar, *Pythian* 4.73-74 (ἦλθε δέ οἱ κρυόεν πυκινῷ μαντεύμα θυμῷ, | πὰρ μέσον ὀμφαλὸν εὐδένροιο ῥηθὲν ματέρος); *Pythian* 4.6ff.; 6.3; 8.59; 11.9; *Nemean* 7.33; Sophocles, *Oedipus Rex* 476ff., 897ff.; (cf. Strabo, *Geography* 9.3.6; Pausanias, *Description of Greece* 10.16.3).

68. Aeschylus, *Septem ante Thebas* 747; *Agamemnon* 1056; *Cheophori* 1036; Euripides, *Orestes* 331.

the sanctuary is of course sacred territory and everything that is in it is 'holy' as well and has to be protected. Thus it is, for example, strictly forbidden to remove wine from the stadium.[69]

The special role of the Delphic oracle is further illuminated by its special status and function in the process of colonization.[70] This involvement in the process of colonisation started as early as the eighth century (Malkin 1987: 22). In general, *poleis* sent an envoy to Delphi to acquire some sort of legitimation for the new colony.[71] As such Delphi's active part in the process added greatly to the influence of this central shrine, as the accumulated votives found at Delphi show.[72]

Despite the popularity of the Greek oracles, there was always a certain danger in consulting them,[73] since hardly any specific questions could be asked (Parker 2000: 77). Furthermore, 'divination fails of its function if its objectivity is not convincingly demonstrated' (p. 78). Generally oracles are sacred and their sayings should not be altered.[74] Herodotus knows about a certain Onomacritus, a chresmologue who got expelled from Athens because he amended the oracles of Musaeus (Herodotus 7.6.3-4). Here we are close to the Deuteronomic stipulations in Deut. 4.2 and 13.1, where it is explicitly stated that the stipulations of God shall not be altered.

5. *Central Place Theory*

The starting point for my social-scientific interpretation of Deuteronomy 12 will be W. Christaller's theory of a *central place* (first developed with regard to mediaeval cities in southern Germany). Prior to him, von Thünen's study 'of the intellectual fiction of the isolated city in a featureless plain demonstrated the theoretical relationship between distance from the centre and increasing economic disadvantage' (Champion 1989: 2). Christaller prefers to speak of 'central places' instead of settlements in his work (Christaller1966: 17), because the word 'place' implies much more than just a settlement for him. He states that 'every place has a certain importance which is usually defined...as the size of the place' (p. 17). However, 'neither area nor population very precisely express the meaning of the

69. *CID* I, 3, see also *CID* I, 9 (Nomima I, 71).

70. On the role of Delphi in the process, see the detailed study by Malkin 1987 and for a catalogue of responses Fontenrose 1978.

71. See for example ML 5 for the foundation of Cyrene.

72. On votives, see Price 1999: 58-63.

73. Nevertheless, it has been possible to put pressure on the Pythia in Delphi to say the right thing (see, e.g., Herodotus 7.140-43), as Flacelière 1965: 63 rightly states: '...but [it] also indicates the extent to which the Delphic priesthood and the Pythia could be influenced by personal pressure, political intrigue and financial generosity...'

74. Plato, *Laws* 738c: οὐδεὶς ἐπιχειρήσει κινεῖν νοῦν ἔχων ὅσα ἐκ Δελφῶν ἢ Δωδώνης ἢ παρ' Ἄμμωνος ἤ τινες ἔπεισαν παλαιοι λόγοι ὁπῃδη τινας πείσαντες, φασμάτων γενομένων ἢ ἐπιπνοίας λεχθείσης θεῶν ('no man of sense—whether he be framing a new State or re-forming an old one that has been corrupted—will attempt to alter the advice from Delphi or Dodona or Ammon, or that ancient sayings, whatever form they take—whether derived from visions or from some reported inspiration from heaven').

importance of the town' (p. 17). Since importance is never a sum but rather a combination of efforts, it would be wrong to link the importance of a place to its population (p. 18). Centrality is then the relative importance of a place with regard to the region surrounding it, or—geographically speaking—'the most important center of any society...will be positioned in the geographical center of that society' (Cohen 2002: 23); a centre is only called a centre if it performs a central function (Christaller 1966: 18-19). Christaller's theory can furthermore be summarized as follows:

> (1) The basic function of a city is to be a central place providing goods and services for a surrounding tributary area. The term "central place" is used because to perform such a function efficiently, a city locates at the center of minimum aggregate travel of its tributary area i.e. central to the maximum profit area it can command.
> (2) The centrality of a city is a summary measure of the degree to which it is such a service center; the greater the centrality of a place, the higher is its "order".
> (3) Higher order places offer more goods, have more establishments and business types, larger populations, tributary areas and tributary populations, do greater volumes of business, and are more widely spaced than lower order places.
> (4) Low order places provide only low order goods to low order tributary areas; these low order goods are generally necessities requiring frequent purchasing with little consumer travel. Moreover low order goods are provided by establishments with relatively low conditions of entry. Conversely, high order places provide not only low order goods, but also high order goods sold by high order establishments with greater conditions of entry. These high order goods are generally "shopping goods" for which the consumer is willing to travel longer distances, although less frequently. The higher order of the goods provided, the fewer are the establishments providing them, the greater the conditions of entry and trade areas of the establishments, and the fewer and more widely spaced are the towns in which the establishments are located. Ubiquity of types of business increases as their order diminishes. Because higher order places offer more shopping opportunities, their trade areas for low order goods are likely to be larger than those of low order places, since consumers have the opportunity to combine purposes on a single trip, and this acts like a price-reduction.
> (5) More specifically, central places fall into a hierarchy comprising discrete groups of centers. Centers of each higher order group perform all the functions of lower order centers plus a group of central functions that differentiates them from and sets them above the low order. A consequence is a "nesting" pattern of lower order trade areas within the trade area of higher order centers, plus a hierarchy of routes joining the centers.
> (6) Even more specifically, with Thünen-type limiting assumptions relating to uniformity of population distribution, the hierarchy may be organized according to (a) a market principle, according to which nesting follows a rule of threes. Deviations from the market principle may be explained by (b) the principles of traffic, which give rise to linear patterns and nesting according to fours, or (c) the socio-political or administrative "separation" principles, with the hierarchy organized according to a rule of sevens, and with low-order twin cities where one would predict a high order place to be located if only the marketing principles were operative. (Berry and Pred 1965: 3-4)

After this brief summary of Christaller's theory, it will immediately become apparent that the application of the model to the biblical and Greek texts has certain difficulties.[75] First of all, Christaller's data are limited and confined to southern mediaeval Germany and of course he is neither a social-scientist nor a historian but an urban geographer.

> Much of this work suffers from being too concerned with the spatial patterning rather than the social reality, and from weakness in moving from one frame of reference to another. Furthermore, the kind of relationships typically analysed in this way has been comparatively small-scale, within a defined zone, whether that is a geographical entity such as an island or river drainage or a historically defined polity, and focused on a single central point, whether a small settlement in relation to the resources in its catchment area or a large urban centre in relation to its hinterland. (Champion 1989: 3)

As far as the critique of the concept of central place theory is concerned, it has been observed by archaeologists and anthropologists, that

> [a]pplications of central place theory by European and American geographers have been primarily concerned with western industrialised societies, and soon it became clear that these models were not necessarily relevant to the needs of archaeologists and anthropologists... The geographer's concept of a 'central place' is therefore extremely narrow, and so we must ask whether archaeologists and anthropologists should extend the use of the term to cover different sorts of societies. (Collis 1986: 38)

We must always remember that '[c]entral-place theory has successfully offered a set of assumptions appropriate to market-based societies in the modern world' (Hodges 1987: 131). But whether these findings are readily transferable to a society of the past, of which our main set of data is a written text, remains to be seen.[76] Also, the theory does not provide an explanation of how the system of a central place originates and develops in the first place (Cohen 2002: 23). Moreover, the theory assumes a constant flow of various goods to the central place to be distributed there, but it never accounts for any physical barriers that might affect and interrupt such flow.[77] Furthermore we should note that

> [a]ll human societies show centralising tendencies, as do some animal societies... Even simple human societies tend to greater complexity than the rest of the animal kingdom in the varying levels of settlement hierarchy... With more complex societies the forms of centralisation become more complex... (Collis 1986: 38)

Christaller was quite aware of the universality of central places when he states in the introductory chapter:

> The crystallization of man around a nucleus is, in inorganic as well as organic nature, an elementary form of order of things which belong together—a centralistic order. This order is not only a human mode of thinking, existing in the human world of imagination and developed because people demand order; it in fact exists out of the inherent pattern of matter. (Christaller 1966: 14)

75. For a critique of Christaller's work, see Beavon 1984: 18-41.

76. On the problem of utilizing literary texts for anthropological research, see Sant Cassia 1991 and Shore 1995.

77. Recent applications of central place theory to Canaanite archaeology (Cohen 2002) have started to modify the original model, by using a conflation of Christaller's theory with attempts to develop a theory that is based on the data from the southern Levant (see Cohen's use of Stager 2001: 625-38).

Thus we need to modify the model. First of all it is necessary to stress that we are dealing with two cultic centres here, which in the case of Delphi are quite remote from any urban centre. As far as Deuteronomy is concerned, ch. 12 does not seem to know of a city attached to the sanctuary, since the text distinguishes between the place of worship/sacrifice (*māqôm*) and the cities (*šeʿārîm* lit. 'gates') where the Israelites will be living.[78] Rather than just speaking of a 'central place' it might be more fitting or accurate to use the opposition of centre and periphery,[79] since it is precisely that which is talked of in Deuteronomy 12. However, we have to bear in mind that

> core and periphery...are not to be elevated to superhistorical forces, operating universally and not in need of specific analysis in any given context. On the other hand, these concepts do provide a general framework within which it is possible to analyse in very precise terms the specific conditions in which the relationships between polities at different levels of economic, political or technological development did, in specific cases, produce changes in those polities. (Champion 1989: 10)

This notion of centre and periphery is of course not absent in Christaller's original theory when he speaks of different hierarchies of centres.[80] But since he only speaks of low and high order places the reader gets the impression that the phenomenon of peripheral existence is not really catered for. We will see in the following part that there has been a certain notion of centre and periphery in the shaping of a sacred landscape in both Israel and ancient Greece.

Despite the fact that the theory has been developed with regard to cities, it is possible to transfer the findings to the sanctuaries of Israel and Greece, since these sacred places functioned as mini-cities or economic centres throughout the ancient world.[81] 'One notable feature of the classical central-place is that they seem to be more often found in agrarian societies, where central places are periodic and traders are mobile' (Smith 1976: 15).

With regard to Deuteronomy 12, the higher good offered at the place where Yahweh's name will dwell is sacrifice, and we find the stipulation that there shall be only one legitimate place of worship four times in this chapter (Deut. 12.1-7, 8-12, 13-14, 26-27a). Also, the reduction of the legitimate places for the cult to just one place *qua* the creation of a centre redefines religious activity in Israel. Also we should remind ourselves that it is highly unlikely that core and peripheries will ever be distributed in an even or simple manner across geographical space (Stoddart 1989). Furthermore, Deuteronomy 12 might just be only the initial step in the creation of a centre. If the single-purposed consumer trip—as advocated by Christaller—is highly unlikely (Smith 1976: 24), we can probably

78. One should also note that the term *šeʿāreykā* serves as *pars pro toto* for the city as a whole (Gertz 1994: 33, 79), as is usually the case in Deuteronomy (see Deut. 5.14; 12.12, 15, 17, 18, 21; 14.21, 27-29; 15.7, 22; 16.5, 11, 14, 18; 17.2, 5, 8; 18.6; 23.17; 24.14; 26.12; 28.52, 55, 57; 31.12); only in Deut. 6.9 = 11.20 is a concrete gate envisaged.

79. On the use of the concept of centre and periphery in archaeology etc., see Rowlands 1987.

80. On Christaller's hierachy of central places, see King 1984: 31-32.

81. See Blenkinsopp 1991; Burkert 1988; Weinberg 1976 and the critique of Weinberg's theory by Williamson 1998.

argue that supplies are attracted to one another, creating an economic centre. Deuteronomy 12 is aware that the 'place' can be far away (12.21; 14.24), thus silently assuming that the land is fairly extensive (12.20; 19.8) as well as the existence of members of the in-group at the periphery. Centralization in Deuteronomy does not mean a centralization of the people in close vicinity to the sanctuary. Passages like 14.24-27 seem to provide stipulations for making the pilgrimage to the central place easier and also seem to know of money. If it is possible to buy sheep, wine, etc. at the central place, the cultic centre is also an economic one. We realize that the single-purpose consumer trip, already mentioned, seems to be highly unlikely. Furthermore, the supply of a high order good such as sacrifice attracts several businesses catering for low order goods, such as animals, etc.

6. *Shaping a Sacred Landscape*

If landscape does not equal nature, it is clear that dichotomies such as public vs. private and sacred vs. profane belong to the landscape or setting of Deuteronomy and that the 'poetics of space' will provide us with information about how the author of the work perceived his (or her) world (Bachelard 1958). On the other hand,

> [t]he concept of sacred implies restriction and prohibition on human behaviour—if something is sacred then certain rules must be observed in relation to it, and this generally means that something that is said to be sacred...must be placed apart from everyday things and places, so that its special significance can be recognised, and rules regarding it obeyed. (Hubert 1994: 11)

Furthermore, sacred sites are sometimes difficult to recognize for outsiders. The 'creation of sacred space' is made possible by selecting certain positions from the vast expanse of the world. These locales become then positions, because it is here that the effects of power are being repeated.[82] It is in this place apart that the divinity resides,[83] but is not necessarily confined to there, since the deity can leave the temple/sacred site and return.[84] Worship, then, generally means to come or to turn to the gods, i.e. entering the sacred sphere (Deut. 12.11-12).[85] We should note that for Deuteronomy and the Deuteronomistic literature generally, '[t]here is not one example...of *God's dwelling* in the temple or the building of a house for God. The temple is always the *dwelling of his name*, and the house is always built for *his name*' (Weinfeld 1972: 193).

In a further step I now need to evaluate what kind of sanctuaries we are dealing with in Deuteronomy 12 and at Delphi. Following F. de Polignac we can distinguish between three different types of sanctuaries in the Greek world:

82. See Knipe 1988: 107 quoting the insights of G. van der Leeuw.

83. See Deut. 12.5; *Homeric Hymn to Demeter* 27-29 (ὁ δὲ νόσφιν | ἧστο θεῶν ἀπάνευθε πολυλλίστωι ἐνὶ νηῶι | δέγμενος ἱερὰ καλὰ παρὰ θνητῶν ἀνθρώπων ['he, however, was seated apart from the gods, in his prayerful temple, receiving fine offerings from mortals']), see also *Iliad* 300-302. For the Old Testament concept of the so called *Shekina*-theology, cf. Janowski 1993: 119-47.

84. Homer, *Iliad* 5.446-47; *Odyssey* 7.81; 8.363.

85. Aristophanes, *Clouds* 306-307.

(a) urban sanctuaries, (b) extra-urban sanctuaries and (c) inter-urban sanctuaries. Since neither Deuteronomy 12 nor the evidence from Delphi suggest that an urban centre is attached to the sanctuary,[86] we can probably disregard type (a).[87] *Extra-urban sanctuaries* can be defined as cultic centres, which 'are administered by the city-state but are located outside the urban space. They too are national monuments but are destined to mark or expand the territorial influence of the city and to act as regional centres for the cult. They thus unite the rustic population under a national cult' (Marinatos 1993: 229). *Inter-urban sanctuaries*, on the other hand, can be defined as being

> located away from major cities and, although they were under the administrative control of their nearby city-states or amphictonies they had an aura of neutrality. They thus formed ideal places for political interaction. They were places where Greeks could meet other Greeks on equal grounds to compete and to agree, to establish superiority in athletics, to read each other's propaganda in the form of dedicatory inscriptions, to sound each other out. (Marinatos 1993: 230)

The classification of Delphi as an inter-urban sanctuary with a distinctive national character is fairly easy and inscriptional evidence supports such a view. Here at Delphi we find dedications from individual states from all over Greece[88] as well as truly national dedications.[89]

However, Deuteronomy 12 does not yet know the concept of a temple. The place which Yahweh will choose is just called *māqôm*, i.e. 'place', so it could just be an altar etc. The same thing can be observed in the Greek world, where

> the temple is not an essential religious part of the Greek sanctuary—it is the altar which is essential. Hence most sanctuaries are of earlier date than their temples, and some never acquired a temple, among them sanctuaries housing far from insignificant cults. (Sourvinou-Inwood 1993: 19)[90]

The building of a temple would then be a step towards monumentalization. 'The altar moved from a central position to an eastward peripheral one, the temple from a westward peripheral to a central one, and the sacrificial area from a westward to an eastward peripheral one' (Sourvinou-Inwood 1993: 10). However, I would note that further stipulations in Deuteronomy clearly envisage the place where Yahweh will choose his name to dwell to be a full blown sanctuary, where priests reside and where it is possible to provide food etc. for the Levites.

The stipulations in Deuteronomy 12 regarding the one central sanctuary put an end to the tradition that patriarchs etc. tend to build an altar after the seizure of a

86. *Māqôm* can de used in the Old Testament to describe the place of human dwelling (see Judg. 7.7; 1 Sam. 2.20) but this is not the case in Deuteronomy.

87. On the question of Phokian settlement at Delphi see Morgan 1990: 106-26.

88. Comp. ML 19; ML 25 (Athens); ML 28 (Gelon of Syracuse); Jeffery 1990: 168.4 (Argive dedication).

89. Cf. the Greek thank offering for the victories in the war against Persia in ML 27 which starts το[ίδε τὸν] | πόλεμον [ἐ]- | πολ[έ]μεον· and continues to list 31 Greek states that have fought against the Persians.

90. On the Greek phenomenon of the *temenos* see Berquist 1967.

land.[91] At the same time the text marginalizes these well known sanctuaries, since it is now forbidden to offer sacrifices there (12.13).[92] Thus the sacred landscape changes.

7. *Conclusion*

We have seen in the course of this study that the concept of central places is well known both in Greece and ancient Palestine. Despite the lack of actual Hebrew vocabulary for the word 'centre', the Bible is familiar with such a concept and the prominence Mt Zion will achieve proves the point. However, this Zion-theology is still absent from the Pentateuch as a whole and the reader gets the impression that the centre in these books of the Hebrew Bible is in fact Mt Sinai (interestingly enough, in those passages of the Hebrew Bible where legal stipulations from the Pentateuch are revised or discussed, these legal stipulations can never be found in the laws promulgated at Mt Sinai).[93]

The sacred landscape of Israel changes with Deuteronomy 12. From now on it is made clear that Yahweh, the God of Israel who has travelled with Israel through history and the wilderness, will choose a permanent dwelling for himself. There is a striking parallel here to Apollo who chooses Delphi from among all the sites in Greece. This motion results into a secularization of the local shrines and altars:

> In draining the local sphere of all cultic content, the authors of Deuteronomy do not leave it as a profane religious void. Instead, they reconzeptualize it in secular terms and give it positive new content. The local sphere continues to have a fundamentally religious structure. One continues to receive divine blessing in the local sphere, although it is now mediated. The compensation for the loss of direct access to the divine, with the eradication of the local altars, does not only take place at the cultic center with the repeated emphasis on the 'joy' available there to the pilgrim. (Levinson 1997: 49)[94]

This change results in the introduction of a strong notion of centre and periphery in Deuteronomy. All the local shrines which have previously been centres themselves are no longer at the centre of religious life. The believer has from now on to embark on a religious journey if he wants to come into direct contact with the divine. The society has to be mobile. Texts like Deut. 18.6-8 may also hint at the fact that there has been a certain migration towards the central sanctuary.[95] We should, however, also note that the vision of the central sanctuary according to

91. See Gen. 12.6-7, 8; 13.18 (Abraham builds altars in Shechem, Bethel and Mamre); Gen. 26.25 (Isaac in Beersheba); Gen. 33.18-20; 35.1-8 (Jacob); Josh. 8.30 (Joshua in Ebal); Judg. 6.24-26 (Gideon); 1 Sam 7.17 (Samuel in Ramah); 1 Sam. 14.35 (Saul).

92. To be precise here one should probably speak, following the insights of Billson (1988) and Germani (1980), of structural marginality, since this form of marginality 'refers to the political, social and economic powerlessness of certain...disadvantaged segments within societies' (Billson 1980: 185).

93. See Isa. 56.1-8; 66.18-24, where Deut. 23.2-9 (ET 1-8) is modified.

94. On the notion of the 'joy' in Deuteronomy, see Braulik 1988: 161-218.

95. On the passage in general, see Dahmen 1996: 287-310, and the critique of Dahmen's view in Otto 1999b.

Deuteronomy 12 also clearly states that this sanctuary is accessible for all the population of Israel. In similar fashion the non-urban sanctuaries of the Greek world provided religious access to the population living on the periphery, i.e. away from the main cities (de Polignac 1995: 112).

The required mobility of the people results in a clustering of economic potential at the central sanctuary. It is here that aspects of the 'central place theory' evaluated above begin to function.

Furthermore, the location of the texts within the Bible as a whole is quite remarkable: the centralization of worship is the first legal stipulation given to Israel in Deuteronomy before the entry into the land. Seizure of territory is only possible if sanctioned by the divine sphere. The same is true for the Greek way of colonization where the Delphic oracle legitimates the new settlement.[96] As such, the new territory becomes automatically sacred.

As far as the classification of the sanctuary according to Deuteronomy 12 is concerned, the text itself suggests that we are dealing with a so-called *inter-urban sanctuary* which is located away from major settlements to which the people from all over the country and its settlements would travel. In the Hebrew Bible this inter-urban sanctuary got rapidly transformed into an urban sanctuary, thus equating the place where Yahweh will choose to dwell with the city of Jerusalem. The comparison with Delphi would then have to be replaced with one using Athens and its acropolis.

BIBLIOGRAPHY

Amandry, P.
1992 'Où était l'Omphalos?', in J.-F. Bommelaer (ed.), *Delphes: Centennaire de la 'Grande Fouille' réalisée par l'Ecole française d'Athène (1892–1903)* (Université des Sciences Humaines de Strasbourg, 12; Leiden: E.J. Brill): 177-205.

Andrews, M.
1999 *Landscape in Western Art* (Oxford History of Art; Oxford: Oxford University Press).

Bachelard, G.
1958 *La poétique de l'espace* (Paris: Presses Universitaires).

Beavon, K.S.O.
1984 *Central Place Theory: A Reinterpretation* (London and New York: Longman).

Berquist, B.
1967 *The Archaic Greek Temenos: A Study of Structure and Function* (Skrifter Utgivna av Svenska Institutet I Athen, 4/XIII; Lund: C.W.K. Gleerup).

Berry, B.J.L., and A. Pred
1965 *Central Place Studies: A Bibliography of Theory and Applications* (Bibliography Series, 1; Philadelphia: Regional Science Research Institute).

Billson, J.M.
1988 'No Owner Soil: The Concept of Marginality Revisited on its Sixtieth Birthday', *International Review of Modern Sociology* 18: 183-204.

96. If a colony is founded without consulting the Delphic oracle it is generally mentioned; see for example Herodotus 5.42, where the Spartan prince Dorieus founds a colony in Lybia.

Blenkinsopp, J.
1991 'Temple and Society in Archaemenid Judah', in P.R. Davies (ed.), *Second Temple Studies*. I. *Persian Period* (JSOTSup, 117; Sheffield: Sheffield Academic Press): 22-53.

Braulik, G.
1988 'Die Freude des Festes. Das Kultverständnis des Deuteronomium—die älteste biblische Festtheorie', in *idem*, *Studien zur Theologie des Deuteronomium* (SBAB, 2; Stuttgart: Katholisches Bibelwerk): 161-218.
1991 *Die deuteronomischen Gesetze und der Dekalog: Studien zum Aufbau Deuteronomium 12–26* (SBS, 145; Stuttgart: Katholisches Bibelwerk).

Burkert, W.
1985 *Greek Religion* (Cambridge, MA: Harvard University Press).
1988 'The Meaning and Function of the Temple in Classical Greece', in M.V. Fox (ed.), *Temple in Society* (Winona Lake, IN: Eisenbrauns): 27-48.

Champion, T.C.
1989 'Introduction', in *idem* (ed.) 1989: 1-21.

Champion, T.C. (ed.)
1989 *Centre and Periphery: Comparative Studies in Archaeology* (One World Archeology, 11; London and New York: Routledge).

Christaller, W.
1950 *Das Grundgerüst der räumlichen Ordnung in Europa: Die Systeme der europäischen zentralen Orte* (Frankfurter Geographische Hefte, 24.1; Frankfurt: W. Kramer).
1966 *Central Places in Southern Germany* (trans. Carlisle W. Baskin; Englewood Cliffs, NJ: Prentice–Hall). First published as *Die zentralen Orte in Süddeutschland* (Jena: G. Fischer, 1933).

Clements, R.E.
1996 'The Deuteronomic Law of Centralisation and the Catastrophe of 587 B.C.E.', in J. Barton and D. Reimer (eds.), *After the Exile: Essays in Honour of Rex Mason* (Macon, GA: Mercer University Press): 5-25.

Cohen, S.L.
2002 *Canaanites, Chronologies, and Connections: The Relationship of Middle Bronze IIA Canaan to Middle Kingdom Egypt* (Studies in the Archaeology and History of the Levant, 3; Winona Lake, IN: Eisenbrauns).

Cohn, R.L.
1981 *The Shape of Sacred Space: Four Biblical Studies* (AAR.SR, 23; Chico, CA: Scholars Press).

Collis, J.
1986 'Central Place Theory is Dead: Long Live the Central Place', in E. Grant (ed.), *Central Places, Archeology and History* (Sheffield: Department of Archeology and Prehistory): 37-39.

Dahmen, U.
1996 *Leviten und Priester im Deuteronomium* (BBB, 110; Bodenheim: Philo).

Dubisch, J.
1995 *In a Different Place: Pilgrimage, Gender, and Politics at a Greek Island Shrine* (Princeton Modern Greek Studies; Princeton, NJ: Princeton University Press).

Eliade, M.
1956 *The Sacred and the Profane* (New York: Harper & Row).
1959 'Methodological Remarks on the Study of Religious Symbolism', in M. Eliade and J. Kitagawa (eds.), *The History of Religions: Essays in Methodology* (Chicago: University of Chicago Press): 1-20.

Fitter, C.
1995 *Poetry, Space, Landscape: Toward a New Theory* (Literature, Culture, Theory, 13; Cambridge: Cambridge University Press).

Flacelière, R.
1965 *Greek Oracles* (trans. Douglas Garman; London: Elek Books).

Fontenrose, J.
1978 *The Delphic Oracle: Its Responses and Operations with a Catalogue of Responses* (Berkeley and London: University of California Press).

Fritz, V.
1977 *Tempel und Zelt. Studien zum Tempelbau in Israel und zu dem Heiligtum der Priesterschrift* (WMANT, 47; Neukirchen–Vluyn: Neukirchener Verlag).

Germani, G.
1980 *Marginality* (New Brunswick: Transaction Books).

Gertz, J.C.
1994 *Die Gerichtsorganisation Israels im deuteronomischen Gesetz* (FRLANT, 165; Göttingen: Vandenhoek & Ruprecht, 1994).

Halpern, B.
1981 'The Centralization Formula in Deuteronomy', *VT* 13: 20-38.

Herrmann, H.V.
1953 *Omphalos* (Münster: Aschendorff).

Hirsch, E.
1995 'Landscape: Between Place and Space', in E. Hirsch and M. O'Hanlon (eds.), *The Anthropology of Landscape: Perspectives on Place and Space* (Oxford Studies in Social and Cultural Anthropology; Oxford: Clarendon Press): 1-30.

Hodges, R.
1987 'Spatial Models, Anthropology and Archaeology', in J.M. Wagstraff (ed.), *Landscape and Culture: Geographical and Archaeological Perspectives* (Oxford: Basil Blackwell): 118-33.

Hölkeskamp, K.J.
1993 'Demonax und die Neuordnung der Bürgerschaft von Kyrene', *Hermes* 121: 404-21.
1999 *Schiedsrichter, Gesetzgeber und Gesetzgebung im archaischen Griechenland* (Historia Einzelschriften, 131; Stuttgart: F. Steiner).

Hölscher, G.
1922 'Komposition und Ursprung des Deuteronomiums', *ZAW* 40: 161-255.

Hubert, J.
1994 'Sacred Beliefs and Beliefs of Sacredness', in D.L. Carmichael, J. Hubert, B. Reeves and A. Schanche (eds.), *Sacred Sites, Sacred Places* (One World Archeology, 23; London: Routledge): 9-19.

Huffman, C.A.
1993 *Philolaus of Croton. Pythagoraen and Presocratic: A Commentary on the Fragments and Testimonia with Interpretative Essays* (Cambridge: Cambridge University Press).

Janowski, B.
1993 '"Ich will in eurer Mitte wohnen": Struktur und Genese der exilischen Shekina-Theologie', in *idem*, *Gottes Gegenwart in Israel* (Neukirchen–Vluyn: Neukirchener Verlag): 119-47.

Jeffery, L.H.
1990 *The Local Scripts of Archaic Greece* (Oxford: Oxford University Press, 2nd edn).

Jost, M.
1992 'Sanctuaires ruraux et sanctuaires urbaines en Arcadie', in O. Reverdin and B. Grange (eds.), *Le sanctuaire grec* (Entretiens sur l'Antiquité Classique, 37; Geneva: Fondation Hardt): 205-39.

King, L.J.
1984 *Central Place Theory* (Scientific Geography Series, 1; Beverly Hills, London and New Delhi: Sage Publications).

Knipe, D.M.
1988 'The Temple in Image and Reality', in M.V. Fox (ed.), *Temple in Society* (Winona Lake, IN: Eisenbrauns): 105-38.

Levinson, B.M.
1997 *Deuteronomy and the Hermeneutics of Legal Innovation* (New York and Oxford: Oxford University Press).

Lohfink, N.
1991a 'Die *ḥuqqîm ûmišpāṭîm* im Buch *Deuteronomium* und ihre Neubegrenzung durch Dtn 12,1', in *idem*, *Studien zum Deuteronomium und zum deuteronomistischen Literatur,* II (SBAB, 12; Stuttgart: Katholisches Bibelwerk, 1991): 229-56.
1991b 'Zur deuteronomischen Zentralisationsformel', in *idem*, *Studien zum Deuteronomium und zur deuteronomistischen Literatur,* II (SBAB, 12; Stuttgart: Katholisches Bibelwerk): 147-77.
1995 'Kultzentralisation und Deuteronomium. Zu einem Buch von Eleonore Reuter', *ZABR* 1: 117-48.
1996 'Fortschreibung? Zur Technik der Rechtsrevisionen im deuteronomischen Bereich, erörtert and Deuteronomium 12, Ex 21,2-11 und Dtn 15,12-18', in T. Veijola (ed.), *Das Deuteronomium und seine Querbeziehungen* (Schriften der Finnischen Exegetischen Gesellschaft, 62; Göttingen: Vandenhoeck & Ruprecht): 127-71.

Maag, V.
1956 'Erwägungen zur deuteronomischen Kultzentralisation', *VT* 6: 10-18.

Malkin, I.
1987 *Religion and Colonization in Ancient Greece* (Studies in Greek and Roman Religion, 3; Leiden and New York: E.J. Brill).
1989 'Delphoi and the Founding of Social Order in Archaic Greece', *METIS* 41: 129-53.

Marinatos, N.
1993 'What were Greek Sanctuaries? A Synthesis', in Marinatos and Hägg (eds.) 1993: 228-33.

Marinatos, N., and R. Hägg (eds.)
1993 *Greek Sanctuaries: New Approaches* (London and New York: Routledge).

Morgan, C.
1990 *Athletes and Oracles: The Transformation of Olympia and Delphi in the Eighth Century* BC (Cambridge Classical Studies; Cambridge: University Press).
1993 'The Origins of Pan-Hellenism', in Marinatos and Hägg (eds.) 1993: 18-44.

Norin, S.
2000 'Die Stätte, die der Herr erwählt', in M. Hengel, S. Mittmann and A.M. Schwemer (eds.), *La Cité de Dieu—Die Stadt Gottes* (WUNT, 129; Tübingen: J.C.B. Mohr [Paul Siebeck]): 99-118.

Otto, E.
1999a *Das Deuteronomium: Politische Theologie und Rechtsreform in Juda und Assyrien* (BZAW, 284; Berlin and New York: W. de Gruyter).

1999b 'Die post-deuteronomistische Levitisierung des Deuteronomiums. Zu einem Buch von Ulrich Dahmen', *ZABR* 5: 277-84.

2001 *Das Deuteronomium im Pentateuch und Hexateuch: Studien zur Literaturgeschichte von Pentateuch und Hexateuch im Lichte des Deuteronomiumsrahmens* (FAT, 30; Tübingen: Mohr-Siebeck).

Parke, H.D., and D.E.W. Wormell

1956 *The Delphic Oracle.* I. *The History* (Oxford: Basil Blackwell).

Parker, R.

1983 *Miasma: Pollution and Purification in Early Greek Religion* (Oxford: Clarendon Press).

2000 'Greek States and Greek Oracles', in R. Buxton (ed.), *Oxford Readings in Greek Religion* (Oxford: Oxford University Press): 76-108.

Perlitt, L.

1994 'Motive und Schichten der Landtheologie im Deuteronomium', in *idem*, *Deuteronomium-Studien* (FAT, 8; Tübingen: J.C.B. Mohr [Paul Siebeck]): 97-108.

Perlman, P.

2000 *City and Sanctuary in Ancient Greece: The Theorodokia in the Peloponnese* (Hypomnemata; Göttingen: Vandenhoeck & Ruprecht).

Plöger, J.G.

1967 *Literarkritische, formgeschichtliche und stilkritische Untersuchungen zum Deuteronomium* (BBB, 26; Bonn: Peter Hanstein Verlag).

Polignac, F. de

1994 'Mediation, Competition, and Sovereignty: The Evolution of Rural Sanctuaries in Geometric Greece', in S.E. Alcock and R. Osborne (eds.), *Placing the Gods: Sanctuaries and Sacred Space in Ancient Greece* (Oxford: Clarendon Press): 3-18.

1995 *Cults, Territory and the Origin of the Greek City State* (Chicago: Chicago University Press).

Price, S.R.F.

1999 *Religions of the Ancient Greek*s (Key Themes in Ancient History; Cambridge: Cambridge University Press).

Reuter, E.

1993 *Kultzentralisation. Entstehung und Theologie von Dtn 12* (BBB, 87; Frankfurt: A. Hain).

Rofé, A.

1972 'The Strata of Law about the Centralization of Worship in Deuteronomy and the History of the Deuteronomic Movement', in *Congress Volume: Uppsala 1971* (VTSup, 22; Leiden: E.J. Brill): 221-26. Reprinted in *idem*, *Deuteronomy: Issues and Interpretation* (Old Testament Studies; London and New York: T. & T. Clark, 2002): 97-101.

Römer, T.

2000 'Du Temple au Livre: L'idéologie de la centralisation dans l'historiographie deutéronomiste', in S.L. McKenzie and T. Römer (eds.), *Rethinking the Foundations: Historiography in the Ancient World and in the Bible. Essays in Honour of John Van Seters* (BZAW, 294; Berlin and New York: W. de Gruyter): 207-25.

Roscher, W.H.

1913 *Omphalos* (Abhandlungen der sächsischen Gesellschaft der Wissenschaften 29.9; Leipzig: A. Hirzel).

1918 *Der Omphalosgedanke bei verschiedenen Völkern, besonders den semitischen* (Berichte der sächsischen Gesellschaft der Wissenschaften, 70.2; Leipzig: A. Hirzel).

Rowlands, M.
1987 'Centre and Periphery: A Review of a Concept', in M. Rowlands, M. Larsen and K. Kristiansen (eds.), *Centre and Periphery in the Ancient World* (New Directions in Archeology; Cambridge: Cambridge University Press): 1-11.

Sack, R.D.
1986 *Human Territoriality: Its Theory and History* (Cambridge: Cambridge University Press).

Sant Cassia, P.
1991 'Authors in Search of a Character: Personhood, Agency and Identity in the Mediterranean', *Journal of Mediterranean Studies* 1: 1-17.

Seferis, G.
1997 'Delphi', in A. Leontis (ed.), *Greece: A Traveller's Literary Companion* (San Francisco: Whereabouts Press): 84-99.

Seitz, G.
1971 *Redaktionsgeschichtliche Studien zum Deuteronomium* (BWANT, 93; Stuttgart: W. Kohlhammer).

Shore, C.
1995 'Anthropology, Literature, and the Problem of Mediterranean Identity', *Journal of Mediterranean Studies* 5: 1-13.

Smith, C.A.
1976 'Regional Economic Systems: Linking Geographical Models and Socioeconomic Problems', in *idem* (ed.), *Regional Analysis*. I. *Economic Systems* (Studies in Anthropology; New York: Academic Press): 3-63.

Sokolowski, F.
1962 *Lois sacrées de cités grecques: Supplement* (Paris: de Boccard).

Sourvinou-Inwood, C.
1990 'What is Polis Religion?', in O. Murray and S. Price (eds.), *The Greek City: From Homer to Alexander* (Oxford: Clarendon Press): 295-322.
1993 'Early Sanctuaries, the Eighth Century and Ritual Space', in Marinatos and Hägg (eds.) 1993: 1-17.

Stager, L.E.
2001 'Port Power in the Early and the Middle Bronze Age: The Organization of Maritime Trade and Hinterland Production', in S.R. Wolff (ed.), *Studies in the Archaeology of Israel and Neighboring Lands in Memory of Douglas L. Esse* (Studies in Ancient Oriental Civilization, 59; Chicago: The Oriental Institute): 625-38.

Stoddart, S.
1989 'Divergent Trajectories in Central Italy 1200–500 BC', in Champion (ed.) 1989: 88-101.

Talmon, S.
1993 'The "Navel of the Earth" and the Comparative Method', in *idem*, *Literary Studies in the Hebrew Bible: Form and Content. Collected Studies* (Jerusalem: Magnes Press; Leiden: E.J. Brill): 50-75.

Terrien, S.
1970 'The Omphalos Myth and Hebrew Religion', *VT* 20: 315-38.

Thünen, J.H. von
1930 [1842] *Der isolierte Staat in Beziehung auf Landwirtschaft und Nationalökonomie*, I (Sammlung sozialwissenschaftlicher Meister, 13; repr. Jena: G. Fischer).

Tilley, C.
1994 *A Phenomenology of Landscape: Places, Paths, Monuments* (Explorations in Anthropology; Oxford and Providence: Berg).

Weinberg, J.
1976 'Die Agrarverhältisse in der Bürger-Tempel-Gemeinde der Achämenidenzeit', in J. Harmatta and G. Komoróczy (eds.), *Wirtschaft und Gesellschaft im alten Vorderasien* (Budapest: no publisher): 473-86. ET in *idem*, *The Citizen–Temple–Community* (JSOTSup, 151; Sheffield: Sheffield Academic Press, 1992): 92-104.

Weinfeld, M.
1972 *Deuteronomy and the Deuteronomic School* (Oxford: Oxford University Press).
1988 'The Pattern of Israelite Settlement in Canaan', in J.A. Emerton (ed.), *Congress Volume: Jerusalem 1986* (VTSup, 40; Leiden: E.J. Brill): 270-83.

Weippert, H.
1980 '"Der Ort, den Jahwe erwählen wird, um dort seinen Namen wohnen zu lassen". Die Geschichte einer alttestamentlichen Formel', *BZ* 24: 76-94.

Wellhausen, J.
1899 *Die Composition des Hexateuchs un der historischen Bücher des Alten Testaments* (Berlin: W. de Gruyter, 3rd edn).

Williamson, H.G.M.
1998 'Judah and the Jews', in M. Brosius and A. Kuhrt (eds.), *Studies in Persian History: Essays in Memory of David M. Lewis* (Achaemenid History, 11; Leiden: Nederlands Instituut voor het Nabije Oosten): 145-63.

Merely a Container? The Ark in Deuteronomy*

Ian Wilson

Many scholars have noted that the presentation of the ark in Deuteronomy is different from that in other parts of the Pentateuch. In particular, they have drawn attention to its portrayal in Deuteronomy as a container for the tables of the covenant, i.e. in contrast to its depiction, particularly in the Priestly writings, as Yahweh's throne/footstool[1] or war palladium.[2]

In general, there have been two responses to such observations. Some scholars see no fundamental discrepancy between the two pictures, considering that the different corpora merely stress different[3] aspects of the same artefact. Others, however, point to a number of contrasts between the two portrayals which they regard as of crucial significance. These include the absence of all reference to either the ark cover or the cherubim[4] and the claimed divesting of the ark of any

* I would like to thank St Deiniol's Library, Hawarden, for a two week Residential Scholarship in 1997 during which some of the research for this article was carried out, and also Dr Almut Hintze, Dr Kasia Jaszczolt, Dr Tom Lundskaer-Nielson and Dr Elizabeth Magba for their helpful suggestions regarding the material relating to idioms.

1. Seow 1992: 391: 'the ark does not appear anywhere in Deuteronomy in connection with the enthronement of YHWH'; Dumermuth 1958: 71: 'die traditionelle Auffassung der Lade als Thron des unsichtbar gegenwärtig gedachten Jahwe im Deuteronomium fehlt'.

2. Terrien 1978: 201: 'the Deuteronomists gave a meaning to the ark that differed dramatically from that of the Holy War tradition. They called the ancient palladium "the ark of the covenant," and they conceived it as a container for the tablets of the Ten Words (Deut. 10:1-5)'; Weinfeld 1972a: 208: 'according to...Deuteronomy...[t]he ark does not serve as God's seat upon which he journeys forth to disperse his enemies (Num. 10:33-6), but only as the vessel in which the tables of the covenant are deposited'; Fretheim 1968: 6: '[t]here is not a word [in Deuteronomy] concerning the role of the ark in holy war, in representing Yahweh, or as the cult object of the central sanctuary'.

3. Davies 1962a: 223: 'the container idea does not exclude the throne idea... Rather...different aspects may be emphasized in different parts of the literature'; de Vaux 1960: 132, ET 1961: 301: 'as extra-biblical documents show, there is no contradiction involved in the vivid contrast presented by the notions of the Ark as a pedestal or throne and of the Ark as a receptacle'; Dürr 1924: 27: '[d]er von der Kritik konstruierte absolute Gegensatz der Auffassungen in den Quellen ist in diesem Sinne *nicht* vorhanden, die verschiedene Hervorhebung der einzelnen Elemente erklärt sich eben aus der verschiedenen Einstellung der Quellen'.

4. Mettinger 1982: 51: 'the Deuteronomistic account of the construction of the Ark (Deut. 10:1-5)...does not mention the cherubim at all. This...would seem to be the result of the conscious suppression of the notion of the God who sat enthroned in the Temple'; Weinfeld 1972a: 208: 'no mention is made of the ark cover (כפרת) and the cherubim which endow the ark with the semblance of a divine chariot or throne'; Clements 1965a: 302: '[in Deuteronomy] there is not one word or hint that [the ark] had anything to do with the cherubim-throne of Yahweh, or that in any fashion whatsoever it symbolized or represented his presence'.

cultic significance.[5] In addition, the appellation 'of the covenant of Yahweh' (i.e. as in 'ark of the covenant of Yahweh') which is used to qualify all four references to the ark outside of Deut. 10.1-5, i.e. in 10.8; 31.9, 25, 26, is frequently viewed as reflecting its function as a container for Yahweh's covenant.[6] This is in contrast to the qualifications 'of Yahweh' or 'of God', which are seen as indicating a connection between the ark and the divine presence.[7] Such scholars deny that the difference is indicative of a mere stressing of different aspects of the ark. Rather, it points to a deliberate and fundamental change in its conception.[8] From being connected with the presence of the deity, it has been demoted to being merely a box.[9]

In fairness, it has to be said that in Deuteronomy the ark's predominant function, i.e. as described in 10.1-5, is that of the container for the second set of tables of the covenant. However, aside from the question as to whether such a portrayal necessarily implies a denial of other possible functions,[10] there is one significant

5. Fretheim 1968: 8: 'the ark...was severed from *all* connection with the cultic life of Israel'; Dumermuth 1958: 75: '[d]ie Lade wird ihrer eigentlichen kultischen Rolle entkleidet' (but see his n. 79); von Rad 1958: 112, ET 1966: 106: '[s]o far as *Deuteronomy* is concerned the ark has no cultic significance'.

6. E.g. Clements 1965b: 96: '[in Deuteronomy's] view the ark was, as its name implied, only a container'; Bernhardt 1964: 1041: '[e]ntsprechend macht die spätere Anschauung [die Lade] zum Aufbewahrungsort der beiden Gesetzestafeln... Daher auch ihre Bezeichnung als... "Bundes-L." oder "L. des Bundes Jahwes" bzw. "Elohims" (Dt 10 8 31 9.25f...)'. Cf. Dus 1964: 242-43.

7. E.g. Cartledge 2001: 70: '[t]itles that emphasize God's presence include the "ark of Yahweh" and the "ark of Yahweh of hosts, who is enthroned on the cherubim"'. Cf. Dibelius 1906: 14-15.

8. Fretheim 1968: 6-7: '[i]t is difficult to conceive how Deuteronomy could have ignored so completely the idea of the ark as the symbol of the presence of God unless it had deliberately set out to do so'; Clements 1965b: 96 n. 2: 'it is hardly conceivable that the Deuteronomists could have ignored its interpretation as a symbol of Yahweh's presence unless they deliberately intended to do so'.

9. Braulik 1986: 98: '[das Dtn] entmythologisiert...die Lade zum bloßen Behälter der Dekalogtafeln (10^{1f})'; Weinfeld 1972a: 208: '[t]he specific and exclusive function of the ark, according to...Deuteronomy, is to house the tables of the covenant (10:1-5)... The holiest vessel of the Israelite cult performs...nothing more than an educational function'; Nicholson 1967: 31: '[the Deuteronomist] has reduced [the ark] to a mere receptacle for the tables of the law and has robbed it of its significance as the throne of the invisibly present Yahweh' (cf. pp. 56, 71, 112); Clements 1965b: 96: '[the ark] became simply a container for the keeping of the law tablets, and had no mysterious significance as a symbol of his presence on earth. Deuteronomy was attempting a complete re-interpretation so far as the ark was concerned'; Dus 1963: 127 [*sic*]: 'im gegenwärtig Dtn...die Lade in ihm sehr wenig vorkommt—dazu nur als der Aufbewahrungskasten der Dekalogtafeln und des Gesetzesbuches (Dtn x 1ff., xxxi 25f.)'; Dumermuth 1958: 72: '[w]o die Lade im heutigen Text des Deuteronomiums explizit erwähnt wird, erscheint sie merkwürdig verändert, abgeblaßt zum bloßen Aufbewahrungsbehälter für die Dekalogtafeln'; von Rad 1958: 112, ET 1966: 106: '[f]or theologians of deuteronomic persuasion the ark has...one single purpose—that of acting as a receptacle for the tables. It has no other rôle'.

10. Cf. McConville 2002: 188: '[t]o claim...that Deuteronomy and Exod. 25–31 have different theologies of the ark is to fall into the fallacy of assuming that every reference to a phenomenon conveys the writer's whole concept of it'; Abba 1962: 886: '[t]he fact that an institution is not mentioned does not necessarily mean that it is unknown; it may equally well imply that it is so well established that it can be taken for granted'; Rowley (1956: 192), commenting on the different portrayals of the Day of the Lord in the Hebrew Bible: '[n]ot all of [its] features...are found in every one of these

piece of evidence bearing on the question of Deuteronomy's conception of the ark, but which so far appears to have been overlooked. This is found in 10.8, which refers to Yahweh setting apart the tribe of Levi 'to carry the ark of the covenant of the Lord, to stand before the Lord to minister to him and to bless in his name'. Now, if the Levites's 'standing before' Yahweh refers to their standing *in his presence*, then this would imply a connection with the ark, since it would seem highly unlikely that the presence before whom the Levites stand would be unconnected with the ark which they also carry. Such a literary juxtaposition of ark 'of the covenant' and divine presence would not be unique. 1 Samuel 4.4 refers to 'the ark of the covenant[11] of the Lord of hosts, who is enthroned on the cherubim',[12] and the latter description is widely understood as referring to the deity's presence associated in some way with the ark.[13]

Most of the remainder of this article will therefore consist of an investigation of the expression 'to stand before...to minister to...', to see whether, in the case of Deut. 10.8, it does in fact refer to the presence of Yahweh localized in proximity to those who carry the ark of his covenant.

1. *Source Considerations*

In giving evidence for the debased role of the ark in Deuteronomy, most scholars adduce only 10.1-5, though some also refer to texts from ch. 31.[14] Rarely do they appeal to 10.8 in support of this view,[15] despite its containing the qualification 'ark *of the covenant* of Yahweh'. This omission may be due to a judgment either that 10.8 adds nothing of significance to the discussion, or, more likely, that it should be excluded on source-critical grounds. While there are those who consider vv. 1-5 and 8-9 to have originated from either the same[16] or else a closely

pictures. This no more indicates that the unmentioned features would be repudiated by the authors than an artist's painting of a man's head and shoulders implies an intention to suggest that he had no legs and feet'.

11. A number of commentators consider the epithet 'of the covenant' to be a later addition to the MT, usually on the basis of its omission from the LXX: Caquot and de Robert 1994: 77; Klein 1983: 37; Stoebe 1973: 131; McKane 1963: 47; Bressan 1954: 104; Driver 1913: 46; H.P. Smith 1912: 33-34; Budde 1902: 34. The insertion, however, is usually attributed to a Deuteronomistic hand and, if correct, would indicate that such an editor had no fundamental objection to juxtaposing references to 'the ark of the covenant' and the divine presence in the same literary context.

12. The occasional commentator considers the qualification 'enthroned on the cherubim' to be a later addition: Bressan 1954: 104; H.P. Smith 1912: 34; Dhorme 1910: 47; Budde 1902: 34.

13. Cartledge 2001: 70; Stolz 1981: 42, 214; McCarter 1980: 106; Haran 1978: 225-26, 256-57; Gehrke 1968: 47; von Rad 1958: 115-16, ET 1966: 109-110; Bressan 1954: 103-104; Goldman 1951: 22; Leimbach 1936: 33; Kirkpatrick 1888: 71.

14. Usually vv. 25-26, but sometimes also v. 9. Preuss (1982: 17, 188), Achtemeier (1978: 21), Schmitt (1972: 102, 122 n. 466), Nicholson (1967: 31, 71, 112) and Clements (1965a: 301-302) include some reference to both, while Seow (1992: 391-92), Kaiser (1969: 112, ET 1975: 132) and Dus (1963: 127 [*sic*]) refer only to vv. 25-26.

15. Exceptions include: Preuss 1982: 17, 188; Schmitt 1972: 102, 122 n. 466.

16. Terrien 1978: 162-63, 174, 215 n. 25; Valentin 1978: 271-73; Peckham 1975: 58; Nicholson 1967: 29-30; Dumermuth 1958: 74; Smend 1912: 252; Klostermann 1907: 261. Cf. Bertholet 1899: 33: '[e]s ist für mich nicht ausgeschlossen, dass es der Verf. von 9 7^{b}–10 5 sei'.

related[17] source, others believe that the two sections come from different hands, with vv. 8-9 usually being attributed to later redaction.[18] This latter view would mean that vv. 8-9 could not be invoked to shed light on the role of the ark portrayed at the beginning of the chapter and also, incidentally, in ch. 31. Thus, before proceeding, it will be necessary to consider the reasons which have been advanced in favour of vv. 8-9 having been written by a hand later than that of vv. 1-5 in order to discern whether they are determinative for the elimination of vv. 8-9 from the discussion.

Reasons for Eliminating 10.8-9 from the Discussion?

Deuteronomy 10.8-9 have been ascribed to a later hand on several grounds. They are sometimes bracketed together with vv. 6-7, with the case for the perceived incongruity of their present position applying to vv. 6-9 as a whole.[19] The suggested reasons can, for convenience, be grouped under several headings, and will be considered in turn:

Literary genre. Some scholars have distinguished vv. 6-9 from their context on the grounds that they are written in narrative rather than speech form.[20] While this is certainly true of vv. 6-7, it is not the case with vv. 8-9 since they refer to 'the Lord *your* God (*'ᵉlōheykā*)'. Puukko (1910) draws this very distinction, but does note that the appositive involves a direct form of address. Nevertheless, on the basis of its absence from the LXX he considers it to be a very late addition,[21] and concludes that the implication that vv. 8-9 come from the same author as 10.1-5 is unfounded since they are merely a short section of narrative.[22] Against this, however, it must be said that there are no variant readings in any of the other ancient versions, and the second person form of address is almost certainly attested at Qumran.[23] Moreover, no recent commentators have sought to emend

17. Nielsen 1995: 115: 'alles [von Dt 9,7–10,11] stammt von einer (oder von zwei) dtr Redaktion(en)'; Steuernagel 1923: 86-87: largely D²b vs. Rd/dtr editors; H.W. Robinson n.d.: 106-107: D² vs. Rᴰ.

18. Preuss 1982: 50; Phillips 1973: 69, 73-74; Seitz 1971: 51, 57, 65-69; von Rad 1964: 56, ET 1966: 79; Lohfink 1963: 290-91; Hölscher 1922: 172 n. 3; Hempel 1914: 140, 175 n. 2, 223. Cf. G.A. Smith 1918: 135.

19. Mayes 1979: 196: '[m]aterial [10.6-9] is here incorporated which clearly disrupts what is basically an artistic deuteronomistic adaptation and elaboration of a deuteronomic account'; Puukko 1910: 94: '10, 6-9...stören empfindlich den Zusammenhang'.

20. Haran 1978: 68 n. 15: '[t]his fragmentary passage...has a narrative, not a rhetorical form, and it breaks the continuity of Moses' oration'; García López 1978: 25: '[d]ans ces versets, il y a changement de personne et, de plus, le récit des versets précédents s'interrompt. En conséquence, on les considère généralement comme un ajout postérieur'. Cf. Rofé 2002: 1; Sonnet 1997: 66, 240, 242.

21. Puukko 1910: 166. The LXX is reflected in the NEB/REB rendering of v. 9b: 'as *he* promised them'.

22. '[W]ir haben es hier mit einem gewöhnlichen, in rein erzählender Form abgefaßten Stück zu tun' (Puukko 1910: 166). Cf. Steuernagel 1900: 36: '[יהוה] אלהיך fehlt LXX, ist also nicht als Beweis zu verwerten, dass v. 8-9 zur Rede Moses gehören'; Bertholet 1899: 33: 'eine Berufung auf [יהוה אלהיך] (v. 9ᵇ) angesichts des Fehlens dieser Worte in LXX von zweifelhaftem Werte'.

23. Baillet (1962: 62) has reconstructed the text of Deut. 10.8-12 from the fragment 2QDeutᶜ, and considers that *yhwh 'lwhykh* was probably in 2Q 'd'après la longueur des lignes'.

the text by removing the reference to the divine name and its appositive, while Wevers (1994: 277) ascribes this particular minus to the LXX having simplified the MT.[24] It would therefore seem safe to infer that the LXX version is attributable to the translator's omission of the divine name from the MT, i.e. rather than to an alternative Hebrew *Vorlage* underlying the Greek text. Furthermore, within vv. 8-9 there is only one instance of Yahweh *your God*, when several would have emphasized the passage's nature as direct speech. This, however, is consistent with the relative paucity of similar appositives within the rest of 9.7–10.11 as a whole, i.e. in contrast to their frequency in the literary contexts immediately before and after.[25]

While not including any first person references to Moses himself (cf. 9.9, 10, 11 *et passim*), vv. 8-9 do refer to 'Yahweh *your* God', and so give the verses a rhetorical, rather than purely narrative form.[26] They can thus be seen as the continuation of Moses' address to the people in vv. 1-5.[27] Consequently, substantial grounds for positing a difference in literary genre between vv. 8-9 and 1-5 of Deuteronomy 10 are lacking.[28]

Content. Some scholars perceive a change of focus.[29] Seitz (1971: 51) views the selection of the Levites as an unexpected reminiscence in this context, while others consider v. 10 to be the actual continuation of vv. 1-5.[30] However, not only is the ark (v. 8) mentioned several times in vv. 1-5 (i.e. in vv. 1, 2, 3 and 5), but the qualification '*of the covenant of Yahweh*' (v. 8) is generally regarded as alluding to the stone tablets placed therein (v. 5) and on which the deity had inscribed the words of his covenant (vv. 2, 4; cf. 9.9-11, 15-17).[31] Moreover,

24. Cf. Christensen (2001: 195), who observes that '[p]rosodic analysis supports MT'. Neither Aejmelaeus (1996) nor Ziegler (1960), in their articles on the LXX of Deuteronomy, comment on 10.9. The former (1993: 86) does indicate, however, that if 'it would have been possible to arrive at the [LXX] translation…from a text identical with the MT…the case is text-critically irrelevant'.

25. The proportions of instances of Yahweh with an appositive are: 9.7–10.5(7), 10-11: 3/33 (9%), 9.1-6: 4/8 (50%), 10.12-22: 7/10 (70%).

26. Polzin (1981: 209) observes that 'the presence of "as the LORD your God said to him" does not indicate the narrator's utterance (since he never uses the second person to indicate the audience for whom he is writing) but rather Moses' reported speech in some kind of direct discourse'.

27. Cf. Polzin 1981: 209: 'in verse 9b, "as the LORD your God said to him" suddenly shifts the report into direct discourse again…Verses eight and nine sound very much like a continuation of Moses' speech in verse five'; Driver 1902: 121: '[a]s the…phraseology show[s] (…note "thy God" in v.[9]), these two verses are a genuine continuation of the discourse of Moses…interrupted by v.[6-7]'; Dillmann 1886: 282-83: 'V. 8f.… (u. zwar als Fortsetzung der Moserede, wie אלהיך V. 9 zeigt)'.

28. 10.1-5 is generally regarded as being Deuteronom(ist)ic. See Wilson 1995: 106.

29. Vermeylen 1985: 202: '[c]es versets [10.6-9] interrompent, en effet, le fil du récit'; García López 1978: 25: 'le récit des versets précédents s'interrompt. En conséquence, on les considère généralement comme un ajout postérieur'.

30. Mayes 1979: 205: '[v]. 5 obviously finds its continuation in v. 10, where the first person singular speech of Moses appears once more; so the intervening verses are secondary'; Fretheim 1968: 3 n. 19a: 'all four verses [i.e. 6-9] are editorial…[b]ecause v. 10 continues directly from vv. 1-5'. Cf. Vermeylen 1985: 202.

31. Von Rad 1958: 112, ET 1966: 106: '[a]t Horeb Yahweh gives Moses the task of making an ark…for the purpose of storing the tables of the law [Deut. 10.1ff.]…and since in deuteronomic circles the term "covenant"…became the technical expression for "decalogue", "Ark of the

mention of those who are charged to carry that same ark and its contents (v. 8) is both consistent with the perspective of 9.7–10.11 as a whole, since the journey to the land still lies in the future (9.28; 10.11),[32] and is related by many scholars to the Levites's role in the Exodus account of the golden calf incident.[33] Such links would appear to belie the need for postulating the work of a different hand.

Vocabulary. Other scholars regard the use of certain expressions as symptomatic of subsequent editorial activity:

1. 'At that Time'. Both Loewenstamm (1992: 43 n. 6) and Seitz (1971: 51) consider that *bāʿēt hahiw'* indicates evidence of later redaction. Plöger (1967: 223), however, queries the notion that it definitely points to literary composition or text expansion, claiming that for source analysis the phrase must be used in conjunction with other evidence.[34] Thus, he and Seitz cite the looseness of 10.8-9 to the preceding context.[35] But, leaving aside the question as to whether looseness *per se* necessarily implies subsequent literary activity,[36] the clear connections between vv. 8-9 and 1-5 (see above) would seem to militate against its being applicable in this instance. In any case, the majority of commentators see sufficient affinities between the two to connect them together.[37] No adequate reason has been found to explain why the expression, either on its own or in combination with other grounds, should be taken to signal a later hand rather than a single author using it to link different events which were considered to occur during the same period.
2. 'Separate'. Weinfeld (1991: 420-21) describes vv. 8-9 as '[a]nother independent pericope about the Levites'. He considers the use of the verb 'separate' (*hibdîl*) instead of 'choose' (*bāḥar*) to be 'characteristic of the priestly literature',[38] but does not appear to draw any source-critical conclusions from this. However, aside from his questionable assumption

Covenant"...became the specifically deuteronomic term for the ark'. Cf. Blenkinsopp 1989: 100; Labuschagne 1987: 220-21; Bernhardt 1964: 1041; Morgenstern 1928: 70; Dürr 1924: 18; Steuernagel 1923: 86.

32. *Re* 10.8-9, Sonnet (1997: 67 n. 78) notes its 'contextual pertinence (ark—carriers of the ark)', while G.A. Smith (1918: 135) refers to the 'natural connection between the mention of the making of the Ark and that of the appointment of its bearers'.

33. Tigay 1996: 106; Mayes 1979: 206; Phillips 1973: 74; Buis and Leclercq 1963: 93; Wright 1953: 398; Driver 1902: 121; Oettli 1893: 50; Dillmann 1886: 282-83. Cf. Brueggemann 2001: 123-24.

34. Cf. DeVries' (1975: 58) comment about the temporal expression *bayyôm hahûʾ*: '[t]he phrase is not in itself a clue to secondary literary accretion'.

35. Seitz 1971: 51; Plöger 1967: 223. Cf. Loewenstamm (1992), who offers no explanation at all.

36. Compared with the presence of contradictory/incompatible material in 10.8-9 which might have constituted plausible evidence for it coming from a different hand to that of vv. 1-5.

37. Most associate the selection of the Levites with the events described at Horeb (vv. 1-5), rather than with the Israelites' subsequent journeyings (vv. 6-7): in addition to those mentioned in nn. 16, 17 and 33, see also Cairns 1992: 109; Haran 1978: 77 n. 25; Davies 1962b: 275; Clamer 1940: 579; Reider 1937: 105; Junker 1933: 57; Morgenstern 1928: 150 n. 182; G.A. Smith 1918: 135. Cf. Braulik 1986: 83; Watts 1970: 230; von Rad 1964: 56-57, ET 1966: 79.

38. Cf. García López 1978: 25, 30, esp. n. 206.

that the two words are synonymous, the verb does occur in several contexts which are generally regarded as being Deuteronom(ist)ic:[39] Deut. 19.2, 7;[40] 29.20 (ET 21)[41] and 1 Kgs 8.53.[42] It is thus clear that the occurrence of 'separate' in Deut. 10.8 cannot be used as the basis for ascribing vv. 8-9 to a different hand from that of vv. 1-5.

Summary. None of the reasons put forward in favour of 10.8-9 originating from an author other than that of vv. 1-5 has been found to be convincing. Neither the perceived differences in literary genre and content nor the possible deductions from vocabulary are persuasive. In fact, a significant body of scholarly opinion, while not necessarily agreeing as to who was responsible, does attribute the two passages to the same or closely related hand(s).[43]

2. *The Significance of* la‘ᵃmōd lipnê yhwh *in Deuteronomy 10.8*

Earlier Views

Deuteronomy 10.8 refers to Yahweh setting apart the tribe of Levi 'to carry the ark of the covenant of the Lord, to stand before the Lord to minister to him (*la‘ᵃmōd lipnê yhwh lᵉšārᵉtô*) and to bless in his name'. Whereas the majority of scholars who comment on the phrase consider that, in this context, *la‘ᵃmōd lipnê* means 'to serve',[44] but do not go on to deal with the immediately following *lᵉšārᵉtô*, there have been those who imply that the two together should be viewed in a unitary way as referring to some form of service.[45] In contrast, there are a

39. 'Deuteronom(ist)ic' is used of material which has been variously identified as either Deuteronomic or Deuteronomistic.

40. Nielsen 1995: 187-88; M. Rose 1994a: 147; Miller 1990: 141, 145; Rofé 1986: 211-13, 217 n. 30, 220-21, 223; Mayes 1979: 48, 283-85; Phillips 1973: 82, 128; Seitz 1971: 242-43; Buis and Leclercq 1963: 140; Cunliffe-Jones 1951: 116; Junker 1933: 85; G.A. Smith 1918: 158, 236; Bertholet 1899: XIX-XX; H.W. Robinson n.d.: 151-52.

41. Otto 2000: 151-52, 156, 181 n. 125; M. Rose 1994b: 551; Cairns 1992: 254; Preuss 1982: 8, 60; Mayes 1979: 46, 359; Phillips 1973: 198-99; Buis and Leclercq 1963: 17, 181, 183; Driver 1902: lxxv-lxxvi; Steuernagel 1900: 107; H.W. Robinson n.d.: 209. Cf. Nicholson 1967: 36.

42. Cogan 2001: 292-93; Fretheim 1999: 48; Buis 1997: 87; Knoppers 1995: 248; DeVries 1985: xlvii, 126; Würthwein 1985: 94, 96; Jones 1984: 197-98; Mayes 1983: 111; Levenson 1981: 159-60, 162; Cross 1973: 278; Dietrich 1972: 74 n. 39; J. Robinson 1972: 98-99, 109; Weinfeld 1972a: 36-37; J. Gray 1970: 203, 215, 226; Jepsen 1956: Übersicht über Quellen und Redaktionen; Montgomery and Gehman 1951: 193-94; Burney 1903: 112; Benzinger 1899: 59; Skinner n.d.: 139, 152. Cf. Nelson 1981: 73.

43. See above, nn. 16 and 17.

44. Mayes 1979: 206: '*to stand before the Lord*: this is synonymous with *to minister*'; Thompson 1974: 146: '[t]he phrase *stand before* is an idiom meaning "wait upon", "serve"'; Clamer 1940: 579: '*se tenir devant Yahweh*, formule usitée pour désigner le service des prêtres'; Reider 1937: 105: '*to stand before the Lord*...i.e. to wait upon and serve Him'; G.A. Smith 1918: 136: '*to stand before the LORD to minister unto him*...Both vbs...are...employed...specially to express religious service'; Driver 1902: 123: '*[t]o stand before*...is a Heb. idiom meaning *to wait upon, to serve*'.

45. Maxwell 1987: 169: 'to "*stand before the Lord to minister to Him*."...this phrase is used to indicate several different kinds of service'; Steuernagel 1900: 36: 'לעמד - לשרתו, als Ein [*sic*] Ausdruck zusammengehörend'; Dillmann 1886: 283: 'das *Stehen vor Gott ihm zu dienen*, mit welcher Formel gewöhnlich der priesterliche Dienst am Heiligthum bezeichnet wird'.

number of (largely) pre-critical scholars who opt for a literal interpretation of the standing, considering (presumably) that each of the two infinitives should be understood separately, and thus that the first describes the physical posture (standing) to be adopted by the Levites when they carry out the second, i.e. ministering to Yahweh.[46] It is this interpretation for which I shall contend in the discussion which follows.

The Old Testament Instances

There are four instances of the collocation *ʿmd lpny* [slot A] *lšrt* [slot B] (‘stand before…to minister to…’) in the Old Testament:

> Moses said to Korah, ‘Hear now, you sons of Levi: is it too small a thing for you that the God of Israel has separated you from the congregation of Israel, to bring you near to himself, to do service in the tabernacle of the Lord, and to stand before the congregation to minister to them (*w^{e}la ^{ʿa}mōd lipnê hāʿēdâ l^{e}šār^{e}tām*)’. (Num. 16.8-9)
>
> At that time the Lord set apart the tribe of Levi to carry the ark of the covenant of the Lord, to stand before the Lord to minister to him (*la^{ʿa}mōd lipnê yhwh l^{e}šār^{e}tô*) and to bless in his name, to this day. (Deut. 10.8)
>
> [The Levites] shall be ministers in my sanctuary, having oversight at the gates of the temple, and serving in the temple; they shall slay the burnt offering and the sacrifice for the people, and they shall stand before them to serve them (*w^{e}hēmmâ yaʿam^{e}dû lipnêhem l^{e}šār^{e}tām*). (Ezek. 44.11)
>
> My sons [i.e. Levites], do not now be negligent, for the Lord has chosen you to stand before him, to minister to him (*la^{ʿa}mōd l^{e}pānāyw l^{e}šār^{e}tô*), and to be his ministers and burn incense to him. (2 Chron. 29.11)

In each of them the first free slot [A] is filled by a noun or pronominal suffix, and the second [B] by the corresponding pronominal suffix. In Deut. 10.8 and 2 Chron. 29.11 Yahweh is the object of the construction, while in Num. 16.9 and Ezek. 44.11 it is the congregation and people respectively.[47]

Preliminary Considerations

Before evaluating the two main possible interpretations of the collocation, it is necessary, first, to demonstrate that all four instances are relevant to the discussion, and secondly, to establish the number of tasks which Deut. 10.8 attributes to the tribe of Levi.

The texts to which appeal can be made. J.-M. Babut (1995: 63, ET 1999: 69), in outlining the steps to be followed when attempting to ascertain the meaning of an expression by componential analysis, limits his investigations to instances ‘for which there is a reasonable certainty that the same stage of the language is represented throughout’.[48] However, of the four methods suggested by him for

46. Brown 1993: 136: ‘*stand*—the posture of a servant’; Poole 1962: 356: ‘*[t]o stand before the Lord*…this being the posture of ministers’. Cf. Benson 1815: 591.

47. It is assumed that this change in object, i.e. from divine to human, makes no difference to the meaning of the collocation. Cf. Healey 1968: 72.

48. Cf. Sawyer 1972: 114: ‘for adequacy as well as convenience, a single point in the development of the language…is to be selected as a starting-point’.

establishing linguistically homogeneous expressions only one would appear to apply to the collocation under discussion. While dating its occurrences requires caution, none of them either '*belong to the same literary unit*' or are linked to a '*single tradition*'. Nevertheless:

> In a more general way, it is possible to investigate whether the contexts of the occurrences reveal similarities in vocabulary and style that would help determine the degree of linguistic homogeneity in the texts under consideration... Here is one of the most valuable tools for establishing a linguistically homogeneous corpus... (Babut 1995: 64-65, ET 1999: 70)

Examination of the known instances of the collocation reveals the following similarities. In all four cases it is represented as occurring within speech, whether by Moses (Num. 16.9; Deut. 10.8, cf. 'your God' in v. 9), Yahweh (Ezek. 44.11) or Hezekiah (2 Chron. 29.11). In each case members of the same tribe, whether designated 'sons of Levi' (Num. 16.8), 'tribe of Levi' (Deut. 10.8) or 'Levites' (Ezek. 44.10; 2 Chron. 29.5) are described as having been selected by the deity in order to 'stand before...to minister to' either himself or the congregation/people. Thus, they are 'separated'/'set apart' (Num. 16.9; Deut. 10.8), 'appointed' (Ezek. 44.14) or 'chosen' (2 Chron. 29.11) both for this purpose and for at least one other normally associated with the operation of the cult. The latter involves service in/of the sanctuary (Num. 16.9; Ezek. 44.11, 14), carrying the ark (Deut. 10.8) or burning incense (2 Chron. 29.11). Finally, while the exact location of the 'standing before...to minister to...' is nowhere spelled out, in all four cases its practitioners have some connection with the sanctuary, be it tabernacle, 'chosen place' or Temple. In Num. 16.9 the Levites do service 'in the tabernacle of the Lord' and in Ezek. 44.11 they are ministers 'in [his] sanctuary, having oversight at the gates of the temple, and serving in the temple' (see also v. 14). In 2 Chron. 29.11 their incense burning presumably also locates their activity in the Temple, while the 'stand[ing] before...to minister to...' in Deut. 10.8 may well be at the 'chosen place', since according to 17.12 that is where the Levitical priest 'stands to minister...to the Lord' ('there', cf. vv. 8-10).

In view, therefore, of the close similarities between the literary contexts of the four instances, there would seem to be little evidence for the collocation in Deut. 10.8 being understood in a way different from that of the other three. It therefore seems reasonable to proceed on the assumption that, despite its occurrence in disparate bodies of literature, the expression has the same meaning in all four cases.[49]

The number of tasks in Deuteronomy 10.8. In considering the duties assigned to the Levites in Deut. 10.8, the question arises as to the number of roles to which the verse refers, whether four:[50]

49. This is not to assert the identity of the various Levites referred to in the four texts, but merely to claim that the collocation has the same sense in each case.

50. As implied by Ringgren 1989: 199, ET 2001: 182; Reider 1937: 105; Morgenstern 1928: 150 n. 182.

1. to carry the ark of the covenant of Yahweh
2. to stand before Yahweh
3. to minister to [Yahweh]
4. to bless in his name

or only to three, i.e. with ‘to stand before Yahweh to minister to him’ (however understood[51]) in some sense representing one basic activity.

Of the four instances of the collocation ‘stand before...to minister to...’, two throw some light on this question of the number of tasks involved. In Num. 16.9 the clause ‘the God of Israel has separated you from the congregation of Israel’ is followed by a group of dependent infinitival clauses, within which the position of the conjunction *wāw* would appear to be significant. Generally, in Hebrew lists, one of two main patterns is observed. Either every item in the series (except the first) is preceded by the conjunction, or only the last is.[52] Moreover, in cases involving infinitive constructs, each of which is introduced by *lāmed*, and where three or more are all subordinated to the same main clause (as in Num. 16.9), the same two patterns, i.e. involving *wāw* attached to either every[53] or only the last[54] item, are the principally occurring ones. In Num. 16.9, however, only the infinitive construct of *‘āmad* has the conjunction. Consequently, if its sequence exemplifies the second of the two patterns, the *wāw* introduces the final member of the series, and the two parts of ‘to stand before the congregation to minister to them’ would appear to be connected in some way.[55]

This deduction is supported by Ezek. 44.11, in which Yahweh specifies the Levites’s area of responsibility by means of a series of third person plural verbs: ‘They shall be (*wᵉhāyû*) ministers in my sanctuary...they shall slay (*hēmmâ yišḥᵃṭû*) the burnt offering...and they shall stand (*wᵉhēmmâ ya‘amᵉdû*) before the people...’ The final reference to ministering, however, is not specified by means of the third person plural verb, ‘and they shall minister to them’ (e.g. *wᵉhēmmâ yᵉšārᵉtûm*), but by the infinitive construct prefaced by *lāmed*, ‘*to* minister to them’ (*lᵉšārᵉtām*). This suggests that the Levites’s ministering is not a fourth activity in addition to those already mentioned, but rather is somehow linked to their standing before the people. Thus, ‘to stand before them to minister to them’ is in some sense one item. This being the case, and, assuming the same basic import, it

51. See next section.

52. Koehler and Baumgartner 1998: 245: ‘ו connects three or more words (phrases); in this case ו precedes every (except the first) or only the last word’. Cf. van der Merwe, Naudé and Kroeze 1999: 298; Clines 1995: 596; Gibson 1994: 36; Waltke and O’Connor 1990: 648; Holladay 1971: 84; BDB, 252.

53. I.e. apart from the first. Cf. Gen. 43.18; Deut. 26.17; Josh. 22.5; 2 Sam. 3.25; 7.23; 11.11; Isa. 10.6; Jer. 1.10a; 18.7; 31.28a; Amos 8.5; Eccl. 5.17 (ET 18), 18 (ET 19); 8.15; Est. 8.11aβ; Dan. 9.24; 11.35; Ezra 7.10; Neh. 8.12; 10.30 (ET 29); 1 Chron. 19.3; 29.19; 2 Chron. 2.13 (ET 14); 31.2.

54. Deut. 11.22; 30.16a, 20a; Judg. 2.19; 1 Kgs 8.58; Isa. 30.2; Est. 3.13a; 7.4; 1 Chron. 23.13.

55. Deut. 10.8 likewise follows the second of the two patterns, since the conjunction is attached to the last item in the series (‘and to bless in [Yahweh’s] name’). This does not, however, rule out the possibility that the previous two infinitives were intended to be read together. Cf. those textual variants (2QDeutᶜ, Samaritan Pentateuch, Vulgate) in which the conjunction also appears before ‘to stand’.

therefore means that only three roles are allocated to the Levites in Deut. 10.8.[56] The two parts of 'to stand before the Lord to minister to him' should thus be considered together, and not as separate activities.

'To Stand before X to Minister to X'—the Problem

Broadly speaking, the exegete is faced with two contrasting, though related, interpretations of the collocation: the figurative, according to which the 'standing before' (either on its own or as part of the whole expression) denotes the Levites's service, and the literal, in which it refers to the posture to be adopted by them when they carry out that service. Although the two readings overlap, in that both view the collocation as stipulating a serving role, they differ inasmuch as the literal also necessitates the spatial proximity to the Levites of the one before whom they stand. In other words, a literal interpretation points to the deity's earthly presence in the immediate vicinity of those who carry the ark. Since such a distinction, according to which 'stand before' (*'āmad lipnê*) can be understood either literally or in the sense of 'serving', is one which is generally recognized both within the standard lexicons[57] and by those studies dealing with the preposition itself (*lipnê*),[58] the attempt to determine which of the two is intended in Deut. 10.8 would appear to be a valid one. However, despite the difficulty of doing do, several aspects of the way the collocation has been understood combine to suggest a means of resolving the issue, i.e. by considering whether the expression is in fact an *idiom*. By this is meant 'a peculiarity of phraseology approved by the usage of a language, and often having a signification other than its grammatical or logical one'.[59] Three factors point to this as a possible way of viewing the collocation: first, its alleged semantic equivalence to the one-word expression 'serve';[60] secondly, the likely existence of an exact literal counterpart[61] resulting

56. This is the conclusion to which the majority of scholars are drawn, for example, Merrill 1994: 200: 'the functions of the Levites—carrying the ark, standing to minister, and pronouncing blessings'; see also Christensen 2001: 196; Polzin 1981: 209; Craigie 1976: 201; von Rad 1964: 57, ET 1966: 79-80; Myers 1961: 24; Cunliffe-Jones 1951: 75; Driver 1902: 122-24; Dillmann 1886: 283; H.W. Robinson n.d.: 107.

57. *ThWAT*, VI: 198-99, 651-53, ET *TDOT*, XI: 182, 608-10; *HALAT*, III: 795, ET *HALOT*, II: 841; *THAT*, II: 458-59; BDB, 763-64.

58. Sollamo 1985: 24-25; Reindl 1970: 32-34; Rabban 1952: 6-7; Nötscher 1924: 86-87.

59. I.e. as narrowly defined by *OED*, sense 3. This is in contrast to the sense referred to by Caird (1980: 109) in his chapter entitled 'Hebrew Idiom and Hebrew Thought': 'it is usually possible to express any given idea in a variety of ways… Yet it often happens that among the possible forms of expression one is regarded as normal usage and characteristic of native speakers of the language, and such normal usage we call idiom'. Cf. *OED*, sense 2.

60. Cf. Fernando 1996: 54: 'certain sequences of words (co-occurrences) over time become composite units (idioms), which then function as if they were single words'; Meier 1975: 165: '[Bally's] second [idiom characterization]…is the…semantic equivalence with a one-word expression'; Chafe 1968: 111: 'the meaning of an idiom is comparable to the meaning of a single lexical item'.

61. Chomsky 1980: 150: '[idiomatic expressions] sometimes have a perfectly reasonable literal meaning if understood as nonidiomatic'; Newmeyer 1972: 296: 'idioms invariably have well-formed literal equivalents'; Weinreich 1969: 68: 'they would not be idioms…because they do not have any literal counterparts'; Chafe 1968: 111: 'an idiom which is well-formed will have a literal counterpart'.

in semantic ambiguity;[62] and thirdly, the more figurative nature of the reading 'serve' in relation to 'stand before to minister to' understood in a literal sense.[63] The advantage of regarding the collocation as potentially idiomatic, rather than merely figurative, is that recourse can then be had to some of the insights gained from the burgeoning literature on idioms, and a conclusion possibly reached as to its precise meaning.

Evidence for an Idiomatic Interpretation?

Frequently associated with idioms are a number of features whose presence could enable a distinction to be drawn between the idiomatic and literal interpretations of any given collocation:

Phonological distinctiveness. Some idioms contain phonological traits, such as alliteration, assonance or rhyme, the memorability of which helps to fix them in the popular consciousness, and so convert them from being a mere nonce form into a habitual collocation.[64] Within the Old Testament, however, only alliteration occurs to any significant extent,[65] but does not feature consistently in the expression being considered. Two of the words, *lpny* and *lšrt*, invariably begin with *lāmed*, but *'md* is not always prefixed by it (in Ezek. 44.11 it occurs as the imperfect/jussive form, *ya'am^{e}dû*).

Contextual distinctiveness. One feature which usually distinguishes an idiom from its literal counterpart is context:

> Context is the crucial variable which leads the speaker/hearer to identify and interpret a given expression as being idiomatic or not... The idiomaticity of forms with their homonymous literal counterparts...springs from *an obvious mismatch between their*

62. 'Ambiguity' in the sense of uncertainty as to what the author meant (Empson 1953: 5). Cf. Weinreich 1969: 60: 'the ambiguity of literal expressions having idiomatic counterparts'; Katz and Postal 1963: 277: 'the semantic ambiguity between [idiomatic meaning] and the compositional meaning'.

63. Nunberg, Sag and Wasow 1994: 492: '[i]dioms typically involve metaphors...metonymies ...or other kinds of figuration'; Chafe 1970: 47: 'the overwhelming tendency is for semantic units and configurations involving concrete, tangible meanings to yield idiomatic units involving more abstract and intangible meanings'.

64. Malkiel 1959: 121-22: 'in numerous languages [a binomial] acquires added strength and appeal if the matching is supported by an extra measure of suggestive outward resemblance between A and B, a token of partial identity which produces a powerful welding effect on the whole'. Cf. Makkai 1975: 26 n. 1: '[t]here are a large number of [English] idioms which exist primarily because of traditional (phonological) rhyming, alliteration, or... There is no denying that such...features... must have contributed heavily to the institutionalization of many a frozen form'.

65. Casanowicz 1894: 30. He refers to instances of assonance and rhyme as 'hardly any' and a 'comparatively small' number, respectively (p. 33). Not surprisingly, neither are present in the four instances under consideration. Assonance is excluded by the absence of any consistent repetition of vowel sounds throughout the collocation—as also is rhyme, and by the same token, because of the lack of recurring syllables (caused by the non-repetition of both vowels and non-initial consonants). Note that the latter is so, regardless of whether the term is limited to instances in which the similarity lies in a stem-syllable (Casanowicz 1894: 33) or broadened to include the so-called 'grammatical' or 'barren' rhymes resulting from inflexional endings (Segert 1992: 172).

> *possible literal interpretation and the context of situation.* Such expressions, therefore, *must* mean something other than what their literal components denote... It is the contextual mismatch which leads the hearer to select the appropriate idiomatic sense.[66]

The idiomatic and literal variants of any given expression generally occur in different and frequently contrasting literary environments.[67] This means that, provided the context contains sufficient information, it should be possible to determine whether a given collocation is to be understood literally or idiomatically, and in the latter case, what is meant. The corollary to this, however, is that the briefer the context the more likely it is to be difficult to determine which of the two senses is intended. In the case of Deut. 10.8, with its use of the collocation 'to stand before...to minister to...', it appears that either interpretation is compatible with the immediately preceding reference to the ark of the covenant. A figurative one is feasible, since those who carry that ark (the Levites) are known to serve the deity,[68] while precedents for the literal interpretation can be found in those ark references in which Yahweh is generally regarded as being in some sense present,[69] and where the notion of standing in that presence would therefore be intelligible. On the other hand, if it could be maintained, on the basis of wider contextual considerations, that Yahweh is portrayed as being absent from the earthly sphere,[70] then no such literal 'standing before' him would be possible, and that particular reading would therefore have to be excluded. In fact, I have argued elsewhere that within Deuteronomy there is considerable evidence for a belief in the earthly presence of the deity.[71] Consequently, the literal interpretation of Deut. 10.8 remains open to consideration.

Keysar (1994: 248-49) has drawn attention to *two* kinds of contextual information which can lead to the distinguishing of the figurative from the literal: that which renders a particular interpretation *plausible*, and that which *eliminates* it.[72] In the case of Deut. 10.8, however, the sole plausibility of the figurative interpretation (serving Yahweh) cannot be demonstrated since the two readings overlap: divine service (*šrt*) is also entailed in its literal alternative.[73] This means

66. Fernando and Flavell 1981: 6. Cf. Cacciari and Tabossi 1988: 680: 'what is peculiar about these [idioms] is that if taken literally they sometimes make no sense but, nevertheless, they do fit in an appropriate context. It is very likely therefore that the detection of this incongruency can play a role in the identification of an idiomatic expression'.

67. Cf. Healey 1968: 94: '[s]uch pairs of homophonous expressions [i.e. idioms and non-idioms] contrast...[in that t]hey occur in at least partly different contexts, that is, they collate with at least some different lexical items'.

68. In addition to the use of *šērēt* in Deut. 10.8 to express the Levitical service of Yahweh, it also occurs in Deut. 17.12; 21.5; Jer. 33.22; Ezek. 40.46; 43.19; 44.15; 1 Chron. 15.2; 23.13 and 2 Chron. 13.10, whether applied to Levites, Zadokites or Aaronides. Other terms are less common: *'ābad 'et-ᵃbōdâ* (Num. 8.11), *ᵃbîdā'* (Ezra 6.18) and *'ābad* (2 Chron. 35.3).

69. E.g. the ark as divine meeting place (Exod. 25.22; 30.6; cf. Lev. 16.2; Num. 7.89) or war palladium (Num. 10.33-36; 1 Sam. 4.1-11; cf. Ps. 132.8; 2 Chron. 6.41).

70. As, for example, would appear to be claimed by those scholars espousing Name Theology.

71. Wilson 1995.

72. 'Plausible' in the sense that elements in the context positively suggest a particular interpretation, i.e. rather than eliminate the alternative.

73. Though the literal one could be seen as entailing a narrower, more prescribed, sphere of service, since it specifies proximity to the one being served.

that any contextual constraints pointing to the plausibility of the former are likely also to be consistent with the latter, and thus that the only way of substantiating the figurative interpretation will be by eliminating the literal.

Unfortunately, the context of Deut. 10.8 provides insufficient information to enable a clear-cut choice to be made between the two possible interpretations. Moreover, neither do those of the three other occurrences of the collocation,[74] each of which involves Levites[75] of one sort or another as its implied subject. This lack of contextual detail can be attributed to the fact that none of the four deals with an actual occurrence of the Levites's actions, from a description of which some idea might have been gained as to what such 'stand[ing] before...to minister to...' entailed. Rather, all four occur as one aspect of a job description, whether as part of a purpose clause introduced by *lāmed*,[76] or as an instruction introduced by the imperfect.[77] In every case the context is minimal, and the required contextual mismatch, which might have led to the elimination of the literal interpretation, is missing. There would therefore appear to be no solid contextual grounds for affirming that Deut. 10.8 should be understood in some kind of figurative/idiomatic sense.

Limited syntactic flexibility. Relative to the changes which its literal counterpart can undergo, there are frequently strict limitations on the number and type of modification which can be carried out on an idiom's internal structure[78] without it ceasing to be an idiom.[79] Moreover, as indicated above, an idiomatic collocation generally occurs in a literary context different from that of its literal alternative. This means that if modification of the idiom causes it to lose its idiomatic denotation, then the resulting expression will be found only in contexts similar to those frequented by the original non-idiomatic collocation. Consequently, the existence of clear differences between the contexts in which the original and modified collocations occur could provide evidence for the former being understood in an idiomatic sense. In the case of Deut. 10.8 there are two texts containing closely

74. But see the discussion of Ezek. 44.11 below, pp. 230-32.

75. See above, p. 220.

76. As in Num. 16.9 ('the God of Israel has separated you...to [*lāmed*] stand before...'), Deut. 10.8 ('the Lord set apart the tribe of Levi...to [*lāmed*] stand before...') and 2 Chron. 29.11 ('the Lord has chosen you to [*lāmed*] stand before...').

77. As in Ezek. 44.11 ('[the Levites] shall stand [*ya'am^{e}dû*] before...').

78. Nunberg, Sag and Wasow 1994: 492: 'idioms [are] characterized by...[i]nflexibility: [they] typically appear only in a limited number of syntactic frames or constructions, unlike freely composed expressions'. Cf. Healey's (1968: 95) observation *re* English idioms: '[t]hey may differ in the expansions and transformations which they undergo, the idiom usually being more limited than the non-idiom'.

79. Gumpel 1974: 1: 'the idiom bears a marked lack in flexibility: any interference with the minutest particle comprising it may cause the whole sense, and as such the idiom, to disintegrate, leaving either a meaningless sentence or one which has reverted to non-idiomatic structure'; note also Chafe 1965: 36: '[u]sually...it is possible to find a transformation of the units contained in the complex [idiomatic] unit where the idiom dissipates, leaving the literal unit as the only possibility'.

similar variants[80] which could be regarded as resulting from modification of the collocation in question:

> Bring the tribe of Levi near, and cause them to stand before Aaron the priest, and they shall minister to him (*wᵉha ʿᵃmadtā ʾōtô lipnê ʾahᵃrōn hakkōhēn wᵉšērᵉtû ʾōtô*). (Num. 3.6)

> The man who acts presumptuously, by not obeying the priest who stands to minister there to the Lord your God (*hā ʿōmēd lᵉšāret šām ʾet-yhwh ʾᵉlōheykā*), or the judge, that man shall die… (Deut. 17.12)

In Num. 3.6 the qal of *ʿmd* (‘stand’) in Deut. 10.8 is replaced by the hiphil (‘cause to stand’)[81] and the purposive *lāmed* (‘to [minister to]’) by the connective *wāw* (‘and [they shall minister to]’).[82] By contrast, in Deut. 17.12 the *lpny* together with its object (‘before the Lord’) is omitted and *šām* (‘there’) inserted between *lᵉšāret* (‘to minister to’) and its object (‘the Lord your God’).[83] Two problems come to mind, however. First, in general, and as already indicated above, it is difficult to envisage usages of the idiomatic and slightly modified (and therefore literal) collocation which would indicate a difference in meaning between them, in view of the fact that both idiomatic and literal versions of the original collocation are able to occupy the same literary context. Secondly, and in particular, both Num. 3.6 and Deut. 17.12 also entail job descriptions for Levites.[84] This means that in practice there is no obvious difference between their contexts and those of Deut. 10.8, Num. 16.9, Ezek. 44.11 or 2 Chron. 29.11. Of course, it could be that the collocation common to these four texts is in fact idiomatic and that its variants in Num. 3.6 and Deut. 17.12 still retain that idiomatic meaning. Nevertheless, it remains the case that there is no clear evidence for an idiomatic usage in Deut. 10.8.

Lexical components lacking their normal meaning. The individual components of an idiom do not normally contribute their literal meaning to that of the whole.[85] However, in the case of Deut. 10.8 known denotations of each half of the collocation overlap to a significant extent with the idiomatic sense, ‘serve’,

80. Increasingly disparate variants occur with neither *lpny* nor a direct object of the verb *šrt*: ‘the priests could not stand to minister because of the cloud’ (1 Kgs 8.11//2 Chron. 5.14) and ‘the Lord your God has chosen [the Levitical priest]…to stand to minister in the name of the Lord’ (Deut. 18.5). See also 2 Chron. 8.14 and 31.2 in which *ʿmd* occurs in the hiphil and is widely separated from the following *lᵉšārēt*.

81. A substitution similar to the one discussed by Binnick 1971.

82. RSV: ‘set them before Aaron the priest, that (*wāw*) they may minister to him’.

83. RSV: ‘the priest who stands to minister there (*šām*) before (*ʾet*) the Lord your God’. The word order (*šām ʾet*) is retained in the Samaritan Pentateuch, Peshitta, Targums and Vulgate, but reversed in the LXX: ἐπί τῷ ὀνόματι (= *ʾet-šām*), rendered as minister ‘in the name of’. Wevers (1995: 285) considers that the LXX reading could have arisen from the MT by metathesis (for other examples involving similar transposition of entire words see Delitzsch 1920: 91-92). However, he suspects that ‘the translator wanted to harmonize with 18:7, but indicated that the text was somewhat different by adding *ἐπὶ* before *τῷ ὀνόματι*’.

84. Num. 3.6: ‘the tribe of Levi’, Deut. 17.9: ‘Levitical priests’.

85. Fernando (1996: 38) refers to ‘pure idioms losing the meaning of their constituent words’; Fraser 1970: 33: ‘no part of the idiom has retained any literal interpretation’.

proposed for the expression viewed as a unit.[86] 'Serve' is not only the literal meaning of *šrt*,[87] but also one of the common figurative renderings of *'md lpny*.[88] Thus, however else it might be classified, the collocation is unlikely to be a full idiom.[89] Moreover, by the same token neither is it likely to be a 'semi-idiom', i.e. one in which 'at least one formative contributes its ordinary lexical meaning'.[90] While either half could be construed as imparting such 'ordinary lexical meaning', the other would not yield the unexpected interpretation necessary for the collocation to be regarded as idiomatic. Alternatively, the meaning of the whole could be equated with that of just one of its components, whether *'md lpny* or *šrt*. Nunberg, Sag and Wasow (1994: 508 n. 20), however, exclude this kind of understanding on the grounds that it entails attributing no meaning whatsoever to one or other of the two elements.[91] It is thus clear that the close similarity between the proposed unitary interpretation of the collocation and known meanings of its two components militates against *'md lpny...lšrt* being granted idiomatic status.

Conclusion. None of the possible idiom characteristics to which appeal could be made by a non-native speaker of Biblical Hebrew has been shown to provide clear evidence for an idiomatic interpretation of the collocation under consideration. It would thus appear that there are no substantial grounds for affirming that 'to stand before the Lord to minister to him' in Deut. 10.8 should be understood in an idiomatic rather than a purely literal sense.[92] I therefore intend to argue that, although linked together, the two verbs in the collocation should be understood separately, with the 'standing before' indicating the physical posture to be adopted by the Levites for the purpose of (*lāmed*) ministering. Several lines of evidence point to such a literal interpretation as the most likely in the case of the collocation in question.

The Known Posture of Levites/Priests when Carrying out Cultic Acts

The data available indicates that when Levites/priests carry out cultic acts, they do so from a *standing* position. While the Korahites stood at the entrance to the tent of meeting with their censers (Num. 16.18), the priests were unable to stand to minister in the Temple, i.e. because of the cloud (1 Kgs 8.11//2 Chron. 5.14).

86. It is not being claimed that these meanings of *'āmad lipnê* and *šērēt* are synonymous either with each other or with the idiomatic sense proposed for the whole, but that there is significant semantic congruity between them.

87. *NIDOTTE*, IV: 256: 'wait on, be an attendant, serve, minister'; *ThWAT*, VIII: 496: 'dienen'; *HALAT*, IV: 1532: 'dienen' (ET *HALOT*, IV: 1662: 'serve'); *TWOT*, II: 958: 'minister, serve'; *THAT*, II: 1019: 'bedienen, dienen'; BDB, 1058: 'minister, serve'.

88. As in Gen. 41.46; Deut. 1.38; 1 Sam. 16.21-22; 1 Kgs 1.2, etc. See also nn. 57 and 58 above.

89. I.e. one 'for which the constituent or series of constituents contains no formatives whose ordinary lexical meaning contributes to the semantic interpretation' (Newmeyer 1974: 327).

90. Newmeyer 1974: 327-28.

91. Note their rejection of Ruhl's analysis of the English idiom 'kick the bucket': '[w]e...believe our analysis to be preferable to the alternative...of assigning *kick* an idiomatic sense meaning..."die", and *the bucket* no sense at all'.

92. *Contra* Maxwell, Steuernagel and Dillmann. Cf. n. 45 above.

Deuteronomy itself refers to 'the [Levitical] priest who stands to minister there to the Lord' (17.12) and to Yahweh's having chosen him 'to stand and minister in [his] name' (18.5).[93] There are no recorded instances of either Levites or priests carrying out cultic activities from a seated (or kneeling) position.[94] Thus, the posture implied by a literal understanding of the 'stand before' of Deut. 10.8, etc. is the only one for which the Old Testament provides independent evidence.

Levites/Priests as the Subject of 'Stand Before' in the Sense of 'Serve'?
There is little clear Old Testament evidence for priests or Levites as the subject of the phrase *'md lpny* (whether qal or hiphil) in the sense of 'service', i.e. of another being, whether human or divine. Of the few occurrences outside of the collocation under investigation,[95] Exod. 9.10, Deut. 18.7[96] and Zech. 3.1, 3 are almost certain to be literal. Ezekiel 44.15 is similar to the four in question,[97] and is likely to be literal in view of Yahweh's presence in the sanctuary and the specifying of those who can/cannot 'come near' to the deity (vv. 13, 15). Jeremiah 15.1 and Ps. 106.23 could well be figurative, but are primarily concerned with intercession or mediation rather than service. This leaves two instances which require some discussion: Num. 8.13a and Judg. 20.28.

Numbers 8.13a. Here, Yahweh instructs Moses to 'cause the Levites to stand before (*w^{e}ha'^{a}madtā...lipnê*) Aaron and before (*w^{e}lipnê*) his sons'. By and large this has been understood literally, though the occasional translation[98] or commentator[99] does interpret it as implying the Levites's service of the priests. On two grounds, however, it would appear that the expression in 8.13a is intended in its literal sense. First, its position within 8.5-19, which divides naturally into two main sections. Verses 6-14 constitute Yahweh's instructions to Moses *re* the procedure for the purification of the Levites prior to the commencement of their service, while vv. 15-19, the commencement of which is signalled by '[a]nd after that (*w^e'aḥ^{a}rê-kēn*)...', gives some indication of the Levites's intended role, together with an explanation of the background to their special relationship to the deity.[100] Within the section as a whole, however, the injunction 'you shall cause

93. Cf. W.H. Rose 2000: 62.

94. Note the absence of furniture for seating inside the tabernacle or either Temple.

95. Including the instance of *he'^{e}mîd lpny* in Num. 3.6.

96. Wilson 1995: 171.

97. '[T]he Levitical priests...shall stand before me to offer me the fat and the blood, says the Lord God'.

98. 'You shall place the Levites in attendance upon Aaron...' (NJPS); 'you shall cause the Levites to attend Aaron...' (RSV).

99. Especially Noth 1966: 62, ET 1968: 68-69: 'here there comes into play the idea expressed in 3.5-10, that the Levites are put at the disposal of the priests for "service" (the expression "to stand *or* be set before someone" usually includes the concept of "serving")'. See also Sturdy 1976: 67 and McNeile 1911: 45.

100. Note that the same structure pertains in the following verses (20-22), which outline the carrying out of these instructions. Verses 20-21 summarize the implementation of the Levites's purification procedure, while v. 22 (beginning '[a]nd after that [*w^e'aḥ^{a}rê-kēn*]...') indicates that they did in fact commence their service in the Tent of Meeting.

the Levites to stand before…' (v. 13a) occurs *before* the part detailing the nature of their task. It would therefore appear that the figurative (i.e. service) interpretation is ruled out, and that the literal is the one intended. Secondly, this conclusion is supported by the sequence of instructions within v. 13 itself, where the Levites's standing before Aaron is required *before* their being offered as a wave offering. Analysis of almost all other Old Testament instances of wave offerings reveals that first of all the making of the offering is mentioned, and then some indication of the fate/purpose of the item being offered.[101] Such an arrangement would also appear to exclude a figurative understanding of v. 13a, since that would entail the ultimate destiny of the Levites (i.e. service) being referred to before the command to offer them as a wave offering, and so reverse the normal order. If, however, this instance is consistent with the general pattern, then it provides further evidence that the literal meaning of the expression is the one intended. I thus conclude that the v. 13a instruction which has to be carried out prior to the wave offering, i.e. causing the Levites to 'stand before Aaron and his sons', refers to the former being brought into close spatial proximity to the latter.[102]

Judges 20.28. This refers to 'Phinehas the son of Eleazar, son of Aaron, standing before it/him (*'ōmēd lᵉpānāyw*) in those days'. In this case, it has to be said that commentators do tend to render the Hebrew in terms of service[103] rather than a literal standing before.[104] In fact, however, both interpretations would appear to make sense, though no one has yet been found to provide any justification for either of them. Moreover, as Zapletal (1923: 293) has pointed out,[105] it is not clear

101. Thus, in Exod. 29.22-25 the waving of the offering is mentioned in v. 24 prior to its burning on the altar in v. 25. Cf. the following, in which the instruction or implementation is listed first, and then its fate or purpose (in parentheses): Exod. 29.26a (26b); Lev. 7.30bβ (31b, 34-35); 8.27 (28), 29a (29b); 10.15a (15b); 14.12 (13-18), 24 (25-29); 23.20a (20b); Num. 5.25abα (25bβ-26a); 6.20aα (20aβ); 8.11a (11b), 21aβ (22b). The one possible exception is Num. 8.15: '[a]nd after that the Levites shall go in to do service at the tent of meeting…and you shall offer them as a wave offering (*wᵉhēnaptā 'ōtām tᵉnûpâ*)'. However, while some commentators consider its two halves to have originated from different hands (Noth 1966: 62-63, ET 1968: 69; Heinisch 1936: 42; von Rad 1934: 95-96; Binns 1927: 51; G.B. Gray 1903: 80-81; Holzinger 1903: XIV; Dillmann 1886: 44), the majority of those who view the verse as a unity tend to interpret the *wāw* of *wᵉhēnaptā* as introducing a dependent temporal clause along the lines of 'when you have offered them as…' (Ashley 1993: 172; Levine 1993: 270; Milgrom 1990: 63 n. 27; Kellermann 1970: 118; Greenstone 1939: 84).

102. In fact, such an understanding brings this instance into line with the general pattern, since, following the instruction to offer the Levites as a wave offering (v. 13), their final fate/destination is then indicated in the following verses in which Yahweh indicates that: 'the Levites shall be mine' (v. 14), '[they] shall go in to do service at the tent of meeting' (v. 15), 'they are wholly given to me…I have taken them for myself' (v. 16), 'all the first-born…are mine… I consecrated them for myself, and I have taken the Levites instead of all the first-born among the people of Israel. And I have given the Levites as a gift to Aaron and his sons…to do the service…at the tent of meeting' (vv. 17-19).

103. Soggin 1987: 292-93: 'ministered'; Hertzberg 1985: 246: 'tat…den Dienst'; Maier 1965: 41: 'diente'; Penna 1963: 238: 'era di servizio'; Vincent 1958: 134: 'desservait'; Zapletal 1923: 291: 'bediente'; Budde 1921: 27: 'Bedienung'; Keil 1863: 346: 'diente'.

104. Boling (1975: 282) translates it as 'stationed before'.

105. 'Ob sich das Suffix in לְפָנָיו auf אֲרוֹן, also auf die Bundeslade, oder auf das הָאֱלֹהִים bezieht, ist nicht ganz klar'. Cf. Martin 1975: 213-14.

to whom or what the suffix refers anyway. A few translations and commentators opt for the deity,[106] the majority for the ark.[107] It would therefore appear that Judg. 20.28 cannot be appealed to as an unambiguous example of *'md lpny* being used in the sense of 'serve'.

Summary. There is thus no certain Old Testament precedent for the phrase 'stand before' being used to express the Levitical/Priestly service of another being. In fact, such service is commonly expressed using the verb *šērēt*, whether of humans[108] or of the deity.[109]

Precedents for a Literal Interpretation

Of the several uses of *'md lpny* found in the Old Testament there are a number of clear instances of its being employed in the literal sense. In 1 Kgs 1.28, for example, when Bathsheba 'stood before' the king, it is apparent both from David's addressing her in v. 30 ('as I swore to you [*lāk*]...saying, "Solomon your son [*b^{e}nēk*]..."') and from her response of obeisance in v. 31 that they are in close proximity to one another, and thus that the 'standing before' is literal.[110] Similarly, in 1 Kgs 22.21 (//2 Chron. 18.20), it is clear both from the implied proximity of 'all the host of heaven' to Yahweh (v. 19) and of the ensuing conversation between the enthroned deity and the spirit that 'stood before' him (vv. 21-22) that the latter is represented as being in the divine presence.

Ezekiel 44.11

Two features of the immediate literary context in which the expression occurs point to it being understood in its literal sense:

The plausibility of the Levites and people being proximate. That it is plausible[111] that the Levites's standing before the people is in their presence, is clear from two pieces of evidence. First, it would appear that the Levites's sphere of operation within the Temple is largely restricted to that part of its precincts to which the people are allowed access. This of itself would imply the spatial proximity of the two groups to one another. Secondly, and more particularly, the Levites are instructed to 'slay the burnt offering...for the people' (v. 11b), an action presumably intended to take place on one of the tables 'in the vestible of the [north] gate' (Ezek. 40.39). Now, although a number of scholars have observed that this instruction and the corresponding one in Leviticus differ in that in the latter it is

106. Block 1999: 561; Woudstra 1965: 128; Arnold 1917: 103; Moore 1908: 434.

107. Hertzberg 1985: 246; Boling 1975: 282; Maier 1965: 41; Penna 1963: 239; Vincent 1958: 134; Burney 1930: 478; Budde 1921: 27 n. 2; Keil 1863: 346, ET 1887: 453.

108. Num. 8.26; 18.2; Ezek. 44.12.

109. Deut. 17.12; 21.5; 1 Sam. 2.11; 3.1; Ezek. 40.46; 43.19; 44.15, 16; 45.4; 1 Chron. 15.2; 23.13.

110. Cf. also Gen. 43.15; Exod. 9.10; Num. 27.2; 1 Kgs 3.16; 2 Kgs 4.12; 5.15; 8.9; Est. 8.4; Dan. 2.2.

111. See p. 224, above, for Keysar's (1994) distinction between the two types of contextual information which can lead to the distinguishing of the figurative from the literal.

the *offerer himself* who kills the sacrifice,[112] nonetheless, it would seem legitimate to assume that, in other respects, features of the ritual were intended to be the same. And in fact, many scholars do appeal to the Levitical laws to shed light on the procedure for burnt offerings in Ezekiel 40–48. Information adduced from Leviticus in this way, whether explicitly or implicitly, include: reference to the entrails and legs as the parts which are to be washed (from Lev. 1.9, 13),[113] the throwing of the animal's blood against the altar (from Lev. 1.5, 11)[114] and the observation that the entire carcass has to be burned (from Lev. 1.9, 13),[115] with no part of it being consumed by the worshipper.[116] In addition, some commentators refer their readers to Leviticus in general,[117] i.e. without specifying any particular aspects of the sacrificial procedure. In view of such precedents, therefore, it would seem reasonable to infer, following Lev. 1.4, that the Levite's killing of the animal would be accompanied by the Israelite making the sacrifice 'lay[ing] his hand upon the head of the burnt offering'.[118] This would clearly constitute a situation where the Levite and individual worshipper would be in close spatial proximity, and thus render plausible the interpretation of 'stand before' in the literal sense.

The Levite/Levitical priest contrast. Further support for this interpretation arises from a comparison of the Levites and Levitical priests in Ezekiel 44. The Levites 'stand before' the people (v. 11), whereas the Levitical priests 'stand before' Yahweh (v. 15).[119] Thus, since the deity is depicted as being present within the Temple (v. 2; cf. v. 4), this means that both the reference to the Levitical priests 'stand[ing] before' Yahweh, and the two 'approaching' verbs used in relation to him,[120] are most reasonably understood in the literal sense of implying the physical proximity of the verbs' subjects and the deity. If therefore, the 'standing before' Yahweh is to be understood in its literal sense in v. 15, it is not unreasonable to assume that the 'standing before' the people in v. 11 is also to be understood in the same way.

112. Block 1998: 630; Allen 1990: 261; Cody 1984: 262; Feinberg 1969: 260; Wevers 1969: 319; van den Born 1954: 259; Cooke 1936: 481.

113. Blenkinsopp 1990: 204; Cody 1984: 202; Carley 1974: 275; Fisch 1950: 275; Cooke 1936: 437; Redpath 1907: 221; von Orelli 1888: 159; Keil 1868: 394, ET 1876: 216.

114. Cooper 1994: 383; Redpath 1907: 237.

115. Biggs 1996: 130; Lind 1996: 329; Allen 1990: 230; Cody 1984: 201; Cooke 1936: 437; Heinisch 1923: 196; Kraetzschmar 1900: 281; Bertholet 1897: 221; Davidson 1892: 327, 328; Lofthouse n.d.: 321.

116. Cody 1984: 201; Hengstenberg 1867: 199, ET 1869: 380.

117. Lind 1996: 329; Blenkinsopp 1990: 204; Redpath 1907: 249.

118. Some scholars equate the 'sacrifice' which the Levites slay for the people (44.11b) with the peace offering: Haran 1978: 61; Cooke 1936: 481; Davidson 1892: 332. Cf. Allen's (1990: 230) comment on Ezek. 40.41. If such an identification is correct, this killing would likewise bring Levite and offerer into close proximity, cf. Lev. 3.2, 8, 13.

119. A contrast noted by Block 1998: 633; Taylor 1969: 271; Zimmerli 1969: 1128, ET 1983: 456; Cooke 1936: 481.

120. *Nāgaš* (v. 13), *qārab* (v. 15). Note that in those verses both verbs are also used in relation to physical cultic objects.

Summary. The likely proximity of Levites and people especially during the slaying of the burnt offering, together with the reasonable presumption that the v. 11 'standing before' is meant in the same sense as that in v. 15, both imply an understanding of the Levites's 'standing before' the people in a literal sense, an interpretation pointing to their spatial proximity one to the other.

Consistency with Deuteronomy

Generally. The literal interpretation is also possible in Deuteronomy, since in both historical and legal sections of the book Yahweh is portrayed as being present on the earth (Wilson 1995). When the incidents described in Deuteronomy 1–3, 4–5 and 9–10 are compared with the corresponding accounts in Exodus and Numbers, no evidence is found for either elimination or even reduction of the notion of divine presence (Wilson 1995: chs. 2–4). Rather, it is clearly expressed in a variety of ways, similar to that found in the tetrateuchal narratives[121] and sometimes fulfilling the same function in the Deuteronom(ist)ic accounts as it does in theirs (Wilson 1995: 199-200). Deuteronomy's terminology alludes to the presence of Yahweh with varying degrees of directness, though with no overall weakening of its mode of expression, i.e. compared to that in Exodus and Numbers. Three ways of denoting God's earthly whereabouts are particularly well attested: his being with/among the people, his going with/among/before them, and his speaking from (*mittôk*) the fire on the mountain (Wilson 1995: 205-209), the latter mode of communication being identical to that from the 'burning bush' (Exod. 3.4) and thus similarly indicative of the divine presence (Wilson 1995: 57-66). Furthermore, when such features do not occur in the Deuteronom(ist)ic accounts, their absence can generally be explained either on the basis of context or in terms of differing emphases within the narratives being compared. Deuteronomy clearly depicts God as being present on the earth, both on the journey to the land and for the giving of the law.

This affirmation of divine presence in the historical chapters of the book finds support in its legal section—particularly from an examination of the usage of the phrase 'before the Lord' (*lpny yhwh*) within Deuteronomy 12–26 (Wilson 1995: chs. 5 and 6). First, apart from the two figurative examples in ch. 24,[122] the majority of instances both mention a location and envisage particular occasions on which the activity 'before the Lord' is to take place—two features suggestive of a *literal* understanding of the phrase (Wilson 1995: 142-46, 156-58). Secondly, the expression is only used to qualify such activities if they occur at the 'chosen place'. Nowhere is it applied to anything carried out 'within [the] towns'. And thirdly, throughout chs. 12–26, it is found that, whereas the use of prepositions in connection with the deity is generally consistent with that in the rest of the Old Testament, in five cases out of thirteen 'before' (*lipnê*) is used *instead of* the one most commonly associated with the particular activity concerned

121. Though with the notable exception of 'descend' (*yārad*) and the range of anthropomorphisms found in Exod. 33.17-23.

122. Verses 4, 13. See Wilson 1995: 142, 157.

(Wilson 1995: 147-53). Thus, the verbs 'rejoice' (*śāmaḥ*), 'say' (*'āmar*) and 'worship' (*hištaḥªwâ*) are all followed by 'before' (*lipnê*) instead of 'in' (*bᵉ*), 'to' (*'el* or *lᵉ*) and 'to' (*lᵉ*) respectively. Such a usage indicates a compliance with Hebrew syntax where little or no choice was involved, but a definite bias in favour of 'before' where more than one preposition was available. This preference increases significantly (in a way that the more usual alternatives would not have done) the incidence in chs. 12–26 of an expression ('before the Lord') whose literal interpretation *requires* the presence of the deity in the vicinity of the one carrying out the activity. Such a choice would be strange in a context in which divine transcendence was of major concern. However, it would be understandable if Yahweh was indeed present at the 'chosen place', since 'before' would be ideal for expressing the thought that the rejoicing, saying and worshipping were to be in immediate proximity to him. Moreover, it would explain the observed restriction of 'before the Lord' to activities carried out at that site, because it was only there that his localized presence was to be found.

Thus, examination of the general characteristics of the phrase 'before the Lord' as it occurs in Deuteronomy 12–26 suggests that, with the exception of the two in ch. 24, the majority of occurrences are to be understood in the literal sense, a conclusion additionally supported by independent evidence from the contexts of the instances involving standing (18.7; 19.17) and saying (26.5) (Wilson 1995: 167-87). Activities qualified by the expression are intended to take place in the immediate vicinity of the deity. They therefore provide evidence for a belief in his localized presence at the 'chosen place'.

It is thus clear that Deuteronomy affirms that God was present on the earth during the wilderness wanderings, on Horeb and at the 'chosen place'. The Deuteronomists, who are generally regarded as being responsible for both penning those same historical sections and incorporating the Deuteronomic law into their history, can thus be assumed to be comfortable with the notion of a deity localized in proximity to the Levites.

In particular. In addition, it needs to be pointed out that the specific activity predicated as occurring 'before Yahweh' in 10.8, i.e. 'standing' (*'āmad*), also occurs 'before Yahweh' in the legal section (in 18.7 and 19.17). Both cases have been argued to be literal, and, as has just been mentioned, in both cases there are specific contextual features which point in the direction of such a literal interpretation. It is striking that, whereas in 19.17 the 'stand[ing] before Yahweh' occurs in a judicial context,[123] in 18.7 it occurs in a *cultic* one which also involves the Levites. Deuteronomy 18.1-8 contains additional information about their duties, but, like 10.8-9, does refer to their ministering (*šērēt*, vv. 5, 7), albeit 'in the name of' rather than 'to' Yahweh, as well as to the prohibition against their having any 'portion or inheritance with Israel' (v. 1, cf. v. 2) on the grounds that 'the Lord is their inheritance' (v. 2).

123. Prescribing the procedure to be followed in the case of a malicious witness.

Verdict

It has been argued that the collocation 'to stand before...to minister to...' is in some sense a unit, however understood. Of the two main interpretations considered, i.e. idiomatic or literal, the idiomatic has not been possible to disprove, but has been shown to have no evidence in its favour. Moreover, the suggestion that 'to stand before' should itself be understood figuratively, i.e. in the sense of 'serve',[124] an interpretation for which the Old Testament provides a number of examples, has been rejected in view of the likely resulting semantic redundancy of one or other of the two halves of the collocation, and the lack of any clear instances of such Levitical/Priestly activity being understood in this way. We are therefore left with the literal interpretation of 'stand before', one for which the Old Testament also contains adequate precedent, and which entails each half of the collocation being given its full weight. While in the case of Deut. 10.8 there is insufficient information in its immediate literary environment to provide evidence for such an understanding, the same collocation occurs in Ezekiel 44, arguably with the same sense, and here a case has been made for the plausibility of 'stand[ing] before' being understood literally. In Deut. 10.8 such an interpretation of the collocation is consistent, first with the known posture of Levites/ priests when they carry out cultic actions both generally and in Deuteronomy, and secondly with that book's affirmation of the earthly presence of Yahweh, not only in battle and on Horeb, but also at the 'chosen place' (Wilson 1995) and thus in the sphere of the cult.

I conclude, therefore, that the evidence is not evenly balanced between an idiomatic/figurative and a literal interpretation of the collocation, but rather is weighted in favour of the literal. If this be granted, then the Levites's 'standing before' the deity indicates that they are ministering to him *in his presence*.

3. *The Ark–Divine Presence Connection*

Given that the Levites stand in the divine presence, it is finally necessary to consider whether the most likely location for that presence is in the vicinity of the ark.

The Ark and the Deity are Both Located at the 'Chosen Place'

The Ark. Although Deuteronomy nowhere spells out the final destination of the ark, it would seem, based on the regular recital of the law at 'the place which [the Lord your God] will choose' (31.9-13), that the latter was envisaged as being its ultimate resting place. The law and ark are connected to such an extent that the whereabouts of one determines that of the other.

1. The Association of the Law with the Ark. The majority of commentators consider 'this law' which is read out at the 'chosen place' (31.11, 12) to be the same as that recorded in the book (*sēper*) mentioned in vv. 24-29,[125] and intended to be kept by the side of the ark (v. 26).

124. See above, n. 88.

125. Two forms of exception to the majority view have been noted. Largely following Staerk (1894: 74-75), some older commentators consider that, although in their present form both passages

2. The Association of the Law with the 'Chosen Place'. In order for the law to be read out there, either the law-book must already be at the 'chosen place', or it must first be taken there. In this connection, the Old Testament contains several other instances of a *sēper* (variously rendered 'book', 'scroll', 'letter') described as being 'read'. In the majority of such cases, the immediate literary context usually indicates that, prior to the perusal of its contents, the *sēper* is first *conveyed* to where the reading is intended to take place. This transfer is represented in one of two ways: either *sēper* is the direct object of an appropriate 'delivery' verb, most often 'bring' (*hēbî'*),[126] but occasionally 'send' (*šālaḥ*);[127] or its implied bearer is represented, by means of 'come' (*bô'*),[128] 'go' (*hālak*)[129] or 'go up' (*'ālâ*),[130] as repairing to where the *sēper* is to be read. There are two instances, however, where no such transfer is reported. In these cases it would appear that the *sēper* is already in close proximity to the one who will read it, and so does not need to be brought, sent or otherwise conveyed to him before he is able to do so. In Deut. 17.18-20 the (future) king is required to make for himself a copy of the law in a book. But once he has done so, the instructions make no reference to its being brought to him so that he is then able to peruse it. Verse 19 reads: 'it shall be with him [*'immô*]', suggesting that it is already in his possession. Secondly, in Josh. 8.30-35 Joshua reads out 'all the words of the law...according to all that is written in the book of the law' (v. 34). The context gives no indication of where he obtains the latter, though it does specify that his hearers were standing 'on opposite sides of the ark' (v. 33). However, given that both this passage[131] and

deal with the law, v. 24 (and presumably v. 26) originally read *haššîrâ hazzō't* ('this song') instead of *hattôrâ hazzō't* ('this law'), with the result that the whole of vv. 16-30 (apart from v. 23) then functioned as a unified introduction to ch. 32: Junker 1933: 121; Steuernagel 1900: 112-13; Bertholet 1899: 93-94. Cf. G.A. Smith 1918: 340-41. Welch (1932: 64), however, accepts the present form of the text, but considers that vv. 24-29 refer to a later development in the function of the law: '[w]hereas that law had once been publicly read each seventh year to the whole people, it was now...to be set aside and form a historical document... The Code is quietly but firmly put upon the shelf'.

126. 2 Kgs 5.6; Est. 6.1; Neh. 8.1, 2; 2 Chron. 34.16.

127. 1 Kgs 21.8, 11; 2 Kgs 5.5.

128. 2 Kgs 22.8-10 (Hilkiah gives the book of the law to Shaphan [v. 8], who then 'comes' to Josiah [v. 9] and reads it to him [v. 10]); Jer. 36.4-8 (Baruch writes upon a scroll [v. 4] and is then ordered to 'go' to the Temple [v. 6] and read it to the people [v. 6, cf. v. 8]); 51.59-64 (Jeremiah writes in a book [v. 60], and then tells Seraiah that when he 'comes' to Babylon [v. 61] he is to read 'all these words' [v. 61]).

129. Jer. 51.59, see the previous note.

130. 2 Chron. 34.14-33 (Shaphan brings and reads the book of the law to Josiah [vv. 16, 18], who then 'goes up' to the Temple [v. 30] and reads it to the people [v. 30]).

131. E.g. Auld 1998: 111: '[t]he paragraph has always been recognized as, in some sense at least, a Deuteronomic text'; Miller and Tucker 1974: 72: '[m]ost recent commentators correctly conclude that the passage...stems primarily from the Deuteronomistic historian'. See also Nelson 1997: 116-19; J. Gray 1986: 43, 94; Soggin 1970: 163, 177, ET 1972: 227, 241-42; Noth 1957: 16, 43, 99, 104, 106, ET 1991: 31, 63, 132, 138, 140; Baldi 1956: 8.

> Deut. 31.24-26a[132] are usually regarded as originating from a similar source (Deuteronomic [school]/Deuteronomistic), it would seem reasonable to suppose that the book from which Joshua reads had been taken from where, according to Deut. 31.26, it was to be put 'by the side of the ark', and that because of its immediate proximity there is no reference to its being conveyed to Mt Ebal for Joshua's use.[133]

In the case of Deut. 31.9-13, there is also no mention of 'this law' being brought, taken or in any way transferred to the 'chosen place' prior to its being recited in the presence of all Israel. In the light of Old Testament usage, the most plausible explanation for this is that the law-book is already there. If this is the case, then, by the same token, the ark, by the side of which 'this book of the law' is intended to be kept (v. 26), must also be located 'at the place which the Lord your God will choose'.

The deity. I have already indicated that the presence of Yahweh, as denoted by the majority of the sixteen instances of 'before the Lord' in chs. 12–16, is localized at the 'chosen place'.[134] It thus appears that Deuteronomy envisages both the deity and the ark as eventually being present in the same location.

The Ark and the Deity are Both Located at the Sanctuary

The 'chosen place' at which both divine presence and ark will ultimately be based is generally considered to refer to the *sanctuary*,[135] i.e. rather than to the settlement in which the sanctuary is situated.[136] Moreover, in view of the presence of

132. E.g. Clifford 1982: 161: '[t]his latter section...is generally considered Deuteronomistic'. See also Tigay 1996: 504; Begg 1983: 97; Preuss 1982: 60-61; Nelson 1981: 124; Mayes 1979: 46, 372, 379; Skweres 1979: 75 n. 320; Levenson 1975: 221; Nicholson 1967: 27, 31, 36; Lohfink 1962: 46; de Tillesse 1962: 32; Noth 1957: 39, ET 1991: 59-60.

133. No instances have been found in which the *sēper* is initially far from the reading site, but is not represented as being transferred there.

134. See above, pp. 232-33.

135. Tigay 1996: xiii: 'Deuteronomy speaks of [God] as dwelling in heaven (26:15); only His name dwells in the sanctuary (e.g., 12:5)'; Braulik 1994: 32: 'YHWH himself is not localized in the earthly temple; his name is present there'; Levenson 1985: 125: '[h]ere [e.g. Deut. 12.5] it is not the case that YHWH dwells in the sanctuary in a literal anthropomorphic sense, but that he places his "name"...there'; Mettinger 1982: 38: '[in] the time of the Exile...we...find...God's... "Name", in conjunction with the sanctuary. This is the case in Deuteronomy'; Weinfeld 1972b: 1018: '[Deuteronomy] resorts...to the phrase "the place where He shall choose to cause his name to dwell"...so as to emphasize that it is God's name...who dwells within the Sanctuary'; McBride 1969: 2: '[a]ccording to Deuteronomy, Israel may approach God at the shrine where he chooses to "establish" or "fix" his name'; Nicholson 1967: 55-56: 'in Deuteronomy...[Yahweh's] name is present in the sanctuary'; Clements 1965b: 94 n. 4: 'the [Deuteronomic] doctrine of Yahweh's name set in Israel's sanctuary'; Dumermuth 1958: 61: '[d]ie Formel: "*Der Ort, den Jahwe erwählt, um seinen Namen daselbst wohnen zu lassen*"...hat man seit jeher auf den Zentralkultort gedeutet'; Noth 1957: 104, ET 1991: 139: 'the formula in the Deuteronomic law which describes the temple as the "dwelling" "chosen" by God for his "name"'; von Rad 1947: 26, ET 1953: 38: 'the assumption of a constant and almost material presence of the name at the shrine'; McNeile 1912: 27: '[t]his sanctuary is described as "the place which Jehovah...shall choose...to put His Name there"'.

136. Note that the ark did eventually find its way to the Jerusalem Temple (1 Kgs 8.1-21).

the covenant tables and law-book which accompany the ark, such a scenario would be consistent with the known ancient Near Eastern practice of preserving important documents in sanctuaries/temples under the surveillance of the associated deity.[137]

4. *Conclusion*

In Deuteronomy, the ark of the covenant is portrayed mainly in its relation to the law. It is depicted primarily as a receptacle within which are contained the two tables of the covenant (10.1-5) and by the side of which is to be kept 'this book of the law' (31.24-26)—an emphasis which may well be reflected in its designation as the ark 'of the covenant' of Yahweh (10.8; 31.9, 25, 26). This is not, however, its only function in Deuteronomy. In 10.8 the Levites's carrying of the ark is mentioned immediately before a reference to their 'stand[ing] before Yahweh to minister to him'. I have considered the significance of the latter and concluded that there are no substantial grounds for understanding it in a figurative/idiomatic sense. Rather, the available evidence suggests that the collocation refers to the posture adopted by the Levites when they minister in the divine presence. The same literary context thus refers both to the ark of the covenant and to cultic activity carried out in the presence of the deity. The two activities are therefore almost certain to be linked. Moreover, while they are clearly intended to take place on different occasions, their literary juxtaposition would seem to render unlikely the view that the author's primary concern was to sever the ark from any connection with the divine presence. Rather, the inclusion of both roles in the same literary context has the effect of inviting such a link to be made. Furthermore, if this be granted, it has also been argued that Yahweh and the ark are both envisaged as eventually being based at the same location, i.e. 'the place which the Lord your God will choose', a phrase generally considered to denote a particular sanctuary. This being the case, it would therefore seem to be highly improbable that the presence before whom the Levites stand would be unconnected with the ark which they also carry. I therefore conclude that, although Deuteronomy is mainly concerned with the ark's function as a container, it does also acknowledge its association with the divine presence.[138] The book's portrayal of the ark is thus consistent with its affirmation of God's earthly presence, not only during the wilderness wanderings and on Horeb, but also at the 'chosen place'.

137. Haran 1978: 255: 'the practice of burying various books, documents, written oaths, and covenants in a special case under the images of gods in temples was common in Egypt and the Hittite kingdom—and apparently throughout the ancient Near East'; de Vaux 1967: 256: '[l]a coutume de mettre des documents dans les sanctuaires sous la garde des dieux est bien attestée dans l'Ancien Orient'; Jirku 1923: 184: '…daß es eine im ganzen AO verbreitete Sitte war, wichtige Urkunden des religiösen, staatlichen und privaten Lebens an geweihten Orten niederzulegen'.

138. Cf. 1 Sam. 4.4; 2 Sam. 6.2.

Bibliography

Abba, R.
1962 'Priests and Levites', in *IDB*, III: 876-89.
Achtemeier, Elizabeth R.
1978 *Deuteronomy, Jeremiah* (Proclamation Commentaries; Philadelphia: Fortress Press).
Aejmelaeus, Anneli
1993 *On the Trail of Septuagint Translators: Collected Essays* (Kampen: Kok).
1996 'Die Septuaginta des Deuteronomiums', in Timo Veijola (ed.), *Das Deuteronomium und seine Querbeziehungen* (Schriften der finnischen exegetischen Gesellschaft, 62; Helsinki: Finnische exegetische Gesellschaft): 1-22.
Allen, Leslie C.
1990 *Ezekiel 20–48* (WBC, 29; Dallas: Word Books).
Arnold, William R.
1917 *Ephod and Ark: A Study in the Records and Religion of the Ancient Hebrews* (Harvard Theological Studies, 3; Cambridge, MA: Harvard University Press).
Ashley, Timothy R.
1993 *The Book of Numbers* (NICOT; Grand Rapids: Eerdmans).
Auld, A. Graeme
1998 *Joshua Retold* (Old Testament Studies; Edinburgh: T. & T. Clark).
Babut, Jean-Marc
1995 *Les expressions idiomatiques de l'hébreu biblique: signification et traduction: un essai d'analyse componentielle* (Cahiers de la Revue biblique, 33; Paris: J. Gabalda). ET *Idiomatic Expressions of the Hebrew Bible: Their Meaning and Translation through Componential Analysis* (trans. Sarah E. Lind; BIBAL Dissertation Series, 5; North Richland Hills, TX: BIBAL Press, 1999).
Baillet, M.
1962 'Textes des grottes 2Q, 3Q, 6Q, 7Q à 10Q', in M. Baillet, J.T. Milik and R. de Vaux, *Les 'Petites Grottes' de Qumrân* (DJD, 3; Oxford: Clarendon Press): 43-164.
Baldi, P. Donato
1956 *Giosuè* (La Sacra Bibbia; Turin: Marietti).
Begg, Christopher T.
1983 'The Tables (Deut. x) and the Lawbook (Deut. xxxi)', *VT* 33: 96-97.
Benson, Joseph
1815 *The Holy Bible, Containing the Old and New Testaments, with Notes, Critical, Explanatory, and Practical,* I: *Genesis–1 Samuel* (London: Wesleyan Conference Office, 8th edn).
Benzinger, I.
1899 *Die Bücher der Könige* (KHAT, 9; Freiburg: J.C.B. Mohr [Paul Siebeck]).
Bernhardt, K.-H.
1964 'Lade', in Bo Reicke and Leonhard Rost (eds.), *Biblisch-Historisches Handwörterbuch* (4 vols.; Göttingen: Vandenhoeck & Ruprecht, 1962–79): II, 1038-41.
Bertholet, Alfred
1897 *Das Buch Hesekiel* (KHAT, 12; Freiburg: J.C.B. Mohr [Paul Siebeck]).
1899 *Deuteronomium* (KHAT, 5; Freiburg: J.C.B. Mohr [Paul Siebeck]).
Biggs, Charles R.
1996 *The Book of Ezekiel* (Epworth Commentaries; London: Epworth Press).

Binnick, Robert I.
1971 'Bring and Come', *Linguistic Inquiry* 2: 260-65.
Binns, L. Elliott
1927 *The Book of Numbers* (Westminster Commentaries; London: Methuen).
Blenkinsopp, Joseph
1989 'Deuteronomy', in Raymond E. Brown, Joseph A. Fitzmyer and Roland E. Murphy (eds.), *The New Jerome Biblical Commentary* (London: Geoffrey Chapman): 94-109.
1990 *Ezekiel* (Interpretation; Louisville, KY: John Knox Press).
Block, Daniel I.
1998 *The Book of Ezekiel: Chapters 25–48* (NICOT; Grand Rapids: Eerdmans).
1999 *Judges, Ruth* (The New American Commentary, 6; Nashville: Broadman & Holman).
Boling, Robert G.
1975 *Judges* (AB, 6A; Garden City, NY: Doubleday).
Born, A. van den
1954 *Ezechiël* (De Boeken van het Oude Testament; Roermond: J.J. Romen & Zonen).
Braulik, Georg
1986 *Deuteronomium 1–16, 17* (Die Neue Echter Bibel; Würzburg: Echter Verlag.
1994 'The Joy of the Feast', in *The Theology of Deuteronomy: Collected Essays of Georg Braulik* (trans. Ulrika Lindblad; BIBAL Collected Essays, 2; N. Richland Hills, TX: BIBAL Press): 27-65.
Bressan, Gino
1954 *Samuele* (La Sacra Bibbia; Turin: Marietti).
Brown, Raymond
1993 *The Message of Deuteronomy* (The Bible Speaks Today; Leicester: IVP).
Brueggemann, Walter
2001 *Deuteronomy* (Abingdon Old Testament Commentaries; Nashville: Abingdon Press).
Budde, Karl
1902 *Die Bücher Samuel* (KHAT, 8; Tübingen: J.C.B. Mohr [Paul Siebeck]).
1921 'Ephod und Lade', *ZAW* 39: 1-42.
Buis, Pierre
1997 *Le Livre des Rois* (SB; Paris: J. Gabalda).
Buis, Pierre, and Jacques Leclercq
1963 *Le Deutéronome* (SB; Paris: J. Gabalda).
Burney, C.F.
1903 *Notes on the Hebrew Text of the Books of Kings* (Oxford: Clarendon Press).
1930 *The Book of Judges* (London: Rivingtons).
Cacciari, Cristina, and Patrizia Tabossi
1988 'The Comprehension of Idioms', *Journal of Memory and Language* 27: 668-83.
Caird, G.B.
1980 *The Language and Imagery of the Bible* (London: Gerald Duckworth).
Cairns, Ian
1992 *Word and Presence: A Commentary on the Book of Deuteronomy* (ITC; Grand Rapids: Eerdmans).
Caquot, André, and Philippe de Robert
1994 *Les Livres de Samuel* (CAT, 6; Geneva: Labor et Fides).

Carley, Keith W.
1974 *The Book of the Prophet Ezekiel* (CBC; Cambridge: Cambridge University Press).
Cartledge, Tony W.
2001 *1 & 2 Samuel* (Smyth & Helwys Bible Commentary, 7; Macon, GA: Smyth & Helwys Publishing).
Casanowicz, Immanuel M.
1894 *Paronomasia in the Old Testament* (Boston: Norwood Press).
Chafe, Wallace L.
1965 'Meaning in Language', in E.A. Hammel (ed.), *Formal Semantic Analysis* (American Anthropologist Special Publication, 67, no. 5, pt. 2: Menasha, WI: American Anthropological Association): 23-36.
1968 'Idiomaticity as an Anomaly in the Chomskyan Paradigm', *Foundations of Language* 4: 109-27.
1970 *Meaning and the Structure of Language* (Chicago: University of Chicago Press).
Chomsky, Noam
1980 *Rules and Representations* (Oxford: Basil Blackwell).
Christensen, Duane L.
2001 *Deuteronomy 1:1–21:9* (WBC, 6A; Nashville: Thomas Nelson, rev. edn).
Clamer, Albert
1940 'Le Deutéronome', *La Sainte Bible* (8 vols.; Paris: Letouzey & Ané, 1940–64): II, 483-742.
Clements, R.E.
1965a 'Deuteronomy and the Jerusalem Cult Tradition', *VT* 15: 300-12.
1965b *God and Temple* (Oxford: Basil Blackwell).
Clifford, Richard J.
1982 *Deuteronomy with an Excursus on Covenant and Law* (OTM, 4; Wilmington, DE: Michael Glazier).
Clines, David J.A. (ed.)
1995 *The Dictionary of Classical Hebrew*, II. ב-ו (Sheffield: Sheffield Academic Press).
Cody, Aelred
1984 *Ezekiel, with an Excursus on Old Testament Priesthood* (OTM, 11; Wilmington, DE: Michael Glazier).
Cogan, Mordechai
2001 *1 Kings* (AB, 10; New York: Doubleday).
Cooke, G.A.
1936 *The Book of Ezekiel* (ICC; Edinburgh: T. & T. Clark).
Cooper, Lamar Eugene, Sr
1994 *Ezekiel* (The New American Commentary, 17; Nashville: Broadman & Holman).
Craigie, Peter C.
1976 *The Book of Deuteronomy* (NICOT; Grand Rapids: Eerdmans).
Cross, Frank Moore
1973 *Canaanite Myth and Hebrew Epic: Essays in the History of the Religion of Israel* (Cambridge, MA: Harvard University Press).
Cunliffe-Jones, H.
1951 *Deuteronomy* (Torch Bible Commentaries; London: SCM Press).
Davidson, A.B.
1892 *The Book of the Prophet Ezekiel* (CBSC; Cambridge: Cambridge University Press).

Davies, G. Henton
1962a 'Ark of the Covenant', in *IDB*, I: 222-26.
1962b 'Deuteronomy', *Peake's Commentary on the Bible* (London: Thomas Nelson): 269-84.
Delitzsch, Friedrich
1920 *Die Lese- und Schreibfehler im Alten Testament* (Berlin: W. de Gruyter).
DeVries, Simon J.
1975 *Yesterday, Today and Tomorrow: Time and History in the Old Testament* (London: SPCK).
1985 *1 Kings* (WBC, 12; Waco, TX: Word Books).
Dhorme, Paul
1910 *Les Livres de Samuel* (EBib; Paris: J. Gabalda).
Dibelius, Martin
1906 *Die Lade Jahves* (FRLANT, 7; Göttingen: Vandenhoeck & Ruprecht).
Dietrich, Walter
1972 *Prophetie und Geschichte: Eine redaktionsgeschichtliche Untersuchung zum deuteronomistischen Geschichtswerk* (FRLANT, 108; Göttingen: Vandenhoeck & Ruprecht).
Dillmann, August
1886 *Die Bücher Numeri, Deuteronomium und Josua* (Kurzgefasstes exegetisches Handbuch zum Alten Testament; Leipzig: Hirzel).
Driver, S.R.
1902 *A Critical and Exegetical Commentary on Deuteronomy* (ICC; Edinburgh: T. & T. Clark, 3rd edn).
1913 *Notes on the Hebrew Text and the Topography of the Books of Samuel* (Oxford: Clarendon Press, 2nd edn).
Dumermuth, Fritz
1958 'Zur deuteronomischen Kulttheologie und ihren Voraussetzungen', *ZAW* 70: 59-98.
Dürr, Lorenz
1924 'Ursprung und Bedeutung der Bundeslade', *Bonner Zeitschrift für Theologie und Seelsorge* 1: 17-32.
Dus, Jan
1963 'Noch zum Brauch der "Ladewanderung"', *VT* 13: 126-32.
1964 'Die Thron- und Bundeslade', *TZ* 20: 241-51.
Empson, William
1953 *Seven Types of Ambiguity* (London: Chatto & Windus, 3rd edn).
Feinberg, Charles Lee
1969 *The Prophecy of Ezekiel: The Glory of the Lord* (Chicago: Moody Press).
Fernando, Chitra
1996 *Idioms and Idiomaticity* (Describing English Language; Oxford: Oxford University Press).
Fernando, Chitra, and Roger Flavell
1981 *On Idiom: Critical Views and Perspectives* (Exeter Linguistic Studies, 5; Exeter: University of Exeter Press).
Fisch, S.
1950 *Ezekiel* (Soncino Books of the Bible; London: Soncino).
Fraser, Bruce
1970 'Idioms within a Transformational Grammar', *Foundations of Language* 6: 22-42.

Fretheim, Terence E.
1968 'The Ark in Deuteronomy', *CBQ* 30: 1-14.
1999 *First and Second Kings* (Westminster Bible Companion; Louisville, KY: Westminster/John Knox Press).
García López, Félix
1978 'Analyse littéraire de Deutéronome, V–XI', *RB* 85: 5-49.
Gehrke, Ralph David
1968 *1 and 2 Samuel* (Concordia Commentary; St Louis: Concordia Publishing House).
Gibson, J.C.L.
1994 *Davidson's Introductory Hebrew Grammar: Syntax* (Edinburgh: T. & T. Clark, 4th edn).
Goldman, S.
1951 *Samuel* (Soncino Books of the Bible; London: Soncino).
Gray, George Buchanan
1903 *Numbers* (ICC; Edinburgh: T. & T. Clark).
Gray, John
1970 *I & II Kings* (OTL; London: SCM Press, 2nd edn).
1986 *Joshua, Judges, Ruth* (NCB; Grand Rapids: Eerdmans).
Greenstone, Julius H.
1939 *Numbers* (Philadelphia: Jewish Publication Society of America).
Gumpel, Liselotte
1974 'The Structure of Idioms: A Phenomenological Approach', *Semiotica* 12: 1-40.
Halpern, Baruch, and Jon D. Levenson (eds.)
1981 *Traditions in Transformation: Turning Points in Biblical Faith* (Festschrift Frank Moore Cross; Winona Lake, IN: Eisenbrauns).
Haran, Menahem
1978 *Temples and Temple-Service in Ancient Israel* (Oxford: Clarendon Press).
Healey, Alan
1968 'English Idioms', *Kivung* 1: 71-108.
Heinisch, Paul
1923 *Das Buch Ezechiel* (Die Heilige Schrift des Alten Testamentes, 8.1; Bonn: Peter Hanstein).
1936 *Das Buch Numeri* (Die Heilige Schrift des Alten Testamentes, 2.1; Bonn: Peter Hanstein).
Hempel, Johannes
1914 *Die Schichten des Deuteronomiums. Ein Beitrag zur israelitischen Literatur- und Rechtsgeschichte* (Beiträge zur Kultur- und Universalgeschichte, 33; Leipzig: R. Voigtländer).
Hengstenberg, E.W.
1867 *Die Weissagungen des Propheten Ezechiel für solche die in der Schrift forschen erläutert* (Berlin: Gustav Schlawitz). ET *The Prophecies of the Prophet Ezekiel Elucidated* (trans. A.C. Murphy and J.G. Murphy; Edinburgh: T. & T. Clark, 1869).
Hertzberg, Hans Wilhelm
1985 *Die Bücher Josua, Richter, Ruth* (ATD, 9; Göttingen: Vandenhoeck & Ruprecht).
Holladay, William L.
1971 *A Concise Hebrew and Aramaic Lexicon of the Old Testament* (Leiden: E.J. Brill).
Hölscher, Gustav
1922 'Komposition und Ursprung des Deuteronomiums', *ZAW* 40: 161-255.

Holzinger, H.
1903 *Numeri* (KHAT, 4; Tübingen: J.C.B. Mohr [Paul Siebeck]).

Jepsen, Alfred
1956 *Die Quellen des Königsbuches* (Halle: Max Niemeyer, 2nd edn).

Jirku, Anton
1923 *Altorientalischer Kommentar zum Alten Testament* (Leipzig: Deichert).

Jones, Gwilym H.
1984 *1 and 2 Kings* (NCB; Grand Rapids: Eerdmans).

Junker, Hubert
1933 *Das Buch Deuteronomium* (Die Heilige Schrift des Alten Testamentes, 2.2; Bonn: Peter Hanstein).

Kaiser, Otto
1969 *Einleitung in das Alte Testament* (Gütersloh: Gerd Mohn). ET *Introduction to the Old Testament* (trans. John Sturdy; Oxford: Basil Blackwell, 1975).

Katz, J.J., and P.M. Postal
1963 'Semantic Interpretation of Idioms and Sentences Containing Them', *M.I.T. Research Laboratory of Electronics Quarterly Progress Report* 70: 275-82.

Keil, Carl Friedrich
1863 *Biblischer Commentar über die prophetischen Geschichtsbücher des Alten Testaments*, I. *Josua, Richter und Ruth* (Leipzig: Dörffling & Franke). ET *Joshua, Judges, Ruth* (trans. James Martin; Edinburgh: T. & T. Clark, 1887).
1868 *Biblischer Commentar über den Propheten Ezechiel* (Leipzig: Dörffling & Franke). ET *Biblical Commentary on the Prophecies of Ezekiel*, II (trans. James Martin; Edinburgh: T. & T. Clark, 1876).

Kellermann, Diether
1970 *Die Priesterschrift von Numeri* 1_1 *bis* 10_{10} (BZAW, 120; Berlin: W. de Gruyter).

Keysar, Boaz
1994 'Discourse Context Effects: Metaphorical and Literal Interpretations', *Discourse Processes* 18: 247-69.

Kirkpatrick, A.F.
1888 *The First Book of Samuel* (CBSC; Cambridge: Cambridge University Press).

Klein, Ralph W.
1983 *1 Samuel* (WBC, 10; Waco, TX: Word Books).

Klostermann, August
1907 *Der Pentateuch. Beiträge zu seinem Verständnis und seiner Entstehungsgeschichte. Neue Folge* (Leipzig: Deichert).

Knoppers, Gary N.
1995 'Prayer and Propaganda: Solomon's Dedication of the Temple and the Deuteronomist's Program', *CBQ* 57: 229-54.

Koehler, Ludwig, and Walter Baumgartner
1998 *A Bilingual Dictionary of the Hebrew and Aramaic Old Testament* (Leiden: E.J. Brill).

Kraetzschmar, Richard
1900 *Das Buch Ezechiel* (HKAT, 3.3.1; Göttingen: Vandenhoeck & Ruprecht).

Labuschagne, C.J.
1987 *Deuteronomium IB* (De prediking van het Oude Testament; Nijkerk: Uitgeverij Callenbach).

Leimbach, Karl A.
1936 *Die Bücher Samuel* (Die Heilige Schrift des Alten Testaments, 3.1; Bonn: Peter Hanstein).

Levenson, Jon D.

1975 'Who Inserted the Book of the Torah?', *HTR* 68: 203-21.

1981 'From Temple to Synagogue: 1 Kings 8', in Halpern and Levenson (eds.) 1981: 143-66.

1985 *Sinai and Zion: An Entry into the Jewish Bible* (New Voices in Biblical Studies; Minneapolis: Winston Press).

Levine, Baruch A.

1993 *Numbers 1–20* (AB, 4A; New York: Doubleday).

Lind, Millard C.

1996 *Ezekiel* (Believers Church Bible Commentary; Scottdale, PA: Herald Press).

Loewenstamm, Samuel E.

1992 'The Formula *Bā'et Hahi'* in the Introductory Speeches in Deuteronomy', in *idem*, *From Babylon to Canaan* (Jerusalem: Magnes Press): 42-50.

Lofthouse, W.F.

n.d. *Ezekiel* (Century Bible; Edinburgh: T.C. & E.C. Jack).

Lohfink, Norbert

1962 'Der Bundesschluss im Land Moab', *BZ* 6: 32-56.

1963 *Das Hauptgebot. Eine Untersuchung literarischer Einleitungsfragen zu Dtn 5–11* (AnBib, 20; Rome: Pontificio Istituto Biblico).

Maier, Johann

1965 *Das altisraelitische Ladeheiligtum* (BZAW, 93; Berlin: Alfred Töpelmann).

Makkai, Adam

1975 'The Cognitive Organization of Idiomaticity: Rhyme or Reason?', *Georgetown University Working Papers on Languages and Linguistics* 11: 10-29.

Malkiel, Yakov

1959 'Studies in Irreversible Binomials', *Lingua* 8: 113-60.

Martin, James D.

1975 *The Book of Judges* (CBC; Cambridge: Cambridge University Press).

Maxwell, John C.

1987 *Deuteronomy* (The Communicator's Commentary, 5; Waco, TX: Word Books).

Mayes, A.D.H.

1979 *Deuteronomy* (NCB; London: Oliphants).

1983 *The Story of Israel between Settlement and Exile: A Redactional Study of the Deuteronomistic History* (London: SCM Press).

McBride, S.D.

1969 'The Deuteronomic Name Theology' (PhD dissertation, Harvard University).

McCarter, P. Kyle, Jr

1980 *I Samuel* (AB, 8; Garden City, NY: Doubleday).

McConville, J.G.

2002 *Deuteronomy* (Apollos Old Testament Commentary, 5; Leicester: IVP).

McKane, William

1963 *I & II Samuel* (Torch Bible Commentaries; London: SCM Press).

McNeile, A.H.

1911 *The Book of Numbers* (CBSC; Cambridge: Cambridge University Press).

1912 *Deuteronomy: Its Place in Revelation* (London: Longmans, Green & Co.).

Meier, H.H.

1975 'The State of Idiomatics', *Dutch Quarterly Review of Anglo-American Letters* 5: 163-79.

Merrill, Eugene H.

1994 *Deuteronomy* (The New American Commentary, 4; Nashville: Broadman & Holman).

Merwe, Christo H.J. van der, Jackie A. Naudé and Jan H. Kroeze
1999 *A Biblical Hebrew Reference Grammar* (Biblical Languages: Hebrew, 3; Sheffield: Sheffield Academic Press).
Mettinger, Tryggve N.D.
1982 *The Dethronement of Sabaoth: Studies in the Shem and Kabod Theologies* (trans. Frederick H. Cryer; ConBOT, 18; Lund: C.W.K. Gleerup).
Milgrom, Jacob
1990 *Numbers* (JPS Torah Commentary; Philadelphia: Jewish Publication Society of America).
Miller, J. Maxwell, and Gene M. Tucker
1974 *The Book of Joshua* (CBC; Cambridge: Cambridge University Press).
Miller, Patrick D.
1990 *Deuteronomy* (Interpretation; Louisville, KY: John Knox Press).
Montgomery, James A., and Henry Snyder Gehman
1951 *The Books of Kings* (ICC; Edinburgh: T. & T. Clark).
Moore, George F.
1908 *A Critical and Exegetical Commentary on Judges* (ICC; Edinburgh: T. & T. Clark).
Morgenstern, Julian
1928 'The Book of the Covenant', *HUCA* 5: 1-151.
Myers, Jacob M.
1961 'The Requisites for Response: On the Theology of Deuteronomy', *Int* 15: 14-31.
Nelson, Richard D.
1981 *The Double Redaction of the Deuteronomistic History* (JSOTSup, 18; Sheffield: JSOT Press).
1997 *Joshua* (OTL; Louisville, KY: Westminster/John Knox Press).
Newmeyer, Frederick J.
1972 'The Insertion of Idioms', *Papers from the Eighth Regional Meeting of the Chicago Linguistic Society*: 294-302.
1974 'The Regularity of Idiom Behavior', *Lingua* 34: 327-42.
Nicholson, E.W.
1967 *Deuteronomy and Tradition* (Oxford: Basil Blackwell).
Nielsen, Eduard
1995 *Deuteronomium* (HAT, 1.6; Tübingen: J.C.B. Mohr [Paul Siebeck]).
Noth, Martin
1957 *Überlieferungsgeschichtliche Studien* (Tübingen: Max Niemeyer). ET *The Deuteronomistic History* (trans. Jane Doull, John Barton, Michael D. Rutter and D.R. Ap-Thomas; JSOTSup, 15; Sheffield: JSOT Press, 2nd edn, 1991).
1966 *Das vierte Buch Mose: Numeri* (ATD, 7; Göttingen: Vandenhoeck & Ruprecht). ET *Numbers* (trans. James D. Martin; OTL; London: SCM Press, 1968).
Nötscher, Friedrich
1924 *'Das Angesicht Gottes schauen' nach biblischer und babylonischer Auffassung* (Würzburg: Wissenschaftliche Buchgesellschaft).
Nunberg, Geoffrey, Ivan A. Sag and Thomas Wasow
1994 'Idioms', *Language* 70: 491-538.
Oettli, Samuel
1893 *Das Deuteronomium und die Bücher Josua und Richter* (Kurzgefasster Kommentar zu den heiligen Schriften Alten und Neuen Testamentes, 2; Munich: Beck).

Orelli, C. von
1888 *Das Buch Ezechiel und die zwölf kleinen Propheten* (Kurzgefasster Kommentar zu den heiligen Schriften Alten und Neuen Testamentes, 5; Nördlingen: Beck).

Otto, Eckart
2000 *Das Deuteronomium im Pentateuch und Hexateuch: Studien zur Literaturgeschichte von Pentateuch und Hexateuch im Lichte des Deuteronomium–rahmens* (FAT, 30; Tübingen: Mohr Siebeck).

Peckham, Brian
1975 'The Composition of Deuteronomy 9:1–10:11', in Joseph Plevnik (ed.), *Word and Spirit* (Festschrift David Michael Stanley; Willowdale: Regis College Press): 3-59.

Penna, Angelo
1963 *Giudici e Rut* (La Sacra Bibbia; Turin: Marietti).

Phillips, Anthony
1973 *Deuteronomy* (CBC; Cambridge: Cambridge University Press).

Plöger, Josef G.
1967 *Literarkritische, formgeschichtliche und stilkritische Untersuchungen zum Deuteronomium* (BBB, 26; Bonn: Peter Hanstein).

Polzin, Robert
1981 'Reporting Speech in the Book of Deuteronomy: Toward a Compositional Analysis of the Deuteronomic History', in Halpern and Levenson (eds.) 1981: 193-211.

Poole, Matthew
1962 *A Commentary on the Holy Bible*, I. *Genesis–Job* (repr., London: Banner of Truth Trust).

Preuss, Horst Dietrich
1982 *Deuteronomium* (Erträge der Forschung, 164; Darmstadt: Wissenschaftliche Buchgesellschaft).

Puukko, A. Filemon
1910 *Das Deuteronomium: eine literarkritische Untersuchung* (BWAT, 5; Leipzig: J.C. Hinrichs).

Rabban, N.
1952 'לפני ה׳', *Tarbiẓ* 23: 1-8.

Rad, Gerhard von
1934 *Die Priesterschrift im Hextateuch* (BWANT, 65; Stuttgart: W. Kohlhammer).
1947 *Deuteronomium-Studien* (FRLANT, 58; Göttingen: Vandenhoeck & Ruprecht). ET. *Studies in Deuteronomy* (trans. David Stalker; SBT, 9; London: SCM Press, 1953).
1958 'Zelt und Lade', in *Gesammelte Studien zum Alten Testament* (TBü, 8; Munich: Chr. Kaiser Verlag): 109-29. ET 'The Tent and the Ark', in *The Problem of the Hexateuch and Other Essays* (trans. E.W. Trueman Dicken; Edinburgh: Oliver & Boyd, 1966): 103-24.
1964 *Das fünfte Buch Mose: Deuteronomium* (ATD, 8; Göttingen: Vandenhoeck & Ruprecht). ET *Deuteronomy* (trans. Dorothea Barton; OTL; London: SCM Press, 1966).

Redpath, Henry A.
1907 *The Book of the Prophet Ezekiel* (Westminster Commentaries; London: Methuen).

Reider, Joseph
1937 *Deuteronomy* (Philadelphia: Jewish Publication Society of America).

Reindl, Joseph

1970 *Das Angesicht Gottes im Sprachgebrauch des Alten Testaments* (Erfurter theologische Studien, 25; Leipzig: St Benno).

Ringgren, Helmer

1989 'עָמַד *'āmad*', in *ThWAT*, VI: 194-204. ET *TDOT*, XI (2001): 178-87.

Robinson, H. Wheeler

n.d. *Deuteronomy and Joshua* (Century Bible; Edinburgh: T.C. & E.C. Jack).

Robinson, J.

1972 *The First Book of Kings* (CBC; Cambridge: Cambridge University Press).

Rofé, Alexander

1986 'The History of the Cities of Refuge in Biblical Law', in S. Japhet (ed.), *Studies in Bible* (trans. Nathan H. Reisner; Scripta Hierosolymitana, 31; Jerusalem: Magnes Press): 205-39.

2002 *Deuteronomy: Issues and Interpretation* (Old Testament Studies; Edinburgh: T. & T. Clark).

Rose, Martin

1994a *5. Mose 12–25: Einführung und Gesetze* (Zürcher Bibelkommentare AT, 5.1; Zürich: Theologischer Verlag).

1994b *5. Mose 1–11 und 26–34: Rahmenstücke zum Gesetzeskorpus* (Zürcher Bibelkommentare AT, 5.2; Zürich: Theologischer Verlag).

Rose, Wolter H.

2000 *Zemah and Zerubbabel: Messianic Expectations in the Early Postexilic Period* (JSOTSup, 304; Sheffield: Sheffield Academic Press).

Rowley, H.H.

1956 *The Faith of Israel* (London: SCM Press).

Sawyer, John F.A.

1972 *Semantics in Biblical Research* (SBT, 24; London: SCM Press).

Schmitt, Rainer

1972 *Zelt und Lade als Thema alttestamentlicher Wissenschaft* (Gütersloh: Gerd Mohn).

Segert, Stanislav

1992 'Assonance and Rhyme in Hebrew Poetry', *Maarav* 8: 171-79.

Seitz, Gottfried

1971 *Redaktionsgeschichtliche Studien zum Deuteronomium* (BWANT, 93; Stuttgart: W. Kohlhammer).

Seow, C.L.

1992 'Ark of the Covenant', in *ABD*, I: 386-93.

Skinner, J.

n.d. *Kings* (Century Bible; Edinburgh: T.C. & E.C. Jack).

Skweres, Dieter Eduard

1979 *Die Rückverweise im Buch Deuteronomium* (AnBib, 79; Rome: Biblical Institute Press).

Smend, Rudolf

1912 *Die Erzählung des Hexateuch auf ihre Quellen untersucht* (Berlin: Georg Reimer).

Smith, George Adam

1918 *The Book of Deuteronomy* (CBSC; Cambridge: Cambridge University Press).

Smith, Henry Preserved

1912 *The Books of Samuel* (ICC; Edinburgh: T. & T. Clark).

Soggin, J. Alberto

1970 *Le Livre de Josué* (CAT, 5a; Paris: Delachaux & Niestlé). ET *Joshua* (trans. R.A. Wilson; OTL; London: SCM Press, 1972).

1987 *Judges* (trans. John Bowden from the Italian; OTL; London: SCM Press, 2nd edn).

Sollamo, Raija
1985 'Den bibliska formeln "Inför Herren/Inför Gud"', *SEÅ* 50: 21-32.

Sonnet, Jean-Pierre
1997 *The Book within the Book: Writing in Deuteronomy* (Biblical Interpretation Series, 14; Leiden: E.J. Brill).

Staerk, Willy
1894 *Das Deuteronomium, sein Inhalt und seine literarische Form: eine kritische Studie* (Leipzig: J.C. Hinrichs).

Steuernagel, Carl
1900 *Deuteronomium und Josua* (HKAT, 1.3; Göttingen: Vandenhoeck & Ruprecht).
1923 *Das Deuteronomium* (HKAT, 1.3.1; Göttingen: Vandenhoeck & Ruprecht).

Stoebe, Hans Joachim
1973 *Das erste Buch Samuelis* (KAT, 8.1; Gütersloh: Gerd Mohn).

Stolz, Fritz
1981 *Das erste und zweite Buch Samuel* (Zürcher Bibelkommentare AT, 9; Zürich: Theologischer Verlag).

Sturdy, John
1976 *Numbers* (CBC; Cambridge: Cambridge University Press).

Taylor, John B.
1969 *Ezekiel* (TOTC; London: Tyndale Press).

Terrien, Samuel
1978 *The Elusive Presence: Toward a New Biblical Theology* (Religious Perspectives, 26; San Francisco: Harper & Row).

Thompson, J.A.
1974 *Deuteronomy* (TOTC; London: IVP).

Tigay, Jeffrey H.
1996 *Deuteronomy* (JPS Torah Commentary; Philadelphia: Jewish Publication Society of America).

Tillesse, Georges Minette de
1962 'Sections "tu" et sections "vous" dans le Deutéronome', *VT* 12: 29-87.

Valentin, Heinrich
1978 *Aaron: Eine Studie zur vor-priesterschriftlichen Aaron-Überlieferung* (OBO, 18; Göttingen: Vandenhoeck & Ruprecht).

Vaux, Roland de
1960 *Les Institutions de l'Ancien Testament*, II (Paris: Cerf). ET *Ancient Israel: Its Life and Institutions* (trans. John McHugh; London: Darton, Longman & Todd, 1961).
1967 *Bible et Orient* (Paris: Cerf).

Vermeylen, Jacques
1985 'Les sections narratives de Deut 5–11 et leur relation à Ex 19–34', in N. Lohfink (ed.), *Das Deuteronomium: Entstehung, Gestalt und Botschaft* (BETL, 68; Leuven: Leuven University Press): 174-207.

Vincent, Albert
1958 *Le Livre des Juges, le Livre de Ruth* (La Sainte Bible; Paris: Cerf, 2nd edn).

Waltke, Bruce K., and M. O'Connor
1990 *An Introduction to Biblical Hebrew Syntax* (Winona Lake, IN: Eisenbrauns).

Watts, J.D.W.
1970 'Deuteronomy', in Clifton J. Allen (ed.), *The Broadman Bible Commentary* (12 vols.; Nashville: Broadman Press): II, 175-296.

Weinfeld, Moshe
1972a *Deuteronomy and the Deuteronomic School* (Oxford: Oxford University Press).
1972b 'Presence, Divine', in *EncJud*, XIII: 1015-20.
1991 *Deuteronomy 1–11* (AB, 5; New York: Doubleday).
Weinreich, Uriel
1969 'Problems in the Analysis of Idioms', in Jaan Puhvel (ed.), *Substance and Structure of Language* (Berkeley and Los Angeles: University of California Press): 23-81.
Welch, Adam C.
1932 *Deuteronomy: The Framework to the Code* (London: Oxford University Press).
Wevers, John William
1969 *Ezekiel* (NCB; London: Thomas Nelson).
1994 'Yahweh and its Appositives in LXX Deuteronomium', in F.G. Martínez *et al.* (eds.), *Studies in Deuteronomy* (Festschrift C.J. Labuschagne; VTSup, 53: Leiden: E.J. Brill): 269-80.
1995 *Notes on the Greek Text of Deuteronomy* (SBLSCS, 39; Atlanta: Scholars Press).
Wilson, Ian
1995 *Out of the Midst of the Fire: Divine Presence in Deuteronomy* (SBLDS, 151; Atlanta: Scholars Press).
Woudstra, Marten H.
1965 *The Ark of the Covenant from Conquest to Kingship* (International Library of Philosophy and Theology: Biblical and Theological Studies; Philadelphia: Presbyterian and Reformed Publishing Company).
Wright, G. Ernest
1953 'The Book of Deuteronomy', in *IB*, II: 309-537.
Würthwein, Ernst
1985 *Das erste Buch der Könige: Kapitel 1–16* (ATD, 11.1; Göttingen: Vandenhoeck & Ruprecht, 2nd edn).
Zapletal, Vincenz
1923 *Das Buch der Richter* (EHAT, 7.1; Münster: Aschendorff).
Ziegler, Joseph
1960 'Zur Septuaginta-Vorlage im Deuteronomium', *ZAW* 72: 237-62.
Zimmerli, Walther
1969 *Ezechiel*, II (BKAT, 13.2; Neukirchen–Vluyn: Neukirchener Verlag). ET *Ezekiel*, II (trans. James D. Martin; Hermeneia; Philadelphia: Fortress Press, 1983).

WHATEVER HAPPENED TO THE ARK OF THE COVENANT?

John Day

Whatever happened to the ark of the covenant? This is a subject that has aroused considerable popular interest in recent years, as a perusal of the Internet and popular religious books shows. However, in contrast to the mass of material on the Internet extending to thousands of web pages (see, e.g., <http://www. mysteries-megasite.com/main/bigsearch/covenant.html> for 250 links) and the considerable number of popular books on the subject (e.g. Dobson 1939; Jeffrey 1990; Hancock 1992; Price 1994; Gray 1997; Bernstein 1998; Boren and Boren 2000; Gardner 2003), much of which are unknown to mainline Old Testament scholars and put forward outlandish viewpoints which imply that the ark still exists, there is, so far as I am aware, no up-to-date and fully comprehensive study of the subject from a modern scholarly, critical point of view. Surprisingly, scholarly books on the ark tend either to devote merely a few lines to the subject (Meinhold 1900: 44; Dibelius 1906: 126; Maier 1965: 80 n. 237; Ritmeyer and Ritmeyer 2000: 72) or fail to discuss it at all (Gressmann 1920; Woudstra 1965; Schmitt 1972).

The kind of material to be surveyed here consists of three types: ancient Jewish and other mediaeval views, modern scholarly critical views (since the nineteenth century), and what one might describe as modern unconventional views. However, I have chosen not to discuss these in three separate sections, since one finds that there are considerable overlaps between these different types of view. Rather, I have chosen to discuss the full range of views in the context of a chronological survey, i.e. the views are discussed in order of the date at which it is proposed that the ark disappeared, starting with the earliest and ending with the latest.

1. *Ark Hidden on Mt Gerizim in the Time of Eli or Moses*

The view that puts the disappearance of the ark at the earliest date is that of the Samaritans. Uniquely, they believe that the Mosaic ark never even reached Jerusalem or the Solomonic Temple, for what was there was merely a replica. The true ark was taken rather to Mt Gerizim, the site of their own sanctuary. Then, according to Samaritan tradition, when the schismatic Eli set up a rival sanctuary at Shiloh complete with rival sacred vessels, including the ark, the Tabernacle and all its contents were hidden by the high priest Uzzi in a cave on Mt Gerizim. This hiding of the cult vessels initiated what the Samaritans regard as a period of divine wrath (*Fanuta*), which will last until true cultic worship, including the hidden Tabernacle with all its vessels, is restored on Mt Gerizim by the eschatological prophet, the *Taheb*. The Samaritan sources which we possess that set out this scenario are mediaeval rather than ancient.[1]

However, already in the first century CE the Jewish historian Josephus (*Ant.* 18.85) attests the Samaritan tradition of the hidden cultic vessels and their future restoration when he reports that during the time of Pontius Pilate in 36 CE a Samaritan promised to lead an assembly to Mt Gerizim where 'he would show them the sacred vessels which were buried there, where Moses had deposited them'. That it should have been Moses who hid the vessels seems puzzling, since Deuteronomy 34 makes it clear that he died before the entry into the promised land west of the river Jordan, and the Samaritans' own traditions which we possess are unanimous in associating the hiding of the vessels with the time of Eli. It is possible, therefore, that Josephus is inaccurate at this point. Alternatively, bearing in mind that our Samaritan sources on the hidden vessels are much later, it is conceivable that Josephus bears witness to an earlier form of the Samaritan tradition which located their hiding in the time of Moses (so Collins 1972: esp. 112), even though this is difficult to reconcile with Deuteronomy 34. It has also been suggested that another first-century CE text, Jn 4.25, already attests the idea that the Samaritan *Taheb* would restore the sacred vessels in the future (cf. Kalimi and Purvis 1994: 683). However, it is not at all obvious that this is what the verse is saying, and the Samaritan woman's words, 'I know that Messiah is coming (he who is called Christ); when he comes he will tell us all things', more naturally refer to a teaching function (cf. the fourth-century CE Samaritan *Memar Marqah* 2.9, 4.11 and 4.12, where it is thrice stated that the *Taheb* 'will reveal the truth' [Macdonald 1963: I, 44, 108, 111]). Kalimi and Purvis cite the RSV rendering, 'he will *show* us all things', but to suppose that this explicitly refers to a visual manifestation of the sacred vessels is not only highly speculative but goes beyond the natural meaning of the Greek verb *anangellein*, 'to tell, proclaim, report'.

No modern scholars see any historicity in the Samaritan viewpoint, which clearly constitutes a later polemical fiction to justify their own claims against the Jews. It seems highly likely that the Samaritan tradition of the hiding of the vessels is modelled on the parallel Jewish legend of the hiding the cultic vessels (see below, sections 9 and 10).

1. Cf., for example, *The Asatir* 11.21-23, 'There will arise a man from the Levites; his name will be 'rzrz son of Fani and the beginning of the strife will be by his hand. And he will add a sanctuary in his days. He will exchange the sanctuary of the Hebrews for a rebellious (strange) sanctuary. He will throw division in the midst of the assembly' (Gaster 1927: 306). *'rzz* is here a cryptogram for Eli, which the Samaritans spell *'yly*. Although Gaster (1927: 160) dated *The Asatir* to 250–200 BCE, more recent scholars regard it as very much later; for example, Ben-Ḥayyim's authoritative study (1943–44) attributes it to the second half of the tenth century CE (cf. Tal 1989: 466). Again in the Samaritan Chronicle No. II (on 1 Samuel §§B, S*–T*), we read, 'So Uzzi gathered together the holy vestments, the golden and silver vessels, the ark of the testimony, the lampstand and altars and all the holy vessels; he placed them in that cave, and no sooner had the High Priest Uzzi left the cave than the entrance of the cave became sealed up by the power of the Lord—blessed is he' (Macdonald 1969: 115).

2. *Ark Taken to Ethiopia in the Time of Solomon*

The earliest date at which it has ever been claimed that the ark disappeared from the Solomonic Temple occurs in what is also the most exotic account of its disappearance. This is to be found in the Ethiopian national epic, the *Kebra Nagast* ('The Glory of Kings'), according to which the ark of the covenant was removed from the Jerusalem Temple to Ethiopia already in the reign of Solomon. The story goes that the queen of Sheba, called Makeda, had sexual intercourse with Solomon when she visited him in Jerusalem, and from this union Menelik was born, who later became king of Ethiopia; from him the Ethiopian royal house is supposed to be descended (right up to Haile Selassie in the twentieth century, according to pious Ethiopians). We read in the epic that when Menelik was grown up he visited his father Solomon in Jerusalem; there, as a result of a conspiracy in which Menelik and his entourage were implicated, Azariah, son of Zadok the priest, carried off the ark from the Temple in Jerusalem, and it was then taken down to Ethiopia, while in its place the Israelites were given a substitute ark. This seeming act of theft is stated to have God's approval, since the Israelites are no longer held worthy to have the divine presence, which is destined now to dwell in Ethiopia.

Modern scholars understandably do not accept the historicity of this story (contrast some popular, unconventional writers, e.g. Jeffrey 1990). For example, it is clear that the land of Sheba from which the queen came is not to be sought in Ethiopia but rather in Saba in the south-west of the Arabian peninsula (modern Yemen). Furthermore, the whole idea of sexual relations between Solomon and the queen of Sheba is clearly a later elaboration of the biblical story. It is also attested in mediaeval Arabic sources and probably derives from a Jewish midrash (Ullendorff 1968: 137), though it is not actually attested in Jewish literature till the eleventh-century *Alphabet of Ben Sira* (Steinschneider 1858: fol. 21b; cf. Ullendorff 1968: 139). The story is ultimately based on an over-imaginative reading of the words of 1 Kgs 10.13, 'And King Solomon gave to the queen of Sheba all that she desired'. The date of the writing down of the Ethiopic text of *Kebra Nagast* in the form that we now have it is the fourteenth century CE, but this is dependent on an earlier Arabic version, which in turn, the work claims, is dependent on a Coptic text. Budge (1932)[2] believed that the earliest form of the *Kebra Nagast* dates from about the sixth century CE, and Hubbard (1956), in his very thorough study of the sources of the work, similarly concurred that a sixth- or seventh-century CE date is indicated. In the light of this it cannot be expected to record genuine historical tradition about the time of Solomon. The point of the work is clearly to glorify Ethiopia as the new Zion, which is represented as inheriting the privileges of the old Zion. Interestingly, the notion that the ark of the covenant was in Ethiopia is already attested in the early thirteenth-century

2. Budge (1932) is still the standard English translation of *Kebra Nagast*. For French translations see Le Roux 1914 and Colin 2002. The earliest complete translation of the work was in German, Bezold 1905. It should be noted that Brooks (1996), in spite of its title, is not an independent scholarly translation from the Ethiopic but follows Budge almost verbatim without acknowledging the fact.

chronicler Abû Ṣâliḥ, an Egyptian of Armenian descent (see Evetts 1895: 287-88 for English translation and 133 for the Arabic text [fol. 105b-106b], cited in Hoberman 1993: 114 and Isaac 1993: 61). Pious Ethiopians believe that the ark is still in Ethiopia in the chapel attached to the Church of Mary Zion in Aksum. Graham Hancock has done much to popularize this view in his book *The Sign and the Seal* (Hancock 1992; cf. Isaac 1993). However, Hancock does not accept the literal truth of the story in the *Kebra Nagast* but believes that the ark disappeared from Jerusalem in the time of Manasseh and was taken down by Judaeans to Ethiopia via Elephantine. His highly unconventional views will be evaluated and rejected below (in section 8 about Manasseh). More recently, Roderick Grierson and S.C. Munro-Hay (1999) have written a wide-ranging book rejecting the view that the object held at Aksum is an actual ark, claiming that it is rather a tablet, which is apparently how many of those who claim to have seen it in the past and the current clergy at Aksum describe it. They do not even totally discount the possibility that the tablet might go back to the Solomonic Temple and seem to give credence to the view found in certain Arab historians that the Jerusalem ark was carried off to Arabia. But these notions are surely as incredible as the idea that the ark of the covenant is in Ethiopia.

3. *Ark Removed by Shishak*

In contrast to the above, the earliest date for the removal of the ark of the covenant from the Temple that modern critical scholars have ever suggested is in the reign of Rehoboam, Solomon's successor and first king of the southern kingdom. This view attributes the loss of the ark to the invasion of Palestine by the Egyptian Pharaoh Shishak, i.e. Shoshenq I, the first ruler of the Libyan twenty-second dynasty, c. 920 BCE. This opinion was first put forward by F. Giesebrecht (so L. Couard 1892: 84; cf. Giesebrecht 1894: 19) and followed by L. Couard (1892: 83-84) in the nineteenth century, and taken up by S. Mowinckel (1930: 272-74) and J. Morgenstern (1960: 185) in the twentieth century, though Mowinckel thought that the lost ark was replaced by another which survived till 586 BCE. Other scholars mention it as one possibility among others (e.g. Eissfeldt 1968: 139, reprinted 1973: 85; Zobel 1973: 85, ET 1977: 373). The biblical account of Shishak's invasion in 1 Kings 14.25-27 states,

> In the fifth year of King Rehoboam, Shishak king of Egypt came up against Jerusalem; he took away the treasures of the house of the Lord and the treasures of the king's house; he took away everything. He also took away all the shields of gold which Solomon had made; and King Rehoboam made in their stead shields of bronze, and committed them to the hands of the officers of the guard, who kept the door of the king's house.

No explicit mention is made here of the ark, however, and this view has therefore generally been rejected. There seem to be four basic objections. First, in his great triumphal relief on the south wall of the hypostyle hall of the temple of Amun at Karnak we possess Shishak's own account of his invasion of Palestine, which lists many individual cities (mostly in the Negev and Northern Israel), but Jerusalem is not one of them. This suggests to most scholars that Shishak passed

Jerusalem by, so that he would not have directly entered the Temple and any tribute paid to him would have been received at a distance, perhaps at Gibeon, the nearest site that is listed (cf. Kitchen 1986: 298; Mazar 1986: 145); consequently, the ark of the covenant is unlikely to have been handed over. Secondly, it seems that the treasures of the Temple to which 1 Kings alludes would not have been hidden in the Holy of Holies, where the ark was, but rather in separate store rooms or treasuries. Thirdly, if Shishak really removed the ark we should expect reverberations of this catastrophic event to be found in the Bible. Fourthly, and following on from this, we find on the contrary that all the indications are that the ark was present in the Jerusalem Temple till about the time of the fall of Jerusalem in 586 BCE. For example, Jer. 3.16 declares, 'they shall no more say, "The ark of the covenant of the Lord". It shall not come to mind, or be remembered, or missed; it shall not be made again. At that time Jerusalem shall be called the throne of the Lord…' This Deuteronomistically edited prose sermon (note, e.g., the Deuteronomistic expression 'ark of the covenant of the Lord') shows that the Jews were grappling with the problem of the disappearance of the ark about the time of the exile, which is passing strange if the ark had in fact been removed several centuries earlier. One may also note 1 Kgs 8.8, which implies that the poles of the ark of the Covenant could still be seen in the Temple 'to this day', presumably at the time of the probable Josianic edition of the Deuteronomistic History, c. 621 BCE.[3] Although it is improbable, one could conceivably argue that the words 'to this day' in 1 Kgs 8.8 are merely quoting an earlier source (just as 2 Chron. 5.9 still cites these words from 1 Kgs 8.8 long after the ark had disappeared), but even on that unlikely scenario the reference 'to this day' suggests that the time of the building of the Solomonic Temple was somewhat remote in time from the original writer, so hardly compatible with a disappearance of the ark already in the tenth century.

Turning away from conventional scholarship, one may note that recently the view that it was Shishak who removed the ark has been followed by Michael Sanders (cf. his web site and his video *Ark of the Covenant*), though he eccentrically identifies Shishak with Rameses III, the twentieth dynasty Pharaoh attributed by all serious scholars to the twelfth century BCE. Sanders detected an object which he believes to be the ark on Rameses III's temple at Medinet Habu and speculates that it was taken to the land of Djahi (referred to in the Harris Papyrus I [ix 1] as the site of a temple of Amun built by Rameses III; cf. *ANET*, 260), which he equates with the modern village of edh-Dhoheriyeh, near Hebron. All this is wild and baseless conjecture. Thus, Rameses III cannot possibly be equated with Shishak, whose name appears to be better preserved in the *ketib* of 1 Kgs 14.25 as Shushak (*šûšaq*; cf. LXX Sousakim), corresponding closely with the name Shoshenq (Susinqu and Shusanqu in Akkadian). Moreover, Djahi was a land, not a village, and in any case the name does not properly correspond with edh-Dhoheriyeh.

3. I am convinced that the double redaction thesis of Cross (1973), Nelson (1981) and others, postulating an initial Josianic and subsequent exilic redaction for the Deuteronomistic History, does greatest justice to the tensions which are manifest within the work.

Finally, on an even more popular level it may be noted that Shishak is also implied to have been the looter of the ark in Steven Spielberg's famous 1981 film *Raiders of the Lost Ark*, a work which doubtless ultimately lies behind some of the increased popular interest in the ark in recent years. There Indiana Jones declares (Lawrence Kasdan and George Lucas, revised third draft screenplay 1979, scene 19), 'An Egyptian Pharaoh stole the Ark from Jerusalem and took it back to the city of Tanis…the Pharaoh had had the Ark hidden in a secret chamber called the Well of the Souls'. Tanis was the capital of the twenty-second dynasty, of which Shishak was the first king, and in the film it is there that Indiana Jones and the Nazis both struggle to gain possession of the ark, which eventually finds its way to a government warehouse in the USA!

4. *Ark Removed by Deliberate Internal Action soon after the Disruption of the United Monarchy*

H. Spieckermann (1989: 93) has fairly recently suggested what appears to be a novel explanation for the disappearance of the ark. He believes that the ark was removed from the Temple soon after the end of the United Monarchy because it had failed as a symbol of religious unity and the traditions associated with it were no longer held in high regard or were no longer needed. He does not elaborate on this explanation in detail, which indeed lacks any real evidence and seems highly speculative. However, in support of his early date for the loss of the ark he claims that the ark goes unmentioned in the Bible for hundreds of years during the monarchical period and finds no authentic pre-exilic testimony to its existence in Israel after the books of Samuel. However, Spieckermann totally fails to discuss some of the relevant texts. For example, no reference is made to Jer. 3.16, which as already noted is inexplicable if the ark had already disappeared hundreds of years prior to the sixth century BCE, and similarly the words 'to this day' in 1 Kgs 8.8 suggest that the ark was present in the Temple much longer than Spieckermann's view supposes. There are also certain implicit ark references in the Psalms which he does not allude to (see Day 2004: 231-34).

5. *Ark Removed by Jehoash*

Proceeding chronologically, the next date for the removal of the ark that has been suggested (by Loenborg 1929; cf. too Eissfeldt 1968: 139, reprinted 1973: 85, as one possibility among others) is the invasion of Jehoash, king of Israel (c. 802–787 BCE) in the time of Amaziah, king of Judah (c. 801–773 BCE), recorded in 2 Kgs 14.13-14 (cf. 2 Chron. 25.21-24). We there read,

> And Jehoash king of Israel captured Amaziah king of Judah, the son of Jehoash, son of Ahaziah, at Beth-shemesh, and came to Jerusalem, and broke down the wall of Jerusalem for four hundred cubits, from the Ephraim Gate to the Corner gate. And he seized all the gold and silver, and all the vessels that were found in the house of the Lord and in the treasuries of the king's house, also hostages, and he returned to Samaria.

Again, we find that there is no mention of the ark, and it seems natural to suppose that it was simply objects from the treasuries that were taken. As in the case of the Shishak hypothesis, we should expect further reverberations in the Old Testament if the ark was removed at this time and other evidence suggests that the ark remained in the Temple till about the end of the monarchy. As noted above, Jer. 3.16 certainly and 1 Kgs 8.8 probably are inexplicable if the ark disappeared this early (cf. too Jewish tradition). Not surprisingly, this view has had little following.

6. *Ark Removed by Ahaz*

Eissfeldt (1968: 139 n. 2, reprinted 1973: 85 n. 2) mentions in passing as one of several suggestions the possibility that Ahaz removed the Ark in connection with the cultic alterations described in 2 Kgs 16.10-18. However, there is no supporting evidence for this conjecture, and, as has already been noted above, Jer. 3.16 certainly and 1 Kgs 8.8 probably are inexplicable if the ark disappeared that early, and tend to support the weight of Jewish tradition that this was nearer the time of the exile.

7. *Ark Removed by Hezekiah*

Both Eissfeldt (1968: 139, reprinted 1973: 85) and Zobel (1973: 403, ET 1977: 373-74) mention in passing as one of several suggestions the possibility that Hezekiah removed the ark in connection with his cultic reforms. However, yet again there is no evidence to support this idea, and Jer. 3.16 certainly and 1 Kgs 8.8 probably, not to mention Jewish tradition, indicate that a date nearer the exile is required.

8. *Ark Removed by Manasseh*

A view that has gained a little more support is that the ark was removed by Manasseh, king of Judah in the seventh century BCE, who is pilloried as the greatest of apostates by the Deuteronomistic historian in 2 Kings 21. This view was already maintained by some scholars in the nineteenth century (Hitzig 1841: 28-29 [1866: 27-28]; Thenius 1849: 420 [1873: 434]) but it has been brought to prominence in the twentieth century by Menahem Haran (1963; 1978: 276-88), and has recently been revived in a new form by Stanley Ned Rosenbaum (2002: 282, 289), as well as forming part of the scenario in the popular, unconventional work of Graham Hancock (1992). Other scholars list it as one possibility among others (e.g. Eissfeldt 1968: 139, ET 1973: 85; Zobel 1973: 403, ET 1977: 374). Haran supposes that the ark was removed in connection with Manasseh's setting up of an image of the goddess Asherah (2 Kgs 21.7), which he thinks occurred in the Holy of Holies. There are, however, various problems with this view, quite apart from the fact that there is not the slightest hint in the biblical text that Manasseh was guilty of any such thing. First, we have no information that the image of Asherah was set up in the Holy of Holies; Deut. 16.21 has a commandment against setting up the Asherah next to Yahweh's altar, which suggests that this was the place where it tended to be located, rather than in the Holy of Holies. It is possible, though, that Deut. 16.21 is thinking of the high places rather than the Jerusalem Temple. In any case, even if Haran were right in supposing that the image of Asherah was set up in the Holy of Holies, there is no reason at all why this should have involved the removal of the ark. It is a fundamental error to suppose that the worship of Asherah would have been regarded as an alternative to that of Yahweh by those, such as Manasseh, who did not belong to the Yahweh alone movement; rather the worship of Asherah would have been closely associated with that of Yahweh, as the Kuntillet 'Ajrud and Khirbet el-Qom finds referring to 'Yahweh and his Asherah' demonstrate. It is for this reason that the Asherah cult was located in Yahweh's Temple and it is extremely likely that she was envisaged as Yahweh's consort, and consequently was not seen as in competition with him by those like Manasseh who worshipped her (cf. Day 2000: 42-67). More recently Stanley Ned Rosenbaum has also suggested that Manasseh removed the ark or at least stripped off its gold covering, not for the reasons given by Haran (though he mistakenly believes that they are), but in order to pay tribute to the Assyrians (Rosenbaum 2002: 282, 289). This is completely speculative.

In recent years the former *Economist* journalist Graham Hancock has publicized the view that the ark was, and indeed still is in Ethiopia in his popular book *The Sign and the Seal: A Quest for the Lost Ark of the Covenant* (Hancock 1992). He accepts that the story contained in the *Kebra Nagast* cannot be historical, and argues rather that the ark was removed from the Temple in the time of Manasseh (following Haran), that it was then taken to Elephantine in southern Egypt where it resided in the Jewish temple, which he claims had been built for this very purpose, and maintains that it was only after this temple's destruction in 410 BCE that it was finally removed to Ethiopia, first to the island of Tana Kirkos for eight hundred years and subsequently to the Church of Mary Zion in Aksum, where he holds—in line with mainline Ethiopian tradition—that the ark now resides. It has already been seen above that there is no evidence for the view that the ark was removed from the Temple in the time of Manasseh: even if the Asherah image was placed in the Holy of Holies (for which there is no evidence), it would in no way have been felt by Manasseh to be incompatible with Yahweh, since Asherah was regarded as Yahweh's consort. Further, there is no evidence that the ark was ever taken to Elephantine. Hancock believes that the fact that Yahweh is said to dwell at Elephantine implies the presence there of the ark, but as Bezalel Porten notes (1995: 76; *contra* Hancock 1992: 440), this is only mentioned once (Porten and Yardeni 1989: II, B.13.2) and, moreover, the text dates from after the destruction of the Elephantine temple in 410 BCE. Furthermore, Porten (1995: 76) notes that the Old Testament can still speak of Yahweh's dwelling in Jerusalem in the post-exilic period when there was no longer an ark in the Temple (he cites Ezra 7.15; cf. Davies 1991 for other examples). Hancock (1992: 440) also appeals to the term 'Lord of hosts' used by the Elephantine Jews in connection with their god Yahu, but as Porten notes, this term (which occurs two or three times at Elephantine, not frequently as Hancock claims) is found numerous times in the Old Testament without any reference at all to the ark (cf. Haggai, Zechariah, Malachi).

9. *Ark Removed or Hidden by Josiah*

The dominant view found in rabbinic writings claims that King Josiah removed the ark from the Temple into a hiding place in the chamber of the wood-store on the Temple Mount in anticipation of the destruction of the Temple (*y. Sheqalim* 6.1.1-2; *b. Yoma* 52b, 53b-54a; *b. Horayot* 12a). (For an alternative rabbinic view see section 11, below.) This view is not taken seriously by modern critical scholars and manifestly smacks of later pious imagination (though it is followed in the popular works of Price 1994; Gardner 2003: 148-49, 241, 260[4]). It is most unlikely that Josiah would have been expecting the destruction of the Temple: the first edition of the Deuteronomistic History dating, apparently from Josiah's reign, is optimistic and it was only the second edition from the exilic period which has the ring of judgment sounding through it. However, the Talmudic scholar, Meir Ish-Shalom (Friedmann) (1904[5]) suggested that Josiah hid the ark on the Temple Mount because the people were going astray after it, and M. Weinfeld (1976: 23 with n. 26) felt this to be a very probable explanation. However, there is no real evidence for this view. Further, if Josiah removed the ark because the people were treating it in an idolatrous way it is surprising that the account of Josiah's reformation fails to mention it, comparable to the way in which the account of Hezekiah's reforms in 2 Kgs 18.4 mentions his removal of another previously hallowed object that was believed to go back to Moses, the bronze serpent Nehushtan. In any case, as has been noted earlier, Jer. 3.16 appears to be part of a post-Jeremianic addition to the text, suggesting that the ark disappeared somewhat later than 621 BCE.

There are some people (not serious scholars, of course) who believe that the ark is still hidden on the Temple Mount and occasional attempts have even been made to discover it there! From 1909–11 the notorious expedition led by Captain Montague Parker undertook tunnelling in the vicinity of the Dome of the Rock in an attempt to discover the Temple vessels, including the ark, but had to beat a hasty retreat when spotted working in the Dome of the Rock, and their actions set off an Arab riot (cf. Dalman 1912; Silberman 1980; 1982: 180-88). More recently, in 1981 a party in search of the ark led by the Chief Rabbi Shelomo Goren and Rabbi Meir Yehuda Getz, who was the Chief Rabbi of the Western wall, explored a tunnel under the Temple Mount starting from Warren's Gate

4. Though Gardner bizarrely dates Josiah to c. 597 BCE and thinks that Jeremiah hid the ark at Josiah's behest, thereby conflating two different traditions. Even more bizarrely, Gardner thinks that the Templars captured the ark from Jerusalem during the Crusades and claims (2003: 271) that the ark is now 'within the aura of the labyrinth of Chartres Cathedral, having moved through the superconducting vortex portal of another parallel dimension of space-time'!

5. I am grateful to Mr Daniel Cochavy of Jerusalem for providing me with a photocopy of this rare Hebrew article.

near the Western Wall but had to stop when the Muslim authorities got wind of it and threatened a riot, and the gate was subsequently sealed up. Certain ultra-orthodox Jews in Israel nowadays support the building of a Third Temple on the Temple Mount and hold that the lost ark of the covenant will be revealed at that time. This view is also put forward by the Christian fundamentalist Randall Price in his popular book *In Search of Temple Treasures: The Lost Ark and the Last Days* (Price 1994).

10. *Ark Hidden by Jeremiah*

Another Jewish view attributed the disappearance of the ark to its being hidden by the prophet Jeremiah shortly before the destruction of the Temple. The earliest version of this tradition goes back to the Jewish historian Eupolemus, whose work dates from about 157 BCE, and whose words were reported in the Greek historian Alexander Polyhistor's *On the Jews* (mid-first century BCE), and are preserved for us in Eusebius's *Praeparatio Evangelica* (9.39.5). This reads:

> Then he [Nebuchadrezzar] seized Jerusalem and captured Jonachim the king of the Jews [seemingly a conflation of Jehoiakim, Jehoiachin and Zedekiah]. He took as tribute the gold and silver and bronze in the Temple and sent them to Babylon, except for the ark and the tablets in it. This Jeremiah preserved. (Trans. F. Fallon in Charlesworth 1985: II, 871)

The best known version of this tradition, however, is that preserved in the Apocrypha in 2 Macc. 2.4-8, which states:

> It was also in writing that the prophet [i.e. Jeremiah], having received an oracle, ordered that the tent and the ark should follow with him, and that he went out to the mountain where Moses had gone up and had seen the inheritance of God. And Jeremiah came and found a cave, and he brought there the tent and the ark and the altar of incense, and he sealed up the entrance. Some of those who followed him came up to mark the way, but could not find it. When Jeremiah learned of it, he rebuked them and declared: 'The place shall be unknown until God gathers his people together again and shows his mercy. And then the Lord will disclose these things, and the glory of the Lord and the cloud will appear, as they were shown in the case of Moses, and as Solomon asked that the place should be specially consecrated'.

The mountain in question here is clearly Mt Nebo, the mountain just east of the river Jordan from which Moses is said to have viewed the promised land in Deuteronomy 34. Next in *The Lives of the Prophets* 2.11-13, generally dated to the first century CE (e.g. D.R.A. Hare in Charlesworth 1985: II, 380-81; contrast Satran 1995, who sees it as Byzantine) we read of Jeremiah:

> This prophet, before the capture of the Temple, seized the ark of the Law and the things in it, and made them to be swallowed up in a rock. And to those standing by he said, 'The Lord has gone away from Zion into heaven and will come again in power. And this will be for you a sign of his coming, when all the gentiles worship a piece of wood'. (Trans. D.R.A. Hare in Charlesworth 1985: II, 388)

One may compare 2 Baruch 6, dating from c. 100 CE, where just before the Temple's destruction Jeremiah's scribe Baruch sees an angel take the sacred vessels from the Temple and swallow them; v. 7 includes the mercy seat (the cover of the ark) and the two tables among the vessels listed, presumably implying the ark (trans. A.F.J. Klijn in Charlesworth 1983: I, 622-23). 4 Baruch 3, dating from the first third of the second century CE, is in turn is dependent on 2 Baruch, and describes how Jeremiah is instructed by the Lord to deliver the sacred vessels to the earth. This he proceeds to do, and the earth swallows them up (trans. S.E. Robinson in Charlesworth 1983: I, 418-19). (On the post-biblical traditions concerning Jeremiah's hiding of the ark generally see Wolff 1976: 61-71.)

Like the view considered above that Josiah hid the ark, this one also has no scholarly following nowadays, and is clearly a later pious fabrication: it is hardly likely that Jeremiah would have hidden the ark, bearing in mind that he was not a member of the Temple staff but rather one who over many years had predicted disaster for the Temple and nation as the just judgment of God. Possibly this tradition arose because of the allusion to the disappearance of the ark in Jer. 3.16-17. However, the unlikelihood of the idea has not stopped one popular British writer (Dobson 1939) from maintaining that Jeremiah hid the ark on Mt Nebo (having previously concealed it on the Temple Mount). It has also not stopped two American explorers from searching for the ark on Mt Nebo, namely Antonia Frederick Futterer in the 1920s and Tom Crotser in the 1980s, the latter of whom even claimed to have discovered the ark there and showed his photographs to a few select individuals. One of these was the respected archaeologist Siegfried Horn, who not surprisingly reported that the alleged ark depicted in the photographs appeared to be a modern construction (Shanks 1983).

Another American explorer who should be mentioned here is Ron Wyatt, who claims (see Gray 1997) that the ark of the covenant was hidden by Jeremiah in the cave in Jerusalem now known as Jeremiah's grotto (so called because Jeremiah is reputed to have been imprisoned and also written the book of Lamentations there). Jeremiah's grotto is opposite Herod's gate and underneath the site known as Gordon's Calvary, which Wyatt unconvincingly holds to be authentic, maintaining that Christ's blood dripped through the rock on to the mercy seat of the ark below. Wyatt even claims to have seen the ark there in 1982 but he failed to produce it for scholarly examination and has since died in 1999. Incidentally, he has also made other incredible claims, such as allegedly discovering Noah's ark, and finding the remains of the Egyptian chariots of the time of the Exodus in the Red Sea, etc.! (For a critique of Wyatt see Price 1994: 152-56.)

Yet another American explorer maintaining that the ark was removed by Jeremiah is Vendyl Jones (see <http://www.vendyljones.org.il>), who believes that the ark was hidden not on Mt Nebo but in a cave near Qumran, and he has spent years searching for it and the other Temple vessels there but without success. He bases his view on an idiosyncratic interpretation of the Qumran Copper Scroll (3Q15), which he believes refers to the burial of the First Temple's sacred vessels. But neither his translation (e.g. rendering *bmškn hmlk'* in 6.11 as 'in[side is the] complete Tabernacle' rather than 'in the residence of the queen') nor his interpretation of the Copper Scroll is shared by the scholarly community. If the Copper Scroll refers to Temple treasures it will be to those of the Second, not First Temple (the script is late Herodian), when there was no ark.

As a further development of the tradition associating Jeremiah with the removal of the ark one should note that the British Israelites, a movement claiming that the Anglo-Saxons are descended from the ancient Israelites, believe that the ark was brought to Ireland by a group led by Jeremiah—including Tamar (Tea) Tephi, a daughter of King Zedekiah, from whom the Irish, Scottish and so eventually British monarchs are supposedly descended—and hidden in an underground chamber at the Hill of Tara in County Meath. British Israelites maintain, in fact, that the name Tara derives from the Hebrew word Torah ('law'), and between 1899 and 1902 they actually dug at the Hill of Tara in an attempt to discover the ark, but the expedition was, not surprisingly, unsuccessful (see Carew 2003; and on the British Israelites more generally, see May 1943; Parfitt 2002: 46-57).[6]

11. *Ark Carried away by the Babylonians under Nebuchadrezzar*

On the surface a plausible explanation is that the ark was carried into captivity by Nebuchadrezzar's Babylonian army following the final fall of the Temple in 586 BCE (so Klamroth 1932: 78; Rudolph 1958: 23) or conceivably at the time of the first captivity in 597 BCE. After all, the evidence tends to suggest that the ark was in the Temple till about this time and we know that Nebuchadrezzar did indeed carry other Temple vessels into captivity (2 Kgs 24.13; 2 Chron. 36.10 for 597 BCE; 2 Kgs 25.13-17; 2 Chron. 36.18; Jer. 52.17-23 [cf. Jer. 27.19-22] for 586 BCE). There is also some later Jewish support for this notion, for we read in 2 Esdras (10.22), as part of the description of the Babylonian conquest, that 'the ark of our covenant has been plundered'. This is also one of the views reported in the Babylonian and Jerusalem Talmuds (*b. Yoma* 53*b*; *y. Sheqalim* 6.1.2). However, what seems to tell against this understanding is the fact that the biblical sources mentioned above do not include the ark among the items removed by Nebuchadrezzar, either in 597 or 586 BCE. (If it was made simply of wood, as Deut. 10.1-5 suggests—contrary to the more elaborate Priestly depiction of Exod. 25.10-22—it might well have escaped the attention of the Babylonians.) Moreover, it is surely significant that when we read in Ezra 1.7-11 of the return of the Temple vessels to Jerusalem following Cyrus's edict, the ark is not among them. This suggests that the ark was not in fact taken into captivity by the Babylonians.

12. *Ark Destroyed by the Babylonians under Nebuchadrezzar*

Probably the most common (though as seen above, far from universal) explanation for the disappearance of the ark among modern critical scholars is that it was destroyed by the Babylonians in 586 BCE in connection with the destruction of the Temple (cf. Dibelius 1906: 126; de Vaux 1960a: II, 128, ET 1961: 299; Maier

6. Recently, Boren and Boren (2000) have written a fantastic work claiming that Jeremiah not only took the ark to Egypt and later to Ireland, but that the ark eventually got taken to America in 1170 CE by Madoc, Prince of Wales and a Templar, who placed it in Sanpete Valley in Utah, where it may well still be!

1965: 80 n. 237; Fretheim 1967: 105 n. 3; Metzger 1985: I, 357), though some concede that its destruction might have taken place either then or in 597 BCE (Fritz 1977: 135, with n. 81), or that it was either burnt or otherwise disappeared in 586 BCE (W.H. Schmidt 1968: 106). The view that the ark was destroyed in 586 BCE certainly seems the most rational explanation. We know that there was no ark in the Second Temple (cf. Josephus, *War* 5.5.5; cf. Tacitus, *Histories* 5.9, and its absence from the list of Temple vessels in 1 Macc. 4), and we have already seen that the ark is neither recorded as having been taken into captivity by the Babylonians nor returned with the other Temple vessels after the exile by the Persian King Cyrus. Even Ezekiel 40–48's vision of the future restored Temple has no ark within it, a vision presumably dating from sometime during the exile.[7] All this suggests that by the time of the exile the ark had disappeared and there appeared to be no prospect of its return, a prospect which there surely would have been if it had been known still to exist. On the other hand, both the Old Testament itself and later Jewish tradition strongly support the view that the disappearance of the ark was somehow connected with the shadow cast by the Babylonian destruction of the Temple.

Thus, whether hidden by Josiah or Jeremiah in anticipation of the Babylonian destruction or plundered by the Babylonians under Nebuchadrezzar, the later Jewish sources are unanimous that it disappeared about that time. As for the Bible itself, 2 Chron. 35.3 implies that the ark still existed in the time of Josiah, but as this verse does not also appear in 2 Kings scholars understandably are uncertain about its historicity. Nevertheless, it certainly provides evidence that in the fourth century BCE, when Chronicles was written, the ark was believed to have still been in the Temple in the time of Josiah. Moreover, that the ark still existed in the Temple in the time of Josiah also seems to be suggested by 1 Kgs 8.8, as has already noted. We there read in the account of Solomon's dedication of the Temple, 'And the poles [of the ark] were so long that the ends of the poles were seen from the holy place before the inner sanctuary; but they could not be seen from outside; and they are there to this day'. Since there was no Temple or ark during the exile, the time of the final redaction of the Deuteronomistic History, we should probably assume that this verse derives from the first edition of the Deuteronomistic History when the Temple was still standing, and this is widely held—rightly in my view—to date from the time of Josiah. The ark is therefore likely to have disappeared sometime between the time of Josiah and 586 BCE and the latter is clearly the natural assumption, when the Temple itself was threatened. Admittedly this particular argument is not totally fool-proof, since, though improbable, it cannot be ruled out that the words 'to this day' might have been taken by the Deuteronomist from an earlier source (just as 2 Chron. 5.9 still cites

7. The Priestly source does, however, have a stipulation for the making of the ark in Exod. 25.10-22. C. Schäfer-Lichtenberger (2000: 238-39 and n. 48) argues on the basis of this that P had expectations of a renewed ark following the exile. This is conceivable but P's ark is set in the context of the Mosaic Tabernacle: are we really to suppose, therefore, that P also envisaged a restored Tabernacle rather than Temple? If not, it is difficult to be confident that he necessarily envisaged a renewed ark.

them long after the ark had disappeared). However, as already noted, even on this scenario, the words 'to this day' suggest a date of writing remote in time from that of the building of Solomon's Temple.

Interestingly, Ezekiel speaks of the cherubim in connection with the Temple in his prophecies from the last decade of the monarchy, and this includes his vision of their departure from the Temple together with the glory of the Lord in Ezek. 11.22-25 (cf. 1 Sam. 4.21-22, which clearly associates the disappearance of the Lord's glory with the earlier temporary loss of the ark to the Philistines at the battle of Aphek, c. 1050 BCE). Note that the glory of the Lord returns to the new Temple in Ezek. 43.1-5, but now without any mention of cherubim. As already noted, another passage which indicates this general period for the loss of the ark is Jer. 3.16-17,

> And when you have multiplied and increased in the land, in those days, says the Lord, they shall no more say, 'The ark of the covenant of the Lord'. It shall not come to mind, or be remembered, or missed; it shall not be made again. At that time Jerusalem shall be called the throne of the Lord, and all nations shall gather to it, to the presence of the Lord in Jerusalem, and they shall no more stubbornly follow their own evil heart.

Interestingly, this verse clearly envisages the loss of the ark, and the fact that it forms part of a prose sermon suggests that it derives from the Deuteronomistic redaction of Jeremiah during the exile (cf. the Deuteronomistic expression 'ark of the covenant of the Lord'). An exilic date is further strongly supported by the fact that the words in question are embedded in a passage that predicts the return from exile and has an eschatological outlook (vv. 14-18). Clearly therefore we catch a glimpse here of the coming to terms with the loss of the ark in the exilic period, which suggests that it had disappeared not long before, presumably in 586 BCE. The words 'it shall not be made again' clearly rule out its merely having been hidden or taken into exile, and presuppose its destruction.

Fortunately, it seems possible to provide more precise documentation for the disappearance of the ark in 586 BCE in a verse that has generally been overlooked in discussions of the fate of the ark, apart mainly from commentaries on Lamentations. In Lam. 2.1 we read, 'How the Lord in his anger has set the daughter of Zion under a cloud! He has cast down from heaven to earth the splendour of Israel; he has not remembered his footstool in the day of his anger.' It is quite probable that this verse refers to the loss of the ark (cf. Kraus 1956: 37; Albrektson 1963: 86). In support of this is the fact that there appear to be three other places in the Old Testament where the expression 'footstool' is used of the ark: 1 Chron. 28.2, Ps. 99.5 and Ps. 132.7. Thus, in 1 Chron. 28.2, it is almost universally accepted that David refers to the ark as a footstool when he declares, 'I had it in my heart to build a house of rest for the ark of the covenant of the Lord, even for the footstool of our God' ('even' being the well attested explicative *waw*). Since the cherubim above the ark constituted Yahweh's earthly throne (cf. 1 Sam. 4.4; 2 Sam. 6.2), it is entirely natural that the ark was conceived as his footstool.[8] Secondly, it seems extremely probable that there is an allusion to the

8. The relationship of the cherubim and ark as throne and footstool is widely accepted (cf. H. Schmidt 1923; de Vaux 1960b; Mettinger 1982: 19-24; Metzger 1985: II, 309-65) and is vividly

ark in Ps. 132.7, where we read, 'Let us go to his dwelling place, let us worship at his footstool!' It is difficult to deny that the ark is intended in the reference to God's footstool here, since, quite apart from the use of this term to denote the ark in 1 Chron. 28.2, it should be noted that the ark is specifically mentioned in both the immediately preceding and following verses. Verse 8 declares, 'Arise, O Lord, and go to your resting place, you and the ark of your might', and v. 6 refers back to the finding of the ark at Kiriath-jearim (Jaar) (cf. 1 Sam. 7.1; 2 Sam. 6.2), when it states, 'Lo, we heard of it in Ephrathah, we found it in the fields of Jaar'. If the 'footstool' simply denoted the sanctuary here with no reference at all to the ark, as some suppose, one wonders why this unusual term should be employed at this precise point.[9] Finally, there is Ps. 99.5, where we read, 'Extol the Lord our God; worship at his footstool! Holy is he!' It is to be noted that the phrase 'worship at his footstool' is identical to that found in Ps. 132.7, so the meaning ought to be the same as there. That it is specifically the ark is further supported by the fact that v. 1 refers to Yahweh's being enthroned on the cherubim: 'The Lord has become king; let the peoples tremble! He sits enthroned upon the cherubim; let the earth quake!' Accordingly, the reference to God's footstool in v. 5 most naturally refers to the ark under the cherubim throne.[10] It is therefore attractive to equate the footstool of Lam. 2.1 with the ark. What further strengthens the case that the word 'footstool' refers to the ark in Lam. 2.1 is the fact that it appears parallel with the term 'splendour' (*tip'eret*), an expression which is certainly used elsewhere of the ark in connection with its earlier loss to the Philistines at the battle of Aphek in Ps. 78.61 (cf. 1 Sam. 4.21-22, which similarly speaks of the loss of the divine glory [*kābôd*] at that time).[11] Psalm 78.61 states, 'He forsook his dwelling at Shiloh, the tent where he dwelt among men, and delivered his power to captivity, his splendour to the hand of the foe'. ('Power' [*'ōz*] is here clearly likewise another term for the ark [cf. Ps. 132.8].) If this interpretation of Lam. 2.1 is correct, we do indeed possess a biblical reference indicating the precise time of the loss of the ark, contrary to what is often supposed (e.g. Noth 1950: 45, ET 1966: 143). However, if the ark did go up in smoke along with the

illuminated by the Ahiram sarcophagus and a plaque from Megiddo (cf. Mettinger 1982: 21-22, figs. 1-2), which both depict a king sitting on a cherub throne with a footstool underneath. The fact that the ark was therefore part of a throne complex is sufficient to explain the language employed in Jer. 3.16-17; it was not itself a throne, for which its name *'ᵃrôn*, lit. 'box, chest', would be inappropriate.

9. Even if the reference were to the sanctuary rather than the ark, as some claim, the context requires that it would be the sanctuary *qua* ark container.

10. The only way to avoid this conclusion would be to suppose that the footstool rather denotes the Temple. But if that were the case the cherubim in v. 1 would have to be the heavenly cherubim. Against that supposition, however, stands the fact that all the other passages referring to Yahweh as 'enthroned on the cherubim' allude to the cherubim in the earthly sanctuary (cf. 1 Sam. 4.4; 2 Sam. 6.2 = 1 Chron. 13.6; 2 Kgs 19.15 = Isa. 37.16; Ps. 80.2, ET 1). Although the last reference might at first appear uncertain, an allusion to the earthly throne in Zion is supported by comparing the language used with that in Ps. 50.2: the former reads, 'You who are enthroned on the cherubim, shine forth', while the latter declares, 'Out of Zion, the perfection of beauty, God shines forth'.

11. The fact that the *tip'eret* is said to have been cast down from heaven to earth may be compared with Isa. 14.12-15 (cf. Dan. 8), where the imagery of casting down from heaven to earth is similarly used to denote an earthly defeat. Yahweh's earthly throne mirrored that in heaven (cf. Ps. 11.4).

rest of the Temple in 586 BCE, it is not surprising that this is not mentioned in 2 Kings 25, since—unlike with regard to cult objects carried into exile—this text does not enumerate any of the objects in the Temple which were simply destroyed.

13. *Conclusion*

In this essay twelve different views about the date of the disappearance of the ark have been examined. The evidence strongly suggests that the ark disappeared about the time of the exile and the most likely explanation is that it was simply destroyed along with the Temple in 586 BCE.

BIBLIOGRAPHY

Albrektson, Bertil
1963 *Studies in the Text and Theology of the Book of Lamentations, with a Critical Edition of the Peshitta Text* (Studia Theologica Lundensia, 21; Lund: C.W.K. Gleerup).

Ben-Ḥayyim, Z.
1943–44 'The Book of Asatir', *Tarbiz* 14: 104-25, 174-90; 15: 71-87, 128 (Hebrew).

Bernstein, Henrietta
1998 *Ark of the Covenant, Holy Grail* (Marina del Rey, CA: De Vorss & Co.).

Bezold, C.
1905 *Kebra Nagast: Die Herrlichkeit der Könige* (Abhandlungen der philosophisch-philologischen königlich Bayerischen Akademie der Wissenschaften, 23.1; Munich: Verlag der königlich Bayerischen Akademie der Wissenschaften).

Boren, Kerry Ross, and Lisa Lee Boren
2000 *Following the Ark of the Covenant, the Treasure of God: Solving the Mystery of Sanpete Valley, Utah* (Springville, UT: Bonneville Books, Cedar Fort Inc.).

Brooks, Miguel F.
1996 *A Modern Translation of the Kebra Nagast (The Glory of Kings)* (Lawrenceville, NJ: The Red Sea Press Inc.).

Budge, E.A. Wallis
1932 *The Queen of Sheba and Her Only Son Menyelek (I)* (London: Oxford University Press [Humphrey Milford], 2nd edn).

Carew, Mairéad
2003 *Tara and the Ark of the Covenant: A Search for the Ark of the Covenant by British-Israelites on the Hill of Tara (1899–1902)* (Dublin: The Discovery Programme and the Royal Irish Academy).

Charlesworth, James H.
1983, 1985 *The Old Testament Pseudepigrapha* (2 vols.; London: Darton, Longman & Todd).

Colin, Gérard
2002 *La Gloire des Rois (Kebra Nagast): Epopée nationale de l'Ethiopie* (Geneva: Patrick Kramer).

Collins, Marilyn F.
1972 'The Hidden Vessels in Samaritan Traditions', *JSJ* 3: 97-116.

Couard, Ludwig

1892 'Die religiös-nationale Bedeutung der Lade Jahves', *ZAW* 12: 53-90.

Cross, Frank Moore

1973 'The Themes of the Book of Kings and the Structure of the Deuteronomistic History', in *idem* (ed.), *Canaanite Myth and Hebrew Epic* (Cambridge, MA: Harvard University Press).

Dalman, G.

1912 'The Search for the Temple Treasure at Jerusalem', *PEFQS* 44: 35-39.

Davies, G.I.

1991 'The Presence of God in the Second Temple and Rabbinic Doctrine', in William Horbury (ed.), *Templum Amicitiae: Essays on the Second Temple Presented to Ernst Bammel* (JSNTSup, 48; Sheffield: Sheffield Academic Press): 32-36.

Day, John

2000 *Yahweh and the Gods and Goddesses of Canaan* (JSOTSup, 265; Sheffield: Sheffield Academic Press).

2004 'How many Pre-exilic Psalms are there?', in *idem* (ed.), *In Search of Pre-exilic Israel: Proceedings of the Oxford Old Testament Seminar* (JSOTSup, 406; London and New York: T. & T. Clark International): 225-50.

Dibelius, Martin

1906 *Die Lade Jahves. Eine religionsgeschichtliche Untersuchung* (Inaugural-Dissertation zur Erlangung der Doktorwürde einer hohen philosophischen Fakultät der Universität Tübingen; Göttingen: Druck der Univ.-Buchdruckerei von E.A. Huth).

Dobson, Cyril C.

1939 *The Mystery of the Fate of the Ark of the Covenant* (London: Williams & Norgate).

Eissfeldt, Otto

1968 'Die Lade Jahwes in Geschichtserzählung, Sage und Lied', in *Das Altertum* 14: 131-45. Reprinted in *idem*, *Kleine Schriften* (Tübingen: J.C.B. Mohr [Paul Siebeck], 1973): V, 77-93.

Evetts, Basil Thomas Alfred (ed.)

1895 *The Churches and Monasteries of Egypt and Some Neighbouring Countries attributed to Abû Ṣâliḥ, the Armenian* (with notes by A.J. Butler; Anecdota Oxoniensia, Semitic Studies, 7; Oxford: Clarendon Press).

Fisher, Milton C.

1992 'The Ark of the Covenant: Alive and Well in Ethiopia?', *Bible and Spade* 8.3: 65-72.

Fretheim, Terence Erling

1967 'The Cultic Use of the Ark in the Monarchial Period' (unpublished ThD thesis, Princeton Theological Seminary).

Fritz, V.

1977 *Tempel und Zelt: Studien zum Tempelbau in Israel und zu dem Zeltheiligtum der Priesterschrift* (WMANT, 47; Neukirchen–Vluyn: Neukirchener Verlag).

Gardner, Laurence

2003 *Lost Secrets of the Ark: Amazing Revelations of the Incredible Power of Gold* (London: Element [HarperCollins]).

Gaster, Moses

1927 *The Asatir: The Samaritan Book of the "Secrets of Moses"* (London: Royal Asiatic Society).

Giesebrecht, Friedrich

1894 *Das Buch Jeremia* (Handkomentar zum Alten Testament; Göttingen: Vandenhoeck & Ruprecht).

Gray, Jonathan

1997 *Ark of the Covenant* (Rundle Mall, Adelaide: Jonathan Gray, P.O. Box 3370).

Gressmann, Hugo

1920 *Die Lade Jahves und das Allerheiligste des salomonischen Tempels* (BWAT, NF 1; Stuttgart: W. Kohlhammer).

Grierson, Roderick, and S.C. Munro-Hay

1999 *The Ark of the Covenant* (London: Weidenfeld & Nicolson).

Hancock, Graham

1992 *The Sign and the Seal: A Quest for the Lost Ark of the Covenant* (London: William Heinemann). Reprinted London: Arrow Books, 1993.

Haran, Menahem

1963 'The Disappearance of the Ark', *IEJ* 13: 46-58.

1978 *Temples and Temple-Service in Ancient Israel* (Oxford: Clarendon Press).

Hitzig, Ferdinand

1841 *Der Prophet Jeremia* (Kurzgefasstes exegetisches Handbuch zum Alten Testament; Leipzig: Weidmannsche Buchhandlung; 2nd edn, 1866).

Hoberman, Barry

1993 'The Ethiopian Legend of the Ark', *BA* 46: 113-14.

Hubbard, David A.

1956 'The Literary Sources of the Kebra Nagast' (unpublished PhD thesis, St Andrews University).

Isaac, Ephraim

1993 'Is the Ark in Ethiopia?', *BARev* 19.4: 60-63.

Ish-Shalom (Friedmann), Meir

1904 'Where is the Ark?', *Ha-Shiloaḥ* 13: 541-49 (Hebrew).

Jeffrey, Grant R.

1990 *Heaven the Last Frontier* (New York: Bantam Books).

Kalimi, Isaac, and James D. Purvis

1994 'The Hiding of the Temple Vessels in Jewish and Samaritan Literature', *CBQ* 56: 679-85.

Kitchen, Kenneth A.

1986 *The Third Intermediate Period in Egypt (1100–650 B.C.)* (Warminster: Aris & Phillips; 2nd edn with supplement).

Klamroth, Erich

1932 *Lade und Tempel* (Güterlsoh: C. Bertelsmann).

Kraus, Hans-Joachim

1956 *Klagelieder (Threni)* (BKAT, 20; Neukirchen–Vluyn: Neukirchener Verlag des Erziehungsvereins, 2nd edn, 1960, 3rd edn 1968).

Le Roux, Hugues

1914 *Makeda reine de Saba, chronique éthiopienne, tr. du 'Gheez'* (Paris: Goupil).

Loenborg, S.

1929 'Die "Silo"-Verse in Gen. 49', *ARW* 27: 376-79.

Macdonald, John

1963 *Memar Marqah: The Teaching of Marqah* (BZAW, 84; 2 vols.; Berlin: Alfred Töpelmann).

1969 *The Samaritan Chronicle No. II (or: Sepher Ha-Yamim): From Joshua to Nebuchadnezzar* (Berlin: W. de Gruyter).

Maier, Johann

1965 *Das altisraelitische Ladeheiligtum* (BZAW, 93; Berlin: Alfred Töpelmann).

May, H.G.

1943 'The Ten Lost Tribes', *BA* 6: 55-60.

Mazar, Benjamin

1986 'Pharaoh Shishak's Campaign to the Land of Israel', in *idem*, *The Early Biblical Period: Historical Studies* (ed. Shmuel Aḥituv and Baruch A. Levine; Jerusalem: Israel Exploration Society): 139-50.

Meinhold, Johannes

1900 *Die 'Lade Jahves'* (Tübingen and Leipzig: J.C.B. Mohr [Paul Siebeck]).

Mettinger, T.N.D.

1982 *The Dethronement of Sabaoth: Studies in the Shem and Kabod Theologies* (trans. Frederick H. Cryer; ConBOT, 18; Lund: C.W.K. Gleerup).

Metzger, Martin

1985 *Königsthron und Gottesthron: Thronformen und Throndarstellungen in Ägypten und im Vorderen Orient im dritten und zweiten Jahrtausend vor Christus und deren Bedeutung für das Verständnis von Ausgaben über den Thron im Alten Testament* (2 vols.; AOAT, 15.1 and 2; Neukirchen–Vluyn: Neukirchener Verlag; Kevelaer: Butzon & Bercker).

Morgenstern, Julian

1960 'The King-God among the Western Semites and the Meaning of Epiphanes', *VT* 10: 138-97.

Mowinckel, Sigmund

1930 'Wann wurde der Jahwekultus in Jerusalem offiziell bildlos?', *AcOr* 8: 257-79.

Nelson, Richard D.

1981 *The Double Redaction of the Deuteronomistic History* (JSOTSup, 18; Sheffield: JSOT Press).

Noth, Martin

1950 'Jerusalem und die israelitische Tradition', *OTS* 18: 28-46. ET 'Jerusalem and the Israelite Tradition', in *idem*, *The Laws in the Pentateuch and Other Essays* (trans. D.R. Ap-Thomas; Edinburgh and London: Oliver & Boyd, 1966): 132-44.

Parfitt, Tudor

2002 *The Lost Tribes of Israel: The History of a Myth* (London: Weidenfeld & Nicolson).

Porten, Bezalel

1995 'Did the Ark Stop at Elephantine?', *BARev* 21.3: 54-57.

Porten, Bezalel, and Ada Yardeni

1986–99 *Textbook of Aramaic Documents from Ancient Egypt Newly Copied, Edited and Translated into Hebrew and English* (4 vols.; Jerusalem: Academon; distributed by Winona Lake, IN: Eisenbrauns).

Price, Randall

1994 *In Search of Temple Treasures: The Lost Ark and the Last Day* (Eugene, OR: Harvest House Publishers).

Ritmeyer, Leen, and Kathleen Ritmeyer

2000 *From Sinai to Jerusalem: The Wanderings of the Holy Ark* (Jerusalem: Carta).

Rosenbaum, Stanley Ned

2002 *Understanding Biblical Israel: A Reexamination of the Origins of Monotheism* (Macon, GA: Mercer University Press).

Rudolph, Wilhelm

1958 *Jeremia* (HAT, 12; Tübingen: J.C.B. Mohr [Paul Siebeck], 2nd edn).

Satran, David

1995 *Biblical Prophets in Byzantine Palestine: Reassessing the Lives of the Prophets* (SVTP, 11; Leiden: E.J. Brill).

Schäfer-Lichtenberger, Christa

2000 '"Sie wird nicht wieder hergestellt werden." Anmerkungen zum Verlust der Lade', in E. Blum (ed.), *Mincha. Festgabe für Rolf Rendtorff zum 75. Geburtstag* (Neukirchen–Vluyn: Neukirchener Verlag): 229-41.

Schmidt, H.

1923 'Kerubenthron und Lade', in *idem* (ed.), *ΕΥΧΑΡΙΣΤΗΡΙΟΝ: Studien zur Religion und Literatur des Alten und Neuen Testaments Hermann Gunkel zum 60. Geburtstage, dem 23. Mai 1922 dargebracht* (Göttingen: Vandenhoeck & Ruprecht): 120-44.

Schmidt, Werner H.

1968 *Alttestamentlicher Glaube und seine Umwelt* (Neukirchener Studienbücher, 6; Neukirchen–Vluyn: Neukirchener Verlag).

Schmitt, Rainer

1972 *Zelt und Lade als Thema alttestamentlicher Wissenschaft: Eine kritische forschungsgeschichtliche Darstellung* (Gütersloh: Gütersloher Verlagshaus Gerd Mohn).

Shanks, Hershel

1983 'Tom Crotser has Found the Ark of the Covenant—or has he?', *BARev* 9.3: 66-69.

Silberman, Neil Asher

1980 'In Search of Solomon's Lost Treasures', *BARev* 6.4: 30-41.

1982 *Digging for God and Country: Exploration, Archeology, and the Struggle for the Holy Land 1799–1917* (New York: Alfred A. Knopf). Reprinted New York: Anchor Books, Doubleday, 1990.

Spieckermann, Hermann

1989 *Heilsgegenwart: Eine Theologie der Psalmen* (FRLANT, 148; Göttingen: Vandenhoeck & Ruprecht).

Steinschneider, Moritz

1858 *Alphabetum Siracidis* (Berlin).

Tal, Abraham

1989 'Samaritan Literature', in Alan D. Crown (ed.), *The Samaritans* (Tübingen: J.C.B. Mohr [Paul Siebeck]): 413-67.

Thenius, Otto

1849 *Die Bücher der Könige* (Kurzgefasstes exegetisch Handbuch zum Alten Testament; Leipzig: Weidmann'sche Buchhandlung; 2nd edn, 1873).

Ullendorff, Edward

1968 *Ethiopia and the Bible* (The Schweich Lectures of the British Academy, 1967; London: Oxford University Press, for the British Academy).

Vaux, Roland de

1958, 1960a *Les Institutions de l'Ancien Testament* (2 vols.; Paris: Cerf). ET *Ancient Israel* (trans. John McHugh; London: Darton, Longman & Todd, 1961).

1960b 'Les chérubins et l'arche de l'alliance. Les sphinx gardiens et les trônes divins dans l'ancien orient', *Mélanges de l'Université Saint Joseph* 37: 91-124. Reprinted in *idem* (ed.), *Bible et Orient* (Paris: Cerf, 1967): 231-59.

Weinfeld, Moshe

1976 'Jeremiah and the Spiritual Metamorphosis of Israel', *ZAW* 88: 17-56.

Wolff, Christian

1976 *Jeremia im Frühjudentum und Urchristentum* (TU, 108; Berlin: Akademie-Verlag).

Woudstra, Marten H.
1965 *The Ark of the Covenant from Conquest to Kingship* (International Library of Philosophy and Theology; Philadelphia: Presbyterian and Reformed Publishing Company).

Zobel, H.-J.
1973 'אֲרוֹן', in *ThWAT*, I: 391-404. ET *TDOT*, I (rev. edn, 1977): 363-74.

Ordeals in the Psalms?[*]

Philip S. Johnston

How can one determine justice in a dispute between two parties where there is no witness or no corroborating evidence? Modern courts agonize to establish the veracity of each party and the validity of circumstantial evidence. Ancient peoples, by contrast, occasionally resorted to what is generally called the 'judicial ordeal', or 'trial by ordeal', or in some recent literature 'supprarational trial'. In this, one or both parties in the dispute was obliged to undergo an ordeal which they might not survive. Those who survived were adjudged innocent and acquitted, those who did not were assumed guilty.

The rationale of the ordeal was an appeal to deity. The gods could see what humans could not, and would surely ensure that justice was done. Hence the definition by T.S. Frymer ([later Frymer-Kensky] 1976: 638): 'Trial by ordeal is an appeal to divine judgment to decide otherwise insoluble cases that cannot be allowed to remain unsolved'. Omniscience was often attributed to deity in the ancient Near East, particularly solar deities, and of course to Yahweh in Israel.[1]

The two reasonably well-attested forms of ordeal in the ancient Near East are the river ordeal and the drinking ordeal. Only the latter features explicitly in the biblical text, in the instance of the woman accused of adultery and obliged to drink 'the waters of bitterness that bring the curse' (Num. 5.18).[2] Nevertheless, both of these forms have been traced in the psalms by different scholars. We will discuss them in turn.

1. *Echoes of a River Ordeal?*

1.1. *River Ordeals*

The river ordeal is well attested for Assyria and Babylonia, occurring in historical and legal texts in Sumerian and Akkadian.[3] In a lengthy survey published in 1982, Bottéro speaks of 'a good hundred items in the Ordeal dossier'.[4] The

* I am very grateful to John Day and Stephanie Dalley for kindly commenting on this paper in draft form, and to colleagues at the Oxford Old Testament Seminar for further useful comments.

1. Cf. van der Toorn 1992: 40.

2. English translation follows NRSV, unless otherwise indicated.

3. Cf. von Soden 1985, ET 1994: 143. Sasson (2001: 49) cites Ur-Nammu laws 10 and 11, which prescribe it.

4. Bottéro 1981: 1010: 'le dossier complet de l'Ordalie compte aujourd'hui une bonne centaine de pièces'.

ordeal is also attested in Elam, Nuzi, Mari and Ḫatti.[5] At Ugarit, the title 'Judge River' possibly echoes this concept, though no river ordeal is explicitly mentioned in the known texts, and 'judge' may simply mean 'ruler' as with the Israelite judges.[6]

At the same time, there are very few extant texts which describe this ordeal in practice. They are as follows, the first three from Mari. (a) Two men accused of treason should undergo the ordeal. If they survive, their accuser will be burned; if not, he will receive their houses and 'people'. (b) Two men and two women from feuding towns should undergo the ordeal. (c) An elder and six women from an aggressive town are taken for the ordeal. The first three survive but the fourth drowns; after this the town renounces its claim and the remaining women are spared. (d) A man accused of murder and his accuser are thrown into the Euphrates, upstream from Sippar, at dawn. It seems that one survived and the other, presumed guilty, drowned. (e) The river 'absolves' one man from the charges of another, as testified by one male and two female witness.[7] These examples show that the river ordeal could be practised in contexts beyond the purely judicial.

While the river ordeal was well known, it is interesting to note the dearth of narrative accounts. The recent encyclopaedic multi-volume *Civilizations of the Ancient Near East* (1995) contains only two references to ordeal of any type outside the Hebrew Bible, both rather general.[8] This may indicate that the practice was less frequent than the legal texts imply, though it may simply reflect the different literary genres.[9]

1.2. *McCarter: A Cosmic River Ordeal is Reflected in the Psalms and Elsewhere*

McCarter (1973) argues that several psalms share 'a common motif which clearly presupposes a situation of judgment by water'. These are six from the psalter: Pss. 18, 66, 69, 88, 124 and 144; plus Jonah 2. He continues (p. 404):

> Each of these contains most or all of the following elements: (1) the psalmist is beset by raging waters; (2) he is surrounded by accusers; (3) he protests his innocence and reliance upon God and beseeches God to deliver him from the waters. If the psalmist is describing a past rescue from the waters, there may be another element: (4) he is drawn out of the waters and set in a safe place.

5. Cf. *CAD s.v. ḫuršānu*; Cardascia 1967: 20. The evidence is surveyed at length in Frymer-Kensky's 1977 PhD dissertation, available only in microfilm despite references to intended publication (cf. Frymer-Kensky 1981: 115 n. 3; 1983: 139 n. 1; Owen 1988: 305 n. 2).

6. Cf. the parallel 'Prince Sea'. For lack of evidence at Ugarit, cf. Curtis 1988: 9; and in Egypt, cf. Montet (*apud* Dossin 1958: 393).

7. Cf. Cardascia 1967; Bottéro 1981. (a-c) Letters to Zimrilim; cf. Dossin 1939 and 1958. (d) Babylonian text extolling the king's judgments, unfortunately damaged where the ordeal is described; cf. Lambert 1965. Lambert identified the king as Nebuchadrezzar, but von Soden (1994: 143 n. 21) corrects this to Nabonidus. (e) All five people are named; cf. Owen 1988.

8. These are: p. 1898 (W. Farber: against witchcraft in Mesopotamia); p. 1963 (H. Kock: the Akkadian and Elamite river god Shazi was one of the lower gods). The index gives two biblical references: p. 2078 (J.M. de Tarragon, on Num. 5) and p. 2051 (van der Toorn: non-specific reference to ordeals by food, drink and fire in Canaan and Israel).

9. Frymer-Kensky (1977: 499-501) concludes from the few descriptions that it took place, so the legal texts should be taken seriously, but that its practice fluctuated over time and place.

This pattern is then illustrated in detail for three psalms (Pss. 18; 69; Jon. 2), 'any one of which might be considered a parade example of the motif in question' (p. 404).

McCarter argues that these passages draw from a mythological concept of river ordeal. The psalmist feels endangered by the rushing cosmic waters which link El's mountain and Mot's abode (1973: 405). He 'clearly conceives of himself as beset by the waters of ordeal in the place of judgment and interrogation' (p. 408). McCarter also proposes that the term *'êd*, normally translated 'calamity' in Job and elsewhere, derives from *'ēd* meaning 'cosmic river', and hence indicates the river ordeal.

McCarter accepts that the Israelites may never have actually practised trial by ordeal (p. 412):[10]

> Indeed the legal material of the Old Testament provides no evidence for a river ordeal in Israelite law. But the existence of the legal institution in Israel need not be assumed. The river ordeal material alludes rather to a mythological background sharing certain concepts with Mesopotamia and probably Canaan.

Hence he concludes (p. 412):

> ...the allusions to the ordeal in the Old Testament are so specific as to be distinguished clearly among the general associations of water and death in which they participate. To the Israelite poet the *cosmic* river ordeal at least was a very viable image... In Old Testament religion, judgment is so pervasive a factor, deliverance from waters or by crossing waters is such a complex theme, that future study of the subject promises to be both complex and exciting.

McCarter's proposal invites close examination of each of its several elements, as will be undertaken below. The theme is certainly complex. Whether this study is suitably exciting will be left to the reader to decide!

1.3. *Was there a Cosmic River Ordeal?*

McCarter (1973) argues for a cosmic river ordeal as follows (p. 407):

> In the cosmology of Mesopotamian myth, the term *ḫuršānu* (Sumerian *ḫuršāg*) referred at once to mountainous regions and to the river ordeal. Mythologically the *ḫuršānu* functions as the place of judgment and interrogation at the entry to the Underworld. In its cosmic aspect the mountain is the place from which judgment is pronounced. At least this is true at Ugarit, where the cosmic mountain of 'Ēl is also referred to by the borrowed term *ḫuršānu*. The connection between the two meanings of *ḫuršānu* is thus an obvious one, insofar as the river ordeal is understood to take place at the foot of the cosmic mountain, the source of the waters and entrance to the Underworld.

However, McCarter's argument is uncertain, for several reasons:

(i) The idea of a cosmic river ordeal is conceptually difficult, even though there is some continuity in various Akkadian texts between earthly and underworld rivers.[11] The river ordeal in this life gives a distinct verdict of innocent or guilty,

10. Similarly de Ward (1977: 17), though she sees echoes, e.g. Ps. 66.12, Isa. 43.2 and the story of crossing the Red Sea.

11. See Frymer-Kensky 1977: 587-613.

resulting in life or death. By contrast, the underworld river is crossed (or sometimes travelled) by all with no judgment involved. The two concepts cannot be easily combined, and McCarter neither notes nor explains these different perspectives.

(ii) The posited link between *ḫuršānu* (as river ordeal) and the underworld is textually uncertain. Indeed, for von Soden, there is no evidence for such a link or for post-mortem judgment.[12] *Ḫuršānu* clearly indicates a judicial verdict in this world. Though the river ordeal was often fatal, *CAD* (*s.v. ḫuršānu*) cites no text which identifies *ḫuršānu* with entrance to the underworld or with its river.[13]

Pope proposed such a link in two texts, but this is dubious in both cases:
(a) In *Ludlul Bēl Nēmeqi* a sufferer portrays recovery as acquittal beside the river of judgment.[14] Here Pope (1955: 70) cites Pfeiffer's translation: 'on the holy river shore (in the underworld) where the (last) judgment of men is manifested'.[15] But Pfeiffer's reconstruction and translation have been superseded. Lambert rearranged the text, removing underworld reference from the immediate context, and translated the line: 'beside the River where the judgment of the people is decided'.[16] The immediate context is one of recovery from illness, while acquittal at the place of ordeal (a suitable location for legal pronouncements) and freedom from slavery (in the following line)[17] are simply metaphors of this. Thus there is no reference here to an underworld river ordeal.
(b) In text *KAR* 143.6-7 a certain messenger goes to a house at the place of the *ḫuršānu* ordeal. For Pope (1955: 70), the messenger is 'on his way to the netherworld'. However, Frymer-Kensky (1983: 138) counters categorically that 'there is no ordeal in this composition', arguing that *ḫuršān* is merely the name of a place.[18]

(iii) The connection between *ḫuršānu* as 'river ordeal' (occasionally divinized) and *ḫuršānu* as 'mountain (region)'[19] is linguistically unclear. For Pope, *ḫuršānu* was originally the underworld mountain, and it later came to mean river ordeal

12. Von Soden 1955: 140: 'Für irgendeine Beziehung zwischen *ḫurš/sān* und der Unterwelt... gibt es vorläufig keinerlei Zeugnis'.

13. *CAD* VI (219, s.v. *ḫubur* A.a) cites the 'Hymn to the Sun-God' ii.6, where Schollmeyer links *ḫubur* with the river ordeal. But Stephens (*ANET*, 388) translates the text entirely differently, without reference to *ḫubur* or the river ordeal. See Frymer-Kensky (1977: 587-613) for further discussion in general and in relation to this Hymn.

14. *i-na i-te-e* ᵈ*nāri (ḫur-šá-an) a-šar deš-en nišī* ᵐᵉš *ib-bir-ru* (Lambert 1960: 54).

15. *ANET*, 437; text III rev., l. 19. Albright (1936: 20) interprets this as 'the River of Death (*nâr Ḫubur*)' and *ḫuršānu* as the mountain of post-mortem judgment. *ANET* orders the tablets: III I, III A, III rev.; the relevant line follows III rev. 5-18, which banish the afflicting demons to the underworld.

16. Lambert 1960: 55; text K 3291 line l. For Lambert (1960: 47), lines assigned letters are not necessarily contiguous. Lambert inserts III I after III rev. 18 (with different labelling); the relevant line then follows III I.51-60, a description of illness. Both changes were accepted by Biggs in the *ANET Supplement* (*ANET*, 600).

17. Regardless of variant translations by Lambert and Biggs (citing Borger).

18. Frymer-Kensky also notes that in the Ninevite version, 'the *ḫuršān* of this text has something to do with the netherworld, and that this text gives a political 'interpretation' of a tale in which Bel went down to the netherworld' (1983: 139). However, this is *ḫuršān* as river, not as river ordeal.

19. Divinized in a god list (ᵈ*Nāru*) and a name (The-*ḫ*.-is-judge). Once it means a siege ramp, cf. *CAD* VI: 254 (b).

by its association with the cosmic river where the dead were judged. Thus 'the actual ordeal was apparently a substitute for the final ordeal at the real *ḫuršān*' (1955: 70). However, Clifford counters that Mesopotamia had no concept of a *Weltberg* or *Unterweltberg*, or of the mountain as a judgment place.[20] Previous scholars assumed that mountains had the same religious significance in Mesopotamian as in West Semitic thought, but many now reject this.[21] As for other views, von Soden (1955: 141) suggested that the river ordeal in seemingly bottomless water was called 'mountain' euphemistically, which is possible if not immediately obvious. Jacobsen (cf. Clifford 1972: 24) proposed that *ḫuršānu* as 'river ordeal' derived from the narrow rock channels through which the swift and turbulent Tigris was forced.[22] This association between rivers and their mountainous source is more immediately recognizable. But it is not unproblematic, since the river ordeal obviously occurred at places like Mari and Sippar where water was neither fast nor turbulent.

Also regarding these terms, Ugaritic *ḫršn* means only 'mountain', not 'river', let alone 'ordeal river'. It occurs in one mythological text, as El's dwelling, and in two administrative texts.[23] None of these concerns judgment.

Thus the proposal of a cosmic river ordeal in Mesopotamian and consequently Israelite mythology is conceptually difficult, textually uncertain, and linguistically unclear.

1.4. *Is a River Ordeal Reflected in the Psalms?*

As noted above, McCarter opens his case by presenting criteria for tracing the ordeal motif in various psalms. These criteria are generally appropriate, but could be refined. In the first, 'raging waters' should perhaps be rephrased as 'deep waters'. The ordeal itself simply required deep water, and the Mesopotamian accounts noted above indicate that it occurred in wide but not necessarily raging or even fast-flowing waters, as at Mari and Sippar. The second criterion, accusers, is unproblematic. The third, however, combines two diverse elements, protestation of innocence and plea for deliverance, obscuring their distinction. Conversely, a relevant criterion would be an echo of the involuntary subjection integral to the river ordeal, for example, 'I was thrown into the waters'. However, McCarter ignores this theme, though perhaps this is unsurprising given that it is totally absent from his selected psalms.

20. Clifford 1972: 9-25. He defines a cosmic mountain as 'involved in the government and stability of the cosmos' (1972: 3), whether real (Mt Zion) or imaginary. McCarter offers no definition.

21. Many also reject Pope's underworld location of El's abode: von Soden 1955: 140-41; Kapelrud 1980: 82; Mullen 1980: 163; Wallace 1985: 98 n. 88.

22. *Ḫuršānu* never means specifically 'narrow rock channels'. Sumerian *ḫuršāg* can mean 'stony, rocky ground', as of mountains or desert (Jacobsen 1970: 30). Jacobsen apparently extrapolates from this to 'rocky substratum' and 'narrow rock channels', but without citing evidence (cf. Clifford 1972: 12-13).

23. Mythological: *KTU* 1.1 II 3, 23; III 12, (16?,) 22, in parallel with *ġr.ks*. The latter is translated 'the mountain of the cup' by de Moor (*ARTU*), 'Mount Throne' by Wyatt (*RTU*). Administrative texts: *KTU* 4.63 III 40 (household census), 4.222.12 (land registry). Also in an Akkadian text at Ugarit: RS 20.24, cf. *Ugaritica* V: 44.

How do the psalms match these criteria? To begin with the so-called parade examples, Psalm 18 has 'torrents of Belial' (NRSV 'perdition', v. 5, ET 4) and mighty waters (v. 17, ET 16), enemies (v. 18, ET 17), affirmation of innocence (v. 21, ET 20), and plea for deliverance with its fulfilment (vv. 7, 17, 20, ET 6, 16, 19). No specific accusation is recorded, but otherwise Psalm 18 matches the stated criteria well. At the same time, neither casual nor careful reading of the psalm suggests that it necessarily echoes trial by ordeal. For one thing, nothing specifically indicates judicial ordeal rather than general distress. For another, the image of drowning and rescue is only one among many: for distress there are also images of hunting (cords of death, snares of Sheol, vv. 5-6, ET 4-5) and of catastrophe (*'êd*, v. 19, ET 18), which McCarter translates as 'river ordeal' (see below); for deliverance there are also images of storm theophany (vv. 8-16, ET 7-15), victorious battle (vv. 32-43, ET 31-42) and kingship (v. 44, ET 43). So the image of drowning and rescue is general rather than specific, just one picture in a vivid kaleidoscope.

Psalm 69, the second key example, similarly has deep waters (vv. 3, 15-16, ET 2, 14-15), enemies (vv. 5, 13, 20-22, ET 4, 12, 19-21), an accusation (v. 5, ET 4), an implicit affirmation of innocence (v. 6, ET 5), pleas for deliverance (vv. 2, 14-19, 30, ET 1, 13-18, 29) and prospective thanksgiving (vv. 31-37, ET 30-36). So Psalm 69 also matches the stated criteria well. Its imagery is less profuse, so arguably the water motif is more central and more evocative of a river ordeal.[24] Yet it too has factors which militate against such a specific echo. First, the psalmist is parched from crying out (v. 4, ET 3), an unexpected symptom if drowning in fresh water. Secondly, he prays for answer 'at an acceptable time' (*'ēt rāṣôn*, v. 14, ET 13), which hardly conveys the urgency of imminent death.[25] Thirdly, the fate wished on the enemies (vv. 23-29, ET 22-28) is that of darkness, desolation and erasure from the book of the living, not that of succumbing to water themselves, as would normally be the case in the river ordeal. All this suggests that the water imagery is general rather than specific, that it connotes being overwhelmed and submerged by difficulties rather than being judicially tried by river ordeal.

Jonah 2 graphically portrays submersion to the depths, as far down as the land whose bars close over forever (v. 7, ET 6), and it is framed by pleas for deliverance and grateful acknowledgment of its provision (vv. 3, 8-10, ET 2, 7-9). It mentions 'those who worship vain idols' (v. 9, ET 8), but without indicating that they have accused the author. And it lacks protestation of innocence. It could certainly reflect the harrowing experience of a river ordeal, but nothing specifically suggests this, and it could equally reflect any experience of drowning.

These three psalms all have water imagery, pleas for divine deliverance, and due acknowledgment of it. But in each case other factors imply a general evocation of drowning, rather than a specific echo of a river ordeal. So, unless *'êd*

24. McCarter underlines the legal terminology in Ps. 69, but Rosenberg (1981: 107-109) notes the absence of legal terminology in many of the others.

25. *'ēt rāṣôn* occurs once elsewhere, in Isa. 49.8, in parallel with 'day of salvation', as a general reference to return from exile. The themes and perspectives are too different for direct comparison. (Cf. Isa. 58.5, *yôm rāṣôn*; 61.2, *šᵉnat rāṣôn*; neither relevant.)

(Ps. 18.19, ET 18) actually means 'river ordeal', none of these three parade examples clearly illustrates the point asserted.

The other four psalms are equally uncertain. Psalm 66, a hymn of praise, pauses to recite a brief catalogue of ways in which God tested his people (vv. 10-12): '...you have tried us as silver is tried. You brought us into the net; you laid burdens on our backs; you let people ride over our heads; we went through fire and through water...' Here, several images of communal hardship are glimpsed in swift succession, with none predominating. There are six different images if fire and water are counted separately, or five if these two are a merism for 'sufferings of every kind'.[26] These images clearly evoke hardship, but it is much less clear that 'going through water' evokes a river ordeal. In any case, the immediate context makes no mention of drowning in deep waters or of accusers, and there is no declaration of innocence or plea for deliverance. The later thanksgiving section does affirm personal innocence and deliverance (vv. 18-19), but this is not directly related to the communal hardships.

Psalm 88 recounts submersion under Yahweh's waves (v. 8, ET 7) as one of several vivid images of despair, and pleads for deliverance. But nothing else in the psalm evokes a watery death, let alone a river ordeal. Also, there are no accusers, and no protestations of innocence.[27] Psalm 124 likewise lacks an affirmation of innocence, as well as a plea for deliverance. It recalls menacing enemies, though as attackers rather than as accusers. It portrays Israel threatened by and delivered from the flooding torrent,[28] yet also delivered from the enemies' teeth and the fowlers' snare (vv. 4-5). Finally, Psalm 144 prays for deliverance from deceitful aliens portrayed as mighty waters (vv. 7-8), and from the cruel sword (v. 11). Thus it mentions deep water, accusers and a plea for deliverance. Also, the psalmist's innocence may be implied by their deceit, but it is not directly affirmed. This psalm fulfils more of McCarter's criteria than many of the others, yet it still hardly requires the river ordeal as a conceptual backdrop. Even here, there is more battle imagery than water imagery (cf. vv. 1, 6, 10, 11), and the psalmist wishes the foes to be routed, not drowned.

	River Ordeal Elements	*Ps. 18*	*Ps. 69*	*Jon. 2*	*Ps. 66*	*Ps. 88*	*Ps. 124*	*Ps. 144*
1.	deep (raging) waters	+	+	+	(+)	+	+	+
2.	accusers	(+)	+				(+)	+
3.	affirms innocence	+	(+)		(+)			(+)
	pleads deliverance	+	+	+		+		+
4.	acknowledges deliverance	+	+	+	(+)		+	
	water is sole image of distress			+				
	'thrown into water'							

In summary, the seven nominated psalms share a motif of menacing water. They each have several related elements, though none has them all: accusers,

26. So Keel 1972: 164, ET 1978: 184; similarly Tate 1990: 150.

27. Further, the psalmist reports but does not record his prayers for deliverance (v. 10). Regarding Ps. 88, Tate (1990: 400) summarizes McCarter approvingly, though without discussion.

28. For Kraus (1978: 848, ET 1989: 441), this refers both to sudden torrents rushing through valleys and to the primaeval flood.

affirmation of innocence, plea for deliverance and acknowledgment of deliverance. In only one is water the sole image of distress (Jon. 2), but it lacks accusation and self-justification. None speaks directly of being thrown into water. Thus there is a recurring motif of the threat of drowning, but insufficient evidence to link this with the river ordeal. McCarter's conclusion that 'the allusions to the ordeal in the Old Testament are so specific as to be distinguished clearly among the general associations of water and death in which they participate' goes well beyond the available evidence.

1.5. *Is a River Ordeal Reflected in Hebrew* 'êd?

In support of his proposal, McCarter also argues that the Hebrew term *'êd* sometimes means 'river ordeal'. The texts concerned lie mostly outside the psalms, but the argument is relevant to the motif under discussion and, if correct, might cause us to re-evaluate the above conclusion.

McCarter first argues that *'êd* (איד), usually translated 'calamity, catastrophe', is really the same word as *'ēd* (אד), since the *yod* in the former is simply a *yod mater*. The latter term occurs twice in the Hebrew Bible, in Gen. 2.6, as the stream which rose from the ground to water the earth, and in Job 36.27, probably as 'mist'.[29] McCarter then interprets both these terms as '(cosmic) River', by extension 'river ordeal' and by further extension 'ordeal' in general. Nevertheless, he asserts, *'êd* 'retains its specific association with the river ordeal' (1973: 409) in several texts, especially in Job.

In response, first, despite their linguistic affinity, the two terms are used distinctly. *'ēd* occurs rarely (only in Gen. 2.6 and 36.27), clearly in aquatic contexts. *'êd* occurs more frequently, mostly in contexts of calamity but not specifically of water.[30] The LXX distinguishes between *'ēd* and *'êd*.[31] Thus, whatever their origin, the words were distinct before the fixation of the MT and the emergence of early versions.

Secondly, *'êd* occurs 24 times, and often cannot mean 'river ordeal'. Expressions parallel to *yôm 'êd* (10 times) and *'ēt 'êd* (once) often indicate disaster, particularly the term *yôm yhwh* (Obad. 15). In prophetic texts *'êd* (10 times) indicates future national punishment and is clearly unassociated with a river ordeal.[32] In psalmodic and wisdom literature *'êd* (14 times) applies to godly and godless alike; and it descends suddenly like a whirlwind, unlike a planned judicial event.[33]

29. Cf. commentaries, e.g. Westermann 1974: 273-74, ET 1984: 200-201; Habel 1985: 511; Wenham 1987: 58-59; Hartley 1988: 479 n. 39; Sarna 1989: 354 n. 8; and briefly Ross 1997: 50, 7e. This *'ēd* is often linked to the Akkadian *edû*, cf. Sæbø 1970. Further discussion in Johnston 1993: 57-59.

30. Cf. Sæbø 1971; Van Dam 1997: 371.

31. *'ēd*: *pēgē* (Gen. 2.6), *nephelē* (Job 36.27); *'êd: hapōleia* (9 times), *hēmera* (3 times), *katastrpohē* (twice), 9 other terms (once each, cf. Santos n.d.).

32. Israel: Jer. 18.17; Ezek. 35.5; Obad. 13 (3 times). Enemies: Jer. 46.21 (Egypt); 48.16 (Moab); 49.8 (Dedan); 49.32 (Kedar, Hazor); Deut. 32.35 (unspecified).

33. Godly: Ps. 18.20 (ET 19)//2 Sam. 22.19; Job 30.12; 31.23. Godless: Job 18.12; 21.17, 30; 31.3; Prov. 1.26, 27 (foolish); 6.15; 17.5; 24.22. Unspecified: Prov. 27.10. (Sæbø 1971 groups the texts as 'national' and 'individual'.) Suddenness: Prov. 1.27; 6.15; 24.22; cf. 27.10.

Parallel expressions in both prophetic and wisdom texts indicate that an *'êd* brings disaster, unlike an ordeal which could result in vindication.[34] So the contexts of use clearly suggest that *'êd* is an unwelcome, calamitous event which is not associated with water.

Thirdly, this interpretation of *'êd* involves further questionable translation in Job. (The texts are reproduced below with the debated terms in italics.)

(a) Job 21.17:

NRSV:	How often is the *lamp* of the wicked *put out*?
	How often does *calamity* come upon them?
McCarter:	How often is the *property* of the wicked *confiscated*?
	And their *ordeal* goes before them?

This repoints *nēr* ('lamp') as *nîr* ('property'), ignoring a common sapiential idiom, and renders *d'k* (normally 'extinguish') as 'confiscate' without support.[35]

(b) Job 21.30:

NRSV:	...the wicked are spared in the day of *calamity*,
	and are rescued in the day of *wrath*.
McCarter:	On the day of *ordeal* the wicked is spared;
	On the day of its *overflowing* they are led along.

The term normally translated 'wrath' (*'ᵃbārôt*, from *'ebrâ*) is a *hapax* here in the plural absolute, but the plural construct occurs twice elsewhere, including later in Job.[36] Although he notes the similar LXX rendering (*orgēs autou*), McCarter finds the term 'problematic' (1973: 409 n. 26),[37] inverts the two final letters to give *'brtw*, and translates it instead as 'overflowing' (presumably from a posited *'ᵃbārâ*). However, while possible, this meaning is unattested elsewhere, the emendation lacks textual support, and the proposal is made simply to support his reinterpretation of *'êd*.

(c) Job 31.23:

NRSV:	For I was in terror of *calamity* from God,
	and I could not have faced *his majesty*.
McCarter:	Then let the *river* of 'El be a fearful thing to me,
	and let me not be stronger than *its rising up*.

This applies *miśśᵉ'ētô* to the posited river, which is quite possible grammatically. But it ignores the verse's opening *kî* and assumes instead a jussive *yᵉhî* (cf. v. 22),

34. Prophetic texts: *'ᵃtidōt* (Deut. 32.35), *rā'â* (Jer. 48.16), *'ᵃwōn qēṣ* (Ezek. 35.5), *pᵉquddâ* (Jer. 46.21), *pqd* (Jer. 49.8), *nēker*, *'bd*, *ṣārâ* (Obad. 12-13). Wisdom texts: *'ᵃbārôt* (Job 21.30), *hawwâ* (Job 30.13), *nēker* (Job 31.3), *paḥad* (Prov. 1.26), *paḥad*, *ṣārâ wᵉṣûqâ* (Prov. 1.27), *pîd* (Prov. 24.22), catalogue of catastrophe (Job 18.12).

35. Cf. *nēr rᵉšā'îm* (here, Prov. 13.9; 24.20), *nērô* (Job 18.6; Prov. 20.20) and *'ôr rᵉšā'îm* (Job 18.5). *d'k* (qal) occurs only of the 'lamp' of the wicked (in these texts) and of hostile armies (once). *d'k* (niphal) occurs of brooks (once) and *d'k* (pual) of enemies (once). This suggests a relatively uniform meaning (cf. BDB).

36. Job 40.11; Ps. 7.7 (ET 6).

37. The term is unproblematic for others: Rowley 1976: 152; Habel 1985: 322-23; Hartley 1988: 320-21. Most ignore McCarter's proposal: Andersen 1976; Grabbe 1977; Gordis 1978; Habel 1985; Hartley 1988; Fohrer 1989.

which is less plausible. Further, the context is Job's ringing declaration of innocence, for which his motivation was partly the fear of God's *'êd*. So the *'êd* is logically a disaster, not an occasion for proving his innocence.

(d) Deuteronomy 32.35, the final text in this section, requires no emendation. McCarter simply interprets 'the day of their *'êd* [NRSV: calamity]' as 'the day of their ordeal'. However, again the immediate context is not one of trial but of judgment: their wine is poisonous, like that of Sodom and Gomorrah, it is the time of Yahweh's vengeance, so 'their foot shall slip'. All this suggests a calamity, not an ordeal.

1.6. *Is a River Ordeal Reflected in Other Hebrew Terms?*

To complete the assessment, we should note that McCarter reinterprets other Hebrew terms in various psalms. In a few places he sees *ḥayyîm* not as 'the living', but as an abbreviation of *mayyîm ḥayyîm*, 'the Living Waters', i.e. 'the cosmic waters that issue from the mountain of Yahweh' (1973: 411 n. 32, *re* Pss. 66.9; 124.3). Similarly he sees *mᵉqôr ḥayyîm*, normally 'the fountain of life', as an abbreviation of *mᵉqôr mayyîm ḥayyîm*, 'the fountain of Living Waters' (in Ps. 36.10, ET 9).

However, these reinterpretations are forced and unconvincing. The terms discussed are common and well-defined: *ḥayyîm* has no explicit water connotations, and *mᵉqôr ḥayyîm* often occurs in contexts with no water associations.[38]

McCarter (p. 409) also finds an ordeal reference in Ps. 32.6.

NRSV:	Therefore let all who are faithful offer prayer to you; at a time of distress, the rush of many waters shall not reach them.
McCarter:	Wherefore let every righteous man offer prayer to you in his time of going forth without cause to the overflowing of the Many Waters. They shall not overcome him!

For this he reinterprets three Hebrew words: *mᵉṣō'* as 'going forth', *raq* as *rêq*, 'without cause', and *ngy* (hiphil) as 'overcome'. But these are all problematic. Admittedly the MT's *mᵉṣō' raq* (lit. 'finding only') is difficult, but the generally accepted emendation to *māṣôq* ('distress') makes sense in the context, and explains the possible corruption to the present text.[39] Instead McCarter emends *mᵉṣō'* to a form of *yṣ'*, presumably *ṣē't* or *ṣē'tô*, whose corruption would be less easy to explain.[40] He reads the proposed *rêq* as the adverb 'without cause'; but elsewhere *rêq* is an adjective ('empty, vain'), while the related adverb is always *rêqām*.[41] And *ngy* never elsewhere means 'overcome' (cf. BDB, *HALAT*). So this reinterpretation involves too much emendation to be convincing.

38. *mᵉqôr hayyîm*: Prov. 10.11; 13.14; 14.27; 16.22 (cf. *mᵉqôr ḥokmâ*, Prov. 18.4).

39. So RSV, JB, NEB, NJB, NRSV, REB, A.A. Anderson 1972: I, 258; Craigie 1983: 264. H. Bardtke (*BHS* note) also suggests *māṣôr*, 'siege'.

40. McCarter does not record the form he proposes. It could possibly be a hophal, which would explain the initial *m*, but the translation offered is active, not passive.

41. E.g. Pss. 7.5 (ET 4); 25.3. Also, *rêqām* (16 times) never occurs elsewhere as a synonym of 'innocent'.

1.7. *Conclusion*

The Israelites were certainly fearful of water. Historiography and psalmody alike testify that they were not natural sailors, and water usually signified danger. Several psalms clearly portray situations of great distress as drowning in water. This could reflect the experience of someone undergoing a river ordeal. However, as argued above, such a judicial ordeal is unlikely to be the reference point of the imagery. There is no evidence for a mythological concept of cosmic river ordeal, nor evidence for such an ordeal practised in Israel, nor evidence in the immediate contexts of the psalms and of other texts proposed. Upon investigation, McCarter's proposal is not convincing.

2. *Elements of a Drinking Ordeal?*

2.1. *Drinking Ordeals*

Another form of ordeal was the drinking ordeal. In this, an accused person would drink a potion and pronounce a self-imprecatory oath. If the potion produced a harmful or fatal effect, the person was declared guilty; if not, they were adjudged innocent.

The best known instance of this is the procedure for a woman suspected of adultery outlined in Num. 5.11-31. Here a suspicious husband takes his wife and an offering to the priest; the priest gives her a potion of water mixed with dust from the floor and loosens her hair; he pronounces an imprecatory oath to which she assents, and records it; she drinks the potion, now called 'bitter water' (or 'water of bitterness', v. 24), and he receives the offering. If she has been unfaithful, she will have 'bitter pain' and become barren; if not, she will be fertile. This text has already received much close scrutiny elsewhere, and will not be further discussed here.[42]

Frymer-Kensky refers to the procedure of Numbers 5 as a self-imprecatory oath rather than an ordeal.[43] Certainly there are several important formal differences, notably the act of swearing and the extended time-frame for a verdict to be established. However, other scholars define the term 'ordeal' more widely to include this procedure also, since in essence it is a suprarational procedure.

There is only scattered evidence for drinking ordeals in the ancient Near East. Frymer-Kensky (1981: 119) argues that at least one set of Elamite texts 'represent a drinking trial in which the litigant drinks a potion while avowing the legitimacy of his claim'.[44] She also notes other evidence of drinking procedures (p. 120): 'Among the Hittites we hear of drinking the rhyton of the life of the god...but the details are not known. At Mari we have a fealty oath...in which minor deities

42. See commentaries, Frymer-Kensky 1984, and their bibliographies.

43. Frymer-Kensky (1981: 120), though her earlier *IDBSup* article accepts the designation 'ordeal' (1976: 639).

44. She discusses indistinct phrases, previously interpreted as indicating a river ordeal, in two sets of texts. Texts in the first set have an obscure sanction–imprecation clause about 'going (up) to the water'. Those in the second set refer to 'taking the waters'; this cannot be a river ordeal, since it is undertaken voluntarily and the alternative outcomes assume survival, so must be a drinking ordeal.

drink a potion of water [mixed] with dust from the gate of Mari.' Neither of these is straight-forward: the Hittite text lacks further information, and the Mari one involves deities rather than humans.[45] Nevertheless, there is sufficient evidence to show that a judicial procedure involving a self-imprecatory oath and a drinking potion was a known practice in several ancient cultures.

2.2. *Temple Ordeals*

In 1927, in a SOTS conference in Oxford, H. Schmidt proposed that the setting for a group of some twenty psalms was a judicial ordeal in the Temple.[46] He started with various extra-psalmic texts: Solomon's prayer concerning one who swears before the altar (1 Kgs 8.31-32), the Deuteronomic appeal to priests and judge at the central sanctuary (Deut. 17.8-9), the woman suspected of adultery (Num. 5), and a protestation of innocence in an Elephantine papyrus. From these he proceeded to the psalms, and found traces in several of an ordeal procedure.[47] This involved holding the accused in custody during the procedure, an oath of innocence, an overnight ordeal, and a morning verdict. Schmidt felt unable to specify the precise nature of this nocturnal ordeal.

However, neither the proposed procedure nor the mining of varied psalms for evidence was widely accepted, as illustrated by subsequent SOTS sponsored reviews of scholarship. Johnson (1951: 201) seemed both bemused by Schmidt's proposal—'its ingenuity can hardly be denied'—and open to its validity—'it should certainly be taken seriously as at least a possible explanation of some of these psalms'. However, for Eaton a generation later (1989: 256), 'Schmidt's linking of psalmody with ordeal trials…is pure speculation. Further, the varied psalms which Schmidt adduces…do not clearly conform to such a setting and are treated rather arbitrarily by Schmidt.'[48]

In 1970 Beyerlin published a reworking and refinement of Schmidt's thesis. He re-examined all the psalms listed by Schmidt, retaining only nine and adding another two,[49] and explaining their formal diversity as due to their reflecting different stages of the ordeal proceedings. He proposed several differences: the litigant was not detained and the ordeal was not necessarily nocturnal; the verdict was given in an early morning cultic theophany, and was followed by a banquet which the winner enjoyed and which the losers had to observe.

This proposal has had some support. Kraus (1979: 165, ET 1986: 132) describes a process whereby the psalmist seeks asylum in the sanctuary, then

45. In Dossin's original translation (*ARM* 10.9), the water is mixed with a lintel and door posts. Frymer-Kensky takes the first of these as 'dust', following Moran. Sasson notes that the text is exceptional, since 'cuneiform literature only occasionally delineates the punishment meted out to contemptuous deities' (1982: 158).

46. Schmidt 1927, expanded in 1928.

47. Schmidt (1927: 150) lists: Pss. 4; 7; 11; 13; 17; 25; 28; 38; 39; 52; 54; 55; 56; 57; 58; 59; 77; 86; 88; 94; 102; 139; plus Hab. 1.1-5. Van der Toorn (1988: 428 n. 4) gives a slightly different list, in two subdivisions: primarily Pss. 3; 4; 5; 7; 17; 26; 27; 31A; 57; 139; 142; also 11; 13; 55A; 56; 59; 94B; 109; 140.

48. Eaton also notes Gunkel's opposition.

49. He retained Pss. 3; 4; 5; 7; 11; 17; 26; 27; 57; and added Pss. 23 and 63.

proceeds to 'the sacral process of judgment proper' including sacrifice, purification rites, incubation in the temple, and a morning verdict pronounced by a priest. However, Eaton (1989: 257) is no more convinced by Beyerlin than by Schmidt:

> The difficulties remain. The psalms in question do not refer with any clarity to such a special situation, and indeed refer to quite other matters (e.g. warfare in Ps. 3). Nothing in tradition points to such a use. The selected psalms do not stand out as a group from other psalms of conflict and entreaty.

Day is similarly unconvinced by both proposals: 'We simply lack the evidence to set the individual lament psalms against the institutional backgrounds that [these scholars] propose' (1990: 29).

2.3. *Van der Toorn: A Temple Drinking Ordeal is Reflected in the Psalms*
Van der Toorn (1988)[50] has recently revived this proposal of a Temple ordeal, with several modifications and one important new element. He focuses on several apparently distinctive aspects of the relevant psalms. First, this is clearly a nocturnal ordeal, since there are 'recurrent references to the sequence of sleeping and waking, a possibly perilous night followed by the long awaited morning' (p. 430). These occur notably in the following:

Ps. 17.3:	If you try my heart, if you visit me by night, if you test me, you will find no wickedness in me.
Ps. 17.15:	As for me, I shall behold your face in righteousness; when I awake I shall be satisfied, beholding your likeness.
Ps. 3.6 (ET 5):	I lie down and sleep; I wake again, for the Lord sustains me
Ps. 139.18:	I awake [margin reading]—I am still with you.
Ps. 4.9 (ET 8):	I will both lie down and sleep in peace; for you alone, O Lord, make me lie down in safety.
Ps. 57.9 (ET 8):	Awake, my soul! Awake, O harp and lyre! I will awake the dawn. (cf. 130.6)

Thus there is a severe nocturnal trial, and the psalmist is in danger of not waking up. Nevertheless, he eagerly anticipates his awaking and consequent acquittal. While the psalmist undergoes the ordeal alone, his accusers may also spend the night in the Temple, though in a different room, hence:

Ps. 57.5 (ET 4):	I lie down among lions that greedily devour human prey; their teeth are spears and arrows, their tongues sharp swords.
Ps. 4.5 (ET 4):	When you are disturbed, do not sin; ponder it on your beds, and be silent.[51]

Similarly, Ps. 5.5-7 (ET 4-6) insists that Yahweh 'destroy[s] those who speak lies' because 'the institutional setting of theses psalms was centered around an ordeal procedure in which the guilty could lose his life' (van der Toorn 1988: 432).

50. Partially summarized in his subsequent (1992) *ABD* entry 'Ordeal'.

51. Ps. 4 'seems to envisage a countercheck procedure by submitting the accusers to an ordeal' (van der Toorn 1988: 432 n. 17).

Secondly, 'In many of the psalms of the accused there is mention of 'beholding the face of the LORD', a *visio Dei* that seems to have coincided with the moment of exculpation' (van der Toorn 1988: 432). Texts cited are (p. 432 n. 18):[52]

Ps. 4.7 (ET 6):	...Let the light of your face shine upon us, O Lord.
Ps. 11.7:	...the upright shall behold his face.
Ps. 17.15:	...when I awake I shall be satisfied, beholding your likeness
Ps. 27.4, 8, 13:	...to behold the beauty of the Lord... Your face, Lord, do I seek...I believe that I shall see the goodness of the Lord in the land of the living.

This experience of God's presence occurred in the morning, and 'was granted only to those who had passed the night safely and were thus proved to be blameless' (van der Toorn 1988: 433). Some texts may be figurative (e.g. Pss. 27.14; 139.18): 'he "sees God", as he senses his nearness' (p. 434). However, the vivid language of Psalm 17 implies a dream theophany, which lingers as the psalmist awakes. The linking of theophany imagery with dawn suggests an 'associative connection' between Yahweh and the sun, as illustrated in terms like 'shine forth' and in the refrain of Ps. 57.6, 12 (ET 5, 11): 'Be exalted, O God, above the heavens. Let your glory be over all the earth.' When the sun rose on the psalmist, 'his trial had ended and he was shown "the path of life", as *coram Deo*, he was saturated with joy (Ps. xvi 11)' (p. 435).

Thirdly, the ordeal, which 'must be personal, potentially life-threatening and take at least several hours to operate' (van der Toorn 1988: 436) was a drinking ordeal with a noxious potion. This would be similar to the potion of Numbers 5, though with more immediate and stronger effect. Elsewhere in the Old Testament there are only allusions to water-drinking ordeals at Marah (Exod. 15.22-26) and following the golden calf idolatry (Exod. 32.20). But there is sufficient supportive evidence from elsewhere in the ancient Near East (see above). The Hebrew Bible testifies more frequently to a wine-drinking ordeal, in the many passages which describe God's cup of wrath. This was a cup full of poisonous wine. Several times in Jeremiah (Jer. 7.14; 9.14, ET 15; 23.15) 'God's punishments are metaphorically described as a trial by ordeal by means of which Israel's guilt is demonstrated' (1988: 439). So the 'cup' mentioned in several of the psalms considered (Pss. 11.6; 16.5; 23.6; cf. Ps. 116.13) is the ordeal itself, not a cup drunk subsequently in celebration (*pace* Beyerlin). '[T]he effect of the cup was dual: judgment upon the wicked, salvation for the righteous' (1988: 441). The cup was drunk as part of a sacrificial meal and was linked to an oath. 'We may therefore safely conclude that the drinking trial by means of wine...is in fact the nocturnal trial that was practised in the case of all the psalms of the accused with an institutional *Sitz im Leben*' (1988: 441-42).

Thus the 'juridico-religious procedure' took the following form for the accused (van der Toorn 1988: 435-36): a rite of purification, admission to the Temple, an oath of innocence (Pss. 7.4-6, ET 3-5; 17.3-5; 26.2; 63.12b, ET 11b), and a nocturnal drinking trial. If the accused survived, there was a morning declaration of innocence ('hearing God's word': Pss. 130.5; 143.8; more obliquely Pss. 3.5b,

52. He also compares Pss. 16.11; 73.20; 143.8; possibly Ps. 63.3 (ET 2).

ET 4b; 16.11a; 27.7b, 11a; cf. Zeph. 3.5) followed by thanksgiving offerings and songs of praise.[53]

2.4. *Is a Temple Drinking Ordeal Reflected in the Psalms?*
Van der Toorn's thesis has several attractive features, and in particular it provides a possible setting for the three striking elements highlighted: sleeping and waking, beholding Yahweh, and the cup. However, closer examination reveals weaknesses regarding each of these three elements as well as in his general approach.

To start with methodology, van der Toorn highlights elements from a number of psalms to illustrate the ordeal procedure. However, unlike Schmidt and Beyerlin, he does not provide a list of psalms thought to reflect this procedure. Some psalms apparently reflect the ordeal directly, perhaps others more obliquely, but no such differentiation is developed. The various psalms quoted can be put in some order of importance, with the most frequently cited as the key psalms (notably Pss. 4, 11 and 17), but this work is left to the reader.[54]

More importantly, no exegesis is provided, even of the most frequently quoted psalms, to show whether the ordeal is reflected in the overall structure and text of the psalm as well as in particular verses. Such exegesis is essential to substantiate the argument presented. So in our assessment we begin by glancing at the first few psalms cited (in canonical order), which include some often cited and therefore key psalms.

There seem to be five crucial elements to the ordeal, as proposed: (1) false accusation, possibly implied by a declaration of innocence; (2) entrance into the Temple; (3) drinking the cup, or at least undergoing a nocturnal trial; (4) spending the night in the Temple; (5) being acquitted, possibly implied by waking, beholding Yahweh in the morning, or a statement of vindication. How well do the proposed psalms reflect these elements?

Psalm 3 has clear references only to sleeping and waking. It mentions foes all around, but no accusation. God answers from his holy hill, but nothing indicates that the psalmist is there, or undergoes any form of trial. So there are two elements of the five. Psalm 3 actually looks like a pre-battle prayer, with the psalmist entreating Yahweh to be his shield against the thousands of enemies, and wanting a good night's sleep before hostilities break out.

Psalm 4 also mentions sleep, but this is the only clear element. Two others are plausible: the mention of lies (v. 3, ET 2) could imply accusations, and prayer to experience the light of Yahweh's face (v. 7, ET 6) could well anticipate vindication. But whether 'right sacrifices' (v. 6, ET 5) imply an oath of innocence, or whether the command to ponder silently on beds is addressed to the accusers elsewhere in the Temple, is less obvious. There is no explicit indication of an

53. Van der Toorn further suggests that the food and drink of the Passover also constituted an ordeal; and that this is later echoed in Paul's description of unworthy partaking of the Lord's supper as 'eating and drinking judgment' on oneself (1 Cor. 11.27-30). This falls outside our immediate concern.

54. Psalms cited: Pss. 3; 4; 5; 11; 17; 26; 27; 55; 57; 139. Psalms noted for comparison: Pss. 16; 73; 80; 143.

ordeal or of overnight presence in the Temple. Instead, the psalmist testifies to great gladness of heart (v. 8, ET 7), a somewhat unexpected emotion if his life is in danger.

Psalm 5 has an opening reference to Yahweh's attentiveness in the morning (v. 4, ET 3) and explicit reference to entering the Temple. But there is no mention of accusation, drinking ordeal or sleeping. So again there are two elements. Psalm 5 reads more like a general prayer for deliverance from enemies, though in less military terms. The posited indices of an ordeal reference are not only meagre; they actually suggest otherwise. In v. 4 (ET 3) the morning is not a time of vindication, but rather of renewed prayer and waiting; and the visit to the Temple is not for the purposes of a trial, but is prompted by Yahweh's love.

Psalm 11 opens with taking refuge in Yahweh, which could mean in the Temple, since it proceeds to note that Yahweh is there. He tests the righteous and wicked, and gives the latter a cup of judgment. Since Yahweh is righteous, the upright will behold his face. Thus there are possible references to Temple, trial and vindication. But there is no hint of false accusation, or of sleeping and waking. This means there are possibly two elements. However, the author takes refuge from ambush and murder, rather than slander, and Yahweh's judgment on the enemies involves firestones and scorching wind, not death in their sleep.

Finally Psalm 17, the most quoted, begins with a plea which implies the psalmist's innocence. It then envisages a nocturnal test, calling for protection for the writer and punishment of his enemies. It concludes with a repeated reference to a morning vision: 'I shall behold your face...beholding your righteousness'. This gives three, perhaps four elements. Of all those cited, this psalm comes closest to indicating the ordeal procedure envisaged. However, even Psalm 17 does not immediately suggest a drinking ordeal in the Temple. There is no reference to the Temple, unless the concluding vision is assumed to occur there. The enemies are characterized as violent despoilers rather than as false accusers. The psalmist avers truthfulness, but not innocence of a supposed crime. As before, the desired fate for the enemies is not nocturnal death but an overthrow which includes their children. In sum, the psalmist prays for vindication and invites God to try him during the night. He calls for vengeance on his enemies, and looks forward to seeing God in the morning. This prayer could reflect an ordeal. But it could equally well reflect a beleaguered psalmist in a non-cultic setting, longing for vindication from his enemies and reassurance from his God.

	Drinking Ordeal Elements	*Ps. 3*	*Ps. 4*	*Ps. 5*	*Ps. 11*	*Ps. 17*
1.	Accusation		(+)			
	Declare innocence		?			(+)
2.	Presence in Temple		?	+	(+)	
3.	Cup				?	
	Test/trial				+	+
4.	Sleep/night	+	+			+
5.	Wake/morning	+		+		+
	Behold Yahweh		(+)		+	+
	Declare vindication					
	Other: Enemies' ordeal		?			

2.5. *Is a Temple Drinking Ordeal Reflected in the Various Elements Noted?* As noted above, van der Toorn's article highlights three elements in particular of what he himself admits, in a telling aside, is an 'enigmatic ordeal procedure' (1988: 440). First, he argues that sleeping and waking imply a nocturnal ordeal, especially when linked with trial by night. But such a link only occurs in Psalm 17. Elsewhere there is little further suggestion that sleeping securely and waking safely imply a judicial ordeal. If one assumes that a cultic setting lies behind each psalm, then sleeping and waking could be oblique references to such an ordeal. But this is a major assumption.

Secondly, he suggests that a morning vision of God is an expression of judicial vindication. This could be the case, but this is not a compelling interpretation either of the relevant verses or of their context. Three of the four psalms cited in this connection have already been discussed above. The other, Psalm 27, certainly illustrates the importance to psalmists of this imagery, whatever it denotes. But it also illustrates the multiplicity of its uses. The psalm has elements which in a different context might reflect the ordeal, but not here. The enemies use weapons, not lies. The Temple is a place of refuge, not of trial. And the desired vision is not linked to the morning, or even to vindication more generally.

Similarly for the *visio Dei* in several psalms noted for comparison. Psalm 16 has a cup, a night encounter and a joyful experience of God's presence. But the cup is expressly Yahweh himself, not some noxious potion, with parallels illustrating this in terms of apportioned land. The night encounter is one of instruction, not approbation. And the experience of God is to be 'forever' (*neṣaḥ*), not just the next morning. Psalm 63 contrasts a sanctuary *visio Dei* (whether past or future) with current experience, but not in an ordeal context. The psalmist longs for God and for rescue, but not explicitly for vindication. And his nocturnal meditation is again joyful, not fearful. Psalm 73 refers to entering the sanctuary, and implies encountering God there, but in the context of pondering the prosperity of the wicked.[55] These psalms show that the motif of seeing or experiencing God occurs in a variety of contexts, and does not particularly suggest vindication following a nocturnal ordeal.

Thirdly and most importantly, there is the cup, the central element in the reconstructed drinking ordeal. The Hebrew term *kôs* occurs rather infrequently outside the psalms: occasionally of a specific physical cup,[56] more frequently in prophetic references to a figurative cup for the wicked.[57] It will herald their ruin; they will drink it to the dregs, stagger and fall. However, these passages strongly imply a cup of judgment, not of trial. There is no sense in which the cup will test those who drink. Rather, they have already been judged guilty, and drinking the

55. Van der Toorn (1988: 433 n. 18) may have cited v. 20 mistakenly, since it refers not to a vision of God but rather to the enemies vanishing as do dreamt characters on awakening.

56. Gen. 40.11 (3 times), 13, 21; 2 Sam. 12.3; 1 Kgs 7.26//2 Chron. 4.5; Prov. 23.32; Jer. 35.5.

57. Isa. 51.17 (twice), 22 (twice); Jer. 25.15, 17, 28; 49.12; 51.7; Lam. 4.21; Ezek. 23.31, 32, 33 (twice); Hab. 2.16. Note expressions: 'cup of consolation' (Jer. 16.7), 'cup of wrath', 'cup of staggering' (Isa. 51.17, 22; Jer. 25.15), 'cup of horror and desolation' (Ezek. 23.33).

cup signifies the onset of their punishment. This is a metaphor not of trial by ordeal, but of sentence following indictment.

There are only five references to a 'cup' in the psalms:

Ps. 11.6:	On the wicked he will rain coals of fire and sulphur; a scorching wind shall be the portion of their cup.
Ps. 16.5:	The Lord is my chosen portion and my cup…
Ps. 23.5:	…my cup overflows.
Ps. 75.9 (ET 8):	For in the hand of the Lord there is a cup… and all the wicked of the earth shall drain it…
Ps. 116.13:	I will lift up the cup of salvation…

Of these, two clearly echo prophetic condemnation of the wicked. In one (Ps. 11.6), the cup consists of scorching wind and burning coals; in the other (Ps. 75.9, ET 8), there is a clear contrast between righteous and wicked, and only the latter drink the cup. Again, this is judgment, not adjudication. Two others speak of a cup which symbolizes blessing. In one (Ps. 16.5), the psalmist chooses Yahweh as his 'cup'; in the other (Ps. 23.5), his cup overflows. Neither image fits a drinking ordeal. And in the fifth text (Ps. 116.13), the psalmist lifts a 'cup of salvation', in response to deliverance. This suggests most naturally a libation offering during the thanksgiving sacrifice (v. 17) in celebration of deliverance already experienced,[58] not a cup to determine whether deliverance would even occur.

Thus the crucial element of the posited Temple drinking ordeal, the cup with its potion, remains conjectural. The few psalmic references to a cup do not refer to a noxious cup drunk as part of a judicial ordeal, including a meal, sacrifice and oath. Instead, these references indicate judgment already determined for the wicked, or blessing already experienced by the righteous.

2.6. *Conclusion*

The concept of a Temple ordeal has waxed and waned since first proposed by Schmidt. Van der Toorn's reworking of it with the added component of drinking a noxious potion draws together various indices from the psalms into a coherent and initially plausible whole. If the relevant psalms necessarily have a cultic *Sitz im Leben* of composition, then these indices could reflect a judicial ordeal, albeit obliquely. But this assumption is an artificial straight-jacket to interpretation. Most of the psalms cited, when studied on their own, give little hint of a judicial background. Even Psalm 17, the strongest example, is not particularly convincing. And the crucial component of the proposed ordeal, the cup with its determinative potion, is notable by its absence from the psalter.

Thus we can conclude overall that there are no obvious echoes of a cosmic river ordeal or of Temple drinking ordeals. The psalms certainly contain many references to ordeals in the general sense of difficult circumstances, but not to ordeals in the technical sense of supra-rational judicial procedures.

58. Cf. Yehawmilk of Byblos lifting up a libation cup before the goddess Ba'alat (B.W. Anderson 2000: 110, erroneously referenced; *ANEP*, pl. 477; *ANET*, 656). I thank John Day for this reference.

BIBLIOGRAPHY

Albright, W.F.
1936 'Zabûl Yam and Thâpiṭ Nahar in the Combat between Baal and the Sea', *JPOS* 16: 17-20.

Andersen, F.I.
1976 *Job* (TOTC; Leicester: IVP).

Anderson, A.A.
1972 *Psalms* (2 vols.; NCB; London: Oliphants).

Anderson, B.W.
2000 *Out of the Depths* (Louisville, KY: Westminster/John Knox Press, 3rd edn).

Beyerlin, W.
1970 *Die Rettung der Bedrängten in den Feindpsalmen der Einzelnen auf institutionelle Zusammenhänge untersucht* (FRLANT, 99; Göttingen: Vandenhöck & Ruprecht).

Bottéro, J.
1981 'L'ordalie en Mésopotamie ancienne', *Annali della Scuola normale superiore di Pisa, Classe di lettere e filosofia* 11.4: 1105-67.

Cardascia, G.
1967 'L'ordalie par le fleuve dans les "Lois Assyriennes"', in G. Wiessner (ed.), *Festschrift für Wilhelm Eilers* (Wiesbaden: Otto Harrassowitz): 19-36.

Clifford, R.J.
1972 *The Cosmic Mountain in Canaan and the Old Testament* (HSM, 4; Cambridge, MA: Harvard University Press).

Craigie, P.C.
1983 *Psalms 1–50* (WBC, 19; Waco, TX: Word Books).

Curtis, A.H.W.
1988 'God as "Judge" in Ugaritic and Hebrew Thought', in B. Lindars (ed.), *Law and Religion* (Cambridge: James Clarke & Co.): 3-12.

Day, J.
1990 *Psalms* (OTG; Sheffield: JSOT Press).

Dossin, G.
1939 'Un cas d'ordalie par le dieu fleuve d'après une lette de Mari', in J. Friedrich, J.G. Lautner and J. Miles (eds.), *Symbolae ad iura orientis antiqui pertinentes Paulo Koschaker dedicatae* (Leiden: E.J. Brill): 112-18.
1958 'L'ordalie à Mari', *CRAIBL*: 387-93.

Eaton, J.H.
1989 'The Psalms and Israelite Worship', in G.W. Anderson (ed.), *Tradition and Interpretation* (Oxford: Clarendon Press): 238-73.

Fohrer, G.
1989 *Das Buch Hiob* (KAT, 16; Gütersloh: Gerd Mohn, 2nd edn).

Frymer, T.S.
1976 'Ordeal', in *IDBSup*: 638-40.

Frymer-Kensky, T.S.
1977 'The Judicial Ordeal in the Ancient Near East' (unpublished PhD dissertation, Yale University).
1981 'Suprarrational Legal Procedures in Elam and Nuzi', in M.A. Morrison and D.I. Owen (eds.), *Studies on the Civilization and Culture of Nuzi and the Hurrians in Honor of Ernest R. Lacheman* (Winona Lake, IN: Eisenbrauns): 115-31.

1983 'The Tribulations of Marduk: The So-Called "Marduk Ordeal Tablet"', *JAOS* 103: 131-41.

1984 'The Strange Case of the Suspected Sotah (Numbers v 11-31)', *VT* 34: 11-26.

Gordis, R.

1978 *The Book of Job* (New York: Jewish Theological Seminary of America).

Grabbe, L.L.

1977 *Comparative Philology and the Text of Job* (SBLDS, 34; Missoula, MT: Scholars Press).

Habel, N.C.

1985 *The Book of Job* (OTL; London: SCM Press).

Hartley, J.E.

1988 *The Book of Job* (NICOT; Grand Rapids: Eerdmans).

Jacobsen, T.

1970 *Toward the Image of Tammuz* (HSS, 21; Cambridge, MA: Harvard University Press).

Johnson, A.R.

1951 'The Psalms', in H.H. Rowley (ed.), *The Old Testament and Modern Study* (Oxford: Clarendon Press): 169-202.

Johnston, P.S.

1993 'The Underworld and the Dead in the Old Testament' (unpublished PhD dissertation, Cambridge University).

Kapelrud, A.S.

1980 'The Relationship between El and Baal in the Ras Shamra Texts', in G. Rendsburg, R. Adler, M. Arfa and N.H. Winter (eds.), *The Bible World: Essays in Honor of Cyrus H. Gordon* (New York: Ktav): 79-85.

Keel, O.

1972 *Die Welt der altorientalischen Bildsymbolik und das Alte Testament* (Zürich: Benziger Verlag; Neukirchen–Vluyn: Neukirchener Verlag). ET *The Symbolism of the Biblical World* (trans. T.J. Hallett; London: SPCK, 1978).

Kraus, H.-J.

1978 *Die Psalmen 60–150* (BKAT, 15.2; Neukirchen–Vluyn: Neukirchener Verlag, 5th edn). ET *Psalms 60–150* (trans. H.C. Oswald; Minneapolis: Augsburg, 1989).

1979 *Theologie der Psalmen* (BKAT, 15.3; Neukirchen–Vluyn: Neukirchener Verlag). ET *Theology of the Psalms* (trans. K. Crim; Minneapolis: Augsburg, 1986).

Lambert, W.G.

1960 *Babylonian Wisdom Literature* (Oxford: Clarendon Press).

1965 'Nebuchadnezzar King of Justice', *Iraq* 27: 1-11.

McCarter, P.K.

1973 'The River Ordeal in Israelite Literature', *HTR* 66: 403-12.

Mullen, E.T.

1980 *The Assembly of the Gods: The Divine Council in Canaanite and Early Hebrew Literature* (HSM, 24; Chico, CA: Scholars Press).

Owen, D.I.

1988 'A Unique Late Sargonic River Ordeal in the John Frederick Lewis Collection', in E. Leichty, M. de J. Ellis and P. Gerardi (eds.), *A Scientific Humanist: Studies in Memory of Abraham Sachs* (Philadelphia: University Museum): 305-10.

Pope, M.H.

1955 *El in the Ugaritic Texts* (VTSup, 2; Leiden: E.J. Brill).

Rosenberg, R.
1981 'The Concept of Biblical Sheol within the Context of Ancient Near Eastern Beliefs' (unpublished PhD dissertation, Harvard University).
Ross, A.P.
1997 'נָהָר', in *NIDOTTE*, III: 46-51.
Rowley, H.H.
1976 *The Book of Job* (NCB; London: Marshall, Morgan & Scott, 2nd edn).
Sæbø, M.
1970 'Die hebräischen Nomina *'êd* und *'ēd*', *ST* 24: 130-41.
1971 'איד *'êd* Unglück', in *THAT*, I: 122-25; ET *TLOT*, I: 92-93.
Santos, E.C. dos
n.d. *An Expanded Hebrew Index for the Hatch–Redpath Concordance to the Septuagint* (Jerusalem: Dugith).
Sarna, N.M.
1989 *Genesis* בראשית (JPS Torah Commentary; Philadelphia: Jewish Publication Society of America).
Sasson, J.M.
1982 'An Apocalyptic Vision From Mari?', *MARI* 1: 151-67.
2001 *Ancient Laws and Modern Problems* (London: Third Millennium Publishing).
Sasson, J.M., *et al.* (eds.)
1995 *Civilizations of the Ancient Near East* (New York: Charles Scribner's Sons).
Schmidt, H.
1927 'Das Gebet der Angeklagten im Alten Testament', in *Old Testament Essays* (London: Charles Griffin & Co.): 143-55. Reprinted in P.H.A. Neumann (ed.), *Zur neueren Psalmenforshung* (Darmstadt: Wissenschaftiche Buchgesellschaft, 1976): 156-67.
1928 *Das Gebet der Angeklagten im Alten Testament* (BZAW, 49; Giessen: Alfred Töpelmann).
Soden, W. von
1955 'Gibt es ein Zeugnis dafür, daß die Babylonier an die Wiederauferstehung Marduks geglaubt haben?', *ZA* 51: 130-66.
1985 *Einführung in die Altorientalistik* (Darmstadt: Wissenschaftliche Buchgesellschaft). ET *The Ancient Orient* (trans. D.G. Schley; Grand Rapids: Eerdmans, 1994).
Tate, M.E.
1990 *Psalms 51–100* (WBC, 20; Dallas: Word Books).
Toorn, K. van der
1988 'Ordeal Procedures in the Psalms and the Passover Meal', *VT* 38: 427-45.
1992 'Ordeal', in *ABD*, V: 40-42.
Van Dam, C.
1997 'איד', in *NIDOTTE*, I: 371.
Wallace, H.N.
1985 *The Eden Narrative* (HSM, 32; Atlanta: Scholars Press).
Ward, E.F. de
1977 'Superstition and Judgment: Archaic Methods of Finding a Verdict', *ZAW* 89: 1-19.
Wenham, G.J.
1987 *Genesis 1–15* (WBC, 1; Dallas: Word Books).
Westermann, C.
1974 *Genesis 1–11* (BKAT, 1.1; Neukirchen–Vluyn: Neukirchener Verlag). ET *Genesis 1–11* (trans. J.J. Scullion; Minneapolis: Augsburg, 1984).

WISDOM PSALMS

Stuart Weeks

Some seventy years after Hermann Gunkel first suggested the existence of a category 'wisdom psalm' (Gunkel and Begrich 1933: 381-97, ET 1998: 293-398) most scholars writing on the subject continue to recognize that certain psalms belong to this genre, but little or no consensus has been achieved either in establishing criteria for membership, or, correspondingly, in identifying a list of wisdom psalms. As a consequence, studies of both the wisdom literature and the psalms have had to contend with a concept that describes neither a definition of form or content, nor any fixed body of material. Norman Whybray has quite rightly noted that 'To write about "the wisdom psalms" is...somewhat akin to making bricks without straw...' (Whybray 1995: 152).

This lack of consensus arises directly from a more basic disagreement about the meaning of the term 'wisdom', which is variously used to refer to a body of literature, a set of ideas and a presumed historical movement. As a result, the psalms in question—and other texts, for that matter—are granted or denied the designation 'wisdom' for different reasons by different scholars, and a 'wisdom psalm', correspondingly, may have been designated as such for any of the following reasons: (1) it uses words, expressions or forms and techniques associated with one or more of the Old Testament wisdom books; (2) it presumes or displays an interest in themes and ideas associated with those books; (3) it is apparently didactic in nature, and can thus be linked to the pedagogical *Sitz im Leben* with which the authors of wisdom literature are themselves often associated.

Although none of these criteria is generally used in isolation, let us for the moment consider each separately as an approach to the issue. Although the most technical, the first, which involves identifying features of a wisdom style, has arguably been the most influential—perhaps because it has an attractive air of objectivity, and seems to offer evidence which is as much statistical as exegetical. A typical example is offered by Kenneth Kuntz's article on wisdom psalms (Kuntz 1974), which draws on R.B.Y. Scott's earlier tabulation of some seventy-seven words supposedly constituting characteristic wisdom vocabulary (Scott 1971: 121), and which also considers 'seven distinct features of psalmic wisdom which may be classified as being rhetorical in character'. These features are: the 'better is *x* than *y*' saying; the numerical saying; the admonition; the direct address to 'sons'; the 'happy is...' saying with *'ašrê*; the rhetorical question; and the simile.

Some of the weaknesses in all this are obvious from the start, and are partly acknowledged even by Kuntz. Taking the 'rhetorical' features first, it is difficult to maintain that any of them are usually, let alone exclusively, features of wisdom literature. Rhetorical questions, for instance, are more common in the prophetic books, and similes are just a common feature of poetic style, as their frequent use in Song of Songs shows clearly. It is similarly difficult to maintain, on grounds of their distribution, that the 'better is…', 'happy is…', or numerical sayings are in some way the exclusive possession of wisdom literature. Indeed, attempts to define them as such frequently end up in circular argumentation, with scholars attempting to show that their use elsewhere is a sign of wisdom influence. Admonitions present a rather different problem, since they have no distinctive form or content of their own: an 'admonition' is simply a command or exhortation, the general character of which is determined by understandings of the context. To say that something is a 'wisdom admonition' is, therefore, not an argument, as such, for wisdom character or influence, but a simple pre-judgment of the issue. Of Kuntz's rhetorical features, then, only the address to sons can usefully be characterized as an element specifically derived from a certain type of wisdom literature. Whether its presence therefore indicates a wisdom character is another matter, but this hardly requires lengthy discussion, as such an address only occurs once in the Psalter anyway (Ps. 34.12).

In passing, we may observe that, if the specific forms noted by Kuntz are unsatisfactory, there is no good reason to suppose that other, better ones can be identified. There is a more general problem here, representing a tendency, by no means confined to Kuntz's article, to believe that wisdom discourse can be recognized from, or even defined in terms of its smallest component parts. That tendency originates in form-critical assumptions about the *Sitz im Leben* of particular forms, and is inextricably linked with attempts to define wisdom through its setting. For the purposes of literary classification, it is of limited usefulness: few, if any types of literature can be defined satisfactorily in such fragmentary terms, and the known types of wisdom composition are no exception.[1] While it may be true that some types of saying or modes of expression are associated with recognized genres—and the direct address to 'sons' may well be an evocation of the classic instruction genre—such associations do not themselves constitute definitions.

Rather different problems beset the use of vocabulary as a guide to the wisdom character of texts, and many scholars have taken a very cautious attitude to this approach, noting significant problems raised both by the association of

1. The point becomes clearer if we look at two types of composition which have strong and obvious association with wisdom literature. The first, 'instructions', present themselves as speeches addressed by one individual to another, whom they are instructing—most commonly the individuals are father and son. The instruction's content has no fixed form or topic. The second type, 'sayings collections', present no such specific context, but instead select, arrange, and probably sometimes compose individual units to create longer poems. It is important to be clear that the individual units are not really the point of these compositions, and that sayings collections are not simple anthologies: the musical concepts of a medley or of sampling are probably closer, and the whole is intended to be greater than the sum of its parts. The units in sayings collections are often irregular in form and length (as in the short collection of Prov. 24.23-34), and may vary considerably in other respects also.

vocabulary with subject matter, and the importance of context for meaning.[2] Such broader considerations aside, there is a more practical problem, in that many of the expressions used to isolate a supposed wisdom style are actually quite common terms. Scott's list includes words like *derek* and *lēb*, so it is little surprise that, when he uses that list, Kuntz ends up rejecting the wisdom character of some psalms despite the presence of many of Scott's words within them.

Some of the sharpest criticism on this point has actually come from Avi Hurvitz (1988), who himself advocates the use of vocabulary for detecting wisdom psalms, but on a much more careful and restricted basis. By finding examples of terms which are used in the wisdom books, but not generally by other books even in very similar contexts, Hurvitz avoids the worst pitfalls of this approach to show persuasively that, for instance, the expression 'turn away from evil' is characteristically a formulation of wisdom literature (pp. 47-49). Even this careful analysis does not, however, offer a panacaea. Because simple coincidence can play a role in the distribution of synonyms or synonymous idioms, Hurvitz's method is only appropriate when we have a fairly substantial collection of texts to compare, and a very marked tendency for one expression to appear principally in the wisdom books. The list of secure examples, therefore, is never going to be very long. More importantly, perhaps, our ignorance of differences in nuance between expressions, and problems of relative dating, make it extremely difficult even to prepare lists of equivalent expressions from which to derive such 'wisdom vocabulary'.

In general, then, attempts to identify wisdom psalms through the enumeration of supposed wisdom forms and expressions are only ever likely to offer quite slender returns. Even if this approach may be able to highlight a small number of secure links with wisdom literature, moreover, it can offer little or no information about the significance of those links, working as it does with such small components of the text.

I originally mentioned three approaches in the quest for wisdom psalms. The other two can be dealt with more briefly. First, thematic criteria for wisdom texts are, if anything, more difficult to establish than forms and expressions, not least because there remain considerable differences of opinion about the themes and ideas of the individual wisdom books. Even were consensus to be achieved, however, we would still face substantial problems of definition. We cannot call something a 'wisdom theme', in any exclusive sense, just because it appears in wisdom literature, even if it appears several times. Were we to do so, then weights and measures, for instance, would be a 'wisdom theme', and we would be talking about the wisdom influence on Ezekiel.[3] If, on the other hand, a wisdom theme has to appear in all the wisdom books, and almost exclusively in those books, then we would have few, if any, such themes. There is a more

2. Crenshaw (1969: 133), for example, observes that, 'When one recognizes that wisdom is rooted in experience, it should be no surprise to discover a common vocabulary among sage, prophet, and priest'. Murphy (1967: 104), noting that the significance of words can shift and change between contexts, makes the rather different point that 'Wisdom language does not constitute wisdom'.

3. Prov. 11.1; 16.11; 20.10, 23. Cf. Deut. 25.13-16; Amos 8.5; Ezek. 45.10.

promising approach in this general area, which I shall consider shortly. For the moment, though, one can say that there are considerable methodological obstacles facing the identification of 'wisdom themes'.

The third of the approaches outlined earlier essentially relies on the identification of a didactic purpose in texts, which permits them to be associated with the presumed didactic purpose and pedagogical setting of wisdom literature. Even leaving aside the considerable historical questions involved, this approach is probably the least satisfactory of all, not least because it requires its own criteria for identifying what is didactic. At one extreme, almost any literature, inasmuch as it involves the communication of ideas, can be called didactic; at the other, it is hard to find precise criteria which allow one to distinguish between wisdom literature and, say, law in this respect. Since the parameters are generally drawn broadly enough to include Job, and the anti-didacticism of Ecclesiastes, descriptions of a text as 'didactic' are rarely more than assertions about its purpose based on quite different criteria.

Behind the whole discussion of wisdom psalms, and relevant to all of these approaches, there is a more fundamental problem, which has generally received less attention: the meaning of the term 'wisdom', when it is applied to texts. 'Wisdom literature' is an old designation, received into modern scholarship essentially as a description of the biblical wisdom books, but now also tied to theories about the origin of those books, and to understandings of the Hebrew word *ḥokmâ* itself. Rather than achieving a more precise definition through its use in scholarship, therefore, the epithet 'wisdom' has become increasingly vague and ambiguous, to the point where it can be used to describe folk proverbs, at one extreme, and ancient scientific or divinatory literature, at the other. The problems involved in identifying wisdom psalms stem not just from technical disputes about methodology, but from the basic lack of definition which also characterizes more general discussions of wisdom.

Before turning to the psalms themselves, therefore, I want to attempt to pin down a reasonable working definition of 'wisdom' as a literary classification, which will at least permit us to derive criteria for the description of texts as 'wisdom literature', and which should clarify just what we mean by such a description. It is a commonplace of modern literary criticism, of course, that genre is not something inherent in texts, so much as something imposed by scholars categorizing texts. That assertion needs to be qualified by the recognition that, for various reasons, writers frequently seek to compose works which conform to particular specifications. The general point is an important one, though: when we seek to define wisdom literature we are creating a classification based on our own criteria, and selecting those criteria to meet our own needs. Let me be clear from the outset, then, that I consider the most useful definition of wisdom literature to be one which can at once incorporate the books of Job and Ecclesiastes, along with the various works collected together in Proverbs, and at the same time distinguish them from other major types of biblical literature. To say that a psalm, or some other text, fits that definition, is therefore to say that it shares whatever distinctive characteristics are shared by the three principal wisdom books.

It is also important to be clear that this definition need not be based on ancient perceptions of genre; indeed, given the scanty evidence for such perceptions, that is anyway unlikely to be a practical way of proceeding. It is perhaps, though, worth spelling out what little we can say. Instructions and sayings collections, two of the most familiar types of composition associated with wisdom literature, are closely related; indeed, many instructions are also sayings collections. The very character of the book of Proverbs, in which the two genres are brought together, along with a small amount of other advice literature, would seem to indicate that they were actively regarded as belonging together. That book, furthermore, links them to the concept of wisdom, not least through the attributions in Prov. 22.17 and 24.23, and the association is further affirmed by Ecclesiastes, both in the epilogue (Eccl. 12.11-12) and in the apparent parody of sayings collections as a source of wisdom (especially Eccl. 7.1-14; 9.17–11.6). Insofar as we can determine an ancient concept of 'wisdom literature', then, it seems to have been linked to the sort of material which we find in Proverbs, primarily sayings collections and instructions. It is impossible to say whether Job, in particular, would have been associated closely with this material, or how Ecclesiastes would have been considered to relate to it. We can observe, though, that it is difficult to locate any concept of a canon of wisdom literature extending beyond Proverbs in Ben Sira or other early Jewish thought,[4] and it seems probable that 'wisdom literature', if it had any meaning at all, would have been taken to be equivalent to 'advice literature'. The ancient classification, so far as we can determine it, is unlikely therefore to prove a suitable basis for our modern one.

That basis is even more unlikely to be found in any proposed *Sitz im Leben* for the literature: even setting aside the problems involved in establishing the existence of an associated movement or context, which I have discussed at length elsewhere (Weeks 1994), little or no literature is usefully defined by its origin in that way.[5]

It is also improbable that a secure definition of wisdom can be founded in any classification of texts by form, although this is a more difficult area. To be sure, some types of composition, such as the instruction, are unique to, or at least strongly associated with the wisdom books in the Old Testament. No one of those books, however, consists entirely of such material, nor does any single such genre characterize all of the wisdom books. While it is possible, then, that we might be able to classify some materials in terms of their wisdom associations, it is difficult to see how we might base an understanding of wisdom literature simply on the formal character of those materials. If we try to define 'wisdom' in this way, we are liable to end up rejecting large parts of each wisdom book, and possibly entire books.

4. As acknowledged by Sheppard 1980: 14-15.

5. Moshe Weinfeld (1972) recognized the problem when he claimed that Deuteronomy shared an origin with wisdom literature, but was not itself wisdom literature; it is probably true, correspondingly, that most scholars would oppose using the term 'wisdom' to describe any surviving administrative documents or teaching materials (such as, for example, the lists of numerals from Kadesh-barnea). Conversely, it seems unlikely that the wisdom designation would be stripped from, say, a section of Proverbs which proved to have originated in quite different circles.

As regards content, we have already seen that the quest for individual wisdom topics raises serious problems of method. There is, however, a broader approach, which offers possibilities. It has long been observed that wisdom literature has a distinctive lack of interest in some of the themes which characterize most other books of the Old Testament, including the history, origins and election of the people, or the covenant and the cult. We might bundle those themes together, indeed, and say that wisdom literature has no specific interest in the relationship between God and his people. That absence is not in itself a useful way of defining wisdom literature. As later texts demonstrate, there is nothing inherent in wisdom literature which precludes consideration of such themes. Equally, to use their absence to define wisdom literature is to admit into the wisdom canon such diverse works as Esther and Song of Songs. What we can say more usefully, though, is that wisdom shows little interest in the relationship between God and people because its primary focus is upon the fate of individuals, not nations. Of course, such an interest in the individual is not itself a wholly distinctive feature of wisdom literature. Wisdom literature's interest, however, can be described more precisely as an interest in the fate of individuals: both the ways in which those individuals are able to shape their future, and the extent to which they are able to do so. Associated with this interest, of course, is a concern with the guidance which individuals can receive, and the authoritativeness of that guidance.

At a basic level, these concerns can be manifested in specific advice about actions which can lead to personal success or failure in particular contexts, but that is only a minor concern in the biblical wisdom books. Within Proverbs, such specific advice coexists with a more substantial quantity of material, in which proper behaviour is commended but not defined. Job and Ecclesiastes, on the other hand, appear to doubt the possibility of learning such proper behaviour as a way of ensuring personal security and prosperity. For Job, this is arguably because the existence of guaranteed results for good behaviour would imply that God could somehow be coerced by humans; for Ecclesiastes, the problem seems similarly to lie in the power of God to do as he wishes, although the book places greater emphasis on the deliberate hiddenness of those wishes, and the absurdity of human attempts to discern them.

Let me be clear, then, that I am not suggesting a definition for wisdom literature that is based on some particular view of how humans should behave: the wisdom books share a common interest in the subject matter, but not a common outlook on it. It is reasonable to ask, though, whether this shared interest does not also imply a shared world-view or theology, so that we can talk of 'wisdom thought' as a distinct entity. It might well be argued that, against a backdrop of historical and prophetic literature, an interest in the individual represents quite a distinctive religious perspective. More particularly, none of the wisdom books seems to consider that the divine will might be mediated through prophecy or the cult, and all of them seem unusually interested in the role of God as creator. Even without speculation based on historical context or presumed foreign influence, a good case can be made for positing the existence of a distinctive wisdom perspective. If so, should that perspective not itself be considered the defining characteristic of wisdom literature?

Biblical scholarship has long since moved on from the idea that Deuteronomistic ideas of theology somehow define Israelite religion, and that 'true' Yahwism must always necessarily have revolved around notions of salvation history or covenant. It is still important, however, to stress that much of the historical and prophetic literature thus deemed normative for Israelite religious thought was composed to meet specific needs, and that those needs probably related to communal, national issues. We cannot assume that the same emphases would have characterized day-to-day religious thought and practice, much of which was surely orientated toward the needs of individuals. The wisdom literature which we have was not obviously composed to meet those needs directly, but its concerns are with that aspect of religion. Where Deuteronomy, say, is broadly concerned with how the community and its members must behave to ensure the survival and prosperity of the people, the wisdom literature is concerned with how individuals discover what they should do to survive and prosper in their own, individual lives, or with exhorting them to follow the guidance which they have received. These are different spheres, but not necessarily contradictory ones, as later wisdom literature, and, perhaps, some parts of Proverbs show. The wisdom literature's interest in individuals, then, need hardly be understood as an expression of heterodox Yahwism: if anything, it probably lies closer to the core business of that religion than do the historical analyses which make up much of the rest of the Old Testament. It need not even, moreover, be understood as evidence for some separate group of authors, unless we seriously wish to assert that someone interested in the religion as a national religion could not also be interested in it as a personal one.

This difference in focus between wisdom and certain other biblical texts may go some way toward explaining a number of the peculiarities which have been identified as products of 'wisdom thought'. We cannot examine that subject in great detail here, but the most significant such idea commonly associated with wisdom literature is that of a creation theology, in which God's role as creator is emphasized instead of his role as national deity of Israel. The waters around this topic have been muddied by spurious claims about inherent retribution or the influence of Egyptian concepts, but the idea originates in a quite proper perception that much of the biblical wisdom literature shows a strong interest in creation. Creation themes, however, are used in different ways by different wisdom books, and their usages do not together self-evidently constitute any single, coherent idea.[6] At best they show creation to be a popular motif in wisdom

6. Prov. 1–9, for instance, uses the place of wisdom in creation to emphasize the close relationship between wisdom and God, and thus the authoritativeness of wisdom in matters regarding the divine will. Job, on the other hand, uses God's creation of the world in the divine speeches, principally to demonstrate divine power and independence, in a way very reminiscent of Second Isaiah; in ch. 28 there is some emphasis on divine power and perspicacity, but the principal point is God's control and monopoly over wisdom from the outset. Ecclesiastes is different again, and portrays God more as a sort of engineer, who has built and continues to maintain a world which works in the particular way which he has designed: the key purpose is to emphasize the way in which restrictions on human understanding are inherent in creation.

literature, something which might be associated loosely with the need to affirm that one can only survive and prosper in the world by conforming to the will of the world's creator. If we detach 'creation theology' from references to creation, and take it to signify little more than an absence of covenantal or salvation-historical concepts in the depiction of divine action, then it is probably true that the wisdom books all represent such a theology, but this is pretty meaningless, and any attempt to specify it further tends only to highlight the theological differences between the individual books.

Serious problems, in fact, confront any attempt to define 'wisdom' as a consistent body of thought, wholly or largely distinct from other Jewish thought. There is simply too much overlap with other literature, and too little coherence between the biblical wisdom books to accomplish this without embracing speculative theories of change and development. While it is possible that the biblical wisdom books embody a shift away from some earlier ideology which was more coherent and distinctive, there are no good grounds upon which to suppose any such thing. In the absence of a distinct, definable and common ideology, their shared interest in particular subject matter remains the only reasonably secure basis for recognizing wisdom compositions.

This is not simply a minimalist position, however slender it appears in contrast to the more elaborate definitions of wisdom which have sometimes been offered. If subject matter is the defining characteristic of wisdom writing, though, it is not the only notable feature of the compositions which we have. It is important to mention, for example, that treatment of this subject matter is commonly associated with a highly poetic, belletristic style, or that certain literary genres and thematic motifs are strongly linked to the discussion of wisdom issues. To some extent, this is simply in line with a common tendency for literary form to correspond to subject matter. It may also, though, reflect certain more precise concerns: the very nature of proverbial sayings or of instructions brings them close to the wisdom interest in authoritative guidance, while highly polished verse is the normal vehicle for important truths in the ancient world, which did not generally share the modern preoccupation with plain-speaking. Important as all these considerations are for understanding wisdom literature, however, they are of limited value for defining or recognizing it: there is more to wisdom literature than its subject matter, but it is the subject matter which makes it wisdom literature.

Let us finally return, then, to the Psalter, with a definition of wisdom in our hand. That definition is not based on specific forms or expressions, but requires a recognition and interpretation of the principal concerns in a text. If a psalm is meaningfully to be described as a 'wisdom psalm', we would expect to find that it has a primary interest in the way individuals act to ensure their future well-being, the guidance they receive in doing so, or the obstacles that they face in deciding how best to act.

It is clear that this definition can be applied to two psalms, 1 and 37, which almost all commentators have taken to be 'wisdom psalms'. Psalm 1 is composed of two contrasting descriptions—of the man who avoids sinners and devotes himself to the Torah (vv. 1-3), and of the wicked (vv. 4-5): the former is like a tree, securely rooted and prosperous, while the latter are like chaff which will be blown away by the wind. Clearly, the intention of the psalm is to commend the behaviour of the good man, and the poem finishes with a promise of divine protection for the righteous, and of annihilation for the wicked. The acrostic Psalm 37 is much longer, and its tone less tranquil, but it makes a similar point: the righteous will be looked after by God, while the wicked will be destroyed. The content of righteousness is again associated indicatively with the reception of divine Torah (v. 31), but specific advice is addressed to the hearer, urging them to trust in God (vv. 3-4, 7), be patient (v. 8), and do good (v. 27). The message is effectively summed up in v. 34: 'Wait for Yahweh and keep to his way'.[7] As in the case of Psalm 1, what makes this text a wisdom text is its concern with the behaviour required for success, a concern expressed through both direct advice and the description of the different fates awaiting the righteous and the wicked.

A third poem, Psalm 49 is rather different from the other two, but has also been accepted by most commentators as a wisdom psalm. It begins with an introduction that explicitly asserts the writer's intention to declaim wisdom. Thereafter, however, the poem does not contrast the fates of the righteous and wicked, but instead takes comfort in the fact that the writer's wealthy persecutors will all die, and not be able to take their wealth with them—an attitude he commends to others. The writer himself expects to be exempted, and ransomed from Sheol by God (v. 16, ET 15), although it is not clear on what basis. If there is any reference here to how one should act, it is probably tied up with the difficult question of 'the poor' in the Psalter, and is certainly not explicit. Indeed, the psalm moves rapidly on from its brief reference to persecution, and most of it seems concerned simply with the general transitoriness of temporal success, as affirmed in the refrain that 'A man does not stay in high repute—he ends up like animals put down'.[8]

This accords with the note in v. 11 (ET 10), that even the wise man will die, and the writer is apparently taking consolation from the fact that his enemies will lose their wealth and social status at death, since their wealth cannot protect them from the normal fate of all humans.[9] He himself, though, apparently hopes to be

7. It is noteworthy that the speaker twice draws on what he claims to have seen himself as a basis for his assertions that the righteous never suffer, while the wicked always perish (vv. 25-26, 35-36). This is rather reminiscent of Ecclesiastes, and more generally of the way in which protagonists assert the authority of their words in some other wisdom literature.

8. Although the general meaning is clear, this refrain in vv. 13 and 21 (ET 12, 20) poses some difficulties. The common translation 'pomp' for *y^e^qār* is misleading: the noun generally indicates high value, and is only otherwise used of human status in Esther (1.4, 20; 6.3, 6, 7, 9, 11; 8.16), where there is no suggestion of overweaning splendour. I take the niphal form of *māšal* to mean 'become like' or 'end up like', in line with the other uses in Pss. 28.1; 143.7; Isa. 14.10. It is noteworthy that all of these uses refer to death. The preposition *k^e^* is strange after that verb: it may be used to indicate that the comparison is not simply with the following noun, but with the whole subsequent clause. I read the refrain as identical in both occurrences, substituting the *yālîn* of v. 13 for *yābîn* in v. 21. The LXX corrects in the other direction, but cf. Ps. 25.13 for a similar expression.

9. This interpretation is not contradicted by the apparent reference to folly in v. 14 (ET 13): *kēsel* here has the sense 'confidence', which is used elsewhere of appropriate confidence in God, so can

saved by God from Sheol, for reasons which he does not explain. This is a long way from the righteous–wicked dichotomy of Psalms 1 and 37, and the writer here is not self-evidently commending any stance or course of action for personal well-being. The psalm is, however, reminiscent of the discussion in Eccl. 3.18-22, which similarly notes the lack of visible difference between humans and animals at death. The point here may be rather different, but I think that the theme may be similar: we are dealing with an anti-wisdom attitude like that of Ecclesiastes. With a nod toward the conventional psalmist's protest against unidentified enemies, the writer makes the point that humans are incapable of their own salvation: whatever they gain in life, even wisdom, they lose at death unless God intervenes. To that extent, it may be right to call this a wisdom psalm: its interest, however, is not in how humans can help themselves, but rather in the constraints on human self-salvation.[10]

There is less unanimous consent to the wisdom character of certain other psalms, but Psalms 32, 34, 112 and 127 have each been accepted by at least several commentators. Of these, Psalm 112 is the least problematic, as it is essentially another description of the benefits which accrue to the righteous man, contrasted in the last verse with the frustration of the wicked. Psalms 32 and 34, on the other hand, both begin with personal testimonies that the writer has been rescued from his troubles by turning to God, followed in each case by an offer to teach—'the way you should go' in Psalm 32, and 'the fear of Yahweh' in Psalm 34. These offers, reminiscent of the introductory exhortations in Proverbs 1–9, are followed by contrasting descriptions of the fates which befall the righteous and wicked. The two psalms are closely related, even though Psalm 34 is an acrostic while Psalm 32 is not, and, again, both easily qualify as wisdom literature on our definition.[11]

The issue is less clearcut for Psalm 127, a Song of Ascent, which is a strange little poem in two parts. The first of these, in vv. 1-2, consists of three sayings about the vanity of undertakings in which God is not involved. The last of these is slightly different from the others, suggesting, as it apparently does, that long hours and anxiety indicate the absence of divine support.[12] The second part of the psalm is simply about the value to oneself of having children, who are a reward from God.[13] In some ways, the psalm resembles a short sayings collection, but it

hardly imply 'foolish confidence', as in RSV's translation. See Ps. 78.7; Prov. 3.26. The term is used of false confidence in Job 8.14; 31.24, so the sense is probably neutral, rather than actively positive. Note that, with most commentators, I see no reference to 'the upright' as a contrasting group in the obscure v. 15 (ET 14).

10. Whybray (1974: 95), usefully notes that the theme, which he takes to be the transitoriness of human life, is 'strongly reminiscent of parts of the book of Job'. I find it difficult to accept the more common assertion amongst commentators, that this psalm is about retribution.

11. Eriksson's recent study of Ps. 34 is willing to accept that it is 'at least in some sense a wisdom poem', although he has some reservations about the definition of the *Gattung* (Eriksson 1991: 76).

12. On the precise sense of the reward in v. 3, see Emerton 1974.

13. The passage is most memorable for its imagery: the children are described as arrows in a quiver.

would be hard to say that it offers any advice, either directly or indicatively.[14] If it is indeed a wisdom psalm, and I think that that is questionable, then it is only because the poem shows an interest in the divine reward to individuals, an interest which characterizes very many psalms.

Where our definition leads to the same results as other approaches, it is usually because those approaches employ thematic or vocabularic criteria which are linked to subject matter. When they do not, matters are rather different. Kuntz, for example, describes Psalm 133 as a wisdom psalm, essentially on the grounds that he considers it to be an 'expanded and picturesque proverb' (Kuntz 1974: 210). I can see no merit for the description in the case of this psalm. Psalm 119, a lengthy acrostic prayer or lamentation, focusing on the writer's devotion to the Torah, has also been viewed as a wisdom psalm by several scholars, most recently Whybray (1997: 33-34).[15] There are several references which probably suggest a knowledge of wisdom literature, but the preoccupation of the poem is not with the Law as guidance, or the benefits which arise from following it, but with the Law itself, so this is not a wisdom psalm. The point is made clear by contrast with another Torah psalm, Psalm 19B, which does note the rewards, albeit briefly, and probably should be considered a wisdom psalm.[16]

It is also difficult to accept as wisdom compositions Psalms 78, 105 and 106, which Mowinckel accepts as, essentially, 'didactic hymns', despite the appeal in Ps. 78.1 to heed the writer's teaching (Mowinckel 1955: 214). That introduction is certainly reminiscent of, say, the introductory appeals in Proverbs 1–9, but it hardly changes the fact that these psalms are closer to the historical books, in their themes and subject matter, than to the wisdom literature.

Along with Ps. 49.2-5 (ET 1-4), in fact, the introduction to Psalm 78 shows very clearly that such reminiscences of advice literature may be imposed quite artificially upon psalms which bear no other resemblance to such literature. On such occasions, we may actually be dealing with little more than a superficial interest in the forms and motifs of advice literature—a sort of wisdom *chic*, which thoroughly undermines any assumption that 'wisdom forms' must indicate a wisdom composition.

My approach has led me to confirm or deny the wisdom character of various psalms which are widely considered to have been wisdom compositions. A number of others have enjoyed little or no such support, but seem clearly to address the subject matter which we have taken to be determinative.[17] The most obvious

14. Despite its interest in individual activity, the first part is almost fatalistic, and the second part clearly presents having children not as something one should do for oneself, to better one's lot, but as something given by God to those he already favours.

15. It is also taken as a wisdom psalm by Munch (1937: 128-31), Perdue (1977: 303) and a few others. Soll (1991: 115-25) has an excellent discussion of the various attempts to describe this as a wisdom psalm, concluding himself that it shows wisdom influence to a limited degree, but is not a didactic or wisdom composition.

16. It is recognized as such by, among others, Munch, Whybray and Perdue.

17. I do not intend to discuss here psalms whose wisdom character is largely contingent upon interpretation of context. The so-called entrance liturgies in Pss. 15 and 24, for instance, are related to wisdom concerns, inasmuch as they offer rewards for ethical behaviour. If they are indeed ritual texts,

candidates deal straightforwardly with retributive ideas, indicating the advantages of righteousness as a way of life. Among these I would include Psalm 25, which Munch (1937: 125-26) accepted chiefly on the basis of its references to teaching, but which has featured on few lists otherwise.[18] This psalm, usually classed as an individual lament,[19] goes beyond the normal self-affirmations to discuss the ways in which God teaches humans to conform to his will and rewards them for doing so.[20] This discussion runs from vv. 8-14, and the acrostic character of the psalm makes it unlikely that we are dealing with a secondary addition to the more traditional sentiments. Among the Songs of Ascent, furthermore, Psalm 125 straightforwardly offers reward for the upright and punishment of the evil, while Psalm 128, more widely recognized as a wisdom psalm,[21] outlines the future prosperity of the man who 'fears Yahweh and walks in his ways'. In a similar vein, Psalm 52 resembles Psalm 1, in terms of both its righteous–wicked contrast, and its use of tree imagery. This psalm has the direct address to the wicked found in some other individual laments, but that hardly rules it out as a wisdom composition (cf., for instance, Prov. 1.22; 6.9).[22]

There has, equally, been very little scholarly interest in the wisdom characteristics of a small group of psalms which focus upon the hiddenness of divine retribution. In Psalm 73, for instance, the writer is tempted to join those who deny divine awareness of the wicked, after seeing their prosperity, but comes to realize that they are indeed punished, and that their apparent success is transient.

Psalm 94 has a similar theme, and is again an affirmation of divine action, over against a claim that God does not see the actions of the wicked.[23] Psalm 10 is also concerned with the problem (notwithstanding its relationship to Ps. 9 as the second half of an acrostic), as, perhaps, is Psalm 14. Of course, there is a link here to broader motifs of divine concealment or delay in the Psalter, but these psalms explicitly address the sort of wisdom problem which preoccupies parts of Job and Ecclesiastes: the effect of the wicked apparently prospering upon the human motivation to be righteous. In connection with this theme, it is also important to mention Psalm 90, which von Rad has compared to Ecclesiastes (von Rad 1957: 452, ET 1962: 453-54). This psalm is slightly different, in that it views the problem not as the prosperity of the wicked, but as the disparity

then this indicates a cultic concern with such issues, parallel to that of the wisdom literature; it is possible, though, that they are to be taken metaphorically, with access to the sanctuary given as an equivalent to dwelling in the land, a perquisite of the righteous.

18. See also Ruppert (1972: 582), who notes the thematic significance of wisdom in the psalm.

19. So Gunkel and Begrich 1933, ET 1998.

20. 'Who is the man who fears Yahweh? He will instruct him in the way he should choose, so that he may live in prosperity himself, and his descendants inherit the land' (vv. 12-13).

21. The psalm is considered a wisdom psalm by, among others, Gunkel, Murphy, and Kuntz.

22. Munch takes Ps. 145 to be a wisdom psalm, and it is true that vv. 17-20 do focus on issues of retribution. I think this is an unusual case, though, of a psalm which simply uses the wisdom affirmations of divine justice as part of a much broader depiction of the divine character.

23. Whybray (1995: 159) has argued that in Ps. 94, 'a section containing wisdom language and ideas has been inserted into a psalm of lamentation (verses 8-14)'. This section clearly picks up the theme of v. 7, however, and is hardly secondary.

between God and humans. The response, however, is much the same: an appeal for God to reveal his work.

I have, then, established that a number of psalms share the distinctive interest of the Old Testament wisdom books in the way individuals act, or know how to act, for their own well-being. Like the wisdom books, these psalms tend to divide into two groups, with some essentially affirming the benefits of righteous behaviour (Pss. 1; 19B; 25; 32; 34; 37; 52; 112; 125; 128), and others addressing the problems associated with recognizing such behaviour or its benefits (Pss. 10; 14; 49; 73; 90; 94). It is important to emphasize, though, that most of these psalms are still recognizably psalms, with connections to other forms, themes and motifs in the Psalter, and that explicit references to advice literature are generally no more than superficial evocations, of a type found elsewhere in biblical literature.

In the single case of Psalm 37, however, we do find a text which demonstrates consistent composition in the style of advice literature, albeit with the superimposition of an alphabetic acrostic structure uncommon in such works. It would not be difficult, indeed, to envisage this psalm as a part of the book of Proverbs, and it seems highly unlikely that its author was unaware of such affinities. It is difficult to know whether vv. 1 and 23a are actually borrowed from the strikingly similar Prov. 24.19 and 20.24a, and the indebtedness may be in the other direction, or to a third source.[24] These close parallels, however, serve to highlight the essential interchangeability, in any case, of most of the sayings in this psalm with similar sayings in the sentence literature of Proverbs, and there is no good reason to doubt that it belongs to the sayings collection genre. At the same time, though, there are certain features, such as the promise that wicked persecutors will be overthrown (esp. vv. 12-13), or the concept of God as a refuge (v. 39),[25] which are strongly reminiscent of other psalms. There is no fixed definition with which to work, but these features, and the inclusion of the piece in the Psalter, suggest that it also belongs to the genre of 'psalm'.

As we turn, finally, to ask what implications there are in the existence of wisdom psalms, Psalm 37 illustrates the important point that genre need not be an exclusive classification, as generic characteristics are not always derived from the same features of a text. This psalm can be a sayings collection, just as sayings collections can be instructions: this is much the same as saying that a sonnet can be a love poem, even though it cannot be a limerick. This overlap of genre is not especially unusual in the biblical literature, and it is generally recognized that a piece can at once be, say, a prophetic oracle and a lament. Discussions of wisdom psalms, on the other hand, tend to assume that their dual nature represents a difficulty—that there is something about a text being a wisdom composition that would generally preclude it from being a psalm, or *vice versa*.

That something lies in a perception that the wisdom psalm represents the meeting point of two quite different traditions: wisdom literature comes from a scribal teaching tradition, and the Psalms from a cultic, Temple tradition. Explanations

24. There is also a strong similarity between Ps. 37.30a and Prov. 10.31a.
25. Cf., e.g., Ps. 31.5 (ET 4); 43.2; 52.9 (ET 7).

for the existence of wisdom psalms are sought, then, in possible areas of physical intersection or historical coalescence between the two. Correspondingly, such psalms have often been associated with the teaching of religious observance in scribal schools, or the work of scribes and schools attached to the Second Temple (Perdue, 1977: 268; Mowinckel, 1955: 206-208). At least one scholar has gone so far as to see a fusion between wisdom and Priestly schools in the early post-exilic period,[26] while many have, more persuasively, pointed to the identification of wisdom with Torah at a later time, with an associated emphasis on Torah-study as a form of worship.[27] Although the last undoubtedly highlights some important issues, all of these attempts to explain the phenomenon of wisdom psalms are highly speculative. Those which appeal to historical process, moreover, fail to explain the occurrence of a similar phenomenon outside Israel (e.g. Lambert 1960: 118-38).

I am not persuaded that any of this is necessary. Even if one accepts the existence of wisdom circles, distinct from other groups in Israel, there is no obvious basis for maintaining that such circles somehow owned the rights to certain words, ideas or literary genres. As it happens, however, I am not convinced that such wisdom circles existed at all, in any meaningful way. Wisdom is not something so diffuse as Whybray's 'intellectual tradition', but nor is it something so precise as a profession, an ideology, or a compositional style. If a general sense is to be defined for the term, many of the same constraints apply that led to our definition for it as a literary classification. It seems likely, therefore, that wisdom should be understood in terms of a set of related issues and concepts, which are the focus of discussion for a body of literature, and with which certain types of composition are strongly associated.

On such an understanding, it might be stranger if we had no wisdom psalms: there is nothing inherently remarkable about a literature of prayer and worship showing a strong interest in divine judgment, and the way in which individuals should behave. Equally, there is no reason why psalms should not share or borrow modes of expression found in other poetic literature with similar concerns, or even lend them to other texts—there is no reason to presume that the traffic was all in one direction.[28] There are some interesting issues arising from explicit evocations of advice literature, especially in those psalms which have no other wisdom associations, but these can probably be addressed in terms of the high status which advice literature appears to have achieved at some relatively late stage. Overall, though, wisdom psalms are not problematic: they simply mark the point at which the interests of two types of writing coincide. In doing so, they remind us that all our distinctions and classification are just a poor approximation to a vibrant and complicated literary culture.

26. Lemaire 1990: 180: 'This [Second Temple] period witnessed a fusion of the royal school tradition with that of the priestly school in the development of a single, national tradition... The priestly tradition became part of the general Israelite wisdom tradition.'

27. See, e.g., Mays 1987; Whybray 1995: 154-55; Fishbane 1990.

28. It is possible that the righteous–wicked contrast, in particular, has its origins outside the advice literature.

Bibliography

Crenshaw, J.L.

1969 'Method in Determining Wisdom Influence upon "Historical" Literature', *JBL* 88: 129-42.

Emerton, J.A.

1974 'The Meaning of *šēnā'* in Psalm cxxvii', *VT* 24: 15-31.

Eriksson, L.

1991 *'Come, Children, Listen to Me!' Psalm 34 in the Hebrew Bible and in Early Christian Writings* (ConBOT, 32; Uppsala: Almqvist &Wiksell).

Fishbane, M.

1990 'From Scribalism to Rabbinism: Perspectives on the Emergence of Classical Judaism', in Gammie and Perdue (eds.) 1990: 439-56.

Gammie, J.G., and L.G. Perdue (eds.)

1990 *The Sage in Israel and the Ancient Near East* (Winona Lake, IN: Eisenbrauns).

Gunkel, H., and J. Begrich

1933 *Einleitung in die Psalmen* (Göttingen: Vandenhoek & Ruprecht). ET *Introduction to Psalms* (trans. J.D. Nogalski; Macon, GA: Mercer University Press, 1998).

Hurvitz, A.

1988 'Wisdom Vocabulary in the Hebrew Psalter: A Contribution to the Study of "Wisdom Psalms"', *VT* 38: 41-51.

Kuntz, J.K.

1974 'The Canonical Wisdom Psalms of Ancient Israel—Their Rhetorical, Thematic, and Formal Dimensions', in J.J. Jackson and M. Kessler (eds.), *Rhetorical Criticism: Essays in Honor of James Muilenburg* (Pittsburgh: Pickwick Press): 186-222.

Lambert, W.G.

1960 *Babylonian Wisdom Literature* (Oxford: Oxford University Press).

Lemaire, A.

1990 'The Sage in School and Temple', in Gammie and Perdue (eds.) 1990: 165-81.

Mays, J.L.

1987 'The Place of the Torah-Psalms in the Psalter', *JBL* 106: 3-12.

Mowinckel, S.

1955 'Psalms and Wisdom', in M. Noth and D. Winton Thomas (eds.), *Wisdom in Israel and in the Ancient Near East: Presented to Professor Harold Henry Rowley* (VTSup, 3; Leiden: E.J. Brill): 205-24.

Munch, P.A.

1937 'Die jüdischen "Weisheitspsalmen" und ihr Platz im Leben', *AcOr.* 15: 112-40.

Murphy, R.E.

1963 'A Consideration of the Classification, "Wisdom Psalms"', in *Congress Volume: Bonn 1962* (VTSup, 9; Leiden: E.J. Brill): 156-67.

1967 'Assumptions and Problems in Old Testament Wisdom Research', *CBQ* 29: 407-18.

Perdue, L.G.

1977 *Wisdom and Cult* (Missoula, MT: Scholars Press).

Rad, G. von

1957 *Theologie des Alten Testaments*, I (Munich: Chr. Kaiser Verlag). ET *Old Testament Theology*, I (trans. D.M.G. Stalker; Edinburgh and London: Oliver & Boyd, 1962).

Ruppert, L.
1972 'Psalm 25 und die Grenze der kultorientierten Psalmenexegese', *ZAW* 84: 576-82.

Scott, R.B.Y.
1971 *The Way of Wisdom in the Old Testament* (New York: Macmillan).

Sheppard, G.T.
1980 *Wisdom as a Hermeneutical Construct* (BZAW, 151; Berlin and New York: W. de Gruyter).

Soll, W.
1991 *Psalm 119: Matrix, Form, and Setting* (CBQMS, 23; Washington, DC: Catholic Biblical Association of America).

Weeks, S.D.E.
1994 *Early Israelite Wisdom* (Oxford: Clarendon Press).

Weinfeld, M.
1972 *Deuteronomy and the Deuteronomic School* (Oxford: Oxford University Press).

Whybray, R.N.
1974 *The Intellectual Tradition in the Old Testament* (BZAW, 135; Berlin and New York: W. de Gruyter).
1995 'The Wisdom Psalms', in J. Day, R.P. Gordon and H.G.M. Williamson (eds.), *Wisdom in Ancient Israel: Essays in Honour of J.A. Emerton* (Cambridge: Cambridge University Press): 152-60.
1997 'Psalm 119—Profile of a Psalmist', in M.L. Barré (ed.), *Wisdom You Are My Sister: Studies in Honor of Roland E. Murphy, O. Carm., on the Occasion of his Eightieth Birthday* (CBQMS, 29; Washington, DC: The Catholic Biblical Association of America): 31-43.

The Zion Tradition and the Editing of the Hebrew Psalter

Susan Gillingham

1. *The Editing of the Hebrew Psalter*

To write about 'the editing of the Hebrew Psalter' implies for the most part a literary interest in the Psalter as a whole. This concern is comparatively recent in psalmic studies: real development dates only from the 1970s, although earlier antecedents are found in J.A. Alexander's and Franz Delitzsch's commentaries on the Psalms, first published in 1850 and in 1860 respectively. Many of the more recent commentators are German, and include C. Barth, J. Becker, F.L. Hossfeld, N. Lohfink, J. Jeremias, K. Koch, M. Millard, J. Reindl, K. Seybold, C. Westermann and E. Zenger; references to these writers will be made later in this study.[1] Significant English and American contributors include J.P. Brennan, W. Brueggemann, D.M. Howard, J.C. McCann, J.L. Mays, P.D. Miller, D.C. Mitchell, N.L de Claissé Walford, G.H. Wilson, J.H. Eaton, A.G. Hunter and R.N. Whybray; and, with a different liturgical bias, M.D. Goulder.[2] Notable French contributors include P. Auffret, E. Beaucamp and J.-M. Auwers.[3] Of the introductions to the history of research into the editing of the Psalter up to the early 1990s, the most useful is probably that by D.M. Howard (1993a).

Most of these scholars have a particular view of what the concerns of the editors were. Some would argue for several independent editorial contributions, found either within the smaller collections or within each of the five books of the Psalter.[4] Others would propose one editorial purpose overall: two frequent suggestions are that this is the work of 'eschatological editors' or 'didactic editors'. Eschatological editing is about the way in which the editors, concerned for the Jewish community as a whole, organized various psalms to show that, despite the

1. Of these, the earliest works are Westermann 1962, ET 1981, and Becker 1975. All the other authors published in the 1980s and the 1990s.

2. M.D. Goulder's work, on Book IV of the Psalter, is the earliest (1975). An early example on the editing of the whole Psalter is Wilson 1984: 337-52. Most English publications date from the late 1980s.

3. Beaucamp 1979 is one of the earliest works in French.

4. Two seminal books in this respect are Seybold and Zenger (eds.) 1994, which has several articles on the smaller collections such as Pss. 15–24 (P.D. Miller), the Asaph psalms (K. Seybold), the Korahite psalms (E. Zenger), and the Enthronement psalms (F.-L. Hossfeld); and McCann (ed.) 1993, with articles on Books I–III and IV–V (G.H. Wilson), Book I (P.D. Miller), Books I–III (J.C. McCann), and the beginning of Book IV (D.M. Howard).

failed national covenant with King David, God's rule over the nations had not failed and soon a new world order would be established where God himself would be acknowledged as king.[5] 'Didactic editing' is about the way the editors, concerned more for the personal needs of individuals within the community, compiled the Psalter to make it more like a reflective prayer book, with wisdom concerns about the right ordering of the world, and with Torah concerns about the means of attaining that order and harmony on the part of each individual.[6]

At first glance, the two views about the editors of the Psalter seem to be quite different. In the former, the editors have more links with the Prophets in their eschatological concerns, whereas in the latter view the editors are closer to the Law and Writings in their didactic concerns. One view sees the Psalter as a public eschatological hymn book; the other, as a private prayer book for personal instruction. It could be argued, however, that the concerns are complementary.[7] For example, didactic psalms and psalms referring to kingship, both Davidic and divine, are often found side by side at critical points in the Psalter: Psalms 1–2; 18–19; 48–49; 72–73; 89–90; 110–11; 144–45 are all important pairs, suggesting that the editors, at least, held both of these concerns together. Several scholars have argued for this dual 'instructional and eschatological' approach.[8]

Regardless of whether the final editing of the Psalter was made with an eschatological or didactic focus, a key concern in this study is whether the editors were working within the confines of the Temple, or outside them. Not surprisingly, scholars are again divided in this respect. E. Zenger and N. Lohfink, for example, taking the view that the Psalter as a whole has an overriding didactic emphasis, argue that many of the psalms are cult-free songs which the editors used to edify personal piety away from the Temple.[9] (Here we may note the much

5. Examples of this view include Wilson 1985, 1992, 1993; Jeremias 1987; Walton 1991; Smith 1992b; Mitchell 1997; and Rösel 1999.

6. Examples of this view include Brennan 1976; Sheppard 1980; Reindl 1981; Ceresko 1990; Lohfink 1990; McCann 1992; Seybold and Zenger (eds.) 1994; Whybray 1996; and Hossfeld and Zenger 1996.

7. The two terms used for the Psalter in Hebrew *tᵉhillîm* (hymns) and *tᵉpillôt* (prayers) could be seen to illustrate the two main concerns of the editors.

8. See Mays 1987; Eaton 1995, and de Claissé-Walford 1997. On the integration of didactic and eschatological themes in Book IV, see Howard 1997: 200-207.

9. See, e.g., Lohfink 1992. Arguing for the private meditative use of many psalms at the time of the editing of the Psalter, he notes that in early Jewish and Christian times the Psalter as a whole was a foundational book for private and personal piety (1992: 4), whereby the readers identified themselves with 'the poor' and saw their opponents as 'the enemies'. This is a development of Lohfink's *Lobgesänge der Armen* (1990: 108-25) except that in the later article Lohfink applies to the redaction of the entire Psalter what he earlier applied to later psalms alone. Lohfink is influenced by E. Zenger, whose publications are frequently quoted in both works. See, for instance, Zenger 1991a, where he argues that the most important influence in the latter stages of the Psalter's compilation is personal piety in a cult-free setting, both in early Judaism and early Christianity. Much of Lohfink's and Zenger's work is a reaction to the predominant cult-functional approach to psalmody in earlier scholarship. Zenger's more recent article (2002), however, does attribute some importance to the Temple and its liturgy, although it still advocates the supreme significance of personal faith above and beyond it.

earlier influence of Gunkel and his category of 'spiritual songs'.[10]) J.C. McCann, J.L. Mays, G.T. Sheppard, G.H. Wilson and R.N. Whybray, in different ways, take this view.[11] Several scholars who take a more eschatological view of the Psalter argue that this theological emphasis developed both within and away from the Temple: commentators include J.H. Eaton and N.L. de Claissé-Walford.[12]

Nevertheless, this study contends that a case can be made for arguing that the editors of the Psalter belonged to Temple circles, and that the Temple and its liturgy was of paramount influence throughout the whole process of the editing. This article thus espouses the view, attributed originally to R. Smend (the elder), that 'The Psalter is the Hymn Book of the Second Temple'.[13] The social context for such editors would be among the priests and scribes of the Second Temple.[14]

10. See Gunkel 1930, ET 1967; Gunkel and Begrich 1928, 1933, ET 1998. For example: 'The most important observation for the psalms is that some of them belong to poetry used in worship, while others do not presuppose the worship service...those psalms which were composed for the cultus are, on the whole, older than those which the pious poet composed for his own use' (1930: col 1611, ET 1967: 5). Also pertinent is Gunkel's analysis of 'Non-liturgical Psalms or 'Spiritual Songs' (1930: cols. 1621-23, ET 1967: 26-29). His views are developed by Hossfeld and Zenger (1996: 336-37) and by Zenger (ed.) 1994, for example: 'That the psalter was not intended as a hymnal either of the second temple or of the synagogues, and is not to be understood as such was already recognised by H. Gunkel... At the turn of the era the psalter was above all the prayer and meditation of those who are called in the psalms the "poor", the "destitute", the "pious", and the "just" who sought in the psalms edification, comfort and hope' (p. 44).

11. See, for example, three papers by J.C. McCann, G.T. Sheppard and G.H. Wilson in the 1992 edition of *Interpretation*. McCann (1992: 121) argues that although the psalms may have originated in the liturgical life of ancient Israel and Judah, they were appropriated, preserved and transmitted to instruct the faithful independently of Temple worship. McCann follows the same argument as Mays (1987), who proposes that earlier issues of cultic function were subordinated by the editors of the Psalter as a whole to questions of content and theology (1987: 12). Sheppard (1992) and Wilson (1992, 1993) take a similar approach: the Psalter as a whole emerged as a book of private prayer. Whybray (1996: 30-35, 118-24) argues slightly differently: although a private 'rereading' of the psalms took place in the second Temple period, for example, the royal psalms being reread messianically, and the psalms about Temple sacrifice being reread to imply a sacrifice of the heart, the Temple and its public worship still played its part.

12. Eaton (1995) examines commentators' views of the kingship psalms (especially Pss. 93, 97 and 99) alongside the same commentators' views of the Torah psalms (Pss. 1, 19 and 119), noting that most scholars agree that the cultic festivals, in their earliest usage, were a natural locus for beliefs about the kingship of God, while in later post-exilic times piety would have assumed a more spiritualized a-cultic dimension. De Claissé-Walford (1997) also focuses on the two theological influences of Torah piety and the kingship of God, taking Pss. 1 and 2 as examples, and having demonstrated that these two themes influenced the shape of all five books of the Psalter, she argues that the editors were not only concerned about liturgical worship but also about the political identity of the Jewish community. Both Eaton's and de Claissé-Walford's views have correspondences with those of scholars who suppose that the origins and development of apocalyptic writing belong more to those at the margins of society than to those from within the Temple, as expressed for example in the 'deprivation theories' of scholars such as P. Hanson, O. Plöger and R.R. Wilson: see the discussion in Cook 1995: 5-12, 29-40.

13. See Auwers 2000: 162 n. 504, who argues that this phrase originated from Smend 1888: 49-50.

14. See Fishbane 1985: 23-43; Smith 1991, 1992b; Millard 1994: 205-12; Creach 1996: 106-21; Davies 1998: 74-88 and 131-34; Auwers 2000: 161-64. Davies identifies the group responsible for the final editing of the whole Psalter as 'temple scribes', whose affiliation with the tribe of Levi made

It would explain the didactic concerns of the editors of the Psalter: given the illiteracy of the ordinary populace, teaching and instruction would have been left in the hands of the 'professionals', so this view has its attraction.[15] It would also explain both the eschatological interests in many psalms, given the close link between God's world rule and his return to Zion in some physical sense: like the post-exilic prophets and some of the earlier apocalyptic writers, and even some of the sectarians at Qumran, the Temple and its liturgy would be seen at the centre rather than marginal to the concerns of these so-called eschatological editors of the Psalter.[16]

Three observations are important at this stage. First, this is not to propose that every composition originally came out of Temple circles. A distinction needs to be made between those psalms which reflect a genuine present experience of Zion at the time of composition, and psalms which have been brought later into Temple liturgy by the editors, who would draw all types of psalms, whether public or private, into a Temple setting.[17] Hence by arguing that the Zion tradition influenced the end of the literary process of the editing of the Psalter, this need not imply that 'Zion' was always a dominant theme in the earliest stages of psalmody. Originally, some of the references to cultic celebrations such as processions and sacrifices, and some uses of myths associated with God's dwelling in a holy place need not always have referred to the Temple in Jerusalem, but to some outlying sanctuary. The publications on the relationship between popular

them 'para-priests'; on this account they would draw all kinds of psalms into their Temple-based collection (pp. 133-34). Mowinckel (1924) was among the first to popularize this idea: reversing Gunkel's theory of psalmody arising from non-cultic circles, Mowinckel saw that the composers of the psalms belonged to pious circles, but composed psalms for official cultic use, with Temple personnel of levitical descent (being Temple singers rather than priests) at a later stage compiling, editing and adding in superscriptions. About Gunkel, Mowinckel observes that he had too low a regard for cultic religion, rather like the ancient prophets and modern liberal Protestant theologians. ('Er schätzt die Kultreligion viel zu niedrig ein, nach der Weise der alten Propheten und die liberalen protestantische Theologen' [1924: 24]). In arguing that the editors of the psalms were of levitical descent, see Mowinckel 1951, ET 1962: II, 85-95, 202-206. For example, '...the psalms which had from early times established themselves by regular use in the temple service would all be included in the Psalter...it must be added that in later Jewish times no psalms were used at the temple service which were not found in the book' (1962: 202). If any psalms were later used privately, this was only because of their popularity in the first instance within a Temple hymn book (1962: II, 204-206).

15. On the low literacy level in the Persian period, see Berquist 1995: 161-76; Carter 1999: 285-324.

16. Views about the prominence of Zion in the Psalms are found in Ollenburger 1987: 13-22, 151-54; Howard 1997: 200-207; Mitchell 1997: 66-89, 292-303; and Hoppe 2000. Examples from prophetic books which exhibit prophetic eschatology, where the theme of God's return to Zion is prominent, include Hag. 1.7-8; 2.1-9; Zech. 1.14, 17; 2.7, 10; 8.2, 3; 9.9, 13; Joel 4.16, 17, 21, ET 3.16, 17, 21; and Isa. 24.23. At Qumran, the *pesharim* on the Psalms offer the clearest examples of this emphasis: see, for example, 4QpPsa (4Q171); 4QFlor (4Q174); 4QCatena A (4Q177); and 11QMelch (11Q13).

17. The complementary relationship between public and private piety in the formation of the Psalter is little different from the composition of hymn books using psalms in the vernacular from the sixteenth century onwards. Luther's 1524 hymn book, Calvin's *Geneva Psalter* of 1551 and 1562, and the English version of the Psalms by Sternhold and Hopkins in 1549 all correspond with this model of individual creativity serving public liturgy.

and official religion by R. Albertz, and on the diversity of cultic life within pre-exilic religion by Z. Zevit, to take just two examples, have shown just how different early use and later adaptation might be.[18]

Secondly, this distinction between popular and official religion is not only a feature of pre-exilic psalmody. Gunkel's 'cult-free' spiritual songs, and Lohfink's 'Lobsänge', as well as Zenger's private meditations, are all deemed to be compositions in a setting away from the Temple in post-exilic times. Moreover, regarding entire collections, K. Seybold argues that the Songs of Ascents and the Asaph psalms had northern non-Temple origins, and were brought into Jerusalem liturgy at a later time, and L.D. Crow contends that the Songs of Ascents were composed in post-exilic times by ordinary Israelites in the northern kingdom making pilgrimage to Jerusalem.[19] This having been said, the earlier or later provenance of particular psalms is less of an issue for this particular study than that of demonstrating the Zion tradition at the final stage of editing.

Thirdly, it is clear that there were times before the final compilation of the Psalter when the term 'Zion' was used to refer not only to a place, but to the people as personifying that place. The period of the exile testifies to this, as passages such as Ezek. 11.16 and Isa. 51.16; 52.1 illustrate in different ways. Furthermore, it is equally clear that after the final compilation of the Psalter the term 'Zion' was still 'democratized' and 'spiritualized' to refer to the community of faith rather than the Temple in Jerusalem: the peoples' sense of being in continual exile (as in Dan. 9.1-27) increased such views. This attitude to the Temple (and hence also to the Zion tradition) was the one taken in the main by the New Testament writers (found, for example, in Jn 2.19-21; 1 Cor. 3.16-17; Eph. 2.21). But such an interpretation of Zion need not negate the literal, physical origins of the tradition. All that this study seeks to demonstrate is that the compilers and editors of the Psalter, who themselves probably understood the Zion tradition in diverse ways, intentionally transformed it into a tradition which usually referred to the Temple.

18. In Albertz's most recent work translated into English (2002a and b: II, 90-100, 101-24), he argues that in the pre-exilic period personal piety in homes and local sanctuaries played a much more important part than is often assumed, and in the post-exilic period, religious services were held in homes and synagogues as well as in the Temple. Nevertheless, he presumes the influence of the Temple personnel in the editing of the Psalter, even though its psalms were used elsewhere, so his views are not at variance with those expressed in this paper. See also Zevit 2001: 668-94, who argues that '...people did not run to shrines or holy places to ask for help, for a favor, or to say thank you, but could do so where they were...' (p. 668). Zevit suggests that a number of psalms were originally addressed to deities other than Yahweh (e.g. Pss. 42–43; 54; 68; 82), but he nevertheless sees that there is a later more orthodox editing which he considers to be 'Jerusalemizing interpolations' creating a 'Yahweh-alone' emphasis (pp. 678-84). Hence, in his regard for the work of Jerusalem editors, Zevit's position is also not far removed from the one taken here.

19. See Seybold 1979; 1996a: 20-21; 1996b, who refers to the 'Zion-Segen-Theologie' (the theology of blessings from Zion) throughout the collection (1979: 268, referring to Pss. 128.5 and 134.3). See also Crow 1996, who argues differently from Seybold in that he sees that the post-exilic editing of this collection took place in Jerusalem, to encourage pilgrimages from the northern villages to the Temple instead.

2. *Establishing the Zion Tradition in the Psalter*

The problem in arguing for a didactic or an eschatological editing of the Psalter is that the theological or linguistic criteria for establishing either schema do not belong uniquely to circles of the wise or the prophets, but are evident in many other traditions as well. By contrast, the Zion tradition can be determined by more specific linguistic criteria (especially in the references to Zion [*ṣiyyôn*] and to Jerusalem [*yᵉrûšālaim*]). And, as argued above, this tradition allows for a broad frame of reference in which many theological traditions contribute, explaining why didactic and eschatological traditions are evident without having to propose different and separate groups of editors.

In terms of linguistic criteria, the obvious starting point is to examine those psalms where the term *ṣiyyôn* and its synonyms are found.[20] The Psalter is one of the few books where the word *ṣiyyôn* is most prevalent. Other than in the Psalms, the only other books where *ṣiyyôn* is used widely are Isaiah[21] and Jeremiah;[22] it also occurs frequently in four of five chapters of Lamentations[23] and also in a few of the minor prophets.[24] It occurs a handful of times in the historiographies,[25] on three occasions equating Zion explicitly with Jerusalem or the 'city of David'.[26]

Not surprisingly, within the Psalms, Zion occurs several times in parallelism with Jerusalem.[27] Some psalms make reference to blessings coming 'from

20. 'Zion Markers' (a term which I owe to Professor J. Day) are often identifiable because of their use in parallelism with *ṣiyyôn*, and include *yᵉrûšālāyim*; *hêkāl* ('temple'); *hêkal qodšᵉkā* ('your holy temple'); *bêt yahweh* ('house of the Lord') or *bêt ᵉlōhîm* ('house of God') or simply *bêtᵉkā* ('your house'); *šaᵃrê ṣiyyôn* ('gates of Zion'), or simply *šaᵃrê* ('gates'), which also refers to the Temple; *ḥᵃṣēreykā* ('your courts') or *ḥaṣrôt yahweh* ('courts of the Lord') and *ḥaṣrôt ᵉlōhênu* ('courts of God'); *har qodšî* ('my holy mountain') or *har yahweh* ('mountain of the Lord'); *miškᵉnôt* ('dwelling place'), usually with a personal suffix; *mᵉqôm qōdeš* ('holy place') or just *qōdeš* ('sanctuary'), also often taking a personal suffix; *'ōhel* ('tabernacle'), again usually with a personal suffix; *mizbēaḥ* ('altar'); and *'îr ᵉlōhîm* ('city of God') or *'îr yahweh* ('city of the Lord'). For a survey of the scope and character of the Zion tradition in the Psalms, see Ollenburger 1987: 13-22, 81-99, and Hoppe 2000: 23-41.

21. Zion references are prevalent throughout all three parts of Isaiah: see Isa. 1.8, 27; 2.3; 3.16, 17; 4.3, 4, 5; 8.18; 10.12, 24, 32; 12.6; 14.32; 16.1; 18.7; 24.23; 28.16; 29.8; 30.19; 31.4, 9; 33.20; 35.10; 37.22, 32; 40.9; 41.27; 46.13; 49.14-15; 51.3, 11, 16; 52.1, 2, 7, 8; 59.20; 60.14; 61.3; 62.11; 64.10; 66.8 (noting that Isa. 51.16 and 52.1 are examples referred to earlier of the Zion tradition applied to the people rather than Jerusalem). Cf. Ollenburger 1987: 104-44, on the Zion tradition in the prophets and in Isaiah in particular; also Hoppe 2000: 57-71, on Isa. 1–39; pp. 99-110, on Isa. 40–55; pp. 128-31, on Isa. 56–66; and pp. 128-31, on Isa. 24–27.

22. See Jer. 3.14; 4.46, 31; 6.2, 23; 8.19; 9.19; 14.19; 26.18; 30.17; 31.6, 12; 50.5, 28; 51.10. Cf. Hoppe 2000: 82-88.

23. See Lam. 1.4, 6, 17; 2.1, 4, 6, 8, 10, 13, 18; 4.2, 11, 22; 5.11, 18. Cf. Hoppe 2000: 88-93.

24. See Amos 1.2 and 6.1; Mic. 1.13; 3.10, 12; 4.2, 7, 8, 10, 11, 13; Zeph. 3.14,16; Obad. 1.17, 21; Zech. 1.14, 17; 2.7, 10; 8.2, 3; 9.9, 13; and Joel 2.1, 15, 23, 32; 4.16, 17, 21 (ET 3.16, 17, 21). Cf. Hoppe 2000: 73-80, on Micah; pp. 80-82, on Zephaniah; pp. 114-18, on Zech. 1–8; pp. 131-35, on Zech. 9–14; and pp. 135-38, on Joel.

25. See 2 Sam. 5.7; 1 Kgs 8.1; 2 Kgs 19.21, 31; 1 Chron. 11.5; 2 Chron. 5.2.

26. 1 Kgs 8.1 ('the city of David, which is Zion'); 1 Chron. 11.5 ('the stronghold of Zion, that is, the city of David'); and 2 Chron. 5.2 ('the city of David, which is Zion').

27. See Pss. 51.20 (ET 18, 'Do good to Zion in your good pleasure: rebuild the walls of Jerusalem'); 102.22 (ET 21, 'So that the name of the Lord may be declared in Zion, his praise in Jerusalem');

Zion' (*mīsṣiyyôn*),[28] others of God residing 'in Zion' (*b^eṣiyyôn*),[29] while others use the memory of Zion as an inspiration for faith.[30] Other psalms use the expression 'Mt Zion' (*har ṣiyyôn*), which is of course the Temple at Jerusalem.[31] Occasionally Jerusalem is used on its own as a synonym for Zion[32] but as well as occurring in parallelism with Zion, Jerusalem is often used along with the 'Temple' (*hêkāl*),[33] the 'house of God' (*bêt yahweh*),[34] the 'city' (*'îr*),[35] or the 'gates' (*ša'^arê*).[36] The terms *hêkāl*, *bêt yahweh*, *'îr*, and *ša'^arê* are often used without reference to Zion, but by the time of the editors it is probable that the reference was to Jerusalem. So, for example, the expression 'holy Temple' (*hêkal qōdeš*)[37] would indicate a Zion tradition in the minds of the Jerusalem editors; so, too, the expression 'his Temple/your Temple' (*hêkālô/hêkāleka*).[38] Even the expression 'house of the Lord' (*bêt yahweh*), from the point of view of the editors, would have been identified as Zion/Jerusalem;[39] and likewise, the expression 'house of God' (*bêt 'elōhîm*), even though it was used in earlier times to indicate other sanctuaries (for example, in Amos 2.8, it probably refers to Bethel[40]). The expression 'your house' (*bêt^ekā*) also implies Zion, if not at the time of the composers, at

125.1-2 ('Those who trust in the Lord are like Mt Zion… As the mountains are round about Jerusalem, so the Lord is round about his people'); 128.5 ('The Lord bless you from Zion! May you see the prosperity of Jerusalem'); 135.21 ('Blessed be the Lord from Zion, he who dwells in Jerusalem'); and 147.12 ('Praise the Lord, O Jerusalem! Praise your God, O Zion!')

28. See Pss. 14.7; 20.3 (ET 2); 50.2; 53.7 (ET 6); 110.2; and 134.3. Pss. 128.5 and 135.21 use *miṣṣiyyôn* in parallelism with Jerusalem.

29. See Pss. 65.2 (ET 1); 76.3 (ET 2); 84.8 (ET 7); 99.2; 102.22 (ET 21). In Ps. 9.12 (ET 11) 'in Zion' is implied in the Hebrew although the prefix is absent.

30. See Pss. 2.6; 48.12-13; 69.36 (ET 35); 87.5; 97.8; 102.14, 17 (ET 13, 16); 126.1; 129.5; 137.1 and 146.10. Other expressions of faith in Zion include the 'daughter of Zion' (*bat ṣiyyôn*) in Ps. 9.15 (ET 14); 'gates of Zion' (*ša'^arê ṣiyyôn*) in Ps. 87.2; 'song of Zion' (*šîr ṣiyyôn*) in Ps. 137.3; 'children of Zion' (*b^enê ṣiyyôn*) in Ps. 149.2; and God's choosing Zion (*kî bāḥar yahweh b^eṣiyyôn*) in Ps. 132.13.

31. See Pss. 48.3, 12 (ET 2, 11); 74.2; 78.68 and 125.1. In Ps. 133.3 the expression 'mountains of Zion' (*har^erê ṣiyyôn*) is a more unusual example.

32. See Pss. 79.3; 122.6 and 137.5, 6 (noting references to Zion in 137.3); also 147.2 (Jerusalem and Zion occur together in v. 12).

33. See Pss. 68.30 (ET 29) and 79.1.

34. See Ps. 116.19.

35. See Ps. 122.3.

36. See Ps. 122.2.

37. See Pss. 5.8 (ET 7); 11.4; 65.5 (ET 4); 79.1; and 138.2 (as in 5.8, ET 7). Ps. 68.30 (ET 29) is also relevant, as this is specifically the Temple at Jerusalem.

38. See Pss. 18.7 (ET 6); 27.4; 29.9; and 48.10 (ET 9).

39. Pss. 27.4 and 116.19 are the best examples, because the term is used in parallelism with the Temple or Jerusalem later in each verse. See also Pss. 23.6 (with its associations with Ps. 27.4); 122.1, 9; and 134.1. Less clear examples, though probably alluding to the Temple, are Pss. 92.14 (ET 13), noting the parallelism with 'the courts', and 26.8.

40. The clearest example is Ps. 84.11 (ET 10), and its setting in the Korahite collection suggests the Temple at least by the time of the editors. Ps. 42.5 (ET 4), with its reference to leading in procession in the 'house of God'), is again a Korahite psalm, and also suggests a specific Temple reference by the time of the editors. Less certain examples are Pss. 52.10 (ET 8), with its reference to being likened to a green olive tree in 'the house of God', and 55.15 (ET 14), which, like Ps. 42, looks to the memory of being in 'the house of God'.

least by the time of the editors.[41] Three times 'gates' (*ša'ᵃrê*) is used in parallelism with Zion or Jerusalem;[42] the other three examples of *ša'ᵃrê* also suggest Zion by the time of the editing of the Psalter.[43] Another term with a clear reference to Zion is 'courts' (*ḥᵃṣērôt*), which we have noted already is found in parallelism with 'gates' or 'Temple' or 'house of God'.[44]

Further cultic terms demonstrate that Zion is implied by the editors. For example, 'the mountain of the Lord', or 'my holy mountain', or 'his holy mountain', or 'your holy mountain' (*har yahweh* or *har qodšî* or *har qodšô* or *har qodšᵉkā*) is used in parallelism with Zion in Psalm 2,[45] and where *har* occurs on its own, the same inference can be drawn.[46] The term 'dwelling place' (*miškᵉnôt*) and the various terms translated as 'habitation' (*mᵉ'ônâ, mā'ôn, nāweh* or *môšāb*) can be given similar interpretations: in all four examples, the allusion is to Zion.[47] The term 'holy place' (*mᵉqôm qōdeš*), or just *qōdeš*, the latter usually translated as 'sanctuary') is also likely to refer to Zion.[48] The term 'tent' (*'ōhel*) is a less certain Zion allusion, although in two cases this is undoubtedly the case.[49] The term *mizbēaḥ* similarly would have implied the altar in the Jerusalem Temple by the time of the editors.[50] The expression 'city of God' (*'îr 'ᵉlōhîm* or *'îr yahweh*) is another synonym for Zion: in one example it is in parallelism with Jerusalem,

41. See Pss. 65.5 (ET 4), noting the reference to the 'holy Temple' and, earlier in the verse, to the 'courts'; and 84.5 (ET 4), because of the context of the rest of the psalm. Less clear are Pss. 69.10 (ET 9), which speaks of 'zeal for your house', 93.5 (which refers to holiness befitting the Lord's house) and 135.2 (which speaks of the 'servants of the Lord' standing in 'the courts of the house of the Lord'), but again by the time of the editors only Zion would be the place implied.

42. See Pss. 9.15 (ET 14); 87.2 (with the parallelism of gates and Zion); and Ps. 122.2, where the parallelism is of gates and Jerusalem.

43. See Pss. 24.7, 9; 118.19, noting the unusual phrase, 'gates of righteousness'; and 100.4 (noting the parallel with 'courts').

44. On courts//gates, see Ps 100.4. On courts//Temple, see Ps. 65.5 (ET 4); on courts//house of God, see Ps 84.11, ET 10 (v. 3, ET 2 also refers to the 'courts of the Lord'); 92.14 (ET 13); 116.19 (where the additional reference to Jerusalem implies a Zion interpretation), and 135.2. Ps. 96.8 is less explicit, although the reference to 'offering' also suggest Temple sacrifice.

45. See Ps. 2.6.

46. See Pss. 3.5 (ET 4); 15.1 (where this occurs alongside *'ōhel*); 43.3 (where it is found in parallelism with *miškᵉnôt*); 48.2 (ET 1), noting here the reference to 'the city of our God' earlier in the verse. The expressions 'hill of the Lord' in Ps. 24.3 and in Ps. 68.17 (ET 16), 'hill of God's abode', are also likely to refer to Zion. Ps. 78.54 is also a similar allusion, although the first word translated as 'mountain' is *gᵉbûl*—the word *har* is found in the next phrase.

47. See Pss. 46.5 (ET 4), noting the parallelism with 'the city of God' in the same verse; 84.2 (ET 1); and 132.5, 7 where the context of the bringing of the ark to the city of David could only mean Zion. Other psalms which do not use *miškᵉnôt* but also imply Zion are Pss. 76.3 (ET 2), using *mᵉ'ônâ*, but with a reference to Zion as well; 68.6 (ET 5, using *mā'ôn*); 79.7 (using *nāweh*); and 132.13 (using *môšāb*, but again in parallelism with Zion).

48. See Pss. 20.3 (ET 2); 24.3; 28.2; 60.8 (ET 6); 63.3 (ET 2); 68.18, 25, 36 (ET 17, 24, 35); 73.17; 74.3, 7 (both verses lamenting the destruction of the sanctuary); 78.69; 96.6; 108.8 (ET 7), a parallel with Ps. 60.8 (ET 6); 134.2; and 150.1.

49. See Pss. 15.1 (where *'ōhel* is in parallelism with *har qōdeš*; 27.6, noting the reference to *hêkāl* in v. 5); and 61.5 (ET 4). (Ps. 78.60 is a good example of *'ōhel* being used with reference to somewhere other than Jerusalem: here the reference is to Shiloh.)

50. See Pss. 26.6; 43.4; 51.21 (ET 19); and 118.27. Ps. 84.4 (ET 3) makes use of the plural form.

in another, with Zion, and the context of the other psalms suggest that Zion is intended.[51] Two psalms speak of God seated above the cherubim (*k^erûbîm*): again, that this referred to Zion from the standpoint of the editors is possible.[52]

A final reference needs to be treated with more care, although again its occurrence in psalms already identified with Zion suggests it also implies a Zion connection: this is the use of the term 'Elyon' or 'Most High God' (*'elyôn*) sometimes used with El or Elohim (*'ēl 'elyôn* or *'^elōhîm 'elyôn*), sometimes used with Yahweh (*yahweh 'elyôn*) and on several occasions used on its own.[53]

The Zion Tradition in the Hebrew Psalter
(asterisks indicate psalms with Zion Markers)

<table>
<tr><td>Book I =
17/41 psalms</td><td>1, 2*</td><td colspan="6">3–41: David
(3*, 5*, 7*, 9*, 11*, 14*, 15*, 18*, 20*,
21*, 23*, 24*, 26*, 27*, 28*, 29*)</td></tr>
<tr><td>Book II =
17/31 psalms</td><td></td><td colspan="2">42–49: Korah
(42*, 43*, 46*,
47*, 48*)</td><td colspan="2">50*
(Asaph)</td><td colspan="2">51–72: David
(51*, 52*, 53*, 55*, 57*,
60*, 61*, 63*, 68*, 69*)</td></tr>
<tr><td>Book III =
11/17 psalms</td><td></td><td colspan="2">73–83: Asaph
(73*, 74*, 76*, 77*,
78*, 79*, 80*, 82*,
83*)</td><td colspan="2"></td><td colspan="2">84–89: Mixed
(84*, 87*)</td></tr>
<tr><td>Book IV =
10/17 psalms</td><td>90
91*
92*</td><td colspan="2">93–100: Kingship
(93*, 96*, 97*,
99*, 100*)</td><td colspan="2">101* (David)
102*
103 (David)</td><td colspan="2">104–106: Hallel
(106*)</td></tr>
<tr><td>Book V =
20/44 psalms</td><td>107*
108* (David)
109 (David)
110* (David)
111</td><td>112–18:
Hallel
(116*,
118*)</td><td>119</td><td>120–34:
Ascents
(122*, 125*,
126*, 129*,
132*, 133*)</td><td>135*
136
137*</td><td>138–45:
David
(138*)</td><td>146–50:
Hallel
(146*, 147*,
149*, 150*)</td></tr>
</table>

Many of these examples occur together in the same psalms; some occur on their own. The table above gives us some idea of the prevalence of the Zion tradition: this is the minimum number of psalms, only using linguistic criteria (for example, the royal psalms 45, 72 and 144 have not been listed because they do not offer a specific Zion reference, although it is clear that they would have been used in the Jerusalem Temple, with their David/Zion associations). Included here

51. For *'îr '^elōhîm*, see Pss. 46.5 (ET 4); 48.2 (ET 1); and Ps. 87.3. For *'îr yahweh*, see Pss. 48.9 (ET 8) and 101.8.

52. See Pss. 80.2 (ET 1) and 99.1.

53. For *'ēl 'elyôn*, see Ps. 78.35; for *'^elōhîm 'elyôn*, see Pss. 57.3 (ET 2) and 78.56. For *'ēl* and *'elyôn* occurring in the same verse or consecutive verses, see Pss. 73.11; 77.11 (ET 10) (with the reference to *'ēl* occurring in the following verse); 106.7; and 107.11; for *'^elōhîm* and *'elyôn* occurring in the same verse, see Pss. 46.5 (ET 4) and 50.14. For *yahweh 'elyôn* occurring together, see Pss. 7.18 (ET 17); 18.14 (ET 13); 47.3 (ET 2); and 97.9. For *yahweh* and *'elyôn* used in the same verse, see Pss. 21.8 (ET 7); 83.19 (ET 18); 91.9; and 92.2 (ET 1). Other references where *'elyôn* occurs entirely on its own are Pss. 9.3 (ET 2); 78.17; 82.6 (with an unusual term, *b^enê 'elyôn*); 87.5 and 91.1. Of these examples, Pss. 7; 18; 21; 57; 77; 82; 83; 91; 106 and 107 are psalms with no other 'Zion Markers'; although *'elyôn* as a term for the God of Jerusalem must have been interpreted as a Zion allusion by the editors, the term must be treated with caution.

are all those psalms which might earlier have referred to another sanctuary, but at the time of editing would have been used to speak of the Temple at Jerusalem.

Before we examine in more detail the editing process in separate collections within the five books, some overall observations are relevant. Seventy-five out of one hundred and fifty psalms bear clear marks of the Zion tradition, if not in the earliest stages of composition, at least in the later stages of editing. This is a count based only upon explicit references. This number of psalms far surpasses those identified by means of the theological criteria which have been used to suggest the didactic and eschatological editing of the Psalms.[54] The Zion tradition occurs in the two most prominent psalm forms. It is found in psalms which celebrate as a present experience God's presence in Zion: these are psalms which have been classified in the main as *hymnic* in form. It is also found in psalms which suggest a longing to return to Zion—psalms which have been classified as *laments* (or in some cases, psalms of confidence attached to or detached from the laments).[55] Furthermore, the Zion tradition is not only often found several times within the same psalm, thus confirming its significance, but also in pairs of psalms, suggesting that the editors deliberately chose to juxtapose psalms with the same terms as part of a 'catchword principle'. Examples include Psalms 2 and 3; 46 and 47; 50 and 51; 65 and 66; 73 and 74; 77 and 78; 82 and 83; 91 and 92; 92 and 93; 128 and 129; 132, 133 and 134; 134 and 135; 146 and 147.[56]

However, linguistic criteria alone cannot determine the full extent of the Zion tradition. Another way of assessing its importance is to look at the placing of this tradition within the smaller collections: it is evident that within each of the five books of the Psalter some of the collections have a deliberate arrangement whereby the Zion tradition is given a central place. The most obvious collection to start with is the Songs of Ascents.

3. *The Songs of Ascents (Psalms 120–34) and the Zion Tradition in Book V of the Psalter*

Almost every scholar who has written about this collection views the Zion tradition as an essential element within it, if not in individual psalms at the time of

54. The number of specifically didactic psalms is perhaps fifteen: the wisdom psalms (37; 49; 73; 112; 127; 128; 139; possibly also Pss. 25; 31; 40; 78; 92) and the Torah psalms (1; 19; 119). To this number might be added some thanksgiving psalms which address the congregation by way of testimony, taking the total up to perhaps twenty-five psalms in all. As for explicitly eschatological psalms (determined more by theological than linguistic criteria), these would include the kingship psalms (47; 93; 96; 97; 98; 99), the last Hallel (Pss. 146–50) and some royal psalms (2; 72; 89; 110; 118; 144) and a few individual laments looking ahead to a future reparation, amounting to just over twenty psalms in all.

55. In this way, the Zion tradition goes far beyond Gunkel's form-critical category of the five Zion Hymns (i.e. Pss. 46; 48; 76; 84; 87; 122), although it certainly includes these.

56. Cf. Pss. 2.6 and 3.5 (ET 4), 'holy hill'; 46.5 (ET 4) and 47.3 (ET 2), 'Most High'; 50.2 and 51.20 (ET 18), 'Zion'; 65.5 (ET 4) and 66.13, 'your house'; 73.17 and 74.3, 7, 'sanctuary'; 77.11 (ET 10) and 78.17, 'Most High'; 82.6 and 83.19 (ET 18), 'Most High'; 91.1, 9 and 92.2 (ET 1), 'Most High'; 92.14 (ET 13) and 93.5, 'house [of the Lord]'; 128.5 and 129.5, 'Zion'; 132.13 and 133.3 and 134.3 and 21, 'Zion'; 134.1 and 135.2, 'house of the Lord'; 146.10 and 147.12, 'Zion'.

their composition, at least in the editing of the psalms within the collection as a whole.[57] The previous outline of the Zion tradition in the Psalter as a whole accords with this observation: it is found explicitly in Psalms 122, 125, 126, 128, 129, 132, 133 and 134 of the collection, and, as will be demonstrated below, the Zion Markers in the psalms hold together this collection as a unified whole.

Psalms 120–134 stand as an independent collection first and foremost on account of the superscription *šîr hamma ʿalôt* appearing consecutively as a title for each psalm.[58] Various suggestions have been offered concerning the meaning of this term, but because they all point in the same direction, that these psalms were either sung 'going up to' Jerusalem or 'at' Jerusalem, and because the precise meaning is unclear, the variant interpretations need not concern us here.[59] In later Jewish tradition, the fifteen psalms were associated with the fifteen steps of the Temple leading from the Court of Women to the Court of Israel, and there are good reasons to accept the proposal that these psalms would have been sung by those making pilgrimage to the Jerusalem Temple.[60] The collection has been termed 'The Fifteen Songs of the Temple Steps'.[61] With the exception of Psalm 132, they are roughly the same length. They display many linguistic similarities;[62] they offer similar unusual formulaic expressions;[63] and they demonstrate

57. See, e.g., Keet 1969; Seybold 1978: 247-68; Mannati 1979; Beaucamp 1979; Auffret 1982; Grossberg 1989; Viviers 1994; Crow 1996: 129-87; Goulder 1997; 1998: 20-113; Satterthwaite 1999: 105-29; Hunter 1999.

58. Ps. 121 has the slightly different heading *šîr lamma ʿalôt*.

59. For a survey of the various meanings, see Keet 1969: 1-17, and Grossberg 1989: 15-19. The most common proposals include an 'ascent' of pilgrims to Jerusalem; the 'going up' of those returning from exile (although the absence of reference to the effects of the exile in Babylon makes this less likely); the 'graded rhythm' in each psalm (in which case, Ps. 132 stands outside this sequence); a reference to the 'series' or 'sequence' of songs, where the ending of one psalm leads in to the next; the pitch of 'high voices' used in the singing of these songs; or the place where the psalms were sung, possibly the Temple steps. The first and last proposals are the most compelling.

60. See the references in the Mishnah (*Middot* 2.5 and *Sukkah* 5.4), quoted in Grossberg 1989: 17.

61. Cf. Sawyer 1967–68: 33. This accords with the LXX translation: *ōdē tōn anabathmōn* may well indicate this practice at the time of the translation.

62. The clearest examples include the affirmative *kî* ('for, because') in Pss. 120.7; 122.5; 123.3; 125.3; 128.2, 4; 130.4, 7; 132.14; 133.3; the expression *hinnēh* ('behold') in Pss. 121.4; 123.2; 127.3; 128.4; 132.6; 133.1; 134.1; the replacing of *ʾašer* ('which') with the shortened form *še* in Pss. 122.4; 123.2; 124.1, 2, 6; 129.6, 7; 133.2, 3; *šām* ('there') to refer to Jerusalem in Pss. 122.4, 5; 132.17; 133.3; *ʿāmad* ('stand') in Pss. 122.2; 130.3; 134.1; *yiśrāʾēl* ('Israel', as the assembled community) in Pss. 124.1; 125.5; 128.6; 129.1; 130.7; *šālôm* ('peace') in Pss. 120.7; 122.6; 125.5; 128.6; and *rabbat* ('too long') in Pss. 120.6; 123.4; 129.1, 2. Further lists can be found in Grossberg (1989: 48-50) and Satterthwaite (1999: 106-107).

63. These include 'Maker of heaven and earth' in Pss. 121.2; 124.8; 134.3 (only elsewhere in Pss. 115.15 and 146.6); 'from this time on and for evermore' in Pss. 121.8; 125.2; 131.3 (only elsewhere in Pss. 113.2; 115.18; Isa. 9.7; 59.21; Mic. 4.7); 'let Israel say' in Pss. 124.1; 129.1; 'peace be upon Israel' in Pss. 125.5 and 128.6; '(may) the Lord bless you from Zion' in Pss. 128.5 and 134.3 (the latter three groups of examples being in this form only in these psalms); and 'let Israel hope in the Lord' in Pss. 130.6 and 131.3. Crow sees these six examples as formulae added into the psalms at the redactional stage (1996: 130-43). This is refuted by Satterthwaite 1999: 108-14.

distinctive poetic techniques.[64] The theme of blessing is clearly evident in at least twelve of the fifteen psalms, so much so that it has been proposed that the Priestly blessing of Num. 6.24-26 may have influenced the editors of this collection.[65]

But even if the collection illustrates a stylistic and linguistic unity, how can we be sure that its theological coherence is in the Zion tradition? There have been several attempts to see a gradual progression, united in the theme of the hope for the restoration of Zion, in this collection, of which that offered by Seybold is perhaps the most helpful (1978: 69-75). The following chart summarizes how this collection might be viewed:

120–22	*123–26*	*127–29*	*130–31*	*132–34*
arrival in Zion	lament and confidence	God's blessing from Zion	penitence and trust	departure from Zion

Psalms 120–34

Psalms 120–22 form the introduction, being a group of psalms referring to the pilgrims' arrival in Jerusalem. The unity of these three psalms may be seen in the ways in which Psalms 120 and 121 begin similarly, in their appeal for help from God, and Psalms 120 and 122 end similarly, with the hope for peace within Jerusalem. Psalm 120 sets the suppliant in a foreign land (see v. 5, where the references to Meshech, near the Black Sea and Kedar, in the Arabian desert, could be read symbolically as the psalmist's alienation in a pagan environment far from the Temple); Psalm 121 is about one whose eyes turn to Jerusalem; Psalm 122 forms the climax, with its focus on fellowship in the Temple. Psalms 133–34 form the conclusion, being a pair of psalms speaking of the departure from the Temple, with its appeal to all 'Israel' to experience God's blessings in Zion (Pss. 133.3 and 134.3). Psalms 123–26 form another group; each psalm here begins the second half with an imperative form usually addressed to God (Pss. 123.3; 124.6 [here a qal passive participle is used, but a call to the congregation to 'bless the Lord' is intended]; 125.4; 126.4). The first two psalms lament (in the mood of Ps. 120.6) the pagan environment (see Pss. 123.4 and 124.2-3 in this respect), and the second two begin with an affirmation of confidence of God's rule over all nations and his presence in Zion (Pss. 125.1; 126.1). Psalms 127–29 reflect on the

64. Viviers (1994: 281-83) has demonstrated that chiasmus is an important element in these psalms, taking Pss. 134 and 121 as the best examples. Hunter (1999: 189) and Grossberg (1989: 26) have shown the importance of what has been termed 'terrace patterns', or step-parallelism, whereby the end of one clause is taken up at the beginning of the next; for example Ps. 121.7-8: 'The Lord will keep you...he will keep your life...'; Ps. 126.2-3: 'The Lord has done great things for them... The Lord has done great things for us'; Ps. 130.5-6: 'I wait for the Lord, my soul waits... my soul waits'. Examples are to be found in every psalm. A refinement of this is the way a distinctive word or phrase is used to link the two ideas: for example, *lûlê* ('if...') in Ps. 124.1, 2; *'ᵃzay* ('then') in Ps. 124.3, 4, 5; and *'āz* ('then') in Ps. 126.2. A detailed assessment is given by Watson 1984: 208-13.

65. See Liebreich 1955. Taking the four phrases 'May the Lord bless you', 'May he protect you', 'May he be gracious to you' and 'May he give you peace', Liebreich finds these evident in twelve of the fifteen psalms (absent only from 124, 126 and 131). The idea is attractive, in that this blessing was apparently spoken by the priests on the Temple steps (see Tosefta, *Soṭah* 7.7). For a refinement of this view, see Grossberg 1989: 50-51.

results of God's blessings from Zion (Pss. 128.5; 129.5). Psalms 130–31 return to the theme of penitence and trust as in Psalms 123–126: the similarities between 130.7 and 131.3 ('O Israel, hope in the Lord') link this pair together. Psalm 132, different from the rest in style and length, is a composite psalm with fragments of some ancient ritual celebrating God's presence in Zion: its pre-exilic origins are clear by the reference to the ark (v. 8) and David's founding of Zion (vv. 1-5, 11-12, 13-18).

Other scholars have grouped this collection in different ways: P. Auffret, for example (1982: 439-531), sees three groups (Pss. 120–24; 125–29; 130–34), noting that the middle psalm in each collection has specific references to Zion (Ps. 122, with vv. 8-9 offering an unusual expression whereby Jerusalem is addressed in the second person singular), or to the Temple (Ps. 127, with its Solomonic superscription) or to David, founder of the Temple (Ps. 132). Another more holistic way of grouping these psalms would be to see Psalm 127 as the centre, with its additional superscription to Solomon, the builder of the Temple, with two psalms with additional Davidic interests on each side (Pss. 122; 124; 131 having Davidic superscriptions, and Ps. 132 being concerned with David's founding of the city).[66] Goulder takes the unity of the collection further still, reading it as a composition by a Levite at the time of Nehemiah, relating mainly to Nehemiah 12, whereby each psalm details one of Nehemiah's attainments in the rebuilding of Jerusalem.[67]

Whichever way this collection is viewed, the predominant impression is that these psalms make good sense when read in succession around the central theme of the restoration of Zion.[68] In this collection, Zion is not associated with warfare, or attributed with any political overtones: the enemies are not violent or warring, but are more those who oppose the faith of Israel. The overall impression is the importance of personal faith and trust in a God who will pour out blessings from Zion. R. Albertz (1997: 95-108) may be correct in observing the 'anti-imperialist' stance in the collection as a whole; but the emphasis on personal faith and trust in God and the apolitical view of Zion hardly makes the collection a threat to Persian rule.

So much for a smaller collection of psalms (120–34) within Book V as a whole; but how might this proposition illustrate the contention that other parts of Book V have also been part of an editing process with the Zion tradition a

66. Hengstenberg (1847: IV. 2, 1-10) observes that 'Yawheh' occurs 24 times in each of these seven psalms (120–26; 128–34), the third psalm of each seven using the form 'Yah' (122.3 and 130.3).

67. See, e.g., Goulder 1998: 20-113. For Goulder, Ps. 120 is Nehemiah's lament at the state of Jerusalem; 121, his journey to the city; 122, his arrival there; 123, his confrontation with opposition; 124, his deliverance; 125, his reforms against usurers; 126, his completion of the walls; 127, his rebuilding of the houses and gardens; 128, the outlying villages coming to Jerusalem; 129, Tobiah's confession; 130, the reforms against the breaking of the Sabbath; 131, the reforms on the mixed marriages; 132, the reforms of the Temple clergy; 133, the procession to the Temple; and 134, the thanksgiving within the Temple.

68. See Satterthwaite 1999: 107, and Hunter 1999: 180. Ps. 126.4, 'Restore the fortunes of Zion', provides an important summary of this thematic unity.

foremost concern? An interesting observation is that in one of the Qumran Psalms scrolls, the collection ends with Psalm 132, while Psalm 133 is found between Psalms 141 and 144, and Psalm 134 before Psalm 151 and after Psalm 140.[69] Psalm 132 is followed by Psalm 119, culminating this Zion collection with a Torah psalm: pilgrimage to Zion leads on to the Torah. (Ps. 119 is then followed by 135 and 136, thus returning back to the Zion theme.) This tells us about how the community at Qumran viewed the link between Torah and Zion, and also suggests that other psalms in Book V (Pss. 140; 141; 144), were seen as connected with Zion.

Goulder sees the Zion theme throughout the whole of Book V: Psalms 107–19 commemorate the rebuilding of the Temple, with reference to Ezra 6, and Psalms 135–50 commemorate Ezra's mission as narrated in Nehemiah 8.[70] This does not allow for the diversity of settings, theological themes and editorial linkages within Book V as a whole: the Zion tradition finds its real locus in Psalms 120–34, and although it is evident throughout the composition of Book V, it is integrated with other themes, as the table below demonstrates:

107	108–10 *David*	111	112–18 *Hallel* (Exodus)	119 *Torah*	120–34 *Ascents*	135 136 137	138–45 *David*	146–50 *Hallel* (creation)

The Separate Collections in Book V (Zion Tradition outside Ascents: Psalms 108; 110; 116; 118; 135; 137; 146; 147; 149; 150)

The explicit use of the Zion tradition in the rest of Book V, as already noted, is found in Ps. 107.11 (the use of *'elyôn*); Ps. 108.7 (an oracle from God's sanctuary); Psalm 110 (linking together the David/Zion themes, as in Ps. 132); Psalm 116 (a psalm of confidence similar in concerns to Pss. 123–26 and Pss. 130–31); Ps. 118.20, 26, 27 (with its references to the gate of the Lord, the house of the Lord, and the altar); Psalm 135 (closely linked in language to Ps. 134, with the terms 'sanctuary' and 'Zion' in Ps. 134.2, 3 and 'courts', 'house of the Lord' and 'Zion' in 135.2, 21); Psalm 137 (a lament on the loss of Zion, akin to Ps. 120, and serving as a theological reflection on the collection of Ascents); Psalm 138 (a thanksgiving psalm with similarities to Pss. 127–29); Psalms 146; 147; 149 and 150 (psalms speaking of God's blessings from Zion, like Pss. 133–34). Hence all of the other psalms with Zion concerns have echoes of linguistic and thematic themes evident in the Songs of Ascents. Taking Book V as a whole, we may note the integration of several basic theological themes: the two Hallel collections (Pss. 112–18; 146–50) celebrate the God of Exodus, who rescues, and the God of creation, who restores; the two Davidic collections (108–10; 138–45) celebrate God's covenant with David; the long Torah psalm (Ps. 119) is a call to obedience to the Law of Moses; and, in their position at the heart of Book V, the Songs of

69. See Sanders 1965: 23; Wilson 1985: 110; Flint 1997: 172-201.

70. See Goulder 1998: 116-209, 212-305, on Pss. 107–19 and Pss. 135–50 respectively. Ps. 137 is the most difficult psalm for Goulder's paradigm, because of its reference to Babylon.

Ascents (120–34) celebrate the God of Zion, who blesses. Almost every significant theological tradition is evident in Book V of the Psalter, and the Zion tradition in the Songs of Ascents is to be found in the very heart of it. Other psalms with Zion themes have not been brought together as another independent collection; nevertheless, their frequent occurrences suggest that the theme of the hope for the restoration of Zion, through trust in the God of Zion, is a dominant motif throughout Book V. The tradition of the restoration of Zion was highly significant in the minds of the editors as they drew together the various independent collections and separate psalms into the whole of Book V.[71]

4. *The Psalms of Korah (Psalms 42–49; 84–85; 87–88) and the Zion Tradition in Books II and III of the Psalter*

As in the Songs of Ascents, the Zion tradition plays a prominent part in the Korahite psalms, collections which are identified by the common term *lībᵉnê qōraḥ* as part of their superscription. Scholars who have written about this collection are all in agreement that, even if the Jerusalem Temple was not the focus at the time of composition, the editing was undertaken by the Korahites of Levitical descent: the affirmation of God's presence in Zion was their key concern.[72]

An overview of the two collections reveals how carefully each has been organized, and indicates that the Zion tradition plays a crucial part in each group. Psalms 42–49, in Book II, are part of the Elohistic Psalter extending from Psalms 42–83, and here it is possible to detect a five-part structure, as the following outline illustrates:

71. In spite of his defence of the didactic and personal influences on the formation of the Psalter, Zenger (1998: 81-82) argues that Book V is a continuation of the theme of 'the vision of the universal kingdom of YHWH, which he will bring about in a great theophany on Zion', begun in Book IV and developed in greater eschatological detail, with calls to celebrate in Zion, throughout Book V.

72. Buss (1963) contends that these psalms were written in the southern kingdom by musicians from the clan of Kohath within the tribe of Levi (1 Chron. 6.22) but away from the Temple, being edited by the Korahites for Temple use during the Persian period. J.M. Miller (1970) also sees the original provenance as not in the Temple, but at sanctuaries such as Arad and Hebron (noting [p. 64] that an ostracon from Arad lists *bᵉnê qōraḥ* ['sons of Korah'] as one of its groups there and proposing [p. 62] that the Korahites were probably a group from Edom who settled among the Calebites [1 Chron. 2.42-50] in the south, supporting the Temple cult, but not part of it). By the Chronicler's day they were resident in Jerusalem, and the pro-Jerusalem stance became a reality as well as an ideal. Peters (1922) contends the psalms were composed in pre-exilic times at Dan, in the far north, but were absorbed into the Temple liturgy in post-exilic times. Goulder (1982) develops Peters' view, and argues that as pre-exilic compositions they were used at a new year festival in the sanctuary at Dan, on account of their references to Jacob (Pss. 44.5, ET 4; 47.5, ET 4; 85.1; 87.2), the reference to Tyre (Ps. 45.13, ET 12) and the descriptions of the north (Pss. 42.7, ET 6; 84.7, ET 6). Nevertheless, Goulder concedes that in post-exilic times they were 'funnelled through the Jerusalem community' (p. 16). Wanke (1966) dates the psalms as post-exilic, and sees that in both composition and editing they were a part of the Temple liturgy, whether encouraging others from afar to make pilgrimage there, or celebrating God's presence in Zion, developing the pro-Zion stance of the post-exilic prophets. Smith (1991) also sees that this is a post-exilic collection due to the liturgical and scribal work of levitical priests, giving a post-exilic impression of the pre-exilic cult.

Pss. 42–43: individual lament, away from Zion, but longing to return
Ps. 44: communal lament, praying for deliverance from national adversity
Ps. 45: ‘in memory of David’: a royal psalm
Ps. 46–48: divine response: psalms confident in God’s presence in Zion (46, 48)
Ps. 49: individual lament (with an additional title *mizmôr*) with didactic appeal

Psalms 84–85, and 87–88, in Book III, are organized in a similar five-fold way:

Ps. 84: individual lament, away from Zion, but longing to return
Ps. 85: communal lament, praying for deliverance from national adversity
[Ps. 86: ‘in memory of David’: Davidic not Korahite superscription]
Ps. 87: divine response: a psalm confident in God’s presence in Zion
Ps. 88: individual lament (with an additional title *mizmôr*) with didactic appeal

These outlines fit well with our earlier list of those psalms which explicitly use the Zion tradition. Zion Markers within these two collections were in Psalms 42–43; 46; 47; 48; and Psalms 84 and 87. In other words, the Zion tradition is clearly evident in the first category of corresponding individual laments, with their longing to be in Zion (42–43 and 84) and in the fourth category of corresponding psalms of confidence which have been termed ‘divine response’ (46, 47, 48 and 87). These two corresponding categories illustrate how the Zion tradition gives each collection its thematic unity, just as in the Songs of Ascents.[73]

As well as this thematic unity, there are several linguistic features which confirm further the interrelationship of these two collections. The *individual laments* Pss. 42.3 (ET 2) and 84.3 (ET 2) refer to *’ēl ḥāy* (‘living God’), a term occurring elsewhere only in Hos. 2.1 (ET 1.10) and Josh. 3.10; *mišk^{e}nôteykā* (‘your dwellings’) occurs in Pss. 43.3 and 84.2 (ET 1) (also as *mišk^{e}nôt* [‘dwelling place’] in Ps. 87.2, and elsewhere only in Ps. 132.5); *bêt ’^{e}lōhîm* (‘house of God’) is found in Ps. 42.5 (ET 4) and *bêtekā* (‘your house’) in Ps. 84.5 (ET 4). In the *Zion hymns*, *‘îr ’^{e}lōhîm* (‘city of God’) occurs in Ps. 46.5 (ET 4), *‘îr ’^{e}lōhênû* (‘city of our God’) in Ps. 48.2 (ET 1) and *‘îr hā’^{e}lōhîm* (‘city of God’) in Ps. 87.3 (elsewhere the term is *‘îr yahweh* [‘city of the Lord’] as in Ps. 101.8); *‘elyôn* is found in Pss. 46.5 (ET 4), 47.3 (ET 2) and 87.5; *har qodšô* (‘his holy mountain’) occurs in Ps. 48.2 (ET 1), and in Ps. 87.1 as *b^{e}har^{e}rê qōdeš* (‘on the holy mountain’); *y^{e}kôn^{e}nehā* (‘he has established it [Zion]’) is found in Pss. 48.9 (ET 8) and 87.5; *’^{e}lōhê ya‘^{a}qōb* (‘God of Jacob) is in Ps. 46.8 (ET 7), and *mišk^{e}nôt ya‘^{a}qōb* (‘dwellings of Jacob’) in Ps. 87.2. In the *communal laments*, *ya‘^{a}qōb* (‘Jacob’) as the people of God is found in Pss. 44.5 (ET 4) and Ps. 85.3 (ET 2); and *ḥesed* (‘steadfast love’) occurs in Pss. 44.27 (ET 26) and 85.11 (ET 10).[74]

In this way, the Korah psalms function like the Songs of Ascents, in that they form an organized collection with internal stylistic unity. Like the Songs of

73. Additional superscriptions unite the psalms within each separate collection: Pss. 42 and 44 are termed *maśkîl*; Ps. 45, as *maśkîl šîr y^{e}dîdôt*; Ps. 46, as *sîr*; Ps. 47, as *mizmôr*; Ps. 48, as *šîr mizmôr*, and Ps. 49, as *mizmôr*. Pss. 84 and 85 are both termed *mizmôr*, while Ps. 87 is termed *mizmôr šîr* and Ps. 88, as *šîr mizmôr*. Other than Pss. 48 and 87, each also has the typically levitical heading *lam^{e}naṣṣēaḥ*.

74. For a more extended survey of verbal similarities, see Zenger 1994a, noting further also ‘concatenation’ links between the psalms within each collection (e.g. *b^{e}laḥas*, ‘in oppression’) in Pss. 42.10 (ET 9) and 43.2; *ya‘^{a}qōb* (‘Jacob’) in Pss. 84.9 (ET 8) and 85.2 (ET 1).

Ascents, they contain not only Zion hymns, but also psalms of lament and confidence, and wisdom and royal psalms, but the Zion tradition provides the focus for the collection as a whole. The editors of the Psalter took these collections, dividing them into two, and chose to open Book II with the first half of the collection and close Book III (adding the royal psalm, Ps. 89) with the second half. The other collections which were their concern in these two books were the psalms of Asaph (with a very different view of Zion, as will be seen below), and the psalms of David (the founder of the Temple and the exemplar of trust in the God of Zion, as in Pss. 51.20, ET 18; 52.10, ET 8; 53.7, ET 6; 55.15, ET 14; 57.3, ET 2; 60.8, ET 6; 61.5, ET 4; 63.3, ET 2; 65.2, 5, ET 1, 4; 68.30, ET 29; 69.10, 36, ET 9, 35 [all these references are in Book II]). In both Books II and III, the Davidic and Zion traditions are closely connected. In Book II, the Korahite collections are set in the midst of psalms with Davidic and Asaph concerns. In Psalms 42–49, Davidic psalms come before the collection (i.e. Pss. 3–41, with the exceptions of Pss. 10 and 33); a royal psalm is found in the middle of the collection (Ps. 45); and an Asaph psalm comes after the collection (Ps. 50). In Book III, the Asaph psalms come before the collection (e.g. Pss. 73–83), a Davidic-headed psalm comes in the middle (Ps. 86) and a royal psalm (Ps. 89) is found at the end. If in Book V the editors were emphasizing the importance of personal trust in the God of Zion, in Books II and III they are emphasizing more a more corporate/national trust in the God of David, the founder of Zion.

5. *The Psalms of Asaph (Psalms 73–83) and the Zion Tradition in Books II and III of the Psalter*

The psalms of Asaph, identified by the common superscription *l*^{e}*'āsāp* in Psalms 50, 73–83, provide important insights into the way the Zion tradition has been edited *into* the collection: here we find a number of psalms which give indications of an origin in the northern kingdom, and the accepted view is that the group as a whole was integrated into the Psalter of the Second Temple from an earlier northern provenance.[75] Perhaps the best illustration of the Zion editing in what looks to be an originally northern psalm is the ending of Psalm 78, which speaks of God's rejection of 'the tent of Joseph' and his choice of 'the tribe of Judah, Mt Zion, which he loves' (vv. 67-68).[76]

Northern influences pervade this collection: four psalms feature 'Joseph' (Pss. 77.16 (ET 15); 78.67; 80.2 (ET 1); and 81.6 (ET 5), and two of these also emphasize the importance of 'Ephraim' (Pss. 78.67; 80.3, ET 2). There are several explicit references to the Exodus tradition (Pss. 77.11-22, ET 10-21; 78.11-53; 80.9-12, ET 8-11; and 81.5-8, ET 4-7, the only occurrences in Books I–III).[77] Even

75. See Buss 1963; Nasuti 1988; Rendsburg 1990; Seybold 1994; Millard 1994: 89-103; Houston 1995; Goulder 1995; 1996; Mitchell 1997: 90-107.

76. See, e.g., Carroll 1971; Campbell 1979.

77. See Goulder (1995: 79-80) who, writing extensively on the northern origins of this collection, notes the marked affinities between Ps. 81 and Deut. 32. Goulder also observes that only the Exodus traditions are prevalent here, not those of Sinai.

when the creation tradition is used in Ps. 74.12-17, this too has close affinities with the parting of the Red Sea as well as with old creation myths. The distinctive references to God as Shepherd (Pss. 74.1; 77.21, ET 20; 78.52; 79.13; 80.2, ET 1; and 83.13, ET 12) again suggest a reflection on the Exodus traditions; indeed, in Psalms 77, 78, and 80 the creation tradition is actually used in the context of the Exodus tradition. The prominence of *ʾēl*, a term used for God especially (although not exclusively) in northern circles, which occurs some nineteen times in the collection (only six times in the Korah collection), in nine of the twelve psalms, again suggests a northern association. The expression *ʾ^{e}lōhê yaʿ^{a}qōb* ('God of Jacob') in Pss. 75.10 (ET 9); 76.7 (ET 6); and 81.2, 5 (ET 1, 4) may be another indication of this.

In contrast to the eleven psalms of Korah (twelve if Ps. 43 is seen as a separate psalm), the twelve psalms of Asaph have a developed theme of God's judgment: if the psalms of Korah illustrate a longing for a deeper experience of God's presence in Zion, the psalms of Asaph lament the absence of God there. The judgment is experienced against Israel (Pss. 50; 77; 78; 80; 81), against Jerusalem (Pss. 74; 79), against the nations (Pss. 75; 76; 83), against the impious (Ps. 73) and even against other gods (Ps. 82). The laments concern national defeat, rather than natural disasters, and the images of Zion here have a more military, warlike context, again in contrast to the more worship-centred picture of Zion evident in the Korah psalms and the Songs of Ascents.

As with the Korah psalms, a careful organization of the psalms within the collection in Psalms 73–83 is evident, as the following outline illustrates:[78]

Ps. 73:	didactic psalm: God's judgment on the impious
Ps. 74:	communal lament
Pss. 75–76:	the divine response (through oracles): God's abode is in Zion
Ps. 77:	individual lament
Ps. 78:	didactic psalm: God's judgment on his own people
Pss. 79–80:	communal laments
Pss. 81–82:	the divine response (through oracles): God's abode is in Zion
Ps. 83:	individual lament

When these outlines are considered in the light of our earlier list of psalms containing explicit references to the Zion tradition, an interesting observation may be made. The Zion tradition is found in all of these psalms *except* Psalms 75 and 81, and both of these form a pair with a psalm where the Zion tradition is most apparent (Pss. 76 and 82). Hence it is clear that, in the editing of the psalms

78. It is hard to explain why Ps. 50 has been split off from the larger collection: one reason may be that its opening provides a commentary on the end of Ps. 51, which is a prayer for the restoration of Zion. Yet its theme of judgment, its oracular material, its use of the Exodus tradition along with its Zion orientation, all link it with Pss. 73–83. It has several linguistic connections, as well: for example, the expression *w^{e}zîz śāday* ('the moving creatures of the field') occurs only in Pss. 50.11 and 80.14 (ET 13); *hôpîʿa* ('shine forth') occurs in Ps. 50.2 and only elsewhere in this collection in Ps. 80.2 (ET 1), although see also Ps. 94.1. Ps. 50.7 ('Hear, O my people, and I will speak, O Israel, I will testify against you') is remarkably similar to Ps. 81.9 (ET 8) ('Hear, O my people, while I admonish you; O Israel, if you would but listen to me').

at least, the Zion tradition is a central feature in this whole collection.[79] This confidence in God's presence in Zion offers a stark contrast with the sense of judgment which pervades the Asaph psalms generally. Examples include Ps. 50.2, 'Out of Zion the perfection of beauty, God shines forth'; Ps. 74.2, 'remember Mt Zion, where thou hast dwelt'; Ps. 76.3 (ET 2), 'His abode has been established in Salem,[80] his dwelling place in Zion'; and Ps. 78.68 'but he chose the tribe of Judah, Mt Zion, which he loves'.

This conflict between faith in the God of Zion and present experience of God's judgment on Israel is an important motif within Book III as a whole, with its conclusion a lament on the destruction of the Davidic dynasty (Ps. 89). Whereas the Davidic and Zion traditions are held together overall in a more confident sense in Book II, the insertion of the Asaph psalms in Book III give this David/Zion appeal a more realistic, judgment-focused orientation. Yet even here, through the inclusion of the more faith-focused second Korahite collection, and through the theme of the ingathering of God's people at Zion in the Asaphite collection, Book III as a whole prepares the way for a fuller expression of God's world rule in Zion, found in the kingship psalms near the beginning of Book IV.[81] To this group of psalms we now turn.

6. *The Kingship Psalms (Psalms 93–100) and the Zion Tradition in Book IV of the Psalter*

Although no superscription unites this collection, most commentators agree that the kingship of God is a unifying theme, but there is some disagreement as to where the collection begins and ends.[82] The analysis below follows D.M. Howard

79. The list of psalms here includes examples of the use of *'elyôn* as well: i.e. Pss. 73.11; 77.11 (ET 10); 82.6; and 83.19 (ET 18).

80. Goulder (1996: 86-88) reads 'Salem' here as a reference to a city near Shechem in the north, and hence sees the reference to Zion as typical Jerusalemite editing of the psalm.

81. Mitchell (1997: 99-107, 166-76) sees that the word *'āsāp* may well be a pun on the idea of the gathering together (the root of the verb in Hebrew is *'sp*) of the people of God, as in Ps. 50.5 ('Gather to me my faithful ones!': *'isᵉpû lî ḥᵃsîdāy*) and so Mitchell interprets the progression from this collection to Book IV in an eschatological sense. Smith (1992b: 409-10) takes a similar view: the Asaph psalms, followed by the Korah psalms and the final lament on the loss of the monarchy in Ps. 89, end the 'historical and temporal' orientation of Books I–III, with Book IV beginning to take on more eschatological dimensions. For a slightly different interpretation, emphasizing less the eschatological aspect, but nevertheless highlighting the continuity between the Asaph psalms and Book IV, see Cole 2000: 231-35, who sees the dominant question in Book III as a lament-type cry 'How long must we suffer?', with the answer to this lament being found in the kingship psalms in Book IV.

82. Gunkel and Begrich (1928–33: II, 94-116, ET 1998: 66-81) view Pss. 47, 93, 96–99 as forming the collection, on the basis of the phrase, 'The Lord is King' (*yahweh mālak*). Westermann (1962: 282, ET 1981: 255) sees the collection as comprising Pss. 93, 95–99, 100. Goulder (1975) argues that the whole of Book IV pertains to the same theme, being a collection of Tabernacles psalms: Ps. 90 opens the liturgy, Pss. 91–104 were sung at morning and evening times during the seven days of the festival, and Pss. 105–106 were added after the exile. Howard (1993b) argues that Pss. 90–94 could be seen as an independent collection added to Pss. 95–100, although in a later work (1997) he takes Pss. 93–100 as a unified collection. Millard (1994: 147-61) sees that Pss. 90–93 form one group, 94–100 another, and 101–106 a final group in Book IV. Wilson (1993b) takes out the psalms he sees as

and takes Psalms 93–100 as the basic unity. This would imply that Psalms 93–94 form an introduction, suggesting a yearning for God's kingship to be established, while Psalms 95–100 develop the theme whereby God's kingship is affirmed as a reality, first over his own people, and finally over the nations of the earth.[83] The following outline sets out this theological progression more clearly.

Ps. 93:	God's kingship is forever
Ps. 94:	God will come to judge the nations of the earth
Ps. 95:	God's people are called upon to acknowledge God as king
Ps. 96:	'Sing to the Lord a new song'
Ps. 97:	God reigns in Zion
Ps. 98:	'Sing to the Lord a new song'
Ps. 99:	God reigns in Zion
Ps. 100:	The whole earth is called upon to acknowledge God as king

Although Psalms 95–100 reflect a more obvious internal structure, the two previous psalms are nevertheless connected to what follows. Psalm 93 (affirming the permanence of God's reign, in contrast to the transience of human life expressed in Pss. 90 and 91) begins with the phrase 'The Lord is king' (*yahweh mālak*), a phrase taken up again in Pss. 96.10; 97.1; 99.1. The end of Psalm 94 and the beginning of Psalm 95 are connected in their references to God as rock (*ṣûr maḥsî* in 94.22; *ṣûr yiš'ēnû* in 95.1). Psalms 94 and 95 both speak of God as 'our God' ('the Lord our God' [*yahweh 'ᵉlōhênû*] in Ps. 94.23; 'our God' [*ᵉlōhênû*] in 95.7). He is the judge of the earth (94.2), and in his hand are the depths of the earth (95.4).

Within Psalms 95–100, Psalms 95 and 100 form the prologue and epilogue on the acknowledgment of God as king, and the four inner psalms form an alternating pattern of celebration and awe at the presence of God. Psalm 95.6-7 calls upon the people of God to worship ('O come let us worship and bow down... For he is our God, and we are the people of his pasture' [*wa'ᵃnaḥnû 'am mar'îtô*]) and Ps. 100.1-3 calls on the whole world to worship ('Make a joyful noise to the Lord, all the lands...know that the Lord is God...we are his people, and the sheep of his pasture' [*'ᵃnaḥnû 'ammô wᵉṣō'n mar'îtô*]). Psalms 96 and 98 both begin with 'Sing to the Lord a new song' (96.1; 98.1), and each calls upon the whole earth to acknowledge Israel's God (96.1; 98.4; both use the expression 'all the earth' [*kol hā'āreṣ*]). Psalms 96.11 and 98.7 both exhort 'Let the sea roar, and all that fills it' (*yir'am hayyām ûmᵉlō'ô*) and each psalm ends with the same refrain 'before the Lord, for he is coming, for he is coming to judge the earth. He will judge the world with righteousness, and the peoples with his truth [or equity]' (Pss. 96.13 and 98.9). Psalms 97 and 99 are also closely connected: each starts with 'The Lord reigns', each sees Zion as rejoicing in God (Pss. 97.8; 99.2), and each ends with reflecting on the holiness of God (Pss. 97.12; 99.9).

alluding to Moses (90; 92; 94; 102; 105–106) and those alluding to David (Pss. 101; 103; 104), which leaves Pss. 93, 95–100 as the kingship collection. Auwers (2000: 50-57) sees Pss. 95–100 as the kernel of the collection.

83. Hossfeld (1994) argues for the inclusion of Ps. 95 in the collection because of its many linguistic and theological links with Ps. 94 before it and Ps. 96 after it.

As for specific Zion Markers within the collection as a whole, Psalms 97 and 99 are the most explicit: 'Zion hears and is glad, and the daughters of Judah rejoice, because of your judgments, O God' (Ps. 97.8) and 'The Lord is great in Zion; he is exalted over all the peoples' (Ps. 99.2). There are other references to Zion in other psalms. Psalm 93 ends with the expression 'Holiness befits your house, O Lord, for evermore' (v. 5). Psalm 96 affirms that 'strength and beauty are in his sanctuary...ascribe to the Lord the glory due to his name; bring an offering, and come into his courts' (vv. 6, 8). And Psalm 100 calls the people to 'enter his gates with thanksgiving, and his courts with praise' (v. 4).

The Exodus tradition is as evident in these psalms as it is in the Asaph psalms. The reference to Moses in the superscription of Psalm 90 and in 90.13, the assertion that Moses and Aaron are prototypes of priests in the Temple in Ps. 99.6, and the reflection on the disobedience of the people under Moses' leadership at Meribah and Massah in Ps. 95.8, all refer back to the God of the Exodus.[84] It is not surprising that some scholars see that this collection fits well with the period of exile, when the Exodus traditions gained a renewed significance: connections between these psalms and Isaiah 40–55, which develops the same traditions of the kingship of God, the Exodus, and God's restoration of Zion, have often been noted.[85]

It may be that the earliest locus for this collection was indeed the exile, or even before that in a new year festival during the period of the monarchy; but, from the point of view of the editors, the function of the Zion tradition in Psalms 93–100 would be to assure the discouraged Second Temple community that Zion was where God's new act of restoration would take place. The longing for Zion and the hope for renewed worship in the Temple link the kingship psalms with the same theme in the Songs of Ascents, the Korah psalms and the Asaph psalms.

Within Book IV as a whole, Zion Markers are found at each side of the collection of kingship psalms. They occur by way of the use of the term *'elyôn* in the two psalms before Psalms 93–100 (Pss. 91.9 and 92.1). They occur again in the two psalms following the collection: Ps. 101.8 refers to 'the city of the Lord' (*'îr yahweh*), and Ps. 102.16 explicitly states, 'For the Lord will build up Zion, he will appear in his glory'.[86] And as well as the reference to *'elyôn* in Ps. 106.7, the last actual verse of Psalm 106, at the end of Book IV, refers to the people being gathered among the nations to give thanks to God's holy name and glory in his

84. See Goulder 1975: 272-73, 285-87, who notes that the Exodus theme continues into the rest of Book IV: Ps. 103.8 is a quotation of Exod. 34.6, and Pss. 105 and 106 are an account of God's great deeds during the time of the Exodus. See also Wilson 1985: 187-88, 215. Tate (1990: xxvi) terms the whole of Book IV 'A Moses Book'.

85. Cf. Creach 1998: 63-76, who notes several linguistic parallels, including those at the beginning and end of both books: e.g. Ps. 90.5-6 and Isa. 40.6-8; Ps. 90.13 and Isa. 40.1; Ps. 106.46-47 and Isa. 54.7; and Ps. 105.10 and Isa. 55.3. See also Jeremias 1987: 121-35, on Pss. 96 and 98 and the relationship with Second Isaiah.

86. On the Zion traditions in this psalm, see Brunert 1996: 179-81, who argues that Ps. 102 is a reassurance to an individual sufferer that the community's hope in the inviolability of Zion continues in spite of appearances to the contrary ('Ps. 102 tröste sich ein einzelner Leidender mit der kollektiven Hoffnung für Zion').

praise (v. 47), a phrase which suggests again that the restoration of God's people in Zion was never far from the editors' concerns.[87]

7. *The Psalms of an Entrance Liturgy (Psalms 15–24) and the Zion Tradition in Book I of the Psalter*

Although Psalms 15–24 have a common element because of the superscription *lᵉdāwid*, this does not provide an exceptional marker in separating these psalms from all the other psalms with the same headings in Book I (only Pss. 10 and 33 are without such a superscription). However, it is possible to detect four smaller collections throughout Book I.[88] Psalms 3–14 may be seen as having some internal unity, with Psalm 8 at the centre (creating a focus to the collection in its affirmation of the glory of God and the dignity of humankind) and five laments on each side, the predominant theme being penitence and lament.[89] Psalms 35–41 suggest a similar group, with Psalm 38 at the centre; here too the dominant theme is lament.[90] Psalms 25–34 indicate a third collection, with Psalm 29 at the heart (creating a focus like Ps. 8, affirming the presence of God in the Temple) with laments (Pss. 26–28) and thanksgivings (Pss. 30–32) set on each side. The linguistic and theological affinities between Psalms 30 and 28, 31 and 27, 32 and 26 suggest that the thanksgivings of Psalms 30–32 may be read as answers to the laments of Psalms 26–28 respectively. The two outer psalms (25 and 34) are also related to each other linguistically and theologically, both being acrostic in form and both being concerned for the plight of the poor and the justice of God: this collection ends more optimistically than the other two collections.[91]

Psalms 15–24 suggest a fourth collection, marked even more than Psalms 25–34 by the theme of confidence in the justice of God. This groups offers perhaps the most convincing internal arrangement, and because the Zion tradition plays a significant part in this collection, it will be the focus of attention here.[92] The outline below reflects how striking this chiastic arrangement is:

Ps. 15:	an entrance liturgy: who shall dwell on God's holy hill?
Ps. 16:	confident trust in God
Ps. 17:	lament for deliverance from personal enemies
Ps. 18:	royal psalm: thanksgiving for victory in battle
Ps. 19:	hymn to God as Creator and giver of the law

87. See Howard 1997: 200-207; in Appendix 4, entitled 'Wisdom and Royalist/Zion Traditions in the Psalter', Howard observes that, far from rejecting a theology of Zion, and emphasizing instead the covenant with Moses and the eschatological coming of God as King, key elements in Book IV as a whole concern Zion, and with it, the Davidic kingdom: these are the necessary earthly expressions of Yahweh's kingdom: '...the psalms as they now stand focus much more on Zion and traditions associated with the monarchy than many scholars have allowed (p. 207).

88. A useful summary of the four collections is found in Auwers 2000: 43-47.

89. Cf. Hossfeld and Zenger 1992: 34-49; Barbiero 1999: 63-188.

90. Cf. Hossfeld and Zenger 1992: 23-34; Barbiero 1999: 543-717.

91. Cf. Hossfeld and Zenger 1994: 375-88; also Zenger 1994b; Barbiero 1999: 325-541.

92. Auffret 1982: 407-38; Hossfeld and Zenger 1993; P.D. Miller 1994: 127-42; Millard 1994: 24-25, 135-37; Gillingham 2002: 68-72.

Pss. 20–21:	royal psalms: prayer and thanksgiving for victory in battle
Ps. 22:	lament for deliverance from personal enemies
Ps. 23:	confident trust in God
Ps. 24:	an entrance liturgy: who shall ascend the hill of the Lord?

There are several linguistic affinities between the corresponding forms of the psalms in this chiasmus. Psalms 16 and 23 provide a good example.[93] So too do Psalms 15 and 24.[94] There are also several clear links between neighbouring psalms.[95] For our purposes, a notable feature is the way in which the Zion tradition has been used within this collection as a whole. It is clearly evident in the psalms at the beginning and end of the collection,[96] it is present in the royal psalms,[97] and it is discernable in Psalm 23, one of the psalms of confidence.[98]

Some scholars propose that the two key themes in this collection are the Torah and the King (e.g. P.D. Miller 1994: 2). These themes are undoubtedly present in the heart of the collection (Pss. 18; 19; 21-22). But the Zion tradition, present at the beginning, middle and end of Psalms 15–24 should not be underestimated: it suggests that the royal tradition and the Torah traditions find their true locus in worship at the Temple.[99]

What of the Zion tradition in the rest of Book I? First, in Psalms 3–14, the first and last psalms offer explicit references to the importance of the Temple (Ps. 3.5, ET 4 has 'he answers me from his holy hill'; and Ps. 14.7 ends with a prayer that 'deliverance for Israel would come out of Zion'). The Zion tradition is also found in Pss. 5.8 (ET 7); 7.18 (ET 17); 9.12, 15 (ET 11, 14) and 11.4. Secondly, in Psalms 25–34, it occurs in Pss. 26.8; 27.4, 6; and 29.9. And Psalm 29, which forms the

93. See, for example, the reference to 'my cup' (*kôsî*) in Pss. 16.5 ('The Lord is my chosen portion and my cup') and 23.5 ('my cup overflows'), the only time that the term is used in the Psalter; see also Ps. 16.10 ('For you do not give me up to Sheol, or let your faithful one see the Pit') and Ps. 23.4 ('Even though I walk through the valley of the shadow of death, I fear no evil'); and Ps. 16.11 ('In your presence there is fullness of joy; in your right hand are pleasures for evermore') with Ps. 23.6 ('Surely goodness and mercy shall follow me all the days of my life, and I shall dwell in the house of the Lord my whole life long').

94. E.g. Ps. 15.1 ('O Lord, who may abide in your tent? Who may dwell on your holy hill?') and Ps. 24.3 ('Who shall ascend the hill of the Lord? And who shall stand in his holy place?).

95. Cf. P.D. Miller 1994: 128-39; also Hossfeld and Zenger 1993: 169-77. Examples include Ps. 15.5 ('those who do these things shall never be moved') and Ps. 16.8 ('because he is at my right hand, I shall not be moved'); Pss. 17.15 and 18.21, 25 (ET 20, 24) on God's gift of 'righteousness' which rewards the suppliant's obedient faith; the references to the 'servant' in the superscription of Ps. 18 ('David the servant of the Lord') and Ps. 19.12 (ET 11, 'moreover by them is your servant warned'). On the affinities between Pss. 22, 23 and 24, see Gillingham 2002: 66-67.

96. Ps. 15.1, with its question concerning who will be admitted to the Temple, followed by a list of conditions to be met by attaining an obedient life (vv. 2-5) matches Ps. 24.3, with its similar question concerning admission to the Temple, and a similar list of requisite moral qualities (vv. 4-6).

97. Ps. 18.7 (ET 6), 'From his temple he heard my voice'; Ps. 20.3 (ET 2), 'May he send you help from the sanctuary, and give you support from Zion'.

98. Ps. 23.6 ('I shall dwell in the house of the Lord forever'), which follows on from an implicit reference to the Temple in Ps. 22.26 (ET 25): 'From you comes my praise in the great congregation'.

99. Barbiero (1999: 324) notes that in Pss. 15–24 pilgrimage to the Temple provides a focal point for sustaining the needs of the people. This is particularly surprising given Barbeiro's main concern with the ways the psalms in Book I serve the needs of 'the pious poor' away from cultic worship in post-exilic times.

climax of the collection, is very much concerned with the awesome presence of God in the Temple.

However, in Psalms 35–41, the Zion tradition is not evident at all. Here the psalms focus much more on the impoverishment and sickness of individual suppliants, in which (through the Davidic superscriptions) the editors have aligned the psalmists' piety to that of David. The absence of any Zion Markers in the latter part of Book I is significant, and gives credence to the views of scholars such as Hossfeld, Zenger and Lohfink that here we might have a collection of psalms focusing on the spiritually and physically poor, marginalized from the life of the Temple.[100] 'Armenfrömmigkeit' ('the piety of the poor') on its own, however, is not the dominant theme throughout the whole of Book I, nor does it continue into Book II. Zion Markers are very much in evidence in the heart of Book I—in Psalms 15–24, and in the psalms which are found just before it (Pss. 9; 11; 14 especially) and in psalms just after it (Pss. 26; 27; 29)—and the Zion Markers are evident again in Psalms 42–49 of Book II, in the Psalms of Korah. So, even if the Zion tradition is absent towards the end of Book I, the editors of Book I and II overall considered as a major concern the importance of Temple worship and God's presence in Zion.

8. *The Zion Tradition at the Beginning and End of the Psalter: Psalms 1–2 and Psalms 146–50*

Scholars who advocate the didactic and the eschatological editing of the Psalter appeal to Psalms 1–2 and 146–50 as evidence of this.[101] Taking Psalms 1–2 together, both being psalms without superscriptions, it is clear that a number of linguistic features unite them.[102] Psalm 1 focuses on wickedness and righteousness in the life of the individual, Psalm 2, on wickedness and righteousness in the life of the nation. Psalm 1 concerns the model Israelite, Psalm 2 the ideal king.[103] The didactic themes are thus apparent in the appeal to instruction in Psalm 1,[104] and the eschatological themes, in the appeal to the kingship of God over the nations, sealed by his decree to the king, in Psalm 2.[105]

Psalms 146–50, also psalms without superscriptions, are connected not only by the call to praise God (*hal*ᵉ*lû yāh*) at the beginning of each one, but also by a number of linguistic features.[106] Like Psalm 2, their theme is that of the kingship

100. See Zenger 1991a; Hossfeld and Zenger 1992: 21-50; Lohfink 1990: 108-25.

101. See Brownlee 1971; Brennan 1980; Wilson 1985: 204-28; Mays 1987; Brueggemann 1991; P.D. Miller 1993; Zenger 1993; Mitchell 1997: 73-74, 83-89; Barbiero 1999: 31-50, 724-25; Høgenhaven 2001; Cole 2002.

102. See *yāšāb* ('sit') in Pss. 1.1 and 2.4; *'ašrê* ('blessed') in Pss. 1.1 and 2.12; *derek* ('way') and *'ābad* ('perish') in Pss. 1.1 and 2.12; *hāgâ* ('meditate' or 'devise, plot') in Pss. 1.2 and 2.1; *nātan* ('give') in Pss. 1.3 and in Ps. 2.8.

103. See P.D. Miller 1993: 85; also McCann 2001.

104. The word 'instruction' is preferred for 'in the law of the Lord' (*b*ᵉ*tôrat yahweh*) in Ps. 1.2, as it holds together both the Torah and the wisdom themes in this psalm. See McCann 1992: 118-20.

105. In pre-exilic times this would imply the ruling monarch, in post-exilic times, the ideal king.

106. See Pss. 145.13 and 146.10, on the everlasting reign of God; Pss. 145.14 and 146.8, on God lifting up those who are falling; Pss. 147.16, 18 and 148.8, in the references to God's word (or

of God over all nations and all creation: the specific links between Psalms 2 and 149 are notable in this respect, where all nations and peoples are seen to come under the judgment of God.[107] Hence an eschatological interpretation of this group of psalms is entirely justified. The didactic interpretation is seen through a number of admonitions in the first two psalms, using wisdom expressions like those in Proverbs (Pss. 146.3-4, 5-7, 8-9; 147.3, 6, 8-11). Psalm 147.19 uses Torah-type language in its reference to the 'statutes and ordinances of Israel', but this is unusual in this collection. Hence the didactic influence in these psalms is less explicitly pervasive than might first appear.

Nevertheless, several scholars would see that didactic and eschatological themes are the dominant concerns of the beginning and ending of the Psalter, and that these indicate the presence of one or both of these themes throughout the Psalter. R.G. Kratz, for example, builds an entire theology of the Psalter on its Torah piety;[108] yet only two other psalms (19B; 119) might be termed 'Torah psalms', and explicit references to the Torah are found only in a handful of other psalms.[109] And yet if one broadens the idea of 'Torah' to mean 'instruction', and so includes all those psalms with wisdom influence in them, as in Psalms 146 and 147, the theme becomes diffuse and difficult to categorize. The same problem is evident with regard to a thoroughgoing eschatological interpretation: only Psalms 93–100, which celebrate the kingship of God, and a handful of royal psalms (Pss. 2; 18; 72; 89; 110; 118; 144) explicitly refer to God's coming again to his people in power and glory.[110] There is of course some merit in seeing Psalms 1–2 and 146–50 as markers for the didactic and eschatological themes in other parts of the Psalter; but it is not the whole story.

What commentators seem to miss is the evidence of the Zion tradition in Psalms 1–2 and 146–50. This may be because it is not explicit in Psalm 1, but the idea of the law being taught in Zion is found in other parts of the Hebrew Bible, and indeed beyond it.[111] It is no coincidence that even in the Psalter, all three

command) sending snow and frost; Pss. 148.14 and 149.2, on Israel's close relationship with God; and Pss. 149.3 and 150.4 on praising God with dancing and tambourine. Articles on this group of psalms (with a preference for their wisdom themes and the piety of the poor) include: Lohfink 1990: 108-10; 1992; Millard 1994: 34-35, 108-109; Zenger 1997; 1998, and the response to Zenger by P.D. Miller 1998, especially on the place of Pss. 146–50 in Book V and the Psalter as a whole. What is notable among these scholars is how little attention is paid to the Zion tradition in this group of psalms.

107. See Pss. 2.1-2 and 149.7-9, on God's judgment of the nations; Pss. 2.6 and 149.2, on Zion inheriting God's promises; Pss. 2.9 and 149.8, on God's judgment with iron (*barzel*); Pss. 2 and 149.8, on God's warning to kings and rulers (Ps. 2.10) and nobles (Ps. 149.8). On the affinities between these two psalms, see Brennan 1980; Cole 2002: 80.

108. Cf. Kratz 1995: 13-18; also Lohfink 1990: 112-14.

109. These include Pss. 37.31; 40.9 (ET 8); 78.5, 10; and 105.45.

110. It could be argued, as does Mays (1987: 10), that the three 'Torah psalms', Pss. 1, 19 and 119, have each been placed alongside psalms with themes which emphasize not only Davidic kingship but, more particularly, the kingship of Yahweh (1/2; 18/19; 118/119). Nevertheless, this only includes six psalms in all.

111. See Isa. 2.3 and Mic. 4.2: 'Out of Zion shall go forth instruction (*tôrâ*)'; 4QFlor 10-14 on 2 Sam 7.14: '...the shoot of David will appear with the teacher of the law...in Zion in the end of

psalms which focus on the importance of the law (Pss. 1; 19B; 119) have been placed next to other psalms which have several Zion Markers (Pss. 2; 18 and 20; 118 and the Songs of Ascents). And it is possible that the reference in Ps. 1.3 to the tree being planted by the water, giving its fruit in due season, may be portraying the righteous person in the Temple, as J.F.D. Creach (1999) argues. Creach cites Ezek. 47.12 and psalms which use the same imagery with reference to the Temple (Pss. 52.10, ET 8 and 92.13-14, ET 12-13) to show how in Ps. 1.3 this suggests an image of obedient piety to the law finding full expression in the stability of the Temple through the metaphor of the tree. However that may be, the Zion tradition is certainly explicit in Ps. 2.6: 'I have set my king on Zion, my holy hill'. And given the close connections between Psalms 2 and 3 (not least in the reference to 'the holy mountain' in Pss. 2.6 and 3.5, ET 4), it could be argued that it is the Zion tradition that provides an overture to these first psalms in the Psalter, culminating in the collection of Psalms 15–24. If the Zion tradition is more significant than has previously been thought, then it is this which holds together both the didactic and the eschatological elements in Psalms 1–2.

Turning to Psalms 146–50, a similar observation could be made. The Zion tradition is found in all but one of these psalms. The importance of giving praise to God in Zion, and the importance of seeing the kingship of God established first and foremost in Zion, pervades the collection. Examples include Pss. 146.10 ('The Lord will reign forever, your God, O Zion, for all generations'); 147.2 ('The Lord builds up Jerusalem') and 147.12 ('Praise the Lord, O Jerusalem! Praise your God, O Zion!': in this last verse, a 'catchword connection' is made with the preceding psalm); 149.1-2 ('Sing to the Lord a new song, his praise in the assembly of the faithful; ...let the children of Zion rejoice in their King') and 150.1 ('Praise God in his sanctuary'). The impression is that all creation is being called upon, throughout Psalms 146–50, to make pilgrimage to Zion to see the presence of God there in all its fullness: this may be as yet an unrealized ideal, and in that sense its eschatological aspect is significant, but the vision is of an actual city in a particular place—Zion.[112]

9. *Conclusion*

We have noted how extensively the editors have integrated the Zion tradition throughout the whole Psalter. In seventy-five psalms, dispersed throughout all five books, the presence of God in Zion is an important focus of faith, whether in the prayers (*t^epillôt*) for the individual, longing to return there, or in the hymns

days'; Ecclus. 24.10-11 (speaking of wisdom, but later in the chapter wisdom is identified with the law): 'In the holy tent I ministered before him, and so I was established in Zion. Thus in the beloved city he gave me a resting place, and in Jerusalem was my domain'; also 2 Esd. 2.40: 'Take again your full number, O Zion, and close the list of your people who are clothed in white, who have fulfilled the law of the Lord'.

112. *Contra* Zenger 1998: 99-100, who argues that the editors of the Psalter were working from a 'post-cultic' perspective, and that the Psalter as whole is about a 'spiritual' pilgrimage to Zion (albeit noting a modification of this view in Keel and Zenger [eds] 2002: 180-206).

(*tᵉhillîm*) of the community, experiencing the presence of God there. The title 'Psalms of David' for the entire Psalter indicates not only the relationship of David and his line with the Psalter as a whole, in a didactic sense (as a model for personal piety) and in an eschatological sense (as a model for an ideal coming king); it speaks too of David as the founder of the Temple (as expressed in 2 Sam. 7) and marks out the Temple as the focal point for the good life and future hope. In an eschatological sense, God will return to his Temple as king, and in a didactic sense, the people will be taught their law in Zion. At the time of the compilation of the Psalter, this is not only a spiritualized pilgrimage, nor is it an other-worldly hope: the compilers' focus is on the Zion tradition as an actual place, with a this-worldly dimension. It would not be surprising if this group of editors and compilers belonged to the same Levitical circles as those who compiled and edited the books of Chronicles: they shared the same vision, and same programme of reform, which at that particular point in time was to reinforce the belief that Zion was the central locus for Judaism, both for the individual and the community as a whole.

BIBLIOGRAPHY

Albertz, R.

1997 'Der jüdische Psalter–ein anti-imperiales Buch?', in R. Albertz (ed.), *Religion und Gesellschaft* (AOAT, 248; Münster: Ugarit-Verlag): 95-108.

2002a 'Religion in Pre-Exilic Israel' (trans. H. Harvey), in Barton (ed.) 2002: 90-100.

2002b 'Religion in Israel During and After the Exile' (trans. H. Harvey), in Barton (ed.) 2002: 101-124.

Alexander, J.A.

1850 *The Psalms, Translated and Explained* (3 vols.; New York: Baker & Scribner).

Auffret, P.

1982 *La sagesse a bâti sa maison: Etudes de structures littéraires dans l'Ancien Testament et spécialement dans les Psaumes* (OBO, 49; Göttingen: Vandenhoeck & Ruprecht).

1995 *Merveilles à nos yeux: Etude structurelle de vingt psaumes dont celui de 1 Ch 16. 8-36* (BZAW, 235; Berlin and New York: W. de Gruyter).

Auwers, J.-M.

2000 *La Composition Littéraire du Psautier: Un Etat de la Question* (Paris: J. Gabalda).

Barbiero, G.

1999 *Das erste Psalmenbuch als Einheit* (Österreichische Biblischen Studien, 16; Frankfurt: Peter Lang).

Barth, C.

1976 'Concatenatio im ersten Buch des Psalters', in B. Benzing, O. Böcher and G. Mayer (eds.), *Wort und Wortlichkeit: Studien zur Afrikanistik und Orientalistik* (Festschrift E.L. Rapp; Meisenheim am Glan: Hain): 30-40.

Barton, J. (ed.)

2002 *The Biblical World*, II (London and New York: Routledge).

Beaucamp, E.

1979 'L'unité du recueil des monteés: Psaumes 120–134', *Studii Biblici Franciscani* 29: 73-90.

Becker, J.
1975 *Wege der Psalmenexegese* (SBS, 78; Stuttgart: KBW Verlag).

Berquist, J.L.
1995 *Judaism in Persia's Shadow: A Social and Historical Approach* (Minneapolis: Fortress Press).

Beyerlin, W.
1979 *Werden und Wesen des 107. Psalm* (BZAW, 153; Berlin: W. de Gruyter).

Brennan, J.P.
1976 'Some Hidden Harmonies in the Fifth Book of Psalms', in R.F. McNamara (ed.), *Essays in Honor of Joseph Brennan* (Rochester, NY: St Bernard's Seminary): 126-58.
1980 'Psalms 1–8: Some Hidden Harmonies', *BTB* 10: 25-29.

Brownlee, W.H.
1971 'Psalms 1–2 as a Coronation Liturgy', *Bib* 52: 321-36.

Brueggemann, W.
1991 'Bounded by Obedience and Praise: The Psalms as Canon', *JSOT* 50: 63-92.
1996 'Psalm 73 as a Canonical Marker', *JSOT* 72: 45-56.

Brunert, G.
1996 *Psalm 102 im Kontext des vierten Psalmenbuches* (SBB, 30; Stuttgart: Katholisches Bibelwerk).

Buss, J.M
1963 'The Psalms of Asaph and Korah', *JBL* 82: 382-92.

Campbell, A.F.
1979 'Psalm 78: A Contribution to the Theology of Tenth Century Israel', *CBQ* 41: 51-79.

Carroll, R.P.
1971 'Psalm LXXVIII: Vestiges of a Tribal Polemic', *VT* 21: 133-50.

Carter, C.E.
1999 *The Emergence of Yehud in the Persian Period: A Social and Demographic Study* (JSOTSup, 294; Sheffield: Sheffield Academic Press).

Ceresko, A.R.
1990 'The Sage in the Psalms', in J.G. Gammie and L.G. Perdue (eds.), *The Sage in Israel and the Ancient Near East* (Winona Lake, IN: Eisenbrauns): 217-30.

Claissé-Walford, N.L. de
1997 *Reading from the Beginning: The Shaping of the Hebrew Psalter* (Macon, GA: Mercer University Press).

Cole, R.
2000 *The Shape and Message of Book III (Psalms 73–89)* (JSOTSup, 307; Sheffield: Sheffield Academic Press).
2002 'An Integrated Reading of Psalms 1 and 2', *JSOT* 98: 75-88.

Cook, S.L.
1995 *Prophecy and Apocalypticism: The Post-exilic Social Setting* (Minneapolis: Fortress Press).

Creach, J.F.D.
1996 *Yahweh as Refuge and the Editing of the Hebrew Psalter* (JSOTSup, 217; Sheffield: Sheffield Academic Press).
1998 'The Shape of Book Four of the Psalter and the Shape of Second Isaiah', *JSOT* 80: 63-76.
1999 'Like a Tree Planted by the Temple Stream: The Portrait of the Righteous in Psalm 1.3', *CBQ* 61: 34-46.

Crow, L.D.
1996 *The Songs of Ascents (Psalms 120–134): Their Place in Israelite History and Religion* (SBLDS, 148; Atlanta: Scholars Press).

Davies, P.R.
1998 *Scribes and Schools: The Canonization of the Hebrew Scriptures* (London: SPCK).

Delitzsch, F.
1883 *Biblischer Commentar über die Psalmen* (BCAT; Leipzig: Dörffling & Franke, 4th rev edn [first published 1860). ET *Biblical Commentary on the Psalms* (trans. D. Eaton; London: Hodder & Stoughton, 1887–89).

Eaton, J.H.
1995 *Psalms of the Way and the Kingdom: A Conference with Commentators* (JSOTSup, 199; Sheffield: Sheffield Academic Press).

Fishbane, M.A.
1985 *Biblical Interpretation in Ancient Israel* (Oxford: Clarendon Press).

Flint, P.W.
1997 *The Dead Sea Scrolls and the Book of Psalms* (Leiden: E.J. Brill)

Gerstenberger, E.S.
1994 'Der Psalter als Buch und als Sammlung', in Seybold and Zenger (eds.) 1994: 1-13.
2001 '"World Dominion" in Yahweh Kingship Psalms': Down to the Roots of Globalizing Concepts and Strategies', *HBT* 23: 192-210.

Gillingham, S.E.
2002 *The Image, the Depths and the Surface: Multivalent Approaches to Biblical Study* (JSOTSup, 354; Sheffield: Sheffield Academic Press): 68-72.

Goldingay, J.
1978 *Songs from a Strange Land: Psalms 42–51* (Leicester: IVP).

Goulder, M.D.
1975 'The Fourth Book of the Psalter', *JTS* 26: 269-89.
1982 *The Psalms of the Sons of Korah* (JSOTSup, 20; Sheffield: JSOT Press).
1990 *The Prayers of David (Psalms 51–72)* (JSOTSup, 102; Sheffield: Sheffield Academic Press).
1995 'Asaph's *History of Israel* (Elohist Press, Bethel, 725 BCE)', *JSOT* 65: 71-81.
1996 *The Psalms of Asaph and the Pentateuch: Studies in the Psalter, III* (JSOTSup, 233; Sheffield: Sheffield Academic Press).
1997 'The Songs of Ascents and Nehemiah', *JSOT* 75: 43-58.
1998 *The Psalms of the Return (Book V, Psalms 107–150): Studies in the Psalter, IV* (JSOTSup, 258; Sheffield: Sheffield Academic Press).

Grossberg, D.
1989 'Songs of Ascents', in *idem*, *Centrapetal and Centrifugal Structures in Biblical Poetry* (Atlanta: Scholars Press): 15-54.

Gunkel, H.
1930 'Die Psalmen', in *RGG*², IV (Tübingen: J.C.B. Mohr [Paul Siebeck]): cols. 1609-27. ET *The Psalms* (trans. T.M. Horner; Facet Books, Philadelphia: Fortress Press, 1967).

Gunkel, H., and J. Begrich
1928–33 *Einleitung in die Psalmen: die Gattungen der religiösen Lyrik Israels* (2 vols.; GHAT; Göttingen, Vandenhoeck & Ruprecht). ET *Introduction to Psalms: The Genres of the Religious Lyric of Israel* (trans. J.D. Nogalski; Macon, GA: Mercer University Press, 1998).

Hengstenberg, E.W.

1847 *Commentar über die Psalmen*, IV.2 (Berlin: Verlag von Ludwig Dehmigte).

Høgenhaven, J.

2001 'The Opening of the Psalter: A Study in Jewish Theology', *SJOT* 15: 169-80.

Hoppe, A.L.J.

2000 'Zion, the City of God: Jerusalem in the Book of Psalms', in *idem*, *The Holy City* (Collegeville, MN: The Liturgical Press): 23-41.

Hossfeld, F.L.

1994 'Psalm 95. Gattungsgeschichtliche, kompositionskritische und bibeltheologische Anfragen', in Seybold and Zenger (eds.) 1994: 29-44.

Hossfeld, F.L., and E. Zenger

1992 '"Selig, wer auf die Armen achtet" (Ps. 41,2). Beobachtungen zur Gottesvolk-Theologie des ersten Davidpsalters', *JBTh* 7: 21-50.

1993 '"Wer darf hinaufziehen zum Berg JHWHs?" Zur Redaktionsgeschichte und Theologien der Psalmengruppe 15–24', in G. Braulik, W. Gross and S. McEvenue (eds.), *Biblische Theologie und gesellschafftlicher Wandel: FS N. Lohfink* (Freiburg: Herder): 166-82.

1994 '"Von seinem Thronsitz schaut er nieder auf alle Bewohner der Erde" (Ps. 33, 14). Redaktionsgeschichte und Komposition der Psalmengruppe 25–34', in I. Kottsieper (ed.), *'Wer ist wie du, HERR, unter den Göttern?' Studien zur Theololgie und religionsgeschichte für Otto Kaiser* (Göttingen: Vandenhoeck & Ruprecht): 375-88.

1996 'Neue und Alte Wege der Psalmenexegese. Antworten auf die Fragen von M. Millard und R. Rendtorff', *BibInt* 14: 332-43.

Houston, W.

1995 'David, Asaph and the Mighty Works of God: Theme and Genre in the Psalm Collections', *JSOT* 68: 93-111.

Howard, D.M.

1993a 'Editorial Activity in the Psalter: A State-of-the-Field Survey', in McCann (ed.) 1993: 52-70.

1993b 'A Contextual Reading of Psalms 90–94', in McCann (ed.) 1993: 108-17.

1997 *The Structure of Psalms 93–100: Their Place in Israelite History* (Winona Lake, IN: Eisenbrauns).

Hunter, A.G.

1999 'Yahweh Comes Home to Zion: The Psalms of Ascents', in *idem*, *Psalms* (OTG; London: Routledge): 173-258.

Jeremias, Jörg

1987 *Das Königtum Gottes in den Psalmen: Israels Begegnung mit dem kanaanäischen Mythos in den Jahwe-König-Psalmen* (FRLANT, 141; Göttingen: Vandenhoeck & Ruprecht).

Keel, O., and E. Zenger (eds.)

2002 *Gottesstadt und Gottesgarten: Zu Geschichte und Theologie des Jerusalemer Tempels* (QD, 197; Freiburg: Herder).

Keet, C.C.

1969 *A Study of the Psalms of Ascents* (London: Mitre Press).

Kratz, R.G.

1995 'Die Tora Davids: Psalm 1 und die doxologische Fünfteilung des Psalters', *ZTK* 93: 13-18.

Levenson, J.D.

1987 'The Sources of Torah: Psalm 119 and the Modes of Revelation in Second Temple Judaism', in P.D. Miller, P.D. Hanson and S.D. McBride (eds.), *Ancient Israelite Religion* (Philadelphia: Fortress Press): 559-74.

Liebreich, L.J.
1955 'The Songs of Ascents and the Priestly Blessing', *JBL* 74: 33-36.
Lohfink, N.
1990 *Lobgesänge der Armen: Studien zum Magnificat, den Hodajot von Qumran und einigen späten Psalmen* (SBS, 143; Stuttgart: Verlag Katholisches Bibelwerk).
1992 'Psalmengebet und Psalterredaktion', *Archiv für Liturgiewissenschaft* 34: 1-22.
McCann, J.C.
1992 'The Psalms as Instruction', *Int* 46: 117-28.
2001 'Righteousness, Justice, and Peace: A Contemporary Theology of the Psalms', *HBTh* 23: 111-31.
McCann, J.C. (ed.)
1993 *The Shape and Shaping of the Psalter* (JSOTSup, 159; Sheffield: JSOT Press).
Mannati, M.
1979 'Les psaumes graduels consitituent-ils un genre littéraire distinct à l'intérieur du psautier biblique?', *Sem* 29: 85-100.
Mays, J.L.
1987 'The Place of the Torah-Psalms in the Psalter', *JBL* 106: 3-12.
Menn, E.
2001 'Praying King and Sanctuary of Prayer, Part I: David and the Temple's Origins in Rabbinic Psalms Commentary (Midrash Tehillim)', *JJS* 52: 1-26.
Millard, M.
1994 *Die Komposition des Psalters: Ein formgeschichtlicher Ansatz* (FAT, 9; Tübingen: J.C.B. Mohr [Paul Siebeck]).
1996 'Von der Psalmenexegese zur Psalterexegese. Anmerkungen zum Neuansatz von Frank-Lothar Hossfeld und Erich Zenger', *BibInt* 4: 311-28.
Miller, J.M.
1970 'The Korahites of Southern Judah', *CBQ* 32: 58-68.
Miller, P.D.
1993 'The Beginning of the Psalter', in McCann (ed.) 1993: 83-92.
1994 'Kingship, Torah, Obedience and Prayer: The Theology of Psalms 15–24', in Seybold and Zenger (eds.) 1994: 127-42.
1998 'The End of the Psalter: A Response to Erich Zenger', *JSOT* 80: 103-10.
Mitchell, D.C.
1997 *The Message of the Psalter: An Eschatological Programme in the Book of Psalms* (JSOTSup, 252; Sheffield: Sheffield Academic Press).
Mowinckel, S.
1924 *Psalmenstudien*. VI. *Die Psalmendichter* (Kristiana: J. Dybwad).
1951 *Offersang og Sangoffer* (Oslo: H. Aschehoug & Co.). ET *The Psalms in Israel's Worship* (2 vols.; trans. D.R. Ap-Thomas; Oxford: Basil Blackwell, 1962).
Nasuti, H.P.
1988 *Tradition History and the Psalms of Asaph* (SBLDS, 88; Atlanta: Scholars Press).
1999 *Defining the Sacred Songs: Genre, Tradition and the Post-Critical Interpretation of the Psalms* (JSOTSup, 218; Sheffield: Sheffield Academic Press).
Ollenburger, B.C.
1987 *Zion, City of the Great King: A Theological Symbol of the Jerusalem Cult* (JSOTSup, 41; Sheffield: Sheffield Academic Press).
Peters, J.P.
1922 *The Psalms as Liturgies* (London: Hodder & Stoughton).

Reindl, J.
1981 'Weisheitliche Bearbeiting von Psalmen: Ein Beitrag zum Verständnis der Sammlung des Psalter', in J.A. Emerton (ed.), *Congress Volume: Vienna 1980* (VTSup, 32; Leiden: E.J. Brill): 333-56.
Rendsburg, G.A.
1990 *Linguistic Evidence for the Northern Origin of Selected Psalms* (SBLMS, 43; Atlanta: Scholars Press).
Ridderbos, N.H.
1972 *Die Psalmen: Stilistische Verfahren und Aufbau mit besonderer Berücksichtigung von Ps. 1–41* (BZAW, 117: Berlin: W. de Gruyter).
Roberts, J.J.M.
1973 'The Davidic Origin of the Zion Tradition', *JBL*: 329-44.
Rösel, C.
1999 *Die messiansiche Redaktion des Psalters: Studien zu Entstehung und Theologie der Sammlung Psalm 2–89* (Calwer Theologische Monographien, 19, Reihe A, Bibelwissenschaft: Darmstadt: Weihert-Druck).
Sanders, J.A.
1965 *The Psalms Scroll of Qumran Cave 11 (11 QPs[a])* (DJD, 4; Oxford: Clarendon Press).
Satterthwaite, P.E.
1999 'Zion in the Songs of Ascents', in R.S. Hess and G.J. Wenham (eds.), *Zion, City of Our God* (Grand Rapids: Eerdmans): 105-29.
Sawyer, J.F.A.
1967–68 'An Analysis of the Context and Meaning of the Psalm-Headings', *TGUOS* 22: 26-38.
Seidel, H.
1982 'Wallfahrtslieder', in H. Seidel and K.-H. Bieritz (eds.), *Das lebendige Wort: Beiträge zur kirchlichen Verkündigung. Festgabe für Gottfried Voigt* (Berlin: Evangelische Verlagsanstalt): 26-40.
Seybold, K.
1978 *Die Wallfahrtspsalmen: Studien zur Entstehungsgeschichte von Psalmen 120–134* (BThS, 3; Neukirchen–Vluyn: Neukirchener Verlag).
1979 'Die Redaktion der Wallfahrtspsalmen', *ZAW* 91: 247-68.
1994 'Das "Wir" in den Asaph-Psalmen. Spezifische Probleme einer Psalmengruppe', in Seybold and Zenger (eds.) 1994: 143-55.
1996a *Die Psalmen* (HAT, 1.5; Tübingen: J.C.B. Mohr [Paul Siebeck]).
1996b 'Jerusalem in the View of the Psalms', in M. Poorthuis and Ch. Safrai (eds.), *The Centrality of Jerusalem: Historical Perspectives* (Kampen: Kok Pharos): 7-14.
Seybold, K., and E. Zenger (eds.)
1994 *Neue Wege der Psalmenforschung* (HBS, 1; Freiburg: Herder).
Sheppard, G.T.
1992 'Theology and the Book of Psalms', *Int* 46: 143-55.
Smend, R.
1888 'Über das Ich der Psalmen', *ZAW* 8: 49-147.
Smith, M.S.
1991 'The Levitical Compilation of the Psalter', *ZAW* 103: 258-63.
1992a 'The Psalms as a Book for Pilgrims', *Int* 46: 156-66.
1992b 'The Theology of the Redaction of the Psalter: Some Observations', *ZAW* 104: 408-12.

Tate, M.E.
1990 *Psalms 51–100* (WBC, 20; Dallas: Word Books).
Viviers, H.
1994 'The Coherence of the *ma'ᵃlôt* Psalms (Pss. 120–134)', *ZAW* 106: 275-89.
Walton, J.H.
1991 'Psalms: A Cantata about the Davidic Covenant', *JETS* 34: 21-31.
Wanke, G.
1966 *Die Zionstheologie der Korachiten in ihrem traditionsgeschichtliche Zusammenhang* (BZAW, 97; Berlin: Alfred Töpelmann).
Watson, W.G.E.
1984 *Classical Hebrew Poetry: A Guide to its Techniques* (JSOTSup, 26; Sheffield: JSOT Press).
Westermann, C.
1962 'Zur Sammlung des Psalters', *Theologia Viatorum* 8: 278-84. ET 'The Formation of the Psalter', in *idem*, *Praise and Lament in the Psalms* (trans. K.R. Crim and R.N. Soulen; Atlanta: John Knox Press, 1981): 250-58.
Whybray, R.N.
1996 *Reading the Psalms as a Book* (JSOTSup, 222; Sheffield: Sheffield Academic Press).
Wilson, G.H.
1984 'Evidence of Editorial Divisions in the Hebrew Psalter', *VT* 34: 337-52.
1985 *The Editing of the Hebrew Psalter* (SBLDS, 76; Chico, CA: Scholars Press).
1986 'The Use of the Royal Psalms at the "Seams" of the Hebrew Psalter', *JSOT* 35: 85-94.
1992 'The Shape of the Book of Psalms', *Int* 46: 129-42.
1993a 'Understanding the Purposeful Arrangement of Psalms in the Psalter: Pitfalls and Promise', in McCann (ed.) 1993: 42-51.
1993b 'Shaping the Psalter: A Consideration of Editorial Linkage in the Book of Psalms', in McCann (ed.) 1993: 72-82.
Zenger, E.
1991a 'Was wird anders bei kanonischer Psalmenauslegung?', in F.V. Reiterer (ed.), *Ein Gott, eine Offenbarung. Beiträge zur biblischen Exegese, Theologie und Spiritualität* (FS N. Füglister; Würzburg: Echter): 397-413.
1991b 'Israel und die Kirche im gemeinsamen Gottesbund. Beobachtungen zum theologischen Programm des 4. Psalmenbuchs', in M. Marcus, E.W. Stegemann and E. Zenger (eds.), *Israel und die Kirche heute. Beiträge zum christlich-jüdischen Dialog* (FS E.L. Ehrlich; Freiburg: Herder): 238-57.
1993 'Der Psalter als Wegweiser und Wegbegleiter. Ps. 1–2 als Proömium des Psalmenbuchs', in A. Angenendt and H. Vorgrimler (eds.), *Sie wandern von Kraft zu Kraft: Aufbrüche, Wege, Begegnungen. Festgabe für Bischof Reinhard Lettman* (Kevelaer: Butzon & Bercker): 29-47.
1994a 'Zur redaktionsgechichtlichen Bedeutung der Korachpsalmen', in Seybold and Zenger (eds.) 1994: 175-98.
1994b 'New Approaches to the Study of the Psalms', *PIBA* 17: 37-54.
1997 '"Daß alles Fleisch den Namen seiner Heiligung segne" (Ps 145, 21). Die Komposition Ps 145–150 als Anstoß zu einer christlich-jüdischen Psalmen–hermeneutik', *BZ* 41: 1-27.
1998 'The Composition and Theology of the Fifth Book of Psalms, Psalms 107–45', *JSOT* 80: 77-102.

2002 '"Ich liebe den Ort, da deine Herrlichkeit wohnt" (Ps. 26.8): Tempeltheologische Semiotisierung des Alltags im Psalter', in O. Keel and E. Zenger (eds.), *Gottesstadt und Gottesgarten: Zu Geschichte und Theologie des Jerusalemer Tempels* (QD, 197; Freiburg: Herder): 180-206.

Zenger, E., and H.L. Hossfeld

1993 *Die Psalmen 1–50* (NEB; Würzburg: Echter).

2000 *Die Psalmen 51–100* (HThKAT; Freiburg: Herder).

Zevit, Z.

2001 *The Religions of Ancient Israel* (London and New York: Continuum).

THE DAY OF ATONEMENT AS A RITUAL OF VALIDATION FOR THE HIGH PRIEST

Deborah W. Rooke

The Day of Atonement is probably one of the best known, and most widely discussed, of the ceremonies of ancient Judaism, partly no doubt because of its appropriation for Christian theology. Many studies have focused on aspects of the Day of Atonement legislation as it appears in Leviticus 16;[1] topics discussed in the scholarly literature include the redactional history and structure of the chapter (Elliger 1966: 202-10; Aartun 1980; Rodriguez 1996), the theology of the sacrifices (Milgrom 1971; Kiuchi 1987: 143-59; Gorman 1990: 75-89, 95-100; McLean 1991), the origins of the rite (or rites) (Zatelli 1998; Carmichael 2000), the significance of the term 'Azazel' (Tawil 1980; Helm 1994; Görg 1995; de Roo 2000), and comparative rites of purification in other ancient Near Eastern cultures (Wright 1987: 15-74; Gane 1998). And indeed, this interest in the Day of Atonement is well placed, because it reflects the importance that was clearly afforded the ceremony by the authors of Leviticus. The laws for the Day of Atonement occupy a central position not only in the book of Leviticus but also in the Pentateuch as a whole; they are clearly the jewel in the crown of the Priestly torah. However, despite the great scholarly interest in the ritual described in Leviticus 16, relatively little appears to have been said about the relationship between the high priest and the Day of Atonement. Such a lack of scholarly comment is a quite remarkable state of affairs, given that this immensely important ceremony can be said to epitomize the role of the high priest as the community's prime mediator between people and deity. It is therefore my intention in this article to remedy that deficiency to some extent, not least because I too have been guilty of it—I devoted the equivalent of merely a single page out of more than three hundred in a monograph on the high priesthood to discussion of the high priest on the Day of Atonement.[2]

One scholar who did give a good deal of attention both to the high priest and to the Day of Atonement is Julian Morgenstern (1881–1976). In a long series of articles published during the first half of the twentieth century, Morgenstern discussed in some detail the development of calendrical usage in ancient Israel, and

1. The following list of studies on various aspects of the Day of Atonement is intended to be illustrative rather than exhaustive. For the reader interested in pursuing any of the aspects referred to, the cited literature itself offers a much fuller bibliography than it is possible or appropriate to provide in the present context.

2. Rooke 2000: 24-25.

suggested a number of reconstructions of the original festal observances that in his opinion lay behind the present Priestly festival calendar in Leviticus and Numbers. One of Morgenstern's primary contentions was that the Day of Atonement in its present form is a very late innovation, dating from no earlier than c. 350 BCE (Morgenstern 1924: 35, 40; 1963: 8), and that originally the tenth day of the seventh month (that is, the autumnal equinox), which is now celebrated as Yom Kippur, had been observed as New Year's Day (1917–18: 31-33; 1924: 22, 28; 1929: 18-19, 37; 1935: 5-13, 146; 1938: 20; 1952–53: 46, 51; 1963: 7, 8, 80). This was immediately preceded by the seven days of the feast of Tabernacles, to which it formed the climax (1917–18: 40-47; 1924: 22, 28; 1935: 5; 1937–38: 10-11).[3] The peculiar date of this New Year's Day was to be accounted for by the change from an original solar[4] to a subsequent luni-solar calendar, which altered both the divisions and the numbering of the months (1924: 71, 75-77; 1935: 5-6).[5] As for the content of the New Year festival on the autumnal equinox, Morgenstern argued that it had consisted of a number of elements: the opening of the eastern gate of the Temple, which was orientated to allow the first rays of the rising equinoctial sun to shine into the heart of the Temple (1929: 17-19, 31-32, 35; 1935: 76; 1952–53: 45-46, 55; 1963: 7-8); the entry of the king (in later times, the chief priest) with a censer into the Holy of Holies at that moment (1924: 41; 1938: 10, 16, 17; 1952–53: 46, 51), in order to kindle in the censer sacred fire from which the outer altar fire was subsequently rekindled (1938: 16, 17, 22);[6] some kind of sanctuary purification rites (1952–53: 41, 44, 46-47, 53); the rite of the Azazel goat (1924: 41, 77; 1935: 10, 80; 1937–38: 11; 1952–53: 47); and the dancing of maidens in the vineyards, which is noted in Mishnah *Ta'an*. 4.8 as part of the Yom Kippur celebrations (1924: 22, 41, 77; 1935: 10, 80).[7] This New

3. Morgenstern's dating of Tabernacles on 3-9/7 and New Year on 10/7 is supported by van Goudoever (1959: 38-42), and more recently by Ulfgard (1998: 37-43).

4. In the light of later scholarship, Morgenstern subsequently argued that the Israelites initially used a pentecontad calendar based on agricultural festivals which was borrowed from the Canaanites, and that the solar calendar, along with the design for the Temple and certain ceremonies which had a solar orientation, was introduced by Solomon as a result of commercial contact with the Phoenicians who observed a solar calendar and religion (Morgenstern 1963: 37-39, 87-91).

5. Morgenstern (1926: 102-107) suggested that the date of 10/7 for New Year's Day came about as a result of the need to harmonize the old solar calendar, under which a year was 365 days, with the new luni-solar calendar, under which a year was 355 days. This explanation was also put forward by Snaith (1947: 131-35, 141), who however thought that the change was from a luni-solar to a solar calendar rather than the other way round.

6. In his later work Morgenstern altered his conception of the nature of the ceremony of the sacred fire, and argued that the fire was rekindled on the altar, which stood in the eastern courtyard of the Temple, by the first rays of the rising equinoctial sun falling upon it (Morgenstern 1963: 38, 90, 98). For a recent evaluation of the ideas about the orientation of Solomon's Temple, upon which Morgenstern's reconstructions depend, see Taylor 1993: 79-86, 161-64, 261-62.

7. In the first volume of his commentary on Leviticus, Milgrom (1991: 1066-67) takes the Mishnah's comment about the dancing maidens as an indicator of the original joyous nature of the Day of Atonement celebrations which were the culmination of the ancient New Year festival. He also refers the reader who wants more details to 'the NOTE on 23.23-25' (Milgrom 1991: 1067), which appears in the third volume of his Leviticus commentary (Milgrom 2001: 2011-19). There, however, he

Year's Day was also the day from which the regnal years of Israelite kings were reckoned (1936: 443, 451, 452, 454; 1938: 24),[8] and indeed, was the day upon which kings were formally inducted into office (1938: 367; 1952–53: 71). Similarly, in the post-exilic period, when the high priest replaced the monarch as the head of the theocratic community, he likewise would have been inducted on the same New Year's Day (1938: 367), and his first official act would have been to enter the presence of Yahweh (1952–53: 71, 72). Finally, Morgenstern argued that these New Year rites were the background against which to interpret a number of other incidents in the Hebrew Bible: the deaths of Nadab and Abihu in Leviticus 10 (1935: 77; 1938: 17-18), the Korahite rebellion in Numbers 16–17 (1938: 18-19, 366; 1963: 26-28), King Uzziah attempting to burn incense and being struck with leprosy in 2 Chronicles 26 (1937–38: 9-12; 1938: 23; 1963: 43, 107-10), and the vision of the high priest Joshua being cleansed and commissioned in Zechariah 3 (1938: 188-89; 1952–53: 71-72; 1963: 93). Morgenstern also suggested that the New Year's Day ceremonial was the background to the argument between Jesus and Joannes, as a result of which Joannes killed Jesus in the Temple (Josephus, *Ant.* 11.297-301) (1938: 365-66).

Now, stimulating though Morgenstern's ideas are, his reconstruction of the New Year celebrations was largely arrived at by a retrojection of Jewish, Christian, ancient Arab, and Moslem tradition, without the Mesopotamian perspective that has been so influential in subsequent discussions of the New Year festival.[9] For this reason I would hesitate to go along with Morgenstern's reconstruction in its entirety; but in two respects I would agree with him, not least because in these two respects I reached the same conclusions independently. I too would argue

denies that the celebrations in the seventh month had anything to do with the new year (Milgrom 2001: 2012-13), and suggests that 1/7 (which he terms the Festival of Alarm Blasts), 10/7 (Yom Kippur) and 15-22/7 (the Festival of Booths) should be taken as originally a single twenty-two-day-long festival complex between the harvest and the rains, that was intended to supplicate God for adequate rain (2001: 2012, 2045-46).

8. In 1936 Morgenstern concluded definitively that throughout the monarchical period the reigns both of Israelite and of Judaean kings were reckoned from the New Year's Day on 10/7 (Morgenstern 1936: 454). However, in the light of subsequent scholarship, he later revised his view and took the position that while the reigns of Judaean kings were reckoned from the New Year's Day on the autumnal equinox (apart from a short period between Joram and Joash), the reigns of Israelite kings were reckoned from a New Year's Day in the spring that arose from the older pentecontad calendar (Morgenstern 1963: 41-43). For more bibliography, and a detailed discussion of the question of how regnal years were reckoned during the monarchy, see Finegan 1998: 245-65.

9. One recent use of the Mesopotamian perspective is in van der Toorn's (1991) discussion of the relationship between the Babylonian Akitu festival and the Israelite New Year festival. It seems that Morgenstern was aware of the proposed parallels between the Israelite and Babylonian New Year festivals, but did not view them favourably. Although he cites Johnson (1935) in support of his own view of the king's sacral status within the nation, he adds, 'I must supplement this reference with the statement that I can go with Johnson but a very little way in his fanciful and arbitrary interpretation of various psalms and in the altogether forced and unsubstantiated conclusions which he draws therefrom' (Morgenstern 1938: 11 n. 28). One wonders whether Morgenstern's own ideas, based on a more conservative Jewish perspective, were developed in conscious opposition to those of his scholarly contemporaries.

that the Day of Atonement as it now stands should be viewed as the high priest's installation day, and that the other five incidents just mentioned should be read in the light of that interpretation. But to say that I agree with Morgenstern in these respects is not to say that I agree with every detail of his reconstruction; and so in what follows I shall attempt to put forward my own view of the matter.

The basic principle that I would like to suggest, then, is that for the high priest the Day of Atonement functions as a yearly ritual confirmation of his high priesthood. The first time he officiates at it, it serves to validate him as high priest; and each subsequent officiation is a revalidation of his position as the community's chief mediator in the ritual sphere. There are a number of reasons for suggesting this, and they will be discussed in turn.

1. *The Day of Atonement Legislation in its Present Narrative Context*

The first reason for suggesting that the Day of Atonement should have such a theological significance for the high priest is the way in which Leviticus 16 is incorporated into the context of the surrounding narrative. This has two elements: its relationship to the story of Nadab and Abihu in Leviticus 10, and its relationship to the narrative of ordination and consecration in Leviticus 8–9. We shall examine these two relationships in turn, beginning with the relationship to the Nadab and Abihu incident in Leviticus 10.

It is often pointed out that the flow of thought in Leviticus 16 follows on from the events of Lev. 10.1-3, where Aaron's two sons Nadab and Abihu offer 'strange fire' to the Lord and are themselves consumed by divine fire. The opening verses of Leviticus 16 (vv. 1-2) refer to the deaths of Nadab and Abihu during their attempt to approach the Lord, so that the instructions that follow in the rest of Leviticus 16 are presented as instructions to Aaron on how to avoid the same fate as his sons. The way the narrative is constructed implies that there is a very practical purpose for giving the Day of Atonement legislation at that particular juncture, namely, the need to cleanse the sanctuary from the pollution caused by the corpses of Nadab and Abihu.[10] But the fact that Aaron can officiate so close to the holiest place—indeed, in the very Holy of Holies—and not be consumed by fire as Nadab and Abihu were, is such a contrast with his sons' fortunes that it must surely be construed as a validation of his priesthood over against theirs.

However, there is more at stake here than simply who does and who does not have the right to serve as a priest. It is noteworthy that Nadab and Abihu lose their lives while attempting to approach the Lord with censers and incense (Lev. 10.1), a ritual act that in the whole of the Pentateuch is only legitimized for one person on one occasion; and that is for Aaron, the high priest, when he enters the Holy of Holies on the Day of Atonement.[11] It is equally striking that for this Day of Atonement ceremony Aaron is commanded on pain of death to use a censer of incense when entering the holy place (Lev. 16.12-13); in other words, the same

10. Milgrom 1991: 1011, 1013; Wright 1992: 75; Gorman 1997: 94. Hartley (1992: 233) speaks of purging 'the pollution of the transgression of Nadab and Abihu'.

11. Harrison (1980: 109) also makes this observation.

action that cost Nadab and Abihu their lives when they carried it out will cost Aaron his life if he *fails* to carry it out. The Nadab and Abihu incident therefore serves as the backdrop for, and contrast to, the Day of Atonement legislation, as is made explicit by the reference to Nadab and Abihu in Lev. 16.1. As the backdrop to the Day of Atonement legislation, it warns of the dangers even to consecrated personnel of attempting to approach the Lord in a way that is not thoroughly sanctioned by him; and when seen in the light of the Day of Atonement legislation, it exemplifies that warning in terms of two men who attempt to carry out duties that properly belong to the high priest when they do not have divine approval for doing so.[12] This may in fact be what is meant by the reference to Nadab and Abihu offering 'strange fire' (*'ēš zārâ*) in Lev. 10.1. The phrase is often taken to mean that the coals used by Nadab and Abihu in their censers were not from the altar but from a profane source which was unacceptable for use in worship.[13] However, the phrase 'strange fire' could also refer to the very fact of them offering incense in censers at all, since the phrase 'strange fire' is followed immediately by the words, 'such as he had not commanded them'.[14] Indeed, not even

12. Several modern scholars understand Nadab and Abihu as usurping the high priest's privileges. Harrison (1980: 109) and Hartley (1992: 133) think that the privilege in question was that of offering incense in the Holy Place, whereas Kiuchi (1987: 81) regards it as entering the Holy of Holies. Nor are these purely modern interpretations. Heger (1997: 63-67) notes that in both Targum Neofiti and Targum of Jonathan for Lev. 16.1 an additional phrase appears after 'the sons of Aaron'; in Neofiti the phrase is 'the high priest' (i.e. Aaron himself), and in Jonathan it is 'the high priests' (i.e. Nadab and Abihu). Heger argues that this indicates that the interpreters saw the incident as reflecting a struggle over the high priesthood: either Nadab and Abihu were contesting the exclusive prerogative of the high priest, or they considered themselves to be high priests. He also notes that in *Sifra, Aḥare Mot* 1.2 Rabbi Yose the Galilaean is quoted as saying that Nadab and Abihu died because they entered the Holy of Holies (Heger 1997: 62 n. 34); similarly, several centuries later Ibn Ezra interprets *b^{e}qorbātām* in Lev. 16.1 as indicating that Aaron's sons brought incense within the veil, which again can be interpreted to mean that they usurped Aaron's high priestly privileges (Heger 1997: 83).

13. So, e.g., Morgenstern 1926: 102; 1963: 6; Haran 1960: 115; Noth 1962: 70, ET 1977: 84-85; Wenham 1979: 155; Harrison 1980: 109; Milgrom 1991: 598; Jenson 1992: 111; Gerstenberger 1996: 117. The idea is not new, being one of a dozen that were propounded by rabbinic interpreters to explain the enigmatic phrase. For more details of the rabbinic interpretations, see Milgrom 1991: 633-34. A variation on this idea is that the fire was kindled according to the practice of non-Yahwistic cults (Porter 1976: 77; Hartley 1992: 132; Budd 1996: 151); indeed, Laughlin (1976: 562-65) suggests that the episode is a polemic against the Zoroastrian fire ritual whereby fire, believed to be sacred, was installed in temples that were built to house it. In contrast to these approaches, Levine (1989: 58) argues that the phrase 'strange fire' refers to the incense rather than to the coals. Uniquely, and untenably, Snaith (1967: 75, 76) argues that the term 'strange' (*zār*) indicates a lay person rather than a priest, and so Nadab and Abihu were lay people trying to act as priests. This view completely ignores the fact that according to Lev. 8 they have just been ordained as priests.

14. Heinisch (1935: 48-49) similarly argues that Nadab and Abihu acted without authorization in bringing an incense offering when no instructions had been given about such offerings by Moses or Aaron. Heger (1997: 67) comments that the stress in the phrase 'such as he had not commanded them' might be on 'them', because only Aaron had been commanded to perform the incense rite. He links this interpretation with the phrase 'strange fire' (*'ēš zārâ*) (Lev. 10.1), which he sees as indirectly expressing Nadab and Abihu's rebellion against Aaron's exclusive privileges: because only Aaron is entitled to make the incense offerings, when Nadab and Abihu attempt to do so they are regarded as 'strangers' (*zārîm*), i.e. illegitimate functionaries, and so whatever they offer will also be deemed

Aaron has yet been commanded to offer incense in a censer, so by the criterion of what has been commanded, anything offered in a censer by anyone would be 'strange fire'.[15]

The second element that forms the backdrop to the Day of Atonement legislation in its present context is the consecration and ordination of Aaron and his sons in Leviticus 8–9. Indeed, the Day of Atonement ceremonial in Leviticus 16 can be seen as the first official duty that Aaron undertakes after his consecration, which in turn could imply that the Day of Atonement is to be regarded as the validation of Aaron's high priesthood, the proof of his ordination and consecration. This then raises the question of how the narrative of ordination and consecration relates to the historical practice of installing high priests. The only description of a full-blown installation ritual is the one given in Leviticus 8–9, where both Aaron and his sons are ordained and consecrated along with the Tabernacle and all its furnishings. However, it is an open question whether the rites described there are a purely fictive initiation of the priesthood as a whole, designed to function as a theological validation of the Aaronide Priestly hierarchy, or whether they are based on actual practice and reflect an elaborate ceremony of preparation for those who would serve at the altar in later (probably post-exilic) times.[16] Assuming that such ceremonies existed and would have occurred at certain designated intervals as appropriate, there is no indication of whether they

'strange' (Heger 1997: 81-82). In this connection, it is worth noting that the MT of Lev. 16.1 implies that Nadab and Abihu's sin was one of presumption, since the verse speaks simply of them drawing near to the Lord and dying, without mention of the 'strange fire': *way^{e}dabbēr yhwh 'el-mōšeh 'aḥ^{a}rê môt š^{e}nê b^{e}nê 'ah^{a}rôn b^{e}qorbātām lipnê-yhwh wayyāmutû*. By contrast, however, the LXX of 16.1 does speak of them offering 'strange fire': καὶ ἐλάλησεν κύριος πρὸς Μωυσῆν μετὰ τὸ τελευτῆσαι τοὺς δύο υἱοὺς Ααρων ἐν τῷ προσάγειν αὐτοὺς πῦρ ἀλλότριον ἔναντι κυρίου καὶ ἐτελεύτησαν. Gradwohl (1963: 292) suggests that the MT of Lev. 16.1 might originally have read *b^{e}haqrîbām 'ēš zārâ* ('when they offered strange fire') instead of *b^{e}qorbātām* ('when they drew near'), but that it was altered to fit the context of the rest of the chapter, which speaks of the appropriate use of legitimate fire from the altar and not 'strange' or illegitimate fire.

15. Laughlin too suggests that Nadab and Abihu might have been 'conceived by the tradition as having tried to offer incense to Yahweh before the instructions were given in Lev. 16.12-13', but sees this as explaining the traditional interpretation of 'strange fire' as fire from an illegitimate source—they offered 'strange' or profane fire because they did not know that they had to use coals from the altar (Laughlin 1976: 561). This interpretation implies that their action would have been legitimate but for the source of fire they used, but it does not take account of the fact that the instructions to Aaron in Lev. 16.12-13 make him the only person in the whole of the Pentateuch, who either before or after the Nadab and Abihu incident is legitimized to offer incense in a censer. In addition, the reference to 'strange fire' (*'ēš zārâ*) in Lev. 10.1 *follows* a more detailed description of Nadab and Abihu's action: 'Now the sons of Aaron, Nadab and Abihu, each took his censer, laid fire in it, and placed incense upon the fire' (*wayyiq^{e}ḥû b^{e}nê-'ah^{a}rōn nādāb wa'^{a}bîhû' 'îš maḥtātô wayyitt^{e}nû bāhēn 'ēš wayyāśîmû 'āleyhā q^{e}ṭōret*, Lev. 10.1a). It therefore seems reasonable to take the subsequent phrase 'and they offered strange fire' (*wayyaqrîbû 'ēš zārâ*, 10.1b) as an evaluative summary that refers to the whole process of bringing incense in a censer, not simply as a description of one of the process's constitutive actions (i.e. putting fire in the censer).

16. For discussion of this matter, see Gerstenberger 1996: 99-114. Gorman (1990: 105) argues that it is difficult to see Lev. 8 as the model for a regularly occurring ordination ritual, both because there would be no-one in normative Israelite society who could fill the role of Moses as depicted in Lev. 8, and because it is difficult to imagine the frequent enactment of a mass ordination ritual.

would have come at a specified time of the year, or whether they would simply have taken place as the need arose.[17] In the narrative world of the Priestly writer, the ceremonies to initiate the priesthood take place during the first eight days of the first month of the year, as part of the whole process of setting up the Tabernacle and initiating the cult (Exod. 40.1-15). This would place the ceremonies in the spring. However, this dating is just as likely to be a Priestly theologization as it is to reflect actual historical practice. The establishment of the cultic apparatus marks the beginning of a new era, which would of course take place at the beginning of a new year; and in P's chronological system, the years are reckoned from the time of the exodus events which mark the birth of the nation and are commemorated in the spring Passover festival (cf. Exod. 12.1-2).

Nonetheless, despite the lack of certainty over the details and timing of any Priestly ordination that might have been a regular feature of Temple ritual, it seems likely that there would have been some sort of ceremony for the high priest at least, because he is distinguished in several texts by being referred to in terms such as 'the one who has been consecrated and anointed'.[18] Additionally, in the instructions given to Moses for the initiation of the priesthood as a whole, Moses is told that Aaron's successors should wear the elaborate high Priestly garments to be anointed and ordained in them (Exod. 29.29),[19] which again indicates a special ceremony for the high priest. And thirdly, at the very end of the narrative of consecration and ordination in Leviticus 8–9, there is an indication that there would have been a special ceremony for the high priest. After all the ceremonies of ordination have been carried out, Moses and Aaron are said to go into the Tent of Meeting and then to come out and bless the people, at which point fire comes forth from the Lord and devours the burnt offering (Lev. 9.23-24). This is a rather strange passage, for several reasons. First, no reason is given for the entry into the tent by Moses and Aaron, and there is no indication of what they might have done in there.[20] Secondly, according to the earlier part of

17. Porter (1976: 62) argues that the ceremonies are derived from contemporary practice and would have been used whenever it was necessary. By contrast with the biblical account, the Qumran Temple Scroll (11QT) apparently envisages an annual consecration of priests at the start of the year (cols. 14-16), though it is unclear whether this annual consecration would also apply to the high priest; Maier (1985: 78) thinks that the 11QT consecration rites would only have applied to the high priest 'when necessary'.

18. Lev. 6.15 (ET 22) refers to 'the priest from among his [Aaron's] sons, who is anointed to succeed him' (*hakkōhēn hammāšîaḥ taḥtāyw mibbānāyw*); Lev. 16.32 speaks of 'the priest who is anointed and consecrated in his father's place' (*hakkōhēn '^{a}šer-yimšaḥ 'ōtô wa'^{a}šer y^{e}mallē' 'et-yādô l^{e}kahēn taḥat 'ābîw*); and Lev. 21.10 describes 'the priest who is chief among his brethren, upon whose head the anointing oil is poured, and who has been consecrated to wear the garments' (*hakkōhēn haggādôl mē'eḥāyw '^{a}šer yûṣaq 'al-rō'šô šemen hammišḥâ ûmillē' 'et-yādô lilbōš 'et-habb^{e}gādîm*). In all three instances it is difficult to interpret the expressions as meaning anyone other than the high priest.

19. *ûbig^{e}dê haqqōdeš '^{a}šer l^{e}'ah^{a}rōn yihyû l^{e}bānāyw 'aḥ^{a}rāyw l^{e}mošḥâ bāhem ûl^{e}mallē'-bām 'et-yādām.*

20. Heinisch (1935: 48) suggests that Moses and Aaron entered the tent to give thanks for past mercies and to pray for continuing divine aid in future. Levine (1989: 57) and Milgrom (1991: 588) refer to two alternative rabbinic traditions: Moses and Aaron entered the tent to pray either for the

Leviticus 9, Aaron has already burned the offerings on the altar, so there would not seem to be anything left to be consumed by divine fire from before the Lord.[21] However, what this passage does seem to do is to establish Aaron's right, over and above that of his sons, to enter the tent; he alone enters with Moses, and none of the other four sons who have been ordained enter with them. It is a rite of entrance that establishes Aaron's right of entry,[22] thereby functioning for Aaron as a rite of passage from lay person to high priest;[23] and the divine fire which consumes the burnt offerings provides dramatic confirmation of Aaron's new status[24] and his right by virtue of that status to enter the tent. This right to enter the tent is then illegitimately claimed by Nadab and Abihu to their cost (Lev. 10.1-3), and is subsequently circumscribed very carefully even for Aaron by the Day of Atonement legislation (Lev. 16). The picture of Moses and Aaron entering the Tent of Meeting at the end of the ceremonies of ordination implies that the final stage of those ceremonies for the high priest involved entering the sanctuary, perhaps even going into the holy place; and when it is noted that the ceremony of Aaron's entry to the sanctuary both on his ordination day and on the Day of Atonement is concluded with burnt offerings,[25] the further implication is that the

appearance of the divine glory or for the emergence of the glory from the tent to ignite the altar. Morgenstern (1938: 14-17) argues that this entry to the tent reflects the climax of the (autumnal) New Year rites, at which the chief priest would enter the sanctuary at sunrise with a censer, and emerge with newly kindled sacred fire in the censer from which to rekindle the altar flame.

21. Noth 1962: 67, ET 1977: 81-82 assumes that the reference to the divine fire consuming the offerings (Lev. 9.24a) is secondary, and is intended to establish the divine origin of the fire that according to Lev. 6.9-13 is to burn perpetually upon the altar. Snaith (1967: 74) suggests that the burnt offering consumed by the divine fire was that of the people, which had been prepared but not consumed (cf. Lev. 9.16). Hartley (1992: 121, 124) argues that the divine fire completes the burning of what was already smouldering on the altar, an apparently traditional explanation which Noth (1962: 68, ET 1977: 82) dismisses as being unworthy of the divine fire. However, Milgrom (1991: 590, 591) comments that animal sacrifices would have taken a long time to burn on the altar, citing the case of the evening *tāmîd* which burned all night (Lev. 6.2). Heinisch (1935: 48) makes a similar point. Porter (1976: 75) thinks that assessing v. 24 as a duplication and therefore secondary is being too literal-minded, and that the verse is a legend of the origin of the perpetual altar fire; but his comment does not answer the objection that there is a duplication in sense between Lev. 9.20 and 9.24.

22. Heinisch 1935: 48; Noth 1962: 67, ET 1977: 81; Hartley 1992: 124, 125.

23. Compare van Gennep's remarks on crossing the threshold between one area and another (van Gennep 1960: 20): '[T]he door is the boundary between the foreign and domestic worlds in the case of an ordinary dwelling, between the profane and the sacred worlds in the case of a temple. Therefore to cross the threshold is to unite oneself with a new world. It is thus an important act in marriage, adoption, ordination, and funeral ceremonies.'

24. So Heinisch 1935: 48.

25. It is true that there is no mention of sacrificial slaughter of animals at the end of the ceremonies of ordination, just the rather cryptic comment about the divine fire consuming the offerings on the altar (Lev. 9.24). However, given that it is the burning on the altar that ultimately defines a slaughtered animal as an offering, it is not unreasonable to view the miraculous consumption in Lev. 9.24 as a metonymic reference to the complete offering process, and therefore as the equivalent of making burnt offerings in Lev. 16.24. The consumption by divine fire is surely just a concretization, for theological and polemical reasons, of Yahweh's acceptance of the offerings, and once that is taken into account there seems to be no reason why the event should not be viewed as both the paradigm for and a reflection of the act of making such offerings in an equivalent situation.

final stage of high priestly ordination would have been the ceremonies of the Day of Atonement.

This view of the Day of Atonement as the climax of high priestly ordination ceremonies could also be supported by the comment at the end of Leviticus 16, to the effect that the ceremonies of the Day of Atonement become the duty of 'the one who is anointed and consecrated as priest in his father's place' (16.32). The mention of being anointed and consecrated in one's father's place would surely have its greatest significance at the time when the anointing and consecration has just taken place;[26] and this way of referring to the high priest is unique to Leviticus 16 (although a somewhat similar expression appears in Lev. 6.15 [ET 22]).[27]

2. *The High Priest's Clothing on the Day of Atonement*

The second major reason for suggesting that the Day of Atonement functions as the high priest's validation—and, equally importantly, his annual revalidation—is the clothing he wears for the rituals that take place on that day. The significance of the elaborate high priestly ceremonial garments as an indicator of the high priest's status is hinted at in the command given to Moses that Aaron's successors should wear them in order to be anointed and ordained (Exod. 29.29). Also, in the Hebrew Bible's only example of a transfer of power between high priests, Eleazar the son of Aaron apparently succeeds to his father's position simply by putting on the garments (Num. 20.23-28). One might therefore expect that for such a distinctive and important duty as the Day of Atonement, the high priest would wear this special attire that has been prepared for him alone, and which is described in Exod. 28.4 as 'holy garments' (*bigᵉdê-qōdeš*). This expectation is heightened by the fact that two of the items of the attire, namely, the ephod and breastpiece, are made of the same type of material as that used for the curtains and the veil of the Tabernacle. The fabric consists of fine linen and blue, purple and red wool, worked together in a manner designated by the Hebrew term *ḥōšēb* which is rendered in the RSV as 'skilfully worked' (Exod. 26.1, 31; cf. 28.6, 15).[28] This is a supremely holy fabric (Haran 1978: 160-61), and its use in the high priest's garments reflects not only his own holiness but also his connection with the holy parts of the Tabernacle (pp. 171, 210-13). It indicates that he alone of all the priests has the right to enter the tent itself to perform ritual acts, instead of merely serving at the altar in the court of the Tabernacle (pp. 206-207, 226-27). Also, both the ephod and breastpiece are adorned with stones engraved with the names of the twelve tribes of Israel (Exod. 28.12, 21), and part of the

26. So Morgenstern 1952–53: 72.

27. See n. 18 above.

28. Haran (1978: 160-60, 167-68) argues that there is a distinction between the fabric used for the Tabernacle veil, for the Tabernacle curtains, and for the high priest's garments, inasmuch as the proportion of wool, linen and other constituent materials differs in each case; he also points out that the fabric used for the Tabernacle veil and curtains is worked with a cherubim design, whereas there are no cherubim on the fabric used for the garments. Nevertheless, despite the differences, all three types of fabric are designated by the term *ḥōšēb* and contain linen and the same three colours of dyed wool, so there is clearly a strong element of similarity between them.

reason why Aaron wears these items when officiating in the sanctuary is to bring the people of Israel to remembrance before the Lord (Exod. 28.12, 29). Hence, it seems only reasonable that on a day such as the Day of Atonement, when atonement is supposedly being made in the Tabernacle for the people, the high priest would wear the garments that symbolize his links with both the Tabernacle and the people. Somewhat surprisingly, however, at the beginning of the ceremony he is instructed to dress himself not in the elaborate high Priestly garments but in plain linen garments (Lev. 16.4). These garments are similar to what the ordinary priests wear, but are described as being made of an even simpler kind of material—they are of plain linen (*bad*), whereas the other priests' garments are said in Exod. 39.27-28 to be made of fine linen (*šēš*) (Haran 1978: 174). Even the high priest's head-dress for this occasion is a plain linen turban (*miṣnepet bad*, Lev. 16.4) instead of the fine linen one that is a part of the ceremonial garments (*miṣnepet šēš*, Exod. 28.39; 39.28). This is then the attire that the high priest wears throughout his stay in the holiest place,[29] as he sprinkles the inner sanctum with the blood of the sacrificial animals in order to purify it, and then dispatches the scapegoat. However, once these rites have been safely carried out, he bathes and changes into 'his garments' (*b^egādāyw*, Lev. 16.24), which can only be the splendid high priestly regalia. In these he carries out the burnt offerings that form the final part of the day's observances.

This scenario raises two questions: first, what is the significance of the plain linen garments on an occasion which would seem to demand the ceremonial garments; and secondly, what does the change in clothing signify? To begin with the first of these questions, some scholars point out that heavenly beings are portrayed as clothed in linen (*bad*) in Ezekiel and Daniel, and conclude that the reason for the high priest wearing plain linen clothing on the Day of Atonement is because, like the heavenly beings, he is coming into the very presence of God.[30] As Haran (1978: 174) puts it, 'These garments serve to indicate a kind of dialectical elevation into that sphere which is beyond even the material, contagious holiness characterizing the tabernacle and its accessories'. Others have assumed that the unadorned linen garments are a symbol of the humility which is appropriate when seeking the expiation of sin before God,[31] or of the high priest's role as the representative of the common people.[32] However, when the high priest's clothing on this occasion is compared with the elaborate ceremonial garments that he wears when officiating in the sanctuary at other times, another

29. Ezekiel similarly prescribes linen as the fabric to be worn by the priests who minister inside the sanctuary, forbidding wool on the grounds that they must not wear anything that would make them sweat (Ezek. 44.17-18). For Ezekiel there is no high priest, so all the priests are able to minister inside the sanctuary.

30. Haran 1978: 174; Wenham 1979: 230; Kornfeld 1983: 63; Milgrom 1991: 1016. Heavenly beings are described as being clothed in linen in Ezek. 9.2, 3, 11; 10.2, 6, 7; Dan. 10.5; 12.6, 7.

31. Snaith 1967: 111; Levine 1989: 101; Hartley 1992: 235-36. Elliger (1966: 212) suggests that the plain linen garments are intended to commend the high priest to God as he seeks absolution for himself and the people.

32. Gorman 1990: 91; 1997: 95; Jenson 1992: 200. Elliger (1966: 212) and Porter (1976: 126-27) also suggest that the linen garments might simply reflect the older garb of the pre-exilic chief priests.

consideration comes to the fore. The stipulation that the high priest should be dressed so plainly means that all of the ritual accoutrements of the ceremonial garments along with their associated significance are denied to him;[33] and this has important ritual consequences for him. The obvious consequence is that he is rendered ritually deaf and dumb while inside the Tent of Meeting. Because he has no breastpiece, he has no Urim and Thummim which would normally rest inside the breastpiece as a symbol of communication between him and Yahweh (Exod. 28.30). Because he has no bells adorning the bottom of his robe, there is no sound as he moves about to reassure the people outside of his well-being, nor to 'communicate' with Yahweh and alert the deity to his presence in the sanctuary. This is despite the fact that in the instructions given to Moses for the ceremonial garments it is specified that Aaron should wear the robe with bells 'when he ministers, and its sound shall be heard when he goes into the holy place before the Lord, and when he comes out, lest he die' (Exod. 28.35).[34] The lack of ephod and breastpiece with their engraved stones also makes him 'dumb' in another sense—he cannot bear the names of the tribes of Israel on his person before the Lord as a reminder to Yahweh of those on whose behalf he officiates (cf. Exod. 28.12, 29). But perhaps the most significant item that he lacks is the gold plate on his forehead, inscribed 'Holy to the Lord', which is intended to absorb the guilt incurred via unintended flaws in the offerings so that the offerings can be accepted by Yahweh (Exod. 28.38).[35] This in turn means that there is no

33. For comments on the significance of the high priest's ceremonial garments, see Rooke 2000: 16-20. Haran (1978: 212-15) regards the wearing of the garments as in itself an act of ritual significance, through which the high priest performs ritual acts on behalf of the people while in the sanctuary.

34. Haran (1978: 218) argues that the mention of the death penalty in conjunction with failure to wear the bell-ridden robe should not be taken to mean that that garment was of particular significance; rather, the intention was that all the garments should be worn whenever the high priest was functioning inside the tent. However, this contradicts what he says a few pages earlier, where he says that Aaron only 'occasionally' adds the Urim and Thummim to the breastpiece (Haran 1978: 213-14). There is no indication in the descriptions of the high priest's garments that the Urim and Thummim are 'optional extras'; and if they do form a part of the ceremonial garments, and the garments all have to be worn together on pain of death whenever the high priest enters the tent, then the Urim and Thummim should be there too.

35. No mention is made of the gold plate in the description of the linen attire that the high priest is to wear on the Day of Atonement; and although it might be thought of as something that did not need to be specified because it would automatically be worn, the way it is presented elsewhere in the text argues against this point of view. In the pattern for the ceremonial garments and the description of their manufacture, it is described as a separate item (Exod. 28.36-38; 39.30-31); and in both the instructions for Aaron's ordination, and the subsequent account of Moses dressing Aaron in the ceremonial garments in order to ordain him, the turban and the plate (also called 'the holy crown') are mentioned quite separately and deliberately (Exod. 29.6; Lev. 8.9). By contrast, no such mention is made of the plate in Lev. 16.4, even though Aaron's head-dress is mentioned; and this gives the strong impression that the plate is not an element of the 'holy garments' to be worn by the high priest during his dangerous sortie into the holiest place. Against this, it might be observed that the list of garments to be donned in Exod. 29.5-6 and Lev. 8.7-9 does not include the linen breeches about which Exod. 28.42-43 is so insistent, but this should not be taken to indicate their absence, since breeches have been stipulated as part of the priests' clothing and so it is simply assumed that they

guarantee that the offerings will be accepted, which makes the whole undertaking much more dangerous and uncertain.

In summary, then, there is a tension between expectation and practice on the Day of Atonement. Not only is this the most important and dangerous ceremony of the year for the high priest—the reference to Nadab and Abihu (Lev. 16.1) and the warnings of the possibility of death in the presence of God (Lev. 16.2, 13) make the danger quite explicit—but the continuing well-being of the community is dependent on the successful performance of the ceremony. Yet when the high priest undertakes this crucial and perilous rite, which is a prerogative due to him because he *is* high priest, he is deprived of everything that marks him out as high priest, and is left vulnerable. It is as if his high priesthood has been annulled, and he is at risk of death by entering the holy place without the symbols of his office.[36] His vulnerability is also underlined by the emphasis in Lev. 16.17 that he must be alone in the Tent of Meeting in order to carry out the ritual, and indeed, by the lack of the names of the tribes of Israel on his garments. The implication of all this is that the ceremonies undertaken while the high priest is dressed in linen are not primarily rituals of mediation for the people, because during those ceremonies the people are not brought to ritual remembrance before Yahweh by their representative. Indeed, given that the high priest is officiating without any of the ritual symbols that mark him out as the people's representative, it is questionable whether he is even functioning as their representative in any ritually meaningful way. Rather, this so-called atonement ceremony is primarily about what the high priest in and of himself can do in the sanctuary; it is a matter between him and Yahweh, and any benefits accruing to the people because of that do so only secondarily.

This understanding of the high priest's role fits well with the point made by a number of scholars, that the Day of Atonement is more accurately regarded as a 'Day of Purgation(s)'. The basis of this theology of purgation is that in the

would have worn them. Similarly, perhaps the golden plate is not mentioned in Lev. 16.4 because it is simply assumed that the high priest will wear it on the Day of Atonement, since it has already been stipulated in Exod. 28.38 that he should wear it at all times. However, if elsewhere breeches (which would not be seen) can be assumed to be part of the priests' clothing without needing to be mentioned, whereas the golden plate (which is highly visible) apparently needs to be specified if it is worn, it is all the more remarkable that Lev. 16.4 does mention breeches but does not mention the golden plate. Under these circumstances, the most natural conclusion is that the plate does not form part of the high priest's holy linen garments for the Day of Atonement (*contra* Rooke 2000: 24-25); and the ritual consequence of this is that he is deprived of the means of absorbing the guilt from unintentionally flawed offerings. This is consistent with Haran's comment that the adverb *tāmîd*, which defines when the golden plate is to be worn (Exod. 28.38), does not mean 'continually', as in many English versions, but 'daily', that is, when the high priest goes into the sanctuary for the morning and evening daily rites (Haran 1978: 214). The Day of Atonement rites are not ordinary daily rites, and so it is not necessarily to be expected that the high priest would wear the golden plate.

36. Gorman (1990: 90-95) speaks of this period as 'marginal time'. Compare also Turner's description of those in a liminal state: 'They may…wear only a strip of clothing, or even go naked, to demonstrate that as liminal beings they have no status, property, insignia, secular clothing indicating rank or role…' (Turner 1969: 95). The loss of status involved in the Day of Atonement rite is one of the primary characteristics of a state of liminality.

normal course of events, the Temple becomes polluted by the impurity generated as a result of the sins and uncleannesses of the Israelites; hence, the function of the rites on the Day of Atonement is to purge the Temple (cf. Lev. 16.16, 18-19), so that it remains habitable for the deity.[37] Similar rites of purgation are attested in neighbouring ancient Near Eastern cultures. By comparison with this, the theologically charged and yet vague notion of 'atonement' fails to appreciate the true significance of the Temple rites because it focuses on the individual or corporate relationship with the deity, and lacks both the sense of impurity as a concrete pollutant that needs to be removed and an understanding of how sacrificial ritual can effect that removal. It also makes it difficult to see how the Day of Atonement might function as the high priest's validation, because it makes the idea of validation dependent upon the high priest being 'good at atoning' but gives no sense of what it means practically speaking to be 'good at atoning'. However, once the Day of Atonement is understood as a Day of Purgation Rites, it becomes much easier to understand how the rites could function as the high priest's validation, because their successful completion depends on the high priest's competence as a ritual actor in carrying out the purgation ceremony, and not on his ability to elicit pity from the deity (which is what is implied by saying that the high priest is good at atoning).[38] If he performs the rites correctly, he will both preserve his life and demonstrate his acceptability to the deity, thus proving his worthiness for the high priesthood.

If this is the meaning of the plain linen clothing, then, the significance of the change of clothing at the end of the purgation rituals (Lev. 16.23-24) becomes clear. Given the commonplace that bathing and changes of clothing often signify a change of status, many scholars have commented that the high priest's ritual of bathing and changing clothes signifies the transition between the sphere of the exceedingly holy and the sphere of the moderately holy. The high priest is moving from having officiated in the inner sanctum, which is highly charged with holiness, to officiating in the courtyard outside the Tabernacle, which is of a

37. See Morgenstern 1952–53: 47-48; Milgrom 1971: 1384-85; 1976; Levine 1974: 75-77; 1989: 99; Wright 1992: 72-74; see also the discussion of purification offerings in Milgrom 1991: 253-61. The sense of communal and personal atonement is present in the current text of Lev. 16, but only as an appendix in 16.29-34, and as Levine (1974: 76) observes, nowhere in the main body of the text (16.3-28) is there mention of the people as direct objects of purification.

38. This paradigm of purgation rather than atonement is also applicable to the ritual of the Azazel goat, a ritual which is incomprehensible without a sense of sin as a malign force (rather like disease) that can be removed by transferring it onto a carrier of some sort. The notion of 'putting the people's sins on the head of the goat' (Lev. 16.21) is meaningless if the sins are viewed as moral lapses, because it is impossible to transfer a moral lapse onto something else. Alternatively, the meaning of the Azazel ritual might be construed as the removal of the impurity that is generated in the people by their moral lapses; but once again, the concept is one of purification rather than of the forgiveness that is implied by the term 'atonement'. In this context, Zatelli's comments on the Azazel rite are illuminating: 'It is important to stress a fundamental feature of this rite: its original nucleus does not aim to appease generic feelings of guilt by means of expiation or substitution. It is a real purgation rite, consisting of the elimination of the impurities which through the transgressions…of a group or a community, have invaded…an important place of worship' (Zatelli 1998: 261). For a comparison of the Azazel goat ritual with other similar ancient Near Eastern rites of purgation, see Wright 1987: 15-74.

lesser degree of sanctity; and so he needs to be careful not to communicate holiness from the inner sanctum to the outer areas. The bathing and change of clothing therefore act as a kind of decontamination from holiness,[39] a ritual airlock, so to speak. However, the change in clothing can also be seen as signifying the personal change in status from potential high priest to confirmed high priest. He earns the right to wear the ceremonial garments by successfully carrying out the atonement ceremony and purifying the Temple without incurring divine wrath in the process.[40] His mediation is accepted; therefore, he can function fully and confidently as high priest, and his assumption of the garments is a declaration of that.

Indeed, the changes of clothing are a visual demonstration of what is happening during the day's ceremonies. Until such time as the rites have been successfully carried out, normal cultic functioning is suspended; and so while the rites are in progress it is inappropriate for the high priest to wear his elaborate high priestly garments which are a part of the mainstream cult. His resumption of the garments indicates the resumption of normal cultic service, including his own status and regular cultic duties as high priest.

3. *The Offerings at the End of the Ceremony*

Further support for interpreting the Day of Atonement as the high priest's validation can be gained from the offerings that are made by the high priest once he has assumed the ceremonial garments after the ceremonies of purification in the holy place. The offerings are two burnt offerings, one for himself and his house, and one for the people (Lev. 16.24). Elsewhere in the Priestly corpus, burnt offerings have two primary associations, both of which are compatible with the understanding of the burnt offering as the most basic form of sacrifice, intended to

39. Porter 1976: 131; Kiuchi 1987: 137; Milgrom 1991: 1048-49; Wright 1992: 73; Hartley 1992: 241-42; Gerstenberger 1996: 223. Snaith (1967: 116) regards the bathing and clothing change as a way of ensuring that Israel is not contaminated with sin (presumably the sin that the high priest has been cleansing by means of the various rites); similarly, Gorman (1990: 93-94) argues that the 'decontamination' is both from the holiness associated with the inner sanctum and from the defilement incurred by 'manipulating' the nation's sin (i.e. using confession and hand-laying to 'place' the sin on the head of the Azazel goat in order to effect atonement).

40. In the context of a discussion of the rites of ordination in Lev. 8 as rites of passage, and of the significance of the clothing that is worn during rites of passage, Milgrom (1991: 569) comments of the high priest's linen clothing on the Day of Atonement, 'he is literally engaged in a rite of passage, entering and exiting the Holy of Holies, into which no man—not even a Moses—may enter'. If Milgrom's understanding of the clothing conventions used on the day of ordination (Lev. 8) is correct, the clothing convention for the high priest on the Day of Atonement is its exact opposite. For their ordination, the liminal state of Aaron and sons is emphasized by them being dressed as priests when they are still lay people and unable as yet to function as priests (p. 569). On the Day of Atonement, however, the high priest's liminal state is reflected by him being dressed in plain garments and being unable to function in his normal cultic capacity despite being the ordained high priest. Milgrom also mentions the idea of the Day of Atonement as a rite of passage in connection with his comment on Lev. 16.4 (Milgrom 1991: 1016), but does not elaborate on how or why the Day of Atonement might be seen as a rite of passage for the high priest.

attract the benevolent attention of the deity.[41] The first association is with rites of passage that mark the movement between states of purity or degrees of holiness, presumably as a way of securing divine approval of the new status and its concomitant implications for the individual's function within the cult. Thus, burnt offerings are made by those who have undergone a specified period of impurity and are now ready to be declared ceremonially pure: by the woman who has given birth, at the end of her specified period of uncleanness (Lev. 12.6); by the leper who has been declared free of the disease (Lev. 14.19, 20); by males or females who have suffered an abnormal genital discharge but are now free of it (Lev. 15.15, 30); and by the Nazirite whose period of separation has been terminated prematurely by defilement through contact with a dead body (Num. 6.11).[42] Also, in the only example of a burnt offering that marks the movement from a higher to a lower status of holiness, the Nazirite offers a burnt offering as part of the ritual that marks the end of his specified period of separation (Num. 6.14).[43] As well as signalling the reversion to normal status following a temporary period of impurity or exceptional purity, burnt offerings are part of the ceremonies that mark permanent movements up the scale of holiness. They are thus included in the ceremonies of ordination for the priests (Exod. 29.18; Lev. 8.18); they are offered by the leaders of all the tribes of Israel for the dedication of the altar (Num. 7.15-88);[44] and they are part of the ceremony whereby the Levites are set apart for the service of the Lord (Num. 8.12). The second major association that burnt offerings have in P is with festivals: burnt offerings are made every morning and evening (Exod. 29.38-42; Num. 28.3-6), and additional burnt offerings are made at all the festivals from the Sabbath to the eight days of the feast of Tabernacles (Num. 29.9-38; cf. also Exod. 23.12, 18). Either or both of these associations could be present in the burnt offerings of Lev. 16.24; however, given that according to Num. 29.11 the day's festal burnt offerings are *in addition to* 'the sin offering of atonement'—presumably all of the offerings described in

41. For comments on the origin and significance of the burnt offering, see Levine 1989: 5-6; Milgrom 1991: 172-77; Jenson 1992: 155-56.

42. All of these rituals require the worshipper to make a sin offering (*ḥaṭṭā't*) as well as a burnt offering (*'ōlâ*). Commenting on the significance of this combination of offerings in the case of the woman who has given birth, Levine remarks, 'The *ḥatta't*, in removing the impurity, restored to the person the right of access to the sanctuary; and the *'olah* that followed immediately upon it symbolized this renewed acceptability. It served as an invocation to God, the first act of worship after being restored to purity. God's acceptance of the *'olah* signaled the readmission of the individual into the religious life of the community' (Levine 1989: 74). However, commenting upon the requirement in Num. 6.11 that the defiled Nazirite offer two turtledoves or pigeons, one for a sin offering and the other for a burnt offering, Milgrom (1990: 47) says that the burnt offering is actually superfluous, since only the purification offering was necessary to purge the sanctuary of the contamination caused by the Nazirite's defilement; the point of having two birds was simply to make an adequate gift for the altar, a point made by Ibn Ezra on Lev. 5.7.

43. Milgrom (1990: 48) notes that this is also a unique example of a purification offering being used in the context of legitimate desanctification.

44. Milgrom (1990: 55, 363-64) argues that the chieftains did not actually offer up the gifts on the day that they brought them, but rather contributed them to a sacrificial store for use in the public cult.

Leviticus 16—'and the continual (i.e. daily morning and evening) burnt offering',[45] the more probable association of these burnt offerings that come as the concluding part of the rite of atonement seems to be with a change of status. As a result of the ceremonies carried out in the holiest place, priesthood, people and Temple have all moved from a state of impurity to one of purity, and the burnt offerings made by Aaron at the end of the rites in the holy place are a confirmation of that new status. However, for the high priest the effect is not only that he has moved from a state of impurity to purity but that he has moved from a state of compromised priesthood to certain priesthood. Hence, the burnt offering has a double significance for him. The status quo has been restored, and he can be high priest for another year.

4. *The Evidence from other Texts*

If, then, as proposed above, the significance of the Day of Atonement for the high priest is that it serves as his annual ritual of validation, there are a number of other texts that can be reinterpreted in the light of it.

a. *The Vision of Joshua the High Priest in Zechariah 3*

One of the most suggestive and yet enigmatic pieces of evidence about the high priest is Zechariah's vision of Joshua son of Jehozadak in Zechariah 3. In the vision Joshua, described as 'the high priest', is shown standing in soiled clothing before the angel of the Lord, apparently being accused by *haśśāṭān*, the Accuser (3.1, 3). The Lord rebukes the Accuser (3.2), and orders Joshua to be reclothed in clean clothing (3.4-5). Joshua then receives an oracle saying, 'If you walk in my ways and observe my service, it is you who shall rule my house and keep watch over my courts, and I will give you right of entrance[46] among those who are standing here' (3.7).

45. Ancient commentators were divided on whether the ram of burnt offering listed as a festal offering in Num. 29.8 was the same as the ram for the people's burnt offering specified in Lev. 16.5. See Wright 1992: 74.

46. The form of the Hebrew word *mahl^{e}kîm* that is rendered 'right of entrance' (RSV 'right of access') is problematic, since it is a *hapax legomenon*. The word is usually taken to be a noun with the sense of 'access' or 'entrance'. However, some exegetes, following the lead of the LXX and Vulgate, have interpreted it as a piel participle meaning 'those who go'; on this interpretation, the promise to Joshua in Zech. 3.7 is that he will have intermediaries between himself and the heavenly court, rather than having direct access to it himself: 'I will give you *those who go* among those who are standing here'. Rose (2000: 82) suggests that such intermediaries would have been 'bearers of revelation, possibly prophets'. For a discussion of the interpretative options, see Rose 2000: 73-82. In the absence of definitive arguments in favour of either interpretation, the 'right of access' option seems more plausible on exegetical grounds, because it is more striking. The vision of Zech. 3 appears to be heralding a new order of things, but to promise a figure of religious authority that he will be granted intermediaries to enable him to ascertain the will of God is nothing new. Far more revolutionary is the claim that Joshua himself will stand in the divine council, and it is perfectly understandable that such an extraordinary development would need to be validated by a prophetic vision.

The image here is one of initiation for Joshua, as is indicated by the change of his clothing.[47] The stripping and reclothing is clearly a symbol of purification, as the text itself makes clear—'behold, I have taken your iniquity away from you' (3.4)—and heralds a change of status for Joshua in terms that imply that he is now the chief mediator of the community. The demand for him to 'walk in my ways and observe my service' (3.7) is the condition upon which his position depends, with the implication that if he fails in this his position will be jeopardized. However, if he fulfils his commission appropriately he will have access to the very presence of God (3.7b); and so being granted access to the divine presence serves as the validation of whether or not the high priest has walked in the ways and kept the service of the Lord. The vision therefore seems to support the idea that it was the high priest's prerogative to function in the very presence of the deity, and that the one who so functioned had divine approval. This is a similar concept as has been argued for in the case of the Day of Atonement ceremonies, although of course it is expressed very differently in Zechariah 3 and in Leviticus 16.

Given that at this stage the Day of Atonement may not even have existed, and that even if it did this vision was apparently dated before the Temple was rebuilt, at a time when any Temple-dependent ceremonies would have been impossible, Zechariah 3 can perhaps be viewed as a contributory element to the Day of Atonement as it later developed.

b. *The Sin of King Uzziah in 2 Chronicles 26*

2 Chronicles 26.16-21, where King Uzziah attempts to burn incense in the Temple but is opposed by the chief priest and is struck with leprosy, may well have the Day of Atonement as its conceptual background.[48] The interpretation of this passage is complicated by the fact that it is an anachronistic mixture of pre- and post-exilic motifs, but it is clearly attempting to rationalize the bald statement of 2 Kgs 15.5 that the Lord struck the king with leprosy. Since leprosy leads to cultic (and social) exclusion, Uzziah is assumed to have committed some sort of cultic sin in order to incur what might be termed a cultic punishment; and the sin is portrayed as attempting to usurp the Priestly privilege of burning incense in the Temple. The scenario is rather forced, because it is clear from Samuel and Kings that the monarch was the chief cultic official in pre-exilic times, and so the idea of Uzziah being barred from officiating in the Temple because he was not of the Priestly family of Aaron is rather ridiculous. The king is said first of all to want to burn incense on the altar of incense (2 Chron. 26.16), but subsequently he is depicted with a censer in his hand for burning the incense (2 Chron. 26.19).

47. Elliger (1967: 122) draws a parallel between Joshua's stripping and reclothing, and Aaron's ordination in Lev. 8.

48. Morgenstern (1938: 6 n. 16) argued that the background was the king's role in the ceremonies of the New Year, as part of which the monarch would enter the innermost sanctuary. Johnstone (1997: II, 167) suggests that the reference in v. 19 to priests in the plural as those who have the right to burn incense may imply that the setting is one of the daily offerings of incense morning and evening. However, according to Exod. 30.7, only Aaron is to burn the daily offerings of incense on the altar of incense, so the reference to 'priests' in the plural burning incense cannot be used to determine the occasion that forms the background to this incident.

According to the P tradition, incense offering on the altar of incense is a high priestly duty (Exod. 30.7), and, as already noted, using a censer is the prerogative of the high priest on the Day of Atonement alone, when he uses it to create the cloud of concealing fragrant smoke in the Holy of Holies (Lev. 16.12-13). Hence, both in wanting to burn incense at all and then in attempting to use a censer to do so, Uzziah is setting out to do what according to Exodus and Leviticus only the high priest is entitled to do. Indeed, if the mention of a censer is taken as a reference to the Day of Atonement ceremony, the incident can be seen as an example of ritual validation being refused to an aspiring cultic mediator in the context of the Yom Kippur observances. Uzziah's punishment for trying to usurp this privilege and for rejecting the rebuke of the chief priest Azariah is pure poetic justice: he is struck with leprosy on his forehead (2 Chron. 26.19), the very place where the high priest wears the gold plate that declares him 'Holy to the Lord'.[49] Thus, Uzziah is permanently invalidated as the community's chief mediator, since he has the sign not of holiness but of defilement on his forehead.

c. *The Korahite Rebellion in Numbers 16–17*

This narrative is interesting in the present context because of the way that incense and censers are used both to determine who can and cannot serve, and to stay the punishment of the people. The Levite Korah, who is presented in Exod. 6.18-21 as a first cousin of Aaron and Moses, heads up a challenge to Moses and Aaron over their claim to a superior status of holiness in the community. In response, Moses proposes that the Korahites and Aaron are to offer incense in censers before the Lord, and the Lord will make plain the man of his choice (16.6-7, 16-17). When they do this, Korah's band of 250 Levites offering incense is consumed by fire. The next day the congregation accuse Moses and Aaron about the loss of life in the episode, and Yahweh punishes the people by sending a plague upon them. Moses immediately tells Aaron to get his censer and go among the people with it; Aaron does so, thereby making atonement for them and stopping the plague.

Although this at first sight looks like a claim to priestly status by non-priestly personnel, the use of censers and incense to determine who is the chosen party implies that Korah is actually challenging Aaron for the high priesthood.[50] This reading is supported by other details in the narrative. In the first place, Korah's challenge is to Moses and Aaron, who are the only two people allowed to go in and out of the Tent of Meeting. Secondly, Moses' reply to Korah's challenge is framed in the singular: 'the one whom he chooses he will bring near to himself' (Num. 16.5), and 'the man whom the Lord chooses is the holy one' (Num. 6.7). This implies that a particular position is at stake, rather than a general issue of status for a whole class of people. Against such a background, the 250 who perish by divine fire can be seen to have tried to claim an inappropriate level of

49. See Johnstone 1997: II, 168-69; Beentjes 2000: 67.

50. Similar readings of this incident may be found in Morgenstern 1938: 18-19, 366; Heger 1997: 72-79. Heger (1997: 78) notes that this interpretation also appears in *Midrash Tanḥuma* (Buber), *Pequdei* 1.

intimacy with the Lord, a level that is reserved for the validated high priest alone, because if censing with impunity is the key to getting close to the Lord then anyone who does it would be able to enter the divine presence.

There are a number of similarities between this episode and the Nadab and Abihu incident. In both cases, the motif of censers and drawing near to the Lord is strongly reminiscent of the high priest's duties on the Day of Atonement; in both cases, the miscreants are cultic personnel, but of a lower grade than Aaron; and in both cases they are consumed by divine fire. In each case, too, the disastrous attempt to draw near is followed by a contrasting narrative that emphasizes Aaron's right to cense and draw near with impunity. Here, the contrasting narrative tells of the people being struck with a punitive plague, and Aaron alone taking his censer and stopping the plague, that is, making atonement for the people, by censing with it among them. The contrast is deliberately striking, that 250 who were not of the Lord's choice succeeded only in getting themselves consumed by fire when they offered incense before the Lord, whereas the one man who is the Lord's choice to offer incense in a censer before the Lord can make atonement for the whole people by that means.

d. *Jonathan Maccabee's Installation as High Priest in 1 Maccabees 10.21*

According to 1 Macc. 10.21, Jonathan Maccabee was designated high priest by Alexander Balas, and he put on the garments at the Feast of Tabernacles in the year 152 BCE. Given the close connection between Tabernacles and the Day of Atonement, it is arguable that Jonathan's inauguration to his high priestly duties was in fact at the Day of Atonement for that year, and that this is the true significance of the comment that he put on the garments at the Feast of Tabernacles. This of course would also be a highly symbolic time at which to take up the high priesthood, indicating as it does a new year, despite the numbering of the months from the spring.

It is interesting that no specific date is given for this installation, other than the generic 'at the Feast of Tabernacles'. This is in contrast with the precise specification of other dates in the book, such as the rededication of the altar on 25 Chislev (1 Macc. 4.52, 59), Simon's cleansing of the Akra on the twenty-third day of the second month (1 Macc. 13.51), and the decree of the people to make Simon their leader and high priest that was passed on 18 Elul (1 Macc. 14.27). The lack of a more precise date, such as 'on the first day of the feast of Tabernacles', for example, could be taken to signify that there was a certain amount of dissatisfaction with Jonathan's preferment; the fact that there is no declaration of public favour for Jonathan as there is for Simon Maccabee later on is often interpreted in this way. However, it could also mean that a given date during the season of Tabernacles was the acknowledged time of year for high priests to be inducted, and so it was unnecessary to specify the date any more precisely.

e. *The Quarrel between Joannes and Jesus in the Temple (Josephus,* Antiquities *11.297-301)*

Josephus's anecdote about the quarrel between the high priest Joannes and his brother Jesus, whereby Joannes, while officiating in the Temple, is provoked by

Jesus and kills him, could be construed as Jesus's challenge to Joannes' mediatory function on the Day of Atonement. Although there is absolutely no evidence in Josephus (or elsewhere, for that matter) as to the precise occasion upon which the murder is supposed to have occurred, the most distinctive occasion on which the high priest would have been serving in the Temple was the Day of Atonement, and this is arguably the most natural association to be made when there is talk about the high priest serving in the Temple. It is therefore conceivable that this is what Josephus has in mind when he sets the incident in the context of the Temple, and also when he decries the slaughter in lurid terms: 'neither among Greeks nor barbarians had so savage and impious a deed ever been committed' (*Ant.* 11.299). Morgenstern (1938: 365-66) thinks that Bagoses' determination to force his way into the Temple is significant, and argues that it was in order to see where his protégé Jesus had died, and that that would have been in the inner place where the high priest would have functioned in the New Year ceremony. In the end, of course, this is all pure speculation, but viewing the incident in the light of a Day of Atonement ceremony that granted ritual validation and therefore important ritual status to the high priest would certainly give a new twist and perhaps more meaning to the incident.

5. *Conclusion*

It has been argued that the Day of Atonement was particularly important to the high priest inasmuch as it would have constituted a yearly validation of his position as the community's chief cultic mediator. Support for this position has been gathered from the narrative structure of Leviticus as it relates to the Day of Atonement legislation, and from elements of the Day itself, namely the high priest's clothing and the sacrifices that are offered. The paradigm has then been applied to several other biblical and para-biblical incidents, with generally positive results.

BIBLIOGRAPHY

Aartun, Kjell

1980 'Studien zum Gesetz über den grossen Versöhnungstag Lv 16 mit Varianten: Ein ritualgeschichtlicher Beitrag', *ST* 34: 73-109.

Beentjes, Pancratius C.

2000 '"They saw that his forehead was leprous" (2 Chr 26.20): The Chronicler's Narrative on Uzziah's Leprosy', in M.J.H.M. Poorthuis and J. Schwartz (eds.), *Purity and Holiness: The Heritage of Leviticus* (Jewish and Christian Perspectives, 2; Leiden: E.J. Brill): 61-72.

Budd, Philip J.

1996 *Leviticus* (NCB; Grand Rapids: Eerdmans; London: Marshall Pickering).

Carmichael, Calum

2000 'The Origin of the Scapegoat Ritual', *VT* 50: 167-82.

Elliger, Karl

1966 *Leviticus* (HAT, 4; Tübingen: J.C.B. Mohr [Paul Siebeck]).

1967 *Das Büch der zwölf kleinen Propheten.* II. *Nahum, Habakkuk, Zephanja, Haggai, Sacharja, Maleachi* (ATD, 25; Göttingen: Vandenhoeck & Ruprecht).

Finegan, Jack

1998 *Handbook of Biblical Chronology: Principles of Time Reckoning in the Ancient World and Problems of Chronology in the Bible* (Peabody, MA: Hendrickson, rev. edn).

Gane, Roy E.

1998 'Schedules for Deities: Macrostructure of Israelite, Babylonian, and Hittite Sancta Purification Days', *AUSS* 36: 231-44.

Gennep, Arnold van

1960 *The Rites of Passage* (London: Routledge & Kegan Paul).

Gerstenberger, Erhard S.

1996 *Leviticus* (OTL; Louisville, KY: Westminster/John Knox Press).

Görg, Manfred

1995 '"Asaselologen" unter sich—eine neue Runde?', *BN* 80: 25-31.

Gorman, Frank H., Jr

1990 *The Ideology of Ritual: Space, Time and Status in the Priestly Theology* (JSOTSup, 91; Sheffield: JSOT Press).

1997 *Divine Presence and Community: A Commentary on the Book of Leviticus* (ITC; Grand Rapids: Eerdmans; Edinburgh: Handsel).

Goudoever, J. van

1959 *Biblical Calendars* (Leiden: E.J. Brill).

Gradwohl, Roland

1963 'Das "fremde Feuer" von Nadab und Abihu', *ZAW* 75: 288-96.

Haran, Menahem

1960 'The Uses of Incense in the Ancient Israelite Ritual', *VT* 10: 113-29.

1978 *Temples and Temple Service in Ancient Israel* (Oxford: Clarendon Press).

Harrison, R.K.

1980 *Leviticus* (TOTC; Leicester: IVP).

Hartley, John E.

1992 *Leviticus* (WBC, 4; Dallas: Word Books).

Heger, Paul

1997 *The Development of Incense Cult in Israel* (BZAW, 245; Berlin and New York: W. de Gruyter).

Heinisch, Paul

1935 *Das Buch Leviticus* (Die heilige Schrift des Alten Testamentes, 1.3; Bonn: Peter Hanstein).

Helm, Rob

1994 'Azazel in Early Jewish Tradition', *AUSS* 32: 217-26.

Jenson, Philip Peter

1992 *Graded Holiness: A Key to the Priestly Conception of the World* (JSOTSup, 106; Sheffield: JSOT Press).

Johnson, Aubrey R.

1935 'The Rôle of the King in the Jerusalem Cultus', in S.H. Hooke (ed.), *The Labyrinth: Further Studies in the Relation between Myth and Ritual in the Ancient World* (London: SPCK): 71-111.

Johnstone, William

1997 *1 and 2 Chronicles* (JSOTSup, 254; 2 vols.; Sheffield: Sheffield Academic Press).

Kiuchi, N.

1987 *The Purification Offering in the Priestly Literature* (JSOTSup, 56; Sheffield: JSOT Press).

Kornfeld, W.

1983 *Levitikus* (Die neue Echter Bibel; Würzburg: Echter Verlag).

Laughlin, John C.H.

1976 'The "Strange Fire" of Nadab and Abihu', *JBL* 95: 559-65.

Levine, Baruch A.

1974 *In the Presence of the Lord: A Study of Cult and some Cultic Terms in Ancient Israel* (SJLA, 5; Leiden: E.J. Brill).

1989 *Leviticus* (JPS Torah Commentary; Philadelphia: The Jewish Publication Society of America).

Maier, Johann

1985 *The Temple Scroll: An Introduction, Translation and Commentary* (JSOTSup, 34; Sheffield: JSOT Press).

McLean, Bradley H.

1991 'The Interpretation of the Levitical Sin Offering and the Scapegoat', *SR* 20: 345-56.

Milgrom, Jacob

1971 'Day of Atonement as Annual Day of Purgation in Temple Times', in *EncJud* (Jerusalem: Keter): V, 1384-87.

1976 'Atonement, Day of', in *IDBSup* (Nashville: Abingdon Press): 82-83.

1990 *Numbers* (JPS Torah Commentary; Philadelphia: The Jewish Publication Society of America).

1991 *Leviticus 1–16* (AB, 3; New York: Doubleday).

2001 *Leviticus 23–27* (AB, 3B; New York: Doubleday).

Morgenstern, Julian

1917–18 'Two Ancient Israelite Agricultural Festivals', *JQR* NS 8: 31-54.

1924 'The Three Calendars of Ancient Israel', *HUCA* 1: 13-78.

1926a 'Additional Notes on "The Three Calendars of Ancient Israel"', *HUCA* 3: 77-107.

1926b 'On Leviticus 10,3', in Cyrus Adler and Aaron Ember (eds.), *Oriental Studies Published in Commemoration of the Fortieth Anniversary of Paul Haupt as Director of the Oriental Seminary of the Johns Hopkins University, Baltimore, MD* (Baltimore: The Johns Hopkins University Press; Leipzig: J.C. Hinrichs): 97-102.

1929 'The Gates of Righteousness', *HUCA* 6: 1-37.

1935 'Supplementary Studies in the Calendars of Ancient Israel', *HUCA* 10: 1-148.

1936 'The New Year for Kings', in Bruno Schindler and A. Marmorstein (eds.), *Occident and Orient: Gaster Anniversary Volume* (London: Taylor's Foreign Press): 439-56.

1937–38 'Amos Studies II: The Sin of Uzziah, The Festival of Jerobeam and the Date of Amos', *HUCA* 12–13: 1-54.

1938 'A Chapter in the History of the High Priesthood', *AJSL* 55: 1-24, 183-97, 360-77.

1952–53 'Two Prophecies from the Fourth Century B.C. and the Evolution of Yom Kippur', *HUCA* 24: 1-74.

1963 *The Fire Upon the Altar* (Chicago: Quadrangle Books).

Noth, Martin

1962 *Das dritte Buch Mose, Leviticus* (ATD, 6; Göttingen: Vandenhoeck & Ruprecht). ET *Leviticus* (trans. J.E. Anderson; OTL; London: SCM Press; rev. edn, 1977).

Porter, J.R.

1976 *Leviticus* (CBC; Cambridge: Cambridge University Press).

Rodriguez, Angel Manuel

1996 'Leviticus 16: Its Literary Structure', *AUSS* 34: 269-86.

Roo, Jacqueline C.R. de

2000 'Was the Goat for Azazel Destined for the Wrath of God?', *Bib* 81: 233-42.

Rooke, Deborah W.

2000 *Zadok's Heirs: The Role and Development of the High Priesthood in Ancient Israel* (Oxford Theological Monographs; Oxford: Oxford University Press).

Rose, Wolter H.

2000 *Zemah and Zerubbabel: Messianic Expectations in the Early Postexilic Period* (JSOTSup, 304; Sheffield: Sheffield Academic Press).

Snaith, N.H.

1947 *The Jewish New Year Festival: Its Origins and Development* (London: SPCK).

1967 *Leviticus and Numbers* (NCB; London: Thomas Nelson).

Tawil, Hayim

1980 ''Azazel the Prince of the Steepe: A Comparative Study', *ZAW* 92: 43-59.

Taylor, J. Glen

1993 *Yahweh and the Sun: Biblical and Archaeological Evidence for Sun Worship in Ancient Israel* (JSOTSup, 111; Sheffield: JSOT Press).

Toorn, Karel van der

1991 'The Babylonian New Year Festival: New Insights from the Cuneiform Texts and their Bearing on Old Testament Study', in J.A. Emerton (ed.), *Congress Volume: Leuven 1989* (VTSup, 43; Leiden: E.J. Brill): 331-44.

Turner, Victor W.

1969 *The Ritual Process: Structure and Anti-Structure* (London: Routledge & Kegan Paul).

Ulfgard, Håkan

1998 *The Story of Sukkot: The Setting, Shaping, and Sequel of the Biblical Feast of Tabernacles* (Beiträge zur Geschichte der biblischen Exegese, 34; Tübingen: Mohr Siebeck).

Wenham, Gordon J.

1979 *The Book of Leviticus* (NICOT; London: Hodder & Stoughton).

Wright, David P.

1987 *The Disposal of Impurity: Elimination Rites in the Bible and in Hittite and Mesopotamian Literature* (SBLDS, 101; Atlanta: Scholars Press).

1992 'Day of Atonement', in *ABD*, II: 72-76.

Zatelli, Ida

1998 'The Origin of the Biblical Scapegoat Ritual: The Evidence of Two Eblaite Texts', *VT* 48: 254-63.

The Temple of David in the Book of Chronicles

John Jarick

The book of Chronicles—especially when read in its own right and not emended to agree with readings in the books of Samuel and Kings—puts forward a picture of the Temple in Jerusalem which is quite startling in a number of respects, and it is the purpose of this paper to explore some of those unique features.

Before painting the picture, however, let me say something about my approach to the canvas. Those who have consulted my recent commentary on 1 Chronicles (Jarick 2002) will be aware of my understanding of the book of Chronicles, but I think it worthwhile for me to note here one or two things of a programmatic nature before drawing attention to the way in which the book treats the Temple.

We are dealing here with a scroll entitled *dibrê hayyāmîm*, and of anonymous authorship. The work itself is generally referred to in English Bibles as 'Chronicles', and the putative author is generally styled 'the Chronicler' in scholarly discussions. However, I prefer to speak of 'the Annals' for the document and of 'the Annalists' for the people responsible for creating that document. The reason for my preference is not simply that many modern English translations render the expression *dibrê hayyāmîm* (when it occurs within the text of the scroll) as 'the Annals', such as the NRSV's 'the Annals of King David' for *dibrê hayyāmîm lammelek dāwîd* (in 1 Chron. 27.24), but also to suggest two aspects which may not be so ably signified by the designations 'Chronicles' and 'the Chronicler'.

Primarily I wish to signal that the book we have access to is not the product of a single author, not even in terms of that historical-critical model which postulates an original Chronicler upon whose foundation various levitical additions were laid or sundry priestly revisions were made. I rather think that the scroll from the first was the product of a collective enterprise of assembling, sifting and refining certain Jerusalemite traditions; that is to say, that a community or guild of tradents was responsible for the composition of these Annals. I could of course speak of 'the Chroniclers' if the collective aspect of authorship was all that I wanted to imply for this work, but I am also attracted to the homophonic relationship between the word 'Annalists', as designating a school of chronographers, and the word 'Analysts', as designating professionals or others who apply analytical skills to their tasks. The people responsible for telling this version of the story of the kingdom of Judah, and within that story devoting an inordinate amount of space to foundation legends of the national Temple, had exactingly analysed the traditions of their people, and they put forward an account that scrupulously insisted on their line of analysis.

No one who reads their work can deny that these 'Annalists' had strident views that they wished to impart in their 'Annals', and that the Temple looms large in their project. Theirs is a 'book of beginnings', looking back to a legendary past. By starting out with Adam and the generations that were believed to have descended from him, they allude to the very beginnings of humankind and in turn to the beginnings of the great divisions of peoples in the known world and the beginnings of the Israelite people itself. By devoting a great swathe of text to their story of King David as founder of the Israelite kingdom and planner of its Temple, as well as to the building and dedication of the Temple by King Solomon, they show that they are most interested in getting across a certain view of the regal and religious system that they advocate. And by drawing the Annals to a close with the invitation from the Persian king for people to 'go up' to Jerusalem, they end with a new beginning—and an implied challenge for their community, to act in accordance with the way the Annalists envisaged things to have been constituted in the earlier beginning of that kingdom and its Temple.

But just what did the Annalists envisage in terms of the Temple, and how does their vision sit with other biblical sources?

1. *Reaching Towards Heaven*

For one thing, the Annalists imagine a Temple that reaches unambiguously heavenwards. Other storytellers in ancient Israel are content to picture a relatively low building, as in 1 Kgs 6.2, where we are told that 'the house that King Solomon built for Yahweh was sixty cubits long, twenty cubits wide, and thirty cubits high'; in other words, the main structure is just half again as high as it is wide, and only half as high as it is long. But in 2 Chron. 3.3-4 we read that 'these were the dimensions Solomon established for building the house of God: the length, in cubits of the old standard, was sixty cubits, and the width was twenty cubits, and the length of the vestibule was the same as the width of the house, namely twenty cubits, and the height was one hundred and twenty cubits'; in other words, the Annalists' Temple appears to be a staggering six times higher than its width and twice as high as its length.

Setting the measurements out in this way may be open to some dispute, so it would be well to look at v. 4 more closely. Much hinges on how we construe the phrase concerning the vestibule, and whether we regard the following phrase concerning a measurement of height as referring to the vestibule alone or to the house as a whole, and indeed whether we are willing to accept that the Annalists intentionally set out such a statistic for the height of their Temple. The Hebrew reads as follows: *wᵉhā'ûlām 'ᵃšer 'al-pᵉnê hā'ōrek 'al-pᵉnê rōḥab-habbayit 'ammôt 'eśrîm wᵉhaggōbah mē'â wᵉ'eśrîm*. The NRSV renders this as 'The vestibule in front of the nave of the house was twenty cubits long, across the width of the house; and its height was one hundred and twenty cubits'. However, just four verses later (in v. 8), when the Hebrew says *wayya'aś 'et-bêt-qōdeš haqqᵒdāšîm 'orkô 'al-pᵉnê rōḥab-habbayit 'ammôt 'eśrîm*, the NRSV says 'He made the most holy place: its length, corresponding to the width of the house, was twenty cubits'. Admittedly the phrase *'ᵃšer 'al-pᵉnê hā'ōrek 'al-pᵉnê rōḥab-habbayit* does not appear quite as elegant as the phrase *'orkô 'al-p^e^nê rōḥab-habbayit*, but in such close proximity they are most naturally seen as variations on a theme, and so something like the wording of the NJPS translation is to be preferred, namely (for v. 4) 'The length of the porch in front [was equal] to the breadth of the house —20 cubits' and (for v. 8) 'its length [was equal] to the breadth of the house—20 cubits'.

Accordingly, I am not persuaded that there is anything so alarming about the expression in v. 4 concerning the horizontal dimensions of the vestibule that we must begin emending the verse to fall more into line with readings in the book of Kings, as NRSV does by speaking of 'the vestibule in front of the nave of the house', which seems rather to be a translation of 1 Kgs 6.3's phrase *w^e^hā'ûlām 'al-p^e^nê hêkal habbayit 'eśrîm 'ammâ 'orkô*. While one can understand the NRSV translation panel's desire to bring the two texts into harmony, it seems to me that the Annalists' words, read within the context of their description of the Temple, carry a different meaning from the phrasing in the Kings context. And so too I am inclined to accept the reading of *mē'â w^e^'eśrîm*, 'one hundred and twenty' cubits for the height of the structure, rather than feeling that it must be brought down to a lower figure in view of the height of just *š^e^lōšîm*, 'thirty' cubits for the Temple depicted in 1 Kgs 6.2. If our quest were for a real First Temple in Jerusalem, then we would doubtlessly prefer the figure given in the book of Kings. As Hugh Williamson rightly remarks, a height of 120 cubits is 'far too high for the first temple' (Williamson 1982: 206), but I would express matters a little differently from him in respect of his comment that 'a hundred and twenty cubits contradicts the expected thirty cubits, which was the height of the rest of the temple'. That 'the height of the rest of the temple' was thirty cubits can unquestionably be said in relation to the figures set out in the book of Kings, which indeed gives a figure of thirty cubits for the height of the Temple, but the book of Chronicles gives no figure for the height of the Temple other than this measurement of 120 cubits. There is mention in 2 Chron. 3.15 that 'in front of the house he made two pillars thirty-five cubits high, with a capital of five cubits on top of each', and when we compare this with 1 Kgs 7.15-16's contention that the pillars were each eighteen cubits high with a capital of five cubits on top of each, we might observe that the Annalists' pillars plus capitals are not only seventeen cubits higher than their counterparts in Kings but are thus also ten cubits higher than the height of the Temple itself in Kings. Again, if our quest were for the real First Temple in Jerusalem, we would presumably prefer the pillar dimensions provided by the book of Kings, but the consistently higher figures presented by the Annalists are telling us something about how they imagined the Temple to be, and it would seem that the lower dimensions conceived by the traditions represented in the book of Kings were simply not high enough for the Annalists' grander vision of the Temple.

It is not clear, however, whether they imagine the entire Temple reaching to the grand heights of 120 cubits, or just the *'ûlām*, the 'vestibule' or entrance-hall being of that height. The punctuation in the NRSV directs readers strongly towards the latter understanding, since it reads as follows:

> These are Solomon's measurements for building the house of God: the length, in cubits of the old standard, was sixty cubits, and the width twenty cubits. The vestibule in front of the nave of the house was twenty cubits long, across the width of the house; and its height was one hundred and twenty cubits. (2 Chron. 3.3-4 NRSV)

This suggests that it is the vestibule that reaches towards heaven, while the main body of the Temple is of an undisclosed height, though presumably constituting a less soaring edifice than the entrance-hall. If we have an eye to the text of Kings, then we might well imagine that the body of the Temple is indeed thirty cubits high. On the other hand, we might, in the more immediate context of the Annalists' Temple-measuring activities, imagine a rather more consistently proportioned Temple of twenty cubits in height above the nave and the holy of holies, given the setting out of other dimensions in which twenty cubits in one direction corresponds to twenty cubits in another direction, such as in the case of the holy of holies, concerning which we are told that 'its length, corresponding to the width of the house, was twenty cubits, and its width was twenty cubits' (2 Chron. 3.8). In some respects I am attracted to the thought that the Annalists' Temple might be constructed in cubes of twenty cubits, since we are told of three segments to their Temple, a holy of holies plus a nave plus a vestibule, and we are told that the *bêt hā'ᵉlōhîm* or 'house of God' was sixty cubits long and twenty cubits wide; accordingly, we might think of three twenty-by-twenty segments making up the ground plan, but the designation of the nave as *habbayit haggādôl* or 'the great house' rather suggests that the sixty-cubit length ought to be applied to that part of the building by itself, with a twenty-by-twenty *bêt-qōdeš haqqᵒdāšîm* or 'holy of holies' and an arguably twenty-by-twenty *'ûlām* or 'vestibule' being added to the back and front respectively of the *bayit gādôl*. The height of either the *bayit gādôl* or the *bêt-qōdeš haqqᵒdāšîm* are then not explicitly expressed, but at least the *'ûlām* stands at 120 cubits.

Now it may be that the Annalists want us to think of the entire complex as reaching those grand heights. After all, their text reads *wᵉ'ēlleh hûsad šᵉlōmōh libnôt 'et-bêt hā'ᵉlōhîm*, 'these were the dimensions Solomon established for building the house of God': *hā'ōrek*, 'the length' such-and-such; *wᵉrōḥab*, 'and a width' of such-and-such, with a vestibule of such-and-such; *wᵉhaggōbah*, 'and the height' such-and-such. It is certainly possible to construe the Annalists' sentence structure as indicating the dimensions of the complete structure in their minds, and not pointing only to the height of the vestibule. However, this may be stretching our imaginations a little too far, even if we concede that we are dealing with an imaginary Temple rather than one that really stood in this form on a Jerusalem hill around the turn of the first millennium BCE. It may strike us as more plausible that the creators of this text thought of a twenty-cubit-square tower standing 120-cubits high at the front of a building stretching back a further sixty cubits and rising to a height of twenty or thirty cubits, rather than that they conjured up the even more imposing image of a building which rose to the height of 120 cubits along its full length of sixty cubits.

But whichever of these pictures most appeals to us, it is clear that a Temple so conceived, a structure which reaches far higher than the extent of its length or breadth, expresses something that is dear to the hearts of many who conceptualize a space for divine–human encounter. The architects and stonemasons of mediaeval Europe would find nothing strange about the Annalists' conceptualization (cf. Rosenau 1979: 99), and nor would the devout citizens of ancient Mesopotamia. Indeed, the book of Genesis records a vignette of the primaeval inhabitants of the land of Shinar saying to themselves, 'Come, let us build ourselves a city, and a tower with its top in the heavens, and let us make a name for ourselves; otherwise we shall be scattered abroad over the face of the whole earth', whereupon God comes down from heaven and scatters them abroad over the face of the whole earth (Gen. 11.4, 8).

The Annalists have the hubris to conjure up in the city of Jerusalem a tower with its top in the heavens, and they have Solomon stand in front of that tower and pray over and over that God may hear in heaven the prayers directed toward that place (2 Chron. 6.21, 23, 25, 27, 30, 33, 35, 39). His ultimate petition concerns the inevitable scattering of the people over the face of the earth:

> If they sin against you—for there is no one who does not sin—and you are angry with them and give them to an enemy, so that they are carried away captive to a land far or near; then if they come to their senses in the land to which they have been taken captive, and repent, and plead with you in the land of their captivity, saying, 'We have sinned, and have done wrong; we have acted wickedly'; if they repent with all their heart and soul in the land of their captivity, to which they were taken captive, and pray toward their land, which you gave to their ancestors, the city that you have chosen, and the house that I have built for your name, then hear from heaven your dwelling place their prayer and their pleas, maintain their cause and forgive your people who have sinned against you. (2 Chron. 6.36-39)

And sure enough, in the unfolding of the Annals, the people are in time spread abroad; indeed, ironically the bulk of them are carried away to the same place where Genesis had sited the primaeval tower (compare 'therefore it was called *bābel*' [NRSV 'Babel'] in Gen. 11.9 with 'he took them into exile in *bābel*' [NRSV 'Babylon'] in 2 Chron. 36.20). But at the end, there is the new beginning, a way back from Babel/Babylon to Jerusalem, when King Cyrus of Persia proclaims that 'Yahweh, the God of heaven, has given me all the kingdoms of the earth, and he has charged me to build him a house at Jerusalem, which is in Judah. Whoever is among you of all his people, may Yahweh his God be with him! Let him go up' (2 Chron. 36.23). The Annalists dare to think that Yahweh's people on earth might reach again for the heavens. Perhaps they think or hope that it will be different next time, or perhaps they fear in their hearts that it will all turn out the same—'for there is no one who does not sin', as their Solomon said—but at least there is an opportunity for better times to come again, and for a rebuilt tower in Jerusalem to point once again to God.

2. *Standing on a Special Mountain*

The second feature that I wish to highlight is that the Annalists imagine their heavenward-reaching Temple as standing on the top of a very special mountain. In itself this should not really surprise us, in that the ancient notion that the interface between heaven and earth was on mountain-tops is a familiar one, and the modern designation of 'the Temple Mount' in Jerusalem is frequently encountered in literature and in news bulletins. And yet these Annals do something with the traditions of ancient Israel that no other biblical writers do. We might almost overlook it, in 2 Chron. 3.1, where the claim is made that 'the house of Yahweh in Jerusalem' was built 'on Mount Moriah'.

Now the only other place in the Hebrew Bible where the place-name 'Moriah' occurs is in a particular part of the story of Abraham. Genesis 22.2 has God saying to Abraham, 'Take your son, your only son Isaac, whom you love, and go to the land of Moriah, and offer him there as a burnt offering on one of the mountains that I shall show you'. The unfolding of the story is well known: Abraham takes his son, his only son Isaac, whom he loves, to a mountain that God shows him, builds an altar there, binds Isaac and prepares to offer him as a burnt offering, only to hear an angelic voice cry out, 'Do not lay your hand on the boy or do anything to him; for now I know that you fear God, since you have not withheld your son, your only son, from me' (v. 12). Abraham then looks up and sees a ram caught in a thicket by its horns, and so he takes the ram and offers it up as a burnt offering instead of his son.

There can be no doubt that the Annalists are thinking of this story of Abraham's near-sacrifice of Isaac in crafting their own story of the beginnings of the Temple in Jerusalem. It is not merely their unique claim that the Temple was built on 'Mount Moriah'. It is also evident that, just as the Genesis narrative depicts a narrowly averted destruction of the people of Israel before they had even begun, so too the Annals depict a narrowly averted destruction of the people of Israel before the site of the Temple is determined in response to the crisis. We read in the Annals that

> Yahweh sent a pestilence on Israel, and seventy thousand persons fell in Israel. And God sent an angel to Jerusalem to destroy it; but when he was about to destroy it, Yahweh took note and relented concerning the calamity, and he said to the destroying angel, 'Enough! Stay your hand.'... David looked up and saw the angel of Yahweh standing between earth and heaven, and in his hand a drawn sword stretched out over Jerusalem. (1 Chron. 21.14-16)

The angel commands David to go up and build an altar at the site; the king does so, and offers burnt offerings on the altar, and then says, 'Here shall be the house of the God Yahweh and here the altar of burnt offering for Israel' (22.1).

Let us note a certain similarity in Abraham's and David's angelic encounters. In the Genesis narrative, we find 'the angel of Yahweh' calling to him from heaven (Gen. 22.11), and we hear the angel speaking as though he is Yahweh himself, commenting—without any introductory formula such as 'Thus says Yahweh'—that 'now I know that you fear God, since you have not withheld your son, your only son, *from me*' (v. 12). Then we read (in v. 14): *wayyiqrā' 'abrāhām šēm-hammāqôm hahû' yahweh yir'eh 'ᵃšer yē'āmēr hayyôm bᵉhar yahweh yērā'eh*. The NRSV is in two minds on the translation of this verse. The main text has it that 'Abraham called that place "The Lord will provide"; as it is said to this day, "On the mount of the Lord it shall be provided"'. An alternative rendering is given in a footnote: 'Abraham called that place "The Lord will see"; as it is said to this day, "On the mount of the Lord he shall be seen"'. The first alternative might seem preferable in view of Abraham's words earlier in the story, in answer to his son's question 'Where is the lamb for a burnt offering?', that *'ᵉlōhîm yir'eh-lô haśśeh lᵉ'ōlâ bᵉnî*, which NRSV renders as 'God himself will provide the lamb for a burnt offering, my son' (Gen. 22.8), though I am attracted to the NJPS rendering, 'God will see to the sheep for his burnt offering, my son'. But it seems to me that the NRSV's second choices, 'the Lord will see' and 'he shall be seen', work particularly well when the story as a whole is viewed in connection with the analogous tale in Genesis 16. In that earlier narrative, Abraham's pregnant slave-girl Hagar encounters 'the angel of Yahweh' at a spring in the wilderness (v. 7), after which she 'called the name of Yahweh who spoke to her, "You are *'ēl rᵒ'î*"', a name which appears to mean 'the God of my seeing', and thus either 'the God who sees me' or 'the God whom I see' or both, and the storyteller has her express (although admittedly in words the later scribes seem to have had some difficulty in transmitting) her wonder that she has seen the One Who Sees. The Hebrew there (in Gen. 16.13) reads *hᵃgam hᵃlōm rā'îtî 'aḥᵃrê rō'î*, which the NRSV translates as 'Have I really seen God and remained alive after seeing him?', but with a footnote remarking that the meaning of the Hebrew is uncertain. The NJPS prefers 'Have I not gone on seeing after he saw me?', though it too notes that the meaning of the Hebrew is uncertain. In any event, these two stories are clearly about 'seeing', and so Abraham's excursion into the land of *môriyyâ*—a name which itself might be taken to mean 'the seeing of Yah'—takes him to the mountain where Yahweh is to be seen: *bᵉhar yahweh yērā'eh.*

And what do we find in the Annals? *Wayyāḥel šᵉlōmōh libnôt 'et-bêt-yahweh bîrûšālaim bᵉhar hammôriyyâ 'ᵃšer nir'â lᵉdāwîd 'ābîhû*, 'Solomon began to build the house of Yahweh in Jerusalem, on Mount Moriah, where Yahweh had appeared to his father David' (2 Chron. 3.1). Note the word *nir'â*, 'he appeared' or 'he was seen', corresponding to the word *yērā'eh*, 'he will be seen' or 'he will appear' in the name Abraham had bestowed upon his mountain. And notice too the same slippage between 'the angel of Yahweh' and Yahweh himself is to be met in the Annalists' depiction of David's encounter with the divine as was noticeable in the Genesis narrative concerning Abraham (and also in the analogous narrative concerning Hagar). At first the Annals tell us that 'David looked up and saw the angel of Yahweh standing between earth and heaven' (1 Chron. 21.16), but then we are told that it was actually Yahweh who had appeared to the father of Solomon, just as Genesis had had Abraham speak of seeing Yahweh on the mountain of Moriah.

In Genesis, as Abraham presumably stood contemplatively for a time on the mountain,

> the angel of Yahweh called to him a second time from heaven, and said, 'By myself I have sworn that, because you have done this, and have not withheld your son, your only son, I will indeed bless you, and I will make your offspring as numerous as the stars of heaven and as the sand that is on the seashore; and your offspring shall possess the gate of their enemies, and by your offspring shall all the nations of the earth gain blessing for themselves, because you have obeyed my voice'. (Gen. 22.15-18)

Is it entirely coincidental that the Annalists speak of Solomon—who in their accounting stands uniquely before God on the same mountain—in terms that seem to echo certain aspects of that divine promise? They say of him that 'King Solomon excelled all the kings of the earth in riches and in wisdom, and all the kings of the earth sought the presence of Solomon to hear his wisdom, which God had put into his mind' (2 Chron. 9.22-23), and they have the queen of Sheba say to him, 'Happy are your people! Happy are these your servants, who continually attend you and hear your wisdom! Blessed be Yahweh your God, who has delighted in you and set you on his throne as king for Yahweh your God. Because your God loved Israel and would establish them forever, he has made you king over them, that you may execute justice and righteousness' (9.7-8).

Something of that assessment of Solomon's wisdom and wealth is also to be found in the book of Kings, but the idea that the king of Israel stood before God on the same mountain as that on which the patriarch of the Hebrews had stood with his son Isaac bound upon an altar is not something that remotely occurred to the compilers of that book. Indeed the writers of Kings do not explicitly state that the Temple is on any hill at all; it might simply be on the same level as the rest of the city of David, as far as their account is concerned. One might even suspect that they deliberately avoid imagining the Temple as being on a high place, since high places are associated with the worship of other gods. In 1 Kgs 11.7-8 they tell us that 'Solomon built a high place for Chemosh the abomination of Moab, and for Milcom [MT Molech] the abomination of the Ammonites, on the mountain east of Jerusalem, and he did the same for all his foreign wives, who offered incense and sacrificed to their gods', and in 1 Kgs 20.23, 28 they tell us scathingly of the Aramaeans' apparent belief that the Israelite God is 'a god of the hills'. Accordingly, the curious failure of the compilers of Kings to situate the Temple on a hill may tell us something of their discomfort about such matters. But for the Annalists matters are very different. Their Solomon builds no other temple or high place than the one dedicated to the name of Yahweh, and he builds it on the same high place that the compilers of Genesis had depicted as the site of Abraham's act of uncompromising faithfulness to the same God.

The Annalists speak of 'the mountain of the house of Yahweh' (2 Chron. 33.15), and they designate that mountain as the Mount Moriah of old (3.1); for them, nothing less than a special mountain could be the appropriate location for this place of interface between heaven and earth. Mount Sinai is not feasibly available to them, though this mountain can replace that one insofar as,

> when Solomon had ended his prayer [of dedication], fire came down from heaven and consumed the burnt offering and the sacrifices, and the glory of Yahweh filled the temple; and the priests could not enter the house of Yahweh, because the glory of Yahweh filled the house of Yahweh; and when all the people of Israel saw the fire come down and the glory of Yahweh on the temple, they bowed down on the pavement with their faces to the ground, and worshipped and gave thanks to Yahweh. (2 Chron. 7.1-3)

The Annalists had already rehearsed this spectacle before the prayer, when the ark of the covenant is brought into the Temple and placed in the holy of holies, for then too 'the house of Yahweh was filled with a cloud, so that the priests could not stand to minister because of the cloud, for the glory of Yahweh filled the house of God' (5.13-14). All of this is evidently calling to mind the depictions of Mount Sinai and the tabernacle in the book of Exodus, where we are told that 'when Moses went up on the mountain, the cloud covered the mountain; and the glory of Yahweh settled on Mount Sinai... Now the appearance of the glory of Yahweh was like a devouring fire on the top of the mountain in the sight of the people of Israel' (Exod. 24.15-17). And again, when 'Moses finished the work [of setting up the tabernacle], the cloud covered the tent of meeting, and the glory of Yahweh filled the tabernacle, and Moses was unable to enter the tent of meeting because the cloud settled upon it, and the glory of Yahweh filled the tabernacle... and the cloud of Yahweh was on the tabernacle by day, and fire was in the cloud by night, before the eyes of all the house of Israel at each stage of their journey' (Exod. 40.34-38).

The Annalists could hardly make it clearer that they regard the mountain and Temple of Jerusalem as standing metaphorically on the ground that the mountain of Sinai and the tabernacle of the wilderness wanderings had once occupied. The compilers of Kings were moderately attracted to this notion too, in that they included in their work the notion of a cloud filling the Temple on the occasion of the ark's deposition into its resting place in the sight of the priests (1 Kgs 8.10-11), but only the Annalists bring into the picture the even grander spectacle of cloud and fire coming down from heaven in the sight of all the children of Israel after the dedicatory prayer of the king. This is in a sense Sinai transplanted, just as it is Moriah reconstituted, in the minds of the Annalists. No site for a Temple could be more authentic and appropriate than this.

3. *Replacing a Rival Site*

Now in the traditions of ancient Israel there was another place that had commanded respect as an authentic and appropriate site for 'the house of God', and that was the place that bore the very name 'Beth-El'. It too had drawn Abrahamic associations, as reflected in Gen. 12.8, where we are told that Abraham 'built an altar to Yahweh and invoked the name of Yahweh' at Bethel. But its great foundation legend claimed nothing less than the imprimatur of the eponymous ancestor of Israel, the patriarch Israel or Jacob himself, who, so the story goes, 'came to a certain place and stayed there for the night... And he dreamed that there was a stairway set up on the earth, the top of it reaching to heaven; and the angels of God were ascending and descending on it' (Gen. 28.11-12). Yahweh speaks to Jacob in the dream, promising him the land on which he lies and offspring to populate it, so when Jacob awakes from his sleep, he exclaims, 'Surely Yahweh is in this place—and I did not know it!... How awesome is this place! This is none other than the house of God, and this is the gate of heaven' (vv. 16-17).

How could this fit into the worldview of the Annalists, who surely imagine that the gate of heaven is on their mountain in Jerusalem, where David had seen the angel of Yahweh standing between earth and heaven and where Solomon and all Israel had seen cloud and fire come down from heaven and embrace the house of God erected there? The simple answer is that it does not, and so the Annalists are studious in scrubbing Bethel from their account. They breathe no word of Bethel's claims to be a holy site, and they mention the place just twice, never with any interesting narrative but merely within lists of towns and territories, first in a list of Ephraimite possessions and settlements (1 Chron. 7.28) and later in a list of obscure towns that King Abijah of Judah takes from King Jeroboam of Israel (2 Chron. 13.19). There is nothing special about the place in either case, which stands in considerable contrast not only with the Genesis legends but also with the twenty appearances of Bethel in the book of Kings, where it features as a continuing rival to the status of Jerusalem as Israel's holiest site.

One looks in vain for any Annalistic parallel to the colourful tales told in Kings of the old prophet in Bethel who hoodwinks a visiting prophet into accepting some hospitality from which he does not return (1 Kgs 13), or of the company of prophets in Bethel who alert the great Elisha to the impending disappearance of his master Elijah (2 Kgs 2), or of the Assyrian-sponsored priest who is sent to Bethel after the dissolution of the northern kingdom in order to teach the new inhabitants how to worship Yahweh (2 Kgs 17.24-28). One even looks in vain for a denunciation of the temple at Bethel, along the lines of 1 Kings 12's account of the breakaway king, Jeroboam, setting up a golden calf at Bethel and appointing non-levitical priests to serve at the altar there. Certainly the Annalists oppose such practices, as they show in a vigorous speech that they place in the mouth of King Abijah of Judah, shouting out to the northerners prior to battle:

> You think that you can withstand the kingdom of Yahweh in the hand of the sons of David, because you are a great multitude and have with you the golden calves that Jeroboam made as gods for you. Have you not driven out the priests of Yahweh, the descendants of Aaron, and the Levites, and made priests for yourselves like the peoples of other lands? (2 Chron. 13.8-9)

The diatribe goes on for some time, but the name 'Bethel' is never enunciated. Might the mention of the specific name in some way dignify Bethel's rival claim to that of Jerusalem?

In one respect, however, it does seem that the Annalists make a nod towards Bethel's claim to have been constituted in the patriarchal age as the definitive dwelling place of Israel's God, and they thereby imply that the claim of Jerusalem to be the true Bethel displaces that of the northern site. The allusion lies in King David's declamation of the Temple site, in 1 Chron. 22.1: *zeh hû' bêt yahweh hā'*^{e}*lōhîm w*^{e}*zeh-mizbēaḥ l*^{e}*'ōlâ l*^{e}*yiśrā'ēl*. The NRSV translates this as 'Here shall be the house of the Lord God and here the altar of burnt-offering for Israel'. I have no strong quarrel with that translation in the context of a narrative sequence in which the Temple is yet to be built on the site where David has as yet constructed only an altar for burnt-offerings, but I would point out that the phrases might more literally be rendered, '*This is* the house of the Lord God, and *this* the altar of burnt-offering for Israel'. I make a point of this in order to draw attention to a certain similarity of expression with the declamation of Jacob in Gen. 28.17, *'ên zeh kî 'im-bêt '*^{e}*lōhîm w*^{e}*zeh ša'ar haššāmayim*, which NRSV renders as 'This is none other than the house of God, and this is the gate of heaven'. There too of course no temple had yet been built on the site, but only—if we accept the narrative sequence of Genesis as we have it—the altar that Abraham had constructed at the place two generations before. Jacob immediately takes the stone that he had been using as a pillow for the night and sets it up as a pillar, pours oil on the top of it, and vows that 'If God will be with me, and will keep me in this way that I go, and will give me bread to eat and clothing to wear, so that I come again to my father's house in peace, then Yahweh shall be my God, and this stone, which I have set up as a pillar, shall be the house of God' (Gen. 28.20-22). The phrase 'it shall be the house of God' is *yihyeh bêt 'ᵉlōhîm*, and its presence shows that the earlier expression regarding the place as being already *bêt 'ᵉlōhîm* does not at all imply that a temple already stands there. Thus I would probably prefer the expressions in 1 Chron. 22.1 to appear in English as 'This is the house of the Lord God, and this the altar of burnt-offering for Israel', to suggest more clearly to the English reader that the phrasing put into the mouth of David in these Annals appears to have been especially crafted by the Annalists to supplant the Bethelite contention that a founder of Israel's traditions had placed the stamp of authenticity on a shrine other than Jerusalem's Temple site. The true *bêt 'ᵉlōhîm* is at Jerusalem, and not at the so-called 'Bethel', is the Annalists' belief; David, and not Jacob, has it right in their eyes.

Sara Japhet has justifiably commented that, in the Mount Moriah text which was discussed earlier, 'Davidic authority' may be seen as superseding 'the ancient traditions of the Abrahamic cult' (Japhet 1993: 552). I might nuance matters a little differently, and say that the Annalists, in having David's vision of Yahweh take place on Mount Moriah, see him as building upon Abrahamic traditions; and I would like to add that they then, in having David mimic the declarative style of Bethel's foundation legend (a matter not raised by Japhet), see him as displacing the ancient traditions of the Bethel cult.

It is a thoroughgoing displacement, in that the Annalists have David do far more than Jacob's paltry little action of setting up his pillow as a pillar. Immediately after he has proclaimed the site for Yahweh's Temple, David embarks on all the preparations necessary for the building of a suitable edifice and for the conducting of appropriate activities in and around the completed structure. He issues orders 'to gather together the aliens who were residing in the land of Israel' (1 Chron. 22.2); he provides 'great stores of iron…as well as bronze in quantities beyond weighing, and cedar logs without number' (vv. 3-4); he calls 'for his son Solomon' and charges him 'to build a house for Yahweh, the God of Israel' (v. 6); and he commands 'all the leaders of Israel' to help Solomon in the task, 'so that the ark of the covenant of Yahweh and the holy vessels of God may be brought into a house built for the name of Yahweh' (vv. 17, 19). None of this is to be found in the books of Samuel or Kings; it is entirely the contention of the Annalists that David designated the Temple site and made all these preparations. The aging David we see in the Kings account is full of bitter and calculating advice to his son Solomon on whom to have executed from among the palace officials, the royal family and the local aristocracy (1 Kgs 2.1-9), but the Annalists' David is tireless in nobler concerns, organizing the Levites for various kinds of service in the Temple complex (1 Chron. 23–26), as well as seeing to the proper organization of a now-peaceful kingdom (ch. 27), and in particular handing over to Solomon a full set of plans for the construction of the Temple (ch. 28) before finally blessing the name of Yahweh in the presence of the assembly of all Israel (ch. 29).

This is an infinitely superior character to that rogue in Genesis who had set up a pillar at Bethel, and it is an infinitely superior character to that rogue in the book of Samuel who commits wanton adultery and proves himself singularly unable to manage a smooth transfer of power to the next generation. The Annalists' David has a voice of singular authority—'This is the house of the Lord God, and this the altar of burnt offering for Israel!'—and the tower of David that inexorably rises up on the site that he designates and in accordance with the plans that he bequeaths to his successor Solomon is an edifice fully worthy of his inexhaustible efforts.

4. *Emerging without Israelite Hands*

There are, however, some intriguing and disturbing unsung efforts that lie underneath this edifice, for the Annalists imagine a Temple for the God of Israel that is built without Israelite hands.

What had the mighty David done immediately after designating the Temple site? He 'gave orders to gather together the aliens who were residing in the land of Israel, and he set [them as] stonecutters to prepare dressed stones for building the house of God' (1 Chron. 22.2). And his successor follows the same policy, for we read some time later that

> Solomon took a census of all the aliens who were residing in the land of Israel, after the census that his father David had taken, and there were found to be one hundred and fifty-three thousand six hundred; from these he assigned seventy thousand as labourers, eighty thousand as stonecutters in the hill country, and three thousand six hundred as overseers to make the people work. (2 Chron. 2.17-18)

The Annalists seem to have no embarrassment in portraying an invidious policy of slave labour under which some of the enslaved are placed in charge of enforcing the enslavement, and they make it explicit in numerical terms that every single one of the non-enfranchised residents of the kingdom are rounded up for the building work.

This represents a considerable variation on the picture in Kings, where we are told that

> King Solomon conscripted forced labour out of all Israel, and the levy numbered thirty thousand men. He sent them to the Lebanon, ten thousand a month in shifts; they would be a month in Lebanon and two months at home... Solomon also had [a further] seventy thousand labourers and eighty thousand stonecutters in the hill country, besides his three thousand three hundred supervisors who were over the work, having charge of the people who did the work... Solomon's builders together with Hiram's builders and the Giblites did the stonecutting and prepared the timber and the stone to build the house. (1 Kgs 5.27-32, ET 13-18)

In the Kings account it is forced labour, to be sure, but it is Israelite labour working together with a workforce from the friendly neighbouring kingdom of Tyre and a contingent of Giblites as well. The assertion in the Annals that the Temple builders are the entire resident alien population of Solomon's kingdom, and nothing but the resident aliens, is a startling picture.

Actually, there are two small caveats to the position just described, in that the Annals do speak of Tyrian workers involved in cutting timber in Lebanon for dispatching to the Jerusalem Temple project though not in bringing the cut timber across Israelite soil to Jerusalem (2 Chron. 2.8, and note v. 16), but one special worker is brought onto the Temple site itself. The latter is the skilled Tyrian craftsman, Huram-abi, whom King Huram of Tyre dispatches to Jerusalem to oversee the engraving and carving work (2 Chron. 2.13-14; cf. 4.11-18). In the Kings account, Solomon sends for a man called Hiram to come from Tyre to take the same leading role in the project (1 Kgs 7.13-45), and many other Tyrians also appear to be on site. But for the Annalists, their Huram-abi is the only exception to the rule that everyone working at the Temple must be a conscripted resident alien; it seems that they are unable to conceive of the resident aliens as being capable of managing entirely from their own inexperienced ranks with the delicate and highly skilled work that Huram-abi is called upon to take charge of, but the project in general can be left in their hands.

Some readers may have a further objection to the idea that the Annals speak only of non-Israelite labour on the Temple project, in that 2 Chron. 2.1-2 had earlier announced that 'Solomon decided to build a temple for the name of Yahweh, and a royal palace for himself. Solomon conscripted seventy thousand labourers and eighty thousand stonecutters in the hill country, with three thousand six hundred to oversee them'. Are these not to be understood as Israelite subjects? Should we edit out the later insertion of resident aliens since this first citation alone is in keeping with the presentation of matters in Kings and so a repetition of the statistics with an alien twist makes for a clumsy text? I think not. On the basis of an approach by Raymond Dillard (Dillard 1987: 5-7, 17-18), it can be argued that this initial mention of the workforce without specification of their citizenship is deliberately taken up by the later application of these statistics specifically to the resident aliens, the two listings of the matter being placed before and after the setting out of the royal correspondence concerning the Temple project. This matches the double arrangement also of the listing of Solomon's wealth, before and after the account of the Temple's construction (2 Chron. 1.1-17 and 9.13-28). Just as the 'twelve thousand horses' counted in at 1.14 are the same set of creatures as the 'twelve thousand horses' counted out again in 9.25, so too the 'seventy thousand labourers' counted in at 2.2 are the same set of workers as the 'seventy thousand' resident-alien 'labourers' counted out at 2.18. At first the unenviable status of the workforce was not specified, but it is underlined at the end.

Now readers with an awareness of the exodus traditions of ancient Israel cannot help but draw to mind a situation once depicted of the Israelites themselves. The book of Exodus begins by picturing the children of Israel, as resident aliens in the land of Egypt, being given the task of building for the 'new king' of that land, who 'set taskmasters over them to oppress them with forced labour; and they built supply cities, Pithom and Raamses, for Pharaoh' (Exod. 1.8, 11). We might imagine that part of the building project was the construction of a temple or two for the Egyptian gods. Well, the boot is most certainly on the other foot in the Annals. The 'new king' in Israel counts the number of resident aliens he has to hand in his kingdom, and he sets them to work on a grand building project in the land of Israel, the construction of the Temple for the Israelite God. Perhaps the Annalists, who do refer to 'Yahweh, the God of Israel', bringing his people 'out of the land of Egypt' (2 Chron. 6.5), imagine that justice is thereby served.

The compilers of these Annals certainly appear to have no misgivings about depicting a tendency on the part of the Israelite kingdom to enslave foreigners, and to state that the Temple-building project depends on the wealth that is forcefully taken from such peoples. Witness the accounts of David's wars of conquests against the surrounding nations in 1 Chronicles 18: 'He defeated Moab, and the Moabites became subject to David and brought him tribute' (v. 2); 'then David put garrisons in Aram of Damascus, and the Aramaeans became subject to David, and brought tribute' (v. 6); 'then he put garrisons in Edom, and all the Edomites became subject to David; and Yahweh gave victory to David wherever he went' (v. 13). Later, when the Ammonite capital city of Rabbah is added to the list of conquests, we are told that David 'brought out the booty of the city, a very great amount, and he brought out the people who were in it, and set them to work with saws and iron picks and axes; thus David did to all the cities of the Ammonites' (20.2-3).

The Annalists give no explicit reason why David should attack all these nations. Perhaps we are meant to think that each of these neighbouring peoples are warlike nations that deserve to be subjugated and have their wealth flowing into Jerusalem, but in any event it is seen as good for the Temple of Yahweh, since materials that are thus brought in will be vital for its construction and outfitting. A note about that is already given not long after the delivery of the divine oracle that 'one of your sons...shall build a house for me' (17.11-12): it is noted (in 18.8) that 'David took a vast amount of bronze' from the cities that he had conquered, and 'with it Solomon made the bronze sea and the pillars and the vessels of bronze'. Thus we are told that Solomon will build the Temple from the material that David accumulates in his wars of conquest, and accordingly in the midst of a narrative of warfare and death and destruction there is a note that the Warrior God who fights for David will himself directly benefit from all those conquests, in the building of his Temple back in Jerusalem.

One more word on the resident aliens who are put to the hard labour of actually building the Temple in these Annals: the compilers of the document are rather keen on statistics, and they tell us that 'Solomon took a census of all the aliens who were residing in the land of Israel, after the census that his father David had taken, and there were found to be one hundred and fifty-three thousand six hundred', all of whom the king promptly set to work (2 Chron. 2.17). This can be compared with the figures given for the earlier census that David had taken of the Israelites themselves, for on that accounting 'in all Israel there were one million, one hundred thousand men who drew the sword, and in Judah four hundred and seventy thousand who drew the sword' (1 Chron. 21.5). In other words, the Annalists' statistics imply that the adult male resident aliens represent ten per cent of the adult male population of the kingdom. It is an intriguing tithe that is given to Yahweh in the pages of the Annals, a slave-labour force of seventy thousand labourers, eighty thousand stonecutters, and three thousand six hundred overseers to bend their backs in the raising up of a monument to the God of the land in which they lived as aliens. Intriguing, too, that David's census had led to the designation of the Temple site, at the place where the angel of Yahweh stopped in his journey of vengeance against David for counting the Israelites, while Solomon's census led to the construction of the Temple with no word of censure from Yahweh. It would appear that it is perfectly acceptable to conduct a census of aliens in order to arrange them into an effective workforce for building the Temple, but it is problematic to have conducted a census of Israelite soldiers, perhaps because that would show a lack of faith in Yahweh fighting Israel's battles. Still, the outcome for Israel is a happy one in the Annalists' story-world, for David's bringing of guilt upon the nation led to the revelation of the place where heaven and earth intersected, and Solomon's marshalling of an alien army of slaves led to the erection of a grand edifice that required no drop of Israelite sweat or blood in its construction.

5. *Arising from a Divine Plan*

There is yet another way in which hands other than Israelite hands may be said to be responsible for the Temple that reaches towards the heavens from the mountain of Jerusalem, and that is to be met with in David's words to his son Solomon (in 1 Chron. 28.19) that *hakkōl bikᵉtāb miyyad yahweh ʿālay hiśkîl kōl malʾᵃkôt hattabnît*. The NRSV translates this as 'All this, in writing at the Lord's direction, he made clear to me—the plan of all the works'. More literally, we might render *bikᵉtāb miyyad yahweh* as 'in writing from the hand of Yahweh', and we might understand the phrase as putting forward a belief that the deity himself had inscribed the Temple plans, as Exod. 31.18 says of the tablets of the covenant: *kᵉtubîm bᵉʾeṣbaʿ ʾᵉlōhîm*, 'written with the finger of God'. It would be no surprise to find so elevated a view among the Annalists, and their repeated use of the term *tabnît* for the Temple plans (1 Chron. 28.11, 12, 18, 19)—a word also used in Exodus (25.9, 40) with reference to the plans for the tabernacle—seems to strengthen the case. Nevertheless, that interpretative possibility should not be overstressed. 'The hand of Yahweh' might more modestly, though still fundamentally importantly in the Annalists' system, refer to divine inspiration on David as he himself personally drew up the plans that he then so carefully handed over to his successor who would be charged with the responsibility of carrying out those plans to the letter.

Needless to say, no such plans, whether written by Yahweh's hand or by David's, are to be seen in the Kings account. Nor is there in that document anything resembling the detailed accounting in the Annals of the divine determination and royal implementation of the roles to be played by various families of priests and Levites once the Temple has arisen above the city of Jerusalem. Such organizational activity takes up several chapters of the Annals, as the venerable King David makes sure first of all that the priests are organized into twenty-four divisions (1 Chron. 24), so that 'their appointed duties' can be effectively managed (vv. 3, 19). The detail is given that they were all organized by means of 'lots' (v. 5), a selection process that appears again in the assigning of other levitical duties, namely the divisions of assistants to the priests (v. 31), the divisions of singer-musicians (25.8) and the divisions of gatekeepers (26.13). Thus the casting of lots is mentioned several times throughout the relevant chapters as the means of organizing the cultic personnel. In this way an emphasis is made that it is not by the decree of the king but rather by the will of the deity that particular clans are assigned particular responsibilities. If a Temple functionary finds that, as a Jakimite, he is in the twelfth division of the priests (24.12), and another finds that, as a Hothirite, he is in the twenty-first division of the singer-musicians (25.28), and yet another finds that, as a Shuppimite, he is a gatekeeper on the western side of the Temple complex, 'at the gate of Shallecheth on the ascending road' (26.16), then each of them can be assured that their lot in life has been determined by divine will. We might say that the hand of Yahweh has written the destiny of each man born into the priestly and levitical families. In all matters concerning the functioning of the Temple, the Annalists assert that it must be 'just so'.

6. *Conclusion*

In summary, then, the book of Chronicles puts forward a somewhat startling picture of the Temple in Jerusalem. The Temple described in these Annals is a tall and thin structure, six times higher than its width, reaching heavenwards from the very mountain where Abraham had been prepared to offer up his son Isaac to the heavens. Tradition (as represented in Genesis) had Abraham naming the place 'Yahweh will be seen'; the Annals narrate that King David indeed sees Yahweh there, whereupon he declares the place to be Israel's true Bethel and embarks on all the preparations necessary for the building of a suitable edifice and for the conducting of appropriate activities in and around the completed structure. Yet no Israelite hand is involved in the construction of this 'tower of David'; the workforce is entirely (apart from a skilled Tyrian craftsman) non-Israelite slave labour under the watchful eyes of non-Israelite overseers, all working to an architectural plan seemingly written by the hand of Yahweh himself. Thus the book of Chronicles depicts a rather different Temple from the one which competing Israelite traditions have handed down to us.

BIBLIOGRAPHY

Dillard, Raymond B.

1987 *2 Chronicles* (WBC, 15; Waco, TX: Word Books).

Japhet, Sara

1993 *I & II Chronicles: A Commentary* (OTL; London: SCM Press).

Jarick, John

2002 *1 Chronicles* (Readings: A New Biblical Commentary; London: Sheffield Academic Press).

Rosenau, Helen

1979 *Vision of the Temple: The Image of the Temple of Jerusalem in Judaism and Christianity* (London: Oresko Books).

Williamson, H.G.M.

1982 *1 and 2 Chronicles* (NCBC; London: Marshall, Morgan & Scott).

1991 'The Temple in the Books of Chronicles', in William Horbury (ed.), *Templum Amicitiae: Essays on the Second Temple presented to Ernst Bammel* (JSNTSup, 48; Sheffield: JSOT Press: 15-31.

Part III

The Temple in Late Second Temple Judaism and in the New Testament

UNDERSTANDINGS OF THE TEMPLE SERVICE IN THE SEPTUAGINT PENTATEUCH

C.T.R. Hayward

The notion that the Septuagint (LXX) may have preserved valuable information about Jewish worship in the period of the Second Temple is by no means new. In a well-known series of essays entitled *The Septuagint and Jewish Worship*, H.St.J. Thackeray attempted to trace the influence of the contemporary synagogue service upon the work of the translators, in line with his theory that the version as a whole had come into being to meet the liturgical needs of Egyptian Jewry.[1] More recently, detailed commentaries on the LXX Pentateuch published in the series *La Bible d'Alexandrie* have drawn attention to the care and precision lavished on the translation of laws relating to the service of the Tabernacle, thus demonstrating the exceptionally high degree of importance attaching to them.[2] The question therefore arises what the translators of the Pentateuch into Greek may have thought that the service of the Tabernacle, which is nothing less than a prototype of the service of the Temple which was offered in their own day, might have signified as a whole. What was its fundamental purpose?

In answering this question, we naturally look to those verses and paragraphs of Scripture where the Greek differs from such text of the Hebrew Bible as is known to us, observing the meanwhile three significant points. First, the LXX's translation may differ from known Hebrew manuscripts because the translators worked from a Hebrew *Vorlage* now lost. Should such turn out to be the case, it would be valuable for our purposes, inasmuch as the information provided by that necessarily hypothetical *Vorlage* would represent a view of the Temple service older than the time of the translators, and one which they have managed to preserve. Secondly, the translators may sometimes mistake a Hebrew word or phrase, and thus 'mistranslate' it. This, too, may be highly informative, and not dissimilar in overall significance from the third point to be considered, namely, the possibility that the translators sometimes deliberately expounded the Hebrew text to convey a meaning which, for whatever reason, they felt compelled to transmit to their readers. Whatever the *direct* cause of a LXX rendering which differs from

1. See Thackeray 1923, and compare his remarks in 1910–11. For critical discussion of his 'liturgical approach' to the version, see Jellicoe 1968: 64-70.

2. See *La Bible d'Alexandrie* in the following five volumes: Harl 1994; Le Boulluec and Sandevoir 1989; Harlé and Pralon 1988; Dorival 1994; Dogniez and Harl 1992. For a good discussion of the methods and principles adopted by the translators, see Olofsson 1990 and 1996.

known Hebrew texts, however, the effect of that translation on readers of the Greek, and its implications, is what will most concern us here. For the version was to be used by Jews who no longer had direct access to the Hebrew Bible; and the precise wording of it, which they came to regard to all intents and purposes as 'the Bible', should throw some light on their appreciation of a subject as central to the Torah as the Temple and its service. Several key passages of the translation confirm this, not least Exod. 25.8, which confronts us with a view of the Tabernacle as a place of divine disclosure.

1. *The Temple as the Place where God is Seen*

The MT of Exod. 25.8 clearly states the reason why the Israelites should construct the Tabernacle, that prototype of the Temple in Jerusalem. They must, says God, present an offering of costly materials, *w*^{e} *'āśû lî miqdāš w*^{e}*šākantî b*^{e}*tôkām*, 'and make for me a sanctuary, so that I may tabernacle among them'. The LXX differs considerably from the Hebrew. The command is addressed to Moses, and its purpose is very striking: *kai poiēseis moi hagiasma kai ophthēsomai en humin*, 'and you shall make for me a holy place, and I shall be seen/appear among you'. The appearance of *hagiasma* here to translate Hebrew *miqdāš* will concern us later: for the moment, we need to examine the treatment of the verb *škn*. The translators can hardly have been unaware that it means to 'tabernacle' or 'dwell'; indeed, every time the root occurs in Genesis they translated it with some form of *katoikein*; and in Num. 14.30; 35.34 they gave it its usual sense of 'dwell in a tent'.[3] Their rendering of this verse is, therefore, arresting. But it is not unique: they again represented *škn* with a verb of seeing at Deut. 33.16, and in so doing begin to disclose something of their purpose. This last verse is part of Moses' blessing of Joseph, which in the MT speaks of 'the favour of the one who dwells in the bush', *r*^{e}*ṣôn šōk*^{e}*nî s*^{e}*neh*. The LXX understood the Hebrew before them to mean *kai ta dekta tō opthenti en tō batō*, 'and the things acceptable to the one who appeared in the bush'. According to LXX Exod. 3.2, it was an angel of the Lord who appeared to Moses out of the bush, in a place designated holy ground at Mt Horeb.[4] The translators, it would seem, wish us to associate in some way the appearance of God in the sanctuary with the appearance of the angel of the Lord to Moses in the burning bush.

It will be recalled that the episode of the burning bush, in both its Hebrew and Greek versions, lays heavy emphasis on the identity of the God there revealed to Moses with the God of the Fathers (Exod. 3.6, 13, 15, 16). Now it is a characteristic of this patriarchal God that he *appears to*, or is *seen by*, his devotees: to give only one example of several to this effect, the MT of Gen. 12.7 notes that the Lord appeared to Abram, *wayyērā' yhwh 'el-'abrām*, a declaration which the

3. See Gen. 9.27; 14.13; 16.12; 25.18; 26.2; 35.22; 49.13; and 3.24 where the Hebrew verb is in the hiphil form with God as subject. See also LXX Num. 5.3; 23.9. God is subject of *škn* five times in Exodus: here at 25.8; and at 24.16; 29.45, 46; 40.35, verses discussed below in sections 2 and 3.

4. LXX Exod. 3.2 reads: 'And there appeared (*ōphthē*) to him an angel of the Lord in a flame of fire from the bush; and he sees that the bush is burning with fire, but the bush was not consumed'.

LXX rendered as *kai ōphthē tō Abram*.[5] The LXX's version of Exod. 25.8, which openly declares that the sanctuary should be made so that God will appear or be seen, thus seems to serve a twofold purpose. First, God's former appearances to the patriarchs are to be continued: the God revealed to Moses as the Lord will continue to appear and be seen, because he is the God of Abraham, Isaac, and Jacob. Secondly, from now on the Lord will be seen, not in a variety of places, but in the one sanctuary, which will be the normal place for the Lord's appearance to Moses, as witness the MT and LXX of Lev. 9.4, 6, 23; 16.2; Num. 14.10; 16.19; and 20.6.

That the Lord is a God who might appear or be seen is evidently important to the LXX translators of Genesis, inasmuch as they introduced the idea into two verses of Scripture where it does not feature in extant Hebrew texts. The first of these is Gen. 16.13, where Hagar designates the Lord as *'ēl r^o'î*, 'a God who sees me', explaining further in opaque and difficult Hebrew *h^agam h^alōm rā'îtî 'aḥ^arê rō'î*, which may be translated as: 'have I indeed up to now seen, after the one who sees me?' This question the LXX translated as *kai gar enōpion eidon ophthenta moi*, 'for indeed I have seen in person the one who appeared to me' (Wevers 1993: 225-26; Harl 1994: 168). Then at Gen. 31.13, where according to the MT God declared to Jacob: 'I am the God of Bethel, where you anointed a pillar', the LXX has put *egō eimi ho theos ho ophtheis soi en topō theou hou ēleipsas moi ekei stēlēn*, 'I am the God who appeared to you in the place of God where you anointed a pillar to me'.[6] But perhaps the most dramatic statement about God's appearing is put into Abraham's mouth at Gen. 22.14, which the LXX has interpreted in a highly distinctive manner.

According to the MT of Gen. 22.13, Abraham on Mt Moriah saw a ram caught in a thicket and offered it as a whole burnt offering in place of his son Isaac. The next verse has him naming the place where this sacrifice was offered *yhwh yir'eh*, to which is appended the note *'^ašer yē'āmēr hayyôm b^ehar yhwh yērā'eh*. If we follow the Masoretic pointing of this note, it may be rendered: 'as it is said to this day, on the mountain of the Lord it (or: he) shall be seen'.[7] Before we consider the LXX of this verse, we must recall that the place of Abraham's offering of Isaac had been definitively determined, within the tradition of the Hebrew Bible itself, as the Temple Mount in Jerusalem: so much is clearly stated in 2 Chron. 3.1. That is to say, the LXX translators were certainly aware that the place where Abraham sacrificed a ram instead of Isaac his son was none other than the Temple Mount in Jerusalem, when they rendered the verse as *kai ekalesen Abraam to*

5. See also MT and LXX of Gen. 17.1; 18.1; 26.2, 24; 35.1, 9; 48.3, where niphal forms of root *r'h* are represented by aorist passives of *horaō*; on which see further Harl 1994: 53-54 and Hanson 1992: 557-68.

6. See Wevers 1993: 502 and Harl 1994: 235, both of whom compare this LXX rendering with the Targum in general. Targum Onqelos reads: 'I am the God who was revealed to you at Bethel', Targums Neofiti and Pseudo-Jonathan offering a very similar rendering.

7. As is often pointed out, another perfectly valid translation of this Hebrew clause would be: 'as it is said this day, on the mountain the Lord shall see, provide', the final word *yr'h* being read as an imperfect qal, 'he shall see'. As we see below, the LXX has certainly opted for an interpretation of the Hebrew which emphasizes the Lord's *appearing*: see Harl 1994: 195.

onoma tou topou ekeinou Kurios eiden hina eipōsin sēmeron en tō orei kurios ōphthē, 'and Abraham called the name of that place "The Lord has seen", so that they may say today: on the mountain the Lord appeared'.[8] It would seem that God's having appeared on that mountain holds special significance: it is an appearance recalled in the present (*today*: the time of the translators themselves?) as a special, even extraordinary, certainly noterworthy event. Presently, we shall discover other LXX verses which leave one in little doubt that for these translators the Temple in Jerusalem, whose prototype is the Tabernacle built by Moses, is the place where now God may be seen, may appear, as he did in ages past to the patriarchs. First, however, we must look at another aspect of the LXX's treatment of the verb *škn* as it appears in the Pentateuch, bearing in mind the biblical datum that the patriarchs were people who called upon the Lord in prayer.[9]

2. *The Temple as the Place where God's Name is Invoked*

At Exod. 29.45 and 46 the translators adopted another important ploy for dealing with *škn* when God is subject, one which they extend into their translation of Deuteronomy to render that book's well-known description of the sanctuary as 'the place which the Lord your God will choose to make his name to dwell there'. This ploy involves taking *škn* as signifying 'to be invoked, called upon'. So at Exod. 29.45, where according to the MT God states *w*^{e}*šākantî b*^{e}*tôk b*^{e}*nê yiśrā'ēl*, 'and I shall tabernacle among the sons of Israel', the LXX has put *kai epiklēthē-somai en tois huiois Israēl*, 'and I shall be invoked, called upon, among the sons of Israel'. In the following verse likewise, the LXX represents God's declaration in MT that he has taken Israel out of Egypt 'so that I may tabernacle in their midst' as *epiklēthēnai autois*, 'to be invoked by them'.[10] Without exception, the LXX represents those verses of Deuteronomy which speak of the place which the Lord has chosen to make his name to dwell there as referring to the place where the Lord's name is to be invoked or called upon.[11]

There can be little doubt that, in adopting this particular explanation of *škn*, the LXX translators are concerned to present the sanctuary as a place of prayer, where God may be called upon directly by his name. Indeed, the sanctuary is presented as a place of prayer *par excellence* in Solomon's famous speech at the

8. Wevers 1993: 324-25, indicates that the *hina* clause here may represent result rather than purpose, and suggests a translation 'so that they say today: in (this) mountain the Lord appeared'; and he acknowledges influence here of the tradition which identified Moriah and Zion.

9. This is particularly true of Abraham: see Gen. 12.8, where Abram calls on the Lord's name after God appears to him; and Gen. 13.4; 21.33, both of Abraham; Gen. 26.25 of Isaac, after a divine appearing (26.24). See further LXX Exod. 33.23, where God tells Moses that his face 'shall not appear to you', and the subsequent event described in Exod. 34.6, when the Lord passes before Moses and 'calls upon the name of the Lord'.

10. For this, MT has *l*^{e}*šoknî b*^{e}*tôkām*. Le Boulluec and Sandevoir 1989: 303 believe the LXX translated thus to avoid anthropomorphism; but this overlooks the observations of Laberge 1985, who demonstrates the close links between God's dwelling in the Temple and the possibility of Israel's calling on his name, a thesis accepted by Dogniez and Harl 1992: 194.

11. See MT and LXX Deut. 12.5, 11; 14.23; 16.2, 6, 11; 26.2, and n. 10 above.

dedication of the Temple recorded in 1 Kgs 8.28-54; and in an oft-quoted proclamation Isaiah (56.7) designated the Temple as a house of prayer for all nations (Wevers 1990: 487). Given this, it comes as something of a surprise to note that the Priestly regulations of the Pentateuch are virtually innocent of any reference to prayer in the sanctuary. Nowhere do we find an order that Moses, Aaron, the priests, or the people should pray in the sanctuary or the Tent of Meeting. Not only is the vocabulary of prayer absent; there is also very little that might even be considered as an oblique or indirect reference to prayer.[12] The translators of the LXX seemingly felt that such an omission had to be redressed.

That they did indeed feel this need is strongly supported by a near-contemporary account of the Temple service preserved by Jesus Ben Sira, in which prayer is specifically singled out as an integral part of the service. Furthermore, LXX Exod. 29.45 and 46, which represent the first occasions in the Pentateuch on which the translators put the passive of *epikalein* for Hebrew *škn*, stand as the climax to the Lord's instructions to Moses about the daily burnt offering in the Temple service, the lamb of the Tamid offering.[13] What Ben Sira describes in his account of the Temple service is almost certainly the Tamid service;[14] and it includes clear reference not only to prayer, but to the invocation of the divine name and to the Priestly blessing, which Ben Sira seems to have regarded as a form of prayer. Some investigation of what he has to say, and its possible significance for the world of the LXX translators, must therefore be our next undertaking.

3. *The Tamid Offering and the Priestly Blessing*

The verses of Ecclesiasticus 50 which most concern us form part of a highly wrought and deeply allusive poetical account of Simon II as high priest officiating in the Jerusalem Temple. This priest, a distinguished representative of the house of Zadok, died around 196 BCE, and was active in the last decades of the third century BCE. Assuming that the translators of the LXX Pentateuch accomplished their work around 250 BCE, the time gap between them and the days of Simon is not long; and it will not be unreasonable to suppose that the Temple service as described less than two generations later than their day by Ben Sira is one which they themselves would have recognized.[15] Ben Sira's poem describes the high priest's appearing, and his ascent to the altar of burnt offering to receive and arrange thereon the sacrificial portions in company with his fellow priests.

12. Aaron's confession of sin over the goat on Yom Kippur (Lev. 16.21) may qualify as a prayer, but it is uttered only once a year. Other possible examples of confession in the sanctuary may be found at Lev. 5.5; Num. 5.7; but the LXX did not consider these verses as referring to prayer, rendering the Hebrew *ydh* with *exagoreuō* on all three occasions.

13. See Exod. 29.38-46. On the rituals involved in the Tamid, see Haran 1978: 205-18 and Milgrom 1991: 388-89, 398-99, 456-57.

14. The older view that Ecclus 50 describes Yom Kippur has largely been abandoned: see Ó Fearghil 1978, and Skehan and di Lella 1987: 550-52.

15. For the date of Simon II, see Schürer 1979: II, 359-60 and 1986: III.1, 201-202; and for the date of the LXX translation, see Tov 1992: 136-37.

Then the priests blow the sacred trumpets, and Ben Sira tells how the people and Simon completed the service. I give here the Hebrew text of Ecclus 50.17-20 as preserved in Ms B from the Cairo geniza:[16]

50.17	*kl bśr yḥdw nmhrw*	*wyplw ʻl pnyhm ʼrṣh*
	lhštḥwt lpny ʻlywn	*lpny qdwš yśrʼl*
50.18	*wytn hšyr qwlw*	*wʻl hmwn hʻrykw nrw*
50.19	*wyrnw kl ʻm hʼrṣ*	*btplh lpny rḥwm*
	ʻd klwtw lšrt mzbḥ	*wmšpṭyw hgyʻ ʼlyw*
50.20	*ʼz yrd wnśʼ ydyw*	*ʻl kl qhl yśrʼl*
	wbrkt yyy bśptyw	*bšm yyy htpʼr*

50.17 All flesh together hastened quickly
And fell on their faces to the ground
To prostrate themselves before the Most High,
Before the Holy One of Israel.

50.18 And the singers gave their voice...

50.19 And all the people of the land gave a ringing shout of joy
In prayer before the Merciful One;
Until he had finished ministering at the altar
And had completed his statutory duties.
50.20 Then he went down and lifted up his hands
Over the whole congregation of Israel:
And the blessing of the Lord was on his lips,
And in the name of the Lord he was glorified.[17]

Here the prayer of the people is evidently a regular, entirely traditional, and uncontroversial part of the Tamid service, in exactly the same way as the psalmody, hymn, or other musical composition performed by the singers: this song, like the prayer before the Merciful One, is not subject of any Pentateuchal command in respect of the liturgy of the sanctuary, but was nonetheless an accepted part of the Temple Service in the days of the Chronicler (Japhet 1993: 420-21; Schaper 2000: 282-85). Ben Sira constantly alludes to Scripture, to the Hebrew Bible, in portraying Simon and the Tamid offering: in and through these Scriptural allusions he contrives to provide us with even more information about the Tamid offering, information which in important particulars relates to matters we have already considered in respect of the LXX. For what particularly informs Ben Sira's words in Ecclus 50.17-20 is Lev. 9.22-24, which speaks of Aaron and Moses blessing the people at the conclusion of a sacrificial offering. According to the MT of Lev. 9.24, the people 'fell upon their faces', *wayyipp*^{e}*lû ʻal-p*^{e}*nêhem* (so Ecclus 50.17) and 'gave a ringing shout of joy', *wyrnw* (so Ecclus 50.9);[18]

16. Hebrew text cited from Beentjes 1997: 90.

17. For the translation, see Hayward 1996: 42-43 and 56-61 for commentary on the verses concerned.

18. This is the only time the verb *rnn* appears in the Pentateuch. The LXX translated it as *exestē*, indicating that the people were beside themselves in amazement. Harlé and Pralon (1988: 121) acutely observe that this Greek verb is used by the LXX at Exod. 19.18, where they record once again that all the people were mightily amazed, *exestē*. This diverges from the MT of Exod. 19.18, which states that all the mountain quaked exceedingly (although some Hebrew manuscripts do read 'the people', and

Lev. 9.22 *q^e^re* tells us that 'Aaron lifted up his hand towards the people and blessed them', *wayyiśśā' 'ah^a^rōn 'et-yādô 'el-hā'ām way^e^bār^e^kēm* (so Ecclus 50.20); and all this represents the climax of his placing of the sacrifical portions upon the altar with the other priests in attendance (Lev. 9.18-21; so Ecclus 50.12-14). We also learn from Lev. 9.23 that, when Moses and Aaron pronounced the blessing over the people, the glory of the Lord *appeared* to all the people: *wayyērā' k^e^bôd yhwh 'el-kol-hā'ām*, which the LXX translated without embellishment. As has often been noted, there are two blessings recorded in this section of Scripture, one given by Aaron alone (Lev. 9.22), the second by Moses and Aaron (Lev. 9.23). Similarly, Ben Sira's account of the service records a twofold blessing (Ecclus 50.20, 21).[19]

Granted that Lev. 9.22-24 informed Ben Sira's account of that part of the service which concerns us, how might the sage have envisaged the appearing of the glory of the Lord, which is central to the scriptural verses which concern him? The answer to this question is most likely supplied by the LXX, which in Num. 6.24-27 presents us with a most striking version of the Priestly blessing, the text of the blessing which Ben Sira would have understood Aaron and Moses to have pronounced over the people during the events recorded in Lev. 9.22-24. In the second clause of this blessing, the priest makes a request as follows: 'may the Lord make his face lighten upon you and be gracious to you'. The LXX here makes the priest beseech God: *epiphanai kurios to prosōpon autou epi se kai eleēsai se*, 'may the Lord make manifest his face over you and be merciful to you'. The LXX has here introduced the language of divine epiphany into the blessing. It is very distinctive, and demands some explanation, especially since the translators of the Pentateuch were very sparing in their use of the verb *epiphainein*, and never used the noun *epiphaneia* or the adjective *epiphanēs*.

On two occasions only outside its translation of the Priestly blessing does the LXX use the verb *epiphainein*, at Gen. 35.7 and Deut. 33.2. The verb is used to speak of God shining forth, appearing, being manifest, and coming into view. The LXX translators will undoubtedly have been familiar with the notion of epiphany from their contact with the Greek-speaking world they inhabited. Among pagan Greeks, epiphanies of the gods in visions to human beings, in extraordinary interventions in human affairs, in sudden and dramatic appearances to bring good fortune or otherwise to promote the well-being of individuals or cities, were almost commonplace, certainly expected, and often recorded in writing by devotees of gods seeking to promote their cults.[20] Such an epiphany, the LXX translators

LXX may have had such a reading as *Vorlage*: see Wevers 1990: 304). All this is significant, given the LXX's tendency to colour its description of the sanctuary with references to Sinai.

19. Like Ben Sira, the Palestinian Targum also introduces prayer into this account of the service: see, e.g., Targum Neofiti of Lev. 9.22, 24, recording that 'Aaron lifted his hands in prayer over the people and blessed them...and all the people...bowed themselves down upon their faces in prayer'.

20. On epiphany and understandings of it in the pagan world, see Daniel 1966: 285, and 283-86 for its distinctive use in the LXX *outside* the Pentateuch, where, Daniel argues, it assumed something like the sense of the rabbinic term *r^e^'îyyâ*, the statutory appearing of a pilgrim at the Temple during the three Festivals. See also and Lane Fox 1986: 102-67, especially 102-23 discussing epiphanies in the pre-Christian period.

believed, had been vouchsafed to Jacob at Bethel: in their version of Gen. 35.7 they note that Jacob built an altar there and called the place Bethel, because there God had manifested himself (*epephanē*) to Jacob. The MT records that God had been revealed to him (Wevers 1993: 579-80). Genesis 35.7 is referring back to the vision granted to Jacob of a ladder fixed on earth and reaching to the heavens, with the Lord standing at its summit, and with angels ascending and descending (Gen. 28.12-13). According to MT Deut. 33.2, the Lord came from Sinai and came forth (*wᵉzāraḥ*) from Seir; he beamed forth from Mt Paran, and came from the myriads of holiness: from his right hand there was a fiery flame (*'ēšdāt*) for them. The LXX translated the word *wᵉzāraḥ* with *kai epephanen*, 'and was manifest'; and they go on to interpret the difficult Hebrew word translated above as 'fiery law' as meaning 'angels', to yield: 'from his right hand there were angels with him'.[21] Both verses help us to understand what the LXX believed an epiphany in Jewish terms might involve: angels should be present; a sacred place or sanctuary recognized in Jewish tradition (Sinai or Bethel) is the proper locale for such a showing forth of divine splendour; and such an appearing of the divinity should be associated with a blessing, as in Deut. 33.1 and Gen. 28.14, and, significantly, Gen. 35.9.

We do not know how many of the LXX translators had been regular worshippers in the Second Temple, and had prostrated themselves in its courts to receive the Priestly blessing. What seems clear, however, is their understanding of that blessing as a petition to God to make manifest his face; and consequently their view of the Jerusalem Temple as a place on a par with Mt Sinai, where God was made manifest to Israel to grant them his Torah in ages past, and with Bethel, the 'house of God' where the ancestor of the Jewish people saw earth and heaven conjoined in the course of an epiphany. Their language of epiphany in the Priestly blessing is consonant with their general view that the sanctuary is a place where God may be seen, or appear to his people, a view examined earlier in this essay; and it also alerts us to the way in which this divine manifestation may, in their view, be expected to take place. For the blessing is given with the utterance of the ineffable name, the tetragram, a point laboured less than two generations later by Ben Sira (Ecclus 50.20). This name may be pronounced with its proper vowels only in the sanctuary, which the LXX occasionally speaks of as *hagiasma*, the very word they used in Exod. 25.8 to define the place where God is to appear or be seen among Israel. This word is not common in the LXX Pentateuch, being represented only nine times outside Exod. 25.8, and it appears to refer to things in the highest grade of holiness.[22] On three of those occasions (LXX Exod. 28.36; 29.6;

21. In this verse, God's epiphany is unambiguously linked with his 'going forth'. The translation may reflect Greek–Egyptian interest in the term *epiphanēs* as a royal title. It was conferred on Ptolemy V (ruled 204–180 BCE), its hieroglyphic equivalent being 'he who cometh forth': see Nock 1972: 154. A century or more after LXX Pentateuch was produced, the author of 2 Maccabees took evident pleasure in recording divine epiphanies in the Jerusalem Temple: see 2 Macc. 2.21; 3.24-30, 54; 14.15; 15.27-34.

22. The LXX uses it at Exod. 15.17; 25.8 of the sanctuary, Hebrew *miqdāš*. Its other uses are all with reference to items holy in the highest degree; at Exod. 28.36; 29.6; 36.37 it is used of the golden plate inscribed with the divine name; at Exod. 29.34; 30.32, 37 of sacred items whose use is strictly

36.37 = MT 39.30) it is found in closest association with the divine name inscribed on the thin golden plate attached to the high priest's head-dress. LXX Exod. 29.6 described the golden plate itself as *hagiasma*. It certainly bore at least the divine name; and LXX Exod. 28.36; 36.37 could be taken as meaning that it bore also the word 'holiness', Hebrew *qōdeš* represented here by Greek *hagiasma*. The Tamid offering which Ben Sira describes has the high priest as its officiant; and the sage is explicit that Simon is vested in the full high priestly attire, the 'garments of glory and beauty' (Ecclus 50.11) so described in Exod. 28.2, 40. When the LXX speaks of the sanctuary as the place of God's 'appearing' or 'being seen', therefore, it appears to have in mind the manifestation of the divine name in the Temple itself, particularly in the course of the Tamid service when the high priest, crowned with the diadem bearing the tetragram, came out of the holy place to bless the assembled Israelites by uttering the expressed name. On hearing the name, the people would fall upon their faces, prostrating themselves in prayer (*m. Soṭah* 7.6; *Yoma* 6.2).

4. *The Temple as the Place where God is Made Known*

In the course of the preceding paragraphs, I have had occasion to refer *en passant* to Mt Sinai, and a brief recapitulation of those references will help prepare the way for the next part of this investigation. First, it will be recalled that it was at Mt Horeb, which is identified in tradition with Mt Sinai, that Moses while standing on 'holy ground' encountered 'the one who appeared in the bush': so LXX Deut. 33.16. Secondly, the God who appeared at Sinai in the bush was identified as the one who characteristically had been in the habit of 'appearing' to Abraham and to Isaac. Thirdly, LXX Deut. 33.2 talks of the Lord's coming forth from Sinai to effect his epiphany from Seir, in the company of angels. Here we may note that LXX Deut. 33.3-4 goes on to speak of Israel as God's people, who are also his sanctified ones, who have received God's words, the Law which Moses gave as a commandment.

Within the most holy recess of the sanctuary which Moses constructs he is told to place the ark of the testimony, which the LXX regularly represents with the phrase *kibōtos tōn marturiōn*, 'ark of the testimonies' (e.g. Exod. 30.6). Alain Le Boulluec and Pierre Sandevoir have rightly observed that the translators, by using the plural 'testimonies' where the Hebrew has the singular, intend to draw their readers' attention to the commandments, particularly those inscribed on the two tablets of the Law which Moses placed in the ark (cf. Deut. 10.1-5). The LXX also speaks of the sanctuary, which the MT can designate the Tent of Meeting, as the Tent of Witness (Le Boulluec and Sandevoir 1989: 43 in respect of ark and Tent). According to the MT of Exod. 25.22; 29.42, 43; 30.6, 36; Num. 17.19, the Lord, speaking in the first person, promises that he will meet with Moses at

confined to the sanctuary; and at Lev. 25.5 of restricted fruit. Some witnesses of LXX Lev. 16.4 use it of the high priest's linen garments worn only on Yom Kippur. On the LXX's use of *hagios* rather than *hieros* to speak of the holy, see the important remarks of Barr 1961: 282-86, reiterated by Harlé and Pralon 1988: 29-30 (against Festugière and Benveniste).

specially designated places within this tent-sanctuary, at its door, before the ark of the testimony, or in the vicinity of the altar of incense. The Hebrew verb used to express this idea of meeting is always a niphal form of the root *y'd*. In every one of these verses except Exod. 29.43 (of which more below), the LXX has translated by speaking of God's making himself known. As an example, one may cite Exod. 30.6, where Moses is told where to place the altar of incense within the sanctuary. The MT of this verse runs as follows: 'And you shall place it in front of the veil which is before the ark of the testimony, before the *kappōret* which is over the testimony where I shall meet with you (*'^{a}šer 'iwwā'ēd l^{e}kā šāmmâ*)'. For the last clause in this verse, the LXX has *en hois gnōsthēsomai soi ekeithen*, which may be rendered as: 'in which (*sc.* the testimonies) I shall make myself known to you from there'. Either the LXX translators had before them a Hebrew *Vorlage* which differs from our MT, reading a niphal form of the root *yd'*, or they have acted in the manner of the later rabbis and availed themselves of the exegetical device *'al tiqrē'*, adopting a reading of the text which suits their own particular exegetical purpose.[23] Whatever the direct cause of their translation, however, its effect is unquestionable: God declares that he will be made known in the sanctuary, often with special reference to the testimonies. The upshot is clear: for the LXX, the sanctuary is the place where God may be made known; and this knowledge is directly related to the presence there of the testimonies, that is the Torah, which Moses received at Sinai. Indeed, in a certain sense the sanctuary has become invested with the properties of Mt Sinai as a place of revelation, as comparison of the MT and LXX of Exod. 29.42-46 will show. Here, the Lord gives final instructions to Moses about the Tamid offering, whose importance for our study has been indicated earlier.

	MT	*LXX*
29.42	A regular whole offering for your generations at the door of the Tent of Meeting before the Lord where I shall meet you to speak to you there.	A continual offering for your generations at the door of the Tent of *Witness* before the Lord, *in which I shall make myself known* to you *from* there so as to speak to you.
29.43	And I shall meet there the sons of Israel; and it shall be sanctified in my glory.	And there I shall *give orders* to the sons of Israel; and *I* shall be sanctified in my glory.
29.44	And I shall sanctify the Tent of Meeting and the altar: and Aaron and his sons I shall sanctify to act as priests to me.	And I shall sanctify the Tent of *Witness* and the altar: and Aaron and his sons I shall sanctify to act as priests to me.
29.45	And I shall dwell among the sons of Israel; and I shall be God for them.	And I shall *be invoked* among the sons of Israel and shall be their God.

23. Wevers (1990: 401 on Exod 25.21 [22], and 486 on Exod. 29.42) is surely correct to argue that the LXX has intentionally interpreted Hebrew *y'd* as *yd'* in all these verses. See also Le Boulluec and Sandevoir 1989: 259, 303, who indicate that the translators seem to have changed 'meet' into 'be known' deliberately, the notion of revelation 'étant probablement plus adapté que celui de rencontre à la mentalité hellénistique' (p. 303).

29.46	And they shall know that I am the Lord their God who brought them out of the land of Egypt so that I might dwell among them. I am the Lord their God.	And they shall know that I am the Lord their God who brought them out of the land of Egypt to *be invoked by them* *and to be their* God.

Many of the LXX's peculiarities in these verses will by now be familiar; but especially telling is their translation in Exod. 29.43 of Hebrew *w*^{e}*nō ʿadtî šāmmâ*, 'and I shall meet there', as *kai taxomai*, which John Wevers explains as meaning 'I will order, i.e. I will give further directions', stating further: 'What is meant is that where God makes himself known so as to speak is where he will be in charge, will give instructions to the Israelites…' (Wevers 1990: 483). In this sense, it might rightly be said that the sanctuary becomes another Sinai, both a holy place and a place where God's will is made known to his people. It should also be reiterated that this sanctuary, where God is made known, is also the place where he may be invoked; he is known in the giving of his commandments, and as these verses make plain, by the manifestation of his holiness through his glory. Thus the LXX declares that it is the Lord himself, not the sanctuary, who will be sanctified in his glory (Exod. 29.43). That glory, the LXX reports, descended on Sinai (Exod. 24.16, where they put *kai katebē* for Hebrew *wayyiškōn*) and later filled the sanctuary (LXX Exod. 40.35).[24] All this is reported to us in a series of verses prescribing the offering of the Tamid service when, as we have seen, the people of Israel prostrated themselves in prayer and received the blessing in the name of the one whom they invoke, who in his sanctuary appears to them as once he appeared to the patriarchs, and makes himself known just as he made himself known to Moses at Mt Sinai with his commandments. The LXX's sense that the sanctuary has a close affinity with Mt Sinai as a place of revelation and divine presence leads directly to the next section of this investigation, the idea of the sanctuary as a place prepared by God.

5. *The Temple as a Place Prepared by God*

In the great hymn of victory which Moses and Israel sang at the sea after their delivery from Egypt, the singers proclaim to God their confidence in his plans for his people, saying to him:

> You shall bring them in and plant them on the mountain of your inheritance:
> The place for your dwelling (*mākôn l*^{e}*šibt*^{e}*kā*) which you have made, O Lord;
> The sanctuary, O Lord, which your hands have established (*kôn*^{e}*nû yādeykā*).
> (MT Exod. 15.17)

24. See Wevers 1990: 487 on LXX Exod. 29.43, where God's statement 'I shall be sanctified in my glory' is discussed. The pronoun *mou* may be either subjective or objective genitive: if the first, the text speaks of God's self-revelation; if the second, it could refer to the glory or praise ascribed to the Lord. Wevers seems to suggest that both senses are intended: if so, we would agree with him. Note that 'glory' is already associated with the name of God in Jewish literature nearly contemporary with the LXX Pentateuch translators: see *1 En*. 8.4; 14.20; 102.3, which speak of God simply as 'the great glory'. The same text refers to the 'throne of glory' (*1 En*. 45.3; 55.4). See further Muñoz León 1983: 147-49 ('glory' in LXX) and 178-80 ('glory' in Ethiopic Enoch).

The LXX form of this verse is very distinctive, not least in those places corresponding to the Hebrew expressions noted above:

> Bring them in, plant them into the mountain of your inheritance:
> Into your ready dwelling-place (*hetoimon katoikētērion sou*)
> which you have constructed, O Lord;
> The sanctuary (*hagiasma*), O Lord, which your hands have made ready (*hētoimasan*).

As the commentators observe, the LXX's decision to render the noun *mākôn*, which means 'place of dwelling, abode', as 'ready', *hetoimos*, was suggested by the verb *kônenû* at the end of the verse, which may indeed mean 'make ready, prepare' (Bissoli 1983; Wevers 1990: 234-45; Le Boulluec and Sandevoir 1989: 176). The Hebrew form of the verse may, and the Greek undoubtedly does, speak of this sanctuary as already in existence; but the effect of the LXX's rendering is to emphasize the already prepared quality of the construction: *hetoimos* in settings which refer to the past (and the Greek translators have used past tenses throughout the verse) may often signify something 'carried into effect, realized'. There are two possible implications latent in this translation. First, the Lord certainly does have a dwelling made ready for him: it has existed from all eternity, and is located in heaven. Although the other books of the Hebrew Bible were translated into Greek some time after the Pentateuch translation was made, it is nonetheless instructive to note that they too use the phrase *hetoimon katoikētērion* at 3 Kgdms 8.39, 43, 49 and parallels in 2 Chron. 6.30, 33, 39; Ps. 32 (33).14; and every one of these verses refers explicitly to the 'prepared, ready dwelling-place' of the Lord as being in heaven. These later translators will have known the Greek Pentateuch; they have evidently associated God's prepared dwelling with heaven; and this suggests that they may have understood the phrase in Exod. 15.17 to refer, in some manner, to a heavenly dwelling. At the same time, however, a mountain is spoken of; and it is legitimate to suggest that the Greek Pentateuch, in translating Exod. 15.17 as it does, may be suggesting to readers the notion that the earthly dwelling of God on Mt Zion in some manner corresponds to or has affinity with the divine residence in heaven.[25] Such a notion will not have been foreign to the readers of the LXX, and may be an important factor in the unusual rendering of this verse, as we shall now see in considering the second point latent in the translation.

This point may be expressed as follows: the translators seem to have regarded the sanctuary as having existed 'from of old'. How long ago the sanctuary of Exod. 15.17 was 'made ready, prepared' the LXX does not tell us; but it is a *hagiasma*, and it is a *hagiasma* which Moses is commanded to make, according to Exod. 25.8. These two verses are the only instances in the LXX Pentateuch of *hagiasma* being used to represent the common Hebrew word *miqdāš*, 'sanctuary'; and the peculiarity of this unusual translation is confirmed and underscored by LXX Exod. 25.9, where Moses is told to make this *hagiasma* according to a *paradeigma* which God has shown to him. The term *paradeigma*, representing

25. So much is evident from the Psalms, which speak on the one hand of God's Temple in Heaven (e.g. Ps. 11.4) and of his Temple in Jerusalem (e.g. Ps. 68.30 [ET 29]).

the Hebrew *tabnît*, is found nowhere else in the entire LXX Pentateuch. It can refer to an architect's blueprint for a building, to a pattern or exemplar of a thing to be made, or to a pre-existing model of some object. The word could conjure up, in the minds of educated Jewish and Greek readers of the LXX, the philosophy of Plato, who had used the word to speak of the heavenly plans and examples of which created things are copies.[26] This is well illustrated by Le Boulluec and Sandevoir in their commentary on LXX Exodus, where they show how Philo would later develop the cosmological significance of the Greek translation of this verse (Le Boulluec and Sandevoir 1989: 253). In fine, the translators' choice of distinctive vocabulary in these verses seems intended to draw attention to the heavenly origin of the sanctuary; and in so doing it casts light on the precise nature of the 'ready, prepared sanctuary' as something associated on the one hand with heaven, and yet at the same time with a mountain which is an earthly reality. The sanctuary is thus like Jacob's ladder at Bethel, firmly planted on earth while at the same time reaching to the heavens; and both these locations are places where, according to the LXX translators, the Lord is made manifest in divine epiphany.

6. *Conclusions*

This brief essay has been able to draw attention only to some of the more important aspects of understandings of the Temple and its service which the LXX communicates to us. Our findings may be presented in summary as follows:

1. The LXX views the Temple as a place where God may be seen, or appear to Israel. Just as once he appeared to the patriarchs (particularly to Abraham on Moriah/Zion) and to Moses (particularly at the bush) in differing locations, so now he may appear in the sanctuary on Zion.
2. The LXX insists that the Temple is a place where God may be invoked by name. It is most certainly a place of prayer. In this way the LXX translators attempt to make up for what they perceive as a lack in the Priestly regulations of the Hebrew Pentateuch.
3. Ben Sira's near-contemporary account of the Tamid indicates that prayer was regarded as an integral part of the service, and that prayer was closely associated with the Priestly blessing. This last the LXX understood as a petition for a divine epiphany. This notion, well known in the Greek world, is sparingly but pointedly employed by the translators in reference to God's appearing from Sinai to give the Torah, and at Bethel to appear to Jacob in a place where heaven and earth meet. Both Sinai and Bethel thus 'colour' the way the translators perceive the Temple.

26. On this word, see Barr 1961: 152-55, where he correctly points out that one cannot be absolutely certain that the *translators* intended to use *paradeigma* in its Platonic sense. This is true; but the word stands out by being used only once in the entire Pentateuch, and it might certainly have invited the very first *readers* of LXX to see in it a Platonic sense. Indeed, it might have been seen by the translators themselves in that sense, inasmuch as Exod. 25.8 speaks of a *heavenly* pattern which Moses is to reproduce on earth.

4. The sanctuary is also, for the LXX, a place where God is made known to Israel. Such revelation is bound up with (*inter alia*) the presence there of the 'testimonies', the commandments enshrined in the Torah.
5. The Temple may be called *hagiasma*, a word restricted by the translators of the Pentateuch to things of the highest degree of sanctity. This word, too, is bound with the divine name inscribed on the head-dress of the high priest, who comes forth in the Tamid service to bless Israel with that same name, the name which is also invoked in prayer in the Temple.
6. In its character of *hagiasma*, the Temple is both a dwelling prepared by God and a structure made by Moses following a pre-existing heavenly blueprint. Thus the translators imply that it links earth and heaven, and is suitable for epiphany.
7. The translators follow the Hebrew Bible in viewing the sanctuary as a place where God's glory may be revealed: they understand that this glory 'descended' at Sinai and 'overshadowed' the sanctuary. There is some indication in their translation of Exod. 29.43, however, that they have begun to associate glory with the divine name, in the manner of other contemporary writers.

This is a rich and varied pattern involving a wide range of ideas, all of which have a long history behind them: they represent, too, opportunities for differing understandings among Jews who worshipped in the Second Temple. Each and every one of them merits further, detailed study; and one is acutely aware of having only skimmed the surface of this subject in the course of this study.

Bibliography

Barr, J.
1961 *The Semantics of Biblical Language* (Oxford: Oxford University Press).

Beentjes, P.C.
1997 *The Book of Ben Sira in Hebrew: A Text Edition of all Extant Hebrew Manuscripts and a Synopsis of all Parallel Hebrew Ben Sira Texts* (Leiden: E.J. Brill).

Bissoli, G.
1983 'Mâkōn-hetoimos. A proposito di esodo 15,17', *Liber Annuus* 33: 53-56.

Daniel, S.
1966 *Recherches sur le vocabulaire du Culte dans la Septante* (Paris: Librairie C. Klincksieck).

Dogniez, C., and M. Harl
1992 *La Bible d'Alexandrie*, V: *Le Deutéronome* (Paris: Cerf).

Dorival, G.
1994 *La Bible d'Alexandrie*, IV: *Les Nombres* (Paris: Cerf).

Hanson, A.
1992 'The Treatment in the LXX of the Theme of Seeing God', in G.J. Brooke and B. Lindars (eds.), *Septuagint, Scrolls and Cognate Writings* (Atlanta: Scholars Press): 557-68.

Haran, M.
1978 *Temples and Temple Service in Ancient Israel: An Inquiry into the Character of Cult Phenomena and the Historical Setting of the Priestly School* (Oxford: Clarendon Press).
Harl, M.
1994 *La Bible d'Alexandrie*, I: *La Genèse* (Paris: Cerf).
Harlé, P., and D. Pralon
1988 *La Bible d'Alexandrie*, III: *Le Lévitique* (Paris: Cerf).
Hayward, C.T.R.
1996 *The Jewish Temple: A Non-Biblical Sourcebook* (London: Routledge).
Japhet, S.
1993 *I and II Chronicles: A Commentary* (OTL; London: SCM Press).
Jellicoe, S.
1968 *The Septuagint and Modern Study* (Oxford: Clarendon Press).
Laberge, L.
1985 'Le lieu que YHWH a choisi pour mettre son nom (MT, LXX, Vg et Targums). Contribution à la critique textuelle d'une formule deutéronomiste', *Estudios bíblicos* 43: 209-36.
Lane Fox, R.
1986 *Pagans and Christians in the Mediterranean World from the Second Century AD to the Conversion of Constantine* (Harmondsworth: Penguin Books).
Le Boulluec, A., and P. Sandevoir
1989 *La Bible d'Alexandrie*, II: *L'Exode* (Paris: Cerf).
Milgrom, J.
1991 *Leviticus 1–16: A New Translation with Introduction and Commentary* (AB, 3; New York: Doubleday).
Muñoz León, D.
1983 *Palabra y Gloria: Excursus en la Biblia y en la Literatura Intertestamentaria* (Madrid: Consejo Superior de Investigaciones Científicas Instituto 'Francisco Suárez').
Nock, A.D.
1972 'Notes on Ruler-Cult I–IV', in Z. Stewart (ed.), *Arthur Darby Nock: Essays on Religions and the Ancient World* (2 vols.; Oxford: Clarendon Press), I: 134-59.
Ó Fearghil, F.
1978 'Sir 50, 5-21: Yom Kippur or the Daily Whole Offering?', *Bib* 59: 301-16.
Olofsson, S.
1990 *God is My Rock: A Study of Translation Technique and Theological Exegesis in the Septuagint* (ConBOT, 31; Stockholm: Almqvist & Wiksell).
1996 'Studying the Word Order of the Septuagint: Questions and Possibilities', *SJOT* 10: 217-37.
Schaper, J.
2000 *Priester und Leviten im achämenidischen Juda: Studien zur Kult- und Sozialgeschichte Israels in persischer Zeit* (FAT, 31; Tübingen: Mohr Siebeck).
Schürer, E.
1973–87 *The History of the Jewish People in the Age of Jesus Christ* (3 vols. in 4; revised G. Vermes *et al.*; Edinburgh: T. & T. Clark).
Skehan, P.W., and A.A. di Lella
1987 *The Wisdom of Ben Sira* (AB, 39; New York: Doubleday).
Thackeray, H.St.J.
1910–11 'Primitive Lectionary Notes in the Psalm of Habakkuk', *JTS* 12: 191-213.
1923 *The Septuagint and Jewish Worship: A Study in Origins* (London: Oxford University Press, 2nd edn).

Tov, E.
1992 *Textual Criticism of the Hebrew Bible* (Minneapolis: Fortress Press).

Wevers, J.
1990 *Notes on the Greek Text of Exodus* (SCSS, 30; Atlanta: Scholars Press).
1993 *Notes on the Greek Text of Genesis* (SCSS, 35; Atlanta: Scholars Press).

Temple and Cult in Apocryphal and Pseudepigraphal Writings from Before the Common Era

Michael A. Knibb

It is hardly a matter of surprise that the Temple, as a major institution in Jewish life, should be mentioned frequently within the writings of the Apocrypha and Pseudepigrapha, whether as a part of the nation's past, or as a contemporary reality, or as an object of future expectation. It is also perhaps hardly surprising that when the Temple is mentioned, it should very often appear as an object of rivalry and contention. The major events of the period that affected the Temple—its desecration in the time of Antiochus IV, the siege of the Temple by Pompey's forces and Pompey's entry into the Temple, and the destruction of the Temple in 70 CE—all provoked a considerable response in the literature of the period, but the Temple formed an object of contention even in writings from before the time of Antiochus IV. Less certainly, the erection of the temple at Leontopolis may also be reflected in some writings (see the references in Collins 1983: 71-72, 78-79, 84; Humphrey 2000: 33-38). In the light of Martin Goodman's contribution to the present volume (pp. 459-68), I have not attempted to take account of documents from the first century CE, but even so, there is still too much material to cover properly, and I intend to focus primarily on documents written before the time of Antiochus IV or under the impact of the desecration of the Temple and the events that followed. That said, while there are obvious practical reasons for treating the Apocrypha and Pseudepigrapha separately, there is something a little artificial in considering any topic in these writings without at the same time taking account of the way it is treated in other contemporary corpora, not least in this context the later writings of the Hebrew Bible and the Scrolls. (Hayward 1996 does discuss a somewhat broader range of texts. He includes two that are discussed here, Ben Sira and *Jubilees*, but his concerns—the inner meaning of the Temple service—is rather different from that of the present study.) It should perhaps be added that the terms 'Apocrypha' and 'Pseudepigrapha' are used here in a purely conventional sense as a matter of convenience.

The treatment of a theme like that of Temple and cult in the Apocrypha and Pseudepigrapha is inevitably bound up with the interpretation of other issues in these documents, including that of dating. While in most cases we can be relatively confident, at least within broad parameters, about where a particular document should be placed, the interpretation of a writing such as 1 Esdras would be considerably facilitated if we knew for certain when it was to be dated. It hardly needs to be said that within the Apocrypha and Pseudepigrapha very different attitudes towards the Temple and cult in Jerusalem are reflected. On the one hand this merely represents a continuation of differences present already within the Hebrew Bible. On the other it provides yet further confirmation of the fact that the Judaism of the period was a very variegated phenomenon.

I

It is convenient to begin with two of the oldest documents within the Apocrypha and Pseudepigrapha that date from more or less the same period, the book of Ben Sira and the *Book of Watchers* (*1 En.* 1–36).

Sirach, as is well known, takes a very positive view of the Temple and the cult in Jerusalem. Most obviously, the book reaches its climax in the glorification of the high priest Simeon (Simeon [Simon] II, the son of Jochanan, high priest in the period around 200 BCE), which forms the final part of the Praise of the Fathers (Ecclus 50.1-24). The beginning of the passage (vv. 1-4) refers to the restoration of the 'house' (Hebrew *bayit*), that is the 'Temple' (Hebrew *hêkāl*), and the fortification of the city in Simon's time, both of which are apparently also mentioned by Josephus (*Ant.* 12.139, 141). Simon is then depicted emerging from the Temple, described here by the three terms 'tent' (*'ōhel*), 'house of the veil' (*bêt happāroket*), and 'sanctuary' (*miqdāš*) (Ecclus 50.5, 11), at the conclusion of the Daily Whole-Offering (cf. Exod. 29.38-42; Num. 28.3-8; for the view that the ceremony is the Daily Whole-Offering, and not the Day of Atonement, cf. Skehan and Di Lella 1987: 550-52; Hayward 1996: 50). The passage describes, in rather exuberant terms, his glorious appearance and his role in the ceremony. His appearance is compared, among other things, with various plants and trees, and with incense (vv. 8-12), and this comparison serves to present Simon as the embodiment of wisdom in that similar comparisons are made in the Praise of Wisdom (Ecclus 24; Hayward 1996: 52, 78).

Earlier in the Praise of the Fathers the glorification of Aaron (Ecclus 45.6-22) and—attached to this—of Phinehas (45.23-25d) stands in sharp contrast to the much more limited attention paid to Moses (44.23f–45.5) and to virtually all the other figures that are mentioned. Much of the passage on Aaron is taken up with a description of his vestments (45.8-13) and with his role in offering sacrifice (45.14-16, 22), while the passage on Phinehas alludes to his role in providing for the sanctuary (*lᵉkalkēl miqdāš*). Both the section on Aaron and that on Phinehas emphasize the belief that the covenant of priesthood made with them was also for their descendants in perpetuity (45.15, 24, where the latter verse alludes clearly to Num. 25.12-13). A prayer on behalf of the contemporary descendants of Phinehas, introduced in each case by 'And now' and by a call to bless the Lord, concludes both the passage dealing with Aaron and Phinehas and that dealing with Simeon (45.24e-26; 50.22-24, Hebrew text). Elsewhere, in Ecclus 7.29-31, the author calls on his readers to fear God and to revere his priests, in particular to give them the portion of the sacrifices due to them.

Apart from these passages, there are brief references in the Praise of the Fathers to the past history of the Temple. In accordance with the traditions preserved in 1 Chronicles (cf. 15.16; 16.4-6; 23.5, 30-32), it is David who organizes the Temple singers and arranges the religious festivals (Ecclus 47.9-10). There are also references to the building by Solomon of the Temple, called here both 'the house' and 'the sanctuary' (Hebrew *bayit* and *miqdāš*, 47.13), the destruction of the holy city (*qiryat qōdeš*) at the time of the exile (49.6), and the rebuilding of the holy Temple (*hêkal qōdeš*) by Zerubbabel and Jeshua (49.12). In view of attitudes in other writings, it is significant that there is no suggestion in Sirach that the rebuilt Temple was unclean or in any way provisional. We should also note here the petition, which forms part of the prayer for the deliverance of the nation (36.1-22), that the Temple (*hêkal*) be filled with the glory of God (36.19). In the poem on wisdom at the end of the book (51.13-30), the author states in the Greek, but not in the Hebrew (11QPs[a]), that he asked for wisdom before the Temple (51.14).

Ben Sira sets out his attitude towards sacrifice in Ecclus 34.21–35.13. On the one hand, sacrifices offered by the lawless and godless, particularly if acquired through the oppression of the poor, are unacceptable; the Most High does not forgive sins for a multitude of sacrifices (34.21-29). Equally, ritual actions performed with an insincere attitude are pointless (34.30-31). In contrast to this, keeping the commandments, and particularly almsgiving, is the equivalent of sacrifice:

> The one who keeps the law makes many offerings;
> one who heeds the commandments makes an offering of well-being.
> The one who returns a kindness offers choice flour,
> and one who gives alms sacrifices a thank-offering.
> To keep from wickedness is pleasing to the Lord,
> and to forsake unrighteousness is an atonement. (Ecclus 35.1-5 NRSV)

Similarly Ecclus 3.30 states, 'As water quenches flaming fire, so alms atones (*t[e]kappēr*) for sin' (Skehan and Di Lella 1987: 162; cf. v. 3).

On the other hand, Ecclus 35.6-13, which is introduced with the words 'Do not appear before the Lord empty-handed, for all that you offer is in fulfilment of the commandment', prescribes the attitude required for an offering to be acceptable and clearly does presuppose an obligation to offer sacrifice. Elsewhere (Ecclus 38.1-15), Ben Sira advises the person who is ill both to pay attention to the physician and to pray to God as the one who heals, to undergo cleansing (by which is also meant adopting a sincere attitude), and to offer sacrifice (38.9-11).

The positive attitude towards the Temple and the cult in Sirach stands entirely in line with one strand of tradition in the Hebrew Bible that is represented, for example, in 1 and 2 Chronicles with its emphasis on the Temple and the cultic institutions. Equally, what is said in Sirach specifically about sacrifice has a parallel in the Hebrew Bible in such passages as Isa. 1.11-17; Hos. 6.6; Amos 5.21-24; or Prov. 15.8; 21.3. But there is one element that is different. In the Praise of Wisdom (Ecclus 24), wisdom describes how, after she had sought without success for a resting place in the world, she was commanded by the Creator of all things to make her dwelling in Jacob. Wisdom then states that she ministered (*leitourgein*) before the Creator in the tabernacle and thereafter was established in Jerusalem, by implication in the Jerusalem Temple:

> In the holy tent I ministered before him,
> and so I was established in Zion.
> Thus in the beloved city he gave me a resting place,
> and in Jerusalem was my domain. (Ecclus 24.10-11 NRSV)

That wisdom is here implicitly depicted as performing a liturgical function (cf. Skehan and Di Lella 1987: 334-35) in the Jerusalem Temple receives support from one element of the imagery with which wisdom praises herself in the following verses:

> Like cinnamon, or fragrant cane, or precious myrrh,
> I give forth perfume,
> like galbanum and onycha and mastic,
> like the smoke of incense in the tent. (Ecclus 24.15, translation adapted from Skehan and Di Lella 1987: 328)

Cinnamon, fragrant cane, and myrrh are three of the ingredients used for the holy anointing oil (Exod. 30.22-25), and galbanum, onycha, and mastic were used to make the incense for the service in the tent (Exod. 30.34-38). Wisdom is then identified with 'the book of the covenant of the Most High God' (Ecclus 24.23), and the effect of attributing to wisdom a liturgical function is to bring together three of the key themes within Sirach: wisdom, law, and temple.

II

At first sight the *Book of Watchers* (*1 En.* 1–36), which can be dated to the latter part of the third or the beginning of the second century BCE, has little concern with the Temple. It is only in the context of the identification of the fragrant tree on the mountain-throne of God (*1 En.* 25.4-6, cf. 24.4-5) that there is a reference to a Temple in Jerusalem (depicted subsequently [26.1] as being at the centre of the earth), although in accordance with the setting of the book the name is not used:

> As for this fragrant tree, no (creature of) flesh has authority to touch it until the great judgment in which (there will be) vengeance on all and a consummation forever. Then it will be given to the righteous and holy. Its fruit {will be} food for the chosen, and it will be transplanted to a holy place by the house of God, the king of eternity. Then they will rejoice with joy and be glad, and they will enter the holy (place); its fragrance (will be) in their bones, and they will live a long life on the earth, such as your fathers lived, and in their days torments and plagues and scourges will not touch them. (*1 En.* 25.4-6, Greek version)

The tree is the tree of life of Gen. 2.9, which is kept from human beings at present (cf. Gen. 3.24), but is to be transplanted in the new age to near the Temple in Jerusalem. Nothing is said in this passage about what view the author took of the Temple in his own day, nor of the Temple in the new age other than that the righteous would enter it. In that age the tree near the Temple, rather than the Temple itself (so Nickelsburg 2001: 315), will be the source of life, a life understood as being very long, as in Isa. 65.19-20, but not eternal. However, insofar as the Temple is associated with the tree understood as the source of life, it may be recalled that the palm trees carved on the inside walls of the Solomonic Temple (1 Kgs 6.29, 32, 35; cf. Ezek. 41.18) have been understood as symbolizing the tree of life (cf. Noth 1968: 125-26). The Temple is the source of life in Ezek. 47.1-12, but the symbolism is different.

Apart from this reference to the Temple in the new age, it is widely recognized that in the account of Enoch's ascent to heaven (*1 En.* 14.8-25), heaven itself is conceived of as a Temple (Himmelfarb 1993: 14-20). The narrative describes how Enoch proceeded from a court or temenos (v. 9) to a 'large house' (vv. 10-14a), and then to a 'larger house', a holy of holies, in which the great glory sat on a high throne (vv. 14b-25). The narrative has been influenced not only by Ezekiel 1, Daniel 7, and Isaiah 6, but also, as Michael Stone originally suggested (cf. Nickelsburg 2001: 254), by Ezekiel 40–44. It may be noted that the term 'sanctuary' (Greek *hagiasma, hagion*) is used of heaven in two passages (*1 En.* 12.4; 15.3) in which the Watchers are condemned for having left heaven. Further, Enoch himself seemingly plays the role of priest of the heavenly Temple, when at the request of the Watchers he intercedes on their behalf (*1 En.* 13.4-5; for priests as intercessors, cf. Ezra 9.5-15; Joel 2.17; Exod. 28.12, 29; for Enoch as priest, cf. Himmelfarb 1993: 25, 45-46; Wright 1997: 199). But intercession is a task that the Watchers ought themselves to have undertaken, and they are accused: 'You ought to petition on behalf of men, not men on behalf of you' (*1 En.* 15.2).

Nickelsburg (2001: 271) suggests that the mention of the intercessory function of the angels at this point may be linked to their role as priests of the heavenly Temple. In any case, it has been argued, particularly by Suter (1979, 2002) and by Nickelsburg (1981; 2001: 230-31; cf. Himmelfarb 1993: 20-23), that the myth of the fall of the Watchers was intended, at least in part, as a criticism of the Jerusalem priests—the earthly counterparts of the priests of the heavenly Temple—of the time of the author. On the one hand, the Watchers are accused of leaving their natural order by marrying the women (*1 En.* 15.3-7), and the offspring of their unions are called 'bastards' (Greek *mazēreoi*, a transliteration of an Aramaic *mamzērîn*) and 'children of fornication' (*porneia*, pointing back to Aramaic *z*ᵉ*nûtā*, *1 En.* 10.9). Further, there are repeated accusations that the Watchers have defiled themselves through their contact with women and with blood (*1 En.* 7.1; 9.8; 10.11; 12.4; 15.4). This concern led Suter to argue that the myth needed to be examined in the light of the rules concerning family purity in the Second Temple period, particularly priestly purity, and that what was at issue was marriages by priests that were regarded as illegitimate, while the emphasis on blood might imply contamination through contact with menstrual blood (cf. the attacks on improper marriages, described as instances of 'fornication' [*z*ᵉ*nût*] in CD 4.12–5.11, and on the defilement of the priests through contact with menstrual blood in *Ps. Sol.* 8.13). On the other hand, the Watchers are presented as subverting one of the traditional roles of priests in that they teach forbidden knowledge (cf. Mal. 2.6-9). This implied criticism of the priesthood in the *Book of Watchers* has been related by Wright to the very strong support of the Jerusalem priesthood in Sirach (cf. Olyan 1987). Wright has used the criticism as part of a case 'that Ben Sira's positive view of the Jerusalem priesthood did not take shape in an ideological vacuum, but that he was deeply engaged in that ongoing war of words [concerning the legitimacy of the Jerusalem priesthood] as one who actively took the side of the Temple priests in polemical opposition against those who criticized them' (Wright 1997: 191; cf. 2002: 182) On this view, the other side of this opposition is represented by the circles that lie behind the *Book of Watchers* (as well as by other writings).

The fact that heaven is conceived of as a Temple in *1 Enoch* 14 makes it very plausible that the criticism of the Watchers is at least in part to be seen as an implied criticism of the Jerusalem priesthood, and Wright's further suggestion of polemical opposition between Ben Sira and the circles behind the *Book of Watchers* is also not unlikely. It is, however, difficult to be precise either about the basis of the criticism of the priests—marriage of priests with foreign women or marriage of priests with Jewish women who were not the daughters of priests (cf. 4QMMT B.75-82; Himmelfarb 2002: 132-34; Ellens and García Martínez 2002: 148-50)—or about the social realities underlying the polemics. The criticism is conveyed through the narrative of the fall of the Watchers, and, as such, it becomes, as Collins has rightly pointed out, 'a paradigm which is not restricted to one historical situation but can be applied whenever an analogous situation arises' (1984: 39).

If the criticism of the Jerusalem priesthood in the *Book of Watchers* is veiled, the same cannot be said of the criticism of the Temple and cult in another section of *1 Enoch*, the *Book of Dreams* (*1 En.* 83–90), or rather in one part of this, the *Vision of the Animals* (*1 En.* 85–90). This section of *1 Enoch*, at least in the form in which we know it, can be dated through the historical allusions in the *Vision of the Animals* to the period before the death of Judas (161 BCE). The vision refers, under the symbolism of a 'house', to the tabernacle in the wilderness period and perhaps at Shiloh (*1 En.* 89.36, 40; Josh. 18.1), although it may be that the wider entity 'the camp' is also envisaged (Tiller 1993: 296-97; Nickelsburg 2001: 381-82). 'House' and 'tower' are then used from *1 En.* 89.50 onwards to refer respectively to Jerusalem and the Temple. The building of the Solomonic Temple is mentioned in *1 En.* 89.50, as well as the presence of the Lord in the Temple and the offering of sacrifice: 'and the Lord of the sheep stood on that tower, and they spread a full table before him'. Thereafter references to the house and the tower refer to the progressive abandonment of Jerusalem and Temple in the pre-exilic period by Israel and Judah (*1 En.* 89.51, 54) and in turn the abandonment of Jerusalem and Temple by God (*1 En.* 89.56).

It is at this point in the narrative that the author introduces the notion of the seventy shepherds to whom the Jewish people are entrusted and who are responsible for the fate of the people until God comes to the earth in judgment. The seventy succeed one another and are divided into four groups corresponding to the periods of Babylonian, Persian, Ptolemaic, and Seleucid rule of Judah, after which the judgment is to take place. The destruction of Jerusalem and the first Temple at the beginning of the Babylonian period is noted in *1 En.* 89.66, the return, and the rebuilding of city and Temple at the start of the Persian period in *1 En.* 89.72, 73. The return and rebuilding are said to occur under the leadership of three of the sheep, most probably Joshua, Zerubbabel, and either Ezra or Nehemiah. Significantly it is said of the Second Temple: 'and they began again to place a table before that tower, but all the bread on it was unclean and was not pure'. This very negative judgment has rightly been compared with the condemnation of the priests and the cult in Malachi 1 and 2, where there is specific reference to offering polluted food on the altar (Mal. 1.7). The condemnation of the cult in the Second Temple period allied with the device of the seventy shepherds and the four world empires forms part of a more widespread pattern of interpretation according to which Judah continued in a state of exile after the return, a state that would only be finally brought to an end with the inauguration of the new age (Knibb 1976: 256-58).

Somewhat surprisingly the desecration of the Temple in the time of Antiochus is not mentioned, but in fact the Temple ('the tower') is not explicitly mentioned after the rebuilding at the beginning of the Persian period. Instead, after the rule of the seventy shepherds has run its course, and after the Lord of the sheep has appeared in judgment, it is noted, in the course of the description of the events of the judgment, that the abyss of fire into which apostate Jews ('the blind sheep') were thrown was on the south of the house, i.e. was south of Jerusalem (*1 En.* 90.26). Thereafter, it is stated that the old house was removed and put in the south of the land, and a new house was erected 'larger and higher than the first one' (90.28-29), in which the Lord of the sheep was present (90.29), and into which all the sheep were gathered (90.33-36). The vision of a New Jerusalem is of course familiar from expectation in the prophets (e.g. Ezek. 40–48; Isa. 54.11-12; 60). Whether a new Temple was implicitly included in the expectation of a New Jerusalem, or whether the presence of God in the house, conceived of thereby as both city and Temple, rendered the need for a traditional Temple in the new age superfluous, remains, as Nickelsburg (2001: 405) observes, uncertain (cf. Tiller 1993: 45-51, 376; VanderKam 1995: 84; Collins 1998: 9-10).

The one other place in the *Book of Enoch* where there is mention of the Temple is in the *Apocalypse of Weeks* (*1 En.* 93.1-10 + 91.11-17), which most probably dates from the pre-Maccabaean period, perhaps about 170 BCE, although it is not certainly attested before the second half of the first century BCE, the date of 4QEn^{g} (4Q212). The whole of world history is divided up in the *Apocalypse* into ten 'weeks' (for the background to the use of the symbolism, cf. Koch 1997), and within this scheme the fifth and sixth weeks (*1 En.* 91.7-8) correspond to the period of the monarchy. The construction of the Temple ('a house of glory and sovereignty') is placed in the fifth week, its destruction and the exile at the end of the sixth: 'and at its end the house of sovereignty will be burnt with fire, and in it the whole race of the chosen root will be scattered'. It appears that the author lived in the seventh week, a time which he describes as being marked by the emergence of a chosen group to whom a special revelation was given (*1 En.* 93.9-10 + 91.11, in which the Aramaic text of 93.10 and 91.11 has been preserved more or less completely):

> (93.9) And after this in the seventh week an apostate generation will arise, and many (will be) its deeds, but all its deeds (will be) apostasy. (93.10, Aramaic) [And at its end] the ch[osen one]s [will] be chosen, as witnesses to righteousness, from the eternal plant of righteousness, [to whom] will be given sevenfold wisdom and knowledge. (91.11, Aramaic) And they will uproot the foundations of violence and the work of deceit in order to carry out [judgment].

The last three weeks cover the events of the end of this age and the inauguration of the new age, and these need not concern us here except to note that a new Temple is erected in the eighth week (*1 En.* 91.12-13): 'And at its end they will acquire riches in righteousness, and the Temple of the [k]in[g]ship of the Great One in his glorious greatness will be built for all generations forever' (v. 13, Aramaic).

What is striking about the *Apocalypse of Weeks* is that the return and the rebuilding of the Temple under Joshua and Zerubbabel are passed over completely, and the whole of the post-exilic period is condemned as one of apostasy. It is only in the events of his own day, and within the group to which he no doubt belongs, that the author sees the period of renewal beginning. And it is as if it would only be in the new age that the Temple would be replaced. The *Apocalypse of Weeks* represents a further example of the view that the state of exile continued long after the return and would only be brought to an end with the inauguration of the new age (Knibb 1976: 259). But it also represents a further example of the criticism of the Jerusalem Temple, cult, and priesthood that is present in the *Vision of the Animals* and, in a veiled form, in the *Book of Watchers*, and it is probable, as Wright suggests in relation to the *Book of Watchers*, that all three sections of *1 Enoch* represent the views of priests and scribes who felt marginalized *vis-à-vis* the ruling priests in Jerusalem (1997: 218).

III

This is perhaps the place to refer briefly to two other writings from the same general period as those we have so far considered, Tobit and *Jubilees*. The first of these, which probably dates from about 200 BCE and stems from the eastern Diaspora, contains two distinct groups of references to the Temple. On the one hand, in the main narrative (Tob. 1–12), Jerusalem is mentioned as the place chosen from all the tribes of Israel 'where all the tribes of Israel should offer sacrifice and where the temple, the dwelling of God, had been consecrated and established for all generations forever' (1.4; all quotations from Tobit are from the NRSV). Tobit twice mentions, as a sign of his piety, that although from the northern kingdom he continued even after the division of the kingdoms to go to Jerusalem for the festivals (1.6-8; 5.14). On the other hand, the hymn and the testament at the end of the book (Tob. 13 and 14) contain references to the Temple from the standpoint of the exile, not just of Israel, which would be appropriate to the situation of Tobit, but also of Judah—the two are not differentiated. The hymn sees the exile as punishment for sin, but asserts that God will again have mercy on them if they repent (13.5-6). The people are urged to acknowledge the Lord so that his 'tent' may be rebuilt (13.10). It looks forward, in language reminiscent of Isa. 54.11-12; 60, to the rebuilding of Jerusalem (Tob. 13.16) and the streaming of the nations to the city (13.11). In the testament Tobit foretells the scattering of 'all of our kindred, inhabitants of the land of Israel', the desolation of the whole land, and the burning and desolation of the Temple (14.4). The text continues:

> But God will again have mercy on them, and God will bring them back into the land of Israel, and they will rebuild the temple of God, but not like the first one until the period when the times of fulfilment shall come. After this they all will return from their exile and will rebuild Jerusalem in splendour; and in it the temple of God will be rebuilt, just as the prophets of Israel have said concerning it. Then the nations in the whole world will all be converted and worship God in truth. (Tob. 14.5-6a)

Here there is a clear statement of the view that the Second Temple only had a provisional character, and this no doubt reflects the critical attitude towards the Second Temple that we have seen in *1 Enoch* (cf. Knibb 1976: 267-68), although the criticism itself is not spelt out. There is a very sharp contrast, as Hayward (1996: 47-48) has pointed out, between the attitude toward the Second Temple reflected in Tobit 14 and the very positive attitude of Ben Sira.

The *Book of Jubilees* has a good deal to say about the Temple service and its meaning (cf. Hayward 1996: 85-107), but refers to the Temple itself in only a few passages. These are of interest both because of their content and because of the circles from which the book stems. VanderKam (2001: 17-21) has argued that cumulatively the evidence suggests that *Jubilees* was composed in the period between 160 and 150 BCE, and he may be right; but because there is no clear reference to the measures imposed by Antiochus IV in 168, it is also possible that it dates from the period shortly before 168 (Nickelsburg 1984: 102-103; Knibb 1989: 16-17, 20).

The main references to the Temple occur in ch. 1. The speech of God to Moses (*Jub.* 1.5-18), which serves as an introduction to the book, begins with a warning that once the people have entered the land, they will forget the commandments of God, turn to foreign gods, and in consequence be sent into exile (vv. 5-13). Verse 10, which may allude specifically to the fate of the northern kingdom, mentions, as one of the causes of the exile, their abandonment of 'my tabernacle, and my temple which I sanctified for myself in the middle of the land so that I could set my name on it and that it could live (there)'. (All translations from *Jubilees* are from VanderKam 1989.) Verse 14 then refers to the period after they were exiled from the land: 'They will forget all my law, all my commandments, and all my verdicts. They will err regarding the beginning of the month, the sabbath, the festival, the jubilee, and the decree'. The passage was no doubt intended in the first instance as a description of the exilic age, but the indication of disputes over the calendar suggests that this verse also had relevance in the time of the author and represented his view of his own age.

The next events mentioned are the repentance of the people, and the gathering of them from among all the nations by God (v. 15). The text continues:

> I will transform them into a righteous plant with all my mind and with all my soul. They will become a blessing, not a curse; they will become the head, not the tail. I will build my temple among them and will live with them; I will become their God and they will become my true and righteous people. I will neither abandon them nor become alienated from them, for I am the Lord their God. (*Jub*. 1.16-18)

Charles (1902: 5) took this as a reference to the Second Temple, but it seems clear that what is really in mind is the Temple of the new age, and that—in a way similar to in the *Apocalypse of Weeks*—we have a further example of the view that the condition of exile had continued beyond the return and would only be brought to an end with the inauguration of the new age (cf. Knibb 1976: 266-67; 1989: 11). That the Temple mentioned here was really understood as the Temple of the new age is confirmed by the references to the Temple later in the chapter, which speak of the revelation to Moses being intended to cover the period 'until the time when my temple is built among them throughout the ages of eternity' (v. 27), or '[until] the time of the new creation when the heavens, the earth, and all their creatures will be renewed..., until the time when the temple of the Lord will be created in Jerusalem on Mt Zion' (v. 29). One of the petitions in Rebecca's blessing of Jacob (*Jub*. 25.14-22) likewise seems to envisage the Temple of the new age: 'May the righteous God live with them; and may his sanctuary be built among them into all ages' (*Jub*. 25.21b).

The one other significant reference to the Temple occurs in the eschatological passage, *Jub*. 23.8-32. The description of the sins of the 'evil generation' (v. 14) includes the statement: 'They will *mention* the great name but neither truly nor rightly. They will defile the holy of holies through the impure corruption of their contamination' (v. 21). VanderKam rightly points out that these faults 'demonstrate that priests, including apparently the high priest (the one who entered the holy of holies), were among the writers' opponents' (2001: 58). References elsewhere in the passage to 'sexual impurity' (where the phrase used points back to an original Hebrew *z*[e]*nût*) and 'contamination' (vv. 14, 17) suggest that what was in mind was marriages that were regarded as illegitimate, and comparison might be drawn with the reference to defiling the Lord's sanctuary that occurs in *Jub*. 30.15, in a context warning against marriage with foreigners. But there are strong indications in the book that *Jubilees* stems from priestly circles, and—as appears to be the case for the *Book of the Watchers* and the other sections of *1 Enoch* considered here—we should no doubt regard the authors as dissident priests who were highly critical of the ruling priestly establishment in Jerusalem.

As a footnote to the above, it may be added that the Garden of Eden, described in *Jub*. 4.26 as one of the four places on the earth that belong to the Lord, and in *Jub*. 8.19 as 'the holy of holies', is implicitly conceived in *Jubilees* to be a sanctuary. This follows, as Hayward (1996: 89) has indicated, from the fact that the law prescribing forty days' purification for a woman before she can enter the sanctuary if she bears a son, but eighty days if she bears a daughter, is derived from the fact that Adam is said to have been brought into Eden on the fortieth day after his creation, but Eve on the eightieth (*Jub*. 3.9-13).

IV

In the final part of this study I would like to turn, much more briefly, to a group of documents that were composed under the impact of the measures taken under the orders of Antiochus IV in 168, particularly the desecration of the Temple, and of the events that followed. Here 1 and 2 Maccabees most obviously deserve consideration. As is well known, for the period down to the death of Nicanor in 161 they cover the same events (although 1 Maccabees then continues down to the death of Simon and accession of John Hyrcanus), but they present very different interpretations of the events.

It is widely recognized that, whatever other purpose lay behind its composition, 1 Maccabees was intended to glorify the Hasmonaeans and, in particular, to legitimize the assumption of the office of high priest by Simon. The narrative reaches its climax in ch. 14 in the hymn praising his reign and the decree that was erected in the Temple confirming the appointment of Simon as leader and high priest forever (v. 41). Attention has often been drawn to the implicit claim that Mattathias and his family were heirs of Phinehas (1 Macc. 2.24, 26, 54), which may be contrasted with what is said concerning Phinehas in Sirach; to the emphasis on the piety of Mattathias and his family; and to the denigration of the leaders who did not obey Judas and his brothers, 'the family of those men through whom deliverance was given to Israel' (5.18-19, 61-62).

The Temple is mentioned nearly sixty times in 1 Maccabees—the words used are predominantly *hagiasma* and *ta hagia*—but it is of interest to observe the pattern of these references. It is of course mentioned frequently (twenty-five times) in the first four chapters, beginning with the narrative of the robbery of the Temple treasures (1 Macc. 1.20-24) and reaching a climax in the narrative of the rededication of the Temple (4.36-59). The distress caused by the actions of Antiochus and of his forces and the reaction they provoked are vividly depicted, but there is no attempt to look for the cause of the events in anything other than the activities of renegade Jews and the decision of Antiochus.

References to the Temple occur rather more sporadically in the remainder of the book, and the emphasis is on the ever-increasing power of the Maccabaean family and on their military success. The Temple is only infrequently mentioned in chs. 5–9. Thereafter, apart from incidental mention of the Temple in one or two passages, there are only, on the one hand, a series of references to the privileges granted to the Temple and to the high priest, and to the support provided for the maintenance of Temple and cult, by successive Seleucid rulers and claimants to the throne (1 Macc. 10.20, 31-35, 39-44; 11.34-35; 15.7, 9); and on the other, a cluster of references in ch. 14, all as part of the justification for the appointment of Simon as leader and high priest, to what he and his brothers had done to preserve the sanctuary and the law. Earlier, Simon himself is recorded as saying to the people: 'You yourselves know what great things my brothers and I and the house of my father have done for the laws and the sanctuary; you know also the wars and the difficulties that my brothers and I have seen' (1 Macc. 13.3, NRSV).

Doran has aptly described 2 Maccabees as 'temple propaganda' (1981: 114) and has argued that throughout the narrative 'the concern is to glorify the defence of the temple and its territory by its patron deity' (p. 75). In contrast to 1 Maccabees, it does offer a theological explanation of the events. The underlying thesis of the book is that the God of the Jews protects his Temple and his people when they are obedient, but that he punishes them for a time when they are disobedient in order to discipline them, but does not withdraw his mercy from them. This thesis is repeatedly illustrated in the three main narrative structures that Doran discerns in the book (2 Macc. 3.1-40; 4.1–10.9; 10.10–15.36). Thus God protected the Temple when Heliodorus was sent to remove the Temple treasures because the laws were observed (2 Macc. 3.1). Then the sequence of events that culminated in the measures of Antiochus and the desecration of the Temple, particularly the activities of apostate Jews, is described in much greater detail than in 1 Maccabees. Significantly these events are interpreted as the disciplining by God of his people for their sins (2 Macc. 5.17-20; 6.12-17; 7.18-19, 32-33), as, for example, in 5.17-18:

> Antiochus was elated in spirit, and did not perceive that the Lord was angered for a little while because of the sins of those who lived in the city, and that this was the reason he was disregarding the holy place. But if it had not happened that they were involved in many sins, this man would have been flogged and turned back from his rash act as soon as he came forward, just as Heliodorus had been, whom King Seleucus sent to inspect the treasury. (NRSV)

It is the sufferings of the martyrs that lead to God again showing mercy (cf. 2 Macc. 7.37). Antiochus dies in agony acknowledging the God of the Jews, and the Temple is recovered and rededicated. Finally, Nicanor's threat to raze the Temple to the ground and his arrogance towards God (2 Macc. 14.33; 15.1-6) are overcome through the prayers of the priests and the piety of Judas. God delivers his people and Temple, and Nicanor is killed.

In view of the importance attaching to the Temple in the narrative, it is perhaps not surprising that it is mentioned some fifty times—proportionately more often than in 1 Maccabees, which is half as long again as 2 Maccabees—and that the references to the Temple are spread fairly evenly through the narrative. (The word used is predominantly *hieron*, to a lesser extent *naos* and variants.) Again in contrast to 1 Maccabees, it is noticeable that the protection and recovery of the Temple and the defeat of their enemies are repeatedly said to have been brought about by divine agency, rather than through human power. Correspondingly, it is the piety of Judas that is emphasized rather than his prowess as a leader. 2 Maccabees, or at least the main body of the book, represents an alternative narrative of the events surrounding the desecration and recovery of the Temple and appears to stem from circles disillusioned with the rule of the Hasmonaeans.

Judith and *3 Maccabees* also deserve consideration as 'alternative narratives', but here it is possible only to offer the briefest of comments on them. The broad similarity between the situation depicted in Judith and that reflected in 1 Maccabees has often been noted, and it seems extremely probable that the figure of Nebuchadnezzar reflects that of Antiochus IV (cf. Otzen 2002: 94-97, 132-34).

Within the narrative we may observe the repeated mention of the threat to Jerusalem and the sanctuary (Jdt. 4.1-3, 12; [5.18;] 8.21, 24; 9.8, 13). In an interesting study entitled 'Judith as Alternative Leader: A Rereading of Judith 7–13', van Henten has interpreted the figure of Judith as an alternative leader in relation to the leadership of Moses and the elders in the wilderness, but also of significance in a contemporary context. Here I can do no more than quote part of his conclusion: 'Against the background of a roughly contemporaneous origin, and the fact that the Maccabees were presented as the leaders exclusively supported by the Lord (1 Macc. 5.62), the figure of Judith may have functioned as a way of releasing criticism against the new Hasmonean dynasty firmly in control at the time' (1995: 252).

3 Maccabees serves as the festal legend of an annual festival of liberation celebrated by the Jewish community in Alexandria and Egypt, and an alternative version of this appears in Josephus, *Apion* 2.53-55. Two main sources can be identified within *3 Maccabees*: a version of the Heliodorus narrative of 2 Maccabees 3 in which it is the Egyptian ruler Ptolemy IV Philopator who unsuccessfully attempts to enter the Temple in Jerusalem; and the festal legend itself, which is concerned with the fate of the Jews in Alexandria and Egypt. In broad outline the plot of *3 Maccabees* is similar to that of 2 Maccabees: an arrogant ruler attempts to enter the Temple in Jerusalem, but is prevented from doing this by God through the prayer of the high priest; the attempt is made to force the Jews to assimilate by participating in the festival of Dionysus (2 Macc. 6.7; *3 Macc.* 2.29-30), and some do so, but the majority refuse and in consequence face immediate extermination; the prayers of the Jews and finally the prayer of the pious Eleazer lead to their being saved through a series of miracles; the arrogant ruler acknowledges the God of heaven as the God of the Jews, and the situation of the Jews is restored and is indeed even better than it was before. It seems probable that *3 Maccabees* was composed in the period of tension between Jews and Greeks in Alexandria that followed the imposition by Augustus in 24/23 BCE of a poll-tax (cf., e.g., Smallwood 1981: 231-32), but it appears that it was written in conscious imitation of 2 Maccabees, and there is much to be said for the view of Tromp that the author 'has moulded the festival legend in accordance with the Heliodorus-pattern' (1995: 321). In any event the narrative of the attempt to enter the Temple by Ptolemy is quite clearly an alternative version of the Heliodorus story in 2 Maccabees 3. Whereas Heliodorus learns his lesson and acknowledges God (2 Macc. 3.35-39), Ptolemy does not until the climax of the events described in the festal legend (*3 Macc.* 6.28; 7.6, 9).

V

Other writings that should be included here for the sake of completeness include the *Letter of Aristeas* and the *Sibylline Oracles*. But here it is possible to mention only 1 Esdras, a writing in which the Temple is above all the focus of attention. The difficulty with 1 Esdras is to know whether it should be regarded as a translation of a more original form of the biblical account of the restoration under Ezra, in which the story of the three young men has been interpolated, perhaps only a fragment of a more complete translation; or whether it should be regarded as a new composition based on Chronicles, Ezra and Nehemiah; for representatives of these two views see Pohlmann (1970) and Williamson (1996). However, it seems most likely that 1 Esdras should be regarded as a new composition, and thus Talshir, for example, has recently argued that 1 Esdras was based on a section of Chronicles–Ezra–Nehemiah, and that the book 'was created for the purpose of retelling the history of the Restoration in such a way that it revolved around the Story of the Three Youths, and its hero Zerubbabel' (1999: 106). In either case the question of purpose arises, and in this connection the 'significant emphasis on the temple' (Myers 1974: 9) seems not without relevance.

The narrative begins with an account of the great Passover celebrated in the days of Josiah, in which it is noted that everything was done in accordance with the commandment of the Lord that was given to Moses (1 Esd. 1.6, cf. v. 11), and that no Passover had been kept like it since the days of Samuel (vv. 20-22). The narrative continues by recounting the death of Josiah and the downfall of Judah, where we may note the mention of the pollution of the Temple in the time of Zedekiah (v. 49), and the fate of the Temple and the Temple vessels (vv. 54-55). The core of the narrative, including the story of the three young men, then describes how permission for the rebuilding of the Temple came to be granted and then withdrawn in the face of the opposition that the attempt to rebuild the Temple aroused, and how eventually the Temple was rebuilt and dedicated, and Passover and the festival of unleavened bread were celebrated (1 Esd. 2–7). The final part of the narrative describes, before the text breaks off abruptly (9.55), the work of Ezra, the problem of mixed marriages, and the reading of the law (8–9).

In view of the emphasis on the Temple, it might be argued that one of the concerns of 1 Esdras was to demonstrate the legitimacy of the restored cult, to show that it was again established as it was in the days of Josiah. But in what context? Here the question of setting and date is raised acutely. It has been suggested that the work has something to do with polemics in the second century between the Jerusalem Temple and the temple at Leontopolis, and that it was intended as a defence of the legitimacy and authority of the Jerusalem Temple (cf. Attridge 1984: 160), and although not without difficulties, this is an attractive suggestion.

Bibliography

Attridge, H.W.
1984 '1 Esdras', in Stone (ed.) 1984: 157-60.

Charles, R.H.
1902 *The Book of Jubilees* (London: A. & C. Black).

Collins, J.J.
1983 *Between Athens and Jerusalem: Jewish Identity in the Hellenistic Diaspora* (New York: Crossroad).
1984 *The Apocalyptic Imagination: An Introduction to the Jewish Matrix of Christianity* (New York: Crossroad).
1998 *Jerusalem and the Temple in Jewish Apocalyptic of the Second Temple Period* (International Rennert Guest Lecture Series, 1; Bar-Ilan University).

Doran, R.

1981 *Temple Propaganda: The Purpose and Character of 2 Maccabees* (CBQMS, 12; Washington, DC: Catholic Biblical Association of America).

Ellens, J.H., and F. García Martínez

2002 'Enochians and Zadokites', *Henoch* 24: 147-53.

Hayward, C.T.R.

1996 *The Jewish Temple: A Non-Biblical Sourcebook* (London: Routledge).

Henten, J.W. van

1995 'Judith as Alternative Leader: A Rereading of Judith 7–13', in A. Brenner (ed.), *A Feminist Companion to Esther, Judith, Susanna* (Feminist Companion to the Bible, 7; Sheffield: Sheffield Academic Press): 224-52.

Himmelfarb, M.

1993 *Ascent to Heaven in Jewish and Christian Apocalypses* (New York and Oxford: Oxford University Press).

2002 'The Book of the Watchers and the Priests of Jerusalem', *Henoch* 24: 131-35.

Humphrey, E.M.

2000 *Joseph and Aseneth* (Guides to the Apocrypha and Pseudepigrapha; Sheffield: Sheffield Academic Press).

Knibb, M.A.

1976 'The Exile in the Literature of the Intertestamental Period', *HeyJ* 17: 253-72.

1989 *Jubilees and the Origins of the Qumran Community: An Inaugural Lecture in the Department of Biblical Studies, King's College London* (London: King's College London).

Koch, K.

1997 'Sabbat, Sabbatjahr und Weltenjahr: die apokalyptische Konstruktion der Zeit', *Ars Semeiotica* 20: 69-86.

Myers, J.M.

1974 *I and II Esdras: Introduction, Translation and Commentary* (AB, 42; Garden City, NY: Doubleday).

Nickelsburg, G.W.E.

1981 'Enoch, Levi, and Peter: Recipients of Revelation in Upper Galilee', *JBL* 100: 575-600.

1984 'Jubilees', in Stone (ed.) 1984: 97-104.

2001 *1 Enoch 1: A Commentary on the Book of 1 Enoch, Chapters 1–36; 81–108* (Hermeneia; Minneapolis: Fortress Press).

Noth, M.

1968 *Könige*, I (BKAT, 9.1; Neukirchen–Vluyn: Neukirchener Verlag).

Olyan, S.M.

1987 'Ben Sira's Relationship to the Priesthood', *HTR* 80: 261-86.

Otzen, B.

2002 *Tobit and Judith* (Guides to the Apocrypha and Pseudepigrapha; London and New York: Sheffield Academic Press).

Pohlmann, K.F.

1970 *Studien zum dritten Esra: Ein Beitrag zur Frage nach dem ursprünglichen Schluss des chronistischen Geschichtswerks* (FRLANT, 104; Göttingen: Vandenhoeck & Ruprecht).

Skehan, P.W., and A.A. Di Lella

1987 *The Wisdom of Ben Sira* (AB, 39; New York: Doubleday).

Smallwood, E.M.

1981 *The Jews under Roman Rule from Pompey to Diocletian: A Study in Political Relations* (SJLA, 20; Leiden: E.J. Brill, 2nd edn).

Stone, M.E. (ed.)
1984 *Jewish Writings of the Second Temple Period: Apocrypha, Pseudepigrapha, Qumran Sectarian Writings, Philo, Josephus* (CRINT, 2.2; Assen: Van Gorcum; Philadelphia: Fortress Press).

Suter, D.W.
1979 'Fallen Angel, Fallen Priest: The Problem of Family Purity in 1 Enoch 6–16', *HUCA* 50: 115-35.
2002 'Revisiting "Fallen Angel, Fallen Priest"', *Henoch* 24: 137-42.

Talshir, Z.
1999 *1 Esdras: From Origin to Translation* (SBLSCS, 47; Atlanta: Society of Biblical Literature).

Tiller, P.A.
1993 *A Commentary on the Animal Apocalypse of 1 Enoch* (SBL Early Judaism and Its Literature, 4; Atlanta: Scholars Press).

Tromp, J.
1995 'The Formation of the Third Book of Maccabees', *Henoch* 17: 311-28.

VanderKam, J.C.
1989 *The Book of Jubilees* (CSCO, 511; Leuven: Peeters).
1995 *Enoch: A Man for All Generations* (Studies on Personalities of the Old Testament; Columbia, SC: University of South Carolina Press).
2001 *The Book of Jubilees* (Guides to the Apocrypha and Pseudepigrapha; Sheffield: Sheffield Academic Press).

Williamson, H.G.M.
1996 'The Problem with First Esdras', in J. Barton and D.J. Reimer (eds.), *After the Exile: Essays in Honour of Rex Mason* (Macon, GA: Mercer University Press): 201-16.

Wright, B.G.
1997 '"Fear the Lord and Honor the Priest": Ben Sira as Defender of the Jerusalem Priesthood', in P.C. Beentjes (ed.), *The Book of Ben Sira in Modern Research: Proceedings of the First International Ben Sira Conference, 28–31 July 1996, Soesterberg, Netherlands* (BZAW, 255; Berlin and New York: W. de Gruyter): 189-222.
2002 'Sirach and 1 Enoch: Some Further Considerations', *Henoch* 24: 179-87.

THE TEN TEMPLES IN THE DEAD SEA SCROLLS*

George J. Brooke

1. *Introduction*

This paper is an attempt to offer a summary overview of the various explicit and implicit descriptions of the Temple in the Dead Sea Scrolls. It is not an attempt at exhaustively portraying the views about the Temple in all the sectarian and non-sectarian compositions found in the caves at and near Qumran, but rather an outline catalogue which describes the range of Temples referred to or implied by those texts. My thesis is that there are ten Temples referred to in the many compositions that have survived in the eleven caves at or near Qumran and that these are variously significant for the Qumran community and its forebears during the two and a half centuries before the fall of what is commonly called the 'Second' Temple. There are several overlaps between the ten Temples, so that in the end the ten can be reduced to three: (1) the earthly Temple in various guises,[1] none of which satisfies divine requirements; (2) heavenly worship which may provide several inklings of a heavenly Temple, but whose overarching significance is that its perfect plan will ultimately be revealed in an earthly counterpart in a new act of divine creation; and (3) the community as temple, a human anticipation of things to come, a *miqdaš 'ādām*.

Making sense of this vast range of material requires some kind of historical overview into which the various literary traditions can be fitted, so as to make a coherent overall theory. This historical overview has certain basic features which will be taken as read and which fall into two categories. The first set of historical pointers concerns Jerusalem. Some textual traditions indicate that before the Maccabaean revolt there were changes in Jerusalem, some of which had an impact on the Temple. After the Seleucid occupation the rededication of the Temple may or may not have satisfied everybody concerned. A common view suggests that at least there were arguments about the priesthood, most especially when the Maccabee Jonathan took the high priesthood upon himself, and that there were significant ongoing disputes about the calendar. A generation later,

* I am grateful to the members of the Oxford Old Testament Seminar for their comments on a preliminary form of this paper, and to members of the New Testament and Second Temple Judaism Seminar of the British New Testament Society, especially C.H.T. Fletcher-Louis, for further helpful suggestions.

1. A useful survey of the biblical and other data on the Temple buildings in Jerusalem can be found in Meyers 1992.

John Hyrcanus undertook to reform some aspects of the Temple, both its buildings and its practices. After various traumas in the first century BCE, including an unwelcome sacrilegious incursion by the Romans under Pompey and the abuse of the treasury by Cassius, Herod engaged in his extensive rebuilding programme which was hardly completed before the catastrophe of 70 CE.

A significant part of the reconstruction of the history of traditions presented here depends on taking seriously the likely dates of the manuscripts in which the evidence is preserved. It is important to attempt to date all the manuscript witnesses to a particular composition; the extant evidence suggests it is necessary to consider not only what may be the earliest attestation of a composition, but also something of when ongoing interest in the composition was generating the need for further copies. Over the years there have been two significant attempts to use the date of the manuscripts to go beyond presenting Qumran or Essene views in a monolithic fashion. Both are worth mentioning briefly as their insights will become relevant as the overview develops.

In the first place for messianism there has generally been an increasingly refined use of the dates of various compositions to assert developments in sectarian expectations. J. Starcky's (1963) initial attempt at outlining a four-stage history of messianism at Qumran has been significantly reviewed and adjusted, with the overall emphasis now suggesting that within the framework of a constant concern for the coming of two messiahs, there were changes and developments concerning how both the priestly and the royal figures were understood.[2] For the latter, it is regularly noted that the royal messiah becomes both significantly more democratic and explicitly more Davidic in compositions which are dated approximately to the late Hasmonaean and Herodian periods.

In the second place, the release of all the copies of the *Community Rule* has provoked the emergence of two schools of thought about the development of the composition and the way in which such developments may reflect real communities. Working principally from the actual dates of the various manuscripts, P.S. Alexander (1996) has outlined a theory in which the community's organization can be envisaged as shifting from more overtly priestly, particularly Zadokite, structures at the start of the first century BCE, to a seemingly more communitarian organization at the end. Against him, S. Metso (1997) has fought a battle on several fronts arguing seemingly on the basis of two maxims, one text-critical (the shorter the earlier) and the other sociological (that sects develop from charismatic beginnings towards institutionalization), that although the only manuscript attestation for the non-priestly community structures is relatively late, the community reflected in those manuscripts must have preceded that found in the Cave 1 form of the *Community Rule*. It is necessary to build on both these examples of using the dates of manuscripts and the reconstruction of literary histories and the communities in the overview of Temple material that follows.

2. See, among others, Oegema 1994; Brooke 1998; Zimmermann 1998: 448-52. On the other hand, confirming earlier opinions, G.G. Xeravits (2002) argues that it is only possible to describe diversity of opinion in the sectarian compositions and no overall line of developing opinion.

2. *The Ten Temples*

1. *The Primordial Temple (Holy of Holies)*

Largely on the basis of the implied allusions to Maccabaean victories in the descriptions of Jacob's wars against the Amorites and the Edomites (*Jub.* 34; 38), such as the mention of the king of Beth-horon and other regional allies (*Jub.* 34.4-7) recalling Judas's defeat of Nicanor at Beth-horon (1 Macc. 7.39-50), and the lack of any hint of a major schism between the author's party and the Maccabees, the book of *Jubilees* is dated sometime between 161 and 152 BCE.[3] Although probably not composed by an Essene, multiple copies, some as late as the turn of the era, have been found in the caves at Qumran, so we may assume that its ideology was both foundational and of ongoing significance for the members of the Qumran community.[4]

Together with its evident concern for the eternal place of the angelic worship that takes place in heaven, the book of *Jubilees* also offers a glimpse of its primordial counterpart on earth as well as other anticipations of how the cult should be practised once the Temple has been built (which is of course the perspective of the author). According to *Jubilees*, aspects of the Temple service were known from the time of Adam. Pre-eminent behind the organization of worship is the keeping of the Sabbath. In 4.26 the author of *Jubilees* states:

> For the Lord has four (sacred) places upon the earth: the garden of Eden and the mountain of the East and this mountain which you are upon today, Mount Sinai, and Mount Zion, which will be sanctified in the new creation for the sanctification of the earth. On account of this the earth will be sanctified from all sin and from pollution throughout eternal generations. (Wintermute 1985: 63)

The garden of Eden is a sacred place, but of what kind? To answer this it is important to notice that according to *Jubilees* Adam and Eve are created outside the garden of Eden and brought to it after forty and eighty days respectively (*Jub.* 3.9, 12), periods which correspond with the laws of Lev. 12.2-5 indicating that Eden was perceived to be a sanctuary. Leviticus 12.2-5 require of a woman a forty days purification if she bears a son and eighty days if she bears a daughter, before she may enter the sanctuary.[5] For C.T.R. Hayward and many other interpreters of *Jubilees* this indicates that a sanctuary was an integral part of creation itself from the outset and that it 'has a good deal to do with the continuing stability and order of creation' (Hayward 1996: 86). *Jubilees* states that Eden is holier than all the rest of the earth (3.12); Noah

> knew that the garden of Eden was the holy of holies and the dwelling of the Lord. And Mount Sinai (was) in the midst of the desert and Mount Zion (was) in the midst of the navel of the earth. The three of these were created as holy places, one facing the other. (Wintermute 1985: 73)

3. 'The latest events to which I can find reference in Jub. are Judas Maccabeus' wars in 161 BC' (VanderKam 1997: 283-84).

4. *Jubilees* seems to be cited as authoritative in the *Damascus Document* (CD 16.3-4; 4Q271 4 ii 5), which seems to have been composed largely in the second century BCE; 4Q218 (4QJub^{c}) is from approximately the turn of the era.

5. 4Q265 implies the same thing; see the discussion by Baumgarten 1994.

In the terms of the book of *Jubilees* Adam and Eve were brought into the holy of holies.

Two issues for our study arise in light of this. First, why should the author of *Jubilees* apply the language of the sanctuary ideally to Eden in the way that he does in the middle of the second century BCE? What is provoking this kind of idealistic throwback? It might be the case that the retelling of Genesis in the context of anticipating right Temple practice has naturally resulted in a sanctification of Eden, of which there are indeed hints in various scriptural texts.[6] But in addition to possibly aligning himself with particular earlier traditions, the author of *Jubilees* may also have had a sense of the political agenda of the Maccabees after the defeat of the Seleucids (despite the ongoing presence of Seleucids in Judaea for another quarter of a century). The sanctification of Eden is a divine guarantee of the political division of the world into three sections with the descendants of Shem, not the Greeks, clearly the rightful heirs of the land of Israel (*Jub*. 8.10-21).

A second issue comes to mind in light of the first. Despite the ongoing authoritative significance of the book of *Jubilees* for the community of the *Damascus Document* and at Qumran, and even the repetition of the forty-day and eighty-day rule in relation to Eden in 4Q265, it seems as if the sectarian texts found at Qumran seldom appeal to Eden as a cultic ideal. Among the few examples of sectarian compositions which do refer to Eden there is one extensive passage in the *Hodayot* (1QH[a] 14[6].12-17), attributed by some to the Teacher and so perhaps composed within a few years of the book of *Jubilees*, which has some echoes of it:

> For Thou wilt bring Thy glorious [salvation] to all the men of Thy Council, to those who share a common lot with the Angels of the Face… They shall send out a bud [for ever] like a flower [of the fields], and shall cause a shoot to grow into the boughs of an everlasting Plant. It shall cover the whole [earth] with its shadow [and its crown] (shall reach) to the [clouds]; its roots (shall go down) to the Abyss [and all the rivers of Eden shall water its branches].[7]

Although Eden is barely mentioned elsewhere in the sectarian scrolls, Adam occurs in a small number of significant texts. In association with language defining the Temple he is mentioned in 4Q174 in the much discussed phrase *miqdaš ʾādām*. I consider that this phrase is a deliberate and brilliant attempt to provide an idiom which includes more than one idea. One of those ideas is an echo of the notion of Eden as sanctuary in the book of *Jubilees*. The *miqdaš ʾādām* is the ‘Temple of Adam’,[8] which can be construed as an actual Temple (perhaps more than just the holy of holies) or as the human (Adamic) community constituted as Eden restored.[9] And why might 4Q174, a composition from the late first century BCE, be reconfirming such an idea together with other cultic aspirations? I

6. Cf. Ps. 46.5 (ET 4); Ezek. 36.35.

7. Some text is restored from the parallel material extant in 4QH[b] [4Q428] 8 1-4.

8. For this rendering see Wise 1994: 174-85.

9. It is possible that the theology of parts of Isaiah was understood as supporting such a viewpoint: see Berges 2002.

suspect that that may have to do with a combination of political and religious factors, some of which I will describe below in relation to other Temples.

2. *The Wilderness Tabernacle*

A second sanctuary assumed or described explicitly among the scrolls is that of the wilderness tabernacle.[10] In addition to the fact that the tabernacle is referred to in numerous scriptural biblical manuscripts found in the Qumran caves, it is also described in the so-called *Reworked Pentateuch* (4Q364-67). However, beyond these scriptural rehearsals of the wilderness tabernacle three points are worth mentioning briefly.

First, the community or communities of the *Damascus Document*, together with those of some other compositions, such as the *Rule of the Congregation* (1QSa), are described as living in camps, and the ideology of the wilderness permeates certain sections of the *Community Rule*, not least with its use of Isa. 40.3's wilderness setting (1QS 8.13-14).[11] If the community at some stage or at all stages of its existence, whether at Qumran or even before occupying the site, identified implicitly and explicitly with Israel in the wilderness, how might it have conceived its focus of worship? The answer to this question is not clear, because the *Damascus Document* seems to allow for the ongoing offering of sacrifices in Jerusalem, not for the keeping of festivals but as performance of Sabbath commitments (CD 11.17-18). Nevertheless, the community behind the *Community Rule* seems to have abandoned the Temple and asserted that its own practices were a sufficient substitute for the Temple's cult. The relationship of the Tent of Meeting to how the community envisaged its worship practices is not clear, but the very impermanence of the tabernacle could have encouraged the movement, or part of it at least, to take the immense spiritual risk of splitting from the actual Temple in Jerusalem when some of the members of the group sought to start again cultically. The community itself is to be an 'everlasting plantation, a holy house for Israel and the foundation of the holy of holies for Aaron' (1QS 8.5-6).

A second matter arises concerning the tabernacle in the wilderness. It is clear from the *Temple Scroll* that many of its regulations in its plan for the Temple derive from the Torah's descriptions of the tabernacle and often from the tabernacle in the first instance, even when there are uses of the descriptions of Solomon's Temple or the proposals of Ezekiel 40–48. As Y. Yadin (1983: 47) commented in his principal edition of 11QT^{a} in relation to the furnishings of the Temple: 'The author expounds of these topics when the biblical text is unclear or fails to provide sufficient detail on how a particular vessel is to be used. He relies in general upon Ex. xxv and Ex. xxxvii, but also uses other sources, including the description of Solomon's Temple.' The need for Torah authentication of the divine prescriptions in the Temple plan of necessity results in the use of wilderness traditions, though the desire to show that the tabernacle also mirrored divine

10. See the detailed overview by Koester 1989: 26-41.

11. On this see, among many other studies, Brooke 1994; Longenecker 1998.

plans for the Temple could have played a part too, since consistency and harmonization of sources are a feature of the editorial processes behind the *Temple Scroll*. Overall one might suppose that noticing the dependence of the *Temple Scroll* on the wilderness traditions of the Pentateuch is further reason to date the scroll to a time when those responsible for its compilation might have been happy to refer back to the wilderness wanderings for a fresh start. The latter half of the second century BCE seems to be just such a time when the Essenes or proto-Essenes and their counterparts dropped their support for the establishment in Jerusalem, a support which many have been seen in the slightly earlier book of *Jubilees*, despite its differences on the calendar.

A third matter relating to the wilderness tabernacle may be discussed in relation to the archaeological remains at Qumran. J.-B. Humbert (1994) has proposed a significant rereading of the remains at Qumran to suggest that cultic issues influenced the reorientation of the site on more than one occasion. Humbert has argued that the Essene occupation of the site in the second half of the first century BCE resulted in the construction of a court for worship, including sacrifices, on the north-western side of the building complex. This court was a trapezoid of approximately 35 × 18 m and has an axis which is oriented precisely towards Jerusalem. Although he does not discuss the significance of the measurements, some support for his reading of the archaeological remains might have been deduced from the fact that the court has the same proportions (2.1) as the courts of the wilderness tabernacle (c. 50 × 25 m; Exod. 27.9-19).

Humbert has further complicated his proposal by suggesting that shortly after the construction of this north-western court the worship centre was moved to the southern side of the site (Locus 77), a room which R. de Vaux, the principal archaeologist of Qumran, had identified as a dining room. Locus 77 is a large room measuring 22 × 4.5 m. If Humbert is right, it is worth noting that this new cultic site does not correspond with any of the scriptural measurements for the tabernacle and its courts. It must be said that among experts the clear identification of any part of the Qumran site with parts of the tabernacle or Temple or their practices remains very much a minority opinion.[12]

3. *The First Temple*

The Temple built by Solomon is assumed in several non-biblical compositions, sectarian and otherwise. This is not the place to rehearse all the references in detail, but by reading between the lines it is clear that the First Temple was evidently understood, with obvious use of hindsight, as essentially flawed. The sixth week in the Enochic *Apocalypse of Weeks*, preserved in Qumran's Cave 4, implies that the failure of the First Temple rests in the way the godless forsook wisdom:

> And thereafter, in the Sixth Week, all in it will become blind, and the hearts of all of them shall godlessly forsake wisdom. And in it a man shall ascend; and at its close, the House of dominion shall be burnt with fire, and in it the whole people (and) the captains of the host shall be dispersed (*1 En.* 93.8). (Black 1985: 86)

12. This is discussed further below, but the majority opinion that there was no animal sacrifice at Qumran has been freshly put by Magness 2002: 105-33.

The text does not display any sympathy for those who had abused the First Temple. The lack of sympathy for the fate of the First Temple may continue to be represented in the type of Judaism to be found in those groups that identified with at least some part of the Enochic view of things.[13]

At Qumran, this seems to be most obviously the case in the exposition of the oracle of Nathan in 4Q174. It is most likely that the multivalent exegesis of the oracle refers in part at least to the First Temple. It was doomed to be surrounded by enemies and eventually destroyed by them: 'And strangers shall lay it waste no more, as they formerly laid waste the Sanctuary of Israel because of its sin'. Although M.O. Wise (1994: 184), for one, has suggested that the reference here is to both the First and Second Temples, it does not seem to me that from the perspective of the author of 4Q174 it is possible to construe the destruction of the First Temple as of a similar sort with the Seleucid occupation of the Temple in 167 BCE or even the Roman entry into the sanctuary in 63 BCE. I remain of the opinion that the referent of 'sanctuary of Israel' in 4Q174 is the First Temple.

However, for completeness' sake, it is also important to recognize that in some places a clear reference to the First Temple in a scriptural source was understood eschatologically. In the *Habakkuk Commentary*, Hab. 2.20, which asserts that the Lord is in his holy Temple, is interpreted eschatologically and made to refer to the Day of Judgment: 'But on the Day of Judgment, God will destroy from the earth all idolatrous and wicked men'. W.H. Brownlee (1979: 215-17) notes the insightful suggestion that the correspondence between the text and interpretation rests in an *'al tiqre'*: in place of *hêkal* in the verse of Habakkuk, the interpreter reads *y^{e}kalleh*, 'will destroy'. But in the context of the Day of Judgment it is clear that the presence of God in the Temple must be read eschatologically, not as a reference to the First temple of Habakkuk which God had long since abandoned.

4. *The Second Temple*

The Second Temple appears in some early sectarian literature to have some valid status.[14] As already mentioned, it seems as if the *Damascus Document*, which we may take to be essentially a composition from the late second century BCE recognizes the basic worth of the Temple, through permitting members to sacrifice there, but it attacks vehemently those connected with running it. On the basis of Isa. 24.17, 'terror, and the pit and the snare are upon you, O inhabitants of the land', Israel's sins are identified as fornication, riches, and profanation of the Temple (CD 4.12-19). To all intents and purposes all three sins may be suitably linked with the Temple, since all three areas involve acts that transgress the distinction between clean and unclean in some way.

4QMMT also supposes that there is still some hope for the Temple as it stands. The composition, probably to be dated to a similar period as the *Damascus Document*, and like the *Damascus Document* also preserved in much later

13. On the complex relationship between the Qumran community and so-called Enochic Judaism, see for heuristic purposes the historical developments described by Boccaccini 1998.

14. A brief overview of what can be known about the Second Temple and its Herodian continuation is outlined in Grabbe 2000: 129-49.

'Herodian' manuscript copies in Cave 4, argues that it is certain laws concerning ritual purity, the role of priests and the sacrificial practices of the Temple that require attention. The dialogical stance of the composition implies that its authors still consider the situation redeemable. However, if the *Temple Scroll* is to be dated to the same period and is in some way to be associated with the cultic reforms of John Hyrcanus,[15] then it is clear that more was at stake for the sectarians than MMT suggests and that Hyrcanus's reforms of the Temple fell far short of what they might have been hoping for. The existence of copies of MMT in 'Herodian' hands also implies that the issues discussed at the time of the break with the Jerusalem Temple were revisited from time to time by members of the community, perhaps at times when there seemed to be the possibility of genuine reform and reconstruction, such as with Herod.

Overall, for the community that resided at Qumran, as for the authors of the *Apocalypse of Weeks*, Daniel and *Jubilees* (all of which are represented in the Qumran library), the problem of the Second Temple rested with those who were running it. The Jerusalem priests and their advisors were the principal causes of the pollution of the Temple, from their otiose calendar to their inept sacrificial procedures, from their usurpation of traditional priestly prerogatives to their insufficient stringency in matters of purity.

5. *The Temple Plan*

The most complete exemplar of the *Temple Scroll* ($11QT^a$) is considered to be in an 'Herodian' hand and so almost certainly belongs to the latter half of the first century BCE or even a little later. Although the *Temple Scroll* may merely reflect general priestly (even Sadducaean) concerns, the significance of such a dating for how the copying out or republication of this elaborate composition might have been an attempt to influence the rebuilding of the Temple being undertaken by Herod will be considered briefly in a later section of this study. The second exemplar from cave 11, $11QT^b$, is generally acknowledged to be in a Hasmonaean hand and so to belong to a previous generation, indicating that the composition certainly antedates the Herodian period. In fact, many scholars have found Y. Yadin's (1983: 386-90) initial arguments concerning the date of the compilation of the scroll persuasive, though there is still room to debate the date and character of the sources that have been used by the redactor or redactors of the compilation. Yadin's key arguments depend upon his recognition that several of the structures described in the *Temple Scroll* also seem to have been part of John Hyrcanus's programme of Temple reorganization, as has already been hinted, which he undertook as part of a wider project of cultic reform and centralization, the most renowned element of which was the destruction of the temple on Mt Gerizim.

The *Temple Scroll*'s Temple plan may have been put together in part to influence John Hyrcanus and as such it may have been partially successful, just as the arguments of MMT may not have fallen entirely on deaf ears. It seems as if there might have been some agreement about some of the Temple's particular

15. As argued by Yadin 1983: 388.

structures, such as the place of slaughter, but that on matters such as the calendar, which permeates the presentation of the festivals in the *Temple Scroll*, there remained a chasm between the composition's redactors and those actually in charge in the Temple.

What Temple does the *Temple Scroll* describe? It seems as if the redactors are acutely aware that nowhere in the Torah is there a description of the way in which the Temple should be built. There may be no surprise at that, since God himself seems to have been against the whole idea until the rise of the monarchy, if the story of Samuel–Kings is to be believed. The *Temple Scroll* seems to contain the plan for the Temple that never was. It was probably envisaged as describing what Solomon's Temple should have looked like, but certainly did not. It filled the role of the plan referred to in 1 Chron. 28.11-19 (NRSV):

> Then David gave his son Solomon the plan of the vestibule of the temple, and of its houses, its treasuries, its upper rooms, and its inner chambers, and of the room for the mercy seat; and the plan of all that he had in mind: for the courts of the house of the Lord, all the surrounding chambers, the treasuries of the house of God, and the treasuries for dedicated gifts; for the divisions of the priests and of the Levites, and all the work of the service in the house of the Lord; for all the vessels for the service in the house of the Lord... 'All this, in writing at the Lord's direction, he made clear to me—the plan of all the works'.

This Temple plan may have its counterpart in heaven, but that is not clearly stated anywhere. Because of the date of its redaction, the *Temple Scroll* can also be taken as being what the Second Temple should have looked like but certainly did not. Later on it could have been what some members of the Qumran community hoped the Herodian reconstruction of the Temple would look like, but again their hopes were unfulfilled.

It is important also to remember that the Temple in the *Temple Scroll*'s major parts is not the eschatological Temple, since the editorial section in column 29 mentions the sanctuary which God himself will establish on the day of creation. The *Temple Scroll* thus really refers to two Temples: the first and most fully described is that which should have been built but never was, neither by Solomon nor by the returnees from exile, neither by Hyrcanus nor by Herod; the second is that which God himself will ultimately create.

6. *The Community as Temple*

Several valuable studies have contributed to the better understanding of how the Qumran community or the movement of which it was a part envisaged itself as a temple community.[16] Briefly put, there seem to have been at least three stages in the community's growing self-awareness in this regard.

In the book of *Jubilees* attention is given to the phrase kingdom of priests and a holy nation (Exod. 19.5-6) at certain key junctures (*Jub*. 16.18; 33.20), though in the end it is the descendants of Levi who are singled out for priestly preferment. Nevertheless, there is recognition that the priesthood can be identified with

16. Most of these studies take their cue from the landmark study by Gärtner 1965.

all of Israel and that like the angels of the Presence and the angels of sanctification who alone keep the Sabbath (*Jub.* 2.18), so Israel alone of all the nations is commanded to keep the Sabbath. For the author of *Jubilees*, as C.T.R. Hayward (1996: 87) comments, through the mark of circumcision 'there is to be a complete correspondence between Israel on earth and the two highest orders of angels in heaven'. The normative status given to what is written in the heavenly tablets results in the acknowledgment of something normative apart from the Torah and its interpreters in Jerusalem. Here may lie the seeds of a community that saw itself as more closely aligned with the divine purposes as practised in heaven than were those of other Jews.

These seeds grow into plants in the expressions of the *Community Rule* where we encounter the well-known passage:

> When these are in Israel, the Council of the Community shall be established in truth. It shall be an Everlasting Plantation, a House of Holiness for Israel, an Assembly of Supreme Holiness for Aaron. They shall be witnesses to the truth at the Judgement, and shall be the elect of Goodwill who shall atone for the Land and pay to the wicked their reward. It shall be that tried wall, that *precious corner-stone*, whose foundations shall neither rock nor sway in their place (Isa. xxviii, 16). It shall be a Most Holy Dwelling for Aaron, with everlasting knowledge of the Covenant of justice, and shall offer up sweet fragrance. It shall be a House of Perfection and Truth in Israel that they may establish a Covenant according to the everlasting precepts (1QS 8.5–10). (Vermes 1998: 109)

The language of this passage allows for a transfer primarily from garden to house, perhaps from the kind of view espoused in the remnant theology of *1 Enoch* and narrated for all Israel in the portrayal of Eden as a sanctuary to the construction of a community set apart in a house and dwelling. The chief characteristic of such a house is its inhabitants and chief among those are its priesthood. In the *Damascus Document*, the *Rule of the Congregation*, and the form of the *Community Rule* found in 1QS the priesthood (the sons of Zadok) has a pre-eminent place in all manner of matters concerning the governance and worship of the community.

While priests remain necessary, in a third stage there seems to have been a rediscovery of the Torah's equal insistence on the priesthood of the whole people of God (Exod. 19.6); there is room for a greater stress on the laicization of priestly ideals, just as the various Cave 4 recensions of the *Community Rule* encourage some scholars to suppose that there was a move away from Zadokite hierarchy to some form of more egalitarian organization.[17] In 4Q174 the oracle of Nathan is interpreted of the community as well. 4Q174 is the sole exemplar for the composition it contains; this might well suggest a late first century BCE date of composition. The key passage depends upon a development of the pun on the word house in 2 Samuel: it refers both to the Temple and also to the messianic offspring of David.

I have argued elsewhere (Brooke 1996, 1999) that the polyvalence of the imagery used in 4Q174 fragment 1, ll. 6-7, should be accepted with little hesitation: 'And he commanded to build for himself a *miqdaš 'ādām* to offer him in it,

17. For details see Brooke 1996.

before him, deeds of thanksgiving'.[18] There is a range of word plays in this exegetical composition: the ambiguity of *miqdaš 'ādām* is its reference both to the Edenic sanctuary of Adam and to the human sanctuary of the community, and the offering of deeds of thanksgiving allows for readers to see the requirement upon them both of right worship and right action ('deeds of the law'). I have already noted that the house in Nathan's oracle is referred to both the Davidic house and also to the eschatological sanctuary of which the community is an anticipation, not least inasmuch as it recalls the Edenic sanctuary where Adam worshipped: the *miqdaš 'ādām* is not just a human temple, a sanctuary made up of men, but a community summoned to live out Adam's cultic calling in the last days. In a single phrase is all of the community's *Urzeit und Endzeit* theology.[19]

When one considers these various references to the community as temple, it emerges that there is a development in the idea that corresponds closely with what we noted in the introductory remarks about the way the various forms of the *Community Rule* may best be understood. It seems at least that from idealized beginnings, something institutional emerged which was gradually transformed into something less hierarchical and more inclusive (at least of men). At every stage in the more explicit sectarian self-understanding the language of the temple could be readily applied to the community itself.

7. *Herod's Temple*

There is no clear reference to Herod's rebuilding programme in any of the scrolls found in the collection at Qumran. It is also well known that the relationship between the Essenes and Herod is difficult to define. It can be argued in line with information in Josephus (*Ant.* 15.373-79) that Herod was favourably disposed towards the Essenes, not least because of the predictions of a certain Essene named Menahem, and that during the supposed abandonment of the site at Qumran, they were able to go about their business unhindered by any form of official persecution.

If such was the case, then it would seem improbable that the Qumran Essenes would not have had some views on or even active engagement with Herod's Temple rebuilding programme. Given the likely 'Herodian' date of the manuscript 11QT[a], a plausible case can be made that such views are to be found in the way in which the lengthy *Temple Scroll* was republished at approximately the time that Herod's rebuilding programme began, perhaps in an attempt to influence what was taking place. It is almost certainly no accident that some of the dimensions and proportions of the Temple courts as listed in the scroll seem to be reflected in the actual dimensions of Herod's Temple.[20] Nevertheless, it is clear

18. There is ongoing debate over whether one should read *ma'ᵃśê tôrâ*, 'works of the law', or *ma'ᵃśê tôdâ*, 'works of thanksgiving', as that which the community offers up. I prefer reading *ma'ᵃśê tôdâ*, that the offering of the community is 'works of thanksgiving', but the striking force of the phrase depends not least upon its readers or hearers perceiving the play on the common idiom *ma'ᵃśê tôrâ*. For detailed discussion of the passage see Kuhn 1994: 202-13.

19. See the elaboration of this in Brooke 1999.

20. See the detailed study by Maier 1989.

that Herod's engineers did not follow the design of the *Temple Scroll* throughout their project; indeed they could not, because of the vast dimensions of the outer court.

Josephus describes how Herod, trying to convince the general population of the integrity of his project, was concerned that building in the sanctuary area should be undertaken by those of suitable priestly pedigree:

> Herod prepared a thousand wagons to carry the stones, selected ten thousand of the most skilled workmen, purchased priestly robes for a thousand priests, and trained some as masons, others as carpenters, and began the construction only after all these preparations had diligently been made by him. (*Ant.* 15.390)

Perhaps some priestly members of the Essene movement were part of this mass group of worker-priests. Whatever the case, the differences between Herod's project and the divinely expressed aspirations of the Qumran group and its wider movement are clearly apparent. If there had been any close encounter between some Essenes and Herod's project, a measure of disillusionment would probably have set in early. Such disillusion might have found its outlet in various ways, by becoming refocused on heavenly worship or redirected eschatologically.

8. *The Heavenly Temple*

As I have already noted, the manuscript evidence for the book of *Jubilees* suggests that it was of influence among the Qumran Essenes or their parent movement throughout the two centuries before the fall of the Temple. It is likely that it was being copied at Qumran during the first century BCE. Its ideology asserts that Israel's true worship is a reflection of the worship of the angels of the Presence and the angels of sanctification, the two classes of angels who alone keep Sabbath with God in heaven (*Jub.* 2.18). At the least there is some kind of correspondence between what was taking place in heaven and the kinds of worship that were being offered on earth. Yet the perspective of the human practices described in *Jubilees* remains earthly; two other compositions provide a clearer glimpse of things in heaven, the Aramaic *New Jerusalem* texts and the more clearly sectarian composition, the *Songs of the Sabbath Sacrifice*, though only the latter seems to speak explicitly of the heavenly Temple

Intriguingly, the manuscript remains of the *Songs of the Sabbath Sacrifice* are exclusively late Hasmonaean or Herodian in date. Although there can be no certainty, it seems to me that there is nothing that requires the composition of the Songs before the middle of the first century BCE. As such, the songs are confirmation of the ongoing and developing interest in some circles in angelic worship. While *Jubilees* envisages heavenly worship with an earthly counterpart, the *Songs of the Sabbath Sacrifice* is less two-sided. It is unclear whether the *Songs* envisage the spiritual transportation of the worshipper to heaven as participant or observer,[21] or whether they encourage earthly worshippers through their attention

21. Cf. García Martínez 1999: 184: 'The complexity and structured organization of the heavenly world that we find in the apocalypses are represented also in the Scrolls, which add a most notable element: the idea that the angels are already living among the members of the community. The

to the sovereignty of God to bring heaven to earth, as argued by D. Dimant (1996: 101): the Qumran 'community aimed at creating on earth a replica of the heavenly world'. Whatever the case,[22] together with the way in which the *Songs of the Sabbath Sacrifice* may compensate for the lack of participation in the worship of the physical Temple in Jerusalem, so their strong focus on the cultic recognition of divine kingship is possibly a positive assertion of the authority of the priesthood as well as an antidote to failed models of kingship on earth, whether that of the Hasmonaeans or of Herod, as well as a provocative comment against those who might put too much hope on a Davidic messiah: the kingship of God as a focus of adoration is more important than attention to any figure who might act as an agent in establishing a kingdom, complete with all of its political machinations and bureaucratic trimmings.

9. *The Qumran Site as Tabernacle/Temple*

If the ongoing and renewed interest in the heavenly Temple was a dominant feature of Qumran ideology in the second half of the first century BCE, then it may have had a counterpart on earth, as Dimant has suggested. In considering the role of the wilderness tabernacle in sectarian Temple ideology, I have already mentioned the reconsideration of the archaeological remains at Qumran by J.-B. Humbert. Whether or not there was a written plan behind the reordering of Qumran, there has been an ongoing minority concern to argue for the practice of animal sacrifices at the Qumran site, thus making it an Essene cultic centre.

Humbert's elaborate proposals are based on his view that when the Essenes occupied Qumran sometime in the middle of the first century BCE, they constructed a court for a sacrificial cult in the north-west of the site oriented towards Jerusalem. Shortly thereafter this cultic site was moved to the southern side of the site. The principal evidence for this rests in a particular interpretation of the pillars in Locus 77 and the interpretation of the location of the small deposits of animal bones in particular places, rather than throughout the site.

Was animal sacrifice practised at Qumran? The majority view, summarized neatly by J. Magness (2002: 105-33), is that there may well have been sacred meals there, but that no animal sacrifice took place at Qumran.[23] The community may have thought of itself as a human sanctuary, a *miqdaš 'ādām*, and some of its compositions may suggest that it believed its worship to be a performance in which humans and angels are joined together in common worship: 'when performing their own liturgy of praise-offerings, the community members also consciously share in that of the highest angels' (Frennesson 1999: 100). Nevertheless, there is no conclusive evidence that the Qumran site itself should be

fellowship with the angels is not restricted to the future but is a reality also of the present and allows participation in the liturgy of the heavenly temple.'

22. A possible third way, that 'the cult is a microcosm of the universe within which the demarcation of sacred space on earth creates an arena within which the human worshippers can participate in the life of heaven', is outlined by Fletcher-Louis 2002: 391; he believes there is no evidence for early Jewish belief in a heavenly Temple.

23. On the possibility that an incense altar was found at Qumran see Elgvin and Pfann 2002.

understood as a cultic centre where there was an alternative sacrificial practice.[24] Rather, as D. Falk (2003) has outlined, the many prayer texts found at Qumran suggest that some of the practices of prayer associated with the Temple in Jerusalem were adapted for use at Qumran. Something similar took place with the development of later synagogue practice. In this way, the prayers from Qumran indicate that cultic life at Qumran was probably more akin to the more democratic ways of synagogues than it was to the hierarchical sacrificial activities of the Temple in Jerusalem.[25] Furthermore, the cultic life of Qumran was probably not that different from that practised by local Essene groups whose activities in particular places may have merited the designation 'house of prostration' (CD 11.21–12.1).

10. *The Temple Not Made with Hands*[26]

Perhaps the earliest reference in the sectarian scrolls to an eschatological Temple of divine origin is to be found in the *Temple Scroll*. In the editorial passage in col. 29, which sums up the offerings which Israel will bring, God says

> I shall accept them and they shall be my people and I shall be for them for ever. I will dwell with them for ever and ever and will sanctify my sanctuary by my glory. I will cause my glory to rest on it until the day of creation on which I shall create my sanctuary, establishing it for myself for all time according to the covenant which I have made with Jacob in Bethel. (Vermes 1998: 200)[27]

Although the correct reading of these lines has been disputed, the emerging consensus would subscribe to the translation given here in which it seems clear that the passage envisages two Temples, the one I have already discussed which remains a pipe-dream, that is, the Temple which should have been constructed but never was, and the one which God has still to create for himself according to the covenant which was made with Jacob at Bethel. This future Temple, not made with hands, is heaven on earth. It seems also to be referred to in 4Q174 where the most likely reconstruction of fragment 1, ll. 2-3 is:

> This (2 Sam. 7.10) refers to the house which he will establish for himself in the last days, as it is written in the book of Moses: The Temple of the Lord, your hands will establish. The Lord will reign for ever and ever. (Exod. 15.17-18)

At different times the community looked to the establishment of a Temple by God himself so that there might be an ultimate remedy for all of Israel's failed attempts at providing a place for the whole of creation in microcosm to celebrate the sovereignty of God.

24. A similar point concerning the spiritualization of the idea of the Temple and its practices is made in the intriguing study by F. Schmidt (1994); he speaks imaginitively of living without the Temple and the move from altar to table.

25. As is contextualized by Binder 1999: 59-63.

26. Helpful comments on the contemporary occurrences of the idea are found in Sweet 1991.

27. The significance in this passage of the covenant with Jacob for identifying the priestly group whose interests are served by such a statement has been described by Rapp 2001: 69-89.

3. *Conclusion*

This quick overview of ten Temples has shown at least two things. First, at any one time the sectarian movement that is best represented by the Qumran community had several aspects to its Temple ideology. For example, at the same time as some community members were arguing for the reform of the Second Temple, others were propounding views which meant that no reform, however sweeping, could satisfy the divine demands as the community understood them.

Second, there seems to be a series of stages in the developing and changing use of Temple language and Temple ideology. Perhaps somewhat idealistic in the immediate aftermath of the Maccabaean successes, an idealism which led to several attempts to reform the actual Temple edifice and its managers, at some time towards the end of the second century BCE the community came to reject the Temple and establish itself as a viable spiritual alternative. Nevertheless, it seems as if Jerusalem was never far away, and two generations later Herod's rebuilding programme may have stimulated renewed interest in the actual Temple. However, perhaps thwarted ambitions in that respect were swiftly compensated by greater attention being given to the community's participation in the worship of the angels and the recollection that only God could and would ultimately create a sanctuary as a worthy dwelling place. All that was anticipated by the community, which may have thought of itself as being the only group which could supply the fully qualified priests to staff such an eschatological edifice; as such it thought of itself as an anticipation of the restored cultic glory of Adam, a *miqdaš ʾādām.*

BIBLIOGRAPHY

Alexander, P.S.
1996 'The Redaction-History of *Serekh ha-Yaḥad*', *RevQ* 17: 437-56.

Baumgarten, J.M.
1997 'Purification after Childbirth and the Sacred Garden in 4Q265 and Jubilees', in Brooke with García Martínez (eds.) 1997: 3-10.

Berges, U.
2002 'Gottesgarten und Tempel: Die neue Schöpfung im Jesajabuch', in O. Keel and E. Zenger (eds.), *Gottesstadt und Gottesgarten: zu Geschichte und Theologie des Jerusalemer Tempels* (QD, 191; Freiburg: Herder): 69-98.

Binder, D.D.
1999 *Into the Temple Courts: The Place of the Synagogues in the Second Temple Period* (SBLDS, 169; Atlanta: Scholars Press).

Black, M.
1985 *The Book of Enoch or I Enoch: A New English Edition* (SVTP, 7; Leiden: E.J. Brill).

Boccaccini, G.
1998 *Beyond the Essene Hypothesis: The Parting of the Ways between Qumran and Enochic Judaism* (Grand Rapids: Eerdmans).

Brooke, G.J.
1994 'Isaiah 40.3 and the Wilderness Community', in Brooke with García Martínez (eds.) 1994: 117-32.

1996 'From "Assembly of Supreme Holiness for Aaron" to "Sanctuary of Adam": the Laicization of Temple Ideology in the Qumran Scrolls and its Wider Implications', *Journal for Semitics* 8.2: 119-45.

1998 'Kingship and Messianism in the Dead Sea Scrolls', in J. Day (ed.), *King and Messiah in Israel and the Ancient Near East: Proceedings of the Oxford Old Testament Seminar* (JSOTSup, 270; Sheffield: Sheffield Academic Press): 434-56.

1999 'Miqdash Adam, Eden and the Qumran Community', in B. Ego, A. Lange and P. Pilhofer (eds.), *Gemeinde ohne Tempel—Community without Temple: Zur Substituierung und Transformation des Jerusalemer Tempels und seines Kultes im Alten Testament, antiken Judentum und frühen Christentum* (WUNT, 118; Tübingen: Mohr Siebeck): 285-301.

Brooke, G.J., with F. García Martínez (eds.)

1994 *New Qumran Texts and Studies: Proceedings of the First Meeting of the International Organization for Qumran Studies, Paris 1992* (STDJ, 15; Leiden: E.J. Brill).

Brownlee, W.H.

1979 *The Midrash Pesher of Habakkuk* (SBLMS, 24; Missoula, MT: Scholars Press).

Dimant, D.

1996 'Men as Angels: The Self-Image of the Qumran Community', in A. Berlin (ed.), *Religion and Politics in the Ancient Near East* (Studies and Texts in Jewish History and Culture; Bethesda, MD: University Press of Maryland): 93-103.

Elgvin, T., in collaboration with S.J. Pfann

2002 'An Incense Altar from Qumran', *Dead Sea Discoveries* 9: 20-33.

Falk, D.

2003 'Qumran and the Synagogue Liturgy', in B. Olsson and M. Zetterholm (eds.), *The Ancient Synagogue from its Origins until 200 C.E.: Papers Presented at an International Conference at Lund University, October 14–17, 2001* (ConBNT, 39; Stockholm: Almqvist & Wiksell International): 404-34.

Fletcher-Louis, C.H.T.

2002 *All the Glory of Adam: Liturgical Anthropology in the Dead Sea Scrolls* (STDJ, 42; Leiden: Brill).

Frennesson, B.

1999 *'In a Common Rejoicing': Liturgical Communion with Angels in Qumran* (Studia Semitica Upsaliensia, 14; Uppsala: Uppsala University).

García Martínez, F.

1999 'Apocalypticism in the Dead Sea Scrolls', in J.J. Collins (ed.), *The Origins of Apocalypticism in Judaism and Christianity* (Encyclopedia of Apocalypticism, 1; New York: Continuum): 162-92.

Gärtner, B.

1965 *The Temple and the Community in Qumran and the New Testament: A Comparative Study in the Temple Symbolism of the Qumran Texts and the New Testament* (SNTMS, 1; Cambridge: Cambridge University Press).

Grabbe, L.L.

2000 *Judaic Religion in the Second Temple Period: Belief and Practice from the Exile to Yavneh* (London: Routledge).

Hayward, C.T.R.

1996 *The Jewish Temple: A Non-Biblical Sourcebook* (London: Routledge).

Humbert, J.-B.

1994 'L'espace sacré à Qumrân: propositions pour l'archéologie', *RB* 101: 161-214.

Koester, C.R.
1989 *The Dwelling of God: The Tabernacle in the Old Testament, Intertestamental Jewish Literature, and the New Testament* (CBQMS, 22; Washington, DC: Catholic Biblical Association of America).

Kuhn, H.-W.
1994 'Die Bedeutung der Qumrantexte für das Verständnis des Galaterbriefs aus dem Münchener Projekt: Qumran und das Neue Testament', in Brooke with García Martínez (eds.) 1994: 169-221.

Longenecker, B.W.
1998 'The Wilderness and Revolutionary Ferment in First-Century Palestine', *JSJ* 29: 322-36.

Magness, J.
2002 *The Archaeology of Qumran and the Dead Sea Scrolls* (Studies in the Dead Sea Scrolls and Related Literature; Grand Rapids: Eerdmans).

Maier, J.
1989 'The Architectural History of the Temple in Jerusalem in the Light of the Temple Scroll', in G.J. Brooke (ed.), *Temple Scroll Studies: Papers Presented at the International Symposium on the Temple Scroll, Manchester, December 1987* (JSPSup, 7; Sheffield: JSOT Press): 23-62.

Metso, S.
1997 *The Textual Development of the Qumran Community Rule* (STDJ, 21; Leiden: Brill).

Meyers, C.
1992 'Temple, Jerusalem', in *ABD*, VI: 350-69.

Oegema, G.
1994 *Der Gesalbte und sein Volk: Untersuchungen zum Konzeptualisierungsprozeß der messianischen Erwartungen von den Makkabäern bis Bar Koziba* (Schriften des Institutum Judaicum Delitzschianum, 2; Göttingen: Vandenhoeck & Ruprecht).

Rapp, H.A.
2001 *Jakob in Bet-El: Gen 35,1–15 und die jüdische Literatur des 3. und 2. Jahrhunderts* (Herders biblische Studien, 29; Freiburg: Herder).

Schmidt, F.
1994 *La pensée du Temple. De Jérusalem à Qoumrân: Identité et lien social dans le judaïsme ancien* (Paris: Editions du Seuil).

Starcky, J.
1963 'Les quatre étapes du messianisme à Qumrân', *RB* 70: 481-505.

Sweet, J.P.M.
1991 'A House Not Made with Hands', in W. Horbury (ed.), *Templum Amicitiae: Essays on the Second Temple presented to Ernst Bammel* (JSNTSup, 48; Sheffield: JSOT Press): 368-90.

VanderKam, J.C.
1977 *Textual and Historical Studies in the Book of Jubilees* (HSM, 14; Missoula, MT: Scholars Press).

Vermes, G.
1998 *The Complete Dead Sea Scrolls in English* (London: Penguin Books).

Wintermute, O.S.
1985 'Jubilees: A New Translation and Introduction', in *OTP*, II: 35-142.

Wise, M.O.
1994 *Thunder in Gemini and Other Essays on the History, Language and Literature of Second Temple Palestine* (JSPSup, 15; Sheffield: JSOT Press).

Xeravits, G.G.
2002 *King, Priest, Prophet: Positive Eschatological Protagonists of the Qumran Library* (STDJ, 47; Leiden: Brill).

Yadin, Y.
1983 *The Temple Scroll*. I. *Introduction* (Jerusalem: Israel Exploration Society, Hebrew University of Jerusalem, Shrine of the Book).

Zimmermann, J.
1998 *Messianische Texte aus Qumran: Königliche, priesterliche und prophetische Messiasvorstellungen in den Schriftfunden von Qumran* (WUNT, 2.104; Tübingen: Mohr Siebeck).

New Voices, Ancient Words: The *Temple Scroll*'s Reuse of the Bible*

Molly M. Zahn

1. *Introduction*

The nature of the *Temple Scroll* (*TS*) is inherently paradoxical. It claims for itself the highest possible sanctity, primacy, and authority—revelation by God to Moses on Sinai. Yet the contents of *TS* are far from unmediated revelation, since much of the Scroll consists of the author's unique reinterpretation of the Pentateuchal legal corpus. Indeed, there is hardly any point in the Scroll where a biblical source of some kind does not lie close at hand. Starting with Yadin's magisterial *editio princeps*,[1] this constant interaction with the Bible has been a focal point of *TS* research. Numerous publications have exponentially increased our understanding of *TS* and the stance of its author with regard to the Bible.[2] It seems, however, that one significant issue involving *TS*'s relationship to the Bible has remained essentially unexplored. In an important early study, Brin observes that the Scroll's continual use of the Bible was intended to make the Scroll appear ancient and authoritative (Brin 1980: 214, 224). Despite this groundbreaking assertion, subsequent studies that examine the Scroll's legal exegesis have given little attention to the paradox of *TS*'s self-presentation. The focus on the Scroll's reuse and reinterpretation of the Bible has tended to obscure the very important fact that the Scroll does not see itself as interpretative or secondary. Instead, it claims to be original, primary law, revealed by God at Sinai. The significance of this claim to the composition of the Scroll, including its reworking of the Bible, should not be overlooked. I would like to argue in this study that the attribution of *TS* to divine revelation has a direct impact on the author's use of the biblical text. The dynamics of the Scroll's use of the Bible cannot properly be understood without taking seriously the Scroll's denial of its interpretative status, and its claim instead to represent the direct word of God.

* The impetus for this article came primarily from work done for a joint article with Bernard Levinson (Minnesota), for whose collaboration in that project and valuable comments on this piece I am most grateful. I would also like to thank John Barton (Oxford), Peter Grund (Uppsala), and Kevin Cathcart (Dublin) for their many comments and suggestions.

1. The original Hebrew edition, *Mᵉgîllat hammiqdāš*, appeared in 1977. Cited in this study is the expanded English translation, Yadin 1977–83.

2. See especially Brin 1980; Kaufman 1982; Wise 1990; Swanson 1995; and the many article-length works of Lawrence Schiffman.

In what follows, I will explore the relationship between *TS*'s use of the Bible and its claim to be Sinaitic. I will first discuss the goal of the author, which in my view was to present an authoritative new version of Sinaitic Torah. I will then take up the important scholarly debate as to how the Scroll's claim to authority should be understood. Next, I will show how the author's reuse of the Bible is not disconnected from the authority claim, but actually advances that claim. An analysis of the most innovative portions of the Scroll, especially the Temple Plan, will demonstrate that the author's extensive reuse of the Bible does not imply that his innovations were merely extrapolations of the biblical text. They were instead independent conceptions that the author phrased in biblical language in order to enhance their authority. Finally, I will examine the implications of *TS*'s use of the Bible for our ideas of revelation, authority, and canon in late Second Temple Judaism.[3]

2. *The Author's Goal: A New Torah*

2.1. *The Problem of the Redacted Pentateuch*

Like much of the interpretative work carried out in the Second Temple and rabbinic periods, *TS* in some fundamental way responds to the problem of the redacted Pentateuch (Levinson and Zahn 2002: 307). On the one hand, the Torah was regarded as the perfect, essential, and incontrovertible expression of God's will to the people of Israel. On the other hand, the Pentateuch as it stood was manifestly an imperfect text, full of ambiguous, contradictory, and repetitive laws. There was thus a substantial gap between the assertions made about the Torah by Second Temple Jews and the reality of the textual artifact itself. The centrality of Torah in Jewish life made exegetical attempts to fill this gap almost inevitable.[4] Such attempts, in the form of rearrangement, clarification, or amplification of the biblical legislation, can be seen in Qumran texts like the *Damascus Document* and 4QMMT as well as in Philo, Josephus, and the Mishnah. Precisely the same concern underlies much of *TS*'s halakhah (Schiffman 1980: 150). Alongside innovations like the plan for a monumental Temple complex and extensive legislation on kingship, the author responds to the canonical Torah by unifying duplicate laws, reconciling contradictory laws, bringing together laws on similar subjects that are scattered throughout the Pentateuch, and clarifying ambiguous laws (Yadin 1977–83: I, 71). His attempts to make the unwieldy redacted Pentateuch readable are in many ways no different from similar attempts by his Second Temple contemporaries.[5]

3. The date of *TS* has been disputed, but the most plausible suggestion places its composition c. 200–150 BCE. For balanced discussions, see García Martínez 1999: 440-44; Crawford 2000: 24-26.

4. On the need for interpretation that arose as the Pentateuch increased in authority and sanctity, see Kugel 1986: 27-39, 67-68, 71; 1997: 3-23; see also Kister 1992: 573.

5. Rearrangement of the biblical laws so as to group them according to topic is evidenced by Philo (*Exposition of the Law*; see Amir 1988: 424-25) and Josephus (*Antiquities*, books 3 and 4; see Altschuler 1982–83: 3-5). This is similar to the topical presentation of legislation in the *Damascus Document* (Baumgarten 2000: 24; Hempel 2000: 34-38) and 4QMMT (Qimron and Strugnell 1994: 147-48), as well as to the organization of the Mishnah by subject. *TS*'s procedure of intertwining

2.2. *The Authority Claim*

Although *TS*'s author shares his drive to understand the Torah as coherent with other early Jewish interpreters, he differs from them in one crucial respect. Despite the derivative nature of much of its halakhah, the Scroll purports to be original revelation, spoken by God to Moses on Mt Sinai. The author sets the stage at the very beginning of the Scroll by redeploying God's exhortation to Moses in Exodus 34. This is when, according to Exodus, Moses reascends Mt Sinai with two new tablets to replace the ones he shattered in the incident of the golden calf (Exod. 32.19). The reuse of Exodus 34 implies to the reader that the setting of *TS* is the same as that of the source text; that is, the mountain of revelation. The setting on Sinai is confirmed later on in the Scroll through reference to 'that which I declare to them on this mountain' (11QT 51.6-7). As this quotation demonstrates, the author also makes clear that God is the speaker of the Scroll's law by voicing much of the text in the first person (Yadin 1977–83: I, 71). He regularly incorporates phrases like 'I, Yahweh' (11QT 45.14) and 'the Temple where I will settle my name' (11QT 45.12). The significance of the first-person voicing becomes especially clear when the Scroll reuses material from the book of Deuteronomy. There, references to God are in the third person, since Moses is speaking to Israel. When the laws of Deuteronomy are incorporated into *TS*, however, the author systematically changes the third-person references to first-person. For example, the frequent Deuteronomic formula, 'When you come into the land that *Yahweh your God* is giving you' (e.g. Deut. 18.9) becomes 'When you come into the land that *I* am giving you' (11QT 60.16). This change is pervasive in those sections of the Scroll that draw upon Deuteronomy, and only fails to occur in a few exceptional instances.[6]

By means of the Sinaitic setting and divine voicing, the author of *TS* presents a unique response to the inconsistencies and limitations of the canonical Torah. In contrast to other interpretative works of the Second Temple period, *TS* actually replaces Torah as it goes along. While other literature identifies itself explicitly as interpretative and creates via commentary a system for reading the redacted Pentateuch as consistent, *TS* solves the problem by styling *itself* as Torah.[7] The

references to multiple biblical sources with similar content or vocabulary also finds many parallels in these texts. For example, 4QMMT B 76-79 combines Lev. 19.19 and Deut. 22.9 (Bernstein 1996: 45-46), and Josephus's laws on war (*Ant.* 4.292-301) integrate material from Deut. 20, 22, and 24 (Altschuler 1982–83: 4).

6. In contrast to the Temple Plan and the sections based on Deuteronomy, much of the legislation in the Festival Calendar (11QT 14–29) and the Purity Laws (cols. 45-51) refers to Yahweh in the third person. This variation formed one of the basic criteria for source division in the early argument that *TS* represents a compilation of discreet non-biblical literary sources; see Wilson and Wills 1982. However, Yadin has offered a much more convincing explanation of the inconsistency: the third-person reference to God occurs in material that has been culled from the Priestly legislation in the Pentateuch. Since it is clear in the Priestly texts, despite this third-person reference, that God is the speaker, the author of the Scroll saw no need to change the references to the first person. See Yadin 1977–83: I, 72. For a full critique of the very common source-critical understanding of *TS*, see Zahn 2001.

7. For a similar point, see Levine 1978: 20.

author's goal, therefore, was to produce a coherent, well-organized legal revelation, encompassing both his own innovations and his interpretation of Pentateuchal law, and to present this revelation as the word of God from Sinai.

2.3. *Pseudepigraph or Torah? The Scholarly Debate*[8]

That *TS* presents itself as direct divine revelation from Sinai has long been recognized as one of the Scroll's characteristic features. However, there has been much debate about how this divine attribution is to be understood. Two questions have become focal points in this discussion. First, does *TS* constitute an example of pseudepigraphy? Second, did the author of *TS* actually intend it to be taken as a new authoritative Torah?

In the *editio princeps* of the Scroll, Yadin continues a debate with Moshe Goshen-Gottstein that began before Yadin's initial publication. Following a public lecture in which Yadin presented *TS* and its contents, Goshen-Gottstein published an article in the Israeli newspaper *Ha-Aretz* arguing that *TS* was a 'halakhic pseudepigraph'. He maintained that it was 'inconceivable that he [the author] was of the opinion that this is a text of the Torah or that others would accept it from him'.[9] Yadin challenged this assumption, and asserted on the basis of the contents and editorial techniques of the Scroll that the author and his community did in fact regard the Scroll as 'a veritable Torah of the Lord' (Yadin 1977–83: I, 392). Therefore, he argued, *TS* is not to be regarded as pseudepigraphic: 'In my opinion there is no warrant for applying the modern concept "pseudepigraph" to a work whose author believed himself to be presenting a true Law' (Yadin 1977–83: I, 392). For both Goshen-Gottstein and Yadin, then, 'pseudepigraph' and 'Torah' are mutually exclusive.

This early debate is rooted on both sides in problematic definitions of pseudepigraphy. On the one hand, Goshen-Gottstein ruled out *a priori* the possibility that *TS* might intend its authority claim seriously, since he considered it 'inconceivable' that a non-biblical text might still be called Torah in the period in which the Scroll was composed. This reasoning is identical to that used in Goshen-Gottstein's earlier argument that the *Psalms Scroll* (11QPs[a]) could not represent a variant version of the canonical book of Psalms, since the scholarly consensus was that the form of the canonical book of Psalms was already fixed by the late Second Temple period (Goshen-Gottstein 1966: 29). Since *TS* cannot have been Torah, Goshen-Gottstein ascribes the fact that God is the text's speaker to pseudepigraphy. His label, 'halakhic pseudepigraph', seems to place the Scroll in the category of midrash halakhah; that is, secondary interpretation of revealed Torah.[10] But this understanding of the Scroll as pseudepigraph (as opposed to

8. My thinking in this section is informed by discussions with Bernard M. Levinson, July 2001.

9. Goshen-Gottstein's article (*Ha-Aretz*, 25 October 1967) is cited according to its quotation by Yadin (1977–83: I, 391).

10. Mink (1987: 46-48) similarly identifies *TS* as a pseudepigraph rather than Torah, and denies that it claims the same authority as the canonical Pentateuch. Instead, according to Mink, the Scroll is an 'example of "the found" in revealed *halakhah*' (p. 48); that is, the Scroll is the product of inspired interpretation on the part of the community, and does not compete with the law, but claims only to

Torah) means that the term 'pseudepigraph' receives an unusual definition: not simply a work attributed to someone other than its actual author, but a falsely attributed work whose attribution is nonetheless not intended to be believed. For if *TS*'s pseudepigraphic attribution to God were to be believed, then the Scroll would constitute Torah.[11] Such a definition of the term 'pseudepigraph' does not seem acceptable.[12]

Yadin, on the other hand, acknowledges that the Scroll's claim to have been revealed on Sinai was meant to be taken seriously: it was to be regarded as Torah. Despite the seriousness of the Scroll's Sinaitic claims, however, Yadin maintains that it is not to be considered pseudepigraphic. His reasoning is that the author of the Scroll actually believed that it represented divinely revealed law. Yadin here responds to a position advanced by Morton Smith with regard to the book of Deuteronomy. Smith asserts that, in modern terms, the book of Deuteronomy was 'blatant pseudepigraphy'.[13] He goes on to suggest that 'It is possible…that the Deuteronomic code was the most influential forgery in the history of the world' (Smith 1972: 208). This language points to what seems to be Yadin's real difficulty: the suggestion that *TS* or Deuteronomy might have been written with the intention to deceive; that they are forgeries or lies. Hence the response that *TS* was not a pseudepigraph: the author had no intention of deceiving his audience, since he believed that what he had written was in fact Torah. Yet Yadin, in his attempt to exculpate *TS*'s author, has provided a definition for 'pseudepigraphy' that is not only extremely subjective, but also impossible to prove. On the one hand, this definition gives 'pseudepigraphy' all sorts of negative connotations by associating it with explicit deception and forgery. On the other hand, it requires an assessment, from the historical distance of thousands of years, of whether or not the real author believed in the truth of his text's pseudepigraphic attribution. In my view, the definition of pseudepigraphy should remain objective and verifiable: pseudepigraphy is writing that is attributed to a figure who is not the real

interpret and supplement it (see also Beckwith 1997: 4). However, while the notion of inspired interpretation is clearly present at Qumran (e.g. in the pesher literature), that notion is foreign to *TS*. The Scroll claims no lateness, no secrecy, no discovery by an inspired interpreter, but rather simply asserts its priority as revelation from Sinai.

11. Schiffman (1999: 121-24) provides an excellent summary of the debate between Yadin and Goshen-Gottstein as to the status of the Scroll as a pseudepigraph and as to whether or not the Scroll was intended as Torah. After turning to a consideration of the role of Moses in the Scroll, Schiffman classifies the Scroll as a 'divine halakhic pseudepigraphon' (p. 131). However, he never returns to his opening discussion to clarify what is meant by this term. It is therefore unclear whether Schiffman intends to espouse the position of Goshen-Gottstein, whereby the Scroll is 'halakhic pseudepigraph' but not authoritative Torah, or whether he means that the Scroll does indeed represent Torah, pseudepigraphically attributed to God at Sinai.

12. See the work of Jeremy Duff, who demonstrates that pseudepigraphy in Second Temple Judaism and in early Christianity cannot be regarded as merely literary fiction or accepted convention. Rather, the available evidence indicates that pseudepigraphic attributions were intended to be believed, and indeed that they were believed. For example, Josephus clearly accepts the pseudepigraphic attribution of the book of Daniel, since he refers to its protagonist as living in the sixth century BCE, not the second (Duff 1998: 172).

13. These are Yadin's words (1977–83: I, 392).

author (see Bernstein 1999: 3). To characterize a work as pseudepigraphic should not be a value judgment, but a description of the literary setting or voicing of a text and/or an author's strategy for authorizing a text.[14]

Two other scholars have also denied that *TS* is pseudepigraphic. Moshe Bernstein correctly recognizes that *TS*'s attribution to God constitutes an authority claim. He points out that the change to the first person is a sign that the author, at some level, wanted to present the Scroll as Torah. However, according to Bernstein, the frequent retention of the third person in the Scroll means that *TS* as a whole is not a pseudepigraph:

> If the author intended to convince his audience that *TS* was the genuine word of God, he failed because he did not maintain the transformation to pseudepigraphon throughout... In my view, the composer's failure to sustain his pretense precludes us from considering the entire work as a pseudepigraphon. (Bernstein 1999: 14-15)

Bernstein seems to advance yet another problematic definition of pseudepigraphy: not only must a work claim to be written by some ancient figure, but that claim must be carried out consistently; what is more, that claim must be successful in convincing people of its sincerity. If the criterion for pseudepigrapha is that they be entirely consistent, however, we would have to reduce drastically the number of texts we classify as pseudepigrapha. Every time an author slipped into his own voice or, say, used a linguistic form common in his own time but unknown in the period in which the text purports to have been written, that text could no longer be considered pseudepigraphic.[15] Further, it does not seem that total consistency was necessary for a work's pseudepigraphic attribution to be believed. The Priestly legal texts of the Pentateuch constitute a particularly pertinent example. The book of Leviticus, for instance, is clearly presented as the words of God to Moses, yet third-person reference to God is frequent.[16] History has shown that, far from failing to convince its readers on account of this inconsistency, Leviticus has achieved its aim of being considered revealed with complete success. The same could probably be said of *TS*, which continued to be copied by the sectarians at Qumran for more than a century after its composition. That they would do this even while believing that the Scroll's Sinaitic claims were false does not seem plausible. Therefore, since the success of pseudepigraphy does not seem to have been dependent upon complete consistency, it should be reasonable to label a text pseudepigraphic simply on the basis of its claims to ancient authorship, even if the fiction thus created is imperfectly maintained.

Michael Wise has also denied that *TS* should be regarded as a pseudepigraph. He claims that the redactor 'conceived of himself as a new Moses'. Hence he 'was not writing in the name of a long-dead hero of the faith, claiming that he had discovered a lost writing which that hero had produced. Rather, his claim

14. For literary voicing as a means of granting authority to a new text, see Fishbane 1985: 257-60; 1988: 350-51; Levinson 1997: 34, 155; Najman 1999: 400-406.

15. Ironically, it is just such slip-ups—such as the anachronistic interjections in Deuteronomy—that allow scholars to identify works as pseudepigraphic in the first place.

16. Morton Smith (1972: 202) argues that these third-person references indicate a pseudepigraphic attempt to frame originally anonymous legislation as divine speech.

was to the same relationship with God that Moses had had' (Wise 1990: 200). This view, however, cannot explain the setting of the text at Sinai. The revelation at Sinai was regarded in Israelite and Jewish tradition as a single historical event, occurring in the time of Moses. By situating itself at Sinai, *TS* also sets itself into the ancient past. Thus, the author of the Scroll could not have conceived of himself as a 'new Moses' in the sense of communicating directly with God, in his own present time. Rather, he in some way regarded himself as privy to that one-time revelation that occurred long ago at Sinai. In that way, the author's claim is exactly parallel to the claims made by the authors of pseudepigraphs. Just as the authors of Enoch and Daniel claimed to have access to the divine revelations given to those ancient biblical figures, so the author of *TS* claims access to God's ancient revelation to Moses at Mt Sinai.

The confusion of terminology in the above debate has resulted in a certain degree of unclarity in the scholarly literature about how the Scroll should be regarded. In fact, it seems clear that *TS* is *both* Torah *and* pseudepigraph, as correctly seen by Levine (1978: 20; see also Swanson 1995: 6-7). Its self-presentation on Sinai and voicing in the first person mean that it is intended as divine revelation of extensive legal material. Since there is no indication that the claim to revelation is not to be taken seriously, the Scroll constitutes Torah. Since the author of the Scroll was not God, the Scroll is a pseudepigraph.[17] It should be noted that this pseudepigraphic claim to come straight from God's mouth essentially gives *TS* a higher status than the Pentateuch, since much of the Pentateuch is mediated to the people by Moses (Wacholder 1983: 31). It even trumps the book of *Jubilees*, which similarly claims to originate from Sinai, since in *Jubilees* the Angel of the Presence mediates God's words to Moses (Levinson and Zahn 2002: 307). The key questions are thus not whether the Scroll is Torah or pseudepigraph, but what precisely is meant by the pseudepigraphic claim to be Torah, what that claim implies about the Scroll's relationship to the canonical Pentateuch, and what difference that claim makes to the composition of the Scroll.

3. *Reuse of the Bible as Support for the Author's Goals*

3.1. *The Scroll's Biblical Voice*

It was mentioned in the introduction that *TS* at nearly every point draws upon a biblical source in some fashion. This constant recourse to the Bible is an integral part of the author's goal of producing an improved version of Pentateuchal law. Yet this is the case not just from a halakhic or hermeneutical perspective—because the biblical text is the source requiring exegetical modification—but because, as Brin pointed out, biblical reuse actually furthers the claims that the author makes for his composition. By redeploying the biblical text, albeit in sometimes drastically altered form, the author creates a biblical voice for the text, a voice worthy of a text that claims to have been spoken by God. This biblical

17. Note that, by this criterion, much of the Priestly source of the Pentateuch is also pseudepigraphic (Smith 1972: 200-203).

persona persists even in the sections of the Scroll that have no discernible biblical source—the redactor mimics the language of the Bible, suppressing the impulse to use linguistic forms more typical of the Hebrew of his own day (Brin 1980: 224).[18] The biblical style implicitly authorizes the text's claim to be revealed on Sinai—after all, it *sounds* like the canonical Pentateuch, that Sinaitic revelation that would have been familiar to its readers.

3.2. *Exegetical Activity as an Authorization Technique*

As shown in the previous section, the author's use of biblical language in general lends credibility to the Scroll's authority claim by granting the text a biblical voice. More specifically, however, I believe that the very act of reworking the biblical text also supports *TS*'s Sinaitic claims. The impact of the author's editorial activity upon the Scroll's presentation as divine pseudepigraph is the result of a particular idea of revelation. As mentioned above, much of the hermeneutical energy expended in the Second Temple period was directed toward solving the problem of the redacted Pentateuch: the fact that the Torah was full of inconsistencies, repetitions, and contradictions. At the root of this struggle lies the notion that scripture, almost by definition, is to be coherent; God's revelation to Israel would never contradict or repeat itself (Kugel 1997: 20; Alexander 2000: 49; Levinson and Zahn 2002: 308; see also Graham 1987: 141). This notion can be played out into the realm of pseudepigraphy: if scripture is expected to be coherent, it follows that any document that would purport to be scripture must exhibit a coherence worthy of a revealed text. On a certain level, the more coherence the text displays, the more plausible its claim becomes.

This I believe is an instructive point with regard to *TS*. The Scroll claims to be Torah. It backs up that claim by producing a coherent, well-organized legal revelation. It brings together laws on similar topics, resolves contradictions between laws, and clarifies ambiguous laws. These rearrangements themselves support *TS*'s authoritative self-presentation, since they increase the consistency and coherence of its legislation. This is especially apparent over against the canonical Torah—for while the Pentateuch is riddled with inconsistency, *TS* presents a

18. Precisely what form of Hebrew would have been natural for the author of *TS* is not easily determined. On the one hand, *TS* shares several linguistic traits with the Hebrew of the Qumran sectarian literature, including a marked tendency toward *plene* spelling, lengthened pronominal suffixes (e.g. *-kâ* for Biblical Hebrew *-kā*), and use of periphrastic verbal forms. On the other hand, several characteristics of Qumran Hebrew are absent in *TS*, such as the spelling *ky'*, the hyperarchaizing pronouns *hw'h* and *hy'h*, and much of the sect's characteristic vocabulary. Such differences support the argument that the Scroll was not composed within the Qumran community; see Schiffman 1980: 147-49; for the linguistic data, compare Yadin 1977–83: I, 25-39. Complicating the issue is the convincing argument of William Schniedewind (1999) that Qumran Hebrew was not a natural stage in the development from Late Biblical to Mishnaic Hebrew, but represented an ideologically motivated 'antilanguage', developed to demarcate the Qumran sect from the surrounding Judaisms and to support the belief that the sect represented the true Israel. As a result, it is hard to tell whether the anachronisms that interrupt the author's imitation of biblical style represent the vernacular Hebrew of the day, which probably closely resembled Mishnaic Hebrew, or an early form of the ideological language of the sect.

version of the Torah that is coherent and free of contradiction (Levinson and Zahn 2002: 308).[19]

Clearly, an objection can be raised at this point. Surely the author's labouring to rearrange and clarify the biblical text also had an halakhic function, and could not have been carried out for the sole purpose of making *TS* seem like scripture.[20] This objection is obviously valid. The author and his community must have been part of an already rich tradition of halakhic exegesis, as is shown by correspondences between the halakhah of *TS* and that of other Second Temple documents, especially the *Damascus Document*, 4QMMT, and *Jubilees*.[21] However, that the author was addressing real interpretative issues does not preclude the possibility that his exegesis also enhanced the Scroll's pseudepigraphic claim. In fact, I would argue that the halakhah of *TS* serves a twofold purpose: every move to smooth out the Torah—iron out contradictions, remove repetitions, clarify halakhic ambiguities—at once serves an interpretative or exegetical purpose and, by creating a more coherent law, bolsters the author's claim that *TS* is Sinaitic. Its halakhah is at once new law and its own pseudepigraphic authorization.

Further, however, the author's two goals—the hermeneutical goal of addressing the inconsistencies in the canonical Torah and the authorial goal of presenting his new compilation as Sinaitic law—are not identical. If my characterization is correct, there is a great amount of overlap. But if reorganization and clarification support the Scroll's pseudepigraphic claims, it is possible that certain editorial changes might serve *only* this purpose. That is, a given change might serve no discernible halakhic function. Instead, it might produce a smoother, more readable text at the purely formal level, thus enhancing the impression that *TS* is a coherent legal revelation.

If this is the case, it would have significant implications for how we understand the author's manipulation of the Bible. Specifically, it would seem to require expanding the categories currently used to classify the Scroll's departures from the biblical text. It seems that, traditionally, such departures either fall into the category of 'textual'—that is, reflecting a difference between the MT and the biblical *Vorlage* of *TS*, or the category of 'exegetical'—meaning the author's deliberate halakhic modifications.[22] Now, a third category, or perhaps a subset of

19. The importance of the Scroll's editorial activity to its authority claim challenges Wacholder's criticism of Yadin for characterizing the Scroll's purpose as primarily editorial (Wacholder 1983: 4). Wacholder understands 'editorial' to mean secondary and interpretative, and therefore accuses Yadin of failing to recognize the Scroll's challenge to and departure from the canonical Torah (p. 30). While it is true that Yadin did not place particular stress upon the Scroll's authority claim vis-à-vis the canonical Pentateuch, he did characterize the Scroll as 'a veritable Torah of the Lord' that was meant to be authoritative (1977–83: I, 392). Furthermore, Wacholder overlooks the extent to which editorial activities like harmonization and conflation actually constituted the means by which the Scroll's author constructed and supported his claim to ultimate divine authority.

20. On the interpretative/halakhic significance of the redactor's exegesis, see Schiffman 1998: 181, 187-88; also 1992a: 567.

21. For a convenient list of these extensive correspondences, see Crawford 2000: 77-82.

22. For an attempt to distinguish between these two types of changes, see Elwolde 1997. In attempting to account for 'exegetical' changes, however, Elwolde does not consider the possibility

the 'exegetical' category, should be defined, so that we can talk about 'formal' or 'literary' changes—modifications that do not appear to have any halakhic significance, but increase the literary coherence of the text.

A few examples will suffice to illustrate that this type of exegetical change does indeed occur. A clear case is found in 11QT 52. There, the author brings together three sacrificial laws from three different sources: the Deuteronomic law forbidding the sacrifice of a blemished animal (11QT 52.3-5//Deut. 17.1), the Priestly law forbidding the sacrifice of an animal and its young on the same day (11QT 52.6-7//Lev. 22.28), and the non-biblical injunction against sacrificing a pregnant animal (11QT 52.5).[23] The two biblical laws use different verbs: Deuteronomy has *zbḥ*, while Leviticus uses the normal Priestly *šḥṭ*, which never occurs in Deuteronomy. The variance reflects the distinct terminology of two different biblical sources, but this modern literary-critical explanation would have been foreign to the author of *TS*. He must have perceived the difference as needless variation. Thus, in conjoining the two laws, he also unifies the vocabulary, changing *šḥṭ* in the Leviticus law to *zbḥ* (Carr 2001: 122). Notably, he construes the intervening non-biblical law of pregnant animals with *zbḥ* as well. The author thereby erases the lexical distinctions that characterize the various Pentateuchal legal sources, and three laws from disparate sources are tied together by means of common vocabulary.[24] This process is illustrated in Fig. 1.

A similar phenomenon occurs in 11QT 48 (Brin 1987: 523-24). The column begins by discussing clean and unclean birds and insects. In the parallel text of Deuteronomy 14, this section is followed by the prohibition of consuming the meat of an animal that died of itself: 'you shall not eat any carcass' (14.21). *TS*'s author incorporates an expanded version of this phrase, but reverses the word order: 'any carcass of flying creature or land animal you shall not eat' (11QT 48.5-6). The direct source for this formulation is found in Ezekiel's Temple Vision: 'any carcass or torn flesh, whether from flying creature or land animal, the priests shall not eat' (Ezek. 44.31). *TS*'s reworking of the biblical stipulations is shown in Fig. 2.

The Scroll's reworking thus presents two departures from the Deuteronomic source text: the specification *b'wp wbbhmh*, 'of flying creature or land animal', and the reversal of the word order. The first of these might well be regarded as a

that a particular variation might be the result of the influence of another biblical source. There is thus no sense of *TS* as an attempt to mediate between the different Pentateuchal legal sources.

23. On this law, see Yadin 1977–83: I, 312-14.

24. Yadin (1977–83: II, 233) maintains that the *šḥṭ* of Lev. 22.28 was replaced by *zbḥ* in order to 'remove any doubt as to the meaning of the command'. Yadin's translation of *zbḥ* as 'kill' implies that he means *TS* wanted to prohibit both sacrificial and secular slaughter of an animal and its young together. But this cannot be the redactor's intention, since the use of *zbḥ* is in fact completely ambiguous. It is true that *zbḥ* does refer to non-sacrificial slaughter in 11QT 53.3, 'and you may kill (*zbḥ*) any of your flock and herd'. However, in the law of blemished animals (52.4), the prohibited *zbḥ* must refer specifically to sacrifice, since non-sacrificial slaughter of blemished animals is expressly permitted in 52.17. Such ambiguity indicates that if the redactor had indeed wished to prohibit all killing of an animal with its young, he presumably would have used a different term (compare the use of the hiphil of *nkh*, 'kill', in the very next law; 11QT 52.6-7).

Figure 1. *Lexical Smoothing in the Sacrificial Laws*

11QT 52.3-7	*Biblical Source*
ולוא תזבח לי שור ושה אשר יהיה בו כול מום רע כי תועבה המה לי	לא תזבח ליהוה אלהיך שור ושה אשר יהיה בו מום כל דבר רע כי תועבת יהוה אלהיך הוא (Deut. 17.1)
ולוא תזבח לי שור ושה ועז והמה מלאות כי תועבה המה לי	
ושור ושה אותו ואת בנו לוא תזבח ביום אחד	ושור או שה אתו ואת בנו לא תשחטו ביום אחד (Lev. 22.28)
ולוא תכה אם על בנים	לא תקח האם על הבנים (Deut. 22.6)

11QT 52.3-7	*Biblical Source*
Do not <u>sacrifice</u> to me an ox or sheep which has any serious blemish, for they are an abomination to me.	Do not <u>sacrifice</u> to Yahweh your God an ox or sheep which has a blemish, anything at all wrong, for it is an abomination to Yahweh your God (Deut. 17.1)
And do not <u>sacrifice</u> to me an ox or sheep or goat which is pregnant, for they are an abomination to me.	<*none*>
And an ox or sheep, it and its young, you shall not <u>sacrifice</u> on the same day, and you shall not kill a mother along with her young.	And an ox or sheep, it and its young, you shall not <u>slaughter</u> on the same day (Lev. 22.28) You shall not take the mother along with the young (Deut. 22.6)

Figure 2: *Syntactical Smoothing in the Dietary Laws*

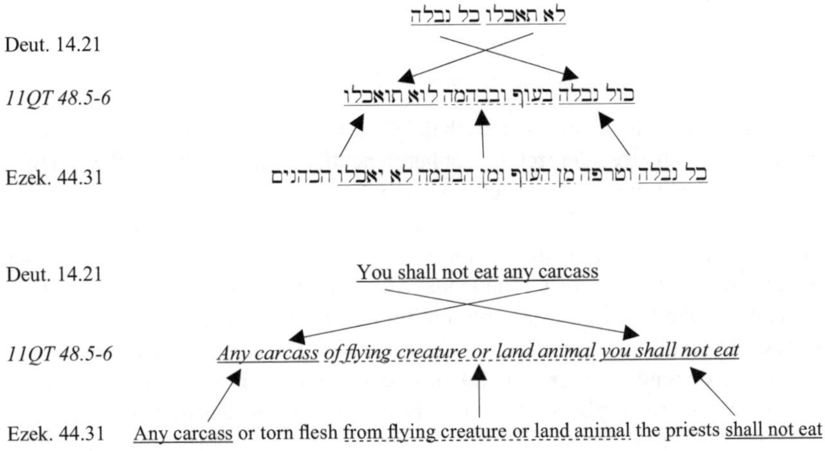
Deut. 14.21
לא תאכלו כל נבלה
11QT 48.5-6
כול נבלה בעוף ובבהמה לוא תואכלו
Ezek. 44.31
כל נבלה וטרפה מן העוף ומן הבהמה לא יאכלו הכהנים
Deut. 14.21
You shall not eat any carcass
11QT 48.5-6
Any carcass of flying creature or land animal you shall not eat
Ezek. 44.31
Any carcass or torn flesh from flying creature or land animal the priests shall not eat

halakhically significant addition meant to clarify the law, but it is hard to imagine that the change in word order effected by redeploying the Ezekiel passage could have any halakhic meaning. Yet this change results in a different sort of harmonization. The syntax of the Ezekiel text, with the prohibited object ('any carcass') preposed in a *casus pendens* (*kol-nᵉbēlâ…lōʾ yōʾkᵉlû*), matches the standard formulation in the dietary laws of both Deuteronomy 14 and Leviticus 11, the two major sources for 11QT 48. The construction 'every (*kōl*) X you shall/shall not eat' occurs four times in Leviticus 11 and six times in Deuteronomy 14.[25] The other construction common in these laws also involves a *casus pendens*: 'this/these/of their flesh you shall (not) eat'. This occurs six times in Leviticus 11 and three times in Deuteronomy 14.[26] In contrast, the straightforward syntax of Deut. 14.21, *lō' tō'kᵉlû kol-nᵉbēlâ*, 'you shall not eat any carcass', occurs only in that verse and in the introduction to the dietary laws in v. 3. Thus, from a syntactical perspective, there is a strong pattern present in the biblical dietary laws that the simple formulation of Deut. 14.21 contradicts. *TS*'s redactor must have perceived this pattern. When he came to incorporate the prohibition upon eating carcasses, he did not simply add the specification 'of flying creature or land animal' to his Deuteronomic source text. He also adapted Deuteronomy's word order to that of Leviticus, Ezekiel, and, indeed, the rest of Deuteronomy 14 as well (see Fig. 2). In other words, he streamlines his text at a purely formal level by levelling the divergent syntax of the biblical prescriptions: the dietary laws in 11QT 48 now uniformly employ the *casus pendens* (ll. 3, 4, 5-6, 6-7).[27]

One last clear example of purely formal change can be mentioned (for details, see Levinson and Zahn 2002). At several points in the Scroll, the author replaces the protasis marker *kî*, 'if', of a biblical casuistic law with the semantically identical conditional, *'im*. Here there can be no question of halakhic or interpretative significance, since the change in no way affects the meaning of the law. Yet the substitution occurs in very specific instances and is clearly intended to provide the Scroll's adaptation of Deuteronomic law with a unified legal syntax.

4. *The Non-Biblical Portions of the Scroll and the Redactor's Independence*

The previous section demonstrates that *TS*'s extensive reuse of the Bible was not motivated strictly by interpretative or hermeneutical concerns, but by the author's desire to present his work as authoritative Torah. In other words, the Scroll's relationship to the Bible is characterized much more by independence than by deference or dependence: the author used the Bible for his own purposes. That observation of the author's independence is significant for our overall understanding of the Scroll. Despite recognition of *TS*'s Sinaitic claim, whereby it rejects any explicit relationship to the canonical Torah, the conception of the Scroll as a dependent work of halakhic exegesis has been relatively common in *Temple Scroll* research. Such a view is implicit in the list of five frequently employed editorial techniques with which Yadin begins his chapter on 'The Composition and Editing of the Scroll':

25. Lev. 11.3, 9b, 41, 42; Deut. 14.6, 9b, 10, 11, 19, 20.

26. Lev. 11.4, 8, 9a, 11, 21, 22; Deut. 14.7, 9a, 12.

27. While Brin (1987: 523-24) notes how the author here conforms the syntax of his Deuteronomic source text to the style of Leviticus and Ezekiel, he does not recognize the extent to which the syntax of Deut. 14.21 also goes against the norm of the rest of Deut. 14.

> [D]rafting the text in the first person with the object of establishing that it is God Himself who is the speaker; merging commands that concern the same subject; unifying duplicate commands, including those that contradict one another; modifying and adding to the commands in order to clarify their halakhic meaning; appending whole new sections. (1977–83: I, 71)

Yadin's language here of 'modifying', 'unifying', and 'appending' points to an understanding of the Scroll according to which the Bible served as the author's conceptual starting point. This model does not conceive of the Scroll as an independent composition, since an independent composition would have nothing to 'modify' or 'unify'—no prior form to which additional material could be 'appended'. To put it another way, Yadin here implicitly presents *TS* as an adaptation or derivation from the canonical Pentateuch, rather than as an independent composition that utilizes the Pentateuch as its major source.

With regard to Yadin's formulation, this difference may seem subtle. It is undeniable, of course, that much of the Scroll does represent the author's reinterpretation of biblical law. However, this model, in which the Bible is the sole point of departure for the Scroll, has been pushed much further. It has been argued that even the most significant departures from the biblical text should be regarded as derived simply and directly from reflection upon the Bible. For example, Phillip Callaway notes that *TS*'s laws on the purity of the Temple City and of Israel (11QT 45–51.5a) 'are not explicit in biblical law, but...can be derived by a simple principle of analogy' (Callaway 1989: 155). Similarly, according to Callaway (p. 158), the new laws in 11QT 57–58 'only make explicit what was already latent' in the biblical law of the King (Deut. 17.14-20). Yadin himself, to give one last example, regards the Scroll's Temple Plan (11QT 3–13, 30–45) as directly derived from the Chronicler's report that God gave to David a plan (*tabnît*) for the Temple (1 Chron. 28.11-19): '...these supplementary sections were compiled and inserted into the scroll because, in the opinion of its author, there was authority for their existence in the biblical text itself' (Yadin 1977–83: I, 83). In his conclusion, Swanson agrees with this position:

> Yadin gave the Scroll its designation, 'Temple Scroll', out of his belief that the material in the Temple Law represented in the author's mind the 'Temple Scroll' described in 1 Chron 28.11-19. We now affirm this thesis. (Swanson 1995: 225; see also Crawford 2000: 34)

The claim that even the most creative portions of *TS* are the product of simple reflection upon the biblical text takes no account of the complete independence with which the author of the Scroll redeployed the Bible. It assumes that since much of *TS* is intimately connected with the text and contents of the canonical Torah, the entire Scroll must have direct biblical roots. Such a claim also fails to give an adequate characterization of the text. A closer look at the law of the King and, in particular, the Temple Plan will demonstrate that these major departures from the biblical text must be regarded as just that—innovations, cast in biblical language and incorporated into *TS*'s Sinaitic revelation in order to provide them with authority.

It is on the basis of their content that the law of the King and the Temple Plan must be judged as innovations. They are simply too different from anything found in the Bible for the model of simple analogical derivation to have any explanatory power. For example, the law of the King includes extensive material on the laws for royal warfare (Schiffman 1988). These include a muster (11QT 57.2-5), rules for apportioning the army when Israel is attacked (11QT 58.3-11), instructions for dividing the spoils in the case of victory (11QT 58.11-15), and rules for offensive warfare (11QT 58.15-21). That this legislation should have been 'latent' in the Deuteronomic law of the King (Deut. 17.14-20) does not seem possible: that law makes no mention at all of the king's traditional duties as commander of the army (Levinson 2001a). Similarly, the Deuteronomic law contains no inkling of *TS*'s stipulation that the king appoint a council of 36 leaders (*nśyy ʿmw*), priests, and levites, apart from whom he shall make no decision (11QT 57.11-15; see Schiffman 1987: 249-52).

In the same way, the attempt to trace the Scroll's Temple Plan back to the *tabnît* of 1 Chronicles 28 does not do justice to the evidence. That *tabnît* is the plan for the Solomonic Temple, revealed by God to David: 'All of it in writing from the hand of Yahweh he showed me' (1 Chron. 28.19). It is clear that, in the Chronicler's mind, the plan is executed properly, and God approves of the new Temple: upon the Temple's completion, God declares to Solomon, 'For now I have chosen and consecrated this house that my name might be there forever and that my eyes and heart might be there for all time' (2 Chron. 7.16).

It is true that the Chronicler's mention of the *tabnît* might well arouse the interest of later interpreters, since the contents of this plan are never spelled out. In other words, the Chronicler maintains that God revealed a Temple plan to David, but the details of that revelation, aside from the summary list in 1 Chron. 28.11-18, were never recorded. It could be imagined that someone might attempt to fill that gap by producing a text that purported to represent God's original revelation to David. But *TS*'s Temple Plan cannot be regarded merely as the result of such harmonistic impulses—its programme is much more tendentious. To begin with, if the Scroll intended to represent the blueprint for the Solomonic Temple, we would expect it to reflect accurately the dimensions and furnishings of that Temple as given in the books of Kings and Chronicles (Schiffman 1996: 571). But this is not the case. The Temple Plan propounded in the Scroll is unique. It draws upon biblical traditions, but uses them selectively, combines their elements in new ways, and sometimes departs from them altogether. The resulting Temple differs from all other descriptions of Israelite or Jewish Temple structures, including the wilderness Tabernacle, the Solomonic Temple, the Temple of Ezekiel's vision, and the Herodian Temple (Schiffman 1996: 570-71).[28] In

28. In his architectural analyses of the Scroll's Temple Plan, Johann Maier argues that the Temple of *TS* does not represent a sectarian literary construction strictly on the basis of biblical sources, but reflects ideal norms current in the 'Jerusalem architectural school' of the time and already attested in earlier Temple plans (1989: 23; 1990: 67-68). While it is important to stress the author's independence from the biblical traditions, and while *TS*'s plan may well have come out of a wider tradition of reflection upon sacred architecture, I am not convinced that there is sufficient

particular, the Scroll's many points of disagreement with the building accounts of Chronicles and Kings make clear that 1 Chronicles 28 does not serve as the basis for the Scroll's Temple Plan.[29] The Scroll's most striking innovation is the organization of the Temple complex into three concentric courts, the outermost of which drastically expands the dimensions of the Temple precinct to 1600 cubits (about half a mile) on each side (Schiffman 1989: 273).[30] 1 Kings does not mention the Temple courts in its building account, but Schiffman considers it most likely that Solomon's Temple had only one court (1989: 278). The account in Chronicles mentions only two courts (2 Chron. 4.9). In neither of these accounts, nor in Ezekiel's Temple Vision, is any idea of concentricity expressed (Schiffman 1989: 270, 279). The Scroll's Temple complex also differs from the Solomonic Temple in several smaller details. For example, the height of the portico or vestibule in *TS* was to be 60 cubits (11QT 4.10), while 2 Chron. 3.4 stipulates 120 cubits, and 1 Kings makes no mention of the height of the portico (Schiffman 1996: 563). Whereas the biblical witnesses know of only three levels of storied structures surrounding the Temple building (1 Kgs 6.5-8; Ezek. 41.5-9), the Scroll requires six (11QT 4.2-5; see Schiffman 1996: 558). Another example pertains to the *menorah*: while the First Temple had ten lampstands (1 Kgs 7.49//2 Chron. 4.7), *TS* calls for only one (Schiffman 1992b: 631).

Given its uniqueness, the Temple Plan of the Scroll actually embodies a move against the Chronicler's Solomonic Temple. As the direct word of God from Sinai, *TS*'s plan represented the ultimate authoritative text. Because of the setting at Sinai, the plan of the Scroll presumably represents, in the Scroll's 'narrative time', the Temple that was to be built in the land after the Israelite conquest. Therefore, it *is* the Temple that Solomon was to have built: the same Temple that the Chronicler maintained was revealed to David. The author of the Scroll was, in effect, describing the version of the First Temple that he thought should have existed (Maier 1989: 23; Beckwith 1997: 12). But the Scroll's revealed Temple Plan could only reflect badly on the Solomonic Temple as depicted in Kings and Chronicles, since it implies that Solomon's Temple did not correspond to God's

evidence to pinpoint such a tradition to a 'Jerusalem architectural school'. More importantly, Schiffman (1989: 281-82) has demonstrated that the author of the Scroll modelled his Temple and its precincts on the Israelite encampment that surrounded the wilderness Tabernacle as depicted in the book of Numbers. Thus, while it is true that the author did not slavishly adhere to the biblical sources and felt free to present an innovative Temple plan, *TS* at the same time presupposes extensive interaction with the biblical Tabernacle and Temple traditions.

29. Swanson takes as proof of *TS*'s dependence upon 1 Chron. 28 the fact that most of the items to be constructed in 1 Chron. 28.11-18 are present in the Scroll's Temple Plan (1995: 225-26). However, the items listed in 1 Chron. 28 would most likely have been expected elements of any Jewish Temple design of the Second Temple period, so their presence in *TS* is unsurprising. On the other hand, the many differences in detail between *TS* and the Chronicler's building account are very difficult to explain if, as Swanson claims, the author took 1 Chron. 28 as his base and was merely providing 'the detail that is lacking from the traditional accounts' (p. 226).

30. These dimensions point to the Temple Plan's theoretical, rather than practical, nature: implementing it would require levelling off Jerusalem's Temple Mount on the west while raising the floor of the Kidron valley on the east by 250 ft (Broshi 1993: 115).

desires for his sanctuary as revealed at Sinai (see also Mink 1987: 44-45). Though, according to the biblical text, the *tabnît* of Chronicles was also divinely revealed, *TS* trumps it in two ways. First, it pushes the revelation back to Sinai, the ultimate source of revelation.[31] Second, despite God's indicating his approval of the Solomonic Temple (2 Chron. 7.16), there is no explicit notice in Chronicles that Solomon built the Temple in precise accordance with the plan revealed by God to his father David. From a hermeneutical point of view, the possibility remains that Solomon did not implement the plan correctly. From this perspective, there would in fact be a relationship between *TS*'s plan and the *tabnît*, but the relationship would be the opposite of that proposed by Yadin and Swanson. Instead of *TS* modelling its plan on the Chronicler's *tabnît*, the Scroll has created a new plan, revealed at Sinai. If God's revelatory voice is consistent, then it follows that the *tabnît* revealed to David must have corresponded to that of *TS*—but then it is the Chronicler's depiction of the details of the *tabnît* in the subsequent building account that does not fit. *TS* has usurped the position of David's *tabnît*, implying as a result that the First Temple was fundamentally flawed from the start, since it did not correspond to divine intention.

One of the motivating forces behind this move may well have been a desire to explain the destruction of the First Temple, and perhaps by extension the Exile and the continued domination of Judaea by conquering powers, as the result of failure on the part of Israel to implement God's cultic commands properly. From the author's historical perspective, the argument is as follows: if the construction and sacrificial plan of *TS* had been implemented from the start, God's blessing would have been assured (11QT 29). The only way to restore that blessing in the present age and make it possible for God to dwell among the people of Israel is to implement correctly God's commands for his Temple given so long ago at Sinai (Schiffman 1996: 571). Rather than being a simple derivation from 1 Chronicles 28, therefore, the Scroll's Temple Plan represents an attempt to reconstrue the contents of that *tabnît* by styling itself as the first and original revelation of God concerning his Temple.

Though the Temple Plan in the Scroll departs from the Chronicler's *tabnît* as regards content, and though its claim to Sinaitic authority implies a move against the Chronicler's *tabnît*, it may be argued that 1 Chronicles 28 nevertheless gave the redactor the biblical basis he needed for composing a divinely revealed Temple Plan. This was the position of Yadin quoted above. However, there is no need to posit such a connection, since the trope of a divinely revealed plan for the Temple or sanctuary occurs at several points in the Hebrew Bible. Besides 1 Chronicles 28, the book of Exodus records that Moses was shown a model (*tabnît*) of the Tabernacle and all its vessels (Exod. 25.9; see also Num. 8.4).

31. If *TS* raises the revelatory status of its Temple vis-à-vis that of Chronicles by depicting it as revealed at Sinai, Chronicles makes precisely the same move vis-à-vis Samuel–Kings: by means of the revelation in 1 Chron. 28, the author grants the Temple a Davidic and divine authority that is absent in Samuel–Kings; compare 2 Sam. 7. (I am grateful to Bernard M. Levinson for bringing this point to my attention.)

Ezekiel's Temple Vision (chs. 40–48) is also presented as revelation, in the form of a tour of the new Temple led by a divine messenger. The tradition of divine revelation of temples and cult objects had very ancient origins in the Near East.[32] It continued into Second Temple and New Testament times, as can be seen from texts like the Qumran New Jerusalem[33] and the New Testament book of Revelation. In depicting his Temple Plan as revealed on Sinai, the author of *TS* may have been drawing specifically on the biblical traditions, especially the tradition that the details for the Tabernacle were revealed to Moses on Sinai. But he may also simply have been participating in a well-developed tradition of attributing temple plans to divine revelation.

The examples of the Law of the King and the Temple Plan illustrate that the author of *TS* was not constrained to use the Bible as his starting point. He drew on biblical material to the extent that it complemented and authorized his own composition, but no more. In a way, such independent and selective use of sources comes as no surprise in a post-biblical composition, since the same phenomenon occurs within the Bible itself. Levinson has demonstrated how Deuteronomy's ambiguous literary relationship with the Covenant Code—close correspondences at some points, but elsewhere complete divergence in content and sequence—results from its authors' independent use of their sources: 'The authors of Deuteronomy used the Covenant Code as a textual resource in order to pursue their own very different religious and legal agenda' (Levinson 1997: 149). Similarly, Japhet and others have shown that Chronicles, far from being a simple ideological rewrite of Samuel–Kings, tendentiously used the Deuteronomistic History as one source among many in its creation of a completely new history of Israel (Japhet 1997: 506-508; Williamson 1982: 21-23; Knoppers 1990: 431-32). *TS*'s melding of biblical sources with completely new material thus has strong precedents within Israelite–Jewish literary tradition.

Although I have argued that the author of *TS* included major innovations as constitutive parts of his new text, I do not intend to portray these innovations as totally independent of any reflection on the Bible. Ideas like the extension of purity laws to the temple city, a personal council for the king, a role for the king in war, and even the procedural and architectural innovations of the Temple Plan itself probably did derive at some level from engagement with the Bible. But this was most likely the engagement of a community or series of communities deeply steeped in the biblical tradition over a period of many years, conditioned by

32. The Sumerian king Gudea was said to have lain down to sleep next to the pile of building materials he had amassed for a temple, and was shown in a dream the precise details of the structure he was to build. No other ancient Near Eastern records survive of the revelation of temple plans, but there are two Hittite dream records in which the king is shown a prototype of the statues that he is to build and consecrate to the deity. There are similar records for two Babylonian kings of the first millennium: Nabû-apla-iddina (ninth century) and Nabonidus (sixth century). See Hurowitz 1992: 168-70; Oppenheim 1956: 193-94, 224.

33. The New Jerusalem contains a utopian blueprint for the city of Jerusalem and the Temple in the manner of Ezekiel: the author receives a tour of the city from an angelic guide. For a description of the text and a comparison with *TS*, see García Martínez 1999.

ideology, social situation, and the influence of many other traditions. By the time these independent (and distinctly non-biblical) perspectives were incorporated into *TS*, the Bible was not the impetus for them, but the means by which they were given legitimacy and authority.

5. *Conclusion: The* Temple Scroll *and the Authority of Torah*

In this study, I have tried to demonstrate the extent to which *TS*'s claim to have been revealed on Sinai directly influenced its composition. The desire to present *TS* as Sinaitic Torah required the author to cloak his entire composition in biblical language. Even the most innovative sections of the Scroll draw upon biblical phraseology or biblical models in order to come across as the word of God. Further, this authorial goal at times prompted exegetical changes or recombinations geared to make the text more coherent and unified. I mentioned earlier that the Scroll gives no indication that its authority claim is not to be taken seriously; therefore it is best to assume that the author was indeed claiming the status of direct divine revelation. In the light of the previous discussion of the Scroll's exegetical techniques, that assumption can now be confirmed. The great lengths to which the author went to make the Sinaitic claim as believable as possible seem to make the conclusion unavoidable that *TS* was indeed intended as authoritative Torah.

This conclusion, however, raises the intriguing question of what that claim to be Torah actually meant in the late Second Temple period, in a society that already had an authoritative, Sinaitic Torah. *TS*'s voicing makes clear that it wanted to be perceived as possessing authority at least equal to, and probably exceeding, the canonical Torah. Yet paradoxically, the Scroll draws all its authority from its competitor. *TS* is dependent upon the authority of the canonical Torah and the authority of Sinai as the source of the canonical Torah, since it is through redeploying Sinai and the language of Torah that *TS* constructs its own authority. In other words, if the Torah did not exist as a recognized authoritative text, *TS* would have no authority (Brooke 1988: 41-42).

On a practical level, then, the author of *TS* was probably not expecting or even hoping that the canonical Torah would somehow disappear. Indeed, in those areas of the law that are covered in only one text but not the other (such as the law of the King and the extended purity regulations in the Scroll), the two texts could exist alongside one another quite comfortably. But in numerous areas there is direct or implied halakhic disagreement (such as whether the purification sacrifice requires accompanying offerings,[34] when to wash and bathe during a seven-day period of purification,[35] and whether intercourse with one's niece is

34. According to the Pentateuchal legislation, a grain and drink offering must be presented with every *'ōlâ*, 'burnt offering', and *zebaḥ*, 'sacrifice' (Num. 15.3-10). The *ḥaṭṭā't*, 'purification offering', does not require a grain and drink offering, and in the sacrificial stipulations for the festivals in Num. 28–29 is always listed after the grain and drink offerings for the other sacrifices (e.g. Num. 28.19-22). In *TS*, however, the position of the *ḥaṭṭā't* is systematically changed so as to include it among the sacrifices requiring grain and drink offerings; see 11QT 17.15; 25.14-15; 28.8-9.

35. See Milgrom 1989: 170-74; 1990: 89-95.

permitted).[36] In these cases, we must surmise that *TS* intended its position to be the authoritative one. At an ontological level, *TS* was indeed trying to usurp the place of the Pentateuch as the most authoritative legal revelation. The author's project of recombining laws and smoothing formulations is an attempt to convey the impression that this new Torah, *TS*, is *better* than the old Torah—more consistent and logical, and more suited to be Israel's primary law.

This assessment, if accurate, has significant implications for our view of the state of the biblical canon in the late Second Temple period. Recent scholarship on the canon has recognized that the bodies of scripture that came to be known as the Prophets and the Writings were very fluid during this period: there was no fixed list of which works were accepted as authoritative and which were not (Barton 1986: 32-43, 61-62; Ulrich 1999: 20-22). But there also seems to be a consensus that that fluidity did not apply to the Torah—that by this period, the shape of the Torah was fixed (Wacholder 1983: 4; Barton 1986: 57; Mink 1987: 47). The evidence of *TS*, however, challenges this consensus. On the one hand, there is little evidence that *TS* or any other work intended to be *included* in the Torah[37]—the shape of the Pentateuch in its current Genesis-to-Deuteronomy format may well have been fixed.[38] On the other hand, perhaps Torah should be defined not as those five specific books, but as the body of revelation given at Sinai (just as the Prophets and Writings were defined as those inspired books not revealed at Sinai). Under this definition, even the Torah was not fixed and closed in the late Second Temple period, since works like *TS* could still claim the status of Sinaitic revelation.[39]

TS thus challenges conventional paradigms in a number of ways. It demonstrates the necessity of rethinking the relationship between exegesis and pseudepigraphy, since here the pseudepigraphic claim to be revealed actually has a major influence on the mechanics of the text's composition and editing, including

36. While the Bible forbids a man from having intercourse with his aunt (Lev. 18.12-13; 20.19-20), it says nothing about intercourse with one's niece. Both *TS* (11QT 66.15-17) and the *Damascus Document* (CD 5.7b-11) extend the prohibition so that it symmetrically applies to niece–uncle intercourse as well. See Levinson 2001b: 231-33.

37. Stegemann has, in fact, claimed that *TS* was intended as a sixth book of the Torah, meant to supplement and update the first five (1988; 1989: 127, 142-43). He therefore dates its composition to the fifth–fourth centuries BCE, after which, he claims, the shape of the Torah was too fixed to allow for an additional book. That *TS* was composed to be a supplemental volume of the Torah, however, seems very unlikely. The tensions between the Scroll's halakhah and that of the Pentateuch, as well as the Scroll's claim to greater revelatory authority than the canonical Pentateuch, instead imply that the Scroll was intended to exist independently of, and most likely in competition with, the canonical Torah.

38. This statement might actually be challenged by works like the *Reworked Pentateuch* (4Q158, 4Q364-367), which comprises a version of Torah with considerable additions and expansions. This text may constitute an alternative edition of the Torah, much like the *Psalms Scroll* (11QPs[a]) represents an alternative edition of the Psalter. For the text of the *Reworked Pentateuch*, see Allegro 1968: 1-6; Tov and Crawford 1994. On 11QPs[a], see Sanders 1965; Barton 1986: 86; Ulrich 1999: 115-20.

39. The book of *Jubilees* represents another example of the same phenomenon, since it also purports to be revealed to Moses on Sinai. For a similar conclusion that does not, however, address the issue of canon, see Swanson 1995: 7.

its reuse of the Bible. The Scroll also bears witness to a more complicated situation regarding the canonization process and the authority of Torah in the late Second Temple period than has commonly been assumed. Finally, *TS* reflects its author's complex conception of revelation, authority, and even history. The locus of revelation was in the past, at the great historical moment when God revealed his will to Moses on Sinai. But the past, in a sense, was not past, and Sinai was not closed, since the author could portray his modern text as a part of that ancient revelation. The dominance of Torah and the authority of Sinai thus did not condemn later interpreters to silence, but invited them to creativity.

> Turn it and turn it again, for all things are contained therein...
>
> *Mishnah Aboth* 5.22

BIBLIOGRAPHY

Alexander, P.S.

2000 'The Bible in Qumran and Early Judaism', in A.D.H. Mayes (ed.), *Text in Context: Essays by Members of the Society for Old Testament Study* (Oxford: Oxford University Press): 35-62.

Allegro, John M. (ed.)

1968 *Qumrân Cave 4: I (4Q158–4Q186)* (DJD, 5; Oxford: Clarendon Press).

Altshuler, D.

1982–83 'On the Classification of Judaic Laws in the *Antiquities* of Josephus and the Temple Scroll of Qumran', *AJS Review* 7-8: 1-14.

Amir, Yehoshua

1988 'Authority and Interpretation of Scripture in the Writings of Philo', in Mulder (ed.) 1988: 421-54.

Barrera, Julio Trebolle, and Luis Vegas Montaner (eds.)

1992 *The Madrid Qumran Congress: Proceedings of the International Congress on the Dead Sea Scrolls, Madrid 18–21 March 1991* (STDJ, 11; 2 vols.; Leiden: E.J. Brill).

Barton, John

1986 *Oracles of God: Perceptions of Ancient Prophecy in Israel After the Exile* (London: Darton, Longman & Todd).

Baumgarten, Joseph M.

2000 'The Laws of the Damascus Document—Between Bible and Mishnah', in Joseph M. Baumgarten, Esther G. Chazon and Avital Pinnick (eds.), *The Damascus Document: A Centennial of Discovery* (STDJ, 34; Leiden: E.J. Brill): 17-26.

Beckwith, R.T.

1997 'The Temple Scroll and its Calendar: Their Character and Purpose', *RQ* 18: 3-19.

Bernstein, Moshe J.

1996 'The Employment and Interpretation of Scripture in 4QMMT: Preliminary Observations', in John Kampen and Moshe J. Bernstein (eds.), *Reading 4QMMT: New Perspectives on Qumran Law and History* (SBL Symposium Series, 2; Atlanta: Scholars Press): 29-52.

1999 'Pseudepigraphy in the Qumran Scrolls: Categories and Functions', in Chazon and Stone (eds.) 1999: 1-26.

Brin, Gershon

1980 'The Bible in the Temple Scroll', *Shnaton: An Annual for Biblical and Ancient Near Eastern Studies* 4: 182-225 (Hebrew).

1987 'Concerning Some of the Uses of the Bible in the Temple Scroll', *RQ* 12: 519-28.

Brooke, George J.

1988 'The Temple Scroll: A Law Unto Itself?', in Barnabas Lindars (ed.), *Law and Religion: Essays on the Place of the Law in Israel and Early Christianity* (Cambridge: J. Clarke): 34-43.

Brooke, George J. (ed.)

1989 *Temple Scroll Studies* (JSPSup, 7; Sheffield: Sheffield Academic Press).

Broshi, Magen

1993 'The Gigantic Dimensions of the Visionary Temple in the Temple Scroll', in Hershel Shanks (ed.), *Understanding the Dead Sea Scrolls: A Reader from the Biblical Archaeology Review* (London: SPCK): 113-15.

Callaway, Phillip R.

1989 'Extending Divine Revelation: Micro-Compositional Strategies in the Temple Scroll', in Brooke (ed.) 1989: 149-62.

Carr, David

2001 'Method in Determination of Direction of Dependence: An Empirical Test of Criteria Applied to Exodus 34,11-26 and its Parallels', in Matthias Köckert and Erhard Blum (eds.), *Gottes Volk am Sinai* (Veröffentlichungen der wissenschaftliche Gesellschaft für Theologie, 18; Gütersloh: Gütersloher Verlag): 107-40.

Chazon, Esther G., and Michael Stone (eds.)

1999 *Pseudepigraphic Perspectives: The Apocrypha and Pseudepigrapha in Light of the Dead Sea Scrolls* (STDJ, 31; Leiden: E. J. Brill).

Crawford, Sidnie White

2000 *The Temple Scroll and Related Texts* (Companion to the Qumran Scrolls, 2; Sheffield: Sheffield Academic Press).

Duff, Jeremy

1998 'A Reconstruction of Pseudepigraphy in Early Christianity' (unpublished DPhil thesis, University of Oxford).

Elwolde, John

1997 'Distinguishing the Linguistic and the Exegetical: The Case of Numbers in the Bible and 11QT^{a}', in Stanley E. Porter and Craig A. Evans (eds.), *The Scrolls and the Scriptures: Qumran Fifty Years After* (JSPSup, 26; Sheffield: Sheffield Academic Press): 129-41.

Fishbane, Michael

1985 *Biblical Interpretation in Ancient Israel* (Oxford: Clarendon Press).

1988 'Use, Authority, and Interpretation of Mikra at Qumran', in Mulder (ed.) 1988: 339-77.

García Martínez, Florentino

1999 'The Temple Scroll and the New Jerusalem', in Peter W. Flint and James C. VanderKam (eds.), *The Dead Sea Scrolls after Fifty Years: A Comprehensive Assessment* (2 vols.; Leiden: E.J. Brill): II, 431-60.

Goshen-Gottstein, Moshe H.

1966 'The Psalms Scroll (11QPs^{a}): A Problem of Canon and Text', *Textus* 5: 22-33.

Graham, William A.

1987 'Scripture', in M. Eliade (ed.), *The Encyclopedia of Religion* (16 vols.; New York: Macmillan): XIII, 133-45.

Hempel, Charlotte

2000 *The Damascus Texts* (Companion to the Qumran Scrolls, 1; Sheffield: Sheffield Academic Press).

Hurowitz, Victor Avigdor

1992 *I have Built You an Exalted House: Temple Building in the Bible in Light of Mesopotamian and Northwest Semitic Writings* (JSOTSup, 115; Sheffield: Sheffield Academic Press).

Japhet, Sara

1997 *The Ideology of the Book of Chronicles and its Place in Biblical Thought* (trans. Anna Barber; Beiträge zur Erforschung des Alten Testaments und des antiken Judentums, 9; Frankfurt: Peter Lang, 2nd edn).

Kaufman, Stephen A.

1982 'The Temple Scroll and Higher Criticism', *HUCA* 53: 29-43.

Kister, Menahem

1992 'Some Aspects of Qumranic Halakhah', in Barrera and Montaner (eds.) 1992: II, 571-88.

Knoppers, Gary N.

1990 'Rehoboam in Chronicles: Villain or Victim?', *JBL* 109: 423-40.

Kugel, James L.

1986 'Early Interpretation: The Common Background of Late Forms of Biblical Exegesis', in J. Kugel and R. Greer, *Early Biblical Interpretation* (Philadelphia: Westminster Press): 11-106.

1997 *The Bible as it Was* (Cambridge, MA: Belknap).

Levine, Baruch

1978 'The Temple Scroll: Aspects of its Historical Provenance and Literary Character', *BASOR* 232: 5-23.

Levinson, Bernard M.

1997 *Deuteronomy and the Hermeneutics of Legal Innovation* (New York: Oxford University Press).

2001a 'The Reconceptualization of Kingship in Deuteronomy and the Deuteronomistic Historian's Transformation of Torah', *VT* 51: 511-34.

2001b 'Textual Criticism, Assyriology, and the History of Interpretation: Deuteronomy 13.7a as a Test Case in Method', *JBL* 120: 211-43.

Levinson, Bernard M., and Molly M. Zahn

2002 'Revelation Regained: The Hermeneutics of *kî* and *'im* in the Temple Scroll', *DSD* 9: 295-346.

Maier, Johann

1989 'The Architectural History of the Temple in Jerusalem in the Light of the Temple Scroll', in Brooke (ed.) 1989: 23-62.

1990 'The *Temple Scroll* and Tendencies in the Cultic Architecture of the Second Commonwealth', in Schiffman (ed.) 1990: 67-82.

Milgrom, Jacob

1989 'The Qumran Cult: Its Exegetical Principles', in Brooke (ed.) 1989: 165-80.

1990 'The Scriptural Foundations and Deviations in the Laws of Purity of the *Temple Scroll*', in Schiffman (ed.) 1990: 83-99.

Mink, Hans-Aage

1987 'The Use of Scripture in the Temple Scroll and the Status of the Scroll as Law', *SJOT* 1: 20-50.

Mulder, Martin J. (ed.)

1988 *Mikra: Text, Translation, Reading and Interpretation of the Hebrew Bible in Ancient Judaism and Early Christianity* (CRINT, 2.1; Assen and Maastricht: Van Gorcum; Philadelphia: Fortress Press).

Najman, Hindy
1999 'Interpretation as Primordial Writing: Jubilees and its Authority Conferring Strategies', *JSJ* 30: 379-410.

Oppenheim, A. Leo
1956 *The Interpretation of Dreams in the Ancient Near East* (Transactions of the American Philosophical Society, 46.3; Philadelphia: American Philosophical Society).

Qimron, Elisha, and John Strugnell (eds.)
1994 *Qumran Cave 4, V: Miqṣat Ma'aśe Ha-Torah* (DJD, 10; Oxford: Clarendon Press).

Sanders, James A. (ed.)
1965 *The Psalms Scroll of Qumrân Cave 11 (11QPs^{a})* (DJD, 4; Oxford: Clarendon Press).

Schiffman, Lawrence H.
1980 'The Temple Scroll in Literary and Philological Perspective', in William Scott Green (ed.), *Approaches to Ancient Judaism*, II (Brown Judaic Studies, 9; Chico, CA: Scholars Press): 143-58.
1987 'The King, His Guard, and the Royal Council in the *Temple Scroll*', *Proceedings of the American Academy for Jewish Research* 54: 237-59.
1988 'The Laws of War in the Temple Scroll', *RQ* 13: 299-311.
1989 'Architecture and Law: The Temple and its Courtyards in the *Temple Scroll*', in Jacob Neusner, Ernest S. Frerichs and Nahum M. Sarna (eds.), *From Ancient Israel to Modern Judaism: Intellect in Quest of Understanding: Essays in Honor of Marvin Fox* (Brown Judaic Studies, 159; 4 vols.; Atlanta: Scholars Press): I, 267-84.
1992a 'The Deuteronomic Paraphrase of the Temple Scroll', *RQ* 15: 543-67.
1992b 'The Furnishings of the Temple According to the Temple Scroll', in Barrera and Montaner (eds.) 1992: II, 621-34.
1996 'The Construction of the Temple according to the Temple Scroll', *RQ* 17: 555-71.
1998 'The Case of the Day of Atonement Ritual', in Michael E. Stone and Esther G. Chazon (eds.), *Biblical Perspectives: Early Use and Interpretation of the Bible in Light of the Dead Sea Scrolls* (STDJ, 28; Leiden: E.J. Brill): 181-88.
1999 'The Temple Scroll and the Halakhic Pseudepigrapha of the Second Temple Period', in Chazon and Stone (eds.) 1999: 121-32.

Schiffman, Lawrence H. (ed.)
1990 *Archaeology and History in the Dead Sea Scrolls: The New York University Conference in Memory of Yigael Yadin* (JSPSup, 8; Sheffield: JSOT Press).

Schniedewind, William
1999 'Qumran Hebrew as an Antilanguage', *JBL* 118: 235-52.

Smith, Morton
1972 'Pseudepigraphy in the Israelite Tradition', in Kurt von Fritz (ed.), *Pseudepigrapha I: huit exposés suivis de discussions* (Entretiens sur l'Antiquité classique, 18; Vandœuvres-Genève: Fondation Hardt): 191-227.

Stegemann, Hartmut
1988 'The Origins of the Temple Scroll', in J.A. Emerton (ed.), *Congress Volume: Jerusalem 1986* (VTSup, 40; Leiden: E.J. Brill): 235-56.
1989 'The Literary Composition of the Temple Scroll and its Status at Qumran', in Brooke (ed.) 1989: 123-48.

Swanson, Dwight D.
1995 *The Temple Scroll and the Bible: The Methodology of 11QT* (STDJ, 14; Leiden: E.J. Brill).

Tov, Emanuel, and Sidnie White Crawford

1994 'Reworked Pentateuch', in Harold Attridge *et al.* (eds.), *Qumran Cave 4, VIII: Parabiblical Texts, Part 1* (DJD, 13; Oxford: Clarendon Press): 187-352.

Ulrich, Eugene

1999 *The Dead Sea Scrolls and the Origins of the Bible* (Studies in the Dead Sea Scrolls and Related Literature; Grand Rapids: Eerdmans; Leiden: E.J. Brill).

Wacholder, Ben Zion

1983 *The Dawn of Qumran: The Sectarian Torah and the Teacher of Righteousness* (Monographs of the Hebrew Union College, 8; Cincinnati: Hebrew Union College Press).

Williamson, H.G.M.

1982 *1 and 2 Chronicles* (NCBC; Grand Rapids: Eerdmans; London: Marshall, Morgan & Scott).

Wilson, Andrew M., and Lawrence Wills

1982 'Literary Sources of the Temple Scroll', *HTR* 75: 275-88.

Wise, Michael

1990 *A Critical Study of the Temple Scroll from Qumran Cave 11* (SAOC, 49; Chicago: Oriental Institute of the University of Chicago).

Yadin, Yigael

1977–83 *The Temple Scroll* (3 vols.; Jerusalem: Israel Exploration Society).

Zahn, Molly M.

2001 'Schneiderei oder Weberei: Zum Verständnis der Diachronie der Tempelrolle', *RQ* 20: 255-86.

THE TEMPLE IN FIRST CENTURY CE JUDAISM

Martin Goodman

Among the many aspects of the Jews and Judaism that seemed odd to non-Jews in the ancient world, worship through offerings and sacrifices in the Temple in Jerusalem was not included. Greeks and Romans found Jews amusing, occasionally admirable, and (sometimes) disgusting, because of their strange customs, such as stopping work on the Sabbath, their distinctive food laws, and the circumcision of males (Stern 1974–84; Feldman 1993). But the attitudes of Greeks and Romans to the Jerusalem Temple in the final century of its existence, after it had been rebuilt magnificently in the Roman manner by Herod the Great, was primarily admiration (Tacitus, *Histories* 5.8.1). To worship through offering sacrificial animals, libations, and incense on special altars in areas consecrated and purified by dedicated priests was standard religious behaviour for almost everyone in the ancient world (Beard, North and Price 1998). It was also not just part but the centre of the religious life of the Jews, a fact whose importance has faded somewhat over the past two millennia as both Jews and Christians (and, later, Muslims) have learned other ways to worship, without a Temple.

The Jerusalem Temple is in fact, or at least should be, much better known than any other temple system in the ancient world precisely because these later Jews and Christians preserved so much evidence about the way that the Temple operated. For no other temple does there survive a record of sacrificial ritual as detailed as the lengthy discussions in the Mishnah and the Tosefta. For no other temple do we have a long first-hand description by a priest who had known the cult from the inside, as Josephus did. The happy chance that so much literary material about the Temple was kept by these two different religious traditions—rabbinic Judaism and Christianity—provides a unique opportunity to gauge in what ways the Temple mattered to ordinary Jews in the generations immediately prior to its destruction (Sanders 1992: 47-169, 305-14; Hayward 1996).

That the Temple was, in some sense at least, of supreme significance to the vast majority of Jews may be surmised from a single traumatic episode which occurred some thirty years before its demise. Both the contemporary philosopher Philo and the (slightly younger) historian Josephus narrate the reaction of Jews worldwide when the crazy emperor Gaius Caligula attempted to install in the Temple a statue of himself so that he might be worshipped there as divine (Schürer 1973: 388-96). Philo, who was in Rome at the time as part of a delegation which had come to the capital to seek redress for his home community in Alexandria in the diaspora after they had suffered pogroms, switched his efforts to try to counter this far more serious threat to the whole Jewish nation. Agrippa I, grandson of Herod the Great, a royal adventurer who had contrived to gain the friendship of Caligula, risked both that friendship and his life by protesting against the sacrilege. The Jews of Judaea and Galilee staged a sit-down strike to prevent a Roman army marching on Jerusalem with the statue. In the event, calamity was averted by the assassination of the tyrant emperor, but not before Jews all over the Roman world had been spurred into collective outrage in a way not recorded either in earlier crises or in the national traumas of the two later great revolts in Judaea in 66–70 and 132–135 CE or the diaspora uprising of 115–117 CE.

Precise details of the appearance of the Temple just before 70 CE are much debated, not for lack of information but because the evidence of Josephus (*Ant.* 15.410-20; *War* 5.184-227; *Apion* 2.102-109) does not cohere in all respects with that in the Mishnah (Avigad 1984). Excavations around the Temple site have brought clarity only to a small selection of the resulting problems of interpretation. The most probable explanation of most of the discrepancies is not that either source is wholly wrong but that the lay-out of the building changed over time (Levine 1994): one extra item of knowledge which is furnished by archaeology is that Josephus's references to structural work on the building having continued almost up to the outbreak of the Great Revolt in 66 CE seem to be correct.

But if details are sometimes hazy, the general picture is not. The Temple was huge compared to other shrines in the Roman empire—rivalled by the great temples of Egypt—for the good reason that whereas devotees of other cults built local shrines, Jews, with few exceptions, directed their pious offerings to just the one place. The main impression in the main courts was space—where the enclosed perimeter of a normal pagan temple had trees, votive offerings and statues, the Jerusalem shrine had a vast piazza for worshippers to gather (Pseudo-Hecataeus in Josephus, *Apion* 1.199), the whole area preserved, according to Philo (*Spec. Laws* 1.74, 156), in a state of exceptional cleanliness. The walls and doors surrounding the court were brightly decorated both with objects dedicated by individuals (such as a golden chain dedicated in memory of his release from captivity by Agrippa I (Josephus, *Ant.* 19.294), or the gilded gate donated by a certain Nicanor according to the Mishnah [*m. Yoma* 3.10]), and with outstanding works of art, such as the golden vine (Josephus, *War* 5.210), which proved sufficiently famous to come to the attention of the gentile historian Tacitus (*Histories* 5.5.5), or the huge purple, blue and scarlet embroidered tapestries on which a panorama of the heavens (excluding the zodiac) was apparently portrayed (Josephus, *War* 5.212-13). It was a sparkling stage set for the worshippers who came to throng the great open space whose size and capacity had been massively increased by Herod's use of modern Roman techniques of vaulting to extend a platform along the side of the hill.

Not that a capacity crowd was normal. On ordinary weekdays, the courts must have felt quite empty, since the daily communal ritual all took place in a restricted area around the court of the priests where the animals were sacrificed, burned and (in some cases) eaten, and the libations were poured. The actors in this solemn ritual were all priests, qualified to serve by inheritance through the male line. Physical impairment would disbar a priest from his duties, but otherwise birth —rather than skill, piety or knowledge—was the only criterion (Schürer 1979: 237-308). Doubtless the caste preserved its own traditions handed down through the generations, but for the great mass of non-Priestly Jews too much was at stake in what the priests did for their conduct to be left entirely without outside scrutiny and (occasionally) interference (Goodman 2000).

The rules of the sacrifices carried out by the priests on behalf of the nation were divinely ordained in the Torah. In marked contrast to pagan cults, in which worshippers themselves decided what they thought the gods wanted and judged their success by what they saw as signs of divine pleasure or displeasure, in the Jerusalem Temple the procedures were laid out by the divine recipient of the offerings, a precise menu with a precise set of times for the meals to be served. In other cults, in times of emergency regular sacrifices could be postponed, with the understanding that the gods would be willing to wait. By contrast, the divine timetable of sabbaths, new moons and festivals cannot be altered by humans (Holladay and Goodman 1986). Hence widespread concern among non-priests that the offerings made by the priests should be carried out in accordance with the divine will, and the disputes among different groups, such as Pharisees, Sadducees and Essenes, on the correct calendar or on matters of intricate cultic detail such as the purity of the priest who carried out the ritual of the red heifer (*m. Par.* 3.7). The extraordinary find at Qumran of multiple copies of *Miqṣat ma‘aśê hattôrâ*, a letter from the Dead Sea sectarians to the High Priest urging him to follow their rulings in such matters, provides evidence of just such attempted interference in the public procedures in the Temple even by a fringe group (Qimron and Strugnell 1994).

Beyond the writing of letters and occasional mass demonstrations, the control by non-priests over the day-to-day running of the Temple was indirect at best, and it is hard to know how often ordinary Jews would go into the Temple precincts for worship. Within Jerusalem, the Temple was the main arena for public meetings of all kinds—it was here, for instance, that the first Jewish Christians preached their message (Acts 2.46-47; 5.21, 42)—but there is no evidence that individuals would go specially to the building for private prayer unless they wished to present a private sacrifice of their own. There was in theory no limit to the number of such sin, guilt and other private offerings one could bring (Sanders 1992: 89-90), buying an animal (usually a bird) from the noisy livestock compounds in the royal portico on the southern edge of the Temple platform and then handing it to a priest, who would carry out the slaughter on your behalf (Sanders 1992; Goodman 1994a). In practice, the fact that no-one, however pious, could bring an offering for every possible sin must have made such offerings essentially voluntary, a matter of individual conscience (or, for the insecure, an issue on which to seek guidance from a religious expert of one persuasion or another). It is a reasonable hypothesis that inhabitants of Jerusalem brought offerings to the Temple more often than those who lived further away, although demonstrating that physical distance created any difference in attitude to the Temple as an institution is not possible (Goodman 1999b).

The experience of the individual worshipper was altogether different on the days of festivals. According to Josephus (*War* 6.420-27), there were 2,700,000 men in Jerusalem for the Passover of 65 CE, to which number should be added women and children. Josephus's figure is not trustworthy, but the impression of a vast crowd such as can still be seen today in Mecca is confirmed by numerous stories about the political volatility of these occasions, which in the first century CE all too often provided opportunity for riots and assassinations (Josephus, *Ant.* 20.186-87). The international flavour of the pilgrim crowd was much boosted in these final years not just because Herod's rebuilding programme had made the Temple a tourist attraction even for non-Jews, but because, following the eradication of piracy by Pompey the Great and the imposition of Roman rule over the whole Mediterranean world, diaspora Jews from all over that world could, and did, travel with a fair degree of safety to Judaea to pay their respects and their dues (Goodman 1999a).

Attendance at such festivals was evidently enjoyable, since there is good evidence that many women and children went up to Jerusalem even though they had no requirement to do so (Safrai 1985). Part of the impact on the individual will have lain in the feelings of anticipation, heightened by the purification procedures which preceded entry into the Temple precincts (Josephus, *Apion* 2.104). On arrival, the worshipper was struck by the imposing architecture, the building towering high above him, the precious metals and stones glinting in the sun (cf. Pseudo-Philo, *LAB* 26)—giving rise in descriptions of the building to recurrent imagery of intense light (Hayward 1996: 15-16). Enmeshed within the crowd, the pilgrim who brought and took to a priest a personal offering would not see much of what happened to 'his' or 'her' animal in the court of priests when it was sacrificed. Women in particular will have had to strain to catch sight of what was going on since they were confined at a further distance, in the court of the women. But perhaps this did not matter, and distance added an element of mystery and power. Cut off from the messy business of the abattoir and butcher, the worshipper could gaze in awe at the practised precision of the priests, who operated 'like angels' (*Jubilees* 30.14), carrying out their duties in complete silence (*Pseudo-Aristeas* 92-95).

Not that the Temple as a whole can have been silent, or even hushed. There was the sound of Levites singing—presumably, given the acoustics of the open-air courtyard, providing background noise rather than hymns with distinguishable words. There were occasional blasts on the trumpet and the constant sound of animals on the way to slaughter. The same animals must have given a distinctive smell to the place, overlain with the scent of roast meat. Incense was of course offered up on the altar, but its scent will hardly have percolated to the outer courts. In the summer heat of Jerusalem all such smells will have dissipated quite rapidly in the open air, as will the tang of human perspiration, hardly avoidable in such a crowd despite the hope expressed by Ezekiel (44.18) that the priests at least should avoid wearing any clothes that cause sweat.

It is easy, with empathy, to imagine the huge emotional impact of the Temple on those who visited it two thousand years ago, but the significance of the Temple went much deeper than just the emotion it elicited from the occasional visitor. The Temple was also an institution of immense importance for those many Jews who were never able to visit the Temple at all because it was too far away. The extreme case was the universal horror, discussed above, at the attempted desecration of the Temple by Gaius Caligula in 40 CE, but, on a more mundane level, ordinary diaspora Jews in Asia Minor, Rome or Babylonia demonstrated their commitment to the public sacrifices for Israel by the annual payment of a half-shekel to Temple funds by each adult male. These payments involved sufficient transfer of wealth to come to the attention of Roman governors (and encourage their rapacity) (cf. Cicero, *Pro Flacco* 28.66-69). Josephus described the existence in Leontopolis in Egypt of a second Jewish temple, which operated for over two hundred years until it was shut down by the Romans in c. 72 CE (*War* 7.420-32; *Ant.* 13.62-73), but it was strikingly not to that temple that the great philosopher Philo looked, despite his proximity to the site, but to Jerusalem. What mattered to Philo, who seems only once to have visited Jerusalem but who devised a complex allegorical interpretation of the details of the Temple ritual, was the *idea* of the Temple cult (Sandmel 1979).

As a result, the destruction of the Temple in 70 CE will have been an appalling disaster for diaspora Jews just as much as for those in Judaea, even if the former had not been caught up in the fighting. They could, and did, provide explanations, both theological and secular, for what had happened (e.g. *4 Ezra*; Josephus, *War* 6.127), but equally crucial was the question of what to do next. The older history textbooks claim that the immediate reaction was to start planning for a Judaism without a temple, a process led by Yohanan b. Zakkai at Yavneh, but such behaviour, farsighted though it turned out to be in practice, is not likely to have been standard among ordinary Jews (cf. Goodman 1994b). For them, the next step was entirely obvious. The Temple had been destroyed, so the task of Jews must be to ensure that, as rapidly as possible, it be rebuilt.

In many ways, such an expectation was wholly reasonable. A rebuilt Temple would not have to be as grand as that of Herod, or even as impressive as the edifice Herod had replaced. Once the site was sufficiently cleared of rubble (a laborious task), the erection of a modest sanctuary and altar would be a simple matter. Plenty of priests survived to officiate, and presumably some still knew what to do. Josephus (*War* 6.268) recorded that people were all too well aware of 'the exactness of the cycle of Destiny' which had delayed the Temple's fall until the precise month and day (as it was supposed) when the Babylonians had destroyed the Temple of Solomon, but in that case they will also have been aware that in due course a new Temple had been built to replace it. Nor was such rebuilding unique to the Jews. When other religious buildings burned down in the Roman world, a not infrequent accident, it was a standard act of pagan piety to permit their re-erection. Emperors before 66 CE freely recognized the worth of the Jewish cult (cf. Josephus, *War* 2.413). Jews might well believe that it would be only a short time before it began again.

Why, then, did it not happen? The answer for at least the next one hundred and fifty years, and perhaps down to the end of late antiquity, does not seem to have been any lessening of desire on the part of the Jews, but the refusal of the Roman state to permit the Jews to behave like all other religious groups within the empire.

The reasons for this unique reluctance by Rome, a reluctance which was to have enormous implications for later Judaism, in fact had, at least in origin, little to do with the Jews at all. In the immediate aftermath of the fall of Jerusalem in 70 CE, the first priority of the Roman emperor Vespasian was not the fate of the Jews but his own position in the Roman state (Levick 1999). Appointed by Nero in 66 CE to the command in Judaea, he had been selected as general over so large a military force precisely because, although he was militarily competent, he was politically insignificant and would therefore pose no threat to the (justifiably) paranoid emperor (Goodman 1987). Nero died in 68 CE following a coup, and was succeeded the next year by no less than four claimants, of whom Vespasian was the last. In practice, Vespasian thus came to power through victory in civil war, but glorying in such an achievement was not best calculated to endear him to his new subjects. Instead he chose, following the precedent of earlier usurpers (notably Augustus), to parade himself as conqueror of foreign enemies dangerous to the state. The only enemies about whom he could possibly make such a claim were the Jews, whom his son Titus subdued in August 70 at great speed, with exceptional ferocity, and with unusual disregard for the loss of Roman soldiers, precisely in order to consolidate as rapidly as possible the propaganda benefits for his imperial image (Goodman 1987: 236).

According to Josephus (*War* 6.238-66) Titus (and presumably also Vespasian) had not intended that the Temple should be burned. Since previous emperors had valued highly the Jews' practice of offering sacrifices in the Temple for the well-being of the emperors themselves, it is not at all unlikely that original Roman war aims involved the re-establishment of the Temple cult under the leadership of pro-Roman high priests such as had cooperated with the Roman state since direct Roman rule was first imposed in Judaea in 6 CE. But once the Temple was destroyed, neither Vespasian nor Titus could safely apologize, since, if the destruction was not portrayed as deliberate, it had to be the product of an incompetent failure of discipline by the commanders on the ground, and would constitute an act of the greatest impiety which would besmirch the record of the new regime.

In any case, no apology was forthcoming. On the contrary, the utensils of the Temple were paraded in their triumph in Rome and displayed as booty in the temple of Pax near the Forum (Josephus, *War* 7.158-62), and all Jews were compelled to pay a symbolic special annual Jewish tax of two denarii to Jupiter Capitolinus in place of the contribution that adult Jewish males had previously sent to Jerusalem (Josephus, *War* 7.218). It must have been hard for the Jews, preoccupied with the aftermath of national defeat, to comprehend the reasons for this Roman recalcitrance, and their growing frustration, culminating in the disastrous defeat of Bar Kochba, can be traced through the next sixty-five years.

In 96 CE the Flavian dynasty founded by Vespasian and Titus came to an end with the murder of Domitian, Titus's younger brother. The new emperor, Nerva, had not been involved in the Judaean war, and the legends on some of his coins, which proclaim a major change in the collection of the Jewish tax, even perhaps its abolition, suggest that he was willing to allow the Jews to return to their earlier state as a protected minority religion within the variegated and multicultural empire ruled by Rome (Shotter 1983). It was almost certainly at this time that Josephus wrote in his last published work, *Contra Apionem* (firmly dated only to between 93 and c. 100 CE), that Jews have only the one Temple in which to worship, using the past tense when referring to the Temple building but the present tense when referring to worship within it (Josephus, *Apion* 2.102-109, 193-199; cf. Bauckham 1996).

The dashing of these entirely reasonable hopes seems to have come about for reasons that, once again, the Jews can hardly have anticipated, or ever fully understood. Nerva was an old man when he became emperor in mid-96 CE, and quite soon after his accession, his bodyguard, the praetorian cohorts on whom he relied for his personal security, compelled him to adopt a suitable son and heir so as to avoid the uncertainty about the succession which had proven so politically damaging in Rome over the past century (Griffin 2000). Nerva chose a young army commander named M. Ulpius Traianus, the future emperor Trajan. As luck would have it, the fortune of Trajan's previously obscure family had been made, like that of Vespasian, some thirty years earlier in the Judaean war, when his father, also called Traianus, had commanded a legion against the Jewish rebels (Alföldy 1998 and 2000). Any hope that the Jewish Temple might be rehabilitated within Roman society was lost.

The long-term consequences were immense. Towards the end of Trajan's rule, in 115 CE, a violent Jewish insurrection erupted in Egypt, Cyrene, Cyprus and Mesopotamia. Our sources of evidence—all either Christian or pagan, since the rabbis were silent on the whole awful affair—give no reason for the uprising, but the obvious cause will have been frustration at the continuing refusal of Rome to allow the Temple to be rebuilt (Goodman 1992; *contra* Horbury 1996).

The final suppression of the revolt in 117 CE coincided with the death of Trajan (Pucci 1981), and his successor, Hadrian, was at first too occupied in securing his own position within the Roman state to have time to deal fully with the Jews. When he did so, eventually, it was in characteristically thorough fashion (Birley 1997). In 130 CE he decided to expunge the name of Jerusalem altogether and to found upon the site of the city a miniature Rome, the Roman colony Aelia Capitolina (Cassius Dio 69.12.1-2). The Jews rebelled 'for the freedom of Jerusalem', as their coins proclaimed, led by Simon bar Kosiba, acclaimed Bar Kochba by his admirers (Mildenberg 1984). But resistance was in vain. In 135 CE the defeated province was renamed Syria Palaestina, Jews were forbidden to remain in their homeland, and the possibility of rebuilding the Temple faded into the distant future (Eck 1999).

This whole sorry tale of frustrated hope attests to the continuing centrality of the Jerusalem Temple in the religious lives of the Jews both in the homeland and in the diaspora even many years after its destruction. Some have argued that the detailed descriptions of the Temple and its rituals found in the Mishnah, redacted some seventy years or so after Bar Kochba, were idealizing and never intended to reflect the real institution (Neusner 1979), but there is no evidence to support this view and it seems more reasonable to assume that the reason for their intense discussions of the way that sacrifices should be offered was that the tannaim generally hoped for a return to temple worship in their own days.

It is difficult to judge precisely when this hope faded and was projected instead on to the future state of Israel in the days of the Messiah, but a point by which at least some Jews appear to have reconciled themselves to life without the Temple may be discerned in the mid-fourth century CE, when, in 362 CE, the emperor Julian, who had once been a Christian but had apostatized to paganism, decided that a good way to infuriate his former co-religionists was to rebuild the Jewish Temple in Jerusalem (Avi-Yonah 1976: 185-207). Rebuilding started, but the attempt eventually came to nothing because Julian died soon after, in 363 CE, while on campaign. The Christian sources narrate in horrified tones the start of rebuilding and the enthusiasm of the Jews, but, so far as is known from surviving manuscripts of rabbinic texts composed in Palestine in the fourth century and later, this was not an enthusiasm shared by the rabbis, who (if the surviving manuscripts give an accurate picture) seem almost totally to have ignored what had happened.

It is possible, then, that at least among the rabbis, by the mid-fourth century hopes for the rebuilding no longer looked to the immediate future. On the other hand, it is certain that the significance of the Temple priests remained powerful for some Jews at least for the rest of late antiquity, as can be seen from the frequent references to the Priestly courses in fifth–sixth century Palestinian synagogue mosaics and the prominence of priests in Palestinian poetry (*piyyûṭ*) of this period (Irshai 2003). Such attitudes may largely have been the product of eschatological expectation, but it is not impossible that they were also practical and mundane. By the twelfth century CE it was possible for Maimonides (*Guide of the Perplexed* 3.32, 46) to refer to the whole system of sacrificial worship as a regrettable stage through which Jews had had to go in order to wean them from worse practices (though even then such an attitude was by no means standard; cf. the view of Nahmanides, *Commentary on Lev.* 1.9), but by then Jews lived in a wholly different world in which neither Christians nor Muslims saw a role for sacrifices. It would be unsurprising if the eventual fading of Jewish hopes for the Temple service to be restored in the immediate non-eschatological future were linked, like so much in Jewish history, to developments in the culture of the surrounding world.

Bibliography

Alföldy, G.

1998 'Traianus Pater und die Bauinschrift des Nymphäums von Milet', *Revue des Etudes Anciennes* 100: 367-99.

2000 'Trajano Padre y la inscripción del nimfeo de Miletos', in J. Gonzalez (ed.), *Trajano: Emperador de Roma* (Rome: L'Erma di Bretschneider): 11-24.

Avigad, N.
1984 *Discovering Jerusalem* (Oxford: Basil Blackwell).
Avi-Yonah, M.
1976 *The Jews of Palestine* (Oxford: Basil Blackwell).
Bauckham, R.
1996 'Josephus' Account of the Temple in *Contra Apionem* 2. 102-109', in L.H. Feldman and J.R. Levison (eds.), *Studies in Josephus' Contra Apionem* (Leiden: E.J. Brill): 327-47.
Beard, M., J.A. North and S.R.F. Price
1998 *Religions of Rome* (2 vols.; Cambridge: Cambridge University Press).
Birley, A.R.
1997 *Hadrian: The Restless Emperor* (London: Routledge).
Busink, Th.A.
1978, 1980 *Der Tempel von Jerusalem* (2 vols.; Leiden: E.J. Brill).
Eck, W.
1999 'The Bar Kochba Revolt: The Roman Point of View', *JRS* 89: 76-89.
Feldman, L.H.
1993 *Jew and Gentile in the Ancient World* (Princeton, NJ: Princeton University Press).
Goodman, M.
1987 *The Ruling Class of Judaea: The Origins of the Jewish Revolt Against Rome, A.D. 66–70* (Cambridge: Cambridge University Press).
1992 'Diaspora Reactions to the Destruction of the Temple', in J.D.G. Dunn (ed.), *Jews and Christians: The Parting of the Ways, A.D. 70 to 135* (Tübingen: J.C.B. Mohr [Paul Siebeck]): 27-38.
1994a 'E.P. Sanders' *Judaism: Practice and Belief*', *SJT* 47.1: 89-95.
1994b 'Sadducees and Essenes after 70 CE', in S.E. Porter, P. Joyce and D.E. Orton (eds.), *Crossing the Boundaries: Essays in Biblical Interpretation in Honour of Michael Goulder* (Leiden: E.J. Brill): 347-56.
1999a 'The Pilgrimage Economy of Jerusalem in the Second Temple Period', in L.I. Levine (ed.), *Jerusalem: Its Sanctity and Centrality to Judaism, Christianity and Islam* (New York: Continuum): 69-76.
1999b 'Galilean Judaism and Judaean Judaism', in W.D. Davies and W. Horbury (eds.), *The Cambridge History of Judaism* (3 vols. so far; Cambridge: Cambridge University Press), III: 596-617.
2000 'Josephus and Variety in First-Century Judaism', *Proceedings of the Israel Academy of Sciences and Humanities* 7.6: 201-13.
Griffin, M.
2000 'Nerva', in A.K. Bowman, P. Garnsey and D. Rathbone (eds.), *The Cambridge Ancient History* (Cambridge: Cambridge University Press, 2nd edn): XI, 84-96.
Hayward, C.T.R.
1996 *The Jewish Temple: A Non-Biblical Source Book* (London: Routledge).
Holladay, A.J., and M. Goodman
1986 'Religious Scruples in Ancient Warfare', *Classical Quarterly* 36: 151-71.
Horbury, W.
1996 'The Beginnings of the Jewish Revolt under Trajan', in H. Cancik, H. Lichtenberger and P. Schäfer (eds.), *Geschichte—Tradition—Reflexion. Festschrift für Martin Hengel zum 70 Geburtstag* (3 vols.; Tübingen: J.C.B. Mohr [Paul Siebeck]): I, 283-304.

Irshai, O.
2003 'The Role of the Priesthood in the Jewish Community in Late Antiquity: A Christian Model?', in C. Cluse, A. Haverkamp and I.J.Yuval (eds.), *Jüdische Gemeinden und ihr christlicher Kontext in kulturräumlich vergleichender Betrachtung (5.-18. Jahrhundert)* (Forschungen zur Geschichte der Juden, 13; Hanover: Verlag Hahnsche Buchhandlung): 75-85.

Jacobson, D.M.
1990–91 'The Plan of Herod's Temple', *Bulletin of the Anglo-Israel Archaeological Society* 10: 36-66.

Levick, B.
1999 *The Emperor Vespasian* (London: Routledge).

Levine, L.I.
1994 'Josephus' Description of the Jerusalem Temple', in F. Parente and J. Sievers (eds.), *Josephus and the History of the Greco-Roman Period: Essays in Memory of Morton Smith* (Studia Post-Biblica, 41; Leiden: E.J. Brill): 233-46.

Mildenberg, L.
1984 *The Coinage of the Bar Kokhba War* (Aarau: Sauerländer).

Neusner, J.
1979 'Map without Territory: Mishnah's System of Sacrifice and Sanctuary', *History of Religions* 19: 103-27.

Pucci, M.
1981 *La Rivolta Ebraica al tempo di Traiano* (Pisa: Giardini).

Qimron, E., and J. Strugnell (eds.)
1994 *Qumran Cave 4, V: Miqṣat Ma'aśe Ha-Torah* (DJD, 10. Oxford: Clarendon Press).

Safrai, S.
1985 *Pilgrimage at the Time of the Second Temple* (Jerusalem: Akademon, 2nd edn [Hebrew]).

Sanders, E.P.
1992 *Judaism: Practice and Belief, 63 BCE–66 CE* (London: SCM Press).

Sandmel, S.
1979 *Philo of Alexandria: An Introduction* (New York and Oxford: Oxford University Press).

Schürer, E.
1973–87 *The History of the Jewish People in the Age of Jesus Christ* (3 vols. in 4; revised G. Vermes *et al.*; Edinburgh: T. & T. Clark).

Shotter, D.C.A.
1983 'The Principate of Nerva, Some Observations on the Coin Evidence', *Historia* 32: 218-23.

Stern, M. (ed.)
1974–84 *Greek and Latin Authors on Jews and Judaism* (3 vols.; Jerusalem: The Israel Academy of Sciences and Humanities).

THE TEMPLE IN THE NEW TESTAMENT

Christopher Rowland

Initially, the early Christians shared the ambivalent relationship to the Temple evident in some circles in the Second Temple period (e.g. Acts 6.7; cf. Mk 14.58; Jn 4.25; McKelvey 1969; Rosenau 1979; Bachmann 1980; Horbury 1990; Brown 1994; Walker 1996; Chilton and Evans 1997; Ådna 2000). Such ambivalence about the Second Temple is not just a Christian phenomenon, however, as it is manifest in passages like *1 En.* 89.73, *Ass. Mos.* 4.5, and *2 En.* 45.3. While most Second Temple texts indicate divine approbation for the Temple (Ecclus 24; *1 En.* 25.46), others suggest a less positive assessment of the successor to Solomon's edifice (*1 En.* 89.73; cf. 91.12-13), itself the subject of an ambiguous oracle in 2 Sam. 7.5-7, 13. Alongside this there was a longing for an eschatological Temple (Tob. 13–14; *Jub.* 1.15-18; 23.8-32; 25; 11QT; cf. Ezek. 36.26-28; Mal. 3.3) or a belief that the heavenly world was the dwelling place for God (*1 En.* 14). This meant that a parallel existed between the heavenly and the earthly in Jewish cosmology, in which the earthly was a pattern of the heavenly (cf. Exod. 25.40). Early Christianity is part of a wider social and theological trend evident in Jewish texts in which cultic language is used in a transferred sense of common life or individual holiness, so that the destruction of the Temple in 70 CE, however catastrophic it might have been, did not leave Jewish groups, of whom the early Christians were one, without the resources to construct a religion which could survive without sacrifice and the ritual of the Temple.

In the New Testament the words used of the Temple are ἱερόν, ναός and οἶκος. At first sight ἱερόν and ναός are used interchangeably in the New Testament. We find ἱερόν used in Mark's Gospel, for example in chs. 11–13, οἶκος in Mk 2.26 and 11.17, and ναός in the Temple saying in 14.58, the allusion to it in 15.29 and the reference to the rending of the veil in 15.39. Ἱερόν is much more common in Luke than ναός (found at Lk. 1.9, 21, 22; 23.45). All the really significant references, theologically, have ναός (Jn 2.19; Acts 17.24; 1 Cor. 3.16, 17; 6.19; 2 Cor. 6.16; Eph. 2.21; 2 Thess. 2.4; Rev. 21.22). It is the word preferred in the Apocalypse (Schrenk 1938: 232-47, ET 1965: 232-47; Michel 1942, ET 1967). Οἶκος is the word used in Stephen's speech in the context of the discussion of Solomon's interpretation of Nathan's oracle in Acts 7.47-49.

1. *The Gospels*

At the centre of Jewish religious life before the First Revolt in 66 CE was the Temple in Jerusalem. The complex of cultic activity carried on there in fulfilment of the cultic regulations of the Torah was a focus of devotion for Jews from all over the world. In the narrative of the last days of Jesus' life in the synoptic Gospels the Temple is a particular focus. The story of the cursing of the fig tree which sandwiches the 'cleansing' is probably a comment on the bankruptcy of the institution. All the Gospels record the fact that Jesus entered the Temple and drove out the traders from the outer court (Mk 11.15-19 and par.). In the Gospel of John the incident is said to have taken place at the beginning of the ministry (Jn 2.13), though it may well have been placed here as part of the structure of argument of the Gospel as a whole (cf. Jn 4.22), in which the divine tabernacling emerges in the early chapters from 1.14 through to ch. 4. The 'cleansing' of the Temple may (at least at this stage, as the situation could have changed after Jesus' rejection by the hierarchy) have been less a protest against the Temple than a summons to reform. The emphasis on the Temple as a house of prayer (Mk 11.17) suggests a rather different role than the primary function of a Temple, to be a place of sacrifice.

There has been much debate over the meaning of this incident. In interpreting it, much depends on the weight one attaches to the quotations from Scripture (Isa. 56.7; Jer. 7.11), and the implied fulfilment of Zech. 14.21 in Jesus' dismissal of the traders. The background is eschatological beliefs about a new Temple, to which the Gentiles would come, reflected in passages like Isa. 2.3, Mic. 4.1-4 and *1 En.* 90.29. It is possible that the dramatic action against the Temple operatives may have symbolized the belief expressed in words elsewhere in the tradition (Mk 14.58; cf. Jn 2.17) that the old Temple had first to be destroyed to make way for the eschatological Temple, though the scriptural glosses suggest a less discontinuous and more reformist sentiment. There may be a hint in John's version of the cleansing that it was seen as a protest against the sacrificial system, for in this version of the story Jesus ejects the sacrificial animals from the Temple also (Jn 2.15). If, however, the Last Supper was a Passover meal, we may suppose that, at least according to the evangelists, Jesus did accept the sacrificial system (Lk. 22.15).

The action against the Temple and the words, which Jesus may have spoken about its destruction, were probably offensive (so Mk 11.18), possibly a reason for their omission from the account of Jesus' life in the Gospel of Luke, where the critique of the Temple is linked with Stephen in Acts 6–7. According to Mk 15.29, Jesus was reproached with his prediction about the Temple in the last moments of his life. While it is not easy to see how any of Jesus' reported words about the Temple could be regarded as blasphemy, except in a very indirect sense, it was the kind of comment which was likely to have caused, at the very least, deep suspicion (e.g. Jn 11.47; cf. Josephus, *War* 2.397). A word against the Temple could have been brought dire consequences for the one who uttered it, as we know happened in the case of another Jesus who predicted the destruction of the Temple and suffered for his pains (Josephus, *War* 6.300-301).

If the initial foray into the Temple seems at first glance, in the versions which have come down to us, to be a plea for reform, the situation is different in the account of the last days in Jerusalem. Before leaving the Temple for the last time,

Jesus gets his companions to note the way in which the widow, out of her poverty, puts in everything she had to live on (Mk 12.44) while the rest contributed out of their abundance. The incident is described without comment. Nevertheless, in the light of Mk 12.40, where the scribes are condemned for devouring widows' houses, the observation that an institution at the heart of Jewish life allows an impoverished widow to give all that she had sits uneasily with the demand in the Torah to care for the widow. If this interpretation seems to be squeezeing too much out of the text, the situation is different in the following verses. It is immediately followed by the eschatological discourse, at the beginning of which (Mk 13.2) Jesus tells his disciples that there will not be left one stone of the Temple on top of another (cf. Lk. 19.47). A prophecy of doom now takes the place of a hope for a different kind of institution found in 11.17 (though the curse on the fig tree probably implies a less hopeful future). The doom-laden prediction (cf. Lk. 19.41-44) is similar to Jeremiah's prediction in Jer. 7.12 (cf. Jer. 26; Mic. 3.12). In the account of his questioning by the high priest in Mk 14.56-58, witnesses report a saying of Jesus, otherwise not recorded in this form in the Gospels, to the effect that Jesus would destroy the Temple and in three days build a Temple not made with hands (Mk 14.58; cf. Mt. 26.61). There is a version of this saying on the lips of Jesus in the Gospel of John (2.19), though it takes the form of a promise by Jesus to rebuild the Temple destroyed by others rather than a promise to destroy and rebuild (cf. Acts 6.14; 7.50). This is then glossed as a reference to the body of Jesus (Jn 2.21-22; cf. 1 Cor 6.19).

The judgment on the Temple and also implicitly its destruction is integral to one of the climactic moments of the synoptic Gospels. At the death of Jesus the veil, which hides the innermost part of the Temple, is torn asunder. This portends doom for the institution and its ideology, which had dominated life, politically, religiously and economically. This moment in the Gospel harks back to the opening chapter, where, at the baptism, a heavenly voice had proclaimed Jesus as God's son and the heavens are rent apart. Heaven and earth are then linked at the rending of the heavens (Mk 1.10 and 15.38). The rending of the veil of the Temple at Jesus' death is by contrast a sign of judgment, not of promise. The juxtaposition of death and rending at the climax of Mark's Gospel means that the moment of defeat of Jesus portends the institution's collapse. It is left to a representative of the Roman military power to recognize in this moment the reign of another sort of king than Caesar. It resembles the situation where in the days of Israel's exile the departure of the divine glory from the Temple was a sign of imminent destruction (Ezek. 1 and 10). But, unlike the prophecy of Ezekiel, there is here no promise that any building would ever again be set apart as a particular place of the divine presence and worship. The extremely compact sequence marks the very start of the 'Christus Victor' doctrine of the atonement in which the defeat of the son of God catches the powers, whether earthly or heavenly, unawares and leads to their discomfiture (1 Cor. 2.9; Col. 2.14-15; 1 Pet. 3.22; cf. Myers 1988; Horsley 2001; Green 1994: 514).

I have deliberately kept the discussion at the level of the New Testament texts as we have them. If I had to try to summarize what relationship these texts had with the last days of the historical Jesus my brief answer would be a fairly conservative one, in that I tend to accept what all the Gospels say about the sense of divine compulsion which led Jesus to go up to Jerusalem to provoke the crisis, which in the end led to his death. In Jerusalem a large popular following in the volatile atmosphere of Jerusalem at pilgrimage time was enough to set him at odds with the priests. In the final days of his life, possibly in the light of the hostility he encountered, he may have uttered prophecies of doom on the Temple and Jerusalem after initially entertaining hopes of reform. There are hints that he might also have begun to contemplate a separate sectarian existence for his followers, with distinctive rites and institutions in the words he uttered at the Last Supper. I think it quite plausible, therefore, that in the last days and hours of his life the *lack* of success of the Jerusalem expedition led Jesus from a more reformist position with regard to the Temple (it should be purified for a new age) to a less optimistic, more sectarian and 'rejectionist' position, in which he asserted that its end was in sight and that it might have no part in the divine plan.

As we have seen, the opening chapters of the Gospel of John include several implicit links between Jesus and the Temple, in which Jesus takes the Temple's place. At the climax of the opening chapter in Jn 1.51, Nathanael is promised a vision which echoes the account of Jacob's vision at Bethel in Gen. 28.12 (Rowland 1984). In this context in which the Son of Man is the intermediary between heaven and earth, the Temple incident is described. The manifestation of divine glory exemplified by the sign at Cana in Galilee means that the locus of that divine glory is now focused pre-eminently, and perhaps exclusively, in the Word become flesh and in the demonstration of glory in the lifting up of Jesus on the cross (Jn 3.14; 12.32-33). As Jesus tells the Samaritan woman, Gerizim and Zion have had their day. True worship is worship in spirit and truth (Jn 4.20-24). The Temple has to take second place to this definitive manifestation of divine glory. The divine presence continues in the community of believers as the Father and the Son make their home with the faithful disciple (Jn 14.23).

The 'tabernacling' of the divine Logos as the definitive presence of the divine glory is a theme which we find in the other Gospels too. A motif right the way through Matthew is that God's presence is found in Jesus (Mt. 1.23; 18.20; 28.19; cf. 25.31-45), for 'one greater than the Temple is here' (Mt. 12.8). The fact that Luke's Gospel begins in the Temple should not disguise that fact that the Temple is linked with the birth of John, whose coming marks the end of the age of the Law and the prophets (Lk. 16.16). The coming of Jesus in humble circumstances is discerned by the inspired insight of Simeon and Anna as they meet the infant Jesus in the Temple. The respect for the institutions of Law and Temple cannot mask the underlying thrust of the Gospel and Acts which moves away from allocating a special role for the Temple as the locus of the divine presence. To return to the Gospel of John: the theme of tabernacling not only has links with wisdom's special location in Israel's institutions (Ecclus 24), for it is also linked with the incarnation of exalted angels in humans, as is evident from the Jewish pseudepigraphon, *The Prayer of Joseph*, quoted by Origen in his commentary on

Jn 1.6 (Smith 1968). Such angelomorphism reminds us that a narrative like the Transfiguration, present as it is in all the synoptic Gospels, offers an account of the presence of the divine glory apart from the Temple and particularly identified with the person of Jesus. These accounts (particularly the one in Matthew) are best interpreted in the light of passages such as Dan. 10.2-9, Rev. 1.13-17, *Apoc. Abr.* 10–11, and *Joseph and Aseneth* 14 (Rowland 1985), and complement the belief that Jesus is 'God with us' (Mt. 1.23), the one who is 'greater than the Temple' (Mt. 12.8).

2. *The Acts of the Apostles*

According to Acts the first Christians continued to worship in the Temple, and this is often taken as an indication of a continued reverence for the Temple. Such continued practice would be understandable, even if the underlying trend was towards a religion which was separate from physical participation in the Temple cult. Life in Jerusalem without reference to participation in the Temple seems unlikely. However, the initial preoccupation with the Temple needs to be set in the context of a narrative in which the divine presence moves with the representatives of the new movements out of Jerusalem to Rome. Gamaliel's words in Acts 5.38-39 express the author's view that the priests and the representatives of the Temple who oppose the emerging Christian movement turn out to be rebels, as the solemn quotation of Isa. 6.9 in the final verses of Acts 28 indicate. Such a rebellion is a particular feature of Stephen's speech in Acts 7.

In this speech about the rebelliousness of the majority of his ancestors he points to Solomon, who built a house for God. In three ways Stephen's speech challenges the divine approbation of the Temple: by making the command to Moses about the tabernacle the result of angelic revelation only; by referring to the implicit disobedience of Solomon; and the suggestion that the Temple was little better than the idolatrous places of the nations.

God's response to the calf in Acts 7.41-42 leads to false worship. The incident of the calf (Exod. 32) leads to God handing the people over to the worship of the host of heaven. The Greek of Amos 5.25-27 is used to prove that it was not to God that Israel sacrificed, but the host of heaven and Moloch. In some ways this passage echoes the theme in Ezek. 20.25-26, where the laws given by God were not good laws but the result of the people's idolatry and disobedience.

In the understated way, which is typical of his speech, Stephen then implicitly questions whether the tent of testimony was really the result of divine revelation. Despite the suggestion of NRSV's translation of the following verse ('Our ancestors had the tent of testimony in the wilderness, as God directed when he spoke to Moses', Acts 7.44) that the cult in the wilderness was the result of divine command, the Greek is more ambiguous. While it would at first sight seem natural to suppose that ὁ λαλῶν refers to God, the last time reference is made to converse between the divine world and Moses in Acts 7.38 it is the angel who speaks with him. Both verses subtly distance God from the ordinances for the wilderness cult, not to mention the Temple in Jerusalem. Angelic mediation in the giving of the

Law is found in *Jub.* 1.27, 3.7, Gal. 3.19, and Heb. 2.2. It is not clear whether the doctrine is being used polemically in Stephen's speech, as all that may be suggested here is that the Law was the product of mediation rather than revelation.

Criticism of an altogether different kind is to be found in the most explicit and stinging criticism of Stephen, directed at Solomon's Temple (Acts 7.46). He points to Solomon as the one who built a house, οἶκος, for God rather than establish the σκήνωμα for the house of Jacob, which is part of the promise to David. David found favour with God and asked God to find a dwelling for the house of Jacob (assuming that οἴκῳ is to be preferred in 7.46). But it was Solomon who built the house. Implicit in this description of Solomon's act is a misunderstanding of what 'dwelling place for the house of Jacob' involved, which was concerned with the promise of the dwelling for Jacob in the land (as seems to be suggested by 2 Sam. 7.10, itself an ambiguous oracle). 2 Samuel 7.13 is merely a prediction of the Temple's construction rather than any approbation of the Temple building. Indeed, the tension between the relative merits of the tabernacle as opposed to a permanent building is one that appears in 2 Sam. 7.6-7 and 1 Chron. 17.6-7 (cf. Isa. 66.1; 1 Kgs 8.27).

The quotation from Isa. 66.1 in Acts 7.49 suggests that Solomon's building of a house for God marked a departure from the divine intention. The introduction of Acts 7.48 suggests a departure from the divine intention. The position of the negative underlines the extent of the misunderstanding by Solomon in his interpretation of the oracle in 1 Kgs 8.20. What is more, the use of χειροποίητος, a word which is almost always linked with idolatry in the Greek Bible (cf. Acts 17.24), stresses the extent of the apostasy (Barrett 1991; 1994: 368-76, esp. 373; cf. Walton 2004). This is a holy place like the high places of the surrounding peoples. So Stephen's speech hints that the heart of Jewish religion is idolatrous, a point which was probably not lost on Stephen's 'hearers' according to the Acts narrative, who reacted violently against what appeared to be a near blasphemous charge. So, while it is true that the early chapters of Acts have the apostles frequenting the Temple, this needs to be set in the context of the narrative as a whole. Stephen's speech is pivotal and provides the reader with new interpretative horizons concerning the providential work of God, which points away from Jerusalem's Temple (where the story in both Luke and Acts begins) to its providential destination at the ends of the earth.

The themes of Stephen's speech have their parallels in other early Christian texts. The idolatrous character of aspects of the religion is also taken up in the *Epistle of Barnabas* (16.7), which parallels some of the themes of Acts 7 (Paget 1994). Jewish cultic worship is condemned, and Barnabas implies that God has rejected that form of worship and compares it to its pagan equivalent (cf. Gal. 4.8-10). The true temple is the human soul in which God dwells, not a building of stone (Paget 1994: 172-74). The polemic we find in Stephen's speech also typifies the emerging Christian polemic against Judaism, if Justin's *Dialogue with Trypho* is anything to go by (Justin, *Dial.* 35). Justin's answer repeats the Stephen tradition that Jews have always been idolaters from the incident of the calf onwards. Without appreciating the extent of acts of martyrdom which took place during the Bar-Kochba revolt, Justin points to Christian acts of resistance against idolatry even to death as proof of Christian rejection of idolatry (*Dial.* 34–35; 46.6-7; cf. Lieu 1996: 115-17).

Finally, in Acts 21.18-26 we find Paul in the Temple with non-Jews bringing the collection (if this is what is referred to in Acts 21.19; cf. 2 Cor. 8–9; Rom. 15.25). Paul is ready to pass a stiff test of his obedience to the letter of the Torah in paying for the release of the Nazirite vows. In this Paul is asked not only to submit to the Law of Moses but also to accept the Temple, as Num. 6.9, 18 indicate. Paul accepts this but the Nazirite vow is hardly completed before Paul is rejected by the mob, an event which leads to his appeal to Caesar and the journey to Rome. Parallel to Jesus in the Gospel, Paul in Acts goes up to Jerusalem, explicitly driven by divine impulse, like Jesus according to Lk. 9.51, and with prophetic warning of the impending rejection (Acts 21.11). In the case of both Jesus and Paul the reception in Jerusalem and the Temple is hostile. The chance is offered and rejected and the message goes to the ends of the earth leaving Jerusalem and its Temple behind. Acts may lack the ominous supernatural voices and portents which herald the destruction of the city in Josephus' account of the years leading up to the First Revolt (Josephus, *War* 6.280). But, like Josephus, who has Jesus son of Ananias predicting a woe on Jerusalem and the Temple (Josephus, *War* 6.300), Luke includes a prediction of the destruction of the city immediately preceding the entrance into the Temple (Lk. 19.41-44). Nothing that happens thereafter, culminating in the rejection of Jesus' emissary, Paul, in Acts 21, does anything to stave off the disaster which is to come.

3. *The New Testament Epistles with Special Reference to Hebrews*

The Pauline letters continue the widespread way in Second Temple Jewish texts in which the transferred sense of temple and cult are applied to lives of service (Rom. 12.1; 1 Cor. 3.16; 6.19; 2 Cor. 6.14–7.1). In 2 Cor. 6.14–7.1 the sense of separation and counter-cultural character of the life of the nascent communities is well captured in what may be an earlier fragment of Pauline theology, influenced by the kind of dualistic ideas we find in the Dead Sea Scrolls. Similarly, according to 1 Cor. 3.17, to destroy God's living temple is as serious a crime as perpetrated by those who defile the Temple, echoing the dire threat found at the entrance to the Temple, mentioned by Josephus and discovered at the end of the nineteenth century ('whoever is caught going beyond the barrier will have himself to blame if death ensues'). In Eph. 2.19-21 temple imagery is used of the way in which the new building of the church emerges with Christ as cornerstone. This parallels the use of the body terminology from 1 Corinthians 12 and Romans 12 in Eph. 4.12, yielding a complex mix of imagery concerning organic and structural growth. Paul occasionally transfers priestly language to his own apostolic task in Rom. 15.15-16. Similarly in 1 Pet. 2.5, 9 and Rev. 1.6 (cf. 5.10; 20.6; Justin, *Dial.* 116.3) we find priestly terminology from Exod. 19.6 applied to the Christian community (cf. Isa. 61.6).

Outside the Pauline corpus the most extended exposition of Christ's relationship to the cultic institutions of the Torah is found in the Epistle to the Hebrews, where the discussion focuses on the tabernacle rather than the Temple. What sets Christ apart from the angels is his sacrifice, which establishes the ultimate link between heaven and earth. A new and living way is opened up (Heb. 10.20), brought about by a body of flesh and blood.

Christ is the one who has passed through the heavens (Heb. 4.14; cf. 6.19; 9.24; 10.19; 12.2) and is now seated at the right hand of the majesty on high (1.5). From Heb. 7.1 onwards the writer explains the significance of the references to the high priesthood of Jesus already hinted at in Heb. 4.14 and 6.20. Jesus was not a high priest of the line of Aaron and was therefore not permitted to officiate in the earthly cult (Heb. 7.11). His high priesthood was according to the order of Melchizedek. His superior office is linked with the superior offering made only once (Heb. 7.27; 9.25; 10.11), unlike the offerings made by the Levitical priesthood which, it is stressed, could not bring into a right relationship with God (Heb. 9.9). Perfection was not to be found in the Levitical priesthood and was merely a shadow of a greater, heavenly reality (Heb. 10.1).

The subtle interweaving of ideas about heavenly high priesthood and superiority to angels has its roots in speculation about the heavenly world and the angelomorphism which is so characteristic of Second Temple Jewish texts (*Apoc. Abr.* 10-11; cf. Exod. 23.20; also Hannah 1998; Hurtado 1988; 2003). The contrasts in Hebrews between the sacrifice of Christ and the sacrifices of the Levitical system and between the heavenly perfection and earthly shadow have been taken as indications of Platonic influence. This is unlikely. Hebrews is dependent on an apocalyptic cosmology to illuminate soteriology whose background is to be found in Jewish apocalypticism and mystical tradition (Attridge 1989; Barrett 1956; Chester 1991; Hofius 1970; 1972; Hurst 1990; Isaacs 1992). Any influence from this quarter may already have infiltrated the emerging apocalyptic tradition with its contrasts between the heavenly world above as the repository of God's ultimate purposes and the world below, where those purposes might be fulfilled. Jewish writings offer evidence that the heavenly cult was something which reflected the activities on earth even to the extent of having a heavenly high priest offering sacrifice. In *b. Ḥag.* 12b, for example, Michael acts as the heavenly priest in one of the highest heavens, Zebul. There is reference to sacrifices made by angels in heaven in *T. Levi* 3.5. There the patriarch ascends to heaven, where God is enthroned in the highest heaven. Before God are the angels 'who minister and make propitiation to the Lord for all the sins of ignorance of the righteous'.

Hebrews 8–10 presupposes a division between earthly and heavenly. According to Heb. 8.5 the earthly shrine was an exact copy of the heavenly. The earthly priests serve merely a copy of the heavenly sanctuary (Heb. 8.5), whereas Christ has entered heaven itself, not the sanctuary which has been made with hands (Heb. 9.24). It is the perfection of the heavenly cult which is the setting for Christ's offering (cf. Heb. 8.5). According to Hebrews, Jesus, by virtue of the sacrifice of himself, was able to enter, not the earthly, but the heavenly sanctuary (Heb. 9.23-24; cf. 9.13). Christ is permitted to go behind the veil into the inner sanctum of heaven and then sit at the right hand of God (Heb. 4.16; 8.1; 12.29), thus becoming the guarantor of the salvation of the faithful (Heb. 6.19-20). Christ's death enabled him to 'ascend' to the divine presence, the climax, in other words, of the ascent of the apocalyptic seer, and he is a pioneer for those who would follow him (Heb. 12.1).

For the author of Hebrews the heavenly sanctuary is the eschatological sanctuary, built (Heb. 8.2) along with the city by God at the end of the age, an age that has now arrived according to Heb. 1.2. The climax of history has now occurred as Jesus is the first to enter the heavenly sanctuary. There is in Hebrews that oscillation between the 'vertical' and the 'horizontal', if one can use spatial metaphors to illuminate the theology of Hebrews. What is above, in heaven, is what is to come and is what will be revealed in the end time; but what is to come is now already revealed (Heb. 9.26) and to which the recipients of the Letter to the Hebrews have access (Heb. 12.22). Even if Hebrews concentrates on the 'vertical' rather than the 'horizontal', the realized rather than the eschatological, the spatial dualism of the apocalyptic and mystical texts facilitates a dialectic, which enables the writer to communicate both the transcendence of present realities and the immediacy of the transcendent in the midst of history.

The cross thus becomes the moment when the unmediated access to God becomes a possibility. Paradoxically the death outside the camp (Heb. 13.12) becomes the place where heaven and earth coincide. Access to the heart of heaven has been achieved by those who follow this heavenly high priest (Heb. 4.16). The cross has become a meeting-point between heaven and earth. The coming together of this age and the age to come (cf. 1 Cor. 10.11) has come at a point when Christ offered sacrifice of himself outside the camp. The place of reproach and rejection turns out to be the very gate of heaven. The moment of the offering of the sacrifice is in history, and yet entrance into heaven takes place at the moment of the death of Jesus 'outside the gate'. The way to the innermost sanctum comes via crucifixion.

In the letter the writer opens up access to the heavenly world for his readers. Like the community of the Dead Sea Scrolls (1QS 11; 1QH 3.20; 11.10) they are offered access to heaven and its inhabitants in the life of this marginal group, to the heavenly Jerusalem itself (Heb. 12.22), and have no need of participation in what the writer considers obsolete rituals. Readers are shown a picture of a heavenly pioneer who opens up access to this other dimension and enters that which transcends the limits of 'the veil of the flesh' to create the possibility of an alternative space for those who, like Jesus, journey with him in search of the eschatological rest, 'outside the camp'.

Hebrews is unequivocal that the religion of the tabernacle (and by implication the Temple also, according to Heb. 9.9) is redundant, made obsolete by a sacrifice which offers access to the very presence of God. Connections have been suggested between Hebrews and Acts 7. But if the reading of Acts 7 adopted in this essay is correct, Stephen's speech is much more radical, for in Hebrews the religion of the tabernacle is simply part of the old aeon (Heb. 1.4). Hebrews is in this sense more 'Pauline' than 'Stephen-like' in its understanding of the past.

4. *The Apocalypse*

The contrasts between heavenly and earthly tabernacle pervade the Apocalypse (Rev. 6.19; 8.3; 11.19; 15.5). In John's vision the tabernacle and Temple are situated in heaven, the source of the divine righteousness (11.19), whose altar is the temporary abode of the souls of those who long for God's vindication (Rev. 6.9-10; cf. 9.13) and who serve God day and night in the Temple (7.15). Compared with the anticipation of the new age in 7.15, John reports that he saw no Temple at the end of his vision (21.22). The explanation offered in the text is that Almighty God and the Lamb are the Temple (v. 22). If a Temple separates off a place of divine presence in the midst of a world, here the divine is immediately present and all-pervasive, which guarantees and identifies holiness (though in Rev. 21–22 the city as a whole becomes a holy precinct outside of which are the unclean, 21.8; 22.15). Revelation 22.11 has indicated there is little need of light because of the radiance of divine glory (cf. Rev. 22.5 and Isa. 60.19). The whole of the city is a space, pervaded with the glory of God and the Lamb. With the establishment of holiness in the midst of the world and in the lives of people of flesh and blood there will be no need for a Temple, either in heaven or on earth, for the tabernacling of God is with humans (Rev. 21.3) and they will see God face to face (Rev. 22.4; Rowland 1998).

If there is a 'story line' to the Apocalypse, it is about the overcoming of the contrasts between 'above' and 'below' and the separation from the divine presence in heaven from earth. The coming of the New Jerusalem from heaven heralds an era when the dwelling of God is with humanity (Rev. 21.3). The climax of the book of Revelation is the description of the New Jerusalem where the throne of God is set and the elect are granted the privilege of seeing God face to face (22.4). In Revelation (and for that matter in the rest of the apocalypses) the vision of God is a glimpse of the divine glory which is hidden in heaven. God's throne in heaven is hidden by the closed door which is opened to the visionary (4.1). That glory and holiness are on earth in the New Jerusalem, where there need be no longer any Temple (21.22).

The reference to the Jerusalem Temple in Revelation 11 led modern historical commentators to see the description of the measurement of the Temple, the inviolability of the sanctuary and the impending threat of the marauding nations, as a Zealot oracle from the days before the fall of Jerusalem to the Romans in 70 CE. Towards the end of the siege the Zealots took refuge in the sanctuary (Josephus, *War* 6.122) and were inspired by the testimony of a prophet who promised deliverance (*War* 6.285-87; Aune 1998: 594-95). Either John's visionary imagination was suffused by the searing impact of this event, or we have here a Jewish oracle stemming from the beleaguered groups in Jerusalem, who put their trust in visions of deliverance; there is an inkling of a similar sort of expectation in Lk. 21.24. This chapter has been linked with prophetic activity down the centuries, as individuals have identified themselves with the witnesses or others have seen their ministry as a fulfilment of the work of the two witnesses, reminding us that the ongoing life of biblical texts like the Apocalypse is a vital part of the interpretations of these texts (Kovacs and Rowland 2004).

5. *Concluding Reflections*

The persistence of the importance of the Temple as a model of the life of the church may be gauged by two examples which point to a rather different kind of appropriation. First, in the early liturgy known as the *Apostolic Tradition of Hippolytus* we find language which leaves us in no doubt that priestly concepts had been transferred to the office of bishop (Rowland 2002; cf. Barker 2003). This is evident in this brief quotation from the prayer at the ordination of the bishop. This manifests a very different notion from the more 'rabbinic' pattern of activity ascribed to the bishop in the Pastoral Epistles, though it has analogies in *1 Clement* 40 and *Did.* 13.3:

> Father, who knowest the hearts of all, grant upon this thy servant whom thou hast chosen for the episcopate to feed thy holy flock and serve as thine high priest, that he may minister blamelessly by night and day, that he may ceaselessly behold and propitiate thy countenance and offer to thee the gifts of thy holy church.

Secondly, when Christianity became the religion of the Roman Empire, things began to change (Kreider [ed.] 2001). Church buildings began to gain in size—something which reflected the growth in the size of congregations, the result of ongoing church growth, and (after 313) of imperial favour. Ecclesiastical buildings became public—hitherto they had been more often domestic, although getting larger—and became beautifully decorated, reflecting imperial iconography. Because of the large congregations, the worship became large-scale rather than relational and communitarian. So there began to emerge a pattern of Christian activity which sits uneasily with the New Testament writers' vision of the common life. At the risk of oversimplification, the life of Christian communities become more akin to the religion of the Temple than the synagogue.

The immediately preceding paragraphs are a reminder that my interest in this discussion is not just a matter of reconstructing the history of ancient religious ideas. The significance of the discussion for New Testament theology has pervaded this essay. The imagery of the Temple was in the theological bloodstream of early Christians and through them became part of Christian identity. Even if at the end of the Second Temple period early Christian writers, like others, were using Temple imagery in a thoroughly transferred sense of their common life, it is clear that religious understanding, determined as it always is by context, came to involve a more literal application of Temple language to the practice of the Christian religion. But in the first century CE things were different. The Qumran sectaries lived in the desert and in their common life created a holy environment where the holy angels assembled and shared their life. The Pharisees had a view of holiness rooted in the practical living in the midst of the variety of human communities, both near to and far from the Temple. The detailed regulations of the Mishnah bear witness to the seriousness of the endeavour of their rabbinic successors to ensure the preservation of a holy space in all aspects of existence. It is that vision which enabled Judaism to survive the destruction of its holy place in 70 CE. The emerging practice of religion based on the synagogue (which could meet anywhere and was not necessarily attached to particular places which were deemed to be holy) was a factor in enabling them to survive the events of 70. In *4 Ezra*, for example, obedience to the divine law is paramount, without land or Temple. Rabbinic Judaism maintained a religion which did not depend on Temple, which in many ways parallels what the early Christian writer, Minucius Felix (*Octavius* 32) says of Christianity in the third century, 'We have no temples; we have no altars'. Minucius Felix is writing in the context of Christianity's arguments with paganism, but his theological inspiration comes from the late Second Temple period and the theological developments of which early Christianity was a part.

Minucius's words can be paralleled in some words of a twentieth-century writer, Karl Barth, writing in the 1920s. In some respects they are an overstatement, but, as is often the case in Barth's writing on the Bible, he manages to capture something of importance in what he writes. The tabernacle/Temple contrast provides him with a way of describing the eschatological contrasts which are so typical of New Testament theology and which encapsulate the underlying thrust of the different New Testament writings in the priority given to Kingdom over church and institution:

> The *church* of the Bible is significantly the tabernacle, the portable tent. The moment it becomes a temple it becomes essentially only an object of attack. One gathers that for the apostles the whole of the Old Testament is summarized in Stephen's apology. Undeniably the central interest of both Testaments is not in the building of the church but in its destruction, which is always threatening and even beginning. In the heavenly Jerusalem of Revelation nothing is more finally significant than the church's complete absence: 'And I saw no Temple therein'. (Barth 1925: 83-84, ET 1928: 72)

In the variety of uses of temple imagery in the New Testament there is a degree of consistency. In the Pauline letters, John 4 and 1 Peter 2 (as in the Dead Sea Scrolls) we find the temple and sacrifice used in a transferred sense of the life of the people of God. In Hebrews the problem with the tabernacle is not so much its important role in the divine economy as the fact that something superior has arrived which has made that which functioned well in the past obsolete. To this extent the words at the opening of the letter, in which the eschatological contrast explains what is distinctive about the offer in the Son, is the hermeneutical guide for understanding the importance of the Temple: 'In many and various ways God spoke of old to our fathers by the prophets; but in these last days he has spoken to us by a Son' (Heb. 1.1). The situation is different in Acts 7, where, as I have suggested, the problem with the Temple is not only that it is obsolete but also that it was an act of rebellion and even idolatry. This places Stephen's speech at the far end of spectrum of attitudes to the Temple in the level of its critique. While the Temple offers an important symbol for the people of God, it is the hope of heaven on earth, anticipated in Christ and in the common life of small groups of men, women and children. Their priority was the temple of the Holy Spirit. So, Immanuel, God with us, who is present 'to the end of the age' (Mt. 28.19) is found where two or three are gathered together in Christ's name (18.20) and in the persons of the hungry, thirsty, naked and imprisoned (25.31-45). Heaven and earth have met in the moment of the death of a crucified man and not in tabernacle or Temple, but outside the camp, a place of shame and reproach (Heb. 13.12-13). The gate of heaven opens up to a solitary visionary on a Greek island, just as the prophet Ezekiel saw the divine glory move from above the cherubim in Solomon's Temple and encountered it in his place of exile by the waters of Babylon. For them all, the Temple had become superfluous as a locus of the divine presence even if it continued to offer the language by which that divine presence in the world could be articulated.

BIBLIOGRAPHY

Ådna, J.
2000 *Jesu Stellung zum Tempel: die Tempelaktion und das Tempelwort als Ausdruck seiner messianischer Sendung* (WUNT, 2.119; Tübingen: J.C.B. Mohr [Paul Siebeck]).

Attridge, H.W.
1989 *The Epistle to the Hebrews* (Hermeneia; Philadelphia: Fortress Press).

Aune, D.E
1998 *Revelation 6–16* (WBC, 52b; Nashville: Thomas Nelson).

Bachmann, M.
1980 *Jerusalem und der Tempel: die geographisch-theologischen Elemente in der lukanischen Sicht des jüdischen Kultzentrums* (BWANT, 9; Stuttgart: W. Kohlkammer).

Barker, M.
2003 *The Great High Priest: The Temple Roots of Christian Liturgy* (Edinburgh: T. & T. Clark).

Barrett, C.K.
1956 'The Eschatology of the Epistle to the Hebrews', in D. Daube and W.D. Davies (eds.), *The Background of the New Testament and its Eschatology* (Cambridge: Cambridge University Press): 363-93.
1991 'Attitudes to the Temple in the Acts of the Apostles', in Horbury (ed.) 1991: 345-67.
1994 *A Critical and Exegetical Commentary on the Acts of the Apostles*, I (ICC; Edinburgh: T. & T. Clark).

Barth, K.
1925 'Biblische Fragen, Einsichten und Ausblicke', in *idem*, *Das Wort Gottes und die Theologie* (Munich: Chr. Kaiser Verlag): 70-78. ET 'Biblical Questions, Insights and Vistas', in *idem*, *The Word of God and the Word of Man* (London: Hodder & Stoughton, 1928): 51-96.

Brown, R.E.
1994 *The Death of the Messiah: From Gethsemane to the Grave. A Commentary on the Passion Narratives in the Four Gospels* (2 vols.; New York: Doubleday).

Chester, A.N.
1991 'Hebrews: The Final Sacrifice', in S.W. Sykes (ed.), *Sacrifice and Redemption: Durham Essays in Theology* (Cambridge: Cambridge University Press): 57-72.

Chilton, B., and C.A. Evans
1997 *Jesus in Context: Temple, Purity, and Restoration* (AGJU, 39; Leiden: E.J. Brill).

Green, J.B.
1994 'The Demise of the Temple as "Culture Center" in Luke–Acts: An Exploration of the Rending of the Temple Veil', *RB* 101: 495-515.

Hannah, D.
1998 *Michael and Christ: Michael Traditions and Angel Christology in Early Christianity* (WUNT, 2.109; Tübingen: J.C.B. Mohr [Paul Siebeck]).
Hofius, O.
1970 *Katapauss: die Vorstellung vom endzeitlichen Ruheort im Hebräerbrief* (WUNT, 11; Tübingen: J.C.B. Mohr [Paul Siebeck]).
1972 *Der Vorhang vor dem Thron Gottes: eine exegetisch-religionsgeschtliche Untersuchung zu Hebräer 6,19f. und 10,19f.* (WUNT, 14; Tübingen: J.C.B. Mohr [Paul Siebeck]).
Horbury, W. (ed.)
1990 *Templum Amicitiae: Essays on the Second Temple Presented to Ernst Bammel* (JSNTSup, 48; Sheffield: JSOT Press).
Horsley, R.
2001 *Hearing the Whole Story: The Politics of Plot in Mark's Gospel* (Louisville, KY: Westminster/John Knox Press).
Hurst, L.W.
1990 *The Epistle to the Hebrews: Its Background of Thought* (Cambridge: Cambridge University Press).
Hurtado, L.
1988 *One God, One Lord: Early Christian Devotion and Ancient Jewish Monotheism* (London: SCM Press).
2003 *Lord Jesus Christ: Devotion to Jesus in Earliest Christianity* (Grand Rapids: Eerdmans).
Isaacs, M.
1992 *Sacred Space: An Approach to the Theology of the Epistle to the Hebrews* (JSNTSup, 73; Sheffield: JSOT Press).
Kovacs, J., and C. Rowland
2004 *Revelation: The Apocalypse of Jesus Christ* (Oxford: Basil Blackwell).
Kreider, A. (ed.)
2001 *The Origin of Christendom in the West* (Edinburgh: T. & T. Clark).
Lieu, J.
1996 *Image and Reality: The Jews in the World of the Christians in the Second Century* (Edinburgh: T. & T. Clark).
McKelvey, R.J.
1969 *The New Temple: The Church in the New Testament* (Oxford Theological Monographs; London: Oxford University Press).
Michel, O.
1942 'ναός', in *TWNT*, IV: 884-95. ET *TDNT*, IV (1967): 880-90.
Myers, C.
1988 *Binding the Strong Man: A Political Reading of Mark's Story of Jesus* (Maryknoll, NY: Orbis Books).
Paget, J.C.
1994 *The Epistle of Barnabas: Outlook and Background* (Tübingen: J.C.B. Mohr [Paul Siebeck]).
Rosenau, H.
1979 *Vision of the Temple: The Image of the Temple of Jerusalem in Judaism and Christianity* (London: Oresko Books).
Rowland, C.
1984 'John 1.51 and the Targumic Tradition', *NTS* 30: 498-507.
1985 'A Man Clothed in White Linen: A Study in the Development of Jewish Angelology', *JSNT* 24: 99-110.

1998 'The Book of Revelation', in *The New Interpreter's Bible* (Nashville: Abingdon Press): XII, 501-743.

2002 *Christian Origins: An Account of the Setting and Character of the Most Important Messianic Sect of Judaism* (London: SPCK, rev. edn).

Schrenk, G.

1938 'ἱερός, τὸ ἱερόν, etc.', in *TWNT*, III: 221-84. ET *TDNT*, III (1965): 221-83.

Smith, J.Z.

1968 'The Prayer of Joseph', in J. Neusner (ed.), *Religions in Antiquity: Essays in Memory of Erwin Ramsdell Goodenough* (Studies in the History of Religions, 14; Leiden: E.J. Brill): 253-94.

Walker, P.W.L.

1996 *Jesus and the Holy City: New Testament Perspectives on Jerusalem* (Grand Rapids: Eerdmans).

Walton, S.

2004 'A Tale of Two Perspectives? The Place of the Temple in Acts', in Simon Gathercole and T.D. Alexander (eds.), *Heaven on Earth: The Temple in Biblical Theology* (Carlisle: Paternoster Press): 135-49.

The Messianic Man of Peace as Temple Builder: Solomonic Imagery in Ephesians 2.13-22

Larry J. Kreitzer

One of the fringe benefits of being a teacher is encountering surprising student howlers in essays or exam scripts. On the internet I recently ran across a collection of these gathered from students in the USA and entitled 'The History of the World according to Student Bloopers'. Two personages who figured in the section on Old Testament history were the Kings David and Solomon. The students had summarized the contributions of these two kings to ancient history in this way: 'David was a Hebrew king skilled at playing the liar. He fought with the Finkelsteins, a race of people who lived in biblical times. Solomon, one of David's sons, had 300 wives and 700 porcupines.' There is an echo of 1 Kgs 11.3 here, but perhaps it is an indication of teenage angst that Solomon is only remembered by our examination student for how many sexual partners he managed to gather in his harem, although what this particular student thought the porcupines were for is anybody's guess.

Apart from the multiplicity of his women, Solomon is generally remembered for three other things, all of which are interconnected: his fabulous wealth, his wisdom as a ruler skilled in international diplomacy and trade,[1] and his building of the Temple in Jerusalem. We see all of these dimensions of Solomon's life being commemorated in the New Testament (Lohse 1964: 459-61, ET 1971: 463-65; Schneider 1993: 257). Thus, Jesus recalls the story of the queen of Sheba being attracted by the wisdom of Solomon when he suggests to the scribes and Pharisees that there is something greater than Solomon in operation within his own life and ministry (Mt. 12.42//Lk. 11.31). Jesus also alludes to the wealth of Solomon when he compares the lilies of the field to Solomon decked out in all his glory (Mt. 6.29//Lk. 12.27). The tradition that Solomon was the king responsible for building the Temple in Jerusalem is also featured in the New Testament. The fact that the portico of the east side of the Court of the Gentiles in Herod's Temple was commonly called 'Solomon's steps' preserves his association with the construction of the Temple (see Jn 10.23; Acts 3.11; 5.12; Josephus, *Ant.* 20.221; *War* 5.185). Perhaps more significantly, Solomon's role in building the Temple is specifically mentioned by Stephen in his death speech in Acts 7.47. Here Stephen uses the construction of the Temple as the culminating event in his

1. Lemaire (1995) discusses the importance of wisdom as a theme in the Solomonic history of 1 Kgs 3–11. Also see Parker 1992.

potted summary of the history of Israel, commencing with Abraham and running down through the rule of Kings David and Solomon (Acts 7.2-47).[2]

Several of these aspects of Solomon's life are also commemorated in later literature associated with his name. Thus, the so-called *Wisdom of Solomon*, an anonymous work probably composed by an Alexandrian Jew in the first century BCE, celebrates Solomon's memory as a wise king and attributes its sapiential material to him.[3] Similarly, the *Testament of Solomon*, also an anonymous work perhaps written by a Greek-speaking Christian in Ephesus[4] toward the end of the first century CE, offers a magic-filled tale about Solomon's building of the Temple.[5]

However, there is a fourth dimension to Solomon's character that needs to be considered: the fact that he is remembered as a 'man of rest/peace'. Certainly his reputation as a 'man of rest/peace' is closely tied up with his construction of the Temple, and indeed it could be argued that it stands as a prerequisite for his role as Temple-builder; but the 'man of rest/peace' motif warrants consideration in its own right. Moreover, Solomon's reputation as the messianic 'man of rest/peace', responsible for the construction of the Temple, offers a promising basis for understanding Jesus Christ as the new Solomon, as I shall attempt to demonstrate. Although Solomon is rarely presented as an important typological figure for later Christian understandings of Jesus Christ himself, there is some evidence, including Josephus, *Ant.* 8.45-49, to suggest that legends of Solomon as a person endowed with magical powers and authority over demons influenced the presentation of Jesus as a healer and exorcist in the gospels.[6] One would have thought that this, coupled with the fact that Solomon was indisputably the anointed 'Son of David', invites a fresh exploration of the contribution that Solomonic imagery makes to the development of Christian reflection about Jesus of Nazareth, who also early on was declared by Christians to be the anointed Son of David (see Rom. 1.3). The fact that Mt. 11.28-30 presents Jesus as wisdom personified and has him speak to all those who are weary and bearing heavy burdens, offering them 'rest' (κἀγὼ ἀναπαύσω ὑμᾶς), may also be relevant in this regard. The point is that both Solomon and Jesus are closely associated not only with God's wisdom, but with the 'rest' that is derived from it.[7]

2. By citing Isa. 66.1-2a in vv. 49-50 Stephen hereby manages to fire a salvo against those who would exalt in Herod's reconstruction of the Solomonic Temple and fail to understand that God does not dwell in buildings made by human hands. In this regard Stephen's speech echoes some of the reservations about the unworthiness of the Temple as a place to contain God which Solomon himself voices in his dedication prayer in 1 Kgs 8.27//2 Chron. 6.18.

3. For more on this, see Horbury 1995: 189-94.

4. Although Schürer (1973–87: III.1, 374) suggests Egypt is the most likely provenance of the work.

5. We shall return to the *Testament of Solomon* below, for it contains one significant, but frequently overlooked, parallel to Eph. 2.20.

6. Berger 1974: 3-9; Duling 1975; Schürer 1973–87: III.1, 375-79, and the literature cited there. Also see Betz 1987: 220-21; Arnold 1989: 32-34.

7. Bowman (1984–85) offers a comparison of Jesus and Solomon as figures illustrating the importance of wisdom in life.

This investigation will be pursued under two main headings. First, we shall summarize the 'rest' (*m^e^nûḥâ*) motif as it is contained in the Old Testament, particularly as it helps us appreciate the unusual description in 1 Chron. 22.9 of Solomon as a 'man of rest/peace' (*'îš m^e^nûḥâ*). Secondly, we shall explore a number of ways in which such Solomonic imagery assists in a rereading of Eph. 2.13-22, a complex christological passage that includes a number of references to 'peace' and 'temple-building'. In this regard it is the unusual statement in Eph. 2.14a ('He himself is our peace [αὐτὸς γάρ ἐστιν ἡ εἰρήνη ἡμῶν]') that serves as our initial focal point. However, as we shall see, there are several other features of the passage which also seem to suggest that an interpretation of Jesus as a new Solomon is one of the ideas underlying the thought of the writer of the letter to the Ephesians.

1. *The 'Rest'* (m^e^nûḥâ) *Motif and the Presentation of Solomon the Temple-Builder as a 'Man of Rest/Peace'* ('îš m^e^nûḥâ)

The theological importance of the Chronicler's depiction of Solomon has been persuasively argued by a number of scholars over the years; Roddy Braun (1973; 1976: 582-86; 1986: 223-25, 269-71), in particular, has given special attention to this theme. Scholarly discussion of Solomon's place in the life of Israel is intimately related to the wider concerns of peace and prosperity for the nation, especially when it is recalled that Solomon's reign is presented by the Chronicler as the pinnacle of Israelite history and his decision to build the Temple in Jerusalem is viewed as the height of the religious life of the people of God. We would do well to recall the Old Testament traditions concerning the rest/peace of Yahweh, which was promised long ago and according to the Chronicler found its culmination in the reign of King Solomon and his building of the Temple in Jerusalem (see the table on pp. 487-88 entitled 'The Use of *hēnîaḥ* and *m^e^nûḥâ* as "Rest"' for a listing and grouping of the texts involved in the following discussion).

The Old Testament idea of 'rest/peace' (*m^e^nûḥâ*) is a concept bearing tremendous theological weight, particularly within the Deuteronomistic History (DtH).[8] Here 'rest' is shown as an integral part of the promises made by Yahweh to his people, and as such it is intimately tied up with the peace that is granted to the nation Israel so used to being surrounded by hostile forces. In Deuteronomy itself, we see the promise of divine 'rest' specifically associated with the future possession of the land of Canaan and the establishment of a central sanctuary there at a

8. This is so whether we postulate, with Martin Noth (1943, ET 1981), a single exilic author, known as the Deuteronomist (Dtr), or detect, with F.M. Cross (1973) and others, a pre-exilic layer which has been revised by a later exilic redactor (Dtr2), or even, with R. Smend (1971), W. Dietrich (1972), T. Veijola (2000), and others, see within the DtH evidence of two or more redactional hands (labelled DtrG, DtrN and DtrP) all writing within the exilic period and reflecting the social and tensions of that time period and offering differing theological perspectives on them. McConville (1992: 67-71) offers a brief summary of the recent scholarly debate as to the formation of the Deuteronomistic History. Also see Knoppers 2000 and Römer and de Pury 2000.

place of God's determining (Deut. 3.20; 12.9-10; 25.19).[9] Within the thought of the Deuteronomist this theological idea of rest is applied to specific individuals whose actions are crucial to the life of the nation. Thus, the promised 'rest' is associated with the time of Joshua (Josh. 1.13, 15; 21.44; 22.4; 23.1), with the peace which comes during the reign of King David (2 Sam. 7.1, 11), and with the peace which characterizes the reign of King Solomon (1 Kgs 5.18, ET 5.4; 8.56).

Table 1. *The Use of* hēnîaḥ *and* m^enûḥâ *as 'Rest'*

A. *The Land of Canaan as a Place of 'Rest' Promised to Moses and the People of Israel*	
Exod. 33.14	He said, 'My presence will go with you, and I will give you rest (*wah^aniḥōtî*)'.
Deut. 3.20	When the Lord gives rest (*yānîaḥ*) to your kindred, as to you, and they too have occupied the land that the Lord your God is giving them beyond the Jordan, then each of you may return to the property that I have given to you.
Deut. 12.9	For you have not yet come into the rest (*m^enûḥâ*) and the possession that the Lord your God is giving you.
Deut. 25.19	Therefore when the Lord your God has given you rest (*b^ehānîaḥ*) from all your enemies on every hand, in the land that the Lord your God is giving you as an inheritance to possess, you shall blot out the remembrance of Amalek from under heaven; do not forget.
Josh. 1.13	Remember the word that Moses the servant of the Lord commanded you, saying, 'The Lord your God is providing you a place of rest (*mēnîaḥ*), and will give you this land'.
Josh. 1.15	Until the Lord gives rest (*yānîaḥ*) to your kindred as well as to you, and they too take possession of the land that the Lord your God is giving them.
Josh. 21.44	And the Lord gave them rest (*wayyānaḥ*) on every side just as he had sworn to their ancestors; not one of all their enemies had withstood them, for the Lord had given all their enemies into their hands.
Josh. 22.4	And now the Lord your God has given rest (*hēnîaḥ*) to your kindred, as he promised them; therefore turn and go to your tents in the land where your possession lies, which Moses the servant of the Lord gave you on the other side of the Jordan.
Ps. 95.11	Therefore in my anger I swore, 'They shall not enter my rest (*m^enûḥātî*)'.
1 Kgs 8.56	Blessed be the Lord, who has given rest (*m^enûḥâ*) to his people Israel according to all that he promised; not one word has failed of all his good promise, which he spoke through his servant Moses.
B. *The Exile from the Land of Israel as a Place where there is no 'Rest'*	
Deut. 28.65	Among those nations you shall find no ease, no resting place (*mānôaḥ*) for the sole of your foot.
Lam. 1.3	Judah has gone into exile with suffering and hard servitude; she lives now among the nations, and finds no resting place (*mānôaḥ*); her pursuers have all overtaken her in the midst of her distress.
Lam. 5.5	With a yoke on our necks we are hard driven; we are weary, we are given no rest (*lō' hûnaḥ-lānû*).

9. Carlson (1964: 99-106) discusses how the idea of 'rest from the enemies round about' is closely connected with the centralization of the Temple cultus in the thought of the Deuteronomist (as can be most readily seen in Deut. 12.1-14 and 2 Sam. 7.1-3). Also see Braulik 1985: 38 on this point.

C. *'Rest' from Surrounding Enemies during the Rules of the Leaders of Israel*	
Deut. 12.10	When you cross over the Jordan and live in the land that the Lord your God is allotting to you, and when he gives you rest (*wᵉhēnîaḥ*) from your enemies all around.
Josh. 23.1	A long time afterward, when the Lord had given rest (*hēnîaḥ*) to Israel from all their enemies all around, and Joshua was old and well advanced in years. (Joshua)
2 Sam. 7.1	Now when the king was settled in his house, and the Lord had given him rest (*hēnîaḥ*) from all his enemies around him. (King David)
2 Sam. 7.11	From the time that I appointed judges over my people Israel; and I will give you rest (*wahᵃnîḥōtî*) from all your enemies. (King David)
1 Kgs 5.18 (ET 4)	But now the Lord my God has given me rest (*hēnîaḥ*) on every side; there is neither adversary nor misfortune. (King Solomon)
1 Chron. 22.18	Is not the Lord your God with you? Has he not given you peace (*hēnîaḥ*) on every side? For he has delivered the inhabitants of the land into my hand; and the land is subdued before the Lord and his people. (King David)
1 Chron. 23.25	For David said, 'The Lord, the God of Israel, has given rest (*hēnîaḥ*) to his people; and he resides in Jerusalem forever'. (King David)
2 Chron. 14.5-6	He built fortified cities in Judah while the land had rest. He had no war in those years, for the Lord gave him peace (*hēnîaḥ*). He said to Judah, 'Let us build these cities, and surround them with walls and towers, gates and bars; the land is still ours because we have sought the Lord our God; we have sought him, and he has given us peace (*wayyānaḥ*) on every side'. (King Asa)
2 Chron. 15.15	All Judah rejoiced over the oath; for they had sworn with all their heart, and had sought him with their whole desire, and he was found by them, and the Lord gave them rest (*wayyānaḥ*) all around. (King Asa)
2 Chron. 20.30	And the realm of Jehoshaphat was quiet, for his God gave him rest (*wayyānaḥ*) all around. (King Jehoshaphat)
D. *Solomon as 'a Man of Rest'*	
1 Chron. 22.9	A son shall be born to you; he shall be a man of peace (*'îš mᵉnûḥâ*). I will give him peace (*wahᵃniḥôtî*) from all his enemies on every side; for his name shall be Solomon, and I will give peace (*šālôm*) and quiet (*šeqeṭ*) to Israel in his days.
E. *The Temple in Jerusalem as Yahweh's 'Resting Place'*	
1 Chron. 6.16	These are the men whom David put in charge of the service of song in the house of the Lord, after the ark came to rest there (*mimmᵉnôaḥ hā'ārôn*).
1 Chron. 28.2	Then King David rose to his feet and said: 'Hear me, my brothers and my people. I had planned to build a house of rest (*bêt mᵉnûḥâ*) for the ark of the covenant of the Lord, for the footstool of our God; and I made preparations for building'.
2 Chron. 6.41	Now rise up, O Lord God, and go to your resting place (*nûḥekā*), you and the ark of your might.
Ps. 132.8	Rise up, O Lord, and go to your resting place (*mᵉnûḥātekā*), you and the ark of your might.
Ps. 132.14	This is my resting place (*mᵉnûḥātî*) forever; here I will reside, for I have desired it.

The reference to the 'rest' granted to God's people Israel in 1 Kgs 8.56 is perhaps the most intriguing of these references, for it arguably represents a reinterpretation of the earlier idea of the conquest of Canaan and equates it instead with the completion of the Temple. As G.H. Jones (1984: 206) puts it: 'The word has been used here because the deuteronomic circle found a new meaning and a new significance for the word in their own particular situation'.[10]

However, an explicit identification of 'rest' and the Temple is by no means clear within the text of 1 Kgs 8.56 itself, and one cannot help but feel that this is an argument based upon the parallel in 2 Chron. 6.41 where a new interpretation of the meaning of Yahweh's 'rest' (*nûḥekā*) as the Temple in Jerusalem is clearly in evidence. This means that in order to understand the complexity of the 'rest' motif within the Old Testament, we need to consider how it is developed within the thought of the Chronicler.

First, it is noteworthy that the Chronicler drops the references to God's 'rest' (*mᵉnûḥâ*) in his parallels to the passages in 2 Sam. 7.1, 11, both of which speak of Yahweh giving *David* rest from his enemies. No doubt the Chronicler makes these alterations in 1 Chron. 17.1, 10 because he wishes to stress *Solomon's* role as the divinely chosen instrument for the building of the Temple.[11] According to Gerhard von Rad (1958: 103-105, ET 1965: 97-99), the concept of 'rest' (*mᵉnûḥâ*) heads off in a new direction within the thought of the Chronicler, who moves the focus away from God giving 'rest' *to* the people of Israel, to God enjoying rest *among* the people of Israel as he settles in Jerusalem among them. We see this, for example, in 1 Chron. 23.25 where David declares: 'The Lord, the God of Israel, has given rest to his people (*hēnîaḥ yhwh ᵉlōhê-yiśrā'ēl lᵉ'ammô*); and he resides in Jerusalem forever'.

This mutuality of 'rest' takes place, above all, as Yahweh settles down to dwell with the ark of the covenant in the Temple sanctuary that Solomon has prepared for him in Jerusalem, the city of his father David. As Solomon says in the final words of his prayer at the dedication of the Temple in 2 Chron. 6.41: 'Now rise up, O Lord God, and go to your resting place (*nûḥekā*), you and the ark of your might. Let your priests, O Lord God, be clothed with salvation, and let your faithful rejoice in your goodness.' This is almost certainly related to the appearance of the term *mᵉnûḥâ* in Psalm 132, where it is used twice in connection with the resting place of the ark of the covenant, a symbol of Yahweh's presence with his people (see 132.8, 14). The same term appears in Isa. 66.1, but to the opposite effect, for the prophet *derides* the suggestion that a temple can be the resting place of Yahweh (*mᵉnûḥātî*) when the heavens are his throne and the earth is his footstool.[12] Such scepticism perhaps echoes the rhetorical question placed on the

10. Also see Braulik 1985: 29-39; Talstra 1993: 247-50.

11. So Williamson 1982: 134-35; Throntveit 1987: 17, 86-88; Japhet 1993: 328. Mention should also be made of 2 Chron. 32.22 (LXX), where an equivalent phrase is used in Greek when the Lord is said to have rescued Hezekiah and given him 'rest from those surrounding him' (καὶ κατέπαυσεν αὐτοὺς κυκλόθεν). The Hebrew verb used in this phrase in 2 Chron. 32.22 is obscure (*wayᵉnaḥᵃlēm*); it is generally regarded as an equivalent to *wayyānaḥ lāhem* ('and he gave rest to them').

12. Levenson (1981: 159) uses the parallel to Isa. 66 as a basis for arguing that 1 Kgs 8.23-53 is 'distinctly Exilic'. Also see Clements 1965: 90-91 on this point.

lips of Solomon in 1 Kgs 8.27, even though Solomon does not explicitly mention the 'resting place' of the Temple itself: 'But will God indeed dwell on the earth? Even heaven and the highest heaven cannot contain you, much less this house that I have built!'

We are now in a position to return more specifically to the characterization of King Solomon himself. Given the close connection between Solomon and the construction of the Temple in Jerusalem as a place for the Lord God to enter into his rest, it is not altogether surprising that Solomon is specifically declared in 1 Chron. 22.9a to be *'îš m^enûḥâ*, 'a man of peace/rest', an unusual phrase found only here in the MT.[13] This declaration is placed on the lips of David as the aging king is engaged in making all of the preparations necessary for the construction of the Temple, including a lengthy speech delivered to the young Solomon (1 Chron. 22.6-16). Within the speech David relates a prophecy given to him by Yahweh about Solomon. Thus we read in 22.9:

> *hinnēh-bēn nôlād lāk hû' yihyeh 'îš m^enûḥâ*
> *wah^aniḥôtî lô mikkol-'ôy^ebāyw missābîb*
> *kî š^elōmōh yihyeh š^emô w^ešālôm wāšeqeṭ 'ettēn 'al-yiśrā'ēl b^eyāmāyw*

> See, a son shall be born to you; he shall be a man of peace. I will give him peace from all his enemies on every side; for his name shall be Solomon, and I will give peace and quiet to Israel in his days.

Moreover, the verse as a whole is significant because it not only describes the son of David in terms of 'rest' (*m^enûḥâ*), but also goes on to speak of Yahweh granting Solomon 'rest' (*wah^aniḥôtî*) from the surrounding enemies, as well as giving 'peace' (*šālôm*) and 'quiet' (*šeqeṭ*) to Israel, and specifically associates all of this with the name 'Solomon' (*š^elōmōh*) itself.[14] No doubt, part of the reason why Solomon can be described as the 'man of rest/peace' has to do with his name *š^elōmōh*, commonly agreed to be associated with the word 'peace' (*šālôm*).[15] In this respect Solomon not only accedes to his father's throne,[16] but peacefully

13. A similar expression, 'a man of peace' (*'îš šālôm*) is found at Ps. 37.37.

14. Riley (1993: 80) describes the verse as a 'fourfold paronomasia upon the name *šelōmōh*'.

15. Myers (1962: 399) describes the name as a caritative form of *šālôm*. Myers (1986: 154) says the word-play between 'Solomon' and 'Shalom' is 'unmistakeable'; Japhet (1993: 398) notes that such a word-play appears nowhere else in the Bible. Ackroyd (1973: 79) suggests that the verse contains *two* word-plays; one on 'Solomon/Shalom' and one involving the two forms of the Hebrew root *nwḥ* in 22.9a. Riley (1993: 78-79) extends this use of paranomasia to include instances where the Hebrew root *šlm* occurs in close proximity to mention of Solomon's name (such as 1 Chron. 18.9 [*sic*]; 29.19; 2 Chron. 5.1 and 8.16). An interesting variation on this explanation associates the name 'Solomon' with the verb 'to make compensation' (*šillēm*), an interpretation which shifts the textual focus to 2 Sam. 12.14-24 where the birth of Solomon to David and Bathsheba can be seen as a 'compensation' for the loss of their first child. For more on this possibility, see Stamm 1960: 285-97; Gerleman 1973: 13; Ishida 1992: 105; Veijola 2000: 345-46. Payne (1988: 566) suggests that 'Solomon' was his throne-name and 'Jedidiah' (in 2 Sam. 12.25 the name given to the child by Nathan the prophet at his birth) was a personal name. Schäfer-Lichtenberger (1995: 227-31) also discusses the significance of the two names.

16. Many commentators have noted the close connection there is in the Chronicler between David and Solomon and suggest that this is modelled on Joshua's succession of Moses. For more on this,

succeeds where his father David could not, for David's reign as king was marked by bloodshed and war, and thus it was deemed far too violent for such a holy task as Temple-building.[17] In short, if Solomon is, for the Chronicler, a 'man of rest/peace', an *'îš m^e^nûḥâ*, then David is by contrast a 'man of wars', an *'îš milḥāmôt*, and indeed he is explicitly declared to be such later on in the narrative in 1 Chron. 28.3.[18]

Just to highlight the 'peaceful' character of Solomon, it is worth noting that he is very rarely ever associated with a military campaign against neighbouring peoples, something that is quite remarkable given what is known about the historical and political turbulence of the time. The only real exception to this is the conquest of Hamath-zobah mentioned in 2 Chron. 8.3, and even here the meaning of the verse is extremely vague: 'And Solomon went to Hamath-zobah, and prevailed over it (*wayyeḥ^e^zaq 'ālеyhā*)'.[19]

In short, it seems undeniable that the Chronicler is intent on stressing the role of Solomon as a 'man of peace', and the theological significance of this may be greater than we often appreciate. One frequently overlooked indication of this significance is the way in which the contrast between David as a 'man of wars' and Solomon as a 'man of peace' has been picked up by other Jewish writers of the first century, notably Josephus and Philo of Alexandria. The divine prohibition against the war-tainted David building the Temple is mentioned by Josephus at several points in his *Jewish Antiquities*. The first of these comes as an editorial comment in *Ant*. 7.92:

see Braun 1976: 586-88; 1986: 222-23; Dillard 1987: 3-4; Williamson 1976; 1982: 155; DeVries 1988; Riley 1993: 76-77, 81-83; Schäfer-Lichtenberger 1995.

17. This tendency to violence is explicitly stated by both the Deuteronomist, who places the explanation for the divine prohibition on the lips of Solomon (1 Kgs 5.17, ET 5.3), and the Chronicler, who places the explanation on the lips of David himself (1 Chron. 22.7-8; 28.2-3). 1 Kgs 5.17 (ET 5.3) suggests that David was so involved with his military campaigns that he simply did not have time to give to the construction of the Temple. Dirksen (1996: 51-56) argues that the Chronicler reinterprets 1 Kgs 5.17 (ET 5.3) and offers what is in effect a theological interpretation for the prohibition against David building the Temple. Kruse (1985: 145) similarly remarks that the reasons given for David's prohibition 'are fanciful products of speculative theology'. Riley (1993: 79-80) helpfully summarizes some of the scholarly discussion about the Chronicler's reasons for presenting David's disqualification by Yahweh in the way that he does.

18. A brief objection might be raised as to the casual way in which 'rest' (*m^e^nûḥâ*) is substituted for 'peace' (*šālôm*) and contrasted with 'war' (*milḥāmâ*) within the argument here. However, both 'peace' (*šālôm*) and 'rest' (*m^e^nûḥâ*) function as opposites of 'war' (*milḥāmâ*). The Chronicler clearly intends a contrast between David as a 'man of wars' and Solomon as a 'man of rest', and there is ample evidence that 'peace' and 'war' were seen as opposites, as Eccl. 3.8 makes clear: 'there is a time for war (*milḥāmâ*) and a time for peace (*šālôm*)'.

19. 2 Chron. 8.4 goes on to say that Solomon also fortified the Syrian town of Tadmor and built store cities in near-by Hamath. Solomon's subjection of Hamath is also mentioned in Josephus, *Ant.* 8.160, although the Deuteronomist makes no mention of any of this in 1 Kgs 9.10-22. It is true that in 1 Kgs 11.14-25 Solomon is said to have faced adversaries in the form of Hadad the Edomite and Rezon the Syrian. However, it has been plausibly suggested that these are fictitious characters created by a post-Deuteronomistic writer to emphasize God's punishment of Solomon for his apostasy. For more on this suggestion, see Edelman 1995.

οὐκ ἐπιτρέπειν δὲ πολλους πολέμους ἠγωνισμένῳ καὶ φόνῳ τῶν ἐχθρῶν μεμιασμένῳ ποιῆσαι ναὸν αὐτῷ.

He (God) could not permit him (David) to construct a Temple for him, because he had fought in many wars and was stained with the blood of his enemies.

A similar declaration is contained in *Ant.* 7.337a, a passage which follows immediately after an account of David gathering together the materials necessary for the building of the Temple. Once again the prohibition against David comes as an editorial comment:

καλέσας δὲ τὸν παῖδα Σολομῶνα κατασκευάσαι τῷ Θεῷ ναὸν αὐτὸν ἐκέλευσε διαδεξάμενον τὴν βασιλείαν, λέγων ὡς αὐτὸν βουλόμενον κωλύσειεν ὁ θεὸς αἵματι καὶ πολέμοις πεφυρμένον

Then he (David) called his son Solomon and bade him build the Temple to God after he should have succeeded to the throne, telling him that he himself had wished to do so, but God had prevented him because of his being stained with blood shed in war.

In *Ant.* 7.371 David himself gives voice to the divine prohibition as he addresses the leaders of the people of Israel with a speech in which he not only commends Solomon to them, but explains why he was not permitted to construct the Temple. Interestingly, in this passage Josephus goes beyond his scriptural source (1 Chron. 28.3), and has David identify Nathan the prophet as God's spokesperson for the divine prohibition:

ἀδελφοὶ καὶ ὁμοεθνεῖς, γινώσκειν ὑμᾶς βούλομαι ὅτι ναὸν οἰκοδομῆσαι τῷ Θεῷ διανοηθεὶς χρυσόν τε πολὺν παρεσκευασάμην καὶ ἀργύρου ταλάντων μυριάδας δέκα, ὁ δὲ θεὸς ἐκωλυσέ με διὰ τοῦ προφήτου Νάθα διά τε τοὺς ὑπὲρ ὑμῶν πολέμους καὶ τῷ Φόνῳ τῶν ἐχθρῶν μεμιάνθαι τὴν δεξιάν, τὸν δὲ υἱὸν ἐκέλυεσε τὸν διαδεξόμενον τὴν βασιλέα κατασκευάσαι τὸν ναὸν αὐτῷ.

Brothers and fellow-countrymen, I wish you to know that with the intention of building a Temple to God I collected a great quantity of gold and one hundred thousand talents of silver; but God, through the prophet Nathan, has kept me from doing so, because of the wars I have fought on your behalf, and because my hand is stained with the blood of the enemy, and he has commanded my son, who will succeed to my throne, to build the Temple to him.

At one point in *Jewish Antiquities* Solomon himself speaks about the prohibition against David building the Temple. This comes in the form of a letter that Solomon writes to King Hiram of Tyre after he (Solomon) succeeds his father David on the throne. Thus in *Ant.* 8.51-52 Solomon speaks of his father's warrior-spirit and then goes on to contrast it with his own peaceful character:

Ἴσθι μου τὸν πατέρα βουληθέντα κατασκευάσαι τῷ Θεῷ ναὸν ὑπὸ τῶν πολέμων καὶ τῶν συνεχῶν στρατειῶν κεκωλεμένον· οὐ γὰρ επαύσατο πρότερον τοὺς ἐχθροὺς καταστρεφόμενος πρὶν ἢ πάντας αὐτοὺς φόρων ὑποτελεῖς πεποιηκέναι. ἐγὼ δὲ χάριν οἶδα τῷ Θεῷ τῆς παρούσης εἰρήνης καὶ διὰ ταύτην εὐσχολῶν οἰκοδομῆσαι τῷ Θεῷ βούλομαι τὸν οἶκον· καὶ γὰρ ὑπ᾽ ἐμοῦ τοῦτον ἔσεσθαι τῷ πατρί μου προεῖπεν ὁ θεός.

Know that my father wished to build a Temple to God, but was prevented by wars and continual expeditions, for he did not leave off subduing his enemies until he had forced them to pay tribute. But I give thanks to God for the peace I now enjoy, and as on that account I am at leisure, I wish to build a house to God, for He indeed foretold to my father that this would be made by me.

This is not to say that Josephus *never* speaks of David enjoying peace during his rule. He does, for example, note in *Ant.* 7.305 that David had a period which was free from war and danger which enabled him to compose songs and hymns in praise of God, as well as making various musical instruments with which the Levites were able to make music in worship.[20] However, the main point seems unmistakable; according to Josephus, David was a 'man of war' whose hands were stained with blood, and this is repeatedly put forward as the reason why David was not allowed to build the Temple in Jerusalem and the task taken over by his son Solomon.

In contrast, Philo of Alexandria mentions Solomon only once in his work, namely in the bizarrely entitled treatise 'On Mating with the Preliminary Studies'. The work is given over to a discussion of the training of the mind through the study of a school curriculum. It uses the story of Abram, Sarah and Hagar found in Gen. 16.1-6 as its scriptural basis, offering an allegorical interpretation of the passage, with Sarah representing the wisdom or virtue which rules a soul, Hagar representing the lower levels of instruction needed for true enlightenment, and Abram representing soul which learns by guided instruction. The reference to Solomon occurs toward the end of the treatise as Philo discusses the value of God's fatherly discipline in the life of the son whom he loves. To illustrate the point he cites Prov. 3.11-12, building no doubt on the traditional belief that the wise King Solomon was the author of the book of Proverbs. What is important for our consideration is the way in which Solomon is introduced to the discussion just prior to the quotation from Proverbs. Philo writes (177):

> τις τῶν φοιτητῶν Μωυσέως, ὄνομα εἰρηνικός,
> ὃς πατρίῳ γλώττῃ Σαλομὼν καλεῖται, φάναι...
>
> One of Moses' disciples, who is named a man of peace,
> which is in our ancestral tongue Solomon, says...

In short, Philo is clearly building on the meaning of Solomon's name, associating it with the Hebrew word 'peace' (*šālôm*), and providing us in the process with a Greek equivalent, namely εἰρηνικός.[21]

20. *Ant.* 7.289 also contains an interesting passage based upon the story of the wise old woman mentioned in 2 Sam. 20.16-22. Here David's pursuit of war against the enemies of the Hebrews is attributed to God himself, albeit in the cause of obtaining eventual peace. The woman says: 'God has chosen kings and commanders to drive out the enemies of the Hebrews and secure them peace from these'.

21. It has often been suggested that, like the name of Solomon, the 'man of peace', the name of the city of 'Jerusalem' itself (*yᵉrûšālaim*), in which the Temple is built, is in some way connected with the Hebrew term *šālôm*, although scholars are generally sceptical about the validity of this popular etymology. However, Josephus, *Ant.* 7.68 seems to suggest that there is a connection along these lines when he says that from the time of Abraham the city of Jerusalem was known as Σόλυμα, which in Hebrew was the equivalent of the Greek term ἀσφάλεια. Clearly this use of 'security' (ἀσφάλεια) implies the Hebrew word *šālôm*. An interesting parallel occurs in 1 Thess. 5.3, where Paul appears to challenge popular perceptions of the stability afforded by the Roman Empire: 'They say "Peace and security (λέγωσιν, Εἰρήνη καὶ ἀσφάλεια)"'. For a summary of recent interpretation of this phrase, see Still 1999: 262-66.

We turn now to the second part of our study and explore the possibility of Solomonic imagery underlying a fascinating paragraph within the letter to the Ephesians.

2. *Solomonic Imagery in Ephesians 2.13-22*

Nearly forty years ago Ernst Käsemann (1966: 288) had this to say about the letter to the Ephesians: 'The entire letter appears to be a mosaic composed of extensive as well as tiny elements of tradition, and the author's skill lies chiefly in the selection and ordering of the material available to him'. What I would like to do here is to suggest—and given the nature of the evidence it can never be more than just a suggestion—that one of those tiny elements of tradition which the writer of Ephesians so skilfully included within his literary mosaic involved the figure of Solomon, son of David. In particular, I want to focus attention on Eph. 2.13-22 because the passage contains three features which, when taken together, appear to triangulate on traditions associated with King Solomon. We now turn to examine these three features in greater detail.

a. *'He is our Peace' (αὐτὸς γάρ ἐστιν ἡ εἰρήνη ἡμῶν) (Ephesians 2.14a)*
Many scholars have argued that Eph. 2.13-18 is a messianic interpretation of several verses from Isaiah, namely Isa. 57.19 (in vv. 13 and 17), 9.5-6 (ET 9.6-7) (in v. 14), and 52.7 (in v. 17).[22] However, it is by no means certain that a messianic interpretation of a montage of texts from Isaiah is what lies at the heart of Eph. 2.13-18. For one thing, it is difficult to see the immediate connection in thought between 'you who once were far off have been brought near by the blood of Christ' in 2.13 and the declaration that immediately follows in 2.14a: 'He himself is our peace' (αὐτὸς γάρ ἐστιν ἡ εἰρήνη ἡμῶν). Generally the connection of thought between the two verses is made by appealing to the theological notion of reconciliation, a peace-making between God and humankind that is achieved by the sacrificial death of Jesus Christ.[23] However, here I would like to propose another way of interpreting 2.13-22, one that attempts to give a different thematic substance to the passage as a whole. In short, I would like to suggest that 2.13-22 is best viewed as a free-standing interpretation based upon traditional imagery associated with King Solomon. The most tantalizing hint of such hermeneutical activity involves the declaration in 2.14a ('He himself is our peace [αὐτὸς γάρ ἐστιν ἡ εἰρήνη ἡμῶν]'), which appears to have as its centre-piece a somewhat veiled word-play on the Hebrew words for 'Solomon' (*šᵉlōmōh*) and 'peace' (*šālôm*). Whether this creative interpretation existed as an earlier hymnic-

22. Stuhlmacher 1986: 187-91; Schnackenburg 1991: 112-18; Moritz 1996: 23-55; Best 1998: 251. Moritz (1996: 31) has some doubts about the allusion to Isa. 9.5-6 (ET 9.6-7) in 2.14a, and suggests that it 'owes more to the attempt to counterbalance the reference to Christ's capacity as the bringer of peace in 17a (ABCB′A′) than to Isa 9.5f'. Lincoln (1982: 26; 1987: 610; 1990: 127) does not think that Isa. 57.19 is necessarily behind the language of 'far and near', but sees this as perhaps arising from later Jewish discussions of proselytism. Also see Martin (1981: 190-92) on this point.

23. See Porter 1993: 698-99, for a summary. Also worth consulting is Martin 1981: 176-88.

liturgical fragment which the writer has taken over and adapted, or whether he composed the whole passage himself, it is now impossible to know for certain, although I tend toward the former hypothesis.[24]

To put the central point in the form of a hypothetical question: Could it be that the (Jewish!) writer of the letter to the Ephesians deliberately wishes to assert that Jesus Christ is, in effect, a new Solomon, and that he composes Eph. 2.14a with precisely that word-play between 'Solomon' (*š*^{e}*lōmōh*) and 'peace' (*šālôm*) in mind? In other words, I am suggesting that by asserting in 2.14a, 'He (Jesus Christ) is our peace', what the writer is doing is making a word-play which (some of his Jewish-Christian) readers would pick up on as 'He (Christ) is *our* Solomon'. We have already noted the close connection between Solomon and the 'rest' (*m*^{e}*nûḥâ*) motif, particularly as it focuses on the description of Solomon as the 'man of peace' (*'îš m*^{e}*nûḥâ*) responsible for building the Temple in Jerusalem where Yahweh himself 'rests' amid his people. But beyond that, there are other indications that a playful juxtaposition of 'Solomon' (*š*^{e}*lōmōh*) and 'peace' (*šālôm*) is occasionally maintained in the MT. For example, in the summary description of Solomon's reign in 1 Kgs 5.4b-5 (ET 4.24b-25) we read:

> *w*^{e}*šālôm hāyāh lô mikkol-*^{a}*bārāyw missābîb*
> *wayyēšeb y*^{e}*hûdâ w*^{e}*yiśrā'ēl lābeṭaḥ 'îš taḥat gapnô w*^{e}*taḥat t*^{e}*'ēnātô*
> *middān w*^{e}*'ad-b*^{e}*'ēr šāba' kōl y*^{e}*mê š*^{e}*lōmōh*
>
> And he had peace on all sides round about him. And Judah and Israel dwelt safely, every man under his vine and under his fig tree, from Dan even to Beersheba, all the days of Solomon.

The passage is most interesting in that it begins with a reference to 'peace' (*šālôm*) and ends with an explicit reference to 'Solomon' (*š*^{e}*lōmōh*), effectively framing the whole description with the Hebrew play on words. The LXX equivalent of 1 Kgs 5.4b-5 (ET 4.24b-25), which comes in the miscellany designated 2.46^{g},[25] reproduces the idea of the Hebrew fairly closely, although it loses the force of similarity of sounds in the Hebrew when it translates 'peace' (*šālôm*) with εἰρήνη:[26]

> καὶ ἦν αὐτῷ εἰρήνη ἐκ πάντων τῶν μερῶν αὐτοῦ κυκλόθεν·
> καὶ κατῴκει Ἰούδα καὶ Ἰσραὴλ πεποιθότες, ἕκαστος ὑπὸ τὴν ἄμπελον
> αὐτοῦ, καὶ ὑπὸ τὴν συκῆν αὐτοῦ, ἐσθίοντες καὶ πίνοντες καὶ ἑορτάζοντες
> ἀπὸ Δὰν καὶ ἕως Βηρσαβὲε πάσας τὰς ἡμέρας Σαλωμών.

24. Many commentators feel that an early Christian hymn or liturgical fragment underlies 2.13-17, although no consensus has been arrived at as to its extent or form, or how much the writer of the letter has added to it. Gnilka (1971: 147-52), for example, reconstructs a nine-line hymn underlying 2.14-18 and takes a number of words and phrases to be redactional additions, including 16a and the whole of v. 18. For more on the hymnic nature of the passage, see Martin 1981: 167-76; Wilhelmi 1987; Lincoln 1990: 127-31; Best 1997: 60-64; 1998: 247-50.

25. The textual expansion and variation in copies of the LXX is considerable at both 3 Kgdms 2.35 and 2.46. Most scholars agree that these so-called miscellanies function as a summary of the reign of Solomon. See Gray 1970: 113-14, for a summary of the matter, and Tov 1999: 549-70, for a more in-depth treatment.

26. There is also a parallel to 1 Kgs 5.4b (ET 4.24b) in 3 Kgdms 5.4b.

> And he (Solomon) was at peace on all sides round about; and Judah and Israel dwelt safely, every one under his vine and under his fig tree, eating and drinking and feasting from Dan even to Bersabee, all the days of Solomon.

One may *perhaps* agree with Emanuel Tov and assume that 2.46^{g} was originally written in Hebrew and that this was then translated into Greek.[27] Whether or not the translator of the LXX was aware of the pun on the Hebrew words *š^{e}lōmōh* and *šālôm* (with which both 1 Kgs 5.4b-5, ET 4.24b-25 and the presumed Hebrew *Vorlage* of 2.46^{g} open and close) does not, at one level, matter very much. The critical point is that the resultant Greek translation of 3 Kgdms 2.46^{g} opens and closes on a suitably 'Solomonic' note, linking together the granting of 'peace' (εἰρήνη) with the person of King Solomon (Σαλωμών) himself. In this respect, 2.46^{g} serves as something of a parallel to Eph. 2.14a in that it demonstrates how closely connected the Greek words 'peace' (εἰρήνη) and 'Solomon' (Σαλωμών) can be. In Eph. 2.14a, however, it can be argued that the *substance* of the pun is still intended, even if its underlying *form* of the Hebrew word-play (on *š^{e}lōmōh* and *šālôm*) has been collapsed into a single Greek word (namely εἰρήνη). And if this is so, it only remains to observe that in christological terms, the assertion that 'He (Jesus Christ) is our peace' could readily be perceived as a typological fulfilment of the idea in 1 Kgs 5.3-5 (ET 4.23-25) of God's granting of 'peace' (*šālôm*/εἰρήνη) on all sides. Not only is this a re-expression of the 'rest' motif so beloved of the Deuteronomistic Historian, but, even more importantly, it also fits well with the Chronicler's identification of Solomon as the messianic 'man of peace'.

A couple of other passing remarks are worth making in respect to Eph. 2.14a. The first is that, given the close connection between the Hebrew name 'Solomon' (*š^{e}lōmōh*) and the Hebrew term 'peace' (*šālôm*), it seems strange that no one (to my knowledge) has ever explored this play on words as a possible backdrop to the curious statement in Eph. 2.14a. There are two reasons for this, it seems to me.

First, Isa. 9.5-6 (LXX) has had a dominant role in setting the interpretative agenda for the verse. To put it bluntly, the evocative language of Isa. 9.5b (ET 9.6b), including (according to Codex Alexandrinus) the powerful description of the messianic king as the 'Prince of Peace' (ἄρχων εἰρήνης), meant that we gave up looking for other background texts.[28] We simply have *assumed* that the messianic imagery from Isaiah 9 underlies Eph. 2.13-18. Another reason is that there has been a lack of appreciation of the overlap of semantic fields of meaning for the two Hebrew terms 'rest' (*m^{e}nûḥâ*) and 'peace' (*šālôm*). Unfortunately, this has meant that the one time in the MT where the Hebrew term *m^{e}nûḥâ* is applied to Solomon, namely 1 Chron. 22.9, has not been fully explored by New Testament scholarship for its potential as an Old Testament text upon which subsequent christological ideas were based.

27. So Tov (1999: 559, 567-68) suggests, based in part on the fact that the Greek translation exhibits a rather literal rendering of Hebrew phrasing. Tov also suggests that the translator of the main text of 1 Kings was also responsible for the two Greek miscellanies.

28. O'Brien (1999: 194) is a case in point: 'the origin of Paul's description of peace as personal is the well-known Old Testament messianic title, "the Prince of Peace" (Isa. 9.6)'.

The second remark to make in passing is that there may well be more than just a play on *two* Hebrew words (*šālôm* and *menûḥâ*) in operation within the passage here. To illustrate the point, I appeal to F.D. Coggan, who half a century ago wrote a short note on the phrase αὐτὸς γάρ ἐστιν ἡ εἰρήνη ἡμῶν in Eph. 2.14a. Coggan put forward the intriguing suggestion that the writer of the epistle may well have had Old Testament sacrificial imagery in mind when describing Christ as 'our peace', and that he used a Hebrew word-play to achieve it. The burden of Coggan's point rested on the fact that forms of the adjective εἰρηνικός, closely related to the term εἰρήνη in the phrase concerned, are regularly used in the LXX to render the Hebrew term *šelem* (*šelāmîm*), generally translated as 'peace offering'.[29]

Coggan's suggestion is certainly novel, even if it is one that has rather fallen on deaf ears as far as New Testament commentators are concerned.[30] Here we simply note that if there is any truth in it at all, it adds another layer of depth and complexity to the word-play underlying Ephesians 2.14a. Not only do we find an explicit declaration regarding 'peace' (*šālôm*), but veiled allusions to both 'peace offerings' (*šelāmîm*) and 'Solomon' (*šelōmōh*). We also need to keep in mind that the Greek adjective εἰρηνικός, which Coggan suggests is so important for communicating the sacrificial dimension underlying the passage as a whole, is precisely the word that Philo of Alexandria gives as his translation equivalent for the name 'Solomon' (*šelōmōh*) (see above).

However, this by no means exhausts the theological significance of the Solomonic imagery contained in Eph. 2.13-22. Let us turn next to consider the significance of the declaration about *Judah and Israel* living together in safety with which both the MT of 1 Kgs 5.5 (ET 4.25) and the Greek miscellany of 1 Kgs 2.46[g] concludes.

b. *'Having Made the Two One' (ὁ ποιήσας τὰ ἀμφότερα ἕν) (Ephesians 2.14b)*

Ephesians 2.14-18 remains one of the most difficult paragraphs in the Pauline

29. Although Coggan's brief note did not list the instances where this happens, it is worth listing places where such a translation equivalent occurs in the LXX. The Greek term εἰρηνικός is used to translate *šelāmîm* in 1 Sam. 10.8; 11.15; 13.9; 2 Sam. 6.17, 18; 24.25; 1 Kgs 3.15; 8.63, 64 (twice); 2 Kgs 16.13; and Prov. 7.14. The same holds true for other Greek versions of the Old Testament. Aquila additionally uses εἰρηνικός to translate *šelāmîm* in Lev. 3.1, 6, 9; 7.13; 3 Kgdms 9.25, while Symmachus and Theodotion follow suit at Lev. 3.1, 6, 9; 7.13. The term εἰρηνικός is also used for *šelāmîm* in 3 Kgdms 2.35[g], part of the Greek miscellanies to the MT; Origen's *Hexapla* also follows suit in its equivalent to this verse, which is found in 3 Kgdms 9.25 (3 Kgdms 9.15-25 does not appear in Codex Alexandrinus, Codex Vaticanus or Codex Sinaiticus; on the other hand, 2.35[f-k], which contains some of the same material, does not appear in Origen's *Hexapla*). What is even more fascinating about 1 Kgs 9.25 is that the MT refers to both 'Solomon' (*šelōmōh*) and 'peace offerings' (*šelāmîm*) in the same verse, similar to the 'Solomonic' declaration made in 1 Kgs 5.3-5 (ET 4.23-25, noted above). The word-association is lost somewhat when it is translated into Greek, as occurs in 1 Kgs 2.35[g] and Origen's *Hexapla* 9.25; in both instances *šelōmōh* becomes Σαλωμών and *šelāmîm* becomes εἰρηνικός. DeVries (1985: lx-lxi) offers a convenient chart showing the order of the parallel texts in the various versions concerned.

30. Best (1998: 251) is simply dismissive of Coggan's proposal: 'There is no reason to see here a reference to the peace offering'.

corpus to unravel, so compressed is the language and so complicated the grammar. Ephesians 2.14-16 consists of one long, rambling sentence of 59 words in Greek, and this is followed in 2.17-18 by another long sentence of 25 words. After the opening declaration in 2.14a that 'He is our peace', the remainder of the first sentence is given over to a series of interlocking phrases describing the decisive actions of Jesus Christ on behalf of humanity. Solomonic imagery might also underlie the declarations made in several of these evocative phrases contained in vv. 14-18. In particular, this is the case with the four phrases which talk about 'both' (τὰ ἀμφότερα)[31] or 'the two' (τοὺς δύο).

> ὁ ποιήσας τὰ ἀμφότερα ἓν (2.14b)
> ἵνα τοὺς δύο κτίσῃ εἰς ἕνα καινὸν ἄνθρωπον (2.15b)
> καὶ ἀποκαταλλάξῃ τοὺς ἀμφοτέρους ἐν ἑνὶ σώματι τῷ Θεῷ (2.16a)
> ἔχομεν τὴν προσαγωγὴν οἱ ἀμφότεροι ἐν ἑνὶ πνεύματι
> πρὸς τὸν πατέρα (2.18)

> Having made both one (2.14b)
> So as to create the two into one new humanity (2.15b)
> And to reconcile both into one new body before God (2.16a)
> Both of us have access in one Spirit to the Father (2.18)

Here we need briefly to consider some of the various ways in which King Solomon is portrayed as ruling over a United Monarchy. In this regard, I would note the intriguing recent contribution of James Linville entitled *Israel in the Book of Kings: The Past as a Project of Social Identity* (1998).[32]

Several passages from the Succession Narrative are important for a consideration of this theme, in that they build upon the tradition that King David was himself said to rule over both Israel and Judah (2 Sam. 5.5).[33] For example, we

31. Too much can be made of the fact that 'both' in 2.14b is neuter in form (τὰ ἀμφότερα), whereas in 2.16b and 2.18 'both' (οἱ ἀμφότεροι) is masculine in form. For example, Lincoln (1990: 129) remarks: 'The neuter formulation τὰ ἀμφότερα is not easy to explain if the passage is treated purely on one level as a straightforward discussion of the relation between Jewish Christians and Gentile Christians'. Lincoln (1990: 140) later attempts to explain the use of the unusual neuter form as 'a remnant of traditional material which originally referred to heaven and earth'. Schnackenburg (1991: 113), on the other hand, suggests that the writer's thought simply progresses from a general picture to the particular; Barth (1974: 263) suggests that the abstract metonyms (such as 'The Uncircumcision' and 'The Circumcision') influenced his diction or that Paul simply used neuter forms in 2.14a to avoid repetition; and Best (1998: 252) proposes that the writer has another neuter noun in mind, possibly γένη or χωρία. An alternative way to explain the use of the neuter form is to link it to the appearance of the phrase 'the commonwealth of Israel' (ἡ πολιτεία τοῦ Ἰσραήλ) in 2.12 and suggest that the writer's own church and the one he is writing to are here both being thought of together as τὰ (ἀμφότερα) πολίτευματα (along the same lines that the city of Philippi is addressed by Paul as a πολίτευμα in Phil. 3.20). In other words, the use of the neuter form τὰ ἀμφότερα in 2.14b is an indication of the *political status* of the churches concerned, while the use of the masculine form τοὺς ἀμφοτέρους in 2.16a focuses on the people who make up those congregations and returns to a more familiar personalized phrasing. For more on my reconstruction of the social circumstances surrounding the writing of Ephesians, see n. 49 below.

32. Linville (1998: 114-54) offers a thorough treatment of this topic and I am dependent upon him for much of the discussion which follows.

33. David's forty-year reign is said to be divided into two parts and centred in two different locations: seven years over Judah from Hebron and thirty-three years over Judah and Israel from

find in 1 Kgs 1.34-35 an interesting passage in which King David declares his intentions for his son Solomon, commissioning Zadok the priest and Nathan the prophet to bring Solomon to Gihon:

> There let the priest Zadok and the prophet Nathan anoint him king over Israel (*melek 'al-yiśrā'ēl*); then blow the trumpet, and say, 'Long live King Solomon!' You shall go up following him. Let him enter and sit on my throne; he shall be king in my place; for I have appointed him to be ruler over Israel and over Judah (*nāgîd 'al-yiśrā'ēl wᵉ'al-yᵉhûdâ*).[34]

Insofar as Solomon is anointed king over Israel he succeeds his father David and can legitimately be described as a 'messianic' figure.[35] There are other instances where Judah and Israel are mentioned together during the time of Solomon's reign. We see this, for example, in 1 Kgs 4.20 where Israel and Judah are said to be as numerous as the sand on the sea-shore, and even more interestingly, given our theme of Solomon and 'peace' (*šālôm*), 1 Kgs 5.5 (ET 4.25) where, during Solomon's reign both 'Israel and Judah dwelt in safety' (*wayyēšeb yᵉhûdâ wᵉyiśrā'ēl lābeṭaḥ*). It is likely that this is an echo of Deut. 12.10, where 'you will dwell in safety' (*wîšabtem-beṭaḥ*) is a parallel expression to 'the Lord God will grant you rest from surrounding enemies' (*yhwh 'ᵉlōhêkem manḥîl missābîb 'etᵉkem wᵉhēnîaḥ lākem mikkol-'ōyᵉbêkem*). However, we see this motif of the United Monarchy most clearly in 1 Kings 8 where Solomon dedicates the Temple to Yahweh, which has been described as 'Solomon's greatest hour'.[36] Here mention of 'your (Yahweh's) people Israel' (*'ammᵉkā yiśrā'ēl*) is found twelve times, including eight occurrences within Solomon's Temple-dedication prayer to Yahweh (1 Kgs 8.30, 33, 34, 36, 38, 41, 43, 52), two occurrences within Solomon's Temple-dedication blessing on the assembled people (1 Kgs 8.56, 59), and one editorial occurrence which is used to conclude the chapter as a whole. In fact the last words of the chapter end on precisely this note and speak of Yahweh demonstrating his goodness 'to his servant David and to his people Israel' (*lᵉdāwid 'abdô ûlᵉyiśrā'ēl 'ammô*) (1 Kgs 8.66).

1 Kings 8.20 is also interesting in that it has Solomon speak of sitting on the 'throne of Israel' (*kissē' yiśrā'ēl*), clearly meaning that he rules over a single nation (consisting of both Israel in the north and Judah in the south). A similar declaration is made about Solomon by the queen of Sheba in 10.9, again with the inference being that 'Israel' is one nation consisting of both the northern Israel and the southern Judah. In short, it seems clear that within the thought of the

Jerusalem. By comparison, in 1 Kgs 11.42 Solomon's reign is also said to be forty years long, all of it from Jerusalem and extending 'over all of Israel' (*'al-kol-yiśrā'ēl*).

34. There is some divergence between the MT and the various Greek versions of the Old Testament concerning the use of 'and Judah' in v. 34 and the order of the phrases ('Israel and Judah' or 'Judah and Israel'?). See Linville 1998: 124-25, for an extended note on this point.

35. Interestingly, this is the only time in Samuel-Kings where a *nāgîd* is said to rule over both Judah and Israel. The term appears 11 times in Samuel–Kings (1 Sam. 9.16; 10.1; 13.14; 25.30; 2 Sam. 5.2; 6.21; 7.8; 1 Kgs 1.35; 14.7; 16.2; 2 Kgs 20.5). It also appears 21 times in 1–2 Chronicles (1 Chron. 5.2; 9.11, 20; 11.2, 7; 12.27; 13.1; 26.24; 27.4, 16; 28.4; 29.22; 2 Chron. 6.5; 11.11, 22; 19.11; 28.7; 31.12, 13; 32.21; 35.8). Linville (1998: 139-49) offers a full discussion of the term.

36. So Linville (1998: 133) describes it.

Deuteronomist there is a deliberate emphasis laid upon the fact that King Solomon reigned over a kingdom consisting of two groups which were at enmity with one another but which had been brought together in order to form a single nation.

However, some scholars have also noted the way in which the Chronicler has similarly brought together both the tribes of the south and the tribes of the north under a combined heading of 'all Israel'. A good example of this is H.G.M. Williamson, who suggests that the Chronicler regards Hezekiah, king of Judah, as a second Solomon in reuniting northern and southern tribes, and that he adapts his sources and constructs his work in such a way as to reflect this.[37] Thus, we note that in connection with the activities of King Hezekiah in inviting the tribes of the north to celebrate Passover in Jerusalem (2 Chron. 30.1-27), a uniting of north and south is accomplished, and the spirit of the great Solomon is invoked. Interestingly, the Chronicler remarks in 2 Chron. 30.26, 'So there was great joy in Jerusalem, for *since the time of Solomon the son of David king of Israel there had been nothing like this in Jerusalem*'. In other words, Solomon is remembered as a king under whom the tribes of the north and the tribes of the south had been united in worship (as we see explicitly declared in 2 Chron. 7.8, where 'all Israel' feasts together following the dedication of the Temple).[38] Similarly, following the Passover celebrations, 2 Chron. 31.1 speaks of 'all Israel' being engaged in throwing down altars dedicated to the Asherim and other gods throughout Judah and Benjamin (the southern tribes) as well as in Ephraim and Manasseh (representing the tribes of the north).

All of which is to say that Solomon is presented by both the Deuteronomistic Historian and the Chronicler as a king reigning over a United Monarchy. Like his father David he rules over both the northern tribes and the southern tribes and forges out of them a single nation, frequently designated as 'all Israel'. The declarations about 'both' (τὰ ἀμφότερα) or 'the two' (τά δύο) in Eph. 2.14-18 follow this precise pattern, although the description of 'northern' and 'southern' tribes gives way to language based on the tension-filled early years of the Christian movement where Jewish/Gentile relations were at issue.[39] In this case the two groups at enmity with one another were two religious categories of people ('Jews' and 'non-Jews') instead of two fractured parts of a political unity ('the North' and 'the South').

A related matter, which may provide another point at which Eph. 2.13-22 demonstrates an underlying Solomonic theme, concerns the way in which foreigners are treated within Solomon's Temple prayer.[40] First, we note that the

37. Williamson 1977: 119-25; 1991: 28-29. Also see Ackroyd 1973: 179-89; Braun 1977; Throntveit 1987: 121-24.

38. So Williamson 1977: 120. The Chronicler is reliant upon a similar declaration in 1 Kgs 8.65.

39. Best (1997: 87-101) offers a good summary of the debate on this question. It is important to note, however, that for the writer of the letter of Ephesians the bitter controversy between Jews and Christians is a matter belonging to a previous generation. In Ephesians what we detect are *echoes* of that controversy.

40. Many have noted that the Chronicler presents an openness toward foreigners. This openness is somewhat at variance with the way that foreigners are treated in Ezra–Nehemiah. On this point, see Newsome 1975: 205-207.

Solomonic 'peace/rest' imagery is inserted into an Isaianic 'frame', as it were, which further develops the 'peace' motif. This basic material of this 'frame' is Isa. 57.19 (which is explicitly cited in v. 17 and alluded to again in v. 13) and Isa. 52.7 (which is alluded to in v. 17).[41] In effect, this means that vv. 17-18 are best viewed as a creative expansion based on the theme of 'peace' (εἰρήνη) being proclaimed to 'those who are far away' (τοῖς μακράν) as well as to 'those who are near' (τοῖς ἐγγύς), with the result that 'both' (οἱ ἀμφότεροι) together are thereby given access to the Father. This distinction between 'the near' and 'the far' in v. 17 is then extended in v. 19, where the traditional language of 'strangers and aliens' (ξένοι καὶ πάροικοι) is set over against descriptions of the Christian readers as 'fellow-citizens' (συμπολῖται) and 'members of the household of God' (οἰκεῖοι τοῦ θεοῦ). It is important to note here that the original context of Isa. 57.19 was a proclamation of divine blessing to *Jews* who were 'in the land' ('those who are near') and Jews who were dispersed in the exile ('those who are far away').[42] The key point here is that the verse from Isaiah originally was proclaiming a vision of a *united Israel*, much as we noted above in connection with the proclamation of a United Monarchy.

What has not been so often noted, however, is that vv. 17-19 also have some remarkable similarities to one of the petitions made by Solomon to Yahweh in connection with his Temple dedication speech. This is the petition regarding foreigners who come to worship at the Temple in Jerusalem, and it is found in 1 Kgs 8.41-43//2 Chron. 6.32-33. The version contained in Chronicles is the more interesting of the two, at least as far as similarities with Eph. 2.17-19 are concerned.[43] The passage reads:

> And every stranger (ἀλλότριος) who is not himself of your people Israel, and who shall have come from a distant land (ἐκ γῆς μακρόθεν) on account of your great name, and your mighty hand and your outstretched arm—when they come and pray toward this place, may you hear from heaven from your prepared dwelling-place (ἐξ ἑτοίμου κατοικτηρίου σου), and do whatever the foreigner (ἀλλότριος) call upon you for, so that all the peoples of the earth may know your name and fear you, as do your people Israel, and that they may know that your name has been called upon the house that I have built.

Now admittedly, the word that is used consistently in the LXX for 'foreigner' within both 1 Kgs 8.41-43 and 2 Chron. 6.32-33 is ἀλλότριος, not the ξένος or πάροικος we noted within Eph. 2.19.[44] However, there is some overlap between the semantic fields of the terms, and both ἀλλότριος and ξένος are used in the LXX to render the same Hebrew word *nokrî*.[45] More importantly, the description

41. Sanders (1965: 217-18) discusses this framing technique.

42. See Lincoln 1982: 26-27; 1990: 146-47; Best 1998: 245; O'Brien 1999: 207, on this point.

43. Lincoln (1990: 149) notes the connection.

44. The term ξένος is also used in 2.12.

45. The Hebrew *nokrî* is rendered by ἀλλότριος in Gen. 31.15; Exod. 2.22; 18.3; 21.8; Deut. 14.21; 15.3; 17.15; 23.20; 29.22; Judg. 19.12; 3 Kgdms 8.41, 43; 11.1, 8; 2 Chron. 6.32, 33; 2 Esd. 10.2, 10, 11, 14, 17, 18, 44; Neh. 13.26, 27; Prov. 2.16; 5.10; 6.24; 23.27; 27.2, 13; Obad. 11; Zeph. 1.8; Isa. 28.21; Jer. 2.21 and by ξένος in Ruth 2.10; 2 Kgs 15.19; Ps. 68.8 (MT 69.9, ET 69.8); Eccl. 6.2; Lam. 5.2.

in 2 Chron. 6.32 of these foreigners as coming from a land which is 'far away' (μακρόθεν) is very similar to the reference to 'those who are far away' (τοῖς μακρὰν) in Eph. 2.17; and the description in 2 Chron. 6.33 of the Temple as 'your dwelling-place' (κατοικτηρίου σου) has its equivalent in the phrase 'the dwelling-place of God' (κατοικτηρίον τοῦ θεοῦ) in Eph. 2.22. In fact, the rare noun κατοικτηρίον, which appears only here and in Rev. 18.2 within the New Testament,[46] is used a number of times within Solomon's Temple dedication speech, always with reference either to the Temple that Solomon built (3 Kgdms 8.13) or to God's dwelling-place in heaven for which the earthly Temple in Jerusalem is a symbolic focal point (3 Kgdms 8.39, 43, 49; 2 Chron. 6.30, 33, 39).[47] One cannot help but wonder if the writer of the letter to the Ephesians is again reliant upon the language and imagery of Solomon's Temple-dedication speech in his use of the term 'dwelling-place' (κατοικτηρίον).[48]

In short, while one would scarcely contest that the primary Old Testament text which is cited in Eph. 2.13-22 is Isa. 57.19, the key question remains *why* the writer of the letter turns to this verse to make his point. I suggest that the Solomonic imagery of 1 Kings 8//2 Chronicles 6 is the reason for this and that the presentation of Jesus Christ as a new Solomon underlies Eph. 2.13-22 as a whole. Indeed, the identification of Jesus Christ as the messianic man of peace in Eph. 2.14a may have been the trigger for the citation of the verse from Isa. 57.19. The citation from Isaiah picks up the theme of a reunited Israel, and thus fits the presentation of Solomon as ruler of a United Monarchy quite nicely. The writer of the letter to the Ephesians turns to the traditional descriptions of Solomon as a Temple-building king who ruled over a unified people in order to stress his point about the need for unity within the congregation he addresses.[49]

We turn now to consider one final intriguing connection between Eph. 2.13-22 and imagery associated with King Solomon. This is found in a little-discussed work known as the *Testament of Solomon*.

46. The verb form κατοικῆσαι appears in Eph. 3.17.

47. See Lincoln (1990: 158); Best (1998: 289); for comments along these lines, see O'Brien 1999: 221. Interestingly, although all these commentators note in passing the account of Solomon's Temple-dedication speech as it appears in 1 Kgs 8, they never mention the parallel in 2 Chron. 6. Clements (1965) provides a solid study of the Old Testament idea of God's dwelling-place in the Temple in Jerusalem.

48. There may also be a connection to another related declaration in 1 Kgs 8.23, where Solomon declares that there is no other like Yahweh the God of Israel, for he is 'God in the heavens above and on the earth beneath' (*ᵉlōhîm baššāmayim mimma'al wᵉ'al-hā'āreṣ mittāḥat*). This is quite an unusual expression, found only two other times in the Deuteronomistic writings (Josh. 2.11 and Deut. 4.39). Could it be that this 'above' and 'below' language is what gives rise to the phrase 'in the heavenlies' (ἐν τοῖς ἐπουρανίοις), an unusual expression found only in Ephesians (1.3, 20; 2.6; 3.10; 6.12)?

49. Scholarly debate about the nature of the congregation being addressed, and the underlying tension between 'we' and 'you' language contained within the letter, is extensive and there is little by way of consensus on the matter. I take the letter to reflect a situation in which a 'daughter-church' (in Hierapolis) is being written to by a Pauline disciple who is a member of the 'mother-church' (in Colossae) in an attempt to patch up differences and heal a rift which has developed between them. See Kreitzer 1997: 37-48, for a fuller discussion of this as an alternative way of assessing the social-setting of the epistle.

3. *The Cornerstone (ἀκρογωνιαῖος) of the Temple: Ephesians 2.20 and the* Testament of Solomon *22.7, 17*[50]

The *Testament of Solomon* is a weird and wonderful document of unknown provenance, uncertain date and contentious authorship.[51] In terms of subject matter, it is a convoluted, magic-filled tale of adventure focusing on Solomon's building of the Temple in Jerusalem. As the tale unfolds there are many unusual, if not bizarre, twists in the story-line which need not detain us here. However, the *Testament of Solomon* does share one important feature with the letter to the Ephesians worth noting briefly. This is its use of the rare word 'cornerstone' (ἀκρογωνιαῖος), a term which also appears in Eph. 2.20 as part of the description of the household of God which has been built upon the foundation of the apostles and prophets, 'Jesus Christ himself being the cornerstone' (ὄντος ἀκρογωνιαίου αὐτοῦ Χριστοῦ Ἰησοῦ).

In fact the *Testament of Solomon* contains *two* intriguing references to the 'cornerstone' (ἀκρογωνιαῖος) of the Temple which Solomon is building in Jerusalem. The first of these is found in 22.7, where Solomon describes his intentions:

> So Jerusalem was being built and the Temple was moving toward completion. Now there was a gigantic cornerstone which I wished to place at the head of the corner to complete the Temple of God.
>
> καὶ ἦν Ἰερουσαλὴμ ᾠκοδωμένη καὶ ὁ ναός συνεπληροῦτο. καὶ ἦν λίθος ἀκρογωνιαῖος μέγας ὅν ἐβουλόμην θεῖναι εἰς κεφαλὴν γωνίας τῆς πληρώσεως τοῦ ναοῦ τοῦ θεοῦ.

The second reference occurs a little further on, after Solomon has sent a servant-boy to capture the Arabian wind demon Ephippus in a wineskin by means of a magic ring which he supplies (22.9-15). The servant-boy is successful in this task and returns from Arabia, depositing the demon-filled wineskin at the entrance to Solomon's Temple. Then we read in 22.17:

> The following day I, Solomon, went into the Temple (for) I was very worried about the cornerstone. (Suddenly,) the flask got up, walked for seven steps, and fell down on its mouth before me.
>
> Τῇ δὲ ἐπαύριον εἰσῆλθον ἐγὼ Σολομῶν εἰς τὸν ναόν. καὶ ἤμην ἐν λύπῃ περὶ τοῦ λίθου τοῦ ἀκρογωνιαίου. καὶ ἀναστὰς ὁ ἀσκὸς καὶ περιπατήσας βήματα ἑπτὰ ἔστη ἐπὶ τὸ στόμα καὶ προσεκύνησέ μοι.

Solomon then exerts his authority over the demon Ephippus and commands him to lift the stone and place it in the corner of the Temple (22.20–23.2). This the demon does, carrying the stone up a flight of stairs and inserting it into the end at the entrance to the Temple (23.3).[52] The bizarre episode concludes with

50. The translation of the *Testament of Solomon* is that of Duling 1983; the Greek text is from McCown 1922.

51. See Duling 1983: 940-44, for a summary of scholarly discussion of these matters.

52. The idea that Solomon managed to build the Temple in Jerusalem by means of demons is picked up in later Christian writing, as *The Testimony of Truth* 9.3.70 from Nag Hammadi illustrates. See Giverson 1972 on this point.

Solomon, in great excitement, quoting the famous passage from Ps. 117.22 (LXX) about the 'stone that was rejected by the builders that became the keystone' and declaring that this scripture has now been fulfilled (23.4).

Very few of the standard commentaries on Ephesians even mention the fact that the term ἀκρογωνιαῖος appears in a document associated with the name of King Solomon.[53] Several of the standard reference dictionaries do not cite *Testament of Solomon* as a place where the term occurs; this is the case for Bauer–Gingrich–Danker's *Greek–English Lexicon of the New Testament and Other Early Christian Literature*[54] as well as Balz–Schneider's *Exegetical Dictionary of the New Testament,*[55] although Lampe's *A Patristic Greek Lexicon* does refer to *Testament of Solomon* 22.7 in its entry for ἀκρογωνιαῖος.[56] However, some of the critical literature published in journals and reference works does occasionally turn to the *Testament of Solomon* when discussing the term. For example, Joachim Jeremias does have a brief note about the reference to the λίθος ἀκρογωνιαῖος in 22.7 within his entry in *TWNT*, I (*TDNT*, I).[57] Here he adduces it in support of his well-known suggestion that the term refers to the final stone which is set in place during the construction of a building, usually over the entrance gate. He cites other parallel expressions from the *Testament of Solomon* to support his contention that λίθος ἀκρογωνιαῖος is a 'capstone' (an *Abschlußstein*, as opposed to a 'cornerstone', a *Grundstein*). These parallel expressions are πτερύγιον τοῦ ναοῦ in 22.8; εἰς τὴν ἀρχὴν τῆς γωνίας ταύτης τῆς οὔσης ἐν τῇ εὐπρεπείᾳ τοῦ ναοῦ in 23.2;[58] and καὶ ἀνῆλθεν εἰς τὸν κλίμακα βαστάζων τὸν λίθων καὶ ἔθετο αὐτὸν εἰς τὴν ἄκραν τῆς εἰσόδου τοῦ ναοῦ in 23.3. Similarly, R.L. McKelvey (1961–62: 357; 1969: 196) offers a full citation of the *Testament of Solomon* 22.7–23.4 within his challenge to Jeremias's interpretation of the meaning of ἀκρογωνιαῖος, although he does not feel that the document supports the idea of a 'capstone' in quite the way Jeremias suggests and fails to contribute meaningfully to the immediate context of Eph. 2.11-22 and its concern over the unity of the Church. Other scholars line up on both sides of this interpretative debate over the imagery implied by the term ἀκρογωνιαῖος, occasionally mentioning the contribution that the *Testament of Solomon* makes to the overall discussion. Thus, the third edition of Martin Dibelius's commentary on Ephesians (1953: 72) cites *Testament of Solomon* 22.7 and 23.3 in passing as support of Jeremias's contention that the term refers to a 'capstone'. Similarly, F.F. Bruce (1973: 231-35) quotes a section from 22.7–23.3 in a short article which essentially adopts Jeremias's position on

53. For example, no mention is made of the *Testament of Solomon* in this regard within the commentaries of Schlier 1958; Houlden 1970; Gnilka 1971; Mitton 1976; Barth 1974; Caird 1976; Stott 1979; Bruce 1984; Schnackenburg 1991; Kitchen 1994; Thurston 1995; Liefield 1997; Perkins 1997; MacDonald 2000.

54. Bauer 1979: 33.

55. See Krämer 1990.

56. Lampe 1961: 66.

57. Jeremias 1933: 793, ET 1964: 792. Also see Jeremias 1942: 279-80, ET 1967: 274-75, where the *Testament of Solomon* is again cited as evidence for his case. Jeremias has since 1925 argued this point in a number of places.

58. Here adopting the longer reading contained in two of the manuscript copies of the work.

the matter (at least as far as the *Testament of Solomon* reference is concerned). A similar point is made in Andrew T. Lincoln's commentary on Ephesians (1990: 154), which again quotes a section from 22.7–23.3,[59] and Best's commentary on Ephesians (1998: 285), which references the passage from 22.7–23.3 without actually citing it.[60] Peter O'Brien (1999: 217) mentions the *Testament of Solomon* in a footnote without giving the verse references,[61] while John Muddiman (2001: 142) makes passing reference to *Testament of Solomon* 22.7–23.3 within his discussion of ἀκρογωνιαῖος, noting that it provides 'unambiguous evidence that this word can be used of a capstone'.[62]

Of course none of this can be used to assert that by including a reference to the 'cornerstone' (ἀκρογωνιαῖος) the writer of the *Testament of Solomon* intends to promote an identification between Jesus Christ and Solomon (that is, between the building that it being constructed and the one responsible for building it). Such an explicit identification is nowhere made within the work, and in any event is rendered questionable given uncertainty as to the provenance of the *Testament* (is it a Jewish or Christian work?). However, an *association* between King Solomon (as Temple-builder) and the ἀκρογωνιαῖος (as the focal-point of the Temple's construction) is certainly expressed within the *Testament*. In other words, there may be some grounds for suggesting that the *Testament of Solomon* offers an intriguing parallel to Eph. 2.20, at least as far as the unusual term ἀκρογωνιαῖος is concerned. We should not overlook the possibility that by making reference in Eph. 2.20 to Jesus Christ as the key component in the Temple, its ἀκρογωνιαῖος, the writer of Ephesians is also deliberately associating him with the person responsible for construction of the first Temple in Jerusalem—Solomon himself. In this sense the story from the *Testament of Solomon* serves as a supportive piece of evidence for my contention that the writer of Ephesians is using Solomonic imagery within his work, particularly in Eph. 2.20-22 where reference is made to Temple-building.

4. *Summary*

I began this study by noting some of the ways in which King Solomon is remembered within the biblical record, with brief attention being given to legends about

59. Lincoln also notes (1990: 444) that οἱ κοσμοκράτορες, another unusual expression found only in Eph. 6.12 within the New Testament, is mentioned twice within the *Testament of Solomon* (in 8.2 and 18.2). For some inexplicable reason, Lincoln vacillates in his dating of the *Testament of Solomon*, describing it here as a 'second-century' document, whereas earlier in his discussion of ἀκρογωνιαῖος in Eph. 2.20 (1990: 154) he describes it as 'from the second *or third century* CE' (my italics).

60. Best also notes (1998: 593) the use of οἱ κοσμοκράτορες in *Testament of Solomon* 8.2 and 18.2 and offers the possibility of a much earlier date for the work when he remarks: 'it is not clear whether the Testament of Solomon predates Ephesians, depends on it, or uses the word independently'. Conybeare (1898: 6) also questions whether we can assume the *Testament of Solomon* imports the phrase from Eph. 6.12.

61. O'Brien simply notes that the *Testament of Solomon*, which he describes as a second- or third-century document, has been adduced in favour of the meaning 'capstone'.

62. Although Muddiman (2001: 142) goes on to suggest that arguments for the idea of ἀκρογωνιαῖος as a 'cornerstone' are more compelling.

his wealth, his renown as a wise ruler, and his part in the construction of the Temple in Jerusalem. I then moved on to consider in more depth a lesser-known motif, namely the description of Solomon as 'a Man of Rest/Peace' (*'îš mᵉnûḥâ*), a declaration explicitly made in 1 Chron. 22.9. This description of Solomon was examined against the larger backdrop of the so-called 'rest' (*mᵉnûḥâ*) motif as it is contained within both the work of the Deuteronomistic Historian and in the writings of the Chronicler. It was also noted how two later Jewish writers of the first century, Josephus and Philo of Alexandria, picked up this Solomonic imagery; in Philo's case Solomon's name is given a translation equivalent of εἰρηνίκος (a 'man of peace'). This Solomonic imagery was then used as the basis for an examination of Eph. 2.13-22 and several parallels in both theme and language were identified. The most important of these involves the phrase found in Eph. 2.14a, where a declaration is made about Jesus Christ: 'He himself is our peace' (αὐτὸς γάρ ἐστιν ἡ εἰρήνη ἡμῶν). I suggested that this phrase has a play on the Hebrew words for 'Solomon' (*šᵉlōmōh*) and 'peace' (*šālôm*) underlying it and that Solomonic imagery unlocks the meaning of the passage as a whole. This in turn suggests that the writer of the letter to the Ephesians is deliberately presenting Jesus Christ as a new Solomon, thereby offering a new avenue of christological expression in the process.

Much of the scholarly discussion about the dynastic promise made through Nathan the prophet to David in 2 Samuel 7 has centred around the nature of the messianic message which the passage seeks to express. The same holds true for some of the post-exilic texts which build upon the ideas contained in 2 Samuel 7, including 1–2 Chronicles. To what extent is the Davidic promise fulfilled in the person of Solomon himself as he builds a Temple in which God can dwell? Or is it more correct to take it that the Chronicler's hopes are pinned on a yet-to-be-revealed future resurgence of the house of David? At times the debate over these two approaches has hardened into a straightforward choice between a theocratic vision and an eschatological one. But should we be required to take theocracy and an eschatological messianism as mutually exclusive alternatives?[63]

In short, perhaps it is not going too far to suggest that for one early Christian thinker, at least, such an either/or choice is resolved somewhat, and that Solomonic imagery is one important means of achieving that resolution.[64] For the writer of the letter to the Ephesians (or at least in the traditions contained in 2.13-22!) it is the appearance of a new Solomon, who reigns and rules in fulfilment of

63. Saebø (1980) argues persuasively that they should not be viewed as such.

64. It is very unusual to find any New Testament commentator who picks up on the Solomonic imagery underlying Eph. 2.11-22. Caird (1976: 61) does head in this direction when he cites 2 Sam. 7.5-11 in connection with Eph. 2.20, but his point is rather the shift in meaning of the word 'house' (οἶκος) rather than a direct reference to Solomon and the ambiguity of 'house' (*bayit*) in the Old Testament passage is seen as a parallel. The commentator who comes closest to explicit mention of Solomon is Martin (1991: 38) who, speaking of 'church growth' as such, remarks: 'It is not measured by statistics or budgets. Rather, it is the growth of a living organism which takes shape by the Spirit's guidance through the circumstances of history and in a fashion drawn from the erection of Solomon's temple (I Kings 6–8).'

the promises made to the household of David, that is all-important. It is Jesus Christ, the new Solomonic 'Man of Peace' who builds the new Temple of the Church, consisting of those who have put their faith in him. He himself is foundational to the very structure of this church, being the cornerstone which holds them all together. In so doing he fashions the believing community into a united people, and the Solomonic ideal of a United Kingdom ruled by a divinely anointed King once again reverberates down the corridors of history.

Walter Brueggemann (2000: 117) recently described Solomon's great Temple-dedication ceremony in 1 Kings 8 in this way: '[The temple] is a great enactment of ecumenism, whereby the city of Jerusalem is able to gather in festive affirmation all the disparate populations of the United Monarchy'. Perhaps the most important legacy of the Solomonic Temple for the Christian Church beginning a third millennium is its challenge to serve as a focal point for the re-enactment of this adventure of ecumenism.

BIBLIOGRAPHY

Ackroyd, P.R.
1973 *I & II Chronicles, Ezra, Nehemiah: Introduction and Commentary* (Torch Bible Commentaries; London: SCM Press).

Arnold, C.E.
1989 *Ephesians: Power and Magic. The Concept of Power in Ephesians in Light of its Historical Setting* (SNTSMS, 63; Cambridge: Cambridge University Press).

Barth, M.
1974 *Ephesians: Introduction, Translation, and Commentary on Chapters 1–3* (AB, 34; New York: Doubleday).

Bauer, W.
1979 *A Greek–English Lexicon of the New Testament and Other Early Christian Literature* (Chicago: The University of Chicago Press, 2nd edn, revised and augmented by F. Wilbur Gingrich and Frederick W. Danker): 33.

Berger, K.
1974 'Die königlichen Messiastraditionen des Neuen Testaments', *NTS* 20: 1-44.

Berry, G.R.
1931 'The Hebrew Word נוח', *JBL* 50: 207-10.

Best, E.
1997 *Essays on Ephesians* (Edinburgh: T. & T. Clark).
1998 *Ephesians* (ICC; Edinburgh: T. & T. Clark).

Betz, O.
1987 'Miracles in the Writings of Flavius Josephus', in Louis H. Feldman and Gohei Hata (eds.), *Josephus, Judaism, and Christianity* (Leiden: E.J. Brill): 212-35.

Bowman, J.
1984–85 'Solomon and Jesus', *Abr-N* 23: 1-13.

Braulik, G.
1985 'Zur deuteronomistischen Konzeption von Freiheit und Frieden', in J.A. Emerton (ed.), *Congress Volume, Salamanca 1983* (VTSup, 36; Leiden: E.J. Brill): 23-39.

Braun, R.L.
1973 'Solomonic Apologetic in Chronicles', *JBL* 92: 503-16.

1976 'Solomon, the Chosen Temple Builder: The Significance of 1 Chronicles 22, 28, and 29 for the Theology of Chronicles', *JBL* 95: 581-90.

1977 'A Reconsideration of the Chronicler's Attitude toward the North', *JBL* 96: 59-62.

1986 *1 Chronicles* (WBC, 14; Waco, TX: Word Books).

Bruce, F.F.

1973 'New Wine in Old Wine Skins: III. The Corner Stone', *ExpTim* 84: 231-35.

1984 *The Epistles to the Colossians, to Philemon, and to the Ephesians* (NICNT; Grand Rapids: Eerdmans).

Brueggemann, W.

2000 *1 & 2 Kings* (Smyth & Helwys Bible Commentary; Macon, GA: Smyth & Helwys).

Caird, G.B.

1976 *Paul's Letters from Prison* (New Clarendon Bible; Oxford: Oxford University Press).

Carlson, R.A.

1964 *David the Chosen King: A Traditio-Historical Approach to the Second Book of Samuel* (Stockholm: Almqvist & Wiksell).

Clements, R.E.

1965 *God and Temple: The Idea of the Divine Presence in Ancient Israel* (Oxford: Basil Blackwell).

Coggan, F.D.

1941–42 'A Note on Ephesians ii.14: αὐτὸς γάρ ἐστιν ἡ εἰρήνη ἡμῶν', *ExpTim* 53: 242.

Conybeare, F.C.

1898 'The Testament of Solomon', *JQR* 11: 1-45.

Cross, F.M.

1973 'The Themes of the Book of Kings and the Structure of the Deuteronomistic History', in *idem*, *Canaanite Myth and Hebrew Epic* (Cambridge, MA: Harvard University Press): 274-89.

Day, J., R.P. Gordon and H.G.M. Williamson (eds.)

1995 *Wisdom in Ancient Israel: Essays in Honour of J.A. Emerton* (Cambridge: Cambridge University Press).

DeVries, Simon J.

1985 *1 Kings* (WBC, 12; Waco, TX: Word Books).

1988 'Moses and David as Cult Founders in Chronicles', *JBL* 107: 619-39.

Dibelius, M.

1953 *An die Kolosser Epheser, An Philemon* (HNT, 12; Tübingen: J.C.B. Mohr [Paul Siebeck], 3rd edn, rev. Heinrich Greeven).

Dietrich, W.

1972 *Prophetie und Geschichte: eine redaktionsgeschichtliche Untersuchung zum deuteronomistischen Geschichtswerk* (FRLANT, 108; Göttingen: Vandenhoeck & Ruprecht).

Dillard, R.B.

1987 *2 Chronicles* (WBC, 15; Waco, TX: Word Books).

Dirksen, P.B.

1996 'Why was David Disqualified as Temple Builder? The Meaning of 1 Chronicles 22.8', *JSOT* 70: 51-56.

Duling, D.C.

1975 'Solomon, Exorcism, and the Son of David', *HTR* 68: 235-52.

1983 'Testament of Solomon', in *OTP*, I: 935-87.

Edelman, D.V.
1995 'Solomon's Adversaries Hadad, Rezon and Jeroboam: A Trio of "Bad Guy" Characters Illustrating the Theology of Immediate Retribution', in Steven W. Holloway and Lowell K. Handy (eds.), *The Pitcher is Broken: Memorial Essays for Gösta W. Ahlström* (JSOTSup, 190: Sheffield: Sheffield Academic Press): 166-91.

Gerleman, G.
1973 'Die Wurzel *šlm*', *ZAW* 85: 1-14.

Giverson, S.
1972 'Solomon und die Dämonen', in M. Krause (ed.), *Essays on the Nag Hammadi Texts in Honor of Alexander Böhling* (Nag Hammadi Studies, 3; Leiden: E.J. Brill): 16-21.

Gnilka, J.
1971 *Der Epheserbrief* (Herders Theologischer Kommentar zum Neuen Testament; Freiburg: Herder).

Gray, J.
1970 *I & II Kings: A Commentary* (OTL; Philadelphia: Westminster Press, 2nd edn).

Horbury, W.
1995 'The Christian Use and the Jewish Origins of the Wisdom of Solomon', in Day, Gordon and Williamson (eds.) 1995: 182-96.

Houlden, J.L.
1970 *Paul's Letters from Prison* (PNTC; Harmondsworth: Penguin Books).

Ishida, T.
1992 'Solomon', in *ABD*, VI: 105-13.

Japhet, S.
1993 *1 & II Chronicles* (London: SCM Press).

Jeremias, Joachim
1933 'γωνία, ἀκρογωνιαῖος, κεφαλὴ γωνίας', in *TWNT*, I: 792-93. ET *TDNT*, I: 791-93 (1964).
1942 'λίθος', in *TWNT*, I: 272-83. ET *TDNT*, IV: 268-80 (1967).

Jones, G.H.
1984 *1 and 2 Kings*, I (NCB; Grand Rapids: Eerdmans).

Käsemann, E.
1966 'Ephesians and Acts', in L.E. Keck and J.L. Martyn (eds.), *Studies in Luke–Acts* (Nashville: Abingdon Press): 288-97.

Kitchen, M.
1994 *Ephesians* (New Testament Readings; Routledge: London).

Knoppers, G.N.
1993 *Two Nations Under God: The Deuteronomistic History of Solomon and the Dual Monarchies* (2 vols.; HSM, 52-53; Atlanta: Scholars Press).
2000 'Introduction', in Knoppers and McConville (eds.) 2000: 1-18.

Knoppers, Gary N., and J. Gordon McConville (eds.)
2000 *Reconsidering Israel and Judah: Recent Studies on the Deuteronomistic History* (Sources for Biblical and Theological Study, 8; Winona Lake, IN: Eisenbrauns).

Krämer, H.
1990 'γωνία, ἀκρογωνιαῖος', in Horst Balz and Gerhard Schneider (eds.), *Exegetical Dictionary of the New Testament* (Grand Rapids: Eerdmans): I, 267-69.

Kreitzer, L.
1997 *The Epistle to the Ephesians* (Epworth Commentaries; London: Epworth Press).

Kruse, H.
1985 'David's Covenant', *VT* 35: 139-64.

Lampe, G.W.H. (ed.)
1961 *A Patristic Greek Lexicon* (Oxford: Oxford University Press).

Lemaire, A.
1995 'Wisdom in Solomonic Historiography', in Day, Gordon and Williamson (eds.) 1995: 106-18.

Levenson, J.D.
1981 'From Temple to Synagogue: 1 Kings 8', in Baruch Halpern and Jon D. Levenson (eds.), *Traditions in Transformation: Turning Points in Biblical Faith* (Winona Lake, IN: Eisenbrauns): 143-66.

Liefeld, W.L.
1997 *Ephesians* (IVP New Testament Commentary Series; Leicester: IVP).

Lincoln, A.T.
1982 'The Use of the Old Testament in Ephesians', *JSNT* 14: 16-57.
1987 'The Church and Israel in Ephesians 2', *CBQ* 49: 605-24.
1990 *Ephesians* (WBC, 42; Dallas: Word Books).

Linville, J.R.
1998 *Israel in the Book of Kings: The Past as a Project of Social Identity* (JSOTSup, 272; Sheffield: Sheffield Academic Press).

Lohse, E.
1964 'Σολομών', in *TWNT*, VII: 459-65. ET *TDNT*, V: 459-65 (1974).

MacDonald, M.
2000 *Colossians, Ephesians* (SP, 17; Collegeville, MN: Liturgical Press).

Martin, R.P.
1981 *Reconciliation: A Study of Paul's Theology* (London: Marshall, Morgan & Scott).
1991 *Ephesians, Colossians, and Philemon* (Interpretation Commentary; Atlanta: John Knox Press).

McCarthy, D.J.
1965 'II Samuel 7 and the Structure of the Deuteronomic History', *JBL* 84: 131-38.

McConville, J.G.
1992 '1 Kings VIII 46-53 and the Deuteronomic Hope', *VT* 42: 67-79.

McCown, C.C.
1922 *The Testament of Solomon: Edited from Manuscripts at Mount Athos, Bologna, Holkham Hall, Jerusalem, London, Milan, Paris and Vienna, with Introduction* (Leipzig: J.C. Hinrichs).

McKelvey, R.J.
1961–62 'Christ the Cornerstone', *NTS* 8: 352-59.
1969 *The New Temple: The Church in the New Testament* (Oxford Theological Monographs: London: Oxford University Press).

Mitton, C.L.
1976 *Ephesians* (NCB; London: Oliphants).

Moritz, T.
1996 *A Profound Mystery: The Use of the Old Testament in Ephesians* (NovTSup, 85; Leiden: E.J. Brill).

Muddiman, J.
2001 *The Epistle to the Ephesians* (Black's New Testament Commentaries; London: Continuum).

Myers, J.M.
1962 'Solomon', in *IDB*, IV: 399-408.
1986 *I Chronicles* (AB, 12; Garden City, NY: Doubleday, 2nd edn).

Newsome, J.D., Jr
1975 'Toward a New Understanding of the Chronicler and His Purposes', *JBL* 94: 201-17.

Noth, M.
1943 'Das deuteronomistische Werk (Dtr)', in *idem*, *Überlieferungsgeschichtliche Studien* (Tübingen: Max Niemeyer): 3-110. ET *The Deuteronomistic History* (JSOTSup 15; Sheffield: JSOT Press, 1981).

O'Brien, P.T.
1999 *The Letter to the Ephesians* (The Pillar New Testament Commentary; Leicester: Apollos).

Parker, K.I.
1992 'Solomon as Philosopher King? The Nexus of Law and Wisdom in 1 Kings 1–11', *JSOT* 53: 75-91.

Payne, D.F.
1988 'Solomon', in *ISBE*, IV: 566-69.

Perkins, P.
1997 *Ephesians* (ANTC; Nashville: Abingdon Press).

Porter, S.E.
1993 'Peace, Reconciliation', in Gerald F. Hawthorne, Ralph P. Martin and Daniel G. Reid (eds.), *Dictionary of Paul and his Letters* (Leicester: IVP): 695-99.

Rad, G. von
1958 *Gesammelte Studien zum Alten Testament* (Munich: Chr. Kaiser Verlag). ET *The Problem of the Hexateuch and Other Essays* (trans. E.W. Trueman Dicken; Edinburgh and London: Oliver & Boyd, 1965).

Riley, W.
1993 *King and Cultus in Chronicles: Worship and the Reinterpretation of History* (JSOTSup, 160; Sheffield: JSOT Press).

Robinson, G.
1980 'The Idea of Rest in the Old Testament and the Search for the Basic Character of Sabbath', *ZAW* 92: 32-42.

Römer, T., and A. de Pury
2000 'Deuteronomistic Historiography (DH): History of Research and Debated Issues', in Albert de Pury, Thomas Römer and Jean-Daniel Maachi (eds.), *Israel Constructs its History: Deuteronomistic Historiography in Recent Research* (JSOTSup, 306; Sheffield: Sheffield Academic Press): 24-141.

Roth, W.
1976 'The Deuteronomic Rest Theology: A Redaction-Critical Study', *BibRes* 21: 5-14.

Saebø, M.
1980 'Messianism in Chronicles? Some Remarks to the Old Testament Background of the New Testament Christology', *HBT* 2: 85-109.

Sanders, J.T.
1965 'Hymnic Elements in Ephesians 1–3', *ZNW* 56: 214-32.

Schäfer-Lichtenberger, C.
1995 *Josua und Salomo: Eine Studie zu Authorität und Legitimität des Nachfolgers im Alten Testament* (VTSup, 58; Leiden: E.J. Brill).

Schlier, H.
1958 *Der Brief an die Epheser: Ein Kommentar* (Düsseldorf: Patmos-Verlag, 2nd edn).

Schnackenburg, R.
1991 *Ephesians: A Commentary* (Edinburgh: T. & T. Clark).

Schneider, G.
1993 'Σολομών, ῶνος', in Horst Balz and Gerhard Schneider (eds.), *Exegetical Dictionary of the New Testament* (Grand Rapids: Eerdmans): III, 257.
Schürer, E.
1973–87 *The History of the Jewish People in the Age of Jesus Christ (175 B.C.–A.D. 135)* (3 vols in 4; revised and edited by Geza Vermes, Fergus Millar and Martin Goodman, Edinburgh: T. & T. Clark).
Smend, R.
1971 'Das Gesetz und die Völker: Ein Beitrag zur deuteronomistischen Redaktionsgeschichte', in H.W Wolff (ed.), *Probleme biblischer Theologie: Festschrift Gerhard von Rad* (Munich: Chr. Kaiser Verlag): 494-509.
Stamm, J.J.
1960 'Der Name des Königs Salomo', *TZ* 16: 285-97.
Still, T.D.
1999 *Conflict at Thessalonica: A Pauline Church and its Neighbours* (JSNTSup, 183; Sheffield: Sheffield Academic Press).
Stott, J.R.W.
1979 *The Message of Ephesians* (Leicester: IVP).
Stuhlmacher, P.
1986 *Reconciliation, Law, & Righteousness: Essays in Biblical Theology* (Philadelphia: Fortress Press).
Talstra, E.
1993 *Solomon's Prayer: Synchrony and Diachrony in the Composition of 1 Kings 8, 14-61* (Contributions to Biblical Exegesis and Theology, 3; Kampen: Kok Pharos).
Throntveit, M.A.
1987 *When Kings Speak: Royal Speech and Royal Prayer in Chronicles* (SBLDS, 93; Atlanta: Scholars Press).
Thurston, B.
1995 *Reading Colossians, Ephesians and 2 Thessalonians: A Literary and Theological Commentary* (New York: Crossroads).
Tov, E.
1999 *The Greek and Hebrew Bible: Collected Essays on the Septuagint* (VTSup, 72; Leiden: E.J. Brill).
Veijola, T.
2000 'Solomon: Bathsheba's Firstborn', in Knoppers and McConville (eds.) 2000: 340-57.
Wilhelmi, G.
1987 'Der Versöhner-Hymnen in Eph 2,14ff', *ZAW* 78: 145-52.
Williamson, H.G.M.
1976 'The Accession of Solomon in the Book of Chronicles', *VT* 26: 351-61.
1977 *Israel in the Books of Chronicles* (Cambridge: Cambridge University Press).
1982 *1 and 2 Chronicles* (NCB; London: Marshall, Morgan & Scott).
1991 'The Temple in the Books of Chronicles', in William Horbury (ed.), *Templum Amicitae: Essays on the Second Temple Presented to Ernst Bammel* (JSNTSup, 48; Sheffield: Sheffield Academic Press): 15-31.

INDEXES

INDEX OF REFERENCES

INDEX OF AUTHORS